D0381010

The Common English Bible

BIBLE DICTIONARY

Nashville

Library of Congress Cataloging-in-Publication Data

CEB Bible dictionary.
p. cm.
ISBN 978-1-60926-024-8 (book - pbk. / trade pbk. : alk. paper) 1. Bible. English--Versions--Common English—Dictionaries. I. Common English Bible (Firm) II. Title: Bible dictionary.
BS440.C43 2011
220.5'2083--dc22
2011013089

Printed in China

11 12 13 14 15 16 17 18—10 9 8 7 6 5 4 3 2 1

Contents

Abbreviations

ANE Ancient Near East
Ant. Josephus, *Jewish Antiquities*
Apoc. Apocryphal/Deuterocanonical books
Aram. Aramaic
b. Indicates reference (e.g. b. Ber. 8a) is from the Babylonian Talmud
BCE Before the Common Era; traditionally BC: before Christ
c. circa
CE Common Era; traditionally AD: Anno Domini: year since the Lord's birth
CEB Common English Bible
cent. century
cf. compare
ch(s). chapter(s)
DSS Dead Sea Scrolls found at Qumran
 1QHa *Thanksgiving Hymns a* of DSS
 1QS *Rule of the Community* of DSS
 3Q15 *Copper Scroll* of DSS
 4Q416 Instruction scroll of DSS
 CD Cairo Genizah copy of the *Damascus Document*
Gk. Greek
Heb. Hebrew
Her. Philo, *Quis rerum divinarum heres sit*
Hist. Polybius, *The Histories*
KJV King James Version
Lat. Latin
LXX Septuagint; Greek translation of the Hebrew Bible
MT Masoretic Text; the Hebrew Bible
m. Mishnah
NT New Testament
NIV New International Version
NKJV New King James Version
NRSV New Revised Standard Version
OT Old Testament
par. parallel
Q Qumran
RSV Revised Standard Version
Syr. Syriac
Tg Targum; Aramaic translation of Hebrew Bible
v(v). verse(s)
Vg Vulgate, standardized Latin version of the Bible
y. Indicates reference (e.g. y. Shev. 9:38d) is from the Jerusalem Talmud

Books of the Bible

Old Testament

Book	Abbreviation
Genesis	Gen
Exodus	Exod
Leviticus	Lev
Numbers	Num
Deuteronomy	Deut
Joshua	Josh
Judges	Judg
Ruth	Ruth
1, 2 Samuel	1, 2 Sam
1, 2 Kings	1, 2 Kgs
1, 2 Chronicles	1, 2 Chron
Ezra	Ezra
Nehemiah	Neh
Esther	Esth
Job	Job
Psalms	Ps
Proverbs	Prov
Ecclesiastes	Eccl
Song of Songs	Song
Isaiah	Isa
Jeremiah	Jer
Lamentations	Lam
Ezekiel	Ezek
Daniel	Dan
Hosea	Hos
Joel	Joel
Amos	Amos
Obadiah	Obad
Jonah	Jon
Micah	Mic
Nahum	Nah
Habakkuk	Hab
Zephaniah	Zeph
Haggai	Hag
Zechariah	Zech
Malachi	Mal

New Testament

Book	Abbreviation
Matthew	Matt
Mark	Mark
Luke	Luke
John	John
Acts	Acts
Romans	Rom
1, 2 Corinthians	1, 2 Cor
Galatians	Gal
Ephesians	Eph
Philippians	Phil
Colossians	Col
1, 2 Thessalonians	1, 2 Thess
1, 2 Timothy	1, 2 Tim
Titus	Tit
Philemon	Phlm
Hebrews	Heb
James	Jas
1, 2 Peter	1, 2 Pet
1, 2, 3 John	1, 2, 3 John
Jude	Jude
Revelation	Rev

Apocrypha (Deuterocanonical Books)

Book	Abbreviation
Tobit	Tob
Judith	Jdt
Esther (Greek)	Add Esth
Wisdom of Solomon	Wis
Sirach	Sir
Baruch	Bar
Letter of Jeremiah	Ltr Jer
Prayer of Azariah	Pr Azar
Susanna	Sus
Bel and the Snake	Bel
1, 2, 3, 4 Maccabees	1, 2,3, 4 Macc
1, 2 Esdras	1, 2 Esdr
Prayer of Manasseh	Pr Man
Psalm 151	Ps 151

Aa

AARON The brother of Moses and Miriam. As God equips Moses for confrontation with Pharaoh, Aaron is provided as his spokesperson (Exod 4:14-16). Elsewhere Aaron functions as an assistant for Moses, so that "Moses and Aaron" work together as a team throughout the conflict with Pharaoh (Exod 5–12). He is also considered the primary ancestor of the Jerusalem priesthood (Exod 28–29; Lev 1–8; Num 6:22-27). His traditional gravesite was Mount Hor in Edom (Num 20:12, 22-29; Deut 10:6). Like Moses, he died outside the land of promise as a punishment (Deut 32:50).

AARONITES Sons or house of Aaron. Descendants of Aaron, who emerged as the sole legitimate claimants to priesthood. Priestly office was not originally limited to Aaronites. Exodus 32 and Num 12; 16–17 witness to rivalries between Aaronites and other groups claiming priestly prerogatives.

AARON'S STAFF Aaron's staff appears alongside the staff of Moses as an instrument of power in the confrontation with Pharaoh and the plagues (Exod 7:8-12, 19; 8:1-2, 5-6, 12-13, 16-17). In Num 17, a staff representing Levi is inscribed with Aaron's name. It blossoms, proving the placement and preeminence of the Aaronites within Levi as the only legitimate priests. It was preserved in the sanctuary as a warning to rival factions.

ABADDON "Destruction." In the OT, it refers to the underworld (Job 26:6; 28:22; 31:12; Ps 88:11; Prov 15:11; 27:20). In the NT, it is personified as Apollyon, the angel of the bottomless pit who reigns as king over the demonic locusts of Rev 9:3-11.

ABAGTHA One of the seven eunuchs assigned to take Vashti to Ahasuerus's banquet in order to display her beauty (Esth 1:10). Eunuchs served as high officials in the Persian court. Abagtha may not have been a literal eunuch, for the word becomes a title as well as a common noun in the Persian period.

ABANA A river, now called Barada, in Syria. Elijah sends Naaman, army captain of King Aram, to cure his leprosy in the Jordan River. Naaman retorts that the Abana and Pharpar Rivers of Damascus are preferable (2 Kgs 5:12).

ABARIM MOUNTAINS A range across the Jordan extending from Mount Nebo to the Arabian Desert (Num 27:12; 33:47-48; Deut 32:49; Jer 22:20). The northern part is also known as Pisgah, identified as the place where BALAAM blessed Israel the second time (Num 23:14), Moses saw the land (Deut 34:1), and Jeremiah hid the covenant chest (2 Macc 2:4-5).

ABBA The transliterated Aramaic word *Abba* appears three times in the NT, always as an address to God and always with the translation "the father." Paul attributes the cry "Abba, Father!" to the spirit in the hearts of believing communities, interpreting it as evidence of their adoption as God's sons and heirs (Rom 8:15; Gal 4:6). Mark 14:36 attributes this cry to Jesus—before Jesus' arrest, he pleads: "Abba, Father, for you all things are possible. Take this cup of suffering away from me. However—not what I want but what you want."

ABDA Adoniram's father (1 Kgs 4:6); Shammua's son among the Levites who returned to Jerusalem after the exile (Neh 11:17; cf 1 Chron 9:16).

ABDEEL "Servant of God." Shelemiah's father, mentioned to identify Shelemiah, who was unable to serve Jehoiakim by arresting Jeremiah and Baruch, since God hid them (Jer 36:26).

ABDI 1. A Levite from the clan of Merari, he was father of Kishi and grandfather of Ethan, appointed as one of the head temple singers by David (1 Chron 6:44 [Heb. 6:29]; 15:17).

2. The Levite father of Kish (2 Chron 29:12).

3. One of the descendants of Elam, who divorced his foreign wife after the people returned from the exile (Ezra 10:26).

ABDIEL "Servant of God." Guri's son and Ahi's father (1 Chron 5:15) in the Gadite tribe's genealogy; mighty warriors whom God favored.

ABDON 1. A minor judge (i.e., a tribal leader in premonarchical Israel [Judg 12:13-15]) from Pirathon (Far'ata) on Mount Ephraim. His wealth was so extreme that he could provide donkeys for each of his forty children and those thirty of his grandchildren who were of riding age. The donkey was a luxury item in ancient Israel's tribal society.

2. A levitical city in the tribal territory of Asher (Josh 21:30).

ABEDNEGO See SHADRACH, MESHACH, ABEDNEGO.

ABEL The second son of Adam and Eve (Gen 4:2), Abel appears only as the brother slain by CAIN because God preferred Abel's offering to Cain's (Gen 4:1-16). Commentators connect the name Abel with the Hebrew noun meaning "vapor, breath" (e.g., Isa 57:13; Ps 144:4), which would denote Abel's ephemeral life, underscored by the absence of any mention of offspring. In Matt 23:35 (Luke 11:51) Abel is the prototype of the murdered innocent. In Heb 11:4 he is portrayed as the first man of faith, recognized as such by God's acceptance of his offering.

ABEL-MEHOLAH A town in the Jordan Valley, south of BETH-SHAN. Abel-meholah was probably the hometown of ADRIEL son of Barzillai, "the Meholathite," who was married to MERAB, the older daughter of Saul (1 Sam 18:19). More notably, it was the hometown of ELISHA (1 Kgs 19:16, 19-20). Gideon and 300 Israelite troops routed a Midianite army in the vicinity of the hill of Moreh, in the Jezreel Valley (Judg 7:1, 19-22), the Midianites fleeing "to the border of Abel-meholah." The third biblical reference, 1 Kgs 4:7-19, presents a system of twelve officials and districts for providing food to the royal household of Solomon. Verse 12 lists it among the official and selected towns of the fifth district.

ABEL-SHITTIM "Meadow" or "brook of the acacias." Campsite on Moabite plains near Jordan River (Num 33:49). See SHITTIM.

ABI "My father." Shortened form of Abijah (2 Kgs 18:2; cf 2 Chron 29:1).

ABI-ALBON One of David's mighty warriors (2 Sam 23:31).

ABIASAPH Descendant of Levi and Korah who, with his household, left Egypt with Moses (Exod 6:24). In 1 Chron 9:19 and 26:1, modifications of the name as "Ebiasaph" and "sons of Asaph" refer to Abisaph's role as a gatekeeper in the temple.

ABIATHAR Great-grandson of ELI and the only priest to survive Saul's command that all the priests in Nob be slaughtered (1 Sam 22:6-19). Abiathar fled to David's camp and took the priestly vest, a powerful reminder of the Shiloh shrine tradition, with him. His presence as David's priest from earliest times was crucial in swinging popular support to David. With David on his deathbed, Abiathar supported Andonijah instead of Solomon as David's successor. Solomon eventually finds a reason to execute all of his rival's supporters except for Abiathar, whom he banishes to Anathoth, outside Jerusalem (1 Kgs 2:13-46).

ABIB First month in Hebrew calendar when Passover was celebrated (Exod 12:21-28; 13:3-10). After the Babylonian exile, it was renamed Nisan.

ABIB, TEL A place in Babylonia in the vicinity of the CHEBAR, where exiles from Judah lived (Ezek 3:15).

ABIDA "(My) father knows." Grandson of KETURAH and Abraham, Abida appears as the fourth of five sons of Midian in the matching genealogical lists of Gen 25:4 and 1 Chron 1:33.

ABIDAN "The (divine) father judges." During the census taken by Moses in the wilderness, Abidan son of GIDEONI represented the tribe of Benjamin (Num 1:11). He led the Benjaminite troops encamped west of the covenant dwelling (Num 2:22; 10:24) and presented offerings for the dedication of the altar (Num 7:60, 65).

ABIEL 1. Abiel, descendant of Benjamin and son of ZEROR, was the father of KISH and the grandfather of Saul (1 Sam 9:1).

2. An Arbathite from BETH-ARABAH (Josh 15:6, 61), Abiel was a member of the "Thirty," a group of warriors who supported David (1 Chron 11:32). In a list of David's mighty men he is called ABI-ALBON (2 Sam 23:31).

ABIEZER "Father is help."

1. A descendant of Manasseh (Josh 17:2). He headed the Abiezerites, the family of GIDEON.

2. A Benjaminite warrior, a native of ANATHOTH, who belonged to a select number of fighters loyal to the throne, bodyguards known as David's warriors (2 Sam 23:27; 1 Chron 27:12).

ABIGAIL Possibly meaning "my (divine) father rejoices."

1. Wife of NABAL the Carmelite, who later marries DAVID; mother of David's son CHILEAB (2 Sam 3:3; Daniel in 1 Chron 3:1). In 1 Sam 25 she appears wise, politically effective, and prophetic. Abigail's intelligence (v. 3), "good judgment" (v. 33), speaking, and hospitality contrast with the churlish Nabal (fool). She acts quickly to placate David's anger at Nabal. Through her speech, Abigail aligns herself with David while diffusing tension and averting violence. In a prophetic proclamation that anticipates Nathan's oracle in 2 Sam 7:11, 16, Abigail assures David that Yahweh will make him "an enduring dynasty" (1 Sam 25:28). After Yahweh strikes Nabal dead, David sends messengers to Abigail and she becomes his wife (1 Sam 25:42).

2. Sister or half sister of David and Zeruiah, and wife of Ithra the Israelite (2 Sam 17:25) or Jether the Ishmaelite (1 Chron 2:17). Absalom appointed her son Amasa commander of the army in place of Joab.

ABIHAIL "The Father is might."

1. Descended from Merari, Abihail is the father of ZURIEL (Num 3:14-39).

2. Wife of ABISHUR from the house of Judah and descended from Jerahmeel (1 Chron 2:29).

3. A Gadite mentioned in the genealogy of 1 Chron 5:11-17.

4. The wife of JERIMOTH, mother of MAHALATH, and daughter of ELIAB (2 Chron 11:18).

5. Father of Queen ESTHER, the wife

of King AHASUERUS; uncle of Mordecai the priest (Esth 2:15; 9:29).

ABIHU A son of Elisheba and Aaron (Exod 6:23; Num 3:2; 26:60; 1 Chron 6:3; 24:1), appointed to priestly service (Exod 28:1). Abihu appears in hierarchy just below Moses and Aaron and with them ascended the mountain and "saw Israel's God" (Exod 24:1, 9-11). Abihu was consumed by fire from Yahweh for offering an unacceptable sacrifice (Lev 10:1-7; cf Num 3:4; 26:61; 1 Chron 24:2).

ABIHUD The third son of BELA, the firstborn son of Benjamin (1 Chron 8:3).

ABIJAH 1. A son of Becher and the grandson of Benjamin (1 Chron 7:8).

2. The daughter of MACHIR (1 Chron 2:21).

3. The second son of SAMUEL (1 Sam 8:2; 1 Chron 6:28 [Heb. 6:13]). Samuel appointed Abijah and his older brother Joel to serve as judges in BEER-SHEBA. However, Abijah and his brother took bribes. Their corrupt behavior led the elders of the nation to demand a king to reign over Israel (1 Sam 8:4-5).

4. A descendant of Aaron, he was one of the leaders of the twenty-four courses or divisions into which the priesthood was divided in the days of David (1 Chron 24:10).

5. A son of JEROBOAM I, and probably the heir apparent of the first king of the northern kingdom. Abijah's death was foretold by the prophet Abijah as part of the announcement of the end of Jeroboam's house (1 Kgs 14:1-18).

6. The second king of Judah after the division of the kingdom. Abijah was the son of REHOBOAM, and grandson of Solomon (1 Chron 3:10).

7. The wife of King AHAZ of Judah and the daughter of Zechariah, Abijah was the mother of King HEZEKIAH (2 Chron 29:1). Her name appears in 2 Kgs 18:2 as Abi, the abbreviated form of the name.

8. One of the twenty-one priests who signed Nehemiah's pledge to keep the law (Neh 10:7 [Heb. 10:8]).

9. A priest who returned from the Babylonian exile with ZERUBBABEL and JESHUA the priest (Neh 12:4).

ABIJAM "Father of the sea." He was the son of Maacah and Rehoboam. He reigned over Judah 915–913 BCE while Jeroboam ruled over the northern kingdom of Israel (1 Kgs 15:1, 7, 8).

ABILENE A region in the Anti-Lebanon mountain range that derived its name from Abila, its chief city, which was located northeast of Mount Hermon, some 18 mi. to the northwest of Damascus on the way to Heliopolis (Baalbek). If Abilene was part of Herod's kingdom, it almost certainly reverted to the descendants of Lysanias after Herod's death, for in ca. 28 CE another Lysanias was ruling over Abilene as tetrarch (Luke 3:1), a reign that is confirmed by epigraphic evidence. At that point, however, the tetrarchy of Abilene could be distinguished from that of Ituraea (Luke 3:1). Abilene subsequently came under the control of Herod Agrippa I (37–44 CE), thanks to his friendship with Gaius and Claudius. Nine years after Agrippa's death, Claudius transferred control of this region to Herod Agrippa II, who retained it in his realm until his death in the 90s, after which it was annexed to the Roman province of Syria.

ABIMAEL One of Joktan's thirteen sons, descendants of Noah's son Shem (Gen 10:21-31) and from whom Abraham descended (1 Chron 1:17-27).

ABIMELECH 1. The king of Gerar in association with Abraham in Gen 20:1-18; 21:22-34; and with Isaac in Gen 26:1-11. In both cases, the patriarch tries to save himself from some perceived threat by claiming his wife is his sister (also Abram in Egypt [Gen 12:10-20]).

2. The son of the judge Gideon/Jerubbaal and a secondary wife (Judg

6:1–8:35), who attempted to establish a monarchy. The text states that Abimelech ruled over Israel for three years, though only Shechem pronounces him king (Judg 9:6, 22).

3. Error for Achishin in the title of Ps 34.

ABINADAB "My father is noble."

1. Father of Eleazar, Uzzah, and possibly Ahio (his brother). Men who moved the covenant chest from Beth-Shemesh to "Abinadab's house [palace/temple], which was on the hill" at Kiriath-jearim (1 Sam 7:1; 1 Chron 13:7), or Baalah (2 Sam 6:2-3).

2. Second son of David's father Jesse (1 Sam 16:8; 1 Chron 2:13).

3. Son of Saul, third- or fourth-born son and sixth child born to Ahinoam (1 Sam 14:49-50; 1 Chron 8:33-39; 9:38-44).

ABINOAM "My father is delight." Barak's father who lived in the city Kedesh in the region Naphtali (Judg 4:6, 12; 5:1, 12).

ABIRAM 1. A Reubenite involved with Korah's challenge of the exclusive priestly leadership of Moses and Aaron (Num 16; also see Num 11–12). God settled the dispute by destroying the rebels, their families, and their possessions.

2. The son of Hiel of Bethel (1 Kgs 16:34), who rebuilt Jericho contrary to divine command; thereby costing his sons' lives (Josh 6:26).

ABISHAG A young Shunammite brought to serve David in his old age (1 Kgs 1:3) either as a nurse, secondary wife, or wife. The text states that David did not know her sexually, which emphasizes his weakened state. She stands in contradistinction to the vocal BATHSHEBA, who inquires about SOLOMON's kingship (1:15) while Abishag watches. After David's death, his older son ADONIJAH requests to marry Abishag (2:17). Solomon interprets this request as a threat to his kingship and orders Adonijah's death (2:22-25).

ABISHAI Son of David's sister Zeruiah, brother of Joab and Asahel (1 Chron 2:13-17). Whereas Joab was commander of David's army, Abishai was chief of its striking nucleus, renowned for his boldness and courage (2 Sam 21:15-17; 23:18-19). Abishai is depicted as David's alter ego, the consistent voice of his dark side, who advocates use of violence to advance David's honor and self-interest (1 Sam 26:8; 2 Sam 16:9; 19:21).

ABISHUA 1. A son of BELA and grandson of Benjamin (1 Chron 8:4).

2. The son of PHINEHAS and great-grandson of Aaron the priest. Abishua was the father of BUKKI. Abishua served as the fourth high priest of Israel (1 Chron 6:4-5 [Heb. 5:30-31], 50 [Heb. 6:35]). He was one of the ancestors of EZRA (Ezra 7:5).

ABISHUR A Judahite of the Hezron family, son of Shammai and brother of Nadab (1 Chron 2:25-33).

ABITAL "My father is dew." One of David's wives, who bore his fifth son Shephatiah (2 Sam 3:4; 1 Chron 3:3).

ABITUB "My father is goodness." One of Shaharaim's two sons, by his wife Hushim (1 Chron 8:11).

ABIUD In Jesus' genealogy, Zerubbabel's son and Eliakim's father (Matt 1:13).

ABNER Army commander under Saul (1 Sam 14:50) who brings David before the king (1 Sam 17:55-57). Abner even enjoys an esteemed place at the king's table alongside David and the king's son Jonathan (1 Sam 20:25). He also functions as the king's bodyguard (1 Sam 26:13-25). Following the death of Saul on Mount Gilboa, Abner plays an instrumental role in elevating Ishbaal as successor to the throne and establishing him at Mahanaim (2 Sam 2:8-9), far removed from David's territory in Hebron. After a rift develops between Abner and Ishbosheth (2 Sam 3:6-11), Abner promotes David's kingship. However, Joab kills Abner. The end of Abner signals the end of opposition to David's eventual kingship over Israel.

ABOMINATION Something that is loathsome to either God or humans.

ABOMINATION OF DESOLATION This phrase is found in the KJV and NRSV, with variations, is derived from Dan 9:27; 11:31; and 12:11; with a parallel in 8:13. The CEB translation in Daniel is "desolating monstrosity." The phrase in Greek appears in 1 Macc 1:54, and again in Matt 24:15 and Mark 13:14. The majority of scholars believe that the abomination of desolation refers to the destructive work of the Seleucid king Antiochus IV Epiphanes. He forced idolatrous practices on the people and desecrated the temple in Jerusalem by placing an altar to Zeus on the altar of entirely burned offering (1 Macc 1:54). Swine, which are unclean according to levitical law, were offered as sacrifices on this pagan altar (2 Macc 6:1-5).

ABRAHAM The primary texts that portray the story of Abraham are recorded in Gen 11:26–25:11. Abraham is the "first" of the Genesis patriarchs and has lived up to the meaning of his name ("the ancestor of a multitude," according to Gen 17:5). His earlier name, Abram (probably "exalted ancestor"), is used exclusively in Gen 11:26–17:5 (Neh 9:7). He is given his new identity in view of a covenant relationship with God (Gen 17:1-8). The formula "The God of Abraham" (e.g., Exod 4:5; 1 Kgs 18:36; 1 Chron 29:18) repeatedly links Israel with Abraham's God. Indeed, Israel is known as "the people of Abraham's God" (Ps 47:9). God's promises to Abraham are repeated to Isaac (Gen 26:3-4, 24) and to Jacob (28:4, 13-14; 35:11-12), through Joseph to the twelve sons of Jacob (50:24), and to Moses and the people of Israel (Exod 6:3-8; 33:1). Moses understands that God's covenant with Abraham takes precedence over the covenant with Israel at Sinai (Exod 32:13), remaining in place in spite of Israel's apostasy. Other texts make similar claims (e.g., Lev 26:42; Deut 4:31; 2 Kgs 13:23; Jer 33:26; Mic 7:20; Gal 3:29). Next to Moses, Abraham is the most frequently named figure from the OT in the NT. Abraham is the ancestor of the Jews (Matt 1:1-2; Luke 13:16; 16:24; 19:9; Acts 13:26; Rom 4:1; 11:1). New Testament writings acknowledge Abraham's centrality in the history of salvation: Abraham receives the covenant and the promise of God's support for his descendants (Luke 1:55, 73; Acts 3:25; 7:2, 17). God is frequently called the God of Abraham and Isaac and Jacob, particularly when God's abiding presence with his people is expressed (Matt 22:32; Mark 12:26 par.; Luke 16:22; 20:38; Acts 3:13; 7:32). Abraham is not important simply as a past example. He is the symbol of future blessing for his true descendants (Matt 8:11; Luke 13:28; 16:19-31; Heb 2:16; 6:13). This blessing is seen as fulfilled in Abraham's descendant Jesus (Matt 1:1–2:17; Luke 3:34; Gal 3:16).

ABRAHAM'S SIDE A metaphorical reference to the familial belonging, honor, and repose the righteous enjoy in the afterlife. The expression occurs only in Luke 16:22. It represents the blessed state of the righteous who join the patriarchs in paradise after death. Transport to Abraham's side or bosom may have an antecedent in the ancient idea of being gathered to one's ancestors (Gen 25:8).

ABRAM "Exalted ancestor." The name of Abraham in Gen 11:26–17:4; 1 Chron 1:27; and Neh 9:7. See ABRAHAM.

ABRON A brook whose towns Holofernes destroyed all the way to the sea (Jdt 2:24).

ABRONAH One of the exodus itinerary sites visited by the Israelites as they traveled between the wilderness of Sinai and Canaan (Num 33:34-35).

ABSALOM "(My) father is peace (or well-being)." Absalom was the third of the sons of DAVID born in Hebron (2 Sam 3:3). Absalom plays a major role in the Succession Narrative of David (2 Sam 9–20; 1 Kgs 1–2). Amnon, Absalom's half brother, raped Absalom's sister Tamar. Absalom's revenge plan resulted in Amnon's death and Absalom's estrangement from David. Absalom later led a failed uprising against David. David ordered his commanders to protect Absalom (2 Sam 18:5), but Joab disregarded the order and killed Absalom.

ABUBUS Father of Jericho's governor Ptolemy, who married Simon Maccabeus's daughter and murdered Simon Maccabeus and his two sons (1 Macc 16:11-16).

ABYSS In the Apocrypha, the abyss is the region of the deep often contrasted with the earth and the heavens (Sir 1:3; 16:18; 24:5, 29; 42:18). In the NT, the abyss is the abode of demons (Luke 8:31) or the abode of the dead (Rev 9:11).

ACACIA A tree or shrub common in the desert areas of Egypt, Arabia, Sinai, and the southern plain. Due to its exceptional durability, acacia radiana was used for the COVENANT CHEST, the furnishings of the COVENANT DWELLING, and the ALTAR (Exod 25–27; 30; 35–38; cf Deut 10:3). Acacia, along with six other desert trees, depicts the imagery of the wondrous renewal of the wilderness (Isa 41:19).

ACCAD A city, Sumerian name Agade, in northern Babylonia, listed in Gen 10:10 among the main cities of the kingdom of Nimrod in the land of Shinar. Possibly founded by Sargon in the 24th cent. BCE, Accad became the dynastic capital until its fall in the 22nd cent. BCE. The city was never rebuilt, and its site has never been identified.

ACCO, AKKO A port city on the coast of Israel, 8 mi. north of Mount Carmel and 30 mi. south of Tyre. It is the best natural port on the coast of Israel, and well situated for inland trade through the Jezreel Valley. The only reference to Acco in the OT is a note in Judg 1:31 that the tribe of Asher "didn't drive out the people living in Acco," an indication that the Canaanite settlement there was well established and strong. The city was conquered by Alexander the Great in his swing through Palestine on the way to Egypt. After his death, it became part of the Seleucid Empire, but was captured for a time by the Ptolemies in the 3rd cent. BCE, who renamed it Ptolemais, as it is called in the books of the Maccabees and in Acts 21:7.

ACCUSER See SATAN.

ACHAIA The Roman province of Achaia, formed after the incorporation of Greece into the Roman Empire (146 BCE), covered the area of the Peloponnese and southern mainland Greece. Corinth, refounded in 44 BCE, became the provincial capital and seat of the Roman governor, which was where Paul encountered Gallio (Acts 18:12).

ACHAICUS Bracketed with STEPHANAS and FORTUNATUS in 1 Cor 16:17 as one of the three long-standing Christian converts from Corinth who traveled to Paul in Ephesus. They caused him delight, provided his spirit "a much needed rest" (16:18), helped compensate for his missing Corinth, and may have brought the letter to which Paul alludes in 1 Cor 7:1.

ACHAN The patriarch of a Judahite

family stoned to death for taking and hiding devoted items from Jericho (Josh 7:1-26).

ACHAR Carmi's son, "who made trouble for Israel" because he had violated the BAN (1 Chron 2:7). Some manuscripts read ACHAN.

ACHBOR 1. Father of the Edomite king BAAL-HANAN (Gen 36:38-39; 1 Chron 1:49).

2. King JOSIAH's courtier who accompanies HILKIAH on his quest to have HULDAH authenticate the Instruction scroll (2 Kgs 22:12-14). This could be the father of ELNATHAN (Jer 26:22; 36:12).

ACHIM Son of Zadok and father of Eliud in Matthew's genealogy of Jesus (Matt 1:14).

ACHIOR Commander of the Ammonite army who is abandoned as a traitor by the Assyrians and taken captive by the people of Bethulia. A Gentile, Achior rehearses Jewish history and theology in impressive detail (Jdt 5:5-22), sides with the Jews in the battle, corroborates Judith's conquest (Jdt 14:5-8), and ultimately converts to Judaism (14:10).

ACHISH 1. The son of MAOCH and king of the Philistine city of GATH (1 Sam 21:10-15) who gives David ZIKLAG. From there David launches attacks against Israel's enemies, while telling Achish that he attacked Judah. The other Philistine lords do not trust David, so Achish sends David away before the Philistines fight the Israelites in Saul's final battle at Mount Gilboa (1 Sam 31).

2. The king of Gath when two servants of SHIMEI flee to Gath (1 Kgs 2:39-40). Shimei's pursuit of these servants leads to his death because he violates his oath to SOLOMON.

ACHOR "Calamity." An inhospitable valley constituting part of the boundary between Judah and Benjamin (Josh 15:7). The valley came to be associated with the execution of Achan and his family (Josh 7:24-26). Both Isaiah and Hosea look to Achor's transformation into a fertile valley as a metaphor of divine restoration (Isa 65:10; Hos 2:15).

ACHSAH The daughter of Caleb who asked for and received springs of water in the southern plain (Josh 15:13-19; Judg 1:12-15).

ACHSHAPH A city-state in the coalition of hostile northern Canaanite kings (Josh 11:1) that became part of the territory of Asher (Josh 19:25).

ACHZIB 1. A town of the tribe of Judah (Josh 15:44). Micah mentions it among several cities of the foothills using paronomasia, or, puns to indicate that Assyria would conquer them before Jerusalem (Mic 1:14).

2. A tell on the Mediterranean coast north of Acco that remained a Canaanite city during the period of the judges (Josh 19:29; Judg 1:31).

ACRE See WEIGHTS AND MEASURES.

ACTS OF THE APOSTLES The Acts of the Apostles narrates the early witness of the church to the resurrection of Jesus, beginning with the events of the Ascension and Pentecost in Jerusalem and continuing through Paul's arrival in Rome. Written by the author of the Gospel of Luke, Acts extends the evangelist's story of God's salvation through Jesus Christ both to the people of Israel and to the Gentiles.

ADADAH A town located on the Edomite boundary of southern Judah (Josh 15:22).

ADAH A woman's name meaning "to adorn."

1. Adah and Lamech were the parents of Jabal, whose descendants

lived in tents and raised livestock (Gen 4:19-20), and Jubal the musician (Gen 4:21). Lamech confesses murder to Adah and his other wife Zillah (Gen 4:23).

2. Esau's Canaanite wife (Gen 36:2).

ADAIAH 1. A native of BOZKATH in Judah (Josh 15:39), the father of JEDIDAH and maternal grandfather of King JOSIAH (2 Kgs 22:1).

2. A member of the levitical family of GERSHOM; son of ETHNI; father of Zerah and an ancestor of ASAPH (1 Chron 6:41 [Heb. 6:26]).

3. Son of SHIMEI (1 Chron 8:21) and one of the leaders of the tribe of Benjamin in Jerusalem before Judah's exile (1 Chron 8:28).

4. Father of MAASEIAH, one of the five commanders of hundreds who joined in a coup against Queen ATHALIAH, usurper of Judah's throne (2 Chron 23:1).

5. Son of JOIARIB and father of HAZAIAH and an ancestor of Maaseiah, who was one of the tribal leaders of Judah in Jerusalem after the exile (Neh 11:5).

6. A priest, son of JEROHAM (1 Chron 9:12; Neh 11:12), probably of the levitical family of Gershom (cf 1 Chron 6:41 [Heb. 6:26]), who returned from exile and settled in Jerusalem.

7. Son of BANI, an Israelite who divorced his Gentile wife after the exile (Ezra 10:29; 1 Esdr 9:30).

8. Son of BINNUI, an Israelite forced to divorce his Gentile wife after the exile (Ezra 10:39).

ADALIA One of Haman's sons hanged on the gallows (Esth 9:8).

ADAM 1. The first man. In the OT, Adam's presence is limited to Gen 2:4–4:26. Yahweh forms Adam ("human") from the ground and places him in the garden. Adam and Eve break Yahweh's one rule against eating the forbidden fruit, and are expelled from the garden and cursed with pain, work, and mortality. In the NT, Paul portrays Adam as a type for Jesus Christ, the "last Adam," who reverses the exile and death brought by the "first" Adam (1 Cor 15:22, 45; Rom 5:14).

2. A city where the Jordan's waters miraculously arose upstream from the Israelites, allowing them to cross the river on dry land (Josh 3:16). Hosea denounces certain priests' disloyalty to Yahweh and murderous activities at the city (Hos 6:7).

ADAMAH A fortified city in the tribe of Naphtali (Josh 19:36). Adamah should not be identified with Adam in Transjordan (Josh 3:16) or with Adami-nekeb (Josh 19:33). Its location remains largely unknown despite suggestions of 7 km west of the Sea of Galilee, at Madon (Josh 11:1; 12:19), and 7 km north of Capernaum.

ADAR Twelfth month in the postexilic Hebrew calendar when completion of the rebuilt temple (Ezra 6:14-16), Purim (Esth 9:1-32), and Nicanor's defeat (2 Macc 15:36) were celebrated.

ADASA Village where Judas Maccabeus defeated the Syrian general Nicanor in 160/161 BCE (1 Macc 7:40-45).

ADBEEL One of Ishmael's twelve sons (Gen 25:13; 1 Chron 1:29).

ADDAN Place in Babylonia whose exiles could not prove their ancestry as Israelites (Ezra 2:59).

ADDAR 1. One of the nine sons of BELA (1 Chron 8:3), the oldest son of Benjamin.

2. A town near the Zin wasteland listed as a southern boundary for the territory allotted to the tribe of Judah (Josh 15:1-4).

ADDER A general term for a poisonous snake (Isa. 59:15).

ADDI 1. A leader of returnees from the Babylonian exile who collectively agreed to divorce their foreign wives (1 Esdr 9:31).

2. An ancestor of Jesus (Luke 3:28).

ADDITIONS TO DANIEL See DANIEL, ADDITIONS TO.

ADDITIONS TO ESTHER See ESTHER, ADDITIONS TO.

ADIDA Town built and fortified by Simon Maccabeus, located in the western foothills (Shephelah) 4 mi. east of Lydda (1 Macc 12:38; 13:13).

ADIEL 1. Father of AZMAVETH, David's royal treasurer (1 Chron 27:25).

2. One of Simeon's tribal leaders (1 Chron 4:36) who led the conquest of GEDOR (1 Chron 4:38-40).

3. A priest qualified to serve in the temple upon returning from exile (1 Chron 9:12).

ADIN The ancestor of 454 Jews (Ezra 2:15; 8:6; Neh 7:20; 10:16) (1 Esdr 5:14) who returned to Jerusalem with Zerubbabel or with Ezra.

ADINA The son of Shiza; a Reubenite leader listed among David's warriors (1 Chron 11:42).

ADMATHA One of the seven officials of Persia and Media who had access to the king Ahasuerus (Esth 1:14). These officials advised the king to banish Queen Vashti, an action that led to the elevation of Esther (Esth 1:19-20).

ADMIN An ancestor of Jesus; Aminadab's father (Luke 3:33).

ADNAH 1. Judahite military commander during the reign of Jehoshaphat (2 Chron 17:14).

2. Manassite who deserted Saul and joined David prior to Saul's death (1 Chron 12:20).

ADONAI, ADONAY "LORD" or "the ruler of the entire earth" was an epithet of "God" (Josh 3:11). The term began as a title; however, Adonai became an alternate name for God, often used in parallelism with Yahweh or as a substitute for it, when Yahweh was deemed too sacred to be pronounced. Subsequently, when the Masoretes added vowel points to the text, the consonants for Yahweh appeared with the vowels for Adonai.

ADONIJAH 1. David's fourth son, born in Hebron by his wife Haggith (2 Sam 3:4). First Kings 1–2 narrates Adonijah's failed bid to succeed DAVID as king of Israel. Adonijah was heir apparent to David's throne, but his younger brother Solomon was a formidable rival. Solomon's mother Bathsheba and the prophet Nathan convince David to declare that Solomon should be anointed king (1 Kgs 1:32-35). Adonijah flees to the temple and refuses to come out without Solomon's promise to spare him. After David's death, Adonijah asks Solomon for David's secondary wife Abishag. Solomon interprets this as a subtle bid for kingship and has Adonijah killed.

2. Judean leader from the time of Jehoshaphat (2 Chron 17:8) and Ezra (Neh 10:16).

3. A leader who set his seal on Ezra's covenant (Neh 10:16).

ADONIKAM The head of a nonpriestly clan returning to Judah from Babylonia in several lists in Ezra–Nehemiah. One list includes those said to come up with Zerubbabel and Joshua during the reign of Darius (Ezra 2:13; Neh 7:18); another, those with Ezra in the reign of Artaxerxes (Ezra 8:13).

ADONIRAM Adoniram, son of Abda, was a Solomonic official in charge of the corvée-force (1 Kgs 4:6; 5:14).

ADONI-ZEDEK "My Lord is righteous" or "My Lord is Zedek." The Jebusite king of Jerusalem who led a coalition of the kings from Jerusalem, Hebron, Jarmuth, Eglon, and Lachish—against Gibeon (Josh 10:1-3).

ADORAIM One of fifteen cities fortified by Rehoboam (2 Chron 11:9). It is the modern Dura, situated about 6 mi. southwest of Hebron.

ADRAMMELECH A deity mentioned in 2 Kgs 17:31. The king of Assyria deported peoples from Babylon, Cuthah, Avva, Hamath, and Sepharvaim, and settled them in the cities of Samaria to replace the Israelites, who had been previously deported to Assyria. Here these peoples continued their worship of foreign gods. While the other groups are simply described as making idols, the Sepharvaites are singled out as the ones who burned children in sacrifice to Adrammelech and Anammelech, the "Sepharvite gods."

ADRAMYTTIUM An ancient port city along the coast of the Roman province Asia (now Turkey). A commercial ship from Adramyttium bound for the Asian coast carried Paul, Aristarchus, and Julius the Centurion from Caesarea to Myra on the first leg of their journey to Rome (Acts 27:2).

ADRIATIC SEA In NT times, the part of the Mediterranean between Crete and Malta, as far as Sicily, was loosely called Adria. This body of water is dangerous for travel in winter due to storms caused by strong northeast winds. On his way to Rome, the apostle Paul traveled on a boat that was "battered by [a] violent storm" (Acts 27:18) and "carried across" (27:27) the Adriatic Sea for two weeks, ending in a shipwreck.

ADRIEL The son of BARZILLAI and husband of either MERAB (1 Sam 18:19) or MICHAL (2 Sam 21:8), King Saul's daughters. DAVID presents Adriel's five sons to the Gibeonites for execution because of Saul's transgression against them, a transgression unrecorded in 1 Sam.

ADULLAM A city in the Judean hills (Josh 15:35) commonly identified with Tell esh Sheikh Madhkûr. Adullam guarded a route from the coastal plain to the highlands of Judea. Fleeing Saul, David hid in "Adullam's fortress" (1 Sam 22:1), which later became a stronghold for him and his men (2 Sam 5:17; 23:13-17; 1 Chron 11:15). Adullam was among the cities fortified by Rehoboam (2 Chron 11:7), and Micah mourns Adullam (Mic 1:15), possibly in anticipation of the invasion of Sennacharib (2 Kgs 18:13; 2 Chron 32:1). Following the exile, Adullam was one of the places where the returning Judeans settled (Neh 11:30). Later, Judas Maccabeus and his army found refuge there during the Maccabean revolt (2 Macc 12:38).

ADULTERY Adultery may be defined as a man having sex with another man's wife, or a married woman having sex with ("lying with") a man other than her husband. The Ten Commandments include a prohibition against committing adultery (Exod 20:14; Deut 5:18). The key to determining if a sexual act is adultery is the woman's marital status. The meaning of the term *wife* includes a woman engaged to be married (Deut 22:23-24). Both parties are condemned to death (cf Lev 20:10; Deut 22:24). In all cases, the subject of the law is the man, and the offense is against another man: a man commits adultery with someone else's wife (fiancée); the woman is called an adulteress.

In Jesus' teachings on divorce, the scope of adultery is expanded: if a divorced man marries another woman, or a man marries a woman who has been divorced by her husband, they commit adultery (Matt 19:9; Mark 10:11-12; Luke 16:18; cf Rom 7:3). Matthew 5:32 extends the category even further: a man who divorces his wife "forces her to commit adultery."

Finally, adultery is used metaphorically. First, 2 Pet 2:14 describes the "false teachers" as "always looking for someone with whom to commit adultery." Here adultery is linked with insatiability, enticement, and greed. Jesus also calls the generation to whom he is preaching "an evil and unfaithful generation." In Matthew (12:39; 16:4), the label is placed on those who ask for a sign, while in Mark (8:38) the "unfaithful and sinful generation" are those who are ashamed of Jesus' words.

ADUMMIM Red rock formations that form the northern boundary of Judah (Josh 15:7). The southern border of the tribe of Benjamin, from En-shemesh to Geliloth, is opposite the ascent of Adummim (Josh 18:17). The site once was a stronghold between Jerusalem and Jericho.

AENEAS A man Peter healed and whose healing converted all residing in Lydda and Sharon (Acts 9:33-35).

AENON Site near Salem where John the Baptist was baptizing while Jesus was in the Judean countryside (John 3:23).

AGABUS A Judean prophet who predicts a worldwide famine during the reign of Claudius (Acts 11:27-30). In response, church elders send relief to the Judean believers through Barnabas and Saul. Agabus also predicts that Paul will be bound by the Jews and delivered to the Romans (Acts 21:10-11).

AGAG, AGAGITE 1. King mentioned in Balaam's third oracle (Num 24:7).

2. King of the Amalekites. SAMUEL orders Saul to devote Agag, the Amalakites, and their possessions to destruction. Saul and the Israelites spare Agag and the finest Amalekite possessions, supposedly for sacrifice to God. God rejects Saul for his disobedience. Samuel executes Agag (1 Sam 15).

3. A term used to describe ESTHER and Mordecai's archenemy HAMAN (Esth 3:1, 10), connecting him to Saul's archenemy Agag, the king of Amalek (just as Mordecai, descendant of Benjamin, is connected to Saul). Haman becomes subject to the divine instructions to wipe out Agag's descendants (1 Sam 15:8).

AGEE Agee the Hararite was the father of SHAMMAH, a warrior among the three (ELEAZAR, Shammah, and Josheb-basshebeth) who commanded under David (2 Sam 23:11).

AGIA Wife of Jaddus and daughter of BARZILLAI (1 Esdr 5:38). The descendants of Agia and JADDUS could not document their descent from the preexilic priesthood (Neh 7:64). David favored Agia's family (2 Sam 17:27; 19:31-39; 1 Kgs 2:7).

AGRIPPA 1. Herod Agrippa I was the grandson of Herod I (and the son of Aristobulus and Berenice). In 41 CE, Agrippa became king of the lands of Samaria and Judea, all the territories once ruled by his grandfather. Acts 12:1-4 maintains that Herod Agrippa had James Zebedee killed "with a sword," a punishment that suggests he held the apostle responsible for civil disorder. Later, he arrested Peter, perhaps again for stirring up apocalyptic expectations (though Peter was miraculously released [Acts 12:6-9]). As a result of these measures, the remaining disciples fled the city, and leadership of the church passed to James the brother of Jesus.

2. Agrippa II arrived as procurator of Judea in 60 CE. Acts uses Agrippa as a witness to Paul's innocence—the king is impressed by the apostle's eloquence and declares that he could have been released had he not appealed to Caesar (Acts 25:13–26:32).

AGUR Agur, "JAKEH's son," is either the proper name or the title (Assembler or Gatherer) of the speaker in Prov 30.

AHAB Ahab was king of northern Israel (ca. 875–854 BCE), succeeding his father Omri. He married Jezebel daughter of King Ethbaal of Sidon. Jehu murdered Ahab's seventy sons in Samaria (2 Kgs 10), and his daughter (or sister) Athaliah ruled Judah prior to her murder (2 Kgs 11:1-16, 20). Ahab was northern Israel's worst king (1 Kgs 16:30, 33; 21:25; Mic 6:16).

AHARAH The third son of Benjamin (1 Chron 8:1).

AHARHEL Son of the Judahite HARUM (1 Chron 4:8).

AHASBAI A Maachathite, the father of ELIPHELET, one of David's mighty warriors (2 Sam 23:34).

AHASHTARITES HAAHASHTARI (1 Chron 4:6) is either the name of one of the four sons of ASSHUR and his wife Naarah from the tribe of Judah, or the name of a Judahite clan, "the Ahashtarites."

AHASUERUS Likely the Persian king Xerxes I, who reigned 486–465 BCE. The most prominent appearance of Ahasuerus is in the book of Esther. In this story Ahasuerus is essentially a fictional construct of a well-known historical figure. There is a brief mention of an Ahasuerus as the father of Darius the Mede in Dan 9:1.

AHAVA Place where Ezra gathered exiled Judahites to embark on their trip from Babylon back to Palestine. The biblical text mentions Ahava only in Ezra 8, once as a town/settlement (v. 15) and twice as a river/canal (vv. 21, 31).

AHAZ Judean king from the 8th cent. BCE, under whom Judah became an Assyrian vassal. According to 2 Kgs 16:2, Ahaz succeeded his father Jotham when he was 20 and reigned sixteen years, from 735 to 15 BCE, although some prefer 743–27 BCE. Following standard regnal formulas, 2 Kgs 16 opens with the indictment that "he didn't do what was right in the Lord's eyes" (v. 2). Instead of emulating his ancestor David, Ahaz followed apostate northern kings and the pagan pre-Israelite inhabitants of the land by sacrificing his son and worshipping at religious shrines that were regarded as illicit by the authors of 1–2 Kgs (2 Kgs 16:3-4).

AHAZIAH 1. Ahaziah (ca. 852–851 BCE) succeeded his father Ahab (1 Kgs 22:40), ruling Israel for two years (1 Kgs 22:51). The text evaluates him negatively because he acts like both parents and worships Baal (1 Kgs 22:52-53).

2. Ahaziah succeeded his father Jehoram (2 Kgs 8:25), ruling Judah for one year (ca. 843–842 BCE). He also is judged negatively for doing what was evil in the sight of the Lord (2 Kgs 8:27).

AHBAN One of the sons of Abishur of Judah in the genealogy of Jerahmeel (1 Chron 2:29).

AHER The Benjaminite father of the Hushites (1 Chron 7:12).

AHI "Brother of Yah." Perhaps an abbreviation of AHIJAH.

1. The name of ABDIEL's son in the Gadite tribe (1 Chron 5:15).

2. One of SHEMER's sons in Asher's tribe (1 Chron 7:34).

AHIAH A leader who supported Nehemiah's reform (Neh 10:26 [Heb. 10:27]).

AHIAM The son of Sharar (2 Sam 23:33) or of Sachar the Hararite (1 Chron 11:35); one of David's "Thirty."

AHIAN One of SHEMIDA's four sons in the tribe of Manasseh (1 Chron 7:19).

AHIEZER "The (divine) brother helps."

1. Son of AMMISHADDAI who represented the tribe of Dan during Moses' census (Num 1:12), presented offerings for the dedication of the altar in

the covenant dwelling (Num 7:66, 71), and led the Danite troops (Num 2:25; 10:25).

2. Head of the Benjaminite archer/slingers who joined David at ZIKLAG (1 Chron 12:3).

AHIHUD "Brother of majesty."

1. SHELOMI's son and a leader of the Asher tribe who received a portion of land according to Moses' allocations (Num 34:27).

2. Son of the Benjaminite GERA or Heglam (1 Chron 8:7).

AHIJAH 1. A priest who accompanied King Saul and his troops when they were at Gibeah, defending Israel against the Philistines (1 Sam 14:3-18). His apparent function was to make inquiries of God.

2. A high official in King Solomon's administration who served as secretary (1 Kgs 4:3).

3. A prophet from Shiloh who gave Jeroboam divine authorization to lead the northern tribes in secession from Davidic rule and foretold the dissolution of the united monarchy (1 Kgs 11:29-39). Ahijah also predicted the death of Jeroboam's son (1 Kgs 14:2-18).

4. The father of Baasha. Baasha became the third king of Israel after he overthrew Nadab the son of Jeroboam I (1 Kgs 15:27, 33; 21:22; and 2 Kgs 9:9).

5. The fourth son of Jerahmeel son of Hezron son of Perez son of Judah by Tamar (1 Chron 2:25).

6. The second son of Ehud son of Bela son of Benjamin (1 Chron 8:7).

7. One of David's renowned warriors (1 Chron 11:36).

8. A Levite in David's time who had charge of the treasuries of God's house, according to the Hebrew of 1 Chron 26:20. However, the Greek reads "their fellow Levites," and this may be the better reading.

AHIKAM The son of Shaphan (2 Kgs 22:12) and father of Gedaliah (2 Kgs 25:22), Ahikam was an official of King Josiah sent to the prophetess HULDAH after the Instruction scroll was found (2 Kgs 22:14; 2 Chron 34:20). Afterward, he protected Jeremiah against JEHOIAKIM and his followers (Jer 26:24).

AHILUD Father of Jeshoshaphat, recorder during the reigns of David and Solomon (2 Sam 8:16; 20:24; 1 Kgs 4:3). Ahilud was also the father of Baana, one of the twelve officers of Solomon (1 Kgs 4:12). Scholars believe that these two Ahiluds were the same person.

AHIMAAZ 1. The son of Zadok, David's chief priest, who plays an important role in the royal house's victory over the rebellious son Absalom (2 Sam 15–18).

2. The father of Saul's wife Ahinoam (1 Sam 14:50).

3. Solomon's son-in-law, one of the twelve district officials (1 Kgs 4:15).

AHIMAN 1. Descendant of Anak (Num 13:22; Josh 15:14; Judg 1:10). Anak was one of the giants called NEPHILIM (Num 13:33; Gen 6:4).

2. A Levite who was one of four gatekeepers in the second temple (1 Chron 9:17).

AHIMELECH 1. A priest of Nob. David tricks Ahimelech into giving him bread and a sword by telling him that Saul had sent David on a secret mission (1 Sam 21:1-9). Saul accuses Ahimelech of conspiring with David (1 Sam 22:9-19). Saul does not believe Ahimelech's genuine protestations of innocence and has all of the priests killed.

2. A Hittite who would not follow David into Saul's camp (1 Sam 26:6).

3. "Abiathar's son Ahimelech," who helped Zadok organize the priestly class (1 Chron 18:16; 24:3-6).

AHIMOTH "My brother is Mot (death)." ELKANAH's son, a descendant of Kohath within the Levite tribe (1 Chron 6:25).

AHINADAB The son of IDDO and one of

Solomon's officers who was in charge of the southern part of Transjordan (1 Kgs 4:14).

AHINOAM 1. Daughter of AHIMAAZ wife of King Saul, mother of JONATHAN, ISHVI, MALCHISHUA, MERAB, and MICHAL (1 Sam 14:49-50).

2. One of DAVID's wives, a Jezreelite. She may be the same woman as Saul's wife Ahinoam (1 Sam 25:43; 27:3; 30:5; 2 Sam 2:2; 3:2; 1 Chron 3:1).

AHIO 1. AMINADAB's (ABINADAB's) son and UZZAH's brother (2 Sam 6:3-4; 1 Chron 13:7) who assisted in carrying the chest of God.

2. ELPAAL's son in the Benjamin tribe (1 Chron 8:14).

3. JEIEL and MAACAH's son in the Benjamin tribe (1 Chron 8:31; 9:37).

AHIRA Son of Enan, leader of the Naphtali tribe, assigned to assist Moses in the census (Num 1:15). Ahira was also in charge of the miltary troops of Naphtali from Sinai to Palestine (Num 10:27).

AHIRAM Ahiram is the third of Benjamin's five sons who would inhabit the land with his family the Ahiramites, according to the census list in Num 26:38. Probable variant spellings are AHARAH, Benjamin's third son (1 Chron 8:1); AHER, father of of the Hushites (1 Chron 7:12); and EHI, the sixth of ten sons of Benjamin (Gen 46:21).

AHISAMACH "My (divine) brother has supported." From the tribe of Dan, Ahisamach was the father of OHOLIAB, one of the skilled workers assigned to design and make the covenant dwelling and its furnishings (Exod 31:6; 35:34; 38:23).

AHISHAHAR One of the sons of BILHAN of the family of Jediael, Ahishahar was a Benjaminite warrior who was the chief of a subclan of Jediael, according to the genealogy found in 1 Chron 7:10-12.

AHISHAR "My brother has sung." Overseer of Solomon's palace household (1 Kgs 4:6).

AHITHOPHEL A counselor of David and supporter of Absalom in his rebellion. Speaking with him "was like asking for a word from God," so he was highly valued first by David and then by Absalom (2 Sam 16:23). When Absalom ignored his advice, Ahithophel knew that the coup would fail, so he committed suicide (17:23).

AHITUB "My (divine) brother is good."

1. Father of AHIJAH in 1 Sam 14:3, but father of AHIMELECH and grandfather of ABIATHAR in 1 Sam 22:9-20.

2. Father of Zadok and grandfather of AHIMAAZ (2 Sam 8:17; 1 Chron 6:7-8, 52-53; 18:16).

3. Father (1 Chron 6:12; Ezra 7:2) or grandfather of a different Zadok (1 Chron 9:11; Neh 11:11).

4. Ancestor of JUDITH (Jdt 8:1).

AHLAB City in the region of Asher where the Canaanites were allowed to remain (Judg 1:31), northeast of Tyre, near the coast; also called Mahalab (Josh 19:29).

AHLAI 1. The son of SHESHAN (1 Chron 2:31). However, 1 Chron 2:34-35 says Sheshan had no sons, only daughters. Perhaps the name Sheshan appears in two different genealogies: the genealogy of the descendants of Jerahmeel (1 Chron 2:25-33) and the genealogy of Seshan's descendants (1 Chron 2:34-41). Or perhaps Ahlai was Sheshan's daughter.

2. The father of ZABAD, one of David's warriors who gave their full support to his kingship (1 Chron 11:41).

AHOAH Son of BELA and grandson of Benjamin in the Benjamin tribe (1 Chron 8:4), the name may have originally been AHIJAH. The same person is referred to as AHIJAH in 1 Chron 8:7.

AHOHI Father of DODO and grandfather of ELEAZAR (2 Sam 23:9).

AHUMAI Ahumai is a descendant of Judah, a son of JAHATH and grandson of REAIAH (1 Chron 4:2).

AHUZZAM "Possessor." A son of Ashhur (1 Chron 4:6).

AHUZZATH Adviser of King Abimelech of Gerar. Ahuzzath and Phicol accompanied their sovereign when he wished to make a covenant with Isaac at Beersheba (Gen 26:26).

AHZAI Son of Meshillemoth, a priest in Jerusalem when Nehemiah rebuilt the city's walls (Neh 11:13).

AI A Canaanite town near Bethel (Gen 12:8; 13:3; Josh 7–8; Ezra 2:28; Neh 7:32; Jer 49:3). Biblical Ai today is almost universally identified with Khirbet et-Tell ("ruin of the tell"), which is located about 9 mi. northeast of Jerusalem. Ai is used as a reference point for the location of Abram's altar at the oak of Moreh. In the biblical narratives the town is most well-known for the conquest account in Josh 7–8 where Yahweh orders Joshua to kill all the inhabitants of Ai except for the livestock and the spoils of the town.

AIAH "Hawk."

1. One of Zibeon's sons (Gen 36:24; 1 Chron 1:40).

2. The father of Rizpah, Saul's secondary wife. She became a pawn in the politics surrounding Saul's reign (2 Sam 3:6-11; 21:8-12).

AIJALON 1. A city allotted to the tribe of Dan (Josh 19:42; Judg 1:35) about 14 mi. northeast of Jerusalem. Joshua commanded the moon to stand still in the Aijalon Valley (Josh 10:12). The army of Saul and Jonathan defeated the Philistines at Aijalon (1 Sam 14:31), which was later fortified by Rehoboam against possible invasion from the northern kingdom (2 Chron 11:10).

2. A city of the tribe of Zebulun where Elon was buried (Judg 12:12).

AKAN Grandson of Seir the Horites. Brother of Bilhan and Zaavan (Gen 36:27). See JAAKAN.

AKKUB 1. Postexilic descendant of David (1 Chron 3:24).

2. The name Akkub also represents the head of a family of postexilic temple gatekeepers (1 Chron 9:17; Ezra 2:42; Neh 7:45; 11:19; 12:25).

3. The head of a family of temple servants (Ezra 2:45).

4. An expounder of the Law (Neh 8:7).

ALEMA Location in Gilead where Judas Maccabeus liberated captive Jews imprisoned by the surrounding Gentiles (1 Macc 5:26, 44).

ALEMETH 1. The grandson of Benjamin through Becher (1 Chron 7:8).

2. Saul's descendant through Jonathan's son Meribbaal (Mephibosheth). In the genealogies he is listed as either the son of Jehoaddah (1 Chron 8:36) or Jarah (1 Chron 9:42).

3. A levitical city in Benjamin (1 Chron 6:60 [Heb. 6:45]).

ALEXANDER 1. A coppersmith who lived in Troas (2 Tim 4:14) and "ruined [his] faith" (1 Tim 1:19-20). In 2 Tim 4:14, Paul refers to him as one who "really hurt me," perhaps as Paul's accuser before the Roman authorities that led to Paul's arrest (cf Acts 21:27).

2. A Jew mentioned in Acts 19:33-34 who tried to make a defense before the crowd in the theater.

3. The son of SIMON of Cyrene (Mark 15:21).

ALEXANDRIA Egyptian city founded by Alexander the Great (331 BCE) situated 14 mi. west of the Canopic branch of the Nile, in between the Mediterranean

Sea and Lake Mareotis. APOLLOS, a Jew "instructed in the way of the Lord" (Acts 18:24-28), came from Alexandria.

ALLAMMELECH Town, possibly situated in the Plain of Acco, given to the Asher tribe (Josh 19:26) when Joshua apportioned the remaining territories (Josh 18:10).

ALLON Name meaning "oak." Simeonite son of Jedaiah and father of Shiphi (1 Chron 4:37); a priest at the time of King Hezekiah.

ALLON-BACUTH Located near Bethel, the burial site of REBEKAH's nurse DEBORAH, was named Allon-Bacuth, which means the "oak of weeping" (Gen 35:8).

ALMODAD The first son of Joktan, a sixth-generation descendant of Shem and one of seventy descendants of Noah (Gen 10:26).

ALMOND. Almonds were one of the gifts sent by Jacob to Egypt (Gen 43:11). Aaron's staff produced almonds overnight as a sign of Yahweh's choice (Num 17:8-13). The cups of the lampstand in the covenant dwelling looked like almond blossoms (Exod 25:33-34; 37:19-20).

ALMS, ALMSGIVING Almsgiving is a benevolent activity for the poor and needy given out of compassion, mercy, and pity. In the OT, there are various forms of relief for the poor, including the prescription of the second tithe for the poor in the third and sixth years of every sabbatical cycle (Deut 14:28-29; 26:12) and the Sabbath law on cultivation of crops, by which God commanded the Israelites to let the land lie unused during the seventh year, so that the poor might get food from it (Exod 23:10-11). In the NT, Jesus exhorts almsgiving in line with the teachings of the OT. According to the Gospels, a disciple of Jesus should give alms (Luke 11:41; 12:33; Matt 6:2-4; 19:21).

ALMUG A type of wood used in the construction of the temple of Solomon brought from Ophir by Hiram of Tyre. It was also used to make harps and lyres for the temple (1 Kgs 10:11-12).

ALOES References in the OT to aloes are most likely based on lign-aloes or eaglewood (Aquilaria agallocha), a tree native to northern Burma and Malaysia. It was used, along with myrrh and cassia, to perfume robes (Ps 45:8 [9]) or, along with cinnamon and myrrh, to freshen the bed (Prov 7:17). While the resin has a distinct and pleasing odor, it is sweeter when burned as incense like frankincense and myrrh (Song 4:14). The NT story of Nicodemus's use of myrrh and aloe to anoint Jesus' body after the crucifixion (John 19:39) refers to another plant (Aloe vera) native to southwest Arabia.

ALPHA AND OMEGA The first and last letters of the Greek alphabet, used metaphorically as God's self-description (Rev 1:8; 21:6) and that of Jesus (Rev 22:13) in the visions of Revelation.

ALPHAEUS 1. Father of Levi the tax collector or customs officer of Herod Antipas (Mark 2:14).

2. In Mark 3:18 (Matt 10:3; Luke 6:15; Acts 1:13), JAMES (sometimes called "the less") son of Alphaeus is distinguished from James son of Zebedee and brother of John. Without convincing evidence, this James has been associated with CLOPAS (John 19:25) or CLEOPAS (Luke 24:18).

ALTAR A place for sacrifice. Offerings were sacrificed at the altar, and the people of God joined in celebrating the divine pleasure in this sacred and communal meal, a feast that they also shared with each other. The Hebrew word for altar, derived from the root meaning "to slaughter," suggests that originally the altar was the place where the slaughter of animals for sacrifice occurred (Gen 22:9). In the Bible, however, animals are never sacrificed on the altar, but offerings of things not slaughtered (grain, wine, incense) are made on altars. Three types of material were used for building altars: earth, stone, and metal. The law on altars in Exod 20:24-26 stipulates three conditions: (a) they are to be built of earth or stone; (b) if from stone, it must be unworked; (c) altars were to be built without steps. No OT laws mention altars made of metal, but there were two in the Jerusalem temple (Exod 27:1-8; 30:1-5; 37:25-28; 38:1-7). In the NT, Revelation speaks of a heavenly altar in the heavenly sanctuary (Rev 6:9; 8:3-5).

ALVAH According to Gen 36:40, Alvah is the name of one of the Esau/Edom tribal chiefs.

ALVAN Ancestor of a Horite subclan in Edom, first son of Shobal and grandson of Seir (Gen 36:23; Alian in 1 Chron 1:40).

AMAL A warrior son of Helem of the tribe of Asher (1 Chron 7:35).

AMALEK, AMALEKITES Amalekites were descendants of Amalek, Esau's grandson born to Eliphaz and his secondary wife Timna (Gen 36:12, 16; 1 Chron 1:36). They are one of the peoples living in and around Canaan and are described as opponents of the Israelites as they moved from Egypt into the wilderness (Exod 17:8-16). They remained enemies after Israel's settlement in the promised land. A deep-seated enmity existed between Amalek and Israel that pervades most references to them.

AMAM A town allocated to the territory of the tribe of Judah (Josh 15:26).

AMANA Mountain located near or in the Lebanon mountains and south of the valley of the Amana River (2 Kgs 5:12 footnote; Song 4:8).

AMARIAH 1. A Levite, high priest (1 Chron 6:7, 52 [Heb. 5:33; 6:37]), and descendant of Aaron, he was the son of MERAIOTH and the father of AHITUB and the grandfather of Zadok the high priest during David's reign.

2. A Levite and high priest and descendant of Aaron through ELEAZAR (1 Chron 6:11 [Heb. 5:37]), the son of AZARIAH (also high priest; 1 Chron 6:10 [Heb. 5:36]) and the father of Ahitub (II) and grandfather of Zadok (II), Amariah appears as an ancestor in EZRA's genealogy (Ezra 7:3; 1 Esdr 8:2; 2 Esdr 1:2).

3. A Levite from the Kohathites clan, Hebron's second son (1 Chron 23:19; 24:23), selected to serve among David's twenty-four Levite divisions.

4. A Levite called "the chief priest," active in the political and religious reforms of JEHOSHAPHAT and appointed to have authority over temple matters (2 Chron 19:11).

5. A Levite, one of the six people King HEZEKIAH appointed to distribute freewill offerings to the Levites living in priestly cities outside Jerusalem (2 Chron 31:15).

6. Son of Hezekiah (possibly King Hezekiah) and father of GEDALIAH and one of the ancestors of the prophet Zephaniah (Zeph 1:1).

7. The son of Shephatiah and father of Zechariah, a Judahite and descendant of the family of PEREZ. After the Babylonian exile, ATHAIAH, a descendant of Amariah, was among those who settled in Jerusalem (Neh 11:4).

8. One of the priests who returned from Babylon with ZERUBBABEL (Neh 12:2), he appears to have been identical with the father of JEHOHANAN, one of the leaders of the ancestral houses in the days of the high priest JOIAKIM (Neh 12:13).

9. A priest among those who signed a postexilic community agreement to keep the Law of Moses (Neh 10:3).

10. A descendant of BINNUI and

one of the Jews who divorced his Gentile wife, whom he had married after the people's return from their exile in Babylon (Ezra 10:42).

AMASA 1. A military leader who led Absolom's troops during the rebellion (2 Sam 17:25). After the uprising had been crushed, David forgave Amasa and put him in charge of the royal troops (19:13). This angered Joab, and when the two men met on the road in pursuit of another rebel, Joab seized Amasa as if to kiss him but then plunged a sword into his gut (20:8-13).

2. An Israelite soldier who opposes the taking of Judean booty in Israel's war with Judah during the time of Ahaz (2 Chron 28:12).

AMASAI 1. A Kohathite listed in the genealogies (1 Chron 6:25).

2. A Benjaminite or Judahite who was chief of David's Thirty (1 Chron 12:18).

3. A priest appointed by David to blow the trumpet in front of the covenant chest (1 Chron 15:24).

4. The father of Mahath, a priest and Kohathite, who took part in the reforms of Hezekiah (2 Chron 29:12).

AMASHSAI A postexilic priest, the son of Azarel and grandson of Ahzai (Neh 11:13). In a parallel account his name occurs as Maasai son of Adiel (1 Chron 9:12). Both lists trace him back to Immer, a levitical priest descended from Eleazar (1 Chron 24:4, 14).

AMASIAH "Yahu has carried." A commander in Jehoshaphat's army, a son of Zichri of Judah (2 Chron 17:16).

AMAZIAH 1. A descendant of DAVID, Amaziah was the ninth ruler of the southern kingdom of Judah ca. 800–783 BCE (2 Kgs 14:1-20). He receives qualified praise: "He did what was right in the LORD's eyes, but not as well as his ancestor King David" (2 Kgs 14:3). He is commended for showing his regard for justice by executing his father's assassins but sparing their children according to Mosaic law (Deut 24:16). After defeating Edom in battle, Amaziah challenges King Joash of Israel (2 Kgs 14:8). They meet for battle at BETH-SHEMESH, 16 mi. southwest of Jerusalem. Amaziah is defeated, abandoned by his troops, and captured.

2. Levitical song leader (1 Chron 6:31-32, 45).

3. Priest at Bethel who informed King Jeroboam of Amos's prophecy (Amos 7:10-13).

AMEN A term of ratification, amen has passed from Hebrew to Greek to English and other languages in transliteration but is often untranslated. The Hebraic root indicates trustworthiness or firmness concerning what is said. Revelation 3:14 designates Christ himself as "the Amen, the faithful and true witness," with the implication that, in Christ, believers find authenticity and the incarnate ratification of God's covenant. First Corinthians 14:16 reveals that to say amen in the Christian assembly is to concur with that which has been spoken by another. This liturgical use of amen arose when no printed prayer books or hymnals existed, but congregational worship in synagogue and church had to actively involve all participants. Therefore, what an individual uttered in prayer or preaching was affirmed by the assembly; a congregational amen was one way of guaranteeing such participation.

AMINADAB 1. The son of Aram and the father of Nahshon (Matt 1:4). The name is elsewhere rendered AMMINADAB.

2. The father of Esther (Add Esth 2:7, 15; 9:29). According to Hebrew manuscripts, Esther's father was ABIHAIL.

AMITTAI The father of Jonah (2 Kgs 14:25; Jonah 1:1).

AMMAH A hill east of Gibeon where

JOAB and DAVID's forces face ABNER and Ishbaal's men. Abner, who killed Joab's brother ASAHEL while attempting to flee from the battle of Gibeon, ironically appeals to Joab to end hostilities because of the close relationship between the two sides (2 Sam 2:24-32).

AMMI Ammi is the second name given to Hosea and GOMER's son (Hos 2:1 [Heb. 2:3]). Originally named Lo-Ammi ("Not My People") by God to reflect the broken covenant with the northern kingdom, the name was modified to Ammi ("My People"), suggesting Israel's restoration.

AMMIEL 1. GEMALLI's son, chosen by Moses as one of the spies (Num 13:12).

2. Father of MACHIR, who housed MEPHIBOSHETH, JONATHAN's son, and later brought food for DAVID, who fled from ABSALOM (2 Sam 9:4-5; 17:29).

3. Father of BATH-SHUA (1 Chron 3:5; perhaps ELIAM, father of BATH-SHEBA [2 Sam 11:3]).

4. OBED-EDOM's sixth son, one of the temple gatekeepers (1 Chron 26:5).

AMMIHUD 1. An Ephraimite, the father of ELISHAMA (Num 1:10; 7:53), leader of the Ephraimites (Num 2:18; 7:48; 10:22).

2. A member of the tribe of Simeon (Num 34:20) who helped Moses apportion Canaan to the tribes.

3. A member of the tribe of Naphtali (Num 34:28) who helped apportion Canaan for Israel's tribes.

4. The father of TALMAI, king of Geshur, with whom Absalom found refuge from King David (2 Sam 13:37).

5. A postexilic Jerusalemite descended from Judah (1 Chron 9:4).

AMMINADAB 1. The father of Elisheba, Aaron's wife (Exod 6:23), and the father of Nahshon, a Judahite leader (Num 1:7; 2:3; 7:12, 17; 10:14). His descendants include BOAZ (Ruth 4:19, 20; 1 Chron 2:10). The genealogies of Jesus include Amminadab (Luke 3:33; AMINADAB in Matt 1:4).

2. A Levite son of Kohath (1 Chron 6:22 [Heb. 6:7]).

3. Son of UZZIEL, who was summoned to move the covenant chest to Jerusalem (1 Chron 15:10-11).

AMMISHADDAI Ammishaddai appears in this text only as the father of AHIEZER, leader of the Danites (Num 1:12; 2:25; 7:66, 71; 10:25). *Shaddai* is often translated as "almighty."

AMMIZABAD Son of BENAIAH, Ammizabad commanded his father's division of 24,000 troops, who were part of the monthly levy (1 Chron 27:6). Benaiah was the commander of the Thirty, also known as David's warriors.

AMMON, AMMONITES A tribal people living east of the Jordan River. A reflection of their history is preserved in the name Amman, the modern capital of Jordan. In the OT the ancestor of the Ammonites is Ben-ammi, a product of an incestuous union between Lot and his two daughters (Gen 19:30-38). The Ammonites play a role in the biblical accounts of wilderness wandering and settlement in the promised land. Indeed, they are noted periodically throughout the historical and prophetic books, though less so in references to the postexilic period. Both Saul and David fight against the Ammonites (1 Sam 11:1-13; 2 Sam 10:1–11:25; 12:26-31). Saul was able to muster an army and defeat the Ammonites led by Nahash.

AMNON 1. The oldest son of DAVID and AHINOAM (2 Sam 3:2). His name, ironically, means "faithful." Amnon rapes and discards his half sister TAMAR (2 Sam 13; a violation of laws in Exod 22:16; Lev 18:9-11; and Deut 22:28-29; 27:22). David refuses to punish him, one of several stories of David's failure to hold himself and his family accountable to

Israelite laws. In retribution ABSALOM, Tamar's full brother, orders his servants to kill Amnon.

2. A son of Shimon in the list of Judahite descendants (1 Chron 4:20).

AMOK A priest and the ancestor of a priestly group who returned to Jerusalem with Zerubbabel from exile (Neh 12:7, 20).

AMON 1. Samaria's governor under King AHAB of Israel. Ahab turned the prophet Micaiah over to Amon and Joash (1 Kgs 22:24-28).

2. King of Judah after the death of his father Manasseh. Although the name means "faithful," Amon, like his father before him, worshipped other gods. Amon came to the throne at the age of 22 and reigned for two years (ca. 642–640 BCE), then was assassinated (2 Kgs 21:19-26; 2Chron 33:21-25).

3. One of Solomon's servants, whose descendants returned from the Babylonian exile (Neh 7:59; "Ami" in Ezra 2:57).

AMORITES A term for people in and around the land of Canaan. On occasion, it is used as a general reference to pre- and non-Israelite inhabitants; at other times it is used to describe a segment, that is, one population group among several inhabiting the land of Canaan before the Israelite settlement in the land.

AMOS Josiah's father; Manasseh's son (Matt 1:10). Manuscript evidence is divided between Amos and Amon. Amos with Asaph (Matt 1:8) symbolizes prophets and psalms within the Davidic genealogy.

AMOS, BOOK OF Among the prophets in ancient Israel, Amos was the first to be associated with a book that preserves his words. For the first time we see an extensive collection of recorded prophecies associated with a prophet. Paradoxically, however, very little personal information is available concerning the prophet himself in contrast to some of the earlier prophetic figures such as Ahijah, Elijah, and Elisha. Because of the paucity of the information, that which is available has been subjected to close scrutiny.

AMOZ Isaiah's father (2 Kgs 19:2, 20; 20:1; 2 Chron 26:22; 32:20, 32; Isa 1:1; 2:1; 13:1; 20:2; 37:2, 21; 38:1). In rabbinical traditions, brother of Judean king Amaziah.

AMPHIPOLIS An ancient city in Macedonia on the east bank of the Strymon River about 3 mi. from the Aegean Sea. On Paul's second missionary journey, Paul and Silas passed through this city and probably preached there, while traveling along the Egnatian Way from PHILIPPI to THESSALONICA (Acts 17:1). This route was the main overland connection between important ports that linked Greece and Italy.

AMPLIATUS A Christian greeted by Paul as "my dear friend in the Lord" (Rom 16:8), whom Paul may have met and befriended in the eastern part of the Roman Empire. The name is typical for slaves or freedmen, which is suggestive of Ampliatus's possible social background.

AMRAM, AMRAMITES 1. The father of Aaron, MOSES, and MIRIAM (Exod 6:20). Amram's father was Kohath, one of Levi's sons (Exod 6:18-20; Num 26:59; 1 Chron 6:2-3 [Heb. 5:27-29]).

2. Amramites were Kohathite Levites whose responsibilities for the sanctuary included caring for the covenant chest and altars (Num 3:27-31; 1 Chron 23:12-13).

3. In Ezra 10:34, one of the priests who promised to reject their foreign wives.

AMRAPHEL King of SHINAR, and one of the four kings led by CHEDORLAOMER in his western campaign against cities in the Dead Sea region

(Gen 14:1, 9). Shinar is a name for Babylon, seen first in the Bible in the genealogy of nations in Gen 10:10 and in the story of the building of the Tower of Babel (Gen 11:1-9).

AMZI 1. A Levite of Merari's family; son of Bani, father of Hilkiah, and grandfather of Amaziah; ancestor of Ethan the musician (1 Chron 6:44-46).

2. A priest, son of Zechariah, an ancestor of Adaiah in Neh 11:12, but not mentioned among Adaiah's ancestors in 1 Chron 9:12.

ANAEL See HANAEL.

ANAH 1. The father of OHOLIBAMAH, one of Esau's Canaanite wives, Anah was son of ZIBEON and grandson of SEIR the Horite (Gen 36:2, 24; 1 Chron 1:40).

2. Anah is also named as a son of Seir (Gen 36:20; 1 Chron 1:38). One of the Horite clans bore Anah's name (Gen 36:29).

ANAHARATH Town given to tribe of Issachar (Josh 19:19) when Joshua apportioned the territories (Josh 18:10). Located south of EN-DOR.

ANAIAH One of six men standing beside Ezra when he read from the Scroll of Moses to the assembly (Neh 8:4). He is one of the leaders of the people who set their seal to the covenant (Neh 10:22).

ANAK, ANAKIM, ANAKITES 1. The son of Arba, named as the ancestor of the Anakim or Anakites (Josh 15:13; 21:11).

2. An area in or around Hebron (also called Kiriath-arba, "the city of Arba") named for Anak. The area is in Judah's central highlands to the middle west of the Dead Sea, south of Jerusalem. Most references name Caleb as the conqueror of Anakite land (Josh 14:12; 15:13-14; 21:12; Judg 1:20). Joshua 21:11 reports that as part of the Levites' allotment of land, the city was settled by Aaronide Kohathites.

3. The inhabitants of Anak called Anakim and Anakites (the sons of Anak, Num 13:22, 28; Deut 1:28; 9:2). The spies to Cannan were frightened by the great stature of the Anakim, who were said to be descendents of the Nephilim (Gen 6:4; Num 13:33). In some places, the Anakim serve as a point of comparison for great height (Deut 2:10, 21).

ANAMIM One of the offspring of EGYPT in the genealogy of nations, the descendants of NOAH, in Gen 10:13; 1 Chron 1:11.

ANAMMELECH A deity worshipped by the people of Sepharvaim who relocated to Samaria after 722 BCE and the reign of Sargon II. In Samaria, Anammelech worship included child sacrifice (2 Kgs 17:31).

ANAN A leader who placed his name on the sealed covenant document (Neh 10:26).

ANANI Elioenai's seventh son (1 Chron 3:24), listed among David's and Zerubbabel's descendants in 1 Chron 3:1-24.

ANANIAH 1. The father of MAASEIAH, whose son AZARIAH participated in repairing the walls of Jerusalem near his own house under NEHEMIAH's leadership (Neh 3:23).

2. A Benjaminite village where Jewish exiles settled upon returning to the land (Neh 11:31-32), probably named for family members of Ananiah living there, hence the NT's name for the town, BETHANY.

ANANIAS 1. Ananias, together with his wife Sapphira, donated profits from a property sale to the Jerusalem church (Acts 4:34–5:1). However, this couple "withheld some of the proceeds" while claiming to contribute the full amount (5:2). When Peter exposed this pretense as a lie against God and the Holy Spirit, Ananias dropped dead on the spot. The same fate befell Sapphira, provoking terror and "trepidation and dread" throughout the congregation (5:5, 11).

2. A disciple of Christ (Acts 9:10) and well-known adherent to the Jewish Law (22:12), Ananias of Damascus was instrumental in transforming Saul of Tarsus from a violent opponent of the early church to its leading missionary (9:1-19; 22:12-16). Guided by a vision of the risen Lord, Ananias met Saul in Judas's house on Straight Street, restored Saul's sight and imparted the Spirit through laying on of hands, directed Saul to be baptized, and relayed his divine commission to be Christ's "witness" (22:15).

3. Appointed high priest by Herod Agrippa II in 48 CE, Ananias the son of Nebedeus presided over the Jewish council that judged Paul after his arrest in the temple (Acts 23:1-5; 21:27–22:29). Upon hearing Paul's confession, Ananias ordered bystanders to strike Paul's mouth (23:1-2). In turn, Paul lashed back at Ananias, invoking God's discipline against "you whitewashed wall" (23:3).

ANASIB Progenitor of a family group of priests who returned to Jerusalem after Darius conquered the Babylonians (1 Esdr 5:24). Nine hundred seventy-two priests descended from Anasib through Jedaiah. Compare Ezra 2:36 and Neh 7:39.

ANATH 1. Anath is a warrior goddess in Canaanite religion, the consort of the storm god Baal, with whom she twice joins to fight against, first, a dragonlike deity of the sea and, second, the Canaanite god of sterility and death.

In the Bible, Anath appears only in a few place-names (Anathoth, Beth-anoth, and Beth-anath) and as part of some personal names (Shamgar son of Anath in Judg 3:31; 5:6; Anathoth; and Anthothijah). Anath's character as a warrior goddess, however, probably influenced the depictions of some of the Bible's warrior women, especially Deborah and Jael in Judg 5. They, similarly to Anath, fight alongside a male deity, Yahweh, who uses the storm as his weapon (Judg 5:4-5, 20-21). The woman of Thebez in Judg 9:50-57 also, like Anath, uses a millstone as a weapon to defeat an enemy.

2. SHAMGAR's father (Judg 3:31; 5:6), although this may be a theophoric rather than a personal name.

ANATHOTH 1. A levitical city within the territory of Benjamin (Josh 21:18; 1 Chron 6:60 [Heb. 6:45]) whose biblical name is preserved in the name of the modern village of Anata and whose probable site is Ras el-Kharrubeth. ABIATHAR was banished to Anathoth by SOLOMON because he supported ADONIJAH (1 Kgs 2:26). The city was the birthplace of the prophet Jeremiah (Jer 1:1; 11:21-23; 29:27; 32:7-9), possibly linking Jeremiah to Abiathar. Anathoth was the native place of ABIEZER (2 Sam 23:27; 1 Chron 11:28) and JEHU, two of David's mighty men. Citizens of Anathoth returned with ZERUBBABEL from Babylonian exile (Ezra 2:23; Neh 7:27; 1 Esdr 5:18).

2. The eighth of the nine sons of BECHER the son of Benjamin (1 Chron 7:8).

3. One of the leaders in the postexilic community who signed a document pledging to keep God's Law (Neh 10:19).

ANCESTOR See FATHER.

ANCIENT ONE In his vision of divine judgment, Daniel sees a celestial court, where a certain "ancient one" sits enthroned to attend to the threat of cosmic chaos represented by terrible monsters arising from the sea (Dan 7:1-14).

ANDREW Andrew is first mentioned in the Gospel of Mark as the brother of Simon Peter (Mark 1:16). He appears twelve times in the NT, four times in the Gospels among the lists of apostles (Mark 3:18; Matt 10:2; Luke 6:14; Acts 1:13), and always among the first four names in these lists (Peter, Andrew,

James, and John). Among the Gospels, Mark and John give Andrew the most attention. In Mark's gospel, Andrew is one of the first disciples to be called by Jesus along with Peter (1:16-18), is present when Jesus cures Peter's mother-in-law (1:29-31), and is among the few (Peter, James, and John) to hear Jesus predict the destruction of the temple (13:3-4).

ANER In Gen 14:13, Aner and his brothers MAMRE and ESHCOL join with Abram against CHEDORLAOMER, king of Elam. Genesis Apocryphan (22:6) describes an active role for the brothers in battle.

ANGEL While Hebrew and Greek words designate messengers both human and heavenly, in the English Bible, angels are spiritual beings.

ANGELS OF THE SEVEN CHURCHES Mentioned only in Rev 1:20 and addressed individually in letters to the churches (Rev 2:1, 8, 12, 18; 3:1, 7, 14), these angels have been identified as guardian angels of the churches and as heavenly personifications of the churches on earth.

ANIAM In Manasseh's genealogy, Shemida's fourth son (1 Chron 7:19).

ANIM A city in the southern highlands near DEBIR, Anim was allotted to Judah (Josh 15:50).

ANKLETS Isaiah 3:18 and Jdt 10:4 describe women wearing anklets—bands of metal that encircled the ankle—along with other JEWELRY (e.g., bracelets, armlets, rings). Anklets were worn to enhance women's beauty and perhaps to attract attention with their tinkling sound.

ANNA 1. In the story of TOBIT, Anna supports her blind husband by weaving (women's work), responds angrily when he challenges the reward she received for her work, weeps when her son leaves them for a long journey, grieves and watches when her son returns late, and rejoices when he returns with a wife. Anna dies at an old age and her son buries her with her husband.

2. Anna's story is narrated as a parallel to Simeon's in Luke's infancy narrative (2:36-38). They both praise God because they recognize Jesus as the Christ, but Anna's words are not included. Anna is described as a prophetess, like Miriam or Deborah in the OT, or like others in Acts who fulfill the prophecy of Joel (Acts 2:17). Luke depicts her as pious, devoted to God, worshipping daily at the temple, praying, and fasting. She is very old, either 84 or widowed for 84 years (thus 105, if she was married at 14, as was customary). The latter is more likely. This characterization is like Judith (Jdt 16:23), and Elizabeth and Zechariah (Luke 1:6-7). Pious, celibate widows like Anna were important in the early church (1 Tim 5:3-16).

3. According to the postbiblical Christian tradition, Anna is the mother of Mary, so the grandmother of Jesus.

ANNAN Family head whose descendants sent their foreign wives and their children away as God's covenant required (1 Esdr 9:32).

ANNAS Annas son of Seth was high priest from 6 to 15 CE. Later, he continued to wield extraordinary power (Luke 3:2), interrogating Jesus (John 18) and serving in the SANHEDRIN (Acts 4).

ANNIAS The progenitor of a family who returned with Zerubbabel and other leaders to Jerusalem after the exile (1 Esdr 5:16).

ANNIUTH A Levite (1 Esdr 9:48). Named Bani in Neh 8:7.

ANNUNCIATION The term *annunciation* is often used in reference to the

Lukan birth narrative, wherein the angel Gabriel announces to the Virgin Mary that she will give birth to Jesus (Luke 1:26-38). The annunciation-type scene is well attested in the Bible and consists of the following elements: The future mother of a biblical hero is described as infertile or barren, or, in Mary's case, a virgin (Gen 16:1; 29:31; Judg 13:2; Luke 1:7).

An ANGEL, a visitor from God, or an oracle announces that the woman will bear a son (Gen 15:4-5; 18:9-15; 30:22; Judg 13:3-7; Luke 1:13-17).

The woman conceives and gives birth (Gen 21:1-7; 30:23; Judg 13:24; Luke 1:24, 57).

The extracanonical Protoevangelium of James narrates a variation of the Lukan annunciation to Mary, and also includes an announcement of Mary's own birth. See MAGNIFICAT.

ANNUNUS One of the priests procured to return to Jerusalem with Ezra in order to serve in the temple (1 Esdr 8:48). He is not included in the par. list in Ezra 8:19, one of several discrepancies between the accounts of Ezra 8 and 1 Esdr 8.

ANOINT Anointing is the application of oil to a person or object by smearing, pouring, or sprinkling. Both the OT and NT refer to common, nonritual, cosmetic or hygienic anointing (see, e.g., Ruth 3:3; 2 Sam 12:20; Ezek 16:9; Amos 6:6; Ps 23:5; Matt 6:17; Luke 7:46). In most of its occurrences in the OT, "anoint" indicates the ritual application of oil to persons or objects to mark or effect a change of identity or status.

ANT This insect crawls into the biblical text only twice, both times in the book of Proverbs (6:6; 30:25), where it is used to illustrate industriousness. There the ant exemplifies a key theme in Wisdom Literature—to be wise and prosperous, one need only observe the order of the natural world, then comport oneself accordingly.

ANTELOPE The antelope is a ruminant with permanent hollow horns that does not fit into the common categories of domesticated bovine animals such as oxen, goats, and sheep.

ANTHOTHIJAH According to Benjamin's genealogy in 1 Chron 8:1-40, he is one of Shashak's sons (8:24).

ANTICHRIST The Antichrist is the adversary of God and Christ that comes in the end times. According to some sources he deceives many into false faith, and according to others he harasses the people of God. The term *Antichrist* is not used in Revelation. It first appears in the Johannine Epistles (1 John 2:18, 22; 2 John 7), and writers from the 2nd cent. CE onward refer to the Antichrist as an agent of Satan, who combines traits of the man of lawlessness (2 Thess 2:1-3), the beast (Rev 13:1-10), and other enemies of God.

ANTI-LEBANON Parallel to the LEBANON range, the Anti-Lebanon mountains run north-south along the border between Lebanon and Syria, peaking to the south at Mount Hermon. In the Bible, only Judith mentions the range by name (Jdt 1:7).

ANTIOCH, PISIDIAN A Roman colony in northern Pisidia. It is located on one of the main Roman roads heading east-west from Ephesus and up the Maeander Valley, and then from Antioch eastward to Iconium and across the Taurus Mountains to Tarsus and Cilicia.

ANTIOCH, SYRIAN Antioch was the name of at least sixteen cities in the Greco-Roman period, five of which were located in SYRIA. The NT mentions Antioch of Pisidia (Acts 13; see ANTIOCH, PISIDIAN) and Antioch of Syria (Acts 6; 11; 13–15; 18; Gal 2; 2 Tim 3). The latter is also known as the Syrian Antioch or Antioch on the Orontes. It was the third-largest city in the Greco-Roman world behind

Rome and Alexandria (Egypt). The city of Antioch is mentioned several times in the NT. The disciples chose seven men, including Stephen and Nicolas from Antioch, to serve the Hellenists (Greek Jews) (Acts 6:5). Some Christians fleeing harassment in Jerusalem, following the stoning of Stephen, traveled as far as Phoenicia, Cyprus, and Antioch. In Antioch some of these refugees preached only to the Jews while others, originally from Cyprus and Cyrene, preached to Greek-speaking Gentiles as well (Acts 11:19-21). This activity resulted in many new converts. When news of this growth reached the Jerusalem leaders, they dispatched Barnabus to assess the situation (Acts 11:22). Finding things in good order, Barnabus then traveled to Tarsus and brought Paul, a native of that city, back to Antioch (Acts 11:25).

The name Christian was first used at Antioch to describe the followers of Christ (Acts 11:26). The Christians of Antioch collected funds for Judean famine relief and sent them with Paul and Barnabus to Jerusalem (Acts 11:27-30).

ANTIOCHIANS Citizens of Antioch.

ANTIOCHUS Antiochus was a frequent name of emperors of the Seleucids. The Seleucid dynasty began with Seleucus I (ca. 312–281 BCE), who was over Alexander's elite guard.

1. Antiochus I Soter (281–261 BCE) was the son of Seleucus I.

2. Antiochus II Theos (261–246 BCE) was the son of Antiochus I and instigator of the Second Syrian War (ca. 260–253 BCE) in which territory was gained in Asia Minor.

3. Antiochus III (223–187 BCE) was the younger brother of Seleucus III, later known as Antiochus the Great.

4. Antiochus IV Epiphanes (175–164 BCE) was the son of Antiochus III. Seleucus IV (187–175 BCE) had a rather undistinguished reign before the throne was taken by his brother Antiochus IV Epiphanes. This figure is infamous in history because of his attempt to suppress Judaism in Judah, and he features prominently in Jewish literature.

5. Antiochus V Eupator (164–162 BCE) was a minor son of Epiphanes who took the throne for a short rule that was more or less dictated by regents at the death of Epiphanes. Antiochus was plotted against by his cousin, the eldest son of Seleucus IV, who murdered him and succeeded to the throne as Demetrius I Soter (162–150 BCE).

It was during the next couple of decades that a new dynasty claimed to be the rightful heir to the Seleucid Empire (some of whose rulers were named Antiochus). The struggle between the two rival dynasties was a godsend to the struggling Maccabean rulership, who used it to establish an independent Jewish state.

6. Antiochus VI, Epiphanes Dionysus (145–142 BCE), was a rival to Demetrius II. In the resulting engagement Demetrius was defeated, and Jonathan Maccabee was able to make gains by throwing his lot in with Antiochus VI. But in 143 Trypho captured and killed both Jonathan and Antiochus VI, taking the throne for himself (ca. 142–138 BCE).

7. Antiochus VII Sidetes (138–129 BCE) was Demetrius's brother. Demetrius's wife Cleopatra sent for his brother to marry her and take the throne as Antiochus VII Sidetes. He attempted to bring Judah, now under the rule of Simon Maccabee, back under Seleucid control, but was defeated by Simon's sons. Some years later he besieged the Jewish ruler John Hyrcanus in Jerusalem in a dispute over Palestinian cities such as Joppa that Simon had taken from the Syrians, but agreement was finally reached. Antiochus VII was killed fighting for the Parthians and succeeded by his brother Demetrius II, who had already been king once before (145–140, 129–126 BCE).

8. Antiochus VIII Grypus (126–96 BCE) succeeded Demetrius and soon

ended Alexander's life. He did not attempt to go against Hyrcanus

9. Antiochus IX Cyzicenus (113–95 BCE) was the half brother of Antiochus VIII, who took the throne as a rival.

10. Antiochus X Eusebes Philopator (ca. 87–84 BCE) was a son of Antiochus IX.

11. Antiochus XI Epiphanes Philadelphus was a son of Antiochus VIII.

12. Antiochus XII Dionysus Epiphanes Philopator Callinicus (ca. 87–84 BCE) was the son of Antiochus XI. During the reign of Alexander Janneus (ca. 86 BCE), Judah was invaded by the army of yet another rival, a son of Antiochus XI. His aim, however, seems to have been only to march through to fight against Arabia.

13. Antiochus XIII Asiaticus (ca. 65–64 BCE) was placed briefly on the throne by the Romans but then removed by Pompey. Asiaticus was the last ruler over the Seleucid kingdom, which now came to an end, though it had been an empire in name only for many years. See DEMETRIUS; EPIPHANES; HASMONEANS; HYRCANUS; LYSIAS; MACCABEES, MACCABEAN REVOLT; SELEUCID EMPIRE; SIMON.

ANTIPAS 1. The second son of Herod I and Malthace, Antipas inherited Galilee and Perea on his father's death in 4 BCE. Footnotes to Luke 3:1 and Matt 14:1 identify him as "tetrach," though Mark 6:14-29 refers to him more loosely as "king." The NT calls him by his family name, "Herod."

2. Herod's Father. See ANTIPATER.

3. A martyr of the church at Pergamum (Rev 2:13).

ANTIPATER 1. Father of Herod the Great (ca. 100–43 BCE).

2. One of two envoys sent by JONATHAN, then by SIMON Maccabeus, to consolidate diplomatic ties with the Romans and the Spartans (1 Macc 12:16; 14:22; Josephus, *Ant.* 13.169). Antipater may have belonged to an ambassadorial family (see 1 Macc 8:17).

ANTIPATRIS Located at the source of the Yarkon River, approximately 12 km (7.5 mi.) east of Tel Aviv, Herod the Great enlarged and changed the name of the ancient city of APHEK to Antipatris to honor his father ANTIPATER in 9 BCE.

ANTONIA, FORTRESS Herod the Great built the Antonia at the northeast terminus of Jerusalem's second wall and named it for his patron Mark Antony. A short north-south wall tied it to the north wall of the temple complex, but later the northern expansion of the temple plaza put the Antonia on the northwest corner of the temple fortifications.

ANUB In Judah's genealogy, he is Koz's son (1 Chron 4:8).

APAME Apame is a secondary wife in the court of the Persian king DARIUS, who, after ZERUBBABEL's discourse on the strength of women, removes Darius's crown from his head, places it on hers, and slaps the king in the face (1 Esdr 4:29-31).

APHEK Aphek is mentioned several times in the Bible as the name of a place (Josh 12:18; 13:14; 19:30; 1 Sam 4:1; 29:1; 1 Kgs 20:26, 30; 2 Kgs 13:17) and refers to varying locations.

Aphek of the Sharon plain (Josh 12:18; 1 Sam 4:1, 12) is about 30 acres and lies at the headwaters of the Yarkon River.

APHEKAH A city in the allotment Joshua gave Judah (Josh 15:53), most likely identical with Aphek (Josh 12:18) and Aphik (Judg 1:31). The king of this royal Canaanite city was defeated by Joshua and the Israelites (Josh 12:7, 18).

APHERRA One of several heads of families who were descendants of Solomon's servants and altogether numbered 372 (1 Esdr 5:34).

APHIAH A Benjaminite ancestor of King Saul (1 Sam 9:1).

APHIK City in the tribe of Asher whose Canaanite inhabitants were not driven out (Judg 1:31). Place of worship of Aphrodite.

APOCALYPSE The Greek term *apocalypse* means "revelation" or "disclosure." An apocalypse consists of visions, auditions, and dreams, whereby the divine world and its secrets are uncovered, revealed, or opened up to the seer.

See APOCALYPTICISM.

APOCALYPTICISM A cluster of religious ideas, some of which were found in revelatory texts like Daniel and Revelation. Apocalypticism is frequently seen as a form of eschatology, with well-defined characteristics: (1) hope for a better world, and with a belief that God's kingdom will break into history, which then leads to history's end; (2) dualism (contrast between the present evil age and a glorious future); exotic symbolism (e.g., Dan 7); (3) an eschatological expectation in which a dramatic transformation of this sinful age will lead to the inauguration of a heavenly kingdom; (4) the stark contrast between the present evil age and the glorious future suggesting a sectarian ethos, in which communities had cut themselves off from wider society and awaited a divine reordering of the world; (5) the imminent end of this world; and (6) a deterministic view of history.

APOCRYPHA, DEUTEROCANONICAL The Apocrypha is a collection of books written by Jewish authors between the 3rd cent. BCE and 1st cent. CE. Their identification as a discrete collection (set apart from the Pseudepigrapha, Dead Sea Scrolls, the works of Philo, etc.) is due largely to the high value placed on these books by Christian readers throughout the millennia and long-standing historic debates concerning their place in the Christian canon. These books include Tobit, Judith, a Greek version of Esther containing additions, the Wisdom of Solomon, Sirach, Baruch, the Letter of Jeremiah, Additions to Daniel, 1 Maccabees, 2 Maccabees, 1 Esdras, the Prayer of Manasseh, Psalm 151, 3 Maccabees, 2 Esdras, and 4 Maccabees.

APOCRYPHA, NT The NT Apocrypha comprises a heterogeneous group of texts initially gathered together by European scholars in the 16th cent. CE. These texts include other gospels and acts of apostles, as well as other documents.

APOLLONIA A Macedonian city named for the Greek god Apollo. Apollonia was centrally located on the Egnatian Way, the Roman-built east-west route for travel from Italy to the province of Asia. Paul and SILAS passed through Apollonia on their way to THESSALONICA (Acts 17:1).

APOLLONIUS 1. Son of Thraseas, governor of Coele-Syria and Phoenicia (2 Macc 3:5), who urged the despoiling of the temple treasury; 4 Macc 4:1-14 makes him the despoiler.

2. Son of Menestheus sent by Antiochus IV Epiphanes to commemorate Ptolemy VI Philometer's coronation in 172 BCE. Jason the high priest acclaimed Apollonius in Jerusalem en route (2 Macc 4:21-22).

3. Mysarch (i.e., commander of Antiochus IV's Mysian mercenaries), possibly to be identified with Apollonius (2) and/or (4). At Antiochus's behest, he seized Jerusalem by trickery in 168/167 BCE and constructed the fortified Akra to house Syrian troops (2 Macc 5:23-26; cf 1 Macc 1:29-36).

4. Governor of Samaria (Josephus, *Ant.* 12.261, 287). Led a campaign against Judas Maccabeus in 166/165 BCE, and lost the battle and his life. Judas took his sword as a trophy (1 Macc 3:10-12).

5. Son of Gennaios, a regional

governor who harassed the Jews (2 Macc 12:2).

6. Governor of Coele-Syria and Phoenicia. On behalf of Demetrius II (not Alexander Balas, as in Josephus, *Ant.* 13.87–88), he fought Jonathan Maccabeus in a major battle near Ashod in 146 BCE, and was decisively defeated (1 Macc 10:69-89).

APOLLOPHANES An Ammonite killed with his brothers Chaereas and Timothy by twenty "young men" in Judas Maccabeus's army at Gazara (2 Macc 10:32-37; 1 Macc 5:6-8).

APOLLOS According to Luke, Apollos was a Jew and a native of ALEXANDRIA, "well-educated and effective in his use of the scriptures" (Acts 18:24). Having received instruction in "the WAY of the Lord," Luke states that "he spoke as one stirred up by the Spirit" and "taught accurately the things about Jesus" (Acts 18:25). This zeal and rhetorical proficiency impressed the Ephesians, who commended him to CORINTH, where he exercised a similar influence over that community (Acts 18:27–19:1). Luke's assertion that Apollos was deficient in the Holy Spirit makes him clearly subordinate to Paul (Acts 18:25*c*-26; cf 19:1-7). This demotion perhaps reflects Apollos's popularity, a fact that Paul himself recognized (1 Cor 1:12; 3:4, 21-22). Because of Apollos's reputation in Corinth, Paul validates his work as a fellow servant of God and a "mentor," but ultimately elevates himself to the role of the Corinthians' father (1 Cor 3:5-15; 4:14-16). Even so, Paul's closing remarks demonstrate that while he and Apollos were in EPHESUS together, the two worked independently (1 Cor 16:12).

APOLLYON The name of the ruler of the abyss in Rev 9:11 and a Greek translation of the Hebrew name ABADDON, which means, literally, "destroyer." Ancient Jewish and Christian writers use many names for the leader of the demons, including SATAN, BEELZEBUL, Mastema, and Semyaza.

APOSTASY The word *apostasy* means "a standing away from" or "rebellion." Though originally referring to political or military rebellion, during the Greco-Roman period the noun also came to mean religious rebellion. It most frequently, particularly in the book of Jeremiah, signifies behavior in which Israel strays from its religious commitments.

APOSTLE Used in the NT, both as a general designation for someone authorized to act on behalf of another, or sent with a commission, and as a distinctive title for particular founding figures and church leaders. Of the nearly 100 appearances of the term, the majority are found in Luke–Acts and in letters attributed to Paul (thirty-four each). In Luke–Acts, apostle is used almost exclusively of the Twelve (usually the group as a whole), both during the time of Jesus and (with Matthias replacing Judas) after the resurrection.

APPAIM Nadab's son and Ishi's father in the genealogy of the clan of Jerahmeel, a descendant of Judah and his daughter-in-law Tamar (1 Chron 2:30-31).

APPHIA A Christian woman mentioned in Paul's greeting to Philemon (Phlm 2) along with ARCHIPPUS as members of Philemon's house church.

APPHUS An appellation for Jonathan Maccabeus, one of Mattathias's five sons (1 Macc 2:5).

APPLE Described as a sweet-tasting (Song 2:3), golden (Prov 25:11), and scented fruit (Song 7:8 [Heb. Song 7:9]), whose tree provides shade (Song 2:3; 8:5) and physical sustenance (Song 2:5; Joel 1:12). Probably, this was an apricot, which was cultivated and grew wild in biblical Palestine and Syria. While the fruit of the tree in the middle of the garden of Eden (Gen 2:9, 17; 3:3-6) is unnamed, tradition designates it as the common apple (see EDEN, GARDEN OF). See APPLE OF THE EYE; FRUIT.

APPLE OF THE EYE Several Hebrew terms are thus translated in the KJV to indicate the eye's pupil or the eyeball, used metaphorically to designate something precious, vulnerable, and deserving of vigilant care (Deut 32:10; Prov 7:2; Ps 17:8; Lam 2:18; Zech 2:8 [Heb. 2:12]).

AQUILA AND PRISCILLA A married couple; business and missionary associates of the apostle Paul.

Priscilla (the diminutive form used in Acts 18:2, 18, 19, 26) or Prisca (Rom 16:3; 1 Cor 16:19; 2 Tim 4:19) is cited before her husband in five of the seven NT references, probably signaling her more prominent role in the early church. Both bear Latin names, and Aquila is identified as a Jewish "native of Pontus" (Acts 18:2). The Pauline Letters and Acts sketch the couple's work and travels across the eastern Mediterranean world, based in Rome, Corinth, and Ephesus.

AR A location in Moab considered a northern Moabite border marker on the edge of Ammonite land along the ARNON River (Num 21:15; Deut 2:18-19). Before Ar was allotted to LOT's descendants, it was the home of the REPHAIM, known for their great stature (Deut 2:9-11, 20). Ar represents Moab's destruction in the poetry of Num 21:28 and Isa 15:1.

ARABAH The Jordan River Valley, including part, or all, of the Dead Sea.

ARAD Arad is a town in southern Palestine mentioned four times in the OT.

ARADUS Island city of north Phoenicia, to whose people the Roman consul Lucius wrote assuring them of the Jews' allegiance (1 Macc 15:23). See ARVAD.

ARAH 1. One of the sons of ULLA from the line of Asher (1 Chron 7:29).

2. The ancestor of a group of exiles who returned with ZERUBABBEL from Babylonian captivity (Ezra 2:5; Neh 7:10; 1 Esdr 5:10).

ARAM, ARAMEANS Semitic peoples who inhabited areas from the Middle Euphrates in Mesopotamia to the Orontes River and DAMASCUS in central and southern SYRIA. They were particularly active from ca. 1200 to 730 BCE. They never formed a unified kingdom but primarily existed as independent states that were loosely connected by language and culture.

ARAMAIC, ARAMAISM Aramaic describes a cluster of closely related dialects that first appear ca. the 9th cent. BCE and continue in use down to today. Aramaic is used in both the OT (Gen 31:47; Jer 10:11; Ezra 4:8–6:18; 7:12-26; Dan 2:4–7:28) and the NT (Mark 5:41; 7:34; 15:34; Matt 27:46; 1 Cor 16:22; Rev 22:20). An Aramaism is an expression in Greek or Hebrew that has been influenced by a typical phrase in Aramaic, marking an author's awareness of both languages.

ARAN Grandson of Seir the Horite and son of Dishan. A chief or a clan of the Horites (Gen 36:28; 1 Chron 1:42). See HARAN; OREN.

ARARAT Ararat refers to the mountainous area in Armenia surrounding Lake Van.

ARAUNAH In 2 Sam 24 it is at the threshing floor of Araunah the Jebusite that Yahweh stops an angel just short of destroying Jerusalem. Upon King David's confession to having taken a census of the people, God tells David to erect an altar at the threshing floor. Araunah appears on the scene, and, recognizing David as the king, offers to give David the threshing floor, the oxen, the wood, and all the other implements for the sacrifice. David declines the gift and insists on paying. Then the sacrifices are made, the destruction is averted, and a severe plague on the people is stemmed.

ARBA Arba was the greatest member of the Anakim, the race of GIANTS (Josh 14:15), and father of Anak (Josh 15:13; 21:11).

ARCHANGEL Meaning "chief angel" or "head angel" (1 Thess 4:16), *archangel* occurs only once in the Bible (Jude 1:9), though the idea is more widespread, and the archangels Michael and Gabriel are named in both testaments.

ARCHELAUS Herod Archelaus was the son of Malthake and Herod the Great. Herod Archelaus himself was exiled to Vienne in southern Gaul (6 CE). See ETHNARCH; HEROD, FAMILY; TETRARCH, TETRARCHY.

ARCHER A soldier armed with bow and arrows, generally found in military contexts.

ARCHEVITES The CEB lists them simply as "the people of [the Mesopotamian city of] ERECH" (Sumerian Uruk) among peoples resettled in and around SAMARIA by OSNAPPAR (probably the Assyrian king Ashurbanipal) who are signatories to REHUM's and SHIMSHAI's letter to the Persian king ARTAXERXES (Ezra 4:9).

ARCHIPPUS A Christian from Colossae greeted as an addressee in Phlm 2 and in the concluding greetings of Col 4:17.

ARCHITE 1. Appellation for HUSHAI, a friend of King DAVID (2 Sam 15:32; 16:16; 17:5, 14; 1 Chron 27:33).

2. Name of a clan living in an area southwest of Bethel and near ATAROTH, whose presence marked the southern boundary of the Joseph tribes (Josh 16:2).

ARCHIVES, ROYAL A section of the royal treasury (Ezra 5:17) where official documents were stored.

ARCTURUS The constellation of stars mentioned in Job 9:9.

ARD In Gen 46:21 Ard is listed as one of Benjamin's ten sons. Yet in Num 26:40 and 1 Chron 8:3, he is listed as a grandson of Benjamin.

ARDAT Field where Ezra received a fourth vision about a mourning woman (2 Esdr 9:26). See ARAD.

ARDON Caleb's son in the list of Judah's descendants (1 Chron 2:18).

ARELI, ARELITES Son of Gad, Jacob and Zilpah's son, who settled in Egypt (Gen 46:16). The progenitor of the Arelites (Num 26:17). See ARIEL.

AREOPAGITE A member of the Council of the Areopagus, the main governing body of Athens. Acts 17 recounts Paul's conversion of DIONYSIUS the Areopagite (Acts 17:34), whose surname implies his membership on the council.

AREOPAGUS See MARS HILL.

ARETAS Dynastic name of a number of Nabatean (Arabian) kings.

1. Aretas I (ca. 170–160 BCE) was the first of the Nabatean dynasts mentioned in the historical record, where an inscription styles him as king. According to 2 Macc 5:8, the high priest Jason was held by him in 168 BCE.

2. Aretas II (ca. 120–96 BCE) pledged to help Gaza fend off the siege of Alexander Jannaeus (Josephus, Ant. 13.358–64).

3. Aretas III "Philhellene" (ca. 87–62 BCE)

was invited by Coele-Syria and Damascus to become their ruler (ca. 84–72 BCE). Aretas became embroiled in territorial disputes with the Hasmoneans. In 82 BCE he defeated Alexander Jannaeus and, later, in the dynastic contest between Hyrcanus II and Aristobulus II, supported the former. In return, Hyrcanus promised to restore twelve cities captured by Alexander (Josephus, *Ant.* 14.18).

4. Aretas IV "Philopatris" (ca. 9 BCE–39 CE) was a long-lived king who presided over a period of notable prosperity in Nabatea. When Herod Antipas expelled his wife, Aretas's daughter, in favor of Herodias, Aretas sent a punitive expedition against him and secured a major victory. According to Josephus, the people regarded Herod's defeat as divine punishment for his execution of John the Baptist (*Ant.* 18.109–19). In 2 Cor 11:32-33 (see Gal 1:15-17), Paul describes his escape from Damascus when "the governor [ethnarch] under King Aretas" sought to capture him. Whether Aretas's ethnarch actually controlled the city or simply oversaw its resident Nabatean colony remains disputed.

ARGOB AND ARIEH The sentence structure in 2 Kgs 15:25 makes it difficult to determine whether Argob and Arieh are two men who had conspired with the captain PEKAH to kill King PEKAHIAH or two men who were assassinated along with King Pekahiah.

ARIARATHES Cappadocian king (163–130 BCE) to whom the Roman consul Lucius wrote a letter assuring him of the Jews' allegiance and requesting him not to join alliances against them (1 Macc 15:22).

ARIDAI Haman's ninth of ten sons, all killed and hanged on the gallows as part of the purging of Jewish enemies (Esth 9:9).

ARIDATHA Haman's sixth of ten sons, all killed and hanged on the gallows as part of the purging of Jewish enemies (Esth 9:8).

ARIEH Killed by Pekah (2 Kgs 15:25). See ARGOB AND ARIEH.

ARIEL 1. Ariel is an obscure name for Jerusalem in Isa 29:1-8.

2. In 2 Sam 23:20 (1 Chron 11:22) Ariel may be a noun referring to a military hero.

3. One of nine leaders mentioned in Ezra 8:16 (Iduel in the par. text of 1 Esdr 8:43).

ARIMATHEA According to all four Gospels, Arimathea was the hometown of Joseph of Arimathea, who provided a tomb for Jesus (Matt 27:57; Mark 15:43; Luke 23:51; John 19:38).

ARIMATHEA, JOSEPH OF See JOSEPH, JOSEPHITES.

ARIOCH 1. The king of Ellasar and one of four kings led by Chedorlaomer in his western campaign against cities in the Dead Sea region (Gen 14).

2. The name of a captain of Nebuchadnezzar's royal guard, who had been sent to kill all the wise men in the country because no one could interpret the king's dream (Dan 2).

3. The name of the king of the Elymeans (i.e., the Elamites) mentioned in Jdt 1:6.

ARISAI One of Haman's sons hanged on the gallows (Esth 9:9).

ARISH, WADI EL See EGYPT, WADI OF.

ARISTARCHUS One of the fellow workers of Paul (Phlm 24). Colossians 4:10 describes him as a "fellow prisoner."

ARK OF NOAH. Floating wooden box that enabled NOAH, his family, and the world's animals to survive the FLOOD.

In Gen 6:14-16 God commands the building of the ark.

ARK OF THE COVENANT See COVENANT CHEST.

ARKESAEUS Persian governor who sat with and advised King Artaxerxes to replace Queen VASHTI (Add Esth 1:14). See ESTHER, ADDITIONS TO.

ARKITE The Arkites are listed among the descendants of Canaan and are likely Phoenician (Gen 10:17; 1 Chron 1:15).

ARMAGEDDON Occurs only in Rev 16:16 as the site of an eschatological battle that prepares the way for the millennium. The term *armageddon* derives from the Hebrew for "mount of Megiddo." Several references to Megiddo occur in the OT. The ancient city of MEGIDDO (Josh 12:21; 17:11; Judg 1:27; 1 Kgs 4:12; 9:15, 27; 2 Kgs 9:27; 1 Chron 7:29) sat on a mound in northwestern Palestine not far from Mount Carmel. Megiddo was adjacent to two major trade routes, one of which carried traffic from Egypt to Syria.

ARMONI A son of Saul and his secondary wife RIZPAH. He and his brother MEPHIBOSHETH die at the hands of the Gibeonites in order to atone for Saul's bloodguilt (2 Sam 21:8-9).

ARMOR OF GOD The armor of God is a rare feature of the larger biblical tradition of divine warfare (e.g., Exod 14–15; Deut 32–33; Pss 18; 68; Hab 3; for armor, see Isa 59:17; Ws 5:17-20). Paul's concept of a believer's spiritual armor of virtues is related (1 Thess 5; Eph 2; 6:10-20; 1 Cor 15:24-26).

ARMOR-BEARER The personal attendant of a king or warrior who performed functions related to warfare. The role occurs eighteen times in the OT but may have evolved into the position of captain.

ARMORY An armory becomes necessary in times of urbanization and growing political and military complexity as the space for the storage and distribution of weapons in times of war or internal crisis (2 Kgs 20:13; Neh 3:19; Isa 39:2; Jer 50:25).

ARMY An organized collection of armed men recruited for large-scale combat. In the OT the term *army* is very common. The Greek equivalent is much less common in the NT, although its presence is certainly presupposed.

ARNA Ancestor of the prophet EZRA (2 Esdr 1:2). Named as ZERAHIAH in a par. list (Ezra 7:4).

ARNAN Arnan appears only in a list of David's descendants (1 Chron 3:21).

ARNI Judah's great-great-grandson (Luke 3:33).

ARNON A stream with a sizable gorge in Transjordan. It runs northwest, then westward to the middle shore of the Dead Sea. The Arnon marked the northern boundary of central Moab (Num 21:13), and the southern boundary of Israel's early tribal territory through the late 9th cent. BCE (Josh 12:1; 2 Kgs 10:33). Israel reportedly captured the land north of the Arnon when they conquered the Amorite king Sihon (Num 21:24).

AROD, ARODITE 1. Arod, listed as the sixth of Gad's seven sons (Arodi [Gen 46:16]).

2. The clan named for Arod according to Num 26:17.

ARODI Listed as the sixth of seven sons of Gad who accompanied JACOB to Egypt (Gen 46:16; Arod [Num 26:17]).

AROER A place-name meaning "crest of a mountain" or "juniper."

1. Aroer on the Arnon, a fortress or a settlement on the northern slope of the Wadi el-Mujib. The biblical river Arnon formed the northern border of Moab. The fortress, on the edge of a canyon (Deut 2:36; 4:48; Josh 12:2; 13:16), gave it a strategic location. Aroer was included in the conquest of the Transjordan area (Deut 2:36; Josh 13:9). It was settled by Gad though it was assigned to Reuben (Num 32:34; Josh 13:16), and it was the beginning point for David's census in Transjordan (2 Sam 24:5). Aroer was the southern border of the Syrian king Hazael (2 Kgs 10:33).

2. Aroer in the Transjordan, modern Amman (Josh 13:25; Judg 11:33), was on the border between Gad and Ammon.

3. Aroer in the arid southern plain west of the Jordan (1 Sam 30:28). David gave loot to the elders of Aroer after he recovered his wives from the Amalekites. Hotham the Aroerite was the father of two of David's mighty men (1 Chron 11:44). In the LXX the place-name appears in Josh 15:22. The location of Aroer in the Davidic period remains unknown but might be Tell Esdar.

4. In the OT, Aroer refers to cities of Aroer located near Damascus (Isa 17:2*a*).

AROM A family head whose unspecified number of descendants relocated themselves to Jerusalem and Judea after the exile had ended (1 Esdr 5:16).

ARPACHSHAD Shem's third son; a grandson of Noah, born two years after the flood (Gen 10:22; 11:10).

ARPAD One of the great cities of Syria (along with Hamath, with which it is always linked; DAMASCUS; and CARCHEMISH) (2 Kgs 18:34, 19:1; Isa 10:9, 36:9, 37:13; Jer 49:23). Arpad fell prey to the Assyrian conquests of the 9th and 8th cent. BCE and was conquered by TIGLATH-PILESER III in 740 BCE.

ARPHAXAD 1. King of Media whom King Nebuchadnezzar defeated and killed (Jdt 1:1-15).

2. Noah's grandson and one of Jesus' ancestors in Luke's genealogy (3:23-38). See ARPACHSHAD.

ARSINOE Sister and consort of Ptolemy IV Philopator, king of Egypt.

ARTAXERXES The name of three Persian kings.

1. Artaxerxes I Longimanus (465–424 BCE), son of Xerxes I. It is generally agreed that Nehemiah came to Jerusalem in the twentieth year of Artaxerxes I (445 BCE; Neh 2:1). Much more disputed is the date of Ezra's arrival. Ezra came to Jerusalem in the 7th year of an Artaxerxes (Ezra 7:8). If under Artaxerxes I, Ezra came in 458; if under Artaxerxes II, Ezra arrived in 398. The principal argument in favor of Ezra's coming to Jerusaleum in 458 is the order suggested by the books of Ezra and Nehemiah.

2. Artaxerxes II Memnon (404–358 BCE). Those who favor a date for Ezra under Artaxerxes II note the mention of a wall (Ezra 9:9), possibly referring to the wall repaired by Nehemiah, and the fact that the high priest in the time of Nehemiah was Eliashib, while in the time of Ezra the high priest was Johanan son of Eliashib (Ezra 10:6). Artaxerxes II reconquered Egypt, which had revolted against Persia in 405.

3. Artaxerxes III Ochus (358–338 BCE). Under Artaxerxes III, Tennes, king of Sidon, revolted ca. 349, but the effect of this revolt on Israel cannot be measured.

ARTEMAS Paul planned to send Artemas, who was a messenger, to signal Titus to meet him at Nicopolis during the coming winter (Titus 3:12).

ARUBBOTH Mentioned as the city of BEN-HESED, one of the twelve officers of King Solomon (1 Kgs 4:10), Arubboth lies between Shaalbim and BETH-SHEMESH on one side and DOR on the other. In Josh 12:17 the king of Hepher is associated with the kings of TAPPUAH, APHEK, and Sharon.

ARUMAH The home of Abimelech, Gideon's son by his Shechemite secondary wife (Judg 8:31). Arumah was Abimelech's home base while he attempted to retain kingship over Shechem (Judg 9:31, 41).

ARVAD An island city on the northwestern Mediterranean coast, north of Tyre, which is associated with today's Ruad. In the biblical genealogies, Arvadites are a tribe of Canaan (Gen 10:18; 1 Chron 1:16). Arvadites came to Tyre's aid as rowers and guards when Babylon attacked (Ezek 27:8, 11).

ARZA Administrator of Elah's palace at Tirzah. When Elah became drunk, Zimri murdered Elah and succeeded him as king (1 Kgs 16:8-10).

ARZARETH The ten tribes of Israel were allegedly deported to Arzareth, a land far beyond the Euphrates River from which they would return in the last days (2 Esdr 13:45-46).

ASA 1. Son of Abijam (or Abijah) and grandson of Rehoboam, he was the third king of Judah after the division of the united monarchy (1 Kgs 15:8; 1 Chron 14:1). He reigned over Judah forty-one years (1 Kgs 15:10). Asa has the second-longest rule among the kings of Judah; only Manasseh reigned longer (2 Kgs 21:1). After his death, Asa was succeeded by his son Jehoshaphat.

2. A Levite, son of Elkanah and father of Berechiah. Berechiah was one of the Levites who lived in the villages of the Netophathites after the people returned from Babylon (1 Chron 9:16).

ASAHEL 1. Brother of JOAB and ABISHAI, and the youngest son of David's sister ZERUIAH (2 Sam 2:18; 1 Chron 2:16). One of the group of "Thirty" (2 Sam 23:24), he was commander of the fourth division of David's army (1 Chron 27:7).

2. One of the Levites whom King JEHOSHAPHAT sent throughout Judah to teach the Law of Moses (2 Chron 17:8).

3. One of the Levites appointed by HEZEKIAH to be in charge of contributions given for the support of the temple (2 Chron 31:13).

4. The father of JONATHAN, one of the few leaders of the postexilic community who opposed Ezra's policy of requiring the men of Judah to send away their foreign wives (Ezra 10:15; 1 Esdr 9:14).

ASAIAH 1. Son of Haggiah (1 Chron 6:30 [Heb. 6:15]) whom David appointed to move the covenant chest from Obed-edom's house to Jerusalem (1 Chron 15:6, 11).

2. Clan leader in the tribe of Simeon who helped drive Ham's descendants from the pastures of Gedor (1 Chron 4:36).

3. One of King Josiah's officials sent to consult the prophetess Huldah concerning the authenticity of the Instruction scroll found in the temple (2 Kgs 22:12, 14; 2 Chron 34:20).

4. A descendant of Judah who returned to Jerusalem after the captivity (1 Chron 9:5).

ASAPH 1. A Levite son of BERECHIAH from the GERSHOM clan (1 Chron 6:39 [Heb. 6:24]; 15:17). Asaph and his descendants became influential musicians in the religious life of Israel. He probably founded a school of singers and musicians who were called "the sons of Asaph" (Ezra 3:10) and played a prominent role in the worship and music of the postexilic community (1 Chron 25:1-2; 2 Chron 20:14; 29:13; Ezra 2:41; Neh 7:44; 11:22). Twelve psalms (Pss 50; 73–83) carry his name in their titles.

2. The father of JOAH, a recorder in the court of HEZEKIAH, king of Judah (2 Kgs 18:18, 37; Isa 36:3, 22), perhaps a

kind of secretary of state who carried out royal decrees.

3. NEHEMIAH came before King ARTAXERXES and requested that Asaph, "the keeper of the king's forest," provide timber for the rebuilding of the temple (Neh 2:8).

4. The son of Abija (Matt 1:7) and the father of JEHOSHAPHAT (Matt 1:8). According to biblical tradition, Abija was the father of ASA, and Jehoshaphat was Asa's son (1 Chron 3:10; 1 Kgs 22:41).

ASAREL One of Jehallelel's four sons in Judah's list of descendants (1 Chron 4:16).

ASARELAH One of ASAPH's four sons whom DAVID designated to prophesy, using musical instruments such as lyres, harps, and cymbals (1 Chron 25:2).

ASCENSION Ascension is a widespread and diffuse category in the ancient world that describes temporary heavenly journeys by seers (either in ecstasy or physically), ascents of heavenly beings who have made earthly appearances, assumptions of the soul at death, and raptures (i.e., bodily translations into the "beyond" as the conclusion of one's life, without the intervention of death).

ASCENT The basic meaning is movement from a lower to a higher elevation. A path or mountain pass is referred to as an "ascent" (Num 34:4; Josh 15:3). Cities were usually built on an elevated location, hence, Judah "went up" to Timnah (Gen 38:12).The journey to Canaan from the desert or from Egypt is described as an ascent (Exod 13:18; 33:1). In both cases, movement is to a higher elevation, but in the biblical traditions, these moves also create a decisive increase in well-being and status. The verb is often used to describe the exodus, usually in the causative form with God as the subject ("This is your God, who brought you up out of Egypt" [Neh 9:18]).

A similar sense applies to personal deliverance from danger.

The verb is often used in conjunction with sacrifice (e.g., Isa 60:7, where sheep and rams "go up for acceptance on my altar," author's trans.). The choice of this verb may relate to the elevation of the animal on the altar or the ascent of the smoke to God in HEAVEN. The depiction of God dwelling in heaven is also assumed when persons are said to go "up" to God (e.g., Moses [Exod 24:1] and Elijah [2 Kgs 2:1]). The Greek verb is used in the NT to describe Jesus' ASCENSION. Even God is said to have "gone up" after vanquishing chaos, in the language of divine enthronement (Ps 47:5 [Heb 47:6]).

Finally, pilgrimages are described as "ascents," because they involve both a journey to a city and a "going up" to God The designation in footnotes of Pss 120–134 as Songs of Ascent reflects their use during pilgrimages.

ASCENT TO HEAVEN Ascent to heaven emerges as an important mode of communication with God in the apocalyptic literature of the Hellenistic and Roman periods. The prophets of the OT heard God's voice, sometimes gazed upon God's presence (Isa 6; Ezek 1), and occasionally were transported from place to place (Ezek 8:2-3; 11:24; 40:1-2). The only prophet in the OT to ascend to heaven is Elijah, who was taken up in a fiery chariot at the end of his life (2 Kgs 2:11); there is no report on his experience. The first Jewish text to describe an ascent to heaven is the Book of the Watchers (1 En. 1–36), one of the earliest of the apocalypses, probably composed in the late 3rd cent. BCE. The hero of its story is Enoch, the antediluvian patriarch who, according to the biblical account, walked with God and then "disappeared because God took him" (Gen 5:21-24; quotation v. 24).

ASENATH An Egyptian woman and daughter of Potiphera the priest of On

(Gen 41:45). Asenath, whose name likely means "belonging to the goddess Neith," is offered in marriage to Joseph by the pharaoh following Joseph's installation as the second in command. The couple has two sons, Manasseh and Ephraim, before the famine in Egypt begins (Gen 41:50; 46:20).

ASHAN Ashan, northwest of BEER-SHEBA, was allotted to the tribe of Judah, then to the descendants of Simeon, whose territory fell within Judah's boundaries (Josh 15:42; 19:7; 1 Chron 4:32). Ashan is also listed among the cities of refuge (1 Chron 6:59).

ASHBEL Ashbel appears in lists of descendants of Benjamin. Genesis 46:21 lists him as the third of ten sons; Num 26:38 and 1 Chron 8:1 as the second of five. First Chronicles 7:6 names JEDIAEL instead of Ashbel among Benjamin's three sons.

ASHDOD Biblical Ashdod, a major Bronze and Iron Age tell in the southern coastal plain of Israel, is located 3.5 mi. southeast of the modern Mediterranean town of Ashdod. The ancient site includes a ca. 20-acre acropolis and ca. 70-acre lower city. It is best known in the Bible as a Philistine town.

Ashdod appears numerous times in the Bible, most notably as one of the five Philistine cities mentioned in Josh 13:3, and served as an important non-Israelite center during the 12th–7th cent. BCE. Biblical Ashdod is infamous as a center for the worship of Dagon. According to 1 Sam 5, the Philistines brought the captured Israelite covenant chest into the temple of Dagon, thus causing the statue of Dagon to fall on his face. Following the chest's arrival, a plague afflicted the residents of Ashdod. Subsequently the chest was sent to Gath and later Ekron, where disasters were also inflicted on their inhabitants.

ASHER, ASHERITES 1. The eighth son born to Jacob through his secondary wife Zilpah. The meaning of the name, "fortunate one," is confirmed by the birth report of the eponymous ancestor (Gen 30:12-13) and the blessed status accorded the tribe in the testamentary benedictions attributed to Moses (Deut 33:24).

2. The ascription of blessing, however, stands in contrast to intimations that the tribe of Asher enjoyed a lesser status than other Israelite tribes, in contrast to the ascription of blessing. In genealogies and tribal lists Asher is grouped with the three other tribes (Gad, Dan, and Naphtali) that traced descent from Bilhah and Zilpah, Jacob's secondary wives.

ASHERAH Asherah, along with Astarte and Anath, was one of the three great goddesses of the Canaanite pantheon. She was particularly known as a mother goddess, the consort of the high father god El.

ASHES The substances remaining after combustion has occurred, whether in domestic ovens, urban conflagrations, or as a result of ritual sacrifices (1 Kgs 20:38; 20:41; 2 Kgs 23:4; Ps 147:16; Job 2:8). Ashes are often mentioned in connection with DUST and sackcloth as signs of MOURNING, grief, and humiliation (2 Sam 13:19; Job 2:8, 12; Isa 61:3; Jer 6:26); the application of ashes to the head and body at times of personal and national crisis, often accompanied by fasting, indicated penitence (Isa 58:5; Ezek 27:30; Jonah 3:6; Esth 4:1, 3; Dan 9:3; Jdt 4:13).

ASHHUR Father of seven sons by Helah and Naarah, descendant of Judah, son of Hezron and his wife Abijah, and founder of the town Tekoa (1 Chron 2:24; 4:5-6).

ASHIMA, ASHIMAH The god worshipped by the people from Hamath who lived in SAMARIA after the Assyrian exile of 722 BCE (2 Kgs 17:30).

ASHKELON Biblical Ashkelon is a large semicircular 150-acre tell facing the

Mediterranean Sea next to the modern city of Ashkelon. Ashkelon is best known in the Bible as one of the Philistine Pentapolis cities, a league of five Philistine centers mentioned in Josh 13:3.

In the Bible, Ashkelon is infamous as the city where Samson killed thirty men to procure their clothes as payment for a wager he had lost to the Philistines (Judg 14:10-19). It was also one of the Philistine cities struck by a plague following the Philistine capture of the covenant chest (1 Sam 6:4, 17). During the final centuries of the Iron Age, Ashkelon was a center for wine production.

ASHKENAZ Gomer's eldest son listed in the Table of Nations (Gen 10:3; 1 Chron 1:6). Ashkenaz represents a geographical area east of the Black Sea, most likely belonging to the Scythians. Jeremiah names them as a threat to Babylon (51:27), and Herodotus describes the Scythians attacking the Cimmerians.

ASHNAH 1. A city in the lowlands of Judah (Josh 15:33). Although the location is uncertain, Aslin is suggested.

2. A city farther south in the lowlands of Judah (Josh 15:43). Modern Idna between Hebron and LACHISH is a possible location.

ASHPENAZ Nebuchadnezzar's official who allowed Daniel and his friends to consume water and vegetables while a part of the royal court (Dan 1:3-4, 7-14, 18).

ASHTAROTH In Deut 1:4; Josh 9:10; 12:4; and 13:12, Moses and the Israelites are said to have defeated King Og of Bashan, who reigned in the towns of Ashtaroth and Edrei, as part of their conquests east of the Jordan before the people crossed over the river and took the territory that became the Israelite heartland. Subsequently, in Josh 13:31, Ashtaroth, along with Edrei, is said to have been assigned to the Machirite clans of the tribe of Manasseh as part of their tribal inheritance. Then, in 1 Chron 6:71 (in OT 6:56), Ashtaroth is said to have been given to the Gershomites as part of the special allotments given throughout Israel to these and other members of the priestly tribe of Levi, who otherwise were landless.

ASHTEROTH-KARNAIM In Gen 14:5, King Chedorlaomer of Elam and three allies defeated a group called the Rephaim in a place called Ashteroth-karnaim. Ashteroth-karnaim is probably identical to the city Ashtaroth mentioned in Deut 1:1; Josh 9:10; 12:4; 13:10, 31; and 1 Chron 6:71, as particularly indicated in Deut 3:11 and Josh 12:4, where King Og of Ashtaroth is identified as one of the last descendants of the Rephaim.

ASHURBANIPAL, ASSURBANIPAL During the reign (668–627 BCE) of Ashurbanipal, the last great Assyrian king, Assyria reached the zenith of its power, expanding its territory from Egypt to Elam. Assyria, however, began to disintegrate toward the end of his reign. It is somewhat ironic that the end of his reign is obscure due to the lack of references and records after 639 BCE, since he is credited with building one of the most extensive libraries in antiquity.

ASHVATH One of Japhet's three sons and a descendant of Asher born to Jacob and Leah's servant Zilpah (1 Chron 7:33).

ASIA In the time of Paul, the Roman province of Asia was bounded on the north by Bithynia and Pontus, on the south by Lycia and Pamphylia, and on the east by Galatia. There were also some very significant and well-established Jewish communities in Asia. We have evidence that at least some of these communities were involved in the lives of their cities, and they clearly had an impact on the development of early Christianity in the province.

According to the Acts of the

Apostles, Paul was active in the province of Asia (Acts 13:1–16:10; 18:19–19:41; 20:6-38). The NT Letters of Colossians, Philemon, and Ephesians give us information about Christian communities in Asia. Believers in Asia are mentioned in a number of other NT documents (Rom 16:5; 1 Cor 16:19; 2 Cor 1:8; 2 Tim 1:15; 1 Pet 1:1; cf 1 Cor 15:32; 16:8; 1 Tim 1:3; 2 Tim 1:18; 4:12).

ASIEL 1. Father of Seraiah, great-grandfather of Jehu, a Simeon chief who sought pastureland in Gedor (1 Chron 4:35).

2. An ancestor of Tobit and member of the tribe of Napthali (Tob 1:1).

3. Scribes who copied books dictated by EZRA (2 Esdr 14:24).

ASMODEUS In Tobit, a wicked demon who kills each of Sarah's seven husbands in the bridal chamber (Tob 3:8; 6:14).

ASNAH A family head whose descendants returned to Jerusalem after the exile (Ezra 2:50; 1 Esdr 5:31). Absent in list in Neh 7:52.

ASP A snake.

ASPATHA One of Haman's sons who were all killed and hanged on the gallows (Esth 9:7). See HAMAN.

ASPHAR A pool in the Tekoa wilderness where Jonathan Maccabeus and Simon Maccabeus camped after escaping from Bachides's murder plot (1 Macc 9:33).

ASPHARASUS One of the exiles whom King Darius allowed to return with Zerubbabel (1 Esdr 5:8), among a list somewhat different from that in Ezra 2:2.

ASRIEL Asriel, a son of Gilead and an Aramean secondary wife, was a descendant of Manasseh listed in Moses' second census taken in the wilderness (Num 26:31). He was also Moses' captain in the wilderness (Num 26:3). Along with other sons of Gilead, Asriel received land to maintain the tribe (Josh 17:2).

ASS The ass, or donkey, was the main beast of burden used in biblical times.

ASSAPHIOTH The ancestral head of a family of temple servants for SOLOMON (1 Esdr 5:33).

ASSHUR 1. Shem's second son (Gen 10:22) is the eponymous ancestor of Assyria.

2. A place located in modern Iraq, the ancient city of Asshur grew first into a nation and then into the Assyrian Empire. See ASSYRIA AND BABYLONIA.

3. The patron god of Assyria does not appear in the Bible except as a theophoric element in the name Esarhaddon (Ezra 4:2).

ASSHURIM 1. Abraham and his wife Keturah's great grandson (Gen 25:3).

2. Tribe who descended from Abraham, Jokshan, and Dedan, residing south of Palestine (Gen 25:1-3).

ASSIR 1. A Levite son of Korah of a Kohathite clan. He was the brother of ELKANAH (Exod 6:24; 1 Chron 6:22 [Heb. 6:7]).

2. A Levite from the Kohathites, the son of ABIASAPH (1 Chron 6:23 [Heb. 6:8]) and the father of TAHATH (1 Chron 6:37 [Heb. 6:22]).

ASSOS A well-fortified coastal city in the Roman province of Asia, north of the island of Lesbos in the Troad. Paul met his companions in Assos after they left TROAS separately by land and sea on their way to MILETUS (Acts 20:13-14).

ASSYRIA AND BABYLONIA Two Mesopotamian kingdoms, both named after their capital cities, that exercised a profound cultural influence on Israel while destroying its political independence. Both kingdoms were located in what is now Iraq. Assyria predates the OT times, but it enters OT history mostly through the Neo-Assyrian Empire beginning in 934 BCE. Babylonia became the more dominant power throughout the 7th cent. and continued to hold sway over Judah and surrounding areas until its defeat by the Persian Empire in 538 BCE. Thus, for most of Israel's and Judah's monarchies, either Assyria or Babylonia represented the great imperial powers of the world, with resources and armies far exceeding the strength of Israel or Judah.

ASTRONOMY, ASTROLOGY The study of the sky, its inhabitants, and their impact upon people on the land below. In the biblical periods, while peasants read the sky as a seasonal, agricultural calendar, city experts (priests, scribes) read the regularities of the sky to set festal calendars and observe predictable social events (horoscopes) concerning societies, cities, and royalty (there were no horoscopes for individuals apart from royalty). These city experts, priests, and scribes were the astronomers/astrologers of the day in Mesopotamia and elsewhere in the circum-Mediterranean.

ASUR Family head whose descendants were among the 372 temple servants who returned after the exile (1 Esdr 5:31). Excluded in Ezra 2:51 and Neh 7:53.

ASYLUM See REFUGE.

ASYNCRITUS A Christian who returned to Rome after the rescinding of the Edict of Claudius or someone Paul addressed in a letter fragment added to Romans (Rom 16:14).

ATAD The threshing floor of Atad became a seven-day mourning site for Joseph and his family as they transported Jacob's body from Egypt to Hebron for burial (Gen 50:10-11).

ATARAH "Crown" or "wreath." Jerahmeel's second wife and Onam's mother in the list of Judah's descendants (1 Chron 2:26).

ATAROTH 1. Located east of the Dead Sea, south of Mount Nebo, and north of the Arnon River; likely the Iron Era site Khirbet Atarus. Numbers 21:21-24 and 32:33 identify it as part of the Amorite land that Israel captured from King Sihon.

2. Elsewhere, Josh 16:2, 7 describe Ataroth as part of the Archites' land, on the eastern border of Ephraim's tribal territory and to the west of the Jordan in the highlands.

ATER 1. A family—Babylonian name Ater, Hebrew name Hezekiah—who returned with ZERUBBABEL from exile (Ezra 2:16; Neh 7:21; 1 Esdr 5:15).

2. A family of gatekeeper returnees (Ezra 2:42; Neh 7:45; 1 Esdr 5:28).

3. A person who signed a postexilic covenant (Neh 10:17).

ATHACH Town in Judah whose people shared in the spoil recovered in David's battle against the Amalekites (1 Sam 30:30).

ATHAIAH Son of UZZIAH and descendant of Judah through PEREZ, Athaiah appears in Nehemiah's list of postexilic inhabitants of Jerusalem (Neh 11:4). Some scholars identify Athaiah as UTHAI from the parallel list in 1 Chron 9:4.

ATHALIAH 1. The daughter of an Israelite king (either Omri or Ahab), the wife of the Judahite king Jehoram, the mother of King AHAZIAH of Judah, and the sole ruler of Judah for more than six years. She is presented as contaminating Judah's allegiance to Yahweh and disrupting the Davidic succession (2 Kgs 8; 2 Chron 21).

2. A son of Jeroham in a census list of the Benjaminite families in Jerusalem (1 Chron 8: 26).

3. Father of Jeshaiah who was among

the returnees from Babylon with Ezra (Ezra 8:7).

ATHARIM A place through which the Israelites enter the arid southern plain. Their presence on the route causes the king of ARAD to take up arms (Num 21:1).

ATHENOBIUS Antiochus VII Sidete's "political adviser" who, on his behalf, demanded that Simon Maccabeus return the cities and the money that he had acquired outside Judea or make monetary restitution for both (1 Macc 15:28-36).

ATHENS The city of Athens and its immediate territory of Attica lie at the south end of the mainland of GREECE. Paul arrived in Athens by sea from Macedonia, presumably arriving at the Piraeus (see PAUL, THE APOSTLE). According to the book of Acts, the city itself was "flooded with idols" (17:16). This reflects the way the city was dominated by the acropolis, which contained a number of sanctuaries, but most notably the Parthenon, the main temple to Athena, the patron deity of the city.

ATHLAI Descendant of Bebai who dismissed his foreign wife as Ezra instructed God's covenant required of him (Ezra 10:28).

ATONEMENT See RECONCILE, RECONCILIATION.

ATONEMENT, DAY OF See DAY OF RECONCILIATION.

ATROTH-BETH-JOAB Located somewhere near BETHLEHEM in Judah, Atroth-Beth-Joab is a town included in HUR's genealogy (1 Chron 2:54).

ATROTH-SHOPHAN Gadites rebuilt the town of Atroth-Shophan east of the Jordan River after it was taken from the Amorite king SIHON (Num 32:35).

ATTAI 1. A member of Judah's tribe who was the son of Egyptian slave Jarha by Sheshan's daughter and was the father of Nathan (1 Chron 2:35-36).

2. A Gaddite warrior who went over to David's side against Saul at the battle of Ziklag (1 Chron 12:11).

3. King REHOBOAM's son by his wife Maachah, who was favored by Rehoboam and also Solomon's grandson (2 Chron 11:20).

ATTALIA A city on the southwestern coast of Asia Minor on the Catarrhactes (Aksu) River, founded by ATTALUS II of PERGAMUM (159–138 BCE) that became the main harbor for the region of PAMPHYLIA. Augustus settled veterans in the city and it became a Roman colony in the 3rd cent. CE. The apostle Paul passed through Attalia at the end of his first missionary journey (Acts 14:25).

ATTALUS The name of three kings of Pergamon. Attalus II Philadelphus (159–138 BCE) promoted the Syrian pretender Alexander Balas (Diod. Sic. 31.32a) and is also a recipient of the letter sent by the Roman consul Lucius proclaiming the Roman alliance with Simon Maccabeus (1 Macc 15:22).

AUGUSTAN COHORT Acts 27:1 refers to the Augustan Cohort. The soldiers named in Acts 27:42 are probably part of this cohort. A cohort, an auxiliary unit that usually ranged from 500 to 1,000 soldiers, was an innovation of Augustus. Similar to a LEGION, it was much smaller and consisted primarily of noncitizens, with the promise of citizenship serving as the chief means of recruitment.

AUGUSTUS Although mentioned only once in the NT (Luke 2:1), Caesar Augustus (b. Sept. 9, 63 BCE–d. Aug. 19, 14 CE) shaped the structures, values, and practices of the imperial world that the followers of Jesus negotiated on a daily basis.

AURANUS Leader appointed by Lysimachus over 3,000 men to quell an uprising of the Jews in Jerusalem (2 Macc 4:40).

AUTHOR OF LIFE Peter's title for Jesus (Acts 3:15) follows the healing of the lame man at Solomon's portico, reminding witnesses that Jesus' name is the source of healing.

AVARAN An appellation with uncertain meaning for Eleazar, Judas Maccabeus's brother, who died while heroically killing King Antiochus IV's elephant (1 Macc 2:5; 6:43-46).

AVEN VALLEY One of the places mentioned in Amos' oracle against Aram (Amos 1:5).

AVENGE *Avenge* means to inflict deserved or appropriate punishment on a perpetrator of wrongs to oneself or others. The corresponding noun is *vengeance*, though that word can also denote revenge, malicious retaliation to repay some wrong.

AVITH In Gen 36:35 and 1 Chron 1:46, Avith appears as the royal residence of the Edomite king HADAD, son of Bedad, credited with defeating the Midianites in Moab.

AVOT, KHIRBET Khirbet Avot is a small site covering about 2 acres in eastern upper Galilee about 7 km west-southwest of Tel Qedesh and 12 km northwest of Tel Hazor. This site, along with other Iron I settlements in the area, is usually identified as part of the territory of Naphtali (Josh 19:32-39).

AVVA One of the towns from which the Assyrian king Sargon moved its inhabitants to repopulate the cities of Samaria after the Israelite deportation (2 Kgs 17:24).

AVVIM, AVVITES 1. A people living near Gaza until the Caphtorim destroyed them, and whose land Joshua's campaigns did not take (Deut 2:23; Josh 13:3).

2. A people deported to SAMARIA by the Assyrians (2 Kgs 17:31).

'AYIN The sixteenth letter of the Hebrew alphabet.

AYYAH A town belonging to the northern tribe Ephraim (1 Chron 7:28). The mention of Aija in Neh 11:31 may be a reference to this same Ayyah.

AZAEL Descendant of EZORA who divorced his foreign wife and put aside their children during Ezra's reform (1 Esdr 9:34).

AZALIAH Meshullam's son, mentioned primarily to identify his son Shaphan, whose reading of the Law motivated Josiah's reforms to set the people apart from pagan cults (2 Kgs 22:3; 2 Chron 34:8).

AZANIAH A Levite whose son Jeshua placed his name on the sealed covenant document (Neh 10:9).

AZAREL 1. One of the Benjamites who joined David at Ziklag (1 Chron 12:6).

2. A Levite son of Heman and head of the eleventh division of temple musicians (1 Chron 25:18).

3. Son of Jeroham and a leader of the tribe of Dan who entered David's service (1 Chron 27:22).

4. One of the descendants of Binnui, who divorced his Gentile wife as part of the religious reform after the Babylonian exile (Ezra 10:41).

5. Son of Ahzai and father of Amashai, one of 128 mighty warriors of the priests who served in the temple under Zabdiel's leadership (Neh 11:13).

6. A priest appointed trumpeter at the dedication of the walls of Jerusalem (Neh 12:36), perhaps the same priest as in number 5 above.

AZARIAH Azariah is the name of numerous individuals in the OT. The name means "Yahweh has helped." The majority of these individuals are found in the books of Chronicles, Ezra, and Nehemiah, and many are associated with the priestly and levitical families.

1. Azariah, son of Zadok, served in the court of Solomon as the high priest (1 Kgs 4:2). That he is listed first among Solomon's officials indicates that Azariah's high priestly role was of great significance.

2. Azariah son of Nathan is another official in Solomon's administration (1 Kgs 4:5). He oversaw the twelve prefects responsible for providing monthly provisions to the palace (1 Kgs 4:7-19).

3. The son of Amaziah and Jecoliah, Azariah was the king of Judah in the first half of the 8th cent. BCE (2 Kgs 15:1-2). He is also referred to as UZZIAH (2 Kgs 15:13).

4. A descendant of Judah, son of Jacob through the lineage of Tamar (Judah's daughter-in-law [Gen 38]) in the genealogical lists of Chronicles (1 Chron 2:8).

5. Another more distant descendant of Judah in the same genealogical list (1 Chron 2:38-39), whose father was Jehu and whose son was Helez.

6. Azariah son of Ahimaaz was a Levite and a descendant of Aaron (1 Chron 6:9 [Heb. 5:35]).

7. Azariah son of Johanan (and father of Amariah) was a grandson of Azariah (6 above). This is probably the same Azariah of Ezra 7:3, although here his father's name is given as Meraioth. The discrepancy can partly be explained by the number of Azariahs and Amariahs in the Chronicles text. The Chronicler identifies him a priest during Solomon's time (1 Chron 6:10 [Heb. 5:36]). Whether or not this was the same Azariah the high priest as in 1 Kgs 4:2 (see 1 above) is uncertain because of the different patronym.

8. Azariah son of Hilkiah was another descendant of Levi through the Aaronid lineage (1 Chron 6:13 [Heb. 5:39]). Being the father of Seraiah, he was also the grandfather of Ezra (Ezra 7:1).

9. Azariah son of Zephaniah was the ancestor of Heman, a Kohathite temple singer during the time of David and Solomon (1 Chron 6:36 [Heb. 6:21]).

10. Among the first returnees from exile was Azariah son of Hilkiah, identified as the chief officer of the temple among the priests (1 Chron 9:11). His patronym is five generations long, perhaps pointing to the importance of his family lineage.

11. Azariah son of Oded is identified as a prophet who encouraged Asa king of Judah to pursue religious reforms (2 Chron 15:1-7). According to the Chronicler, as a result of Asa's successful reforms, Judah enjoyed a period of peace.

12. A son of Jehoshaphat, king of Judah (2 Chron 21:2). He was killed by Jehoram his brother when he succeeded his father to the throne (2 Chron 21:3-4).

13. Another son of Jehoshaphat (2 Chron 21:2). Like his brother of the same name, he was killed by Jehoram (2 Chron 21:3-4).

14. Azariah son of Jehoram, one of the commanders of hundreds who assisted Jehoida in revolting against and deposing Queen Athaliah of Judah and installing Joash in her stead (2 Chron 23:1).

15. The son of Oded, another commander of hundreds who assisted Jehoida in the revolt (2 Chron 23:1).

16. Azariah is identified as the chief priest who led eighty other priests in preventing King Uzziah from making an incense offering on the incense altar of the temple (2 Chron 26:17, 20). The tension between a priest and a king in the cultic role is one that can be found elsewhere in Samuel and Kings.

17. Azariah son of Johanan was one of the Ephraimite chiefs who stood with the prophet Oded in preventing the army of Israel from bringing Judahite captives

into Samaria following Pekah's defeat of Ahaz (2 Chron 28:12).

18–19. Two Levites who participated in the cleansing of the temple under King Hezekiah (2 Chron 29:12). The first, identified as the father of Joel, was a descendant of Kohath; and the second, the son of Jehallelel, hailed from the family of Merari.

20. The chief priest and chief officer of the temple during Hezekiah's reign (2 Chron 31:10, 13).

21. Azariah son of Maaseiah was one of those who repaired the section of the Jerusalem wall next to his house (Neh 3:23-24).

22. One of the leaders of the exiles who returned to Judah from Babylon under the leadership of Zerubbabel (Neh 7:7).

23. A Levite who assisted the people in understanding the Torah read by Ezra (Neh 8:7).

24. One of the priests who set his seal on the covenant that the returnees from exile made to bind themselves to the commandments of Yahweh (Neh 10:2 [Heb. 10:3]).

25. A leader who took part in the dedication of the wall of Jerusalem (Neh 12:33). It is uncertain whether or not he is the same Azariah who repaired a section of the Jerusalem wall (see 21 above).

26. Azariah son of Hoshaiah was one of two men who rejected Jeremiah's prophetic message not to go down to Egypt after the destruction of Jerusalem (Jer 43:2). Instead, they forcibly took a group of people from Judah, including Jeremiah and Baruch, to Egypt.

27. One of the three friends of Daniel, who was given the Chaldean name Abednego (Dan 1:6-7, 11, 19; 2:17). Together with Daniel, Hananiah, and Mishael, he consumed only vegetables and water rather than defile himself by eating royal food. Threatened with the fiery furnace for refusing to worship the golden image that the king made, he and his friends stood firm (Dan 3). In the LXX tradition, Azariah is attributed with a prayer. See AZARIAH, PRAYER OF; DANIEL, ADDITIONS TO.

AZARIAH, PRAYER OF A communal confession of Israel's sinfulness (see Dan 9:4-19; Ezra 9:6-15; Neh 9:6-37; Bar 1:15–3:8). The prayer appears in Greek texts of Dan 3 (between vv. 23 and 24) in Codex Chisianus and in Theodotion (see SEPTUAGINT). The prayer is divided into two parts (3:26-37 and 3:38-45): a contrast between God (3:26-38) and the community (3:29-37) in the first; and a description of the people's needs (3:38) and desire to worship and obey (3:39-41), concluding with a plea for divine help (3:42-45), in the second.

AZARU According to 1 Esdr 5:15, 432 of his descendants returned from exile in Babylon to Jerusalem and Judea. For a similar list, see Neh 10:17-18.

AZAZ Bela's father in Reuben's (i.e., Judah's) genealogy (1 Chron 5:8).

AZAZEL 1. The goat used in DAY OF RECONCILIATION rituals (Lev 16:8, 10, 26). Azazel could mean "scapegoat" or indicate the animal's destination (a sharp or rugged place).

2. A demon named Azazel, leader of angels who corrupt humankind, is bound and buried under sharp rocks in the desert (1 En 8:1-4; 10:4-6). See SACRIFICES AND OFFERINGS.

AZAZIAH 1. A Levite who played the lyre as the COVENANT CHEST entered Jerusalem (1 Chron 15:21).

2. The father of Hoshea, Ephramite chief officer under King David (1 Chron 27:20).

3. A temple overseer during HEZEKIAH's reign (2 Chron 31:13).

AZBUK Nehemiah's father who ruled part of Bethur and helped rebuild the Jerusalem wall after the exile (Neh 3:16).

AZEL Father of six sons, Eleasah's son, and a descendant of Saul's son Jonathan, mentioned in the list of Benjamin's descendants (1 Chron 8:37-38; 9:43-44).

AZETAS A family head mentioned with Kilan whose descendants returned from the exile (1 Esdr 5:15).

AZGAD Azgad's descendants are among returnees to Jerusalem with ZERUBBABEL (Ezra 2:12; Neh. 7:17; 1 Esdr 5:13) or with EZRA (Ezra 8:12; 1 Esdr 8:38). Azgad also appears among those signing a sealed commitment to the Law (Neh 10:15).

AZIEL A Levite harp player who performed for the procession of the covenant chest to Jerusalem (1 Chron 15:20). See JAAZIEL.

AZIZA One of Zattu's six sons who sent away his foreign wife and their children following Ezra's instructions concerning the people of the land (Ezra 10:27).

AZMAVETH 1. A warrior from BAHURIM, one of David's mighty men known as the "Thirty" (2 Sam 23:31; 1 Chron 11:33), and father of JEZIEL and PELET (1 Chron 12:3).

2. The second of the three sons of JEHOADDAH (1 Chron 8:36), a descendant of King Saul through JONATHAN.

3. The son of ADIEL and overseer of David's royal treasury (1 Chron 27:25).

4. Levitical singers from this Benjaminite village, also known as BETH-AZMAVETH (Neh 7:28), participated in the dedication of Jerusalem's walls (Neh 12:29). Forty-two descendants of Azmaveth were among those who returned with ZERUBBABEL from Babylonian captivity (Ezra 2:24).

AZMON A town in the area of Canaan's southern boundary (Num 34:4-5). Joshua 15:4 mentions the town as being within the southern extent of Judah's tribal allotment.

AZNOTH-TABOR Landmark, perhaps a town, that forms the western boundary of the land allotted to the Naphtali tribe (Josh 19:34).

AZOR The only biblical reference to Azor, son of Eliakim and father of Zadok, is in Matthew's genealogy of Jesus (Matt 1:13-14).

AZOR, TEL Tel Azor is located approximately 6 km southeast of Jaffa.

AZRIEL 1. Head of a Manassehite family in Transjordan (1 Chron 5:24).

2. Father of Jerimoth and chief of the tribe of Naphtali under King David (1 Chron 27:19).

3. Father of Seraiah and one of those sent by King Jehoiakim to arrest Jeremiah and Baruch (Jer 36:26).

AZRIKAM 1. A Benjaminite and the first of the six sons of Azel; a descendant of King Saul's son Jonathan (1 Chron 8:38; 9:44).

2. An officer in charge of Ahaz's palace, killed by Zichri, "an Ephraimite warrior" who served in the army of Pekah, king of Israel, when the northern kingdom attacked Judah (2 Chron 28:7).

3. A Levite from the clan of Merari, he was the son of Hashabiah and father of Hasshub and grandfather of Shemaiah, who was one of the Levites in charge of the outside work of the temple after the exile (1 Chron 9:14; Neh 11:15).

4. The last named of the three sons of

Neariah and a descendant of Zerubbabel and David (1 Chron 3:23).

AZUBAH 1. The mother of King Jehoshaphat and daughter of Shilhi (1 Kgs 22:42; 2 Chron 20:31).

2. Caleb's first wife, who bore him three sons (1 Chron 2:18-19).

AZZAN Moses appointed PALTIEL son of Azzan to represent Issachar among the leaders who helped allot land to the tribes (Num 34:26).

AZZUR 1. One of the names written on a sealed commitment to the Law (Neh 10:17).

2. Father of Jeremiah's rival Hananiah (Jer 28:1).

3. Father of Jaazaniah whom Ezekiel, in a vision, sees among a group of twenty-five men (Ezek 11:1).

Bb

B Letter symbolizing the 4th-cent. manuscript Codex Vaticanus.

BAAL In the OT the word occurs both as a noun meaning "lord, master, husband," and as the proper name of a deity. Used in the second sense, Baal is the pagan god most frequently mentioned in the Bible and the archetypical rival of Yahweh; the classic indictment of the Israelites says that, instead of serving Yahweh, they "worshipped," "followed," or "have gone after" Baal or the Baals (Deut 4:3; Judg 8:33; 1 Kgs 18:18; Jer 2:23; 9:14).

See BAALATH; BAALATH-BEER; BAAL-BERITH; BAALE-JUDAH; BAAL-GAD; BAAL-HAMON; BAAL-HANAN; BAAL-HAZOR; BAAL-HERMON; BAAL-MEON; BAAL-PEOR; BAAL-PERAZIM; BAAL-SHALISHAH; BAAL-TAMAR; BAAL-ZEBUB; BAAL-ZEPHON.

BAAL, KING OF TYRE Two kings of Tyre who carry the name "Baal."

1. Baal I was king of Tyre during the reigns of the Assyrian kings Esarhaddon (680–669 BCE) and Assurbanipal (668–627 BCE). In 677 Esarhaddon defeated Sidon and gave Baal the cities of Marubbu and Sarepta (ZAREPHATH) that had belonged to Sidon. The treaty between Esarhaddon and Baal obliges the Tyrian king to strict political loyalty to his Assyrian overlord; however, Baal apparently was able to maintain a certain measure of independence while officially a vassal of Esarhaddon and Assurbanipal.

2. Baal II was a contemporary of Nebuchadnezzar II (604–562 BCE). He is the successor of Ittobaal III.

BAAL, PERSON 1. A man listed in the Reubenite genealogy (1 Chron 5:5-6) as a contemporary of the Assyrian king Tiglath-Pileser III (744–727 BCE).

2. A Benjaminite who was the brother of KISH, Saul's father. He was from Gibeon (1 Chron 8:30; 9:36).

BAAL, PLACE See BAALATH-BEER.

BAALAH The term, associated with several places in Judah, means "lady" or "mistress"; the identity of the deity is unknown.

1. A location, also known as Kiriath-Jearim, along the boundary of Judah's tribal territory (Josh 15:9; 1 Chron 13:6).

2. A town located in the southern part of Judah (Josh 15:29). In the list of Simeonite towns in Judah, it is called BALAH (Josh 19:3; 1 Chron 4:29, BILHAH).

3. A mountain mentioned in the list of locations along Judah's tribal boundary (Josh 15:11).

BAALATH A place located in Dan (Josh 19:44). It appears in lists of Solomon's construction projects (1 Kgs 9:17-18; 2 Chron 8:5-6). The term is common in west Semitic languages as the name of a goddess.

BAALATH-BEER A town marking the border of the tribal territory of Simeon (Josh 19:8). It is called Baal in 1 Chron 4:24-33. It is generally assumed that these are the same.

BAALBEK The ancient city of Heliopolis is located near the modern Baalbek and lies between Mount Lebanon and the Anti-Lebanon mountain range.

BAAL-BERITH A deity worshipped in Israel during the time of the judges, particularly in the region of Shechem. The name occurs once in reference to the Israelites' worship of this deity after the death of Gideon (Judg 8:33), and once in reference to the deity's temple in Shechem (Judg 9:4).

BAALE-JUDAH Location of the covenant chest of God before being moved to Obed-edom and then Jerusalem (2 Sam 6:2). Same as Kiriath-Jearim (2 Sam 6:21).

BAAL-GAD A location in the Baqah Valley at the foot of Mount Hermon (Josh 11:17; 12:7; 13:5).

BAAL-HAMON The unknown location of a vineyard of King Solomon in Song 8:11.

BAAL-HANAN A personal name.

1. An Edomite ruler (Gen 36:38-39; 1 Chron 1:49-50).

2. An official of King David (1 Chron 27:28).

3. The ruler of the Phoenician city of Arvad mentioned on the Assurbanipal Prism.

BAAL-HAZOR A locality near Ephraim (2 Sam 13:23) commonly identified with the highest top of Mount Ephraim. If Hazor is the name of the mountain peak, BAAL is the Syrian storm god, and the town owes its name to the veneration of Baal as lord of the mountain.

BAAL-HERMON A mountain at the border of the hill country of Lebanon (Judg 3:3) mentioned as part of the territory of the tribe of Manasseh (1 Chron 5:23). See HERMON, MOUNT.

BAALIS A 6th-cent. BCE Ammonite king (Jer 40:14).

BAAL-MEON A place in Moab (Num 32:38; Ezek 25:9; 1 Chron 5:8) also known under the names Beth-baal-meon (Josh 13:17), Beth-meon (Jer 48:23), and Beon (Num 32:3).

BAAL-PEOR Baal-peor is both a place-name (Hos 9:10) and the name of a deity (Num 25:3-5). According to Num 25:1-9, the people of Israel participated in the sacrificial cult of Baal-peor at the invitation of the Moabite women. The event took place at Shittim in the plains of Moab northeast of the Dead Sea. The biblical information on Baal-peor is limited; it is said that he was the god of Moabite women (Num 25:2); that his cult included a sacrificial meal in honor of the dead (Num 25:2; Ps 106:28); and it is intimated that his worship had aspects of sexual debauchery (Num 25:1, 6-8). According to Num 31:16, it was BALAAM, the man of nocturnal visions (Num 24:3-4), who had incited the Moabite women to invite the Israelite men to join them in the festivities for Baal-peor. Other texts do not make the connection between Balaam and Baal-peor.

BAAL-PERAZIM A location south of Jerusalem remembered for David's victory over the Philistines (2 Sam 5:18-20; 1 Chron 14:9-11). Perazim is the name of a mountain between Jerusalem and Bethlehem (Isa 28:21). A connection with Perez the ancestor of David is unlikely.

BAALSAMUS In 1 Esdr 9:43, someone who assisted Ezra in the public reading of the Law scroll (MAASEIAH in Neh 8:4).

BAAL-SHALISHAH A town, most likely located in the Jordan Valley or on the slopes opposite Gilgal, from which a man came to meet Elisha (2 Kgs 4:42). The name is connected to "the land of Shalishah" (1 Sam 9:4) that Saul passed through searching for his father's donkeys.

BAAL-TAMAR The place of the Israelites' victory over the Benjaminites. The site is located between Gibeah and Bethel (Judg 20:33).

BAAL-ZEBUB According to the account of 2 Kgs 1, the Israelite king Ahaziah sent messengers to consult "Ekron's god Baalzebub" concerning whether or not he would recover from a wound suffered during a fall.

BAAL-ZEPHON In the OT, Baalzephon occurs as the name of a place in the Egyptian delta (Exod 14:2, 9; Num 33:7). The location is unknown.

BAANA 1. The son of Ahilud, one of Solomon's twelve prefects responsible for supplying provisions for the palace one month of each year. He represented the regions Taanach, Megiddo, and Bethshean (1 Kgs 4:12).

2. The son of Hushai, another prefect of Solomon, responsible for the regions Asher and Bealoth (1 Kgs 4:16).

3. The father of Zadok, one of those who repaired a portion of Jerusalem's walls during the days of Nehemiah (Neh 3:4).

BAANAH A variant of Baana.

1. One of the two sons of Rimmon the Benjaminite. He and his brother Rechab were captains of Saul's son Ishbosheth's raiding bands. They murdered Ishbosheth and brought his head to David, thinking that they would be rewarded but, to their great disappointment, David ordered their hands and feet to be cut off and their mutilated bodies to be hanged as a public warning against regicide (2 Sam 4:2-12).

2. The father of Heleb ("Heled" in 1 Chron 11:30) from Netophah, one of the thirty mighty men of David (2 Sam 23:29).

3. One of the leaders who returned from Babylonian exile with Zerubbabel (Ezra 2:2; Neh 7:7). He could be Baana #3 (1 Esdr 5:8).

4. One of the leaders who, with Nehemiah the governor, set his seal on the firm covenant to observe the Law of Moses, perhaps the same person who returned from the exile.

BAARA In Benjamin's genealogy, a wife whom Shaharaim dismissed, perhaps a Moabite, who apparently bore him no children (1 Chron 8:8-11). It is not mentioned whether she returned to her family.

BAASEIAH A Levite descendant of the Koharthites and an ancestor of ASAPH, who served in the temple by singing (1 Chron 6:25). See MAASEIAH.

BAASHA The third king of Israel after its succession from Davidic rule in Jerusalem (ca. 902–886 BCE). Of the tribe of Issachar, Baasha performed the first in a series of coups d'état in Israel when he overthrew NADAB son of Jeroboam I of Ephraim, while the latter laid siege to the Philistine city of GIBBETHON (1 Kgs 15:27-28). Baasha, in a prolonged military dispute with King ASA of Judah (1 Kgs 15:16, but cf 2 Chron 16:1, which implies a dispute of short duration toward the end of Asa's long rule), attempted to move Israel's border to within 9 km of Jerusalem by fortifying RAMAH. Asa outmaneuvered him by bribing BEN-HADAD of Damascus to attack Israel from the north. With Baasha's attention diverted in this way, Asa returned the border northward by fortifying Geba and Mizpah (1 Kgs 15:22; cf Jer 41:9).

BABEL Genesis 11:1-9 records the OT's version of how Babylon received its name. The inhabitants of the earth/land all speaking one language, come together in a plain in Shinar to build a city whose showpiece is a tower reaching heavenward/skyward (vv. 1-4). Yahweh, upon inspection, is dismayed. Yahweh takes the action necessary to end this project (vv. 5-9). Yahweh confuses the common language (vv. 7, 9), thus ending the possibility of verbal communication among the builders, and then scatters them well beyond the borders of Shinar.

BABYLON City in southern Mesopotamia, located on a branch of the Euphrates, 59 mi. (90 km) southwest of Baghdad. Babylon rose to prominence early in the 2nd millennium BCE.

The OT contains more than 300 references to Babylon, the region of Babylonia, or its inhabitants, as well as forty-nine references to the ethnically precise term "Chaldea/n/s." Because of its international and cultural significance, and its role later in destroying Jerusalem and deporting large portions of its citizens, Babylon came to carry theological significance in the Bible even beyond its obvious historical importance. The city itself came to symbolize ungodly power.

The word Babylon occurs fourteen times in the NT: four times in Matthew's genealogy of Jesus, once in Acts, once in 1 Peter, and eight times in Revelation. In Matthew's genealogy the references to Babylon help organize the lineage of Jesus into three historical periods: Abraham to David, David to the Babylonian exile, and the exile to Jesus the Messiah (Matt 1:11, 12, 17). The Babylonian exile began in the early 6th cent. BCE and marked the end of Israel's Davidic monarchy that ruled from Jerusalem. First Peter mentions Babylon once, but here the term is a political metaphor for Roman rule.

More than half the NT references to Babylon come in the book of Revelation, where the term also serves as a metaphor for Rome. Revelation's attitude toward the Roman Empire is summarized in Rev 14:8 when an angel proclaims, "Fallen, fallen is Babylon the great! She made all the nations drink the wine of her lustful passion."

BABYLONIA See ASSYRIA AND BABYLONIA.

BACA VALLEY The Baca Valley may be an unknown geographical location that pilgrims to the Jerusalem temple passed through, or a symbolic expression of the pilgrims' sorrow turned to joy along the way (Ps 84:6).

BAGOAS Holofernes's personal steward, a EUNUCH, who delivered HOLOFERNES's dinner invitation to JUDITH, and was first to find him beheaded the next morning (Jdt 12:11; 14:14-18).

BAHARUM Town of origin of AZMAVETH, one of David's warriors (1 Chron 11:33), although Azmaveth's town is named BAHURIM in 2 Sam 23:31.

BAHURIM A Benjaminite village near Jerusalem, Bahurim may correspond to modern Ras et-Tmim or Khirbet Ibqe'dan. MICHAL's husband PALTIEL followed her weeping as far as Bahurim when she returned to King DAVID (2 Sam 3:16). Bahurim was also the residence of Shimei son of Gera, who cast stones at David and later begged for mercy (2 Sam 16:5; 19:16; 1 Kgs 2:8). Jonathan and Ahimaaz also hid in Bahurim (2 Sam 17:18). AZMAVETH, a member of David's guard, was probably from Bahurim (2 Sam 23:31; 1 Chron 11:33).

BAITERUS A family head whose descendants returning from the exile numbered 3,005 (1 Esdr 5:17). Absent from lists in Ezra 2:3-35 and Neh 7:8-38.

BAKBAKKAR A Levite descendant of ASAPH living in Jerusalem after the exile had ended (1 Chron 9:15). Absent from the parallel list in Neh 11:16.

BAKBUK A family head whose descendants were of the Nethinim, temple servants, who returned to Jerusalem after the exile (Ezra 2:51; Neh 7:53).

BAKBUKIAH A Levite who led prayer (Neh 11:17), stood opposite the Levites in charge of the songs (Neh 12:9), and guarded the storehouses (Neh 12:25). See BUKKIAH; MATTANIAH.

BALAAM Balaam is a non-Israelite prophet or seer featured in Num 22–24 as the one who blessed Israel in defiance of King BALAK of Moab, who had hired him to curse Israel (see MOAB, MOABITES).

New Testament references to Balaam are uniformly negative, portraying him as a prototype of false prophets and teachers in the NT period (2 Pet 2:15; Jude 11; Rev 2:14).

BALADAN Father of the Babylonian king Merodach-baladan (i.e., Marduk-apaliddina), whose envoys King HEZEKIAH allowed to tour all his storehouses (2 Kgs 20:12).

BALAH In Josh 19:3, the tribe of Simeon receives the town of Balah inside Judah's territory as an allotment. The text implies a location south and east of BEER-SHEBA.

BALAK King of Moab, son of ZIPPOR. Fearing the Israelites, Balak sends for BALAAM, the seer, to curse the Israelites. Balaam curses the Moabites instead (Num 22–24). References to Balak also appear in Josh 24:9; Judg 11:25; Mic 6:5; and Rev 2:14.

BALAMON A town in Samaria. In a field between this town and Dothan, Judith's husband Manasseh was buried (Jdt 8:3).

BALANCES Balances, or scales, were necessary in the world before coinage for each transaction in precious metals (especially silver and gold), since the sole way of determining their value was by weight. Throughout the Bronze and Iron ages, balances were constructed of two pans, suspended by cords from a horizontal beam. The beam was suspended from its middle and either held by hand (in small balances or hand balances), or mounted on a vertical beam (in large balances). The OT does not detail the process of weighing but stresses its moral aspect. This is expressed by the terms "false balances" and "dishonest scales" as opposed to "fair scales" and "honest balances" (e.g., Amos 8:5; Prov 11:1; 16:26; Ezek 45:10).

See WEIGHTS AND MEASURES.

BALAS, ALEXANDER See EPIPHANES.

BALDNESS Head hair loss (baldness) can be natural ("a receding hairline") as in Lev 13:40-41; or intentional ("shaven heads"), as a sign of mourning mentioned likely without approval by the prophets (Isa 22:12), but forbidden to priests (Lev 21:5) and Israelites as well (Deut 14:1); or signaling the end of a Nazirite vow (Num 6:18). Natural baldness does not render one unclean unless associated with a skin problem (Lev 13:42-44).

See HAIR, HAIRS.

BALM *Balm* is a nonspecific term for a variety of medicinal and aromatic mixtures made from olive oil and various resins. Many of these resins were extracted from trees and scrubs found in the semiarid regions of Transjordan, Arabia, and southern Egypt, and this might explain their presence among the goods traded by the Ishmaelites, who were carrying gum, resins, and balm from Gilead to Egypt (Gen 37:25).

BALSAM David is commanded to approach the enemy from the rear near a stand of "balsam trees" (2 Sam 5:23-24; 1 Chron 14:14-15). It is not clear which species of tree or shrub is meant, with mulberry and mastic terebinth suggested.

BALTHASAR The name provided in church traditions for one of the MAGI (Matt 2:1-12). See MELKON.

BAMOTH-BAAL A town on the plateau east of the Jordan near Mount Nebo, exact site uncertain, serving as a stopping place on the Israelite trek from Egypt (Num 21:19-20; 22:41). See NEBO, MOUNT.

BAN The "ban" ("devoted thing," "devoted to destruction") is a category or status encompassing things or people consecrated irrevocably into God's ownership and unavailable for secular use. Leviticus 27:21, 28-29 applies this status to fields, animals, and enslaved people as a result of voluntary dedication. Things that were banned became priestly property according to Num 18:14 and Ezek 44:17. People who were banned were put to death (Exod 22:19; Lev 27:29).

BANI A name similar to BUNNI and BINNUI, all of which are easily confused. The Hebrew can also be understood as the term "son of," so that in a number of places the LXX chooses that meaning rather than the name Bani (e.g., 2 Sam 23:36).

1. A Gadite, one of David's "Thirty" heroes (2 Sam 23:36).

2. The son of Shemer, a descendant of Merrari the son of Levi, and one of the ancestors of Ethan the son of Kishi (1 Chron 6:46).

3. One of the sons of PEREZ son of Judah (1 Chron 9:4), one of the ancestors of Uthai son of Ammihud, who was in Jerusalem in Nehemiah's time.

4. Among those who returned to Judah with Zerubbabbel after the exile (Ezra 2:10; 1 Esdr 5:12; Neh 7:15).

5. Among those who married foreign women (Ezra 10:29, 34, 38; 1 Esdr 9:30, 34).

6. Returnees from Babylonia to Judah with Ezra (Ezra 8:10).

7. Among those who sealed Ezra's covenant (Neh 10:13-15).

8. Among those who assisted Ezra in organizing the people and helping them understand the Instruction (Neh 8:7).

9. The ancestor/family line of Uzzi, overseer of the Jerusalem Levites of the order of Asaph (Neh 11:22).

10. The ancestor/family line of Rehum, a Levite who contributed money for repairing a section of the Jerusalem wall (Neh 3:17).

11. A Levite (group or individual) who took part in the Festival of Booths at the time of Ezra (Neh 9:4-5).

BANNAS One of the ancestors of the seventy-four Levites who returned with Zerubbabel to Jerusalem (1 Esdr 5:26), but not included in Ezra 2:40.

BANNER The most common method of identification for troops on the march or in combat was the battle standard, or banner. The OT mentions a variety of uses for such banners. They serve as rallying points in battle (Ps 60:4; Isa 11:10, 12; possibly Zech 9:16). They signal advancing danger or the beginning of a battle or siege (Jer 4:6; Isa 18:3; Jer 51:12, 27; also used metaphorically in Num 26:10).

BANQUET Banquets were events that were used to mark important social and religious occasions throughout the historical periods and cultural contexts referenced by the Bible. Diners reclined on couches and enjoyed a luxurious repast while being attended to by servants (pictured negatively in Amos 6:4-6; see Plato's Symposium for the Greek archetype). The custom appears to have arisen in the ANE, but was quickly adopted by the Greeks (ca. 6th cent. BCE) and later by the Romans and came to dominate throughout the Greco-Roman world. In the NT, Jesus is always pictured as reclining at meals (e.g., Mark 4:15; 6:39; 8:6; 14:18). Prior to the adoption of the custom of reclining, there are references to sitting at a banquet as the common posture in the ancient Mediterranean world. See FEASTS AND FASTS; MEAL CUSTOMS; WINE.

BANQUET HALL A banquet hall was a chamber containing couches and tables for a reclining meal (Esth 7:8; Amos 6:4-7; also Jer 16:5-8). In the Greco-Roman world, dining rooms for reclining banquets were found at pagan temples (1 Cor 8:10) and other locations including private homes (Mark 2:15).

BAPTISM A rite of immersion in water.

BAPTIST, JOHN THE See JOHN.

BAPTIZE To immerse in water, in relation to the baptism of John, Jesus and his disciples, Jewish ritual immersion (Luke 11:38; Mark 7:4), and of the Holy Spirit (Mark 1:8 et al.). See BAPTISM; JOHN.

BARABBAS This enigmatic character appears in Jesus' Roman trial in all four Gospels (Matt 27:16; Mark 15:7; Luke 23:19; John 18:40): Pilate offers to release one prisoner as part of a Passover amnesty; the Jewish crowd, stirred up by the chief priests, choose Barabbas rather than Jesus.

BARACHEL A Buzite, father of Elihu (Job 32:2, 6).

BARACHIAH Father of Zechariah in Matt 23:35. Spelled Berechiah in Zech 1:1. Also called Jehoida (2 Chron 24:20-22) and Jeberechiah (Isa 8:2). See BERECHIAH.

BARAITA A technical term in the Babylonian Talmud to designate a Tannaitic tradition, which is not included in the Mishnah.

BARAK The son of Abinoam from Kedesh in Naphtali (Judg 4). Barak was called by DEBORAH to follow the order of Yahweh to raise 10,000 men from the tribes Naphtali and Zebulun in order to lead them to war against SISERA, supreme commander of the Canaanite forces suppressing Israel. Despite Yahweh's assurance that Sisera would be delivered into Barak's hands, Barak was willing to obey only if Deborah confirmed her faith in the promised victory by attending the campaign. Deborah's song (Judg 5)—sung by Deborah and Barak—is a poetical depiction of Israel's victory from a slightly different angle. Hebrews 11:32-34 mentions Barak among the ancestors who were commended for their faith.

BARBARIAN Paul uses the term in this manner to describe people who are speaking foreign languages (Col 3:11).

BARIAH Son of Shemiah, whose ancestry can be dated back to Zerubbabel and King David (1 Chron 3:22).

BAR-JESUS A Jewish "false prophet" and magician, also known as ELYMAS, who served procounsul Sergius Paulus (Acts 13:6-11). Bar-Jesus' opposition to Paul and Barnabas resulted in Paul's inflicting blindness upon him, demonstrating Paul's power and authority in the Holy Spirit at the beginning of his first missionary trip.

BAR JONAH, BARJONA See JONAH, BAR; PETER, THE APOSTLE.

BARKOS A family head whose descendants were among the 392 temple servants, called the Nethinim, who returned to Jerusalem after the exile (Ezra 2:58; Neh 7:55).

BARLEY A crucial part of the ancient farmer's pantry, though it takes a backseat to the WHEAT that the biblical record frequently pairs with it (e.g., Deut 8:8; Ezek 4:9; Joel 1:4; and Job 31:40). Barley finds little favor in the sacrificial system where it appears once (Num 5:15), costs one-third the price of wheat (Rev 6:6), and feeds the horses (1 Kgs 4:28). Barley's secondary importance reflects its relative yield and dietary contribution.

BARNABAS Also named Joseph, a prominent apostle and associate of Paul in Antioch of Syria, Cyprus, and Asia Minor. See esp. Acts 4–15 and Gal 2:1-10.

BARODIS A family head whose descendants were among the 372 temple servants, called the Nethinim, who returned after the exile (1 Esdr 5:34; not found in Ezra 2:57; Neh 7:59).

BARREN, BARRENNESS Barrenness describes a woman who is physically unable to bear children.

BARSABBAS Two characters in Acts.

1. Joseph (also called Justus)—one of two men nominated to replace Judas Iscariot among the apostles (Acts 1:23).

2. Judas—distinguished as a leader and prophet among the Jerusalem fellowship. One of a group sent to announce the church's decisions concerning Gentile believers (Acts 15:22-33).

BARTACUS Father of King Darius's secondary wife named Apame, to whom the young man Zerubbabel refers (1 Esdr 4:29).

BARTHOLOMEW In the Synoptic Gospels (Matt 10:3; Mark 3:18; Luke 6:14) and Acts (Acts 1:13), Bartholomew is one of the Twelve, associated with either Philip or Matthew. Bartholomew is never mentioned in the Gospel of John. Bartholomew is usually identified with Nathanael of Cana (John 21:2).

BARTIMAEUS A blind beggar healed by Jesus as the latter exits Jericho (Mark 10:46-52). Thereafter, Bartimaeus follows Jesus, presumably into Jerusalem. Similar stories are found in Matt 20:29-34, which mentions two anonymous blind men healed upon leaving Jericho, and in Luke 18:35-43, wherein Jesus heals one blind man upon entering Jericho. See BLINDNESS.

BARUCH The son of Neriah was Jeremiah's scribe and a member of a prominent Judean family. Baruch appears only in the book of Jeremiah (32:12-16; 36; 43:1-7; 45). He served Jeremiah by performing standard scribal duties: certifying land transactions, writing down the prophet's words, and presenting Jeremiah's divine oracles to the people and the royal court.

BARUCH, BOOK OF This apocryphal text is attributed to Baruch, the son of Neriah and secretary to JEREMIAH, although most scholars think the book was written not in the purported time of the Babylonian exile but sometime during the 2nd cent. BCE. The book nonetheless explores the theme of exile, defined as the consequence of disobeying God's law (4:12), and clearly elaborated in the book's four parts.

BARZILLAI 1. A Meholathite whose son, Adriel, married either MERAB (1 Sam 18:19) or MICHAL (some Hebrew and Greek manuscripts, 2 Sam 21:8).

2. A Gileadite from Rogelim who gave David provisions in Mahanaim after Absalom's revolt (2 Sam 17:27; 19:31-40). David ordered Solomon to take care of Barzillai's sons (1 Kgs 2:7).

3. A priest who took the name of

his father-in-law Barzillai the Gileadite. His descendants could not prove their priestly lineage (Ezra 2:61; Neh 7:63). According to 1 Esdr 5:38, the priest's name was JADDUS, husband of Barzillai's daughter AGIA.

BASEMATH 1. Esau's wife. Esau's genealogy identifies her as the daughter of Ishmael, the sister of Nebaioth (Gen 36:3), and the mother of Reuel and several clans (Gen 36:13, 17). In the Esau story, however, Basemath is the daughter of ELON the Hittite (Gen 26:34; Esau's wife ADAH is given this ancestry in the genealogy). Ishmael's daughter in the narrative is Mahalath (Gen 28:9), who is omitted in the genealogy.

2. A daughter of SOLOMON who was married to AHIMAAZ, Solomon's official over the district of Naphtali (1 Kgs 4:15).

BASHAN Bashan (Batanae in the Roman world, today roughly corresponding with the Golan Heights) is a region that rests generally north of the Yarmuk River, south of Mount Hermon, and east of the Sea of Galilee until reaching the desert and the basalt lava beds of the northwest Arabian Desert. An important agricultural center, Bashan runs about 20 mi. (30 km) east to west, and about 40 mi. (65 km) north to south. After rising about 2,600 ft. out of the Galilee basin, Bashan is a flat region of rich, fertile soil, whose 20–24 in. of annual rainfall support forests and grasslands, making it famous in the ancient world for its livestock and trees.

BATH A volume measure of liquid equal to the dry measure ephah (Ezek 45:11, 14). Perhaps a bath was about 21–23 L. See WEIGHTS AND MEASURES.

BATHING Bathing in the Bible is performed for various reasons: simple hygiene, as in the case of Pharaoh's daughter (Exod 2:5) or the cleaning of a newborn (Ezek 16:4; soap was extracted from both vegetable and mineral alkali); refreshment and relaxation (2 Sam 11:8; Ezek 23:40; Song 4:2; 5:3; Ruth 3:3); hospitality shown toward guests by washing their feet (Gen 18:4; Judg 19:21; John 13:5); and after an experience of strong emotion (Gen 43:31; 2 Sam 12:20). Most instances of bathing occur in connection with ritual purification.

BATHSHEBA Wife of Uriah and later of David; mother of Solomon. Listed as "the wife of Uriah" in the genealogy in Matt 1:6. Bathsheba is identified in 2 Sam 11:3 as the daughter of Eliam (Ammiel in 1 Chron 3:5) and wife of URIAH the Hittite, who served in David's army. David commits adultery with Bathsheba in 2 Sam 11. In 1 Kgs 1–2 Bathsheba is vocal and active in events that secure Solomon's accession to the throne over his older half brother ADONIJAH.

Bathsheba is among five women included in the Gospel of Matthew's genealogy of Jesus (Matt 1:6).

BATH-SHUA 1. Canaanite wife of the patriarch Judah and mother of his sons ER, ONAN, and SHELAH (1 Chron 2:3).

2. Daughter of AMMIEL, wife of DAVID, and mother of SOLOMON (1 Chron 3:7). The LXX and Vulgate have BATHSHEBA in this verse.

BATTERING RAM A war implement used to breach gates, walls, and fortifications. Originally soldiers crashed tree trunks against city gates, but vulnerability to counterattacks and improved fortifications gave rise to battering rams mounted on massive four-wheeled carriages, surrounded with armor and topped with archers' towers. Either as the nosecone of the carriage or suspended from the roof of the structure, this metal-tipped ram in concert with other weaponry and tactics (Ezek 4:2; 21:22; 26:9; Isa 22:5) could decide the outcome of battles. Israel employed them in Joab's siege of Abel of Beth-maacah (2 Sam 20:15).

BATTLE The violent confrontation of two large and opposing armies at a specific location in the course of extended hostilities. In biblical times pitched battles involved the clash of armies composed of light and heavy infantry, and archers, with occasional use of slingers, chariotry, and cavalry. Limited communication eliminated control of battles beyond the opening charge.

When one line broke and ran (2 Kgs 14:11-12), discarding their heavy weapons and armor, heavy casualties resulted (Ps 18:37-42). Decisive battles often affected the outcome of a war, giving victory and control to one army over another and its territory. In biblical and related literature, the final encounter between good and evil is seen as a pitched battle.

BATTLEMENTS Fortification, enclosure, or corner tower constructed atop city walls, especially casemate style—double walls connected by internal partition walls—to provide protection and a platform for observation and counterattacking (Zeph 1:16; 3:6).

BAZLITH The founder of a family group included among the Nethinim (probably families of non-Israelite origin, as may be deduced from their names listed in Ezra 2:43-55; Neh 7:46-57; 1 Esdr 5:31) who returned to Judah from the exile (Neh 7:54).

BEALIAH One of the mighty Benjaminite warriors who fought with King David at Ziklag (1 Chron 12:5).

BEALOTH 1. A town in the southern plain included among Judah's tribal allotment in land conquered by Joshua (Josh 15:24).

2. A western Galilee town in Solomon's ninth administrative district (1 Kgs 4:16). See BAALATH-BEER.

BEARD Israelite men typically wore beards, depicted in Egyptian and Mesopotamian art as curly, but not unkempt. In Israel, the beard was a symbol of manhood, to be shaved only in purification rites, such as those relating to skin diseases (Lev 13:29-30; 14:9).

BEAST A term for an animal, often one that is unfamiliar or frightening.

BEATITUDES This literary form in the biblical material declares God's favor on present circumstances, actions, or practices, and/or God's future reversal or transformation of or salvation from present oppressive circumstances. Beatitudes also often express an implicit imperative or exhortation for humans to live consistently with God's justice. The most well-known "beatitudes" occur at the beginning of the Sermon on the Mount (Matt 5:3-12; Luke 6:20*b*-21).

BEAUTIFUL GATE Gate of Herod's temple courts where Peter and John healed a lame man (Acts 3:2, 10).

BEBAI 1. The ancestor of 623 exiles who returns with Zerubbabel from the exile (Ezra 2:11; 1 Esdr 5:13; Neh 7:16 instead indicates 628). Other decendants return with Ezra (Ezra 8:11; 1 Esdr 8:37). Some of Bebai's descendants appear in the list of men who dismiss their foreign wives (Ezra 10:28; 1 Esdr 9:29).

2. One of the leaders of the people who sets his seal to an agreement to observe the Torah (Neh 10:15 [Heb. 10:16]).

BECHER The father of Zemirah, Joash, Eliezer, Elioenai, Omri, Jeremoth, Abijah, Anathoth, and Alemeth (1 Chron 7:8). Two genealogies place Becher as the second son of Benjamin (Gen 46:21; 1 Chron 7:6), but he is replaced by ASHBEL in other genealogies (Num 26:38; 1 Chron 8:1).

BECORATH A Benjaminite ancestor of Saul, Israel's first king. Zeror's father and Aphiah's son (1 Sam 9:1).

BEDAD Father of Hadad, an Edomite king or chief (Gen 36:35; 1 Chron 1:46).

BEDAN 1. The son of ULAM of the tribe of Manasseh, of whom nothing else is known (1 Chron 7:17).

2. In the MT of 1 Sam 12:11, an otherwise unknown Israelite leader mentioned alongside JERUBBAAL (GIDEON), JEPHTHAH, and either SAMSON (LXX) or SAMUEL (MT).

BEDEIAH One of Bani's descendants who sent his foreign wife and their children away as Ezra instructed (Ezra 10:37; 1 Esdr 9:34).

BEELIADA One of the thirteen sons of David born in Jerusalem (1 Chron 14:7). His name appears as ELIADA in the parallel lists (2 Sam 5:16; 1 Chron 3:8).

BEELZEBUL Jesus' opponents refer to him, and also to the ruler or prince of demons, as "Beelzebul" (Matt 10:25; 12:24, 27; Mark 3:22; Luke 11:15, 18-19), with the claim that Beelzebul was his means of exorcising demons.

BEER The Hebrew word for "well" (Gen 26:15-32). During the Israelites' wilderness wandering, after they left Moab and traveled along the Arnon River they came to a place called "Beer" (Num 21:16), and they celebrated it as Yahweh's gift to Israel (21:17-18). Its precise location remains unknown. JOTHAM fled to Beer from his brother Abimelech's rampage against all of Jerubaal's sons (Judg 9:21).

BEERA Zophah's eleventh son and a descendant of Asher (1 Chron 7:37).

BEERAH A chieftain and a son of Reuben. He was taken into exile by Tilgath-pilneser of Assyria (1 Chron 5:6).

BEER-ELIM A city in Moab (Isa 15:8). Possibly the same as BEER (Num 21:16).

BEERI 1. The father of Esau's wife Judith, a Hittite (Gen 26:34).

2. The name of the father of the prophet Hosea (Hos 1:1).

BEER-LAHAI-ROI The spring where Sarai's slave Hagar saw God (Gen 16:14). Its name "The Well of the Living One (who) Sees Me" came from Hagar's encounter with El-Roi (The God Who Sees Me). Hagar was the first person in the biblical text to identify God with a name. The well was located in an oasis somewhere in the wilderness of Kadesh-Barnea, near Bered, a place-name found only in this story. In Gen 24:62, the name refers to a town or village attached to a well. After Abraham died, the epic story says that Isaac settled at Beer-lahai-roi (Gen 25:11).

BEEROTH Beeroth, whose name means "wells," was one of several Hivite towns in the territory of Benjamin. By pretending they had traveled from a far distance, Beerothites made peace with Joshua and were thus spared, but were later forced to cut wood and carry water for Israel's worship (Josh 9:17-27; see HIVITES).

BEEROTH-BENE-JAAKAN The Israelites depart from this area in the northeastern part of the Sinai for Moserah where Aaron dies (Deut 10:6).

BEER-RESISIM Middle Bronze Age I settlement in the southern plain where people subsisted on a mixed economy of grazing, farming, and trading of copper and other goods.

BEER-SHEBA The city of Beer-sheba, part of the territorial inheritance of Simeon, is the southernmost city of the land of Israel, and a frequent site in the stories about Abraham, esp. Gen 21–28.

BEESHTERAH One of the Transjordanian levitical cities located in the tribal territory assigned to Manasseh (Josh 21:27).

BEHEMOTH In Job 40:15, a large beast.

BEL "Lord," an alternative name for an Akkadian deity. The Babylonian god Marduk is the Bel of Isa 46:1; Jer 50:2; 51:44; and the story of Bel and the Snake.

BEL AND THE SNAKE The apocryphal story Bel and the Snake is the last of three extended Additions to the book of Daniel in the Greek and Latin versions of the Bible (the other two are the Prayer of Azriah and the story of Susanna). Bel and the Snake consists of two tales. Perhaps the account of how Daniel exposes the false god Bel and destroys the snake-like idol of Bel worshipped by the Babylonians was stimulated by Jer 51:34-35, 44 (*see* BAAL). Both stories present a polemic against idolatry.

BELA 1. The first son of Benjamin, who is consistently listed as such in all the genealogies of Benjamin (Gen 46:21; Num 26:38; 1 Chron 7:6; 8:1), despite the fluidity of Benjaminite genealogies.

2. The son of Beor, the first king to reign in Edom (Gen 36:32). Because of his patronymic, the Targum identified Bela with Balaam, "Beor's son." The LXX instead identified him with Balak, king of Moab.

3. The son of Azaz, a Reubenite who lived in Aroer, the southernmost region of the territory of Reuben (1 Chron 5:8-9).

4. Another name for ZOAR, one of five allied cities in the Dead Sea region that fought against an eastern coalition of four kings (Gen 14:2).

BELL The high priest wore bells attached to the lower hem of his long blue "robe for the vest" (Exod 28:31-35; 39:25-26), which provided a visual and aural confirmation of the priest's ritual significance.

BELNUUS A postexilic Jew, descendant of Addi, according to 1 Esdr 9:31 (compare Ezra 10:31). See BINNUI.

BELOVED DISCIPLE "Beloved Disciple" is an abbreviated form of "the disciple whom Jesus loved," a phrase that appears in some form five times in John (13:23; 19:26; 20:2; 21:7, 20). Based on the reference to the disciple's testifying and writing about "these things" (21:24), ancient writers typically associated the traditional author of the Gospel, John the son of Zebedee, with the Beloved Disciple. However, few scholars would make this connection now. Beyond the traditional approach, there have been multiple suggestions regarding the Beloved Disciple's identity. Possible candidates proposed include Lazarus, Andrew, Philip, Nathanael, Thomas, the rich young ruler, and even Judas Iscariot. A few scholars have even proposed Mary Magdalene as the disciple in question.

BEL-SHAR-USUR See BELSHAZZAR.

BELSHAZZAR In Dan 5:2, 11, 13, 18, 22 and Bar 1:11-12, Belshazzar ("Bel protect the king") is the son of the Neo-Babylonian king Nebuchadnezzar, but cuneiform documents and inscriptions state that Belshazzar was the son of the last Neo-Babylonian ruler, Nabonidus.

BELTESHAZZAR The Babylonian court name given DANIEL by Nebuchadnezzar (Dan 1:7). See SHADRACH, MESHACH, ABEDNEGO.

BELTETHMUS A Persian officer in Judah (1 Esdr 2:16, 25). Rather than a proper name, it may be a title for a chancellor or royal deputy as in Ezra 4:8-9, 17.

BEN-ABINADAB One of Solomon's twelve governors who "supplied the king and his palace with food." Each "would provide the supplies for one month per year" (1 Kgs 4:7-19). He was in charge of

Naphath-dor, the coastal area around the port city of Dor, in the northern part of the plain of Sharon. Ben-abinadab was married to Solomon's daughter Taphath (1 Kgs 4:11).

BENAIAH 1. A military leader during David's reign who ultimately came to be army commander during Solomon's reign. The son of the priest (1 Chron 27:5) Jehoiada of Kabzeel (2 Sam 23:20), a town of unknown location, but probably in southern Judah near Edom (Josh 15:21), Benaiah gained prominence during the latter part of David's reign as the commander of "the Cherethites and the Pelethites," usually understood as mercenary Cretans and Philistines (2 Sam 8:18; 20:23; 1 Chron 18:17; see CHERETHITES AND PELETHITES). He became a member of David's elite warriors, "the Thirty," but not of the inner circle, "the Three" (2 Sam 23:22-23). If Benaiah's son Jehoiada succeeded Ahithophel as David's counselor (1 Chron 27:34), then Benaiah would have been a mature, experienced military man before Solomon's reign.

2. A warrior from Pirathon in the area of Ephraim, a member of David's elite military group "the Thirty" (1 Sam 23:30; 1 Chron 11:31). He led the army division that served in the eleventh month (1 Chron 27:14).

3. A Simeonite clan leader who was among those who secured pastureland by conquering the Meunim near Gedor in the central hills of Judah at the time of King Hezekiah (1 Chron 4:34-41).

4. One of the Levites who played the upper-register harp (Alamoth) at the installing of the covenant chest in Jerusalem (1 Chron 15:18, 20).

5. A "Levite of the line of Asaph," grandfather of Jahaziel, who, possessed by the spirit of Yahweh, roused King Jehoshaphat and Judah to prevail over a coalition of Ammonites, Moabites, and Edomites (2 Chron 20:14).

6. A priest among those who blew trumpets to herald the bringing of the chest to Jerusalem (1 Chron 15:24). David appointed him and Jahaziel to blow trumpets regularly before the chest containing the covenant of God (1 Chron 16:6).

7. One of the Levites who assisted Conaniah in collecting and storing tithes and contributions brought to the temple in Jerusalem at the time of King Hezekiah (2 Chron 31:13).

8. Father of Pelatiah, an official in Jerusalem whose advice with respect to the threat from Babylon was opposed by Ezekiel. While Ezekiel castigated Pelatiah and his associates for their violence, Pelatiah died (Ezek 11:1, 13).

9. A descendant of Parosh forced by Ezra to put away his foreign wife (Ezra 10:25; 1 Esdr 9:26).

10. A descendant of Pahath-moab forced by Ezra to put away his foreign wife (Ezra 10:30).

11. A descendant of Bani forced by Ezra to put away his foreign wife (Ezra 10:35).

12. A descendant of Nebo forced by Ezra to put away his foreign wife (Ezra 10:32; 1 Esdr 9:36).

BEN-AMMI "Son of my people; son of my kin." The name Lot's younger daughter gave to her son who was born from her incestuous encounter with her father after the destruction of Sodom and Gomorrah (Gen 19:38).

BEN-DEKER The "son of Deker" is one of twelve prefects over Solomon's districts of Israel (1 Kgs 4:9). Ben-Deker's district comprises a small territory in the western foothills within the allotment of Dan.

BENE-BERAK A city in the southern location of the area allotted to the tribe of Dan (Josh 19:45).

BENEDICTION Although basically a synonym of "blessing," benediction is most often used to designate liturgical invocations for bestowal of divine favor upon worshippers; and, especially in Jewish prayers, formulaic ascriptions of praise to God for benefactions received (e.g., Exod 32:29; Prov 10:6; Isa 65:8; Sir 3:8; Gal 3:14; Rev 5:13).

1. The most familiar example of a liturgical benediction is the priestly blessing in Num 6:24-26 (cf Lev 9:22; Sir 50:20-21).

2. Doxological benedictions of God are a feature of Jewish prayer, as exemplified by the "Eighteen [Benedictions]" that follow major petitions in the daily synagogue service. Scriptural examples of such petitions are the doxologies that conclude major parts of the Psalter (41:13 [Heb. 41:14]; 72:18-19; 89:52 [Heb. 89:53]; 106:48) and introductory praises in several NT Epistles (Eph 1:3; 2 Cor 1:3; 1 Pet 1:3). See BLESSINGS AND CURSINGS.

BENE-JAAKAN Between the Wilderness of Sinai and the Reed Sea (Num 33:31-32). In Deuteronomy it is located near the site of Aaron's death (10:6).

BEN-GEBER Ben-Geber governed RAMOTH-GILEAD, the sixth of Solomon's twelve regional districts (1 Kgs 4:13), each of which supplied royal court provisions one month a year (1 Kgs 4:7). Ben-geber was probably the same as GEBER son of URI, the officer over the land of Gilead (1 Kgs 4:19).

BEN-HADAD In the OT, the name appears as a general dynastic reference to Aram-Damascus in Jer 49:27 and Amos 1:4, but elsewhere designates at least two individual Aramean kings (see ARAM, ARAMEANS).

BEN-HAIL Jehoshaphat's officer commissioned to teach the Judeans from the Instruction scroll (2 Chron 17:7).

BEN-HANAN Son of Shimon and a descendant of Judah (1 Chron 4:20).

BEN-HESED Of Solomon's twelve regional administrators, Ben-Hesed governed the third district, including ARUBBOTH, Soco, and HEPHER in west Manasseh (1 Kgs 4:10). Each district supplied royal court provisions one month a year (1 Kgs 4:7).

BEN-HINNOM See HINNOM, VALLEY OF.

BEN-HUR One of Solomon's twelve officers who each provided Solomon and his household food for one month of the year (1 Kgs 4:8).

BENINU A levitical signatory of the covenant renewal under Ezra (Neh 10:13 [Heb. 10:14]).

BENJAMIN, BENJAMINITES 1. The youngest son of Jacob (Gen 35:18), and the eponymous ancestor of the Israelite tribe that occupied the highland region between Ephraim and Judah.

2. The son of Bilhan and great-grandson of the patriarch Benjamin, according to a late genealogical list (1 Chron 7:10).

3. One of the many Israelite males on a list of those who pledged to put away their foreign wives and bring a guilt offering in response to Ezra's proclamation that the Israelites had broken faith with God through intermarriage with foreigners (Ezra 10:32).

4. An official of Judah who participated in the dedication of the walls of Jerusalem during the time of Nehemiah (Neh 12:34). He is probably the same individual who is reported to have labored to repair a section of the wall (Neh 3:23).

5. The tribe of Benjamin takes its name from the son of Jacob (see 1 above). Although a minor tribe in terms of population and territory, Benjamin plays a prominent role in Israel's history and literature. The book of Joshua elaborates the campaigns waged against cities within Benjamin (Josh 2:1–10:15). Ehud, the first judge whose exploits are elaborated in detail, is a Benjaminite (Judg 3:12-30), and Benjamin is at the center of the outrageous events of rape,

murder, and internecine war that conclude Judges (Judg 19–21). The tribe also figures significantly in the rise of the Israelite monarchy. A Benjaminite (Saul) becomes Israel's first king, another (Abner) facilitates the transference of the kingdom to David after Saul's death, and a third (Sheba) leads an insurrection against David.

BENJAMIN GATE Probably located in the northeast part of the land of Benjamin (Jer 37:13; 38:7; Zech 14:10), it may correspond to the postexilic PARADE GATE or Sheep Gate (Neh 3:31-32). The Upper Benjamin Gate of Jeremiah's confinement (Jer 20:2) may be at the temple courts.

BEN-ONI Rachel's name for Benjamin, which she gave him as she died in childbirth (Gen 35:18). See BENJAMIN, BENJAMINITES.

BEN-ZOHETH A Judahite, son of Ishi, or the term should be translated "and the son of Zohith" (1 Chron 4:20).

BEON A town or pastoral region in northern Moab sought as territory by the Gadites and the Reubenites (Num 32:3).

BEOR 1. Father of Balaam, who was summoned by the king of Moab to curse the Israelites (Num 22:5; 31:8; Deut 23:5; Josh 13:22; 24:9; Mic 6:5; 2 Pet 2:15).

2. Father of the Edomite king Bela (Gen 36:32; 1 Chron 1:43).

BEQA A measure of weight, half-shekel (approx. 6 g), mentioned once in the Bible in relation to the "sanctuary shekel" (Exod 38:26).

See WEIGHTS AND MEASURES.

BERA King of Sodom who rebelled against Chedorlaomer but was defeated; Abram's nephew Lot was among the captured (Gen 14).

BERACAH One of David's band of insurgent archers from Saul's tribe Benjamin (1 Chron 12:3).

BERACAH, VALLEY OF The place where the Judahites praised God for delivering them from their enemies (2 Chron 20:26).

BERAIAH One of the nine sons of SHIMEI of the tribe of Benjamin (1 Chron 8:21).

BEREA A town north of Jerusalem where Bacchides and Alcimus camped with their soldiers after they had beseiged Jerusalem (1 Macc 9:4). Judas's forces were located at Elasa (1 Macc 9:5). Judas fell in battle and was buried in Modein by his brothers Jonathan and Simon.

BERECHIAH 1. Son of ZERUBBABEL (1 Chron 3:20).

2. ASAPH's father (1 Chron 6:39 [Heb. 6:24]; 15:17).

3. Gatekeeper of the covenant chest during David's reign (1 Chron 15:23), possibly the same as above.

4. ASA's son (1 Chron 9:16).

5. MESHILLEMOTH's son and an Ephraimite chief (2 Chron 28:12).

6. Father of MESHEZABEL and son of MESHULLAM (Neh 3:4, 30) whose granddaughter married the son of TOBIAH the Ammonite (Neh 6:18).

7. Son of IDDO and father of ZECHARIAH (Zech 1:1, 7). However, Iddo is Zechariah's father in Ezra 5:1; 6:14; Neh 12:16. The Zechariah son of BARACHIAH mentioned by Jesus (Matt 23:35) further complicates the issue of identity (see Isa 8:2 and 2 Chron 24:20-22).

BERED 1. A grandson of Ephraim, younger son of Joseph (1 Chron 7:20). The name BECHER appears in a parallel register (Num 26:35-36). However, it lists Becher as a son of Ephraim.

2. The well of Beer-lahai-roi was

supposedly located between Kadesh and Bered (Gen 16:14).

BERENICE See BERNICE.

BERI The fourth of the eleven sons of ZOPHAH of the tribe of Asher (1 Chron 7:36).

BERIAH, BERIITES 1. The fourth son of Asher (Gen 46:17; 1 Chron 7:30-31) and the eponymous ancestor of the Beriites (Num 26:44).

2. The Asherite Beriah's descendants (Num 26:44).

3. A son of Ephraim, so named because "misfortune had come to his house" (1 Chron 7:23).

4. A son of ELPAAL (1 Chron 8:12-13) or EBER.

5. Fourth son of SHIMEI, a Levite (1 Chron 23:10).

BERNICE Born in 28/29 CE, the oldest daughter of Agrippa I, Julia Bernice was both a member of the Jewish royal family and a Roman citizen.

BEROEA 1. Modern Verria, a city in southwestern Macedonia on the river Astraeus. Paul and Silas fled to Berea, 80 km/50 mi. southwest of THESSALONICA, to escape Jewish agitators (Acts 17:10, 13). Berean Jews were "more honorable" and also more exacting in their verification of Paul's message from the Scriptures (17:11). Paul's colleague Sopater was a Berean (20:4).

2. Aleppo in northern Syria, made into a Macedonian city by Seleucus Nicator between 381 and 281 BCE. Menelaus, the renegade high priest, was executed there at the order of Antiochus Eupator by being hurled into a tower of ashes (2 Macc 13:1-8; Josephus, *Ant.* 12.385).

BEROTHAH A town mentioned along with Hamath and Damascus as marking Israel's northern boundary in Ezekiel's vision (Ezek 47:16). Sometimes identified with Beirut. Probably the same as Berothai.

BEROTHAI Following successful battles against neighboring areas, David takes bronze from Berothai and BETAH, towns of King HADADEZER of ZOBAH in modern Lebanon, as spoils of victory (2 Sam 8:8). This city may be the same as BEROTHAH.

BERYL The tenth stone in the high priest's embroidered chest pendant (Exod 28:20; 39:13). Beryl, a member of the hexagonal crystal mineral group that includes emerald, has a variety of colors with light green to bluish-green being prominent.

BESAI A family head whose descendants were among the temple servants, called the Nethinim, who returned after the exile (Ezra 2:49; Neh 7:52).

BESCASPASMYS Descendant of Addi who dismissed his foreign wife as Ezra instructed God's covenant required him (1 Esdr 9:31). See MATTANIAH.

BESODEIAH Father of Meshullam who joined Joiada in the repairing of the Old Gate when they returned to Jerusalem after the exile (Neh 3:6).

BET The second letter of the Hebrew alphabet.

BETA The second letter in the Greek alphabet.

BETAH One of the towns in King Hadadezer's kingdom from which King David took bronze after defeating him (2 Sam 18:8). See TIBHATH.

BETEN Town situated within the land Joshua gave to the Asher tribe (Josh 19:25) when he apportioned the remaining territories. See ASHER, ASHERITES.

BETHABARA Location of John's baptismal activities beyond the Jordan (John 1:28), according to some inferior manuscripts. The better-attested reading, BETHANY, has been accepted in recent translations. May be the same as BETH-BARAH or BETH-NIMRAH.

BETH-ANATH A town Joshua allotted to the Naphtalites (Josh 19:38). Its Canaanite inhabitants became forced labor (Judg 1:33). Perhaps located east of Acco. See NAPHTALI, NAPHTALITES.

BETH-ANOTH A town with its villages that had been allocated to the Judah tribe (Josh 15:59). Located southwest of Jerusalem. See JUDAH, JUDAHITES.

BETHANY The ministries of Jesus and John the Baptist are associated with two places named Bethany.

1. Bethany near Jerusalem appears several times in the NT. Bethany was on the Mount of Olives (Mark 11:1), fifteen stadia (1.75 mi.) from Jerusalem (John 11:18).

2. The Gospel of John refers to the place where John the Baptist conducted his ministry as "across the Jordan in Bethany" (1:28).

BETH-ARABAH One of the towns marking the border between the allotments of Benjamin and Judah (Josh 15:6; 18:18).

BETH-ARBEL A town whose destruction by SHALMAN must have been notorious for its level of brutality (Hos 10:14), serving as an analogy to the coming catastrophe upon Bethel for the Israelites' failure to seek the Lord (see BETHEL, SHRINE).

BETH-ASHBEA A Judean town probably located in the western foothills (1 Chron 4:21).

BETHASMOTH See AZMAVETH.

BETH-AVEN Perhaps an older name for the town AI, east of Bethel (Josh 7).

BETH-AZMAVETH Named in Neh 7:28. See AZMAVETH.

BETH-BAAL-MEON Town in northern Moab (Josh 13:17). See BAAL-MEON; MOAB, MOABITES.

BETH-BARAH A town near the Jordan River, between its valley and the Esdraelon Plain. The town marked one of the boundaries of the area that the Ephraemites, led by Gideon, took from the Midianites (Judg 7:24). John the Baptist may have baptized the crowds here. See MIDIAN, MIDIANITES.

BETHBASI A village located southeast of Bethlehem, about 3 mi. northeast of Tekoa (modern Khirbet Beit Bassi), to which Jonathan, Simon, and followers retreated from Bacchides (1 Macc 9:62).

BETH-BIRI A town belonging to the tribe of Simeon prior to the time of David (1 Chron 4:31). See BETH-LEBAOTH; SIMEON, SIMEONITES.

BETH-CAR An unknown site between Mizpah and Philistine territory, where Samuel's army defeated the Philistines (1 Sam 4:11).

BETH-DAGON 1. A village listed as part of Judah's inheritance of uncertain location in the western foothills (Josh 15:41).

2. A village of uncertain location belonging to the tribe of Asher in northern Israel east of CARMEL (Josh 19:27).

3. Common name for a temple to the Philistine god DAGON.

BETH-DIBLATHAIM Among the named towns in JEREMIAH's oracle against Moab (Jer 48:22).

BETH-EDEN An ancient Aramean kingdom in MESOPOTAMIA, located on both sides of the EUPHRATES RIVER south of Carchemis. Words of God through Amos condemn the ruler (scepter) of Beth-Eden (Amos 1:5).

BETH-EGLAIM A town 8 mi. from Gaza.

BETH-EKED Traveling through Beth-eked of the Shepherds on his way from Jezreel to SAMARIA, JEHU and his forces slaughtered forty-two relatives of King AHAZIAH of Judah at a nearby pit (2 Kgs 10:12-14).

BETHEL, SHRINE The name of two places mentioned in the OT: a town in Benjamin and Ephraim, mentioned more often than any place except Jerusalem; and a town in Judah (1 Sam 30:27, possibly the same as Bethul [Josh 19:4]; and Bethuel [1 Chron 4:30]), exact location unknown.

BETH-EMEK Town northeast of Acco in the northern part of the land that Joshua allotted to the Asher tribe.

BETHER Bether, a town in the hill country of Judea about 7 mi. southwest of Jerusalem, was included in a list of cities allotted to Judah (Josh 15:59 LXX).

BETHESDA In Jerusalem at the end of the Second Temple period, located north of the temple compound, this pair of large pools with five colonnades is probably the Probatica mentioned in John 5:2.

BETH-EZEL A town in the western foothills (Mic 1:11).

BETH GADER Town in Judah, founded by HAREPH (1 Chron 2:51).

BETH-GAMUL A town in the tableland of Moab (Jer 48:21, 22-24), probably located east of Dibon.

BETH-GILGAL Town near Jerusalem (Neh 12:29). Some Levite singers lived there.

BETH-HACCHEREM Mentioned in Jer 6:1 as the location of a fire beacon. Later it appears as one of five districts, or district capitals, of the province of Judah, ruled by MALCHIJAH son of Rechab during the Persian Period (Neh 3:14).

BETH-HAGGAN Town toward which Jehu pursued King Aziah (2 Kgs 9:27). Located in Issachar's territory but allotted to the Levites. Same as EN-GANNIM (Josh 19:2; 21:29).

BETH-HARAM A Gadite town in the Rift Valley east of the JORDAN RIVER, northeast of the DEAD SEA (Num 32:36; Josh 13:27).

BETH-HARAN See BETH-HARAM.

BETH-HOGLAH A town in the territory of Benjamin, bordering Judah (Josh 15:6; 18:19, 21) and located near a spring west of the Jordan, southeast of Jericho.

BETH-HORON A levitical twin city, including Lower Beth-horon and Upper Beth-horon, assigned in Josh 21:22 and 1 Chron 6:68 [Heb. 6:53] to Ephraim on its border with Benjamin (Josh 16:3, 5; 18:13-14).

BETH-JESHIMOTH One of the final dwelling sites of the Israelites before crossing the JORDAN RIVER into Canaan. Identified in four verses (Num 33:49; Josh 12:3; 13:20; Ezek 25:9), it is located in the ARABAH on the eastern side of the Jordan River.

BETH-LE-APHRAH A town in the western foothills.

BETH-LEBAOTH A town among the allotment to Simeon in Josh 19:6 and lies within the bounds of Judah's territory in the arid southern plain. Joshua 15:32 names this town simply "Lebaoth," while 1 Chron 4:31 refers to it as Beth-biri.

BETHLEHEM 1. A city in Judah 10 km south of Jerusalem, located on a spur running east from the watershed. Bethlehem is the setting for the book of Ruth and the birthplace of Ruth and Boaz's descendant David (ca. 1000 BCE). Samuel anointed David king in Bethlehem (1 Sam 16:1-13), and David made his home there (1 Sam 17:12, 15; 20:6, 28). The Philistines put a garrison in Bethlehem (2 Sam 23:14-16; 1 Chron 11:16-18) that remained until David established his capital in Jerusalem. David's grandson Rehoboam fortified Bethlehem (2 Chron 11:6). No traces of the wall have been found, but the excavations have not been complete or systematic.

Joseph and Mary were natives of Bethlehem, where they had a "house," according to Matthew (Matt 2:11). Luke concurs that Jesus was born in Bethlehem, "David's city" (Luke 2:4-7).

2. A town in Zebulun (Josh 19:15; Judg 12:8-10).

3. A town in Ephraim where Ibzan, a judge of Israel, lived (Judg 12:8, 10).

4. A descendant of Caleb (1 Chron 2:51, 54; 4:4). See DAVID; JEROME; MESSIAH, JEWISH.

BETHLOMON Ancestor of 123 descendants who returned to Jerusalem and Judea when CYRUS ended the Babylonian EXILE (1 Esdr 5:17).

BETH-MAACAH A clan or territory that later became part of the town name Abel of Beth-Maacah (2 Sam 20:14-15).

BETH-MARCABOTH A town in the tribal allotment for Simeon (Josh 19:5) in the south-central area of Judah, it is also listed as one of the towns inhabited by the families of SHIMEI and his brothers, sons of MISHMA and grandsons of Simeon (1 Chron 4:31).

BETH-MEON A town in Moab located east of the Jordan (Jer 48:23) and mentioned on the Moabite Stone. Usually called BAAL-MEON.

BETH-MILLO An administrative center and residence of the king for Shechem (Judg 9:6, 20) and Jerusalem (2 Kgs 12:21).

BETH-NIMRAH A city in the eastern Jordan Valley, conquered from Sihon, given to the tribe of Gad and built by them (Num 32:3, 36; Josh 13:27).

BETH-PAZZEZ A town in the territory of the tribe of Issachar, probably east of Mount Tabor (Josh 19:21).

BETH-PELET A town located in southern Judah near Edom and allocated by Joshua to Judah's tribe (Josh 15:27). Also, one of the towns where the returning exiles resettled (Neh 11:26). Possibly located southeast of Beer-sheba.

BETH-PEOR "House of Peor," a Transjordanian site referenced four times in the OT. Deuteronomy 3:29 and 4:46 place Israel "in the valley opposite Beth-Peor" prior to entrance into Canaan, while Deut 34:6 locates Beth-Peor "in Moabite country" when referencing the burial place of Moses.

BETHPHAGE A small village outside Jerusalem at the MOUNT OF OLIVES.

BETH-RAPHA Son of ESHTON in Judah's genealogy (1 Chron 4:12).

BETH-REHOB A town or region in Syria north of Dan and south of Hamath, also called "Rehob, near Lebo-hamath," the northernmost sojourn of the spies sent by Moses (Num 13:21). Ammonites hired Syrian mercenaries from Beth-rehob and ZOBAH to battle King David (2 Sam 10:6-19). The Syrian King HADADEZER (vv. 16, 19) is called "Rehob's son" (2 Sam 8:3, 12). The tribe of Dan captured Laish "in the Beth-rehob Valley" (Judg 18:28).

BETHSAIDA Bethsaida, north of the Sea of Galilee, is a regular site of Jesus' ministry. Bethsaida is the initial objective of Jesus' journey in Mark 6:45, although his boat eventually lands in the region of Gennesaret (6:52). The healing of the blind man in Mark 8:22-26 occurs in Bethsaida, and Luke places the feeding of the 5,000 in Bethsaida (9:10). According to John 1:44, Philip, Andrew, and Peter come from Bethsaida.

BETH-SHAN Beth-shan lies 15 mi. south of the Sea of Galilee in the fertile Beth-shan Valley. The site is situated along an ancient international road system that connects Transjordan with the Mediterranean Sea at the strategic crossroads where the Jordan and Jezreel Valleys meet. In the books of Joshua and Judges, Beth-shan and the surrounding towns are described as belonging to the territory of Issachar but were assigned to the tribe of Manasseh, who failed to drive out the Canaanite inhabitants of Beth-shan (Josh 17:11-12; Judg 1:27). Beth-shan is also mentioned as a city in the fifth district established by King Solomon (1 Kgs 4:12).

BETH-SHEAN See BETH-SHAN.

BETH-SHEARIM Southern Galilean town, first known as Besara.

BETH-SHEMESH 1. City in the northeastern western foothills that was located in the Sorek Valley to the west of Jerusalem on the border with Philistia. Joshua 19:41 lists Beth-shemesh as part of the Danite inheritance and describes the town as one of those located along the Sorek Valley as it comes out of the Judean hill country. Beth-shemesh is the first place in Judah that the covenant chest travels when it is returned from Philistia (see 1 Sam 6:9-15).

2. Town in Issachar (Josh 19:22) located to the south of the Sea of Galilee near the Jordan River north of Jarmuth and south of Jabneel.

3. Town in Naphtali (Josh 19:38) that Judg 1:33 describes as still occupied by the Canaanites. Also mentioned in the late execration (Egyptian) texts from the Middle Bronze Age.

4. A town in Egypt mentioned in the MT of Jer 43:13, but the LXX of Jer 50:13 has the Greek equivalent of Heliopolis.

BETH-SHITTAH This is the town where the Midianites fled after Gideon and the Israelites defeated them (Judg 7:22).

BETH-TAPPUAH Listed with Hebron among the towns of Judah in the central hill country (Josh 15:53), Beth-tappuah likely is, or is very near, the modern village of Taffuh, just west of Hebron in the West Bank.

BETH-TOGARMAH Place equivalent to Togarmah (Ezek 27:14; 38:6).

BETHUEL 1. Bethuel was the son of NAHOR, Abraham's brother (Gen 22:20-23). He was called an Aramean of PADDAN-ARAM (Gen 25:20) and was the father of LABAN and REBEKAH (Gen 24:24; 28:5).

2. Bethuel the town was located in the south of Judah (1 Chron 4:30). In the par. list of Josh 19:4, the name appears as Bethul.

BETHULIA The hometown of the book of Judith's namesake and heroine. The location of Bethulia is north of Jerusalem in the Samarian hill country, near Dothan.

BETH-ZAITH The location of Bacchides's camp after his withdrawal from Jerusalem during an attempt to suppress the revolt of JUDAS (1 Macc 7:19).

BETH-ZATHA Reliable manuscripts locate Jesus' healing in John 5:2 at Beth-zatha, a place otherwise unknown. Other manuscripts have BETHSAIDA, Belzetha, and Bethesda.

BETH-ZECHARIAH A location near

Jerusalem identified in 1 Macc 6:32-33 as the site of a battle between Judas's army and a large Seleucid force (including thirty-two elephants).

BETH-ZUR A fortress city located 20 mi. south of Jerusalem (2 Macc 11:5) on the road to Hebron. Beth-zur was included within Judah's allotment (Josh 15:58). Beth-zur occurs in the genealogy of Caleb (1 Chron 2:45), suggesting that the Calebite clan settled or expanded into the named cities. REHOBOAM fortified Beth-zur and fourteen other cities for the defense of Judah (2 Chron 11:5-12).

BETOLIO The ancestral head of fifty-two who returned with their leaders, wives, children, and servants to Jerusalem after the EXILE (1 Esdr 5:21).

BETOMASTHAIM A town mentioned twice in the book of Judith (Jdt 4:6; 15:4), although once with the variant spelling Betomesthaim, described as close to BETHULIA in the Samarian hill country.

BETONIM A city east of the Jordan in the northern part of the allocation to the tribe of Gad (Josh 13:26).

BEULAH This is a figurative name for Zion representing the future prosperity of JERUSALEM. The name, a form of a verb that often means "to marry," occurs in Isa 54:1 and 62:4 and is translated "married" by most English versions.

BEYOND THE JORDAN A general term for the mountain ranges and valleys east of the river Jordan, the fertile hill country of Moab ranging from the tablelands of Madeba extending to the Zered River, southwest of the DEAD SEA (Deut 1:5), with the land of Manasseh in the north, the land of Gad and the land of Reuben to the south (Josh 13). See BETHABARA; JORDAN RIVER.

BEYOND THE RIVER The term "beyond the river" takes its reference from the Euphrates and could refer to the area east (1 Kgs 14:15) or west (Ezra 4:10) of the river depending on the location of the speaker. As reflected in Ezra, the term designated a satrapy that included Syria-Palestine during the Persian period.

BEZAI 1. One of those who sealed Ezra's covenant (Neh 10:18).

2. A family group of 323 members (Ezra 2:17; 1 Esdr 5:16) or 324 (Neh 7:23) that returned to Judah with Zerubbabel after the exile.

BEZALEL 1. Son of URI, a Judahite, a skilled artisan endowed with the spirit of God (Exod 31:2). He and OHOLIAB were responsible for constructing the COVENANT CHEST, the COVENANT DWELLING, and all its furnishings (Exod 31).

2. A son of PAHATH-MOAB (Ezra 10:30), one of the returnees who had to divorce their foreign wives and send away their children.

BEZEK 1. Saul mustered his troops at Bezek before his successful defense of JABESH-GILEAD from the Ammonites led by NAHASH (1 Sam 11:8). This Bezek is often identified with Khirbet Ibzek, north of Shechem.

2. In Judg 1:4-5, Bezek refers to a place and (1:5-7) to a person, Adoni-bezek (master/lord of Bezek), who was defeated, along with the Canaanites and the PERIZZITES, by the tribes of Judah and Simeon.

BEZER The Asherite Zophah's son (1 Chron 7:37). Also a city of refuge in Reubenite territory (Deut 4:43; Josh 20:8), rebuilt by King Mesha.

BICHRI Known in the OT only as the father of SHEBA (2 Sam 20:1-22), he is a Benjaminite whose name is related to that of a tribe of Bichrites loyal to Saul instead of DAVID (2 Sam 20:14).

BIDKAR King Jehu's aide who threw Joram's dead body on Naboth's ground to fulfill God's oracle (2 Kgs 9:25).

BIER A stretcher used for carrying a deceased human body in a funeral procession (2 Sam 3:31; Luke 7:14).

BIGTHA An attendant among King Ahasuerus's seven eunuchs who were requested to bring him Queen Vashti (Esth 1:10). Possibly same as BIGTHAN.

BIGTHAN One of King Ahasuerus's eunuchs. With Teresh he guarded the king. After Mordecai revealed their plot to kill King Ahasuerus, the king had them both executed (Esth 2:21; 6:2). Possibly same as BIGTHA.

BIGVAI 1. One of the Jewish leaders who returned to Judah with Zerubbabel (Ezra 2:2; Neh 7:7). Another seventy-two males of this family returned with Ezra (Ezra 8:14; 1 Esdr 8:40).

2. One who sealed Ezra's covenant (Neh 10:16-17).

BILDAD Bildad the Shuhite, ELIPHAZ, and ZOPHAR are friends who gather to offer Job dialogue in three cycles in the central poetic portion of the book. Bildad's speeches (Job 8; 18; 25) often support the view that the wicked, not the righteous, suffer. See SHUAH, SHUHITE.

BILEAM A town within Manasseh's allotted section that was reassigned along with its pasturelands to some of the Kohathites (1 Chron 6:55). Joshua 17:11 lists Ibleam instead.

BILGAH Aaronite designated head of the fifteenth division of priests by David (1 Chron 24:14). A priest who returned with Zerubbabel (Neh 12:5, 18).

BILGAI Mentioned as one of the priests who placed his name on the sealed covenant document (Neh 10:9). Probably same as Bilgah.

BILHAH Bilhah, LABAN's servant given to RACHEL at her marriage to JACOB (Gen 29:29), bore Jacob two sons, Dan and Naphtali at Rachel's behest. Bilhah is later mentioned as having sexual relations with Reuben, disqualifying him from his inheritance as Jacob's oldest son (Gen 35:22; 49:4).

BILHAN 1. Eldest son of Ezer the Horite, a subbranch of Edomites (Gen 36:27).

2. Eldest son of Jediael, a Benjaminite (1 Chron 7:10).

BILSHAN "Inquirer." One of the leaders of the Jews who returned to Judah with ZERUBBABEL after the exile (Ezra 2:2; Neh 7:7; 1 Esdr 5:8).

BIMHAL This name occurs only once (1 Chron 7:33).

BINEA A Benjaminite descendant of King Saul. He is Moza's son and the father of Raphah (or Raphaiah), Eleasah, and Azel (1 Chron 8:37; 9:43).

BINNUI Name of a person and a clan-group in the postexilic period. The person known as Binnui appears as one of the citizens helping to build the wall of Jerusalem under Nehemiah's direction (Neh 3:24). In Neh 10:10 he is identified as a Levite, as is the case in Neh 12:8. His son Noadiah appears among a list at Ezra 8:33. The name also appears to designate a clan or family group in a list of such groups at Ezra 10:30. It also appears at 10:38, though there is some textual evidence for another name, "Bani." The group also appears in a listing at Neh 7:15.

BIRD OF PREY One of the prime characteristics of the fauna of Israel/Palestine is its vast abundance of birds of prey (eagles, vultures, hawks, falcons, etc.). This was evidently the case in biblical times as well. Probably due to their frequent contact with carcasses, all large carrion eaters among the birds were considered ritually unclean, and hence inedible (Lev 11:13-19; Deut 14:12-18). See BIRDS OF THE BIBLE; EAGLE; NIGHTHAWK; VULTURE.

BIRDS OF THE BIBLE The area of Israel and Palestine is home to more than 300 species of birds. Many of the Bible's references to them are with generic terms, and a number of the specific types of birds are impossible to identify. The unclean birds listed in the virtually identical passages of Lev 11:13-19 and Deut 14:12-18 can all be termed "birds of prey" (in a wide sense), since they feed either on live prey (fish, in several cases) or on carcasses. In the OT, all birds are wild, but in NT times, people had begun to keep domestic fowl.

See EAGLE; OWL; VULTURE.

BIRKET EL-HAMRA See SILOAM.

BIRSHA King of the city of Gomorrah against whom the kings of Shinar, Ellasar, Elam, and Goiim waged war (Gen 14:2, 8, 10-11).

BIRTHRIGHT The special privilege assigned to the oldest offspring of any father. This meant, in the first place, that he inherited two portions, that is, double the portions for the other males. (Females inherited only when there were no males.) See Deut 21:15-17; on females, Num 27:1-11.

BIRZAITH In 1 Chron 7:31, Birzaith was the son of MALCHIEL, an Asherite. See ASHER, ASHERITES.

BISHLAM Possibly the title of a Persian official (Ezra 4:7).

BISHOP The term designates a person who exercises a function of oversight; within the NT an individual oversees a community of believers. The oldest NT text to speak about the overseer/bishop/supervisor is the greeting of Paul's Letter to the Philippians, which is addressed "to all those in Philippi who are God's people in Christ Jesus, along with your supervisors and servants" (Phil 1:1). The letter does not further specify whom these persons were nor what function they may have exercised. Luke's version of Paul's farewell address to the elders of the church at Ephesus urges them to "watch yourselves and the whole flock, in which the Holy Spirit has placed you as supervisors, to shepherd God's church" (Acts 20:28). Combined with Phil 1:1, Acts 20:28 suggests that the overseer was a feature of the Pauline churches. Although bishops/overseers were frequent in early churches, the NT references may refer more to a function than a fixed office within the churches. Titus 1:5-9 and 1 Tim 3:1-8 indicate some characteristics and qualifications of bishops.

BITHIAH Pharaoh's daugher; mother of Miriam, Shammai, and Ishbah; and wife of Mered, a descendant of Judah (1 Chron 4:18).

BITHYNIA A coastal province located in the northwest corner of Asia Minor, Bithynia was named for one of the Thracian tribes who settled there, subduing some of the native tribes, before the 8th cent. BCE. Paul planned to enter Bithynia, probably to reach Nicaea and/or Nicomedia in the western portion of the province, but he felt compelled to travel to Troas instead (Acts 16:7). Nonetheless, 1 Peter bears witness to a 1st-cent. Christian community there, since Bithynia is one of the five provinces to which the letter is addressed (1:1).

BITTER HERBS The term occurs in three biblical passages. Two of the passages deal with the foods to be eaten at Passover. Exodus 12:8 says, "That same night they should eat the meat roasted over the fire. They should eat it along with unleavened bread and bitter herbs." The rules for eating the meal at the second Passover, one month after the first, again require consuming the meat together with unleavened bread and bitter herbs (Num 9:11). Apart from these two verses, the word is found only in Lam 3:15.

BITUMEN Also translated pitch or tar.

BIZIOTHIAH A town near Edom's boundary that lay within the territory assigned to Judah.

BIZTHA An attendant among King Ahasuerus's seven eunuchs who was requested to bring him Queen Vashti (Esth 1:10).

BLASPHEMY Blasphemy, something said in disrespect against God, was strictly prohibited (Exod 22:27; Lev 24:10-23; 1 Kgs 21:13; 2 Kgs 19:3; Isa 37:3; Job 2:9-10). Sometimes actions can also be called blasphemy, as in the building of the golden calf (Neh 9:18, 26).

In the NT, blasphemy is most often seen in verbal remarks. Jesus is charged by his opponents with blaspheming when taking the divine prerogative of forgiving sins, an act that is seen as an imposition on God's unique glory and authority (Mark 2:7; cf Luke 7:37-50).

BLASTUS Blastus was a chamberlain who controlled access to Herod AGRIPPA I's private quarters (Acts 12:20).

BLESSINGS AND CURSINGS Also commonly identified as "benedictions and maledictions," the verbal statements that express and enforce the COVENANT between God and humans, or other expressions of divine providence.

BLINDNESS A loss or lack of sight that was considered total and permanent.

BLOOD Because blood is the substance through which the Israelites believed both humans and animals have God's gift of LIFE (Gen 9:4; Lev 17:11), blood has a sacred quality, and the Israelites were prohibited from consuming blood.

BLOODGUILT "Bloodguilt" was coined by early Bible translators to translate the Hebrew word "blood" when it meant "responsibility for felonious homicide."

BOANERGES A Hebrew or Aramaic term of uncertain etymology ascribed to JAMES and JOHN by Jesus (Mark 3:17). The narrator renders the word into Greek as "sons of thunder," suggesting that they either spoke boldly and vigorously, experienced a sudden awakening, or perhaps even survived a lightning strike.

BOAT Boats were small vessels powered by either rowing or small sails and used in smaller lakes and rivers, generally for fishing or local transportation. Jesus and the disciples were regularly associated with boats, and Jesus even used one as a platform for speaking to a crowd (Mark 4:1).

BOAZ Boaz is a kinsman of Naomi's dead husband Elimelech (Ruth 2:1). He "redeems" (rescues) Naomi and her widowed daughter-in-law Ruth from poverty by marrying Ruth. Thus, Naomi can claim Ruth's child Obed as her dead husband's heir, keeping the family "name" and the family's property rights "alive" (see Lev 25).

BOCHERU One of Azel's six sons and a descendant of Saul, Israel's first king from the tribe of Benjamin (1 Chron 8:38; 9:44).

BOCHIM Place west of the Jordan above Gilgal where the Israelites wept after the Lord's messenger reprimanded them for breaking God's command (Judg 2:1-5).

BODYGUARD. An individual or group charged with the protection of another, particularly of a king.

BOIL Medically, a boil is a painful pus-filled bump under the skin.

BOND An idea represented by a variety of Hebrew and Greek terms referring to either physical (chains, shackles) or metaphorical (oppression, restriction) restraints as well as special unifying connections or oaths, often legal or covenantal obligations.

BOOK In antiquity a book generally took the form of scrolls that had been attached end to end. In the Roman period, wooden tablets, which had been laced together, also came into use. Known as a codex, this proved to be easier to use than unrolling a long scroll. By the early Christian era, sheets of papyrus or leather parchment emerged to replace the wooden tablets. Such papyri and parchments were bound together, making a collection of writings much lighter and more manageable. Most of the early Christian documents that survive from the 2nd and 3rd cent. were constructed in the form of a codex.

BOOTH A temporary building set up in the fields during harvesttime; also the name of a harvest holiday celebrated in the autumn. These booths are to remind the Israelites that they dwelled in booths as they traveled from Egypt to the land of Israel (Lev 23:42-43). The holiday is still celebrated to this day with those observing it most rigorously by sleeping and eating in the booths. The holiday lasts for seven days with a festival day at the beginning and the end of the week. During the Second Temple period it concluded with the Water Drawing Ceremony. See BOOTHS, FEAST OR FESTIVAL OF; COVENANT DWELLING.

BOOTHS, FEAST OR FESTIVAL OF Each major festival in the OT represents a week of harvest in the spring, in the summer, and in the autumn. Spring brings early grain, especially barley, and is also time to move the flocks on from one pasture to another. Summer sees the larger grain-harvest of wheat. Autumn is the last time of gathering for the cycle, and the grapes, olives and nuts of that season make it the most joyous time of all.

BOSOR 1. A city in Gilead where JUDAS Maccabeus rescued besieged Jews (1 Macc 5:26, 36). Located 40 mi. east of the Sea of Galilee, it is likely the site of modern Bosra al Harir.

2. A scribal error for BEOR in 2 Pet 2:15.

BOTTLE A word regularly used to describe various containers.

BOTTOMLESS PIT Transcendent abode of demons, beasts, their king Abaddon (Rev 9:1-2, 11; 11:7; 17:8; 20:1), and the dead. See ABYSS.

BOUNDARY STONE Stone markers indicated the extent of privately owned fields and separated tribes. Israel's legal and wisdom traditions regarded the displacement of such landmarks as a reprehensible crime (Deut 19:14; 27:17; Prov 22:28; compare Hos 5:10). Landgrabs could be affected by surreptitiously relocating a landmark, but more likely tactics would be economic pressure against the poor (Isa 5:8; Mic 2:2) and legal chicanery (1 Kgs 21), making widows and orphans classic victims (Prov 15:25; 23:10).

BOW See RAINBOW.

BOW AND ARROW A bow is a strong, flexible, narrow piece of material, bent to form an arc, with a cord secured to both ends of the arc, from which the user shoots projectiles (arrows) consisting of (1) a lightweight, straight shaft made of reed or a strip of wood, (2) a stone, bone, or metal tip, and (3) a feathered tail.

Bows and arrows were used for hunting, target practice, and as military weaponry. They enabled archers to maim or kill, to set a city or ship on fire, or to send messages from a distance. Archers carry quantities of arrows (ca. 25–30 arrows) in quivers.

BOWELS Among several terms that refer either to specific body parts or to internal organs in general (Num 5:22; 2 Chron 21:15; Acts 1:18; 2 Macc 9:5-6). The same terms are variously translated as entrails, inmost parts, HEART, and body.

BOWLS Vessels made of pottery, wood, or stone, depending upon their religious or household context.

BOZEZ Name of one of two rocky crags between which Jonathan and his armor-bearer passed to reach the Philistine garrison (1 Sam 14:4). Located between Geba (Saul's camp) and Michmash (the Philistines' camp).

BOZKATH 1. A town in the western foothills included among Judah's tribal allotment in the land conquered by Joshua (Josh 15:39).

2. Home of King JOSIAH's maternal grandfather ADAIAH (2 Kgs 22:1).

BOZRAH 1. A city in Moab, probably the same as BEZER, a Reubenite city of refuge (Jer 48:24).

2. An important city in northern Edom, identified with the modern Busayra/Buseirah in southern Jordan. In prophetic oracles, Bozrah is a symbol for all of Edom (Isa 34:6; 63:1; Jer 49:13, 22; Amos 1:12; the KJV translation "Bozrah" in Mic 2:12 is better understood as "pen" or "fold"). Bozrah is mentioned as the home of King JOBAB in Edomite king lists (Gen 36:3; 1 Chron 1:44).

3. A city in the BASHAN, in southern Syria. Judas Maccabeus captured the city, which is mentioned in a list of cities by Tutmose III and in the Amarna Letters, in the 2nd cent. BCE (1 Macc 5:26, 28).

BRAID Elaborate, fashionable plaiting of hair that is considered ostentatious and immodest for Christian women (1 Tim 2:9; 1 Pet 3:3).

BRAMBLE The term used to describe a spiky shrub of entwined vines. The most likely species referred to is the European boxthorn (Lycium europaeum). In Judg 9:14 the bramble is used as a metaphor for the lowest in society in contrast to the olive tree, fig tree, and grapevine. Bramble in Luke 6:44 is a metaphor for the inherent nature of individuals saying that the bramble ("a bad tree") will not bear good fruit.

BRANCH "Branch" describes an heir or descendant of the Davidic king.

BRAZIER A portable firepot used for indoor heating during the cold months. Used when King Jehoiakim burned Jeremiah's scroll (Jer 36:22-23).

BREAD Bread made from cereals, but can also refer to food in general.

BREAD OF PRESENCE Sometimes translated as showbread (in Exod 35:13; 1 Kgs 7:48), the Bread of Presence refers to the two stacks of six unleavened breads (symbolizing the twelve tribes of Israel) that were weekly placed by the high priest on the golden table in the temple in the vicinity of the covenant dwelling (1 Chron 9:32; Num 4:7).

BREASTPLATE Chest armor made of leather, metal, or a combination of the two, used throughout the Near East as early as the 3rd millennium BCE (1 Kgs 22:34; 2 Chron 18:33). The breastplate evolved into a two-piece cuirass, which protected the back. The Romans wore the molded metal cuirass.

God puts on righteousness like a breastplate (Isa 59:17; echoed in Wis 5:18). Paul adapts the theme to represent the spiritual warfare waged by Christians (Eph 6:14; 1 Thess 5:8).

BRETHREN Brothers. See BROTHER, BROTHERHOOD.

BRICK One of the three primary building materials in the ANE, along with wood and stone. Bricks were lighter than stone, and required less labor for large structures. Almost any combination of sand, silt, and clay mixed with binders can be used to produce bricks.

BRIDE OF CHRIST A metaphor for the church (see CHURCH). Paul promises the Corinthian community in marriage as a virgin presented to Christ (2 Cor 11:2). Revelation announces the wedding of the church as bride to the Lamb (Rev 19:7; 21:2, 9; 22:17). Deuteropauline tradition likens the relationship of husband and wife to that of Christ and the church (Eph 5:23-25).

BRIDEGROOM Bridegroom refers variously to: (1) a man betrothed but not yet married, (2) a man celebrating his wedding feast, and (3) a husband, already married. Jesus calls himself a bridegroom (Matt 9:15; Mark 2:19-20; Luke 5:34-35; John 3:29; Gos. Thom. 104), even though, by tradition, he was never married.

BRIDESMAIDS In Matt 25:1-13, ten virgins serve as bridesmaids who go out to meet the BRIDEGROOM.

BRIER Vegetation of little or no value. Briers describes Israel's enemies (Ezek 28:24). In Mic 7:4 and Isa 5:6; 7:23-25; 55:13, brier describes the people, the land, and their lack of worth.

BROAD WALL The name refers to a west or northwest section of the JERUSALEM wall that was "abandoned" or not repaired in the postexilic restoration because it was still standing (Neh 3:8; 12:38).

BRONZE An alloy of copper and tin. During the OT period copper was mined in the East Wadi Arabah (see COPPER) by the Edomites. Bronze is a relatively strong alloy, and therefore continued to be used for the production of weapons and armory, long after iron came into use (1 Sam 17; 2 Sam 22:35; 1 Kgs 4:13; 14:27). It is often mentioned—sometimes together with iron—as a symbol of strength (Deut 33:25; Job 20:24; Jer 1:18). Bronze and iron weapons remained in use side by side until the end of the Persian period.

BRONZE AGE An archaeological period spanning 3300–1200 BCE that draws its name from the use of BRONZE becoming common in the production of utensils, jewelry, and weapons. The Bronze Age is typically divided into "Early Bronze" (3300–2000 BCE), "Middle Bronze" (2000–1550 BCE), and "Late Bronze" (1550–1200 BCE). In the areas of Israel and Jordan, this period marked the beginning of more urban and complex societies. The end of the Bronze Age is marked by destruction layers at various sites in the region, though there was continuous occupation into the Iron Age at some sites.

BROOK A small stream that has water only after rains and is dry most of the year is known today as a wadi.

BROOM The broom tree (Retama raetam) is a bush native to the desert and hill country of Israel and its neighbors. Its branches are used in the manufacture of brooms.

BROTH Liquid prepared by stewing meat in water. Gideon served this substance along with bread and meat to God's messenger (Judg 6:19-20). In response to the messenger's instruction, Gideon poured out the broth as a libation offering. See also the negative use of "broth of unclean meat" (Isa 65:4). See MEAL CUSTOMS.

BROTHER, BROTHERHOOD Siblings (brothers and sisters) had important functions within antiquity's family systems. Central sibling obligations were to strive for harmony, to offer mutual social and practical support, and to defend family interests, such as honor and finances.

Siblings have central roles in the OT and the Apocrypha: Cain and Abel (Gen 4:1-16); Esau and Jacob (Gen 25:19–35:29); Rachel and Leah (Gen 29–30); Joseph and his brothers (Gen 37–50); Moses, Miriam, and Aaron (Exod 1–7; 15:20-21); and the Maccabean brothers (4 Macc 8:1–14:10). Siblings should nourish close relations (Prov 18:24), be in agreement (Ps 133:1; Prov 17:17), and love each other (Lev 19:16-17). However, reality often differed from ideals: the OT describes tensions (Ps 50:20; Jer 9:4) and cases of serious conflict (Gen 4:8; 37:20). The winners were not always those deserving victory (Gen 27–28); yet the OT portrays God as high-minded even toward evildoers (Gen 4:15).

Sibling terms were also used figuratively, of fellow Israelites (Deut 15:11-12; Ps 22:23), colleagues (Num 8:23-26; 2 Chron 29:34), political allies (1 Kgs 9:13; Amos 1:9; 1 Macc 12:6-7), friends (2 Sam 1:26), and lovers (Song 4:9-10). Members of Qumran called each other brothers (1QS VI, 8–10). Israel could be depicted as a family or a siblingship (brotherhood) with God as father (Hos 2; Mal 2:10).

Scholars have devoted more attention to sibling relationships in the Greco-Roman period than in the earlier centuries. With the increasing trend toward urbanization, in Greco-Roman antiquity sibling groups appear to have become smaller, consisting of two to three persons. Usually, brothers and sisters inherited on an equal footing, and primogeniture was not practiced. Since parents often died before all their children were adults, siblingship was the longest familial relationship.

The basic characteristics of OT siblingship recur in the NT. In particular, siblings were expected to display emotional closeness, leniency, and forgiveness. Sibling relations did not imply equality of gender and status, but unity despite differences, with the obligation of the stronger and the weaker to mutual support. As in OT times, conflict occurred, particularly between brothers, often manifesting itself in quarrels over inheritance (Luke 12:13-15). The prominence of sibling groups in the NT shows the importance of family relations for the spread of the gospel: Peter and Andrew (Mark 1:16 par.), James and John (Mark 1:19 par.), Martha, Mary, and Lazarus (John 11:1-44). Siblings also occur in Jesus' parables: the two sons (Matt 21:28-32), and the prodigal and his brother (Luke 15:11-32). Jesus is depicted as having brothers and sisters (Mark 3:31; John 7:3; Acts 1:14). He also refers to sibling relations on other occasions, particularly in cases of family disruption (Mark 13:12 par.).

Paul consistently addresses Christians as siblings whether they are his coworkers or simply church members. Paul describes Christ as "first of many brothers and sisters" (Rom 8:29). Siblingship implies putting Christian love into practice (Rom 12:9-13; 1 Thess 4:9-12), welcoming weaker believers (Rom 14:1–15:13; 1 Cor 8:1–11:1), not condemning or taking one's Christian siblings to court (1 Cor 6:1-11), and treating those who are social inferiors as siblings (Phlm 15-16).

BUCKET A container, often leather, used to draw water from cisterns and wells (John 4:11). The water it holds is used metaphorically to emphasize the prosperity of Israel (Num 24:7) and the insignificance of other nations (Isa 40:15; 2 Esdr 6:56).

BUKKI Probably a shortened form of BUKKIAH.

1. Representing the tribe of Dan, Bukki was one of the twelve delegates who divided up the land of promise among the tribes (Num 34:22).

2. Son of ABISHUA, an Aaronite (1 Chron 6:5).

See PRIESTS AND LEVITES.

BUKKIAH One of the sons of HEMAN who was commissioned by DAVID to prophesy with musical instruments (1 Chron 25:4). He was the leader of the sixth division of musicians (1 Chron 25:13).

BUL The eighth Hebrew month (October–November), later known as Marcheshvan. The month when construction of the temple was completed (1 Kgs 6:38).

BULL The offering of bulls as SACRIFICES AND OFFERINGS or as gifts was a central part of Israelite worship. Bulls were considered the pride of the herd in the Israelite sacrificial system.

Without becoming necessarily syncretistic or idolatrous, the Israelites used bulls as poetic symbols of power. Yet the danger of syncretism was present, because the religion of Israel's Canaanite neighbors included bull cults dedicated to the chief god of the Canaanite pantheon, El, and his son Baal, representing virility, fertility, the weather, and war. The prophets denounced the use of bull icons in the northern kingdom as marks of apostasy (Amos 4:4; 5:5; 7:9; Hos 2:18; 8:4-6; 10:5; 12:11; 13:2).

See CALF, GOLDEN; SACRIFICES AND OFFERINGS.

BULRUSH A marsh plant (Isa 58:5).

BULWARK Fortifications (towers, pillars, and foundations) for strength and security.

BUNAH The Judahite Jerahmeel's second son (1 Chron 2:25).

BUNNI 1. A Levite who heard Ezra's reading of the Instruction scroll (Neh 9:4).

2. A chief of the people who made a covenant with EZRA and others to observe the Mosaic laws (Neh 10:15).

3. The levitical ancestor of SHEMAIAH who agreed to live in Jerusalem (Neh 11:15).

BURDEN Used in both the OT and the NT in the literal sense of a weight or load to be borne, burden is regularly used in a figurative sense in the OT to refer to (1) sins and iniquity, (2) external oppression, (3) cares and strife, or (4) responsibilities and tasks of daily life. The most common Hebrew word for "burden" in the OT is also rendered "oracle" or "prophecy" (e.g., Isa 13–23; Jer 23; 2 Kgs 9:25).

BURIAL The placement of a deceased human body in a tomb or in the earth.

BUSH, BURNING Moses sees a burning bush that is not destroyed by the fire (Exod 3:2-4; see also Deut 33:16]). In the NT the bush is mentioned in Mark 12:26 and Luke 20:37. Stephen mentions it in his sermon where Moses appears as a deliverer rejected by his people (Acts 7:30, 35; see Exod 2:14). The bush is located in Horeb at the site of future worship, covenant making, and revelation of Law.

BUSHEL A vessel large enough to cover a lamp and conceal its light (Matt 5:15; Mark 4:21; Luke 11:33 RSV). It should not be thought of in these contexts first as a unit of measure, but as a measuring vessel or domestic utensil. As a unit of measure, a bushel was equivalent to approximately 8 quarts (1 peck) dry measure, substantially smaller than today's bushel. See WEIGHTS AND MEASURES.

BUZ 1. Son of MILCAH and NAHOR, Abraham's brother (Gen 22:21).

2. A family listed among the clans of Gad during the divided kingdoms (1 Chron 5:14). Job's friend, ELIHU, was a BUZITE (Job 32:2).

3. A nation-state upon whom Jeremiah prophesied God's wrath (Jer 25:23).

BUZI Father of the priest and prophet Ezekiel (Ezek 1:3).

BUZITE Someone from Buz (Jer 25; Job 32:2, 6). See DEDAN; TEMA.

Cc

CAESAR Originally the personal name of the Roman dictator Gaius Iulius, who was murdered in 44 BCE. Caesar was taken up as the family name of his adopted heir Octavian (Augustus) and thereafter came to designate each successive Roman emperor. Caesar (NRSV translates "emperor") appears in the NT, particularly the Gospels and Acts, often in contrast to the rule of God or Jesus (e.g., Matt 22:17-21). Emperors established laws, judged cases, functioned as the final court of appeals, and served as the high priest of the Augustan system of Roman religion.

CAESAREA MARITIMA Midway between Haifa and Tel Aviv stands the remains of a port city built by Herod the Great. The city became the political center of the Roman and Byzantine province called Palestina Prima. The fifteen biblical references to the city all occur in the book of Acts. Caesarea also became the center of ecclesiastical administration during the Byzantine Period, eclipsing even Jerusalem until the latter was designated as a patriarchate in the 6th cent CE.

Caesarea played a significant role in the development of early Christianity. Philip came from Jerusalem to evangelize the city (Acts 8:40). Cornelius, the first Gentile convert, was a centurion stationed at Caesarea. Peter came from Jerusalem to baptize him (Acts 10). Cornelius's conversion initiated the process that transformed Christianity into a world religion with an identity distinct from Judaism. Paul passed through the city several times (e.g., Acts 9:30; 18:22; 21:8). He was imprisoned there for two years before being sent to Rome for trial (Acts 23–26).

CAESAREA PHILIPPI Caesarea Philippi is mentioned twice in the NT: Matt 16:13 and Mark 8:27. Both texts identify the place as the setting for Peter's confession of Jesus as the Messiah.

CAIAPHAS Joseph Caiaphas was the Jewish high priest who interrogated Jesus and handed him over to Pilate. The longest serving high priest of the 1st cent. CE, Caiaphas was deposed in 37.

CAIN Son of ADAM and EVE (Gen 4:1), and rival with his brother ABEL for God's favor (Gen 4:1-16).

CAINAN Noah's great-grandson; an ancestor of Jesus (Luke 3:36; LXX of Gen 10:24; 11:12).

CALAH Mentioned in Gen 10:11-12 as one of the cities built by NIMROD, situated on the Tigris River about 35 km downstream from NINEVEH.

CALAMOLALUS Along with Ono, his 725 descendants were among the exiles returning from Babylon (1 Esdr 5:22). The name may be a corruption from combining Lod and Hadid (Ezra 2:33; Neh 7:37).

CALCOL Son of Zerah and grandson of TAMAR and Judah, Calcol belonged to a guild of musicians known as "the children of MAHOL," whom Solomon is said to have exceeded in wisdom (1 Chron 2:6; 1 Kgs 4:31 [Heb 5:11]).

CALEB, CALEBITES 1. Caleb the son of Jephunneh is one of the spies sent to evaluate whether Israel could take the "promised land" from the Canaanites (see CANAAN, CANAANITES). He is listed among the Judean delegation to this task (Num 13:6); however, he and his brother Othniel are said to be "Kenizzite" (Num 32:12, Josh 14:6, Judg 3:9-11), descendants of Kenaz the grandson of Esau (Gen 36:15), and thus Edomite.

2. The name also belongs to Caleb the son of Hezron in the line of Perez, Judah's son by his daugher-in-law Tamar (1 Chron 2:18-20).

CALEB-EPHRATHAH Town in Gilead where Hezron died.

CALF Young calves were considered a culinary delicacy and were prepared for special meals. According to the biblical story, when the three guests came to Abraham to announce the imminent birth of Isaac, he offered them a meal including a young calf, fresh milk, and baked goods (Gen 18:6-8). Calves, specially selected for fattening (Jer 46:21; Amos 6:4), were served on particular occasions, as mentioned when Saul visited the spiritualist woman at En-Dor (1 Sam 28:24). Young calves were also considered choice animals for sacrifice (Lev 9:2; 16:3; Num 7). In several instances, the calf is used as a symbol of peaceful conditions (Isa 27:10) and coexistence (Isa 11:6). On the other hand, the behavior of this young animal is used as a metaphor for misbehavior (Jer 31:18).

Canaanite religion used the bull and calf as symbols of divinity, and this influenced Israelite religion. The story of the golden calf (Exod 32) is one expression of this influence. Another example is the erection of calves by Jeroboam in Dan and Bethel (1 Kgs 12:28-29). This particular event reverberates in 2 Kgs 10:29 and 17:16. In reality, the bronze bull statuette from the bull site in the Samaria highlands is a remnant of such cultic use of the bull in early Israelite religion.

CALF, GOLD Ancient Near Eastern bull and calf icons were used as symbols of fertility or war. Bull icons were dedicated to El, the chief god of the Canaanite pantheon. Icons were also used as pedestals, with a god astride them or with no god visible (see BULL). The biblical texts associated with the story of the golden calf (Exod 32; Deut 9; 1 Kgs 11–12; Hosea) reflect diverse political and religious interests in the cent. following the division of Solomon's kingdom (ca. 920 BCE), possibly including differences between followers of Moses and those of Aaron. Traditional interpreters have long considered the episode as a sign of the Israelites' betrayal of the covenant.

CALNEH, CALNO Mentioned in Isa 10:9 alongside CARCHEMISH, Hamath, ARPAD, and DAMASCUS (and with Hamath in Amos 6:2), Calno/Kullania is probably the same as the neo-Hittite state of Unqi/Pattina whose capital was Kinalua.

CALVARY The Vulgate translation for "skull," the place of Jesus' crucifixion. See GOLGOTHA.

CAMEL'S HAIR John the baptizer "wore clothes made of camel's hair, with a leather belt around his waist" (Mark 1:6; Matt 3:4), probably an allusion to Elijah (2 Kgs 1:8). The prophet's "shaggy coat" (Zech 13:4) is probably related to Elijah's dress.

CANA A city of Galilee. In the NT, Cana is mentioned only in the Gospel of John (2:1-11; 4:46; 21:2).

CANAAN, CANAANITES 1. Ham's son and the grandson of Noah (Gen 9:18-27; 10:6). He is the eponymous ancestor of the Canaanite people. Noah curses Canaan to be literally "a slave of slaves" among his kin (Gen 9:22, 25-27).

2. A noun for "trader" or merchant (e.g., Hos 12:8; Prov 31:24; Job 40:30). The association of commerce with Canaanites continues with the mercantile power of the Phoenicians in the Iron Age.

3. In the Bible there are numerous references to the land of Canaan and to its inhabitants. *Canaan* and *Canaanite* were terms still used in the NT (Acts 7:11; 13:19). As a geographical term, *Canaan* refers to the eastern Mediterranean coastal area approximating the modern states of Lebanon and Israel (inclusive of the disputed territories), and parts of Syria such as its southern coast and lower reaches of the Orontes Valley. In the OT, Canaan is depicted as both the land of promise and the location of a corrupting culture.

CANANAEAN An appellation for Jesus' disciple Simon (Matt 10:4; Mark 3:18) that differentiates him from Simon Peter and indicates his affiliation with the Zealots. See ZEALOT.

CANDACE Candace is not a proper name but the hereditary royal title for the Ethiopian queen mother. In the NT, the Candace is the employer of the Ethiopian eunuch treasurer converted by Philip (Acts 8:26-40).

CANOPY A shelter used as protection from the elements in the ANE. Unlike a tent or meeting tent, a canopy is an overhead covering, made of fabric or wood, rather than one with sides.

CAPERNAUM Capernaum was the center of Jesus' Galilean ministry (Matt 4:13; 8:5; 17:24; Mark 2:1; 9:33; Luke 4:23, 31; 7:1; John 2:12; 4:46; 6:17, 24, 59). The town reached its peak during the late Roman and Byzantine periods, with an estimated size of 13 acres and a population of ca. 1,500 people.

CAPHAR-SALAMA The site of a battle between the Seleucid general Nicanor and Judas Maccabeus (1 Macc 7:31).

CAPHTOR, CAPHTORIM In Gen 10:14 Caphtorim is mentioned as the seventh offspring of EGYPT. The Caphtorim, inhabitants of Caphtor (Deut 2:23), displaced the Avvim along the southern coast of Israel near Gaza. According to Amos (9:7), Caphtor is the place from which the PHILISTINES originally came, and Jeremiah (47:4) called it an island.

CAPPADOCIA A major region of central Asia Minor, extending at its largest from the Taurus Mountains and the Euphrates in the south to the Black Sea in the north and from the upper Euphrates in the east to the Halys River and Lake Tuz in the west. In 17 CE, Cappadocia became a Roman province, which is mentioned in the Bible in Acts 2:9 and 1 Pet 1:1.

CARABASION Descendant of Bani who dismissed his foreign wife, as Ezra instructed him (1 Esdr 9:34).

CARAVAN The caravan is a group or company (Gen 37:25; Job 6:18; Isa 21:13) that carried merchandise long distances with the use of pack animals for transport. The Hebrew word is related to both the traveler and to the journey's route (Judg 5:6). Israelite caravans primarily used donkeys to transport goods from one tribal area to another.

CARCHEMISH A major city of northern Syria, located ca. 100 km (62 mi.) northeast of Aleppo, near the major crossing of the upper Euphrates River. Carchemish is also mentioned in the Bible in 2 Chron 35:20; Jer 46:2; and 1 Esdr 1:25 as the site of a famous battle in 605 BCE in which the Babylonian king Nebuchadnezzar defeated the waning forces of the Assyrians and their Egyptian allies, led by Pharaoh Neco II.

CARKAS An attendant among King Ahasuerus's seven eunuchs, who were requested to bring him Queen Vashti (Esth 1:10).

CARMEL Carmel is known for the DAVID and NABAL episode (1 Sam 25:2-40), as the birthplace of HEZRO, one of David's soldiers (2 Sam 23:35; 1 Chron 11:37), and ABIGAIL, whom David later married (1 Sam 25:40; 27:3; 2 Sam 2:2; 3:3). Also called Khirbet Kurmul, the city is located in the Hebron hills in Judah northeast of Khirbet Susiya and north of Moan (Ilan and Amit). See CARMEL, MOUNT.

CARMEL, MOUNT Because of its abundant flora, Carmel, meaning "vineyard," "garden-land," or "fruitful" (Isa 10:18; 16:10), may be used as a metaphor for beauty and fertility (Song 7:5; 2 Kgs 19:23; Isa 35:2; 37:24). Conversely, in the absence of flora during drought, Carmel is a metaphor for desolation (Isa 33:9). Mount Carmel was the meeting place between ELIJAH and the prophets of BAAL and ASHERAH (1 Kgs 18:19-40) and later a sanctuary for Elijah (2 Kgs 2:25; 4:25).

CARMI 1. Son of Reuben, ancestor of the Carmites (Num 26:6; Gen 46:9; Exod 6:14; 1 Chron 5:3).

2. Judahite father of Achan (Josh 7) or Achar (1 Chron 2:7), who violated Joshua's ban during the conquest of Jericho.

3. Probably Caleb instead of Carmi (1 Chron 4:1).

CARPENTER A skilled artisan who works with wood, stone, or metals. Only two carpenters are specifically mentioned in the NT—Joseph and Jesus (Matt 13:55; Mark 6:3).

CARPUS A resident of Troas, with whom Paul had left his cloak, some books, and some parchments (2 Tim 4:13). According to Eusebius (*Hist. eccl.* 4.15), a different Carpus was a bishop of Gurdos and Lydia, and martyred in Pergamum ca. 170 CE.

CARSHENA One of King Ahasuerus's officals from Persia and Media, who advised him to replace Queen Vashti (Esth 1:14, 21).

CART The Hebrew word for cart is derived from the word *round*, and can refer to both two- and four-wheeled vehicles, generally pulled by oxen. The same word can be used for cart or wagon. Joseph sent wagons to fetch his father's family (Gen 45:19, 21, 27; 46:5). Judith loads the spoils from Holofernes's camp onto her carts (Jdt 15:11).

Carts often had a sacral function: The Philistines placed the COVENANT CHEST on a new cart for its return to Israel, pulled by two milch cows (1 Sam 6:7-14). Later, David placed the chest on a new cart in an aborted attempt to bring it to Jerusalem (2 Sam 6:3; 1 Chron 13:7).

In ancient Israel, carts were typically made of wood (1 Sam 6:14), but HIRAM of Tyre reportedly cast ten four-wheeled items of bronze for use in the temple (1 Kgs 7:27-37). The typical word for cart, however, is not used, and whether the elaborately decorated furnishings were movable is uncertain.

Isaiah (28:27-28) and Amos (2:13) employed the image of cart wheels, used for threshing grain, as a symbol of divine judgment.

CASIPHIA An unidentified site in Babylonia near the AHAVA River where the temple servants lived during the exile (Ezra 8:17). Before returning to Judah, EZRA sent a delegation to "IDDO, the leader at the place named Casiphia," to recruit servants for the priests in the second temple (8:17).

CASSIA Cassia bark (Cinnamonum cassia) was brought to the Mediterranean from Asia (Ezek 27:19). In Egypt it was part of mummification mixtures, and in ancient Israel it was used in anointing oil (Exod 30:24) and fragrances to adorn the robes of royalty (Ps 45:8 [Heb 45:9]).

CATERPILLAR Bible translations often apply "caterpillar" (butterfly and moth larvae) erroneously to the Hebrew words that likely refer to nymphal stages of locusts, while labeling proper caterpillars as worms.

CATHOLIC EPISTLES The Catholic Epistles include James, 1–2 Peter, 1–2–3 John, and Jude. Although this collection is known by different names ("General Epistles" and "Non-Pauline Letters"), the rubric catholic was used to title this collection because of its universal or "catholic" address and its theological unity.

CATHUA Family head whose descendants were among the temple servants, called the Nethinim, who returned after the exile (1 Esdr 5:30).

CATTLE The collective term *cattle*, which refers to domesticated quadrupeds, specifically bovine animals, is used in the NRSV to translate a variety of Hebrew terms. This can create confusion, since there are other related terms such as *herd*, *flock*, *sheep*, and *oxen*. During biblical times, cattle were used mostly as beasts of burden and for traction, rather than for milk and meat. The latter two were only incidental use. Cattle were also raised for their by-products, such as dung, bones, and hide.

BULLs were a symbol of power and fertility. Bulls are mentioned in the OT numerous times, usually in connection with sacrifices. Sometimes the Bible uses the bull as symbol for Yahweh. The female of the species is mentioned significantly fewer times and mostly metaphorically. In Gen 41, cows appear in Pharaoh's dream, symbolizing good and bad agricultural years. In Hos 4:16, Israel is compared to a stubborn cow.

Cows were harnessed for work. The biblical account mentions that they were used for pulling the wagon, bringing back the covenant chest from Philistia to Judah (1 Sam 6), and they were sacrificed when they reached their destination. When the red cow was selected for the "red heifer ritual," she was supposed to be "without defect, which is flawless, and on which no yoke has been laid" (Num 19:2).

CAUDA An island, also called Clauda, near the southern coast of Crete, which Paul's party passed during a violent windstorm en route to Rome (Acts 27:16). It is probably modern Gaudos, approximately 24 nautical mi. south of Crete.

CAVE Biblical and archaeological evidence shows that caves were places where people lived, took refuge, hid property, or buried the dead. Mountains, wadis, and valleys, all with caves, provide natural shelter across the interior of Israel from the highlands of the Galilee to the Dead Sea. Artificial caves could also be hewn out of the rocky terrain.

CEDAR Like pines, cedars (Cedrus libani) have needlelike leaves clustered on short branch shoots. Cedars of Lebanon probably never grew within the bounds of present-day Israel but were abundant on the high LEBANON mountain ridge to the north.

Historically, the cedar of Lebanon was one of the most important building materials in the Near East. The most famous cedar building, although not the largest, was the temple built by Solomon (1 Kgs 6). In addition, Solomon built a magnificent home for himself entirely out of cedar (1 Kgs 7) that took thirteen years to complete, six more years than the temple. Earlier, David had built a house out of cedar (2 Sam 7:2). While cedarwood is fragrant and attractive, its chief value lies in being the only tree in the region abundant and large enough for big buildings.

CENCHREAE The eastern seaport of Corinth 6 mi. distant. The church was directed by Phoebe (Rom 16:1), and Paul sailed from there to Ephesus (Acts 18:18).

CENSER A gold, copper, or bronze vessel holding coals from the altar fire with INCENSE on top, producing a sweet smell (Lev 10:1; 16:12; Num 16:46; Ezek 8:11). The censer was part of the test for Korah and others who mumbled against Moses and Aaron (Num 16:1-39). An angel in John's vision placed fire in a censer and threw it to earth, causing thunder, lightning, and earthquakes (Rev 8:3-5).

CENSUS A census in the Bible is the enrollment and numbering of a group of people, tribe, or nation for various purposes: the numbering of the seventy members of Jacob's clan who came to Egypt in the time of Joseph (Gen 46:26-27; Exod 1:1-7), taxation for ritual or governmental purposes (Exod 30:13-16; 38:24-26; Luke 2:1-5), assignment of cultic duties to clans of priestly Levites (Num 3:1-39), reckoning the number of Levites available as substitutes for Israel's firstborn males (Num 3:40-51), military counting of troops for war (Num 1:3; 26:2; 2 Sam 24:1-9; 1 Chron 21:1-6), distribution of the land of Canaan according to the size of Israelite tribes and clans (Num 26:3-56), and the counting of former exiles who returned from Babylon to Judah (Ezra 2:1-67). The three most significant census-taking events in the Bible are the wilderness census lists in Num 1 and 26, David's census in 2 Sam 24 and 1 Chron 21, and the census associated with Jesus' birth in Luke 2.

CENTURION A centurion was a ranking officer in the Roman army, usually the commander over a company of 100 men or fewer. The word appears in the NT twenty-five times.

CHABRIS Gothoniel's son and a magistrate of Bethulia to whom Judith presents her plan to deliver their city (Jdt 6:15; 8:10; 10:6).

CHADIASANS Possibly former residents of Kedesh. Along with the Ammidians, they returned to Jerusalem from exile with Zerubbabel and other leaders (1 Esdr 5:20).

CHAEREAS Ammonite commander of the stronghold Gazara, and brother of Timothy, both of whom were defeated and killed by Judas Maccabeus and his men (2 Macc 10:32-38).

CHAFF In the agricultural economy of the biblical world, a major task was winnowing, or separating grains from their stalks and chaff by using a pitchfork to toss the harvested crops into the air, where the wind blew the chaff away. This image is used metaphorically to describe God driving away Israel's enemies as if they are chaff (Pss 1:4; 35:5; Isa 17:13; 29:5) or, most famously, Jesus coming with a winnowing fork in his hand to separate out the evil, or chaff, which will be burned from the good in unquenchable fire (Matt 3:11-12; Luke 3:16).

CHALDEA, CHALDEANS A region in Babylonia and its inhabitants. The designation for the inhabitants, Chaldeans, is used in the Bible to refer to the last dynasty of Babylon (626–539 BCE), whose second king, Nebuchadnezzar II, conquered Jerusalem in 597 and 586 BCE, deporting many Judeans into Babylonian exile. The Chaldeans are mentioned in Isa 47–48; Jer 50–51; Ezek 11:24; 16:29; 23:15-16; 2 Kgs; Ezra; and Daniel.

See ASSYRIA AND BABYLONIA.

CHALKSTONES A metaphor for the fragility of idolatrous altars (Isa 27:9), because limestone, when heated, will convert into lime and break easily.

CHAOS In the biblical worldview, an orderly creation is surrounded by forces of chaos. These forces are primarily described as turbulent waters (Pss 77:16; 93:3; Jer 5:22), and they are occasionally personified as a chaos dragon, Leviathan

(Ps 74:14; Isa 27:1), Rahab (Ps 89:10; Job 26:12), or a Sea/River (Job 7:12; Hab 3:8).

To create the ordered world, God had to restrain these primordial waters of chaos, in some traditions by a cosmic battle to subdue the chaos dragon (Pss 74:12-17; 89:6-15; Job 26:5-14). In the account of creation in Gen 1:1–2:4*a*, God divides the primordial waters (1:2), holding half of them back behind the firmament or sky, and the other half beyond the earth as seas (1:6-10). To prevent the world from collapsing back into chaos, as it did in the great flood (Gen 7:11; 8:2), God held these turbulent waters at bay behind boundaries (Job 38:8-11; Ps 104:5-9; Prov 8:27-29). The NT author of Revelation went beyond his OT ancestors to claim that God would one day eliminate the waters of chaos entirely (Rev 21:1).

CHAPHENATHA A section of the Jerusalem wall that Jonathan Maccabeus rebuilt (1 Macc 12:37). This section may be the "second district" mentioned in 2 Kgs 22:14.

CHARAX Town, east of the Jordan, where the Jews called the Toubiani lived (2 Macc 12:17).

CHARCOAL Common fuel made from wood (Isa 44:12; 54:16) and used symbolically in Ps 11:6; Prov 26:21; John 18:18; and 21:9.

CHAREA The name for HARSHA in 1 Esdr 5:32.

CHARGERS Spirited warhorses, an emendation of cypresses in Nah 2:3. See also Isa 31:1; Jer 8:6; Rev 6:2, and HORSE.

CHARIOT Two- or four-wheeled horse-drawn vehicles, used in both civilian and military contexts, primarily to transport passengers.

See HORSE; WAR, IDEAS OF.

CHARISMA A singular noun meaning "gift," or specifically "gift of healing," or "salvation," or "celibacy." The word appears in various forms in the Pauline tradition (Rom 1:11; 5:15-16; 6:23; 11:29; 12:6; 1 Cor 1:7; 7:7; 12:4, 9, 28, 30-31; 2 Cor 1:11; 1 Tim 4:14; 2 Tim 1:6), and once in 1 Pet 4:10.

See FRUIT OF THE SPIRIT; SPIRITUAL GIFTS.

CHARITY Word used in the KJV to mean "love," and the term is still familiar in traditional Christian wedding rituals (which draw from 1 Cor 13). See SPIRITUAL GIFTS.

CHARMIS A city magistrate of Bethulia (Jdt 6:15; 8:10; 10:6).

CHASM In Luke's parable of the rich man and LAZARUS, the rich man has his fortunes reversed because he fails to heed Moses and the prophets. He is forced to dwell in "the place of the dead," separated by the chasm from reward at ABRAHAM'S SIDE (Luke 16:19-31).

CHEBAR The river (or canal?) at Tel-Abib in the Chaldeans' region, where the prophet Ezekiel received a vision (Ezek 1:3; 3:15, 23; 10:15, 20, 22; 43:3).

CHEDORLAOMER The king of Elam who appears as the leader of a group of kings (Tidal, Amraphel, and Arioch) from the West, who wage battle against five "cities of the plain" in southern Israel, including Sodom and Gomorrah (Gen 14:1-2).

CHELAL An Israelite who was among the returning exiles who were forced by Ezra to give up their foreign wives (Ezra 10:30).

CHELLEANS Inhabitants of the area north of the Rassisites and the Ishmaelites (Jdt 2:23), probably in the eastern portion of Palestine near the Arabian Desert.

CHELOUS A town name appearing only once in the biblical corpus (Jdt 1:9) where its mention with JERUSALEM, BETHANY, Kadesh, and the river of Egypt suggests a southern location.

CHELUB 1. A Judahite in the Chronicler's genealogy (1 Chron 4:11), the brother of Shuah and the father of Mehir.

2. Father of David's officer Ezri, who was in charge of the field workers (1 Chron 27:26).

CHELUBAI See CALEB, CALEBITES.

CHELUHI A descendant of Bani. Ezra forced him and other men to send away their foreign wives and their children, as part of the effort to increase homogeneity in the community of returned exiles in Judea (Ezra 10:35).

CHEMOSH The national deity of the Moabites, whom the OT calls "people of Chemosh" (Num 21:29; Jer 48:46). Solomon built a SHRINE for Chemosh (1 Kgs 11:7; 2 Kgs 23:13), for which he is doomed (1 Kgs 11:33).

CHENAANAH 1. Father of Zedekiah, Jehoshaphat's court prophet, repudiated in 1 Kgs 22 and 2 Chron 18.

2. A Benjaminite in the genealogy of 1 Chron 7:10, which differs from 1 Chron 8:1-40. Genealogies for Zebulun and Dan are missing in 1 Chron 4–8, but it is improbable that 1 Chron 7:6-12 originally was a genealogy of Zebulon.

CHENANI A Levite who supported Ezra's promulgation of the Law (Neh 9:4).

CHENANIAH 1. A Levite who directed the music at the celebration of David's installation of the COVENANT CHEST in Jerusalem (1 Chron 15:22, 27).

2. An Izharite appointed by David for civil duties (1 Chron 26:29).

CHEPHIRAH A Hivite city (Josh 9:17), allotted to Benjamin's tribe (Josh 18:26). Its residents' descendants returned from exile (Ezra 2:25; Neh 7:29).

CHERAN Seir's grandson. A chief or clan of the Horites (Gen 36:26; 1 Chron 1:41).

CHERETHITES AND PELETHITES The Cherethites and the Pelethites served as DAVID's palace guard under the charge of BENAIAH (2 Sam 8:18; 20:23; 23:23). They remained loyal to David in the most difficult circumstances during his reign.

CHERITH, WADI A stream where ELIJAH hid from AHAB and JEZEBEL during the drought in Israel. He remained there until the spring dried up (1 Kgs 17:2-7).

CHERUB 1. A Babylonian city and former home of some of the returnees to Jerusalem with Zerubabbel (Ezra 2:59; Neh 7:61). Those arriving from Cherub could not be confirmed as Israelites.

2. Cherub is a personal name in 1 Esdr 5:36.

CHERUBIM See WINGED CREATURES.

CHESALON A city on Judah's northern boundary and west of Jerusalem. It was also called Mount Jearim (Josh 15:10).

CHESED Abraham's nephew (Gen 22:22).

CHESIL A city in southern Judah near Edom (Josh 15:30). It is possibly the same as Bethul (Josh 19:4), Bethuel (1 Chron 4:30), and Bethel (1 Sam 30:27).

CHEST Container for collecting money for temple repairs (2 Kgs 12:9-10; 2 Chron 24:8-11) and for holding temple treasures (1 Esdr 1:54).

See also COVENANT CHEST.

CHESULLOTH City in the territory allotted to Issachar's tribe (Josh 19:18).

It is probably identical with Chisloth-Tabor (Josh 19:12) and Tabor (1 Chron 6:77).

CHEZIB Birthplace of Shela, third son of Judah and his Canaanite wife Shua (Gen 38:5). Possibly same town as Cozeba and ACHZIB.

CHIDON Name of the town or the owner of the threshing floor where Uzzah died (1 Chron 13:9). A parallel text refers to the threshing floor as Nacon's (2 Sam 6:6). See NACON; UZZAH.

CHILD, CHILDREN In the OT, children signified divine blessing. God blessed Adam and Eve to be fruitful and multiply (Gen 1:27-28). God promised Abraham many descendants (Gen 15:1-5). Blessed was the man with many children (Ps 127:3-6) and bitter was barrenness (1 Sam 1–2; see BARREN, BARRENNESS).

Children were highly valued for their potential roles: contributing to the material well-being of the family, carrying on the family name, perpetuating the covenant nation's unique identity and purpose from one generation to the next. Children were integrated from an early age into family and nation—dedicated to God, and, in the case of males, circumcised on the eighth day (Luke 2:21; see CIRCUMCISION).

Children had to outgrow their ignorance, foolishness, and inexperience in order to fulfill their roles. Thus the stress on children's education. Proverbs 1–9 focuses on parental instruction in wisdom to wean a child from adverse qualities. Children participated actively in familial and communal worship, asked questions concerning the rites observed, and repeatedly listened to the explanations of their elders, and so learned the covenant people's way of life and the underlying narrative of Yahweh's redemption (Exod 12:26-27; Deut 4:9-10). By contrast, when God chose mere youths as instruments of God's purposes, divine sovereignty and power were emphasized (e.g., 1 Sam 16:11-13).

Children's central obligation was to honor their parents (Exod 20:12). The child's obedience formed the basis of a morally and economically viable family, while insolent or violent treatment of parents was condemned (Prov 15:20; 19:26). Parental discipline was seen as necessary out of love—never anger—to save a child from destruction, and could take a harsh, physical form supposedly suited to children's irrationality (Prov 13:24; 19:18).

The perspective on childbearing in the NT is different from that in the OT. Jesus pronounces a woe (not a blessing) on the woman who is pregnant or nursing in the coming eschatological destruction (Mark 13:17). Similarly, Paul points to the impending crisis as the reason not to enter into marriage (except to avoid sexual sin), which involves one in obligations (toward spouse and children) that distract from devotion to the Lord; and Paul never commends procreation to those already married (1 Cor 7:1-40). It is unclear whether 1 Tim 2:15, "A wife will be brought safely through giving birth to their children, if they both continue in faith, love, and holiness, together with self-control," promises salvation on the basis of childbearing (viewed positively) and other commendable acts, or salvation despite having to go through painful childbearing (viewed negatively) as the continuing effect of sin.

Jesus' teaching that disciples are to love him more than father or mother, son or daughter, envisions conflict between parents and children over Jesus, and undermines their traditional mutual obligations (Matt 8:21-22; 10:34-37; Luke 9:59-62; 12:51-53; 14:26 contrast the emphasis on Jesus' obedience to both heavenly Father and earthly parents in Luke 2:41-51). Jesus' description of those who do the will of God as "my brother, sister, and mother" (Mark

3:31-35), however, implies that parent/child obligations are now located within this broader family. If children or parents lose the benefits of the patriarchal family as a result of Jesus' call to follow him, they gain even more by joining God's family: "one hundred times as much now . . . brothers, sisters, mothers, children" (Mark 10:28-30). Further, Jesus' disciples are to welcome little children (not just their own) in his name, following his example.

In striking contrast to children's social inferiority, Jesus teaches that children are models for entering God's reign. In Mark 10:13-16 (par. Matt 19:13-15; Luke 18:15-17), Jesus becomes indignant when the disciples try to prevent people from bringing little children to him (presumably because they were not under obligation to keep the Law in anticipation of the Messiah's blessings), and instead Jesus takes them in his arms and blesses them, for "God's kingdom belongs to people like these children" (Luke 8:16). Children's objective, humble state and corresponding attitude suit them for membership in God's reign, which comes to those who simply need or desire it (1 Pet 2:2). Children's innocence or another positive trait is not implied (compare the realistic views of children in Matt 11:16; Luke 7:32; 1 Cor 3:1-2; 13:11; Gal 4:1, 3; Eph 4:14; Heb 5:13). To enter God's reign one must become like a child: humble.

See CHILDREN OF GOD; FATHER; MARRIAGE.

CHILDREN OF GOD The concept of a familial relationship between humans and God reaches back to ancient mythology and was developed variously in different eras of biblical history. It came to be used metaphorically to designate a special or privileged spiritual relationship to God. References to "children of God" or "sons of God" occur in both covenantal and apologetic contexts as they define the identity of particular peoples and communities.

The divine sonship of Israel was focused in the king, through the corporate solidarity of the people, and the king's identity as the son of God extended to all of Israel (2 Sam 7:14; 1 Chron 17:13; 22:10; 28:6). To the king the Lord promised, in a psalm that was probably composed for a coronation, "You are my son; today I have become your father" (Ps 2:7). The king of Israel was therefore the "one born first . . . the high king of all earth's kings" (Ps 89:27). God's covenant was not with the king per se but with the people of Israel.

The prophets and the later books of the OT begin to emphasize the divine sonship of individual Israelites, "children of the living God" (Hos 1:10), which comes to the fore in the Wisdom Literature. Sirach counsels: "Be like a parent to orphans, and take care of their mothers as for your own wife or husband. Do this, and you will be like a child of the Most High" (4:10).

Divine sonship in a unique sense is reserved for Jesus throughout the NT. Jesus is called both the child of God (Matt 12:18; Acts 3:13, 26; 4:27, 30) and God's son. In sayings attributed to Jesus, those who may be called children of God have a knowledge of God, which has led them to assume ethical qualities that show they are becoming like their divine Father. Peacemakers are blessed because they will be called children of God (Matt 5:9), and those who love their enemies may be called children of God (Matt 5:45).

Paul uses several related phrases: "God's children" (Rom 8:16, 21; 9:8); "children of God" (Phil 2:15), "God's sons" (Rom 8:14, 19), "children from/of the promise" (Rom 9:8; Gal 4:28), "children" (Rom 8:17), "Abraham's children/descendant(s)" (Rom 9:7-8; Gal 3:16, 19, 29), and "heirs" (Rom 8:17; Gal 3:29; 4:1, 7).

Sonship to God is the result of salvation (Gal 3:26). As children of God by faith in Jesus Christ, believers are not sons "by flesh" but "by spirit" (Rom

8:1-11; Gal 4:29) and enjoy freedom from bondage (Rom 8:21; Gal 4:22-23, 26, 30, 31; 5:1). As these references indicate, one of Paul's concerns is to show that believers in Christ are heirs of the promise to Abraham. They and not Abraham's physical descendants are the true children of God.

"Children of God" appears in 1 John 5:2; and "God's children" appears three times in 1 John (3:1-2, 10). In Johannine usage the children of God are those who believe in Jesus, have been born from God, practice love for each other, keep Jesus' teachings, do righteousness, and claim a hope in Christ for their future relationship with God, their Father. See BAPTISM; CHILD, CHILDREN; FATHER; FATHER'S HOUSE; HOLY SPIRIT; GOD'S SON.

CHILEAB Second son of David, born in Hebron of Abigail, Nabal's widow (2 Sam 3:3). In 1 Chron 3:1, the name given to Daniel.

CHILION Son of the Bethlehemites Naomi and Elimelech, who migrated to Moab. Chilion and his brother Mahlon married the Moabites Orpah and Ruth (Ruth 1:2; 4:9).

CHILMAD A Mesopotamian city whose merchants traded with Tyre (Ezek 27:23). It is mentioned with Sheba and Asshur and is located near modern Baghdad.

CHIMHAM Son of Barzillai the Gileadite, who supplied David with food after David left Jerusalem during Absalom's rebellion. Barzillai asked that the reward David offered him go instead to Chimham, who apparently received a parcel of land near Bethlehem.

CHINNERETH, CHINNEROTH Chinnereth is the inland Sea of Galilee that supplies the vast majority of the water flowing into the JORDAN RIVER. In the OT the site also appears to be a city on the sea's western shore, mentioned in the list of Naphtali's towns (Josh 19:35; 1 Kgs 15:20). The city may have given its name to the sea it adjoined (Num 34:11; Deut 3:17), or the sea, shaped like a harp and thus named, may have given its name to the city on its shore.

CHIOS An island of approximately 850 sq. km situated in the eastern part of the Aegean Sea, approximately 10 km from Asia Minor, and a city on the eastern coast of that island. Ancient sources note the locale's reputation for prosperity, quality wines, and claims (contested by others) of being Homer's birthplace. The Bible mentions Chios once, during the course of Paul's voyage back to Jerusalem in Acts 20:15, when his sailing party arrives "opposite Chios" to pass the night anchored within the relatively sheltered waters between the city and the mainland.

CHISLEV See KISLEV.

CHISLON The father of Elidad, who was appointed by Moses to represent the tribe of Benjamin in the distribution of Canaan among the Israelite tribes (Num 34:21).

CHISLOTH-TABOR Called CHESULLOTH in Josh 19:18, Chisloth-Tabor was a village on Zebulun's border with Issachar (Josh 19:12).

CHITLISH The exact location of Chitlish is unknown, although Josh 15:40 lists the town as near LACHISH in Judah's tribal allotment.

CHLOE Chloe is mentioned only in 1 Cor 1:11 in a reference to Chloe's people. Chloe was likely a wealthy business woman from EPHESUS whose "people" were probably business agents (perhaps freedpersons or slaves) acting for her. Those agents brought disquieting news of the Corinthian church to Paul, notably about serious splits (1:10-17;

3:5-23), triumphalism that devalued the cross (1:18–3:4; 4:8-13), and immorality (5:1–6:20).

CHOBA In Jdt 4:4 Choba appears in a list of Israelite cities to the north of Jerusalem that were alerted to an imminent attack by the Assyrian army.

CHORAZIN With Bethsaida and Capernaum, Chorazin was a town denounced by Jesus for not changing their hearts and lives after witnessing his deeds of power (Matt 11:21; Luke 10:13).

CHORBE A family head whose descendants returned from exile (1 Esdr 5:12). See ZACCAI in Ezra 2:9 and Neh 7:14.

CHOSAMAEUS A descendant of Canaan who was forced by Ezra to put away his foreign wife and his children (1 Esdr 9:32).

CHRIST Most frequently used in the NT to refer to Jesus (531 times). Christ is a transliteration of a Greek adjective meaning "anointed (with oil or ointment)," and often used to mean "anointed one." The term Christ became early a typical designation for Jesus, so much so that it functioned as a proper name for him, thus "an apostle of Jesus Christ" (e.g., 1 Pet 1:1). Since the 1st cent. followers of Jesus have been labeled "Christian" (Acts 11:26).

The term bore no religious significance in secular Greek. Its importance in the NT stems from Jewish texts, where it referred to the fulfillment of God's promises regarding the eternal rule of a king from the line of David (see MESSIAH, JEWISH). Each of the NT writers employs the term *Christ* for Jesus.

CHRONICLES, FIRST AND SECOND BOOKS OF Chronicles begins with the first human (1 Chr 1:1); depicts the totality of Israel in genealogical form (1 Chr 1–9); upholds the united monarchy of David and Solomon as an unprecedented era of harmony, success, and national solidarity (1 Chr 10 – 2 Chr 9); recounts the history of the Judahite monarchy as an uneven period, a time of both success and failure (2 Chr 10–36); and concludes with the welcome news of Cyrus the Great's decree ending the Babylonian exile.

CHRYSOLITE The second stone in the high priest's chest pendant (Exod 28:17; 39:10) and the seventh stone (literally "gold stone") in New Jerusalem's foundation wall (Rev 21:20). It is compared to wisdom (Job 28:19); it appears as one of the gems of Eden adorning the king of Tyre (Ezek 28:13). Some English translations render the Hebrew as topaz, a common, clear, gold-colored gem. Currently in mineralogy, chrysolite is an interchangeable term for olivine, a green gemstone.

CHRYSOPRASE The tenth stone in New Jerusalem's foundation wall (Rev 21:20). Chrysoprase's colors vary from apple-green to yellowish-green.

CHURCH The church according to the NT is the community gathered in Jesus' name to worship God and serve others. Rooted in the Jesus movement, the church took shape through faith in the saving significance of Jesus' death and resurrection, and found expression in various Christian communities. The NT canon bears witness to the unity and diversity of church life and organization during the 1st cent. CE.

CHUZA According to Luke, Chuza was an official in HEROD ANTIPAS's court and husband to one of Jesus' benefactors, JOANNA (8:3). The term used to describe his position suggests that he was not an ordinary administrator but a high-ranking, powerful retainer, possibly manager of Herod's estate.

CILICIA A region and Roman province, forming the southern part of Turkey to the south of the Taurus mountain range, and facing the island of Cyprus. To the north lay Galatia and Cappadocia, to the west Lycia and Pamphylia (see Acts 27:5), and to the east Syria. There were two main parts to the region: Cilicia Tracheia ("Rugged"), a mountainous region in the west, and the fertile Cilicia Pedias ("Plain") to the east (Ezek 27:11).

Tarsus was one of the main cities of the region (see Acts 21:39, 22:3).

CIMMERIANS An ancient people for whom Gomer may be an eponym (Gen 10:2; 1 Chron 1:5).

CIRCUMCISION An operation performed on males—infants, children, and adults—to remove all or a portion of the foreskin. The Pentateuch stipulates the circumcision of every Hebrew male on the eighth day after birth (Gen 17:10-11; Lev 12:2-3), every slave of an Israelite (Gen 17:12-13; Exod 12:44), and aliens who resided permanently within Israel if they desired to celebrate and eat the Passover (Exod 12:48).

Circumcision was not practiced exclusively by the Israelites. The prophet Jeremiah (9:25-26) lists "Egyptians or Judeans, Edomites or Ammonites, Moabites or the desert dwellers who cut the hair on their foreheads" as being circumcised.

CISTERN A pit or well used for water storage, vital for survival in the arid Palestine region. Cisterns were generally bulbous or pear-shaped cavities of varying sizes, normally chiseled (Deut 9:11; Neh 9:25; 2 Chron 26:10) into limestone bedrock for the primary purpose of water storage.

CITY Sedentary communal existence, with basic social institutions and shared building projects. In ancient times, most cities were small, perhaps hundreds or a few thousand people. Early Christianity grew most readily among some of the largest cities of the Roman Empire.

CITY GATE The gate was the most vulnerable part of a city's defenses (Isa 28:6), so a typical gate consisted of two to four pairs of "piers" and intervening pairs of "chambers."

CITY OF PALM TREES Another name for JERICHO (Deut 34:3; 2 Chron 28:15). As one of the oldest cities in the world, Jericho grew up around a spring (Elisha's spring) that nourished a date-palm grove, earning the town this epithet.

CITY OF REFUGE Cities of refuge were established in Israel to offer protection for those who had inadvertently killed another human being (Exod 21:12-14). The retaliatory justice of Israel's kinship system demanded a life for a life. The six cities designated in Josh 20:8-9 were strategically located so that none lay outside a day's journey from any point in Israel.

The concept of asylum in the ANE was generally associated with sanctuaries. The covenant scroll (see COVENANT SCROLL) reflects this perspective through legislation that allows a killer to flee to a place appointed by God if the murder was not premeditated (Exod 21:12-14; Num 35:9-29; Deut 4:41-43, 19:1-3).

CITY OF SALT Khirbet Qumran, the City of Salt, was one of the six cities of Judea listed in Josh 15:61-62. It is situated in wilderness and was inhabited several times beginning in the Iron Age and lasting until the Bar-kokhba revolt.

CITY OF THE SUN An Egyptian city, probably HELIOPOLIS (Isa 19:18; Jer 43:13).

CLAUDIA Probably Roman, perhaps a leader of the Christian community, mentioned in 2 Tim 4:21 as sending greetings to TIMOTHY.

CLAUDIUS Born on Aug. 1, 10 BCE, in Lugdunum (Lyons), Gaul, Tiberius

Claudius Nero Germanicus was recognized by the senate as Rome's emperor on Jan. 25, 41 CE. His reign would extend until his death (possibly by murder) on Oct. 13, 54 CE.

CLAY A natural type of sediment or soil composed of minerals (as well as many impurities), which are plastic and sticky when wet, but hard and indestructible when heated to a high temperature. Clay is best known for the making of pottery. Clay is sometimes used as a metaphor for humans (Job 10:9; Isa 45:9; 64:8; Jer 18:6; Rom 9:19-21; see also Sir 33:13).

CLAY TABLETS Clay tablets were the primary writing medium for the cuneiform texts from Mesopotamia and adjacent areas from at least the 4th through the 2nd millennium BCE.

CLEOPAS In Luke 24:13-32 Cleopas and another disciple of Jesus walk to Emmaus and are joined en route by the risen Jesus. He may or may not be CLOPAS, the husband of Mary recorded in John 19:25 as standing near Jesus' cross.

CLOAK Translation of several Hebrew and Greek words referring to an outer garment.

CLOPAS Clopas is mentioned in John 19:25 in association with Mary, who is said to be the sister of Mary, Jesus' mother. He is sometimes equated with Alphaeus (Matt 10:3; Mark 3:18; Luke 6:15) and Cleopas (Luke 24:18).

CLOUD, CLOUDS Clouds sometimes bear rain (Exod 19:9; Eccl 11:3; Job 26:8; 38:22-38; Luke 12:54). Clouds are also a metaphor for communication between heaven and earth (Ps 18:10-11; Joel 2:2).

CLOUD, PILLAR OF See COLUMN OF CLOUD AND LIGHTNING.

CNIDUS A Greek port town in the region of Caria on the southwestern tip of Asia Minor, past which Paul sailed on his way to Rome (Acts 27:7), turning southward toward Crete after winds blew him off course.

COAT OF MAIL A coat of mail is body armor of joined metal plates that are worn by warriors and horses.

COELE-SYRIA The geographic designation of this term varies greatly in the sources and over time. In its strictest geographical definition, it is the Greek name for the Beqaʿ Valley between the LEBANON and ANTI-LEBANON mountains in southern Syria. It is located north of Palestine in modern-day Lebanon (1 Esdr 4:48; cf Amos 1:5 [Valley of Aven]; compare Josh 11:17, 12:7 [Valley of Lebanon]).

COL-HOZEH 1. Father of Shallum (Neh 3:15).

2. Ancestor of Maaseiah who lived in Jerusalem after the exile (Neh 11:5).

COLLECTION, THE Paul organized a large ecumenical collection for the poor in the Jerusalem churches in various Christian communities under his control between 48 CE and 57 CE. His various references to this ambitious venture indicate that it was not just an "ordinary" fund-raising project (1 Cor 16:1-4; 2 Cor 8-9; Gal 2:10; Rom 15:25-27). The collection had far-reaching implications for all the parties involved, since it served as a concrete means to give expression to the unity between Jewish and Gentile Christians.

COLOSSAE Access from the Aegean coast into the interior of Asia Minor (Anatolia is modern Turkey) was provided by river valleys. One of the most important was the Meander, running east from near Ephesus. About 100 mi. upstream it was joined by the river Lycus, whose valley provided the most accessible route to the central plateau and served as a major artery of east-west communication during the Greek and Roman periods. The fertile Lycus Valley also encouraged settlement, and supported three prominent cities—Laodicea and Hierapolis, with Colossae a further 10 mi. upstream.

Four or five centuries before the time of the NT, Colossae had been populous, large and wealthy, its wealth due both to its position on the main road from Ephesus and Sardis to the Euphrates and to its wool industry. But by the early years of the Roman Empire, its significance had been much reduced, in contrast to Laodicea (an administrative and financial center) and Hierapolis (famous for its hot mineral springs). Christianity had been established there by Epaphras, a native of Colossae (Col 4:12).

COLOSSIANS, LETTER TO THE The church of Colossae was founded probably in the second half of the 50s CE. It was not established by Paul himself, although he may have passed nearby on his journey through Phrygia to Ephesus (Acts 18:23; 19:1), since Colossae lay on or close to one of the main East-West routes through Anatolia. Its foundation seems rather to have been the result of evangelism by Epaphras (Col 1:6-7), who was a native of Colossae and who may have been responsible for the evangelism of the Lycus Valley cities (Col 4:13). Presumably Epaphras was converted by Paul during Paul's sojourn in Ephesus (Acts 19:8-10), as also another resident of Colossae—Philemon (Phlm 19); that Philemon also lived in Colossae is almost universally inferred from the par. between Col 4:9-14 and Phlm 23-24. If so, the founding of the church in Colossae may provide the only clear example of Paul's likely tactic of establishing an evangelistic center in a major city (here Ephesus) from which an individual or teams of evangelists would go out to cities within striking distance from Ephesus.

COLUMN OF CLOUD AND LIGHTNING The column of cloud by day and of lightning (NRSV has "fire") by night first occurs in Exod 13:21-22, an appearance of the Lord guiding Israel through the wilderness (the same pillar with two aspects, Exod 14:24). Exodus 14:19 equates the column with the accompanying messenger (see Exod 23:20). The Lord communicates with Moses in the cloud, which descends at the entrance of the meeting tent (e.g., Exod 33:9-11). This cloud, associated with the covenant chest, directs Israel's route through the wilderness (Num 10:33-36).

COMFORTER See COMPANION.

COMING OF CHRIST See PAROUSIA; SECOND COMING.

COMMANDMENT Commandments, such as the TEN COMMANDMENTS, are directly addressed injunctions concerning matters of moral gravity. Not limited in duration or to a particular person, they are incumbent on all individuals of the addressed class for an unlimited duration. The speaker assumes responsibility for the addressee's behavior, and, by implication, the addressee's welfare. The addressee owes the speaker compliance.

COMMANDMENTS, TEN See TEN COMMANDMENTS.

COMMUNION This term, literally "sharing," is used in the NT for the sharing of believers in fellowship together and with God. It is most common in Paul (e.g., "called by him to partnership with his Son" [1 Cor 1:9]; see also Phil 3:10; 2 Cor 13:13), and is especially connected with the common meal or Lord's Supper, where Christians "share" in the "body" and "blood" of Christ (1 Cor 10:16) in a manner that is comparable, in Paul's mind, to the table fellowship of pagans with their deities, and which, therefore, Christians should avoid (1 Cor 10:21). See COVENANT, OT AND

NT; EUCHARIST; LAST SUPPER, THE; LORD'S SUPPER.

COMMUNITY OF GOODS The sharing of resources by the early Christ movement, seen most explicitly in Acts 2:42-47; 4:32-37, and which may be referred to in the word KOINONIA. These texts depict the importance to the community of the selling of possessions and the even distribution of resources (especially food, although note Acts 6:1ff.).

COMPANION The CEB translation of a word variously translated as "counselor" (KJV) and "comforter" (NIV). In the NT it appears only in the Johannine literature. In the Gospel of John it is Jesus' name for the Holy Spirit, whom the Father (or Jesus) will send to the disciples to be Jesus' presence in the world after his return to the Father (14:16, 26; 15:26-27; 16:7*b*-11, 12-15). In 1 John it describes Jesus' role for the sinner (2:1). See PARACLETE.

CONANIAH 1. A Levite, Hezekiah's chief officer in charge of contributions and tithes (2 Chron 31:12-13).

2. A levitical chief under King Josiah (2 Chron 35:9).

CONCUBINE See SECONDARY WIFE.

CONDUIT See JERUSALEM.

CONFIRMATION The rite in the ancient church in which baptized people received laying on of hands and anointing with oil for obtaining the Holy Spirit. Although anointing with oil and laying on of hands at or after baptism is not explicitly witnessed in the NT, precedent for it was found in Mark 1:10, where Jesus receives the Holy Spirit at his baptism; Acts 8, where the Spirit comes upon new believers when the apostles lay hands on them; and Acts 10:38, where Jesus is said to be anointed with the Spirit.

CONSCIENCE Conscience is important to moral theology and practice. However, the Bible's contribution to this notion is not easily determined. There is no corresponding term in Hebrew, and where the Greek word translated by conscience is used by the NT, an older sense of self-consciousness, especially awareness of one's guilt or negative feelings, may be all that is required by the text.

CONSECRATE In the OT and NT, consecration entails setting someone or something apart from others of their class. Usually consecration elevates its object's status vis-à-vis God and is equivalent to making its object holy.

CONTRIBUTION FOR THE SAINTS See COLLECTION, THE.

CONTRIBUTIONS See COLLECTION, THE.

CONVERSION Conversion usually involves turning from one way of living to a different way of living. The OT focuses on the religious and social obligations of Israelites.

New Testament conversion is also understood as turning from one way of living to a different way of living. This transformation almost always involves turning to God (Acts 15:3, 19-20; Gal 4:8-9), and it is frequently associated with changing hearts and lives (Acts 3:19; 26:20). The Synoptic Gospels present the inbreaking of "God's kingdom" as the impetus for this transformation. Both John the Baptist and Jesus demand changes in the way people live their lives.

Since Acts depicts the growth of the early church, it is full of conversion stories (2:41-42; 4:4; 8:26-40; 9:35, 42; 10:1–11:18). While Paul never recounts a conversion experience like the one portrayed in Acts (9; 22; 26), he does frequently mention being "called" by God (Gal 1:11-17). Paul presents conversion as a divine calling (1 Cor 7:17-24) responded to with obedient faithfulness

(Rom 1:5-6). While there is indeed much ambiguity regarding what conversion actually entails, it is clear that the biblical notion of conversion involves a change in lifestyle that results from (re)turning to the biblical God.

CONVOCATION, HOLY Literally, this phrase might be rendered "holy proclamation." Usage shows that its purpose was to announce the arrival of a festival day. Hence, the term is idiomatic for the day itself: the "holy convocation" or "sacred occasion" when Israel was called from its usual labors to public celebration and worship. The Sabbath itself is named as a "holy occasion" (Lev 23:3). Seven festal days are so designated in Lev 23: the first and seventh days of Unleavened Bread (vv. 7-8), Weeks (v. 21), the first day of the seventh month (v. 24), the Day of Reconciliation (v. 27), and the first and eighth days of Booths (vv. 35-36). See FEASTS AND FASTS.

COPPER A metal. When alloyed with tin it produces BRONZE. In the OT, the Hebrew words are usually translated as "bronze," since they refer to objects made of bronze. Deuteronomy 8:9 refers to the actual mining of copper, describing the land "where you will mine copper from the hills." Job 28:2 mentions that "rock is smelted into copper."

In the NT, the word *copper* is generally used in the meaning of bronze coins (Matt 10:9; Mark 12:42; Luke 21:2).

COR See KOR.

CORBAN Corban primarily denotes a gift or sacrificial offering that is consecrated to God. In later Judaism it also introduces a vow dedicating something to God, declaring it holy by separating it from the secular sphere so that others may not benefit from it. Corban appears in the NT only in Mark 7:11, where Jesus is arguing with the Pharisees over purity practices, thus over the nature of holiness. See SACRIFICES AND OFFERINGS; SANCTIFY, SANCTIFICATION.

CORIANDER SEED The seed of the coriander plant (Coriandrum sativum), which is also known as cilantro and Chinese parsley, is used as a spice. Its greens may have been one of the BITTER HERBS. The term is used only in the OT to describe the appearance of MANNA (Exod 16:31; Num 11:7).

CORINTH City commanding the isthmus linking the Peloponnese to mainland Greece. Paul worked with Prisca and Aquila for eighteen months while founding the church there (spring 50 to late summer 51 [Acts 1:1-18]). He made two subsequent visits (2 Cor 12:14; 13:1), on the second of which he wrote Romans. He wrote a series of letters to the community, two of which have been lost (1 Cor 5:9; 2 Cor 2:4).

CORINTHIANS, FIRST LETTER TO THE The letter of Paul traditionally known as *The First Epistle to the Corinthians* was not the first letter that Paul wrote to Christians in Corinth. In 1 Cor 5:9 he writes, "I wrote to you in my [previous] letter not to associate with immoral persons." Paul had a sustained interaction with them through oral reports and letters. He first arrived in Corinth en route from Athens in 49 or 50 CE, and ministered there for eighteen months during the proconsulship of Gallio (51–52 or 50–51). Paul wrote the "previous" letter (of 1 Cor 5:9) from Ephesus, on hearing a disquieting report of developments. In the spring or summer of 54 he wrote 1 Corinthians in part in response to an oral report of "splits" from "Chloe's people" (1:11; *see* CHLOE), as well as other reports. He reacts to these reports in 1:10–6:20. Paul also received a letter of inquiry from Corinth, to which he responds in 7:1–14:40. Some postulate another (third) "intermediate" letter (or part of a letter) between 1 and 2 Corinthians. If this is correct, 1 Corinthians would be Paul's second letter to Corinth, and 2 Corinthians would be his fourth.

In broad terms 1 Corinthians embodies six general segments of discussion: Chapters 1–4 expound the causes and cures of "splits" within the Christian community in Corinth (1:10–4:21). Chapters 5–6 convey Paul's further response to oral reports. Chapters 7–10 take up the letter from Corinth. Chapter 7 concerns marriage, celibacy, widowhood, and singleness (7:1-40). Chapters 8–10 concern "food sacrificed to idols" (8:1). Chapters 11–14 address aspects of public worship. Chapter 15 expounds the resurrection of the dead.

CORINTHIANS, SECOND LETTER TO THE Second Corinthians is the Pauline letter with the most complicated set of historical, social, and communal elements behind it. It was most likely written in stages to the church in Corinth. Questions of Paul's apostolic authority and mission echo in and against such issues as a Corinthian misunderstanding of Paul's travel intentions, his harsh treatment of disloyalty, his desire to engage the church in the collection for Jerusalem, and the presence of a Jewish-Christian opposition to Paul. A profound theological presentation of Christian existence holds the whole together.

CORMORANT A large fishing bird.

CORNELIUS A Roman army officer stationed in Caesarea and evangelized by the apostle Peter in the book of Acts. The strategic importance of Cornelius's encounter with Peter is suggested by its threefold iteration: an extensive initial account in Acts 10:1-48 reinforced by Peter's flashbacks in 11:1-18 and 15:7-11.

CORNERSTONE *Cornerstone* is an architectural term that has figurative meanings and messianic nuances in the NT. The usage implies that a cornerstone is a primary stone in the building's foundation.

COS Cos lies in the Aegean Islands known as the South Sporades, off the southwest coast of Turkey, and was noted on the sea journey between Miletus and Rhodes (Acts 21:1).

COSAM An ancestor of Jesus, tracing him back to Adam (Luke 3:28).

COUNCIL, THE COUNCIL, COUNCIL HOUSE Terms used for judicial entities in various social, political, and religious contexts. In the OT, Yahweh the God of Israel holds the highest place of judgment among a "divine council" (Ps 82:1) or assembly of heavenly beings or "holy ones" (Ps 89:7). At times, divinely commissioned human beings, such as prophets, may also "stand" in the heavenly council in order to receive special instructions for God's people (Jer 23:18-22; Amos 3:7).

Rulers in the biblical world typically had a royal council or advisory court comprised of military commanders and diplomatic officials (2 Kgs 9:5; 25:19; Jer 52:25; 1 Esdr 2:17; Jdt 6:1, 7; 2 Macc 14:5; 4 Macc 17:17; Acts 25:12).

In the NT, "council" designates any local tribunals before which Jesus' followers may be examined and summoned to testify (Matt 10:17; Mark 13:9).

Most frequently in the NT, "council" refers to "the council" or SANHEDRIN, the supreme Jewish court in 1st-cent. Jerusalem. In the Sermon on the Mount, Jesus warns that anyone who slanders a fellow Jew "will be in danger of being condemned by the governing council" (Matt 5:22). Jesus himself is interrogated and disciplined by the high Jerusalem council on the eve of his crucifixion (Matt 26:57-68; Mark 14:53–15:1; Luke 22:66-71; John 18:12-27), as are Peter, John, Stephen, and Paul in the book of Acts (4:1-22; 5:17-41; 6:12-15; 22:30–23:10, 28).

COUNSEL, COUNSELOR The Hebrew and Greek words have a dual meaning that is often reflected in English translations. They mean to counsel or advise, but also to put that advice into motion (i.e., to plan). Counselor sometimes appears to be an official position in the OT (1 Chron 26:14; 27:33; Ezra 7:28; Job 3:14). However, a variety of people give counsel, including prophets (Num 24:14; 1 Kgs 1:12), elders (1 Kgs 12:6), parents (Exod 18:19), and the people more broadly (2 Chron 20:21; 30:23). God is described as the preeminent counselor (Isa 28:29; Jer 32:19). God's decrees (Ps 119:24), Wisdom (Prov 8:14), and the messianic figure of Isa 9:6 and 11:2 share the divine quality of providing counsel. To be successful, human counsel must coincide with God's counsel (Prov 21:30). Absalom (2 Sam 15–17) and Rehoboam (1 Kgs 12) are examples of leaders who choose bad advice over good, although their choices complete God's plan. Elsewhere, God's counsel supersedes what humans have planned (Ps 33:10-11; Isa 8:10; 19:11, 17). The words appear less often in the NT. Jewish leaders are said to counsel together to kill Jesus (Matt 26:4; John 11:53). God's counsel or plan remains supreme (Acts 5:39; Rom 11:34; Eph 1:11).

COURT OF THE GENTILES The area of the Jerusalem temple where Gentiles who conducted themselves reverently were permitted to enter. It was an open area surrounded by porches or cloisters. This court was the location of the merchants and the money changers whom Jesus drove from the temple.

COURTYARD Enclosed areas separate from but immediately surrounding a house, a palace, or the Jerusalem temple. See HOUSE, HOUSEHOLD; TEMPLE, JERUSALEM.

COUSIN The English term translates, more literally, "the son/daughter of his/her uncle" (Lev 25:49; Esth 2:7; Jer 32:8-9, 12). Cross-cultural parallels suggest that "uncle" could refer to any male relative of the preceding generation, so these are not necessarily "first cousins.

COVENANT, BOOK OF THE See COVENANT SCROLL.

COVENANT, MOSAIC See COVENANT, OT AND NT.

COVENANT, NEW See COVENANT, OT AND NT.

COVENANT, OT AND NT A covenant is a formal commitment made by one party to another party, or by two parties to each other; its seriousness is normally undergirded by an oath and/or rite undertaken before God and/or before other people.

The first covenant is made by God to NOAH, his descendants, and thus with all future humanity, including all other living creatures (Gen 6:18; 9:8-17). The covenant is a one-sided commitment on God's part, by which God undertakes never again to flood the earth and thus destroy life on earth.

Yahweh first makes a covenant with Abraham to give the land of Canaan to his descendants (Gen 15:18-20). In God's second covenant with Abraham (Gen 17), the focus of the covenant lies on the promise of offspring. Like the Noah covenant, this Abraham covenant issues entirely from God's initiative but leaves ambiguous the relationship between divine commitment and human obligation.

In Exod 6:6-8, Yahweh had referred to delivering Israel from serfdom, establishing the mutual relationship, and taking them to the land. When they reach Sinai, in Exod 19:1-8 Yahweh points out that the first undertaking has been fulfilled; it is therefore possible to move onto the second. This will involve Israel's keeping God's covenant. The phrase recurs from Gen 17:9-10, and the people could understandably reckon that Yahweh is simply reasserting the demand for circumcision; this might link with the ease with which they agree, "Everything that the LORD has said we will do" (Exod 19:8). Actually, it will become clear that keeping the covenant will now have much broader implications.

In his "last words" David says that God "made an eternal covenant with me, laid out and secure in every detail" (2 Sam 23:5). The narrative has not recorded this, though one could see Yahweh's promise in 2 Sam 7 as covenantlike.

Beyond the calamity of exile Yahweh declares the intention of making a new covenant with both Judah and Ephraim (Jer 31:31-34). It will be new because the thing Yahweh intends to do is different; it is new as the Sinai covenant was new over against the Abraham covenant.

The NT shows rather little explicit interest in covenant, though in the broader sense the concerns of covenant are embedded in the theological thinking of the NT. Luke 1:72 declares that Jesus came because God "remembered his holy covenant" and the Gospel of Mark casts Jesus' death in light of OT covenant: "My blood of the covenant . . . is poured out for many" (Mark 14:24). According to the Gospels, Jesus came to fulfill the covenant. The reference to "pouring out" and to "many" suggests a link with Isa 53 and thus ultimately with the "covenant to the people" in Isa 42:6; 49:8. The Jesus covenant will benefit the world more spectacularly than the previous versions of the covenant did.

Apostles such as Paul saw themselves as "ministers of a new covenant," whose novelty lies in its being "not based on what is written but on the spirit" (2 Cor 3:6). Hebrews develops the notion of the new covenant most systematically (see esp. Heb 8–9).

COVENANT CHEST The Hebrew word, which designated a box or chest, became primarily associated with a sacred cult object kept in the covenant dwelling or the temple, indicating the presence of God in the midst of Israel. Nearly a third of all references to the chest are in the books of Samuel. Since the Chronicler uses the books of Samuel as a source, those designations of the chest reflect the ones used in 1 and 2 Samuel. Many have regarded the reference in 1 Sam 4:4 (see 2 Sam 6:2; 1 Chron 13:6) as the fullest and most ancient name for the chest: "the chest containing the covenant of the LORD of heavenly forces, who sits enthroned on the winged heavenly creatures." The chest is emblematic of the relationship between God and Israel as covenant partners. The Priestly tradition in the Pentateuch, which includes the detailed description of God's instructions for and the fashioning of an elaborate gold-covered chest, refers to this sacred object solely as the "chest containing the covenant."

COVENANT DWELLING The portable tent sanctuary constructed by the people of Israel in the Wilderness of Sinai according to instructions given by God to Moses on Mount Sinai after God's conclusion of a covenant with Israel (Exod 25–31; 35–40). Together with its cultic personnel and its rituals, it constitutes the archetype of OT worship.

COVENANT SCROLL This title for the collection of Laws in Exod 20:22–23:33 comes from Exod 24:7. The collection contains provisions governing altars to Yahweh (Exod 20:23-26), a collection of "judgments" covering crimes against persons and property (Exod 21:1–22:17), religious and moral transgressions (Exod 22:18-20, 28-31) intermixed with duties to the poor and vulnerable (22:21-27), and a table of holy times and festivals (23:10-19), followed by instructions for departure from Sinai/Horeb. Both the style and content suggest this code is the oldest in the Pentateuch.

COZBI Daughter of the Midianite chief

Zur who married the Israelite Zimri. Both were slain by the priest Phineas, thereby averting a plague (Num 25:6-15).

COZEBA Town in Judah's highlands (1 Chron 4:22). Possibly the same place as Achzib (Josh 15:44) and Chezib (Gen 38:5).

CRATES The deputy commander of the Seleucid citadel in Jerusalem. Sostratus, the commander of the Jerusalem citadel, appointed Crates to rule in his absence, while he and the high priest Menelaus traveled to meet King Antiochus Epiphanes. Crates led a band of Cyprian mercenaries (2 Macc 4:29).

CREATION The biblical concept of creation encompasses the entire world of nature, including humanity, and views this world as brought into being and sustained by God.

Genesis 1–3 is the most sustained biblical account of creation. When creation is described in other biblical literature, it is characterized as an integrated whole, and it plays a foundational role in the biblical story. The Psalms contain some of the most detailed accounts of creation outside of Genesis. Typically, psalmists describe God's establishment of larger cosmic orders as the context or foundation for God's establishment of the order of the historical sphere, so that cosmic orders are closely connected, for example, to the Law (Pss 19; 93), to religious ritual (Ps 24), to the exodus and settlement (Ps 136), to the establishment of the Davidic dynasty (Ps 89), and to the rebuilding of Zion (Ps 74). The praise of God at the heart of the Psalms is expressed not just by human beings but by all members of creation (Pss 96–98; 145; 148; 150). When God delivers the climactic speech in the book of Job from the storm wind, God speaks about God's activity in all of creation, especially in those realms out of human reach (Job 38:1–42:6).

In his letter to the Romans, Paul describes the realm of nonhuman creation as sharing the fallen fate of humanity and its longing for redemption (Rom 8:18-25). When he says "Creation was subjected to frustration" (v. 20), that "the whole creation is groaning together and suffering labor pains" (v. 22), and that "the creation itself will be set free from slavery to decay and brought into the glorious freedom of God's children" (v. 21), Paul appears to make the claim that nonhuman nature together with human nature acquired a fatal defect as a result of human sin (Gen 3:14-19).

CREATOR See CREATION.

CRESCENS 1. An associate of PAUL, THE APOSTLE who left him for GALATIA (2 Tim 4:10), or as a few manuscripts read, Gaul. The reference may not be wholly positive, as Crescens's departure is part of a theme emphasizing associates' abandoning of the imprisoned Paul.

2. Crescens the Cynic is mentioned by Justin Martyr as an opponent he refuted in public debate (*2 Apol.* 2.3). Later tradition explicitly blames Crescens for having brought about Justin's death.

CRETE Crete is a large island forming the southern boundary to the Aegean. The Minoans, made famous through the excavation of Knossos, inhabited the island during the 2nd millennium BCE. OT references to CAPHTOR (Deut 2:23; Jer 47:4; Amos 9:7) have been linked to Crete. Paul sailed along the southern side of Crete on his way to Rome (Acts 27:7-16). A series of Christian communities was established on the island during the 1st cent. CE, and these formed the context for the epistle to Titus.

CRIB A feeding trough or stall for the domesticated donkey (Isa 1:3) and oxen.

CRISPUS A ruler of the SYNAGOGUE in CORINTH who, with "his entire household," was baptized by Paul personally (Acts 18:8; 1 Cor 1:14).

CROSS "The cross" refers to the Roman instrument of Jesus' death and thus serves also as shorthand for his death in its salvific and theological significance.

The word *cross* appears in the NT twenty-eight times, while the verb *crucify* appears fifty-four times, each with both literal and metaphorical uses. In the Gospels, the word *cross* refers to the cruel, degrading, and torturous device of execution—reserved for slaves, insurgents, and similar types—to which Jesus was nailed. It refers also, by extension, to the lifestyle of disciples, who are called to follow Jesus in the self-denial, service, and sacrificial love that led to his crucifixion (Mark 8:34). In the letters, *cross* and *crucify* point at times to the stark historical reality (Phil 2:8; Heb 12:2), but more often—and even in the historical references—the real focus is on the ironic reality that this Roman instrument of taking life was God's means of giving life.

CROWN The English translation of several Hebrew and Greek words for a type of headdress worn by kings, officials, and priests. It is also used metaphorically for a person's position or as a prize.

CROWN OF THORNS According to the Gospels, the soldiers carrying out Jesus' crucifixion "twisted together a crown of thorns and put it on him" (Mark 15:17). The crown, meant to resemble the laurel wreath worn by Caesar, is part of the mockery of Jesus. This mockery includes a purple cloak, a reed (symbolizing the scepter), and personal address as a so-called king (Mark 15:18-19).

CRUCIBLE A crucible is a melting pot, made of pottery, often used for liquefying silver and other refining. It is used in Prov 17:3 and 27:21 as a metaphor for the judging of a person.

CRUCIFIXION Crucifixion was a form of execution practiced in late antiquity, whereby a person was tied or nailed to a pole or cross and left to hang.

CUBIT A major measure of length, roughly the length of a human arm from the forearm to the tip of the middle finger (ca. 52 cm). See WEIGHTS AND MEASURES.

CUCUMBER The word for cucumber appears in Num 11:5 when Israel yearned for the cucumbers they had to eat in Egypt. These may have been muskmelons.

CUMIN Cumin, of the carrot family, is a bitter-tasting seed that was used to season stews and to flavor bread. Isaiah's parable on proper agricultural methods illustrates the force involved in plowing, harvesting, and threshing: even cumin is struck with sticks to separate the seeds. Jesus ridicules the Pharisees (Matt 23:23) for their concern with the items of the tithe (dill, anise, and cumin) while failing to obey the foundation of the Law (justice, mercy, and faith; compare Hos 6:6 and Mic 6:8). See PLANTS OF THE BIBLE; SPICE.

CUN A city belonging to King Hadadezer from which David took much bronze (1 Chron 18:8).

CUP A vessel out of which one may drink, or the actual drink. Joseph used a cup for drinking and divination (Gen 44).

Cups are symbols of enjoyment and blessing, a metaphor for salvation (Pss 16:5; 23:5). A cup also stands for an act of kindness, as the donation of a cup of cold water in Jesus' name will be rewarded by God (Matt 10:42; Mark 9:41).

A cup is filled with an intoxicating liquid that acts like a poison and is a metaphor for God's fury (Isa 51:17, 22; Rev 14:10). When Jesus speaks of the cup that he must drink (Mark 10:38-39; John 18:11), he refers to the suffering that he must undergo. That he prays to God to remove it (Matt 26:39; Mark 14:36; Luke 22:42) indicates that he interprets it to be symbolic of the wrath of God that he must bear.

A cup is shared after the breaking of bread at the Last Supper that symbolizes Jesus' blood poured out in sacrifice to establish a new covenant (Matt 26:27-28; Mark 14:23-24; Luke 22:20).

CUPBEARER A wine taster and trusted royal adviser in Egyptian (Gen 40:1-23), Israelite (1 Kgs 10:5; 2 Chron 9:4), Assyrian (Tob 1:21-22), Persian (Neh 1:11), and other ancient Near Eastern courts. At times, Jews held this prominent position in foreign lands. According to the book of Tobit, Ahikar (Tobit's nephew) served as cupbearer and chief financial officer for the Assyrian kings Sennacherib and Esar-haddon (Tob 1:21-22; 2:10; 11:18; 14:10); and Nehemiah leveraged his position as cupbearer to the Persian ruler Artaxerxes to secure an appointment as governor of Judah during the period of postexilic reconstruction.

CURSE The meaning varies in different contexts. Curse often denotes an utterance spoken to consign a person (or object) to harm or deprivation. Sometimes it takes the form of a prayer to God or decree from God to bring disaster. It regularly denotes the opposite of blessing, often in the context of the covenant.

CURTAIN OF THE TEMPLE See VEIL OF THE TEMPLE.

CUSH, CUSHITE 1. Cush, the eponymous ancestor of the nation that shares his name, appears in Gen 10:6-9 and 1 Chron 1:8-10, where he is described as the eldest son of Noah's son Ham. He is presented as the primogenitor of several significant North African tribes. In the Genesis account the major Mesopotamian kingdoms are also ascribed to his lineage.

2. Cush is also the name of a certain Benjaminite mentioned as a source of anxiety for King David in the header of Ps 7:1. No further details about Cush's identity or the cause of David's complaint can be discerned in biblical narratives.

3. Cush is often conflated with modern ETHIOPIA, a land to the southeast of the biblical country.

CUSHAN The term *Cushan* occurs once in the psalmlike prayer of Hab 3:7 (See CUSHAN-RISHATHAIM).

CUSHAN-RISHATHAIM Cushan-rishathaim is mentioned four times in Judg 3, twice in v. 8 and twice in v. 10. In the extant text he is identified as "king of Aram-naharaim," literally "king of Aram of the two rivers."

CUSHI 1. Great-grandfather of Jehudi, an official in Jehoiakim's court (Jer 36:14).

2. Father of the prophet Zephaniah (Zeph 1:1).

CUTHA A temple servant whose descendants are included in a list of returnees from the Babylonian exile, released by Darius and led by ZERUBBABEL (1 Esdr 5:32).

CYAXARES King of Media who destroyed Nineveh and captured its residents (Tob 14:15). Cyaxares is called AHASUERUS in some manuscripts.

CYPRUS Paul visited this Mediterranean island during a missionary journey (Acts 13:4), as did Barnabas and John Mark after parting ways with Paul over a disagreement about retaining John Mark in their work (see Acts 15:39).

CYRUS Cyrus (II) the Great established the Persian Empire (539–ca. 531 BCE) during a seminal period in the history of the Jews and the development of Judaism. Ezra and Isaiah credit Cyrus with freeing the Judean exiles in Babylon and allowing them to return home (Ezra 1:1-8; Isa 45:1) to rebuild the temple at Jerusalem (Isa 44:28; Ezra 3:7; 4:3-5; 5:13-17; 6:3-5).

Dd

DAGON A prominent ANE deity described in the OT as the national god of the PHILISTINES. The OT relates stories concerning temples of Dagon in Gaza (Samson's death, Judg 16), Ashdod (the capture of the covenant chest, 1 Sam 5:1-5; so also 1 Macc 10:83-84; 11:4, where Azotus = Ashdod), and Beth-shan (the display of Saul's head, 1 Chr 10:10, based on the par. in 1 Sam 31:9), none of which have been confirmed by archaeology. Sites named Beth-Dagon in Judah and Asher (Josh 15:41; 19:27) suggest that other temples of Dagon once stood within those tribal territories. Theologically, the story in 1 Sam 5 is notable for establishing the power of Israel's God over Dagon, as Dagon's statue is reported to have fallen over and broken into pieces in the presence of the covenant chest.

DAISAN One of the heads of ancestral houses that Darius sent back to Jerusalem after the exile. The descendants of Daisan were among the temple servants (1 Esdr 5:31).

DALMANUTHA A region referenced only in Mark 8:10 (with variations such as Magdala and Magada).

DALMATIA A region on the eastern Adriatic named after the Dalmatae (Delmatae), an Illyrian tribe that emerged as Rome's major regional enemy after the decline of the Illyrian kingdom (2 Tim 4:10).

DALPHON One of HAMAN's ten sons who were hanged (Esth 9:7, 13). The etymology and meaning are uncertain.

DAMARIS Pairing of Paul's female Athenian convert Damaris (Acts 17:34) with DIONYSIUS demonstrates Luke's affinity for both women and men.

DAMASCENE Name used to designate the fertile area of DAMASCUS produced by the Barada River. The Ghuta oasis and the district called the Merj are found within this area.

DAMASCUS A city located ca. 150 mi. northeast of Jerusalem that became the capital of a powerful Aramean kingdom in the 10th–8th cent. BCE. The city existed as a significant regional center into the Roman period. The Aramean kingdom centered in Damascus was one of the most dominant states in Syria-Palestine during the monarchical period, especially 900–730 BCE (see ARAM, ARAMEANS). The city appears in the NT as the location associated with the encounter of Saul of Tarsus with the risen Jesus. Damascus sits in one of the most fertile regions in Syria-Palestine and was known in the ancient world for its waters, gardens, and orchards (see 2 Kgs 5:12). Damascus had a powerful influence on Israel and Judah. The Umayyad Mosque in present-day Damascus, for example, likely stands on the ancient site of the temple of the god Hadad, after which Ahaz of Judah is said to have modeled an altar in Jerusalem (2 Kgs 16:10-16; compare 2 Chron 28:23). The city often competed with Samaria for control of regions like Dan (see DAN, DANITES) and RAMOTH-GILEAD, and at times exercised political dominance over both Samaria and Jerusalem. At other times, Damascus was Israel's strongest ally against other foes.

DAN, DANITES 1. The fifth son of JACOB through Rachel's servant BILHAH. The name, meaning "he has judged," is explained by the patriarch's birth narrative, during which RACHEL signifies the birth of a son born through her servant Bilhah as a divine judgment on her behalf (Gen 30:3-6). As such, the patriarchal narratives identify Dan as the first of the four sons born to the servants of Jacob's wives (the other sons are Napthali, Asher, and Gad; see Gen 35:25; 46:23; Exod 1:4).

2. The Israelite tribe that traced its descent through Dan. Tribal lists and traditions reflect the same grouping of Dan, Napthali, Asher, and Gad (Num 13:12-25; Deut 33:20-25), although the absence of Gad in many cases indicates that the organizational scheme may have more to do with geography than genealogy. This is particularly apparent in Priestly literature, where tribal Dan is most commonly grouped only with Asher and Napthali, the tribes that, with Dan, occupied the northernmost region of Israel (Num 1:38-39; 2:25-26; 7:66-71; 19:25; 26:42-43; cf 1 Chron 12:35). An exception to this scheme is Dan's grouping with the Joseph tribes, Benjamin, and Naphtali (the children attributed to Rachel) in a list of tribal leaders from David's census (1 Chron 27:22 [Heb. 27:24]).

DANCING Dancing is a form of religious worship and community celebration in biblical texts. Community celebrations constitute religious dance in the sense that public rituals and festivals are part of communal worship.

Dancing and music form important elements of Israelite religious worship. Both singers and dancers praise God (Ps 87:7). As well, dance includes musical accompaniment (Pss 149:3; 150:3). For example, David's procession to bring the covenant chest of God to Jerusalem includes singing, dancing, and music (2 Sam 6; 1 Chron 15). As part of this procession, David wears a linen vest and dances "with all his strength before the LORD" (2 Sam 6:14). David's wife Michal admonishes him for what she perceives as shameless behavior, but he rebukes her (2 Sam 6:20-22).

Dance may be employed in idolatrous worship. For instance, Joshua hears what he assumes is the noise of warfare when he and Moses return from Mount Sinai. Instead, he and Moses find the Israelites singing and dancing as they worship the golden calf (Exod 32:17-19). Also, in a contest at Mount Carmel, Elijah makes fun of the prophets of Baal who limp about the altar as they pray to Baal to answer them (1 Kgs 18:21, 26).

Dancing is considered to be the opposite of mourning. For example, Ecclesiastes contrasts weeping and mourning with laughing and dancing (Eccl 3:4). In a psalm of thanksgiving, the psalmist exclaims, "You changed my mourning into dancing!" (Ps 30:11 [Heb. 30:12]). Conversely, in a communal lament the people ask the Lord to remember the calamities that have befallen them and complain, "Our dancing has changed into lamentation" (Lam 5:15).

Instances of dancing in the NT do not involve religious worship. Yet, as in the OT, dancing involves rejoicing and festivity. For instance, in the parable of the prodigal son, as the elder son approaches home, he hears singing and dancing in celebration of the younger son's return (Luke 15:25). Also, at the birthday party of Herod Antipas, his stepdaughter, the daughter of Herodias, dances for him and his guests (Matt 14:6; Mark 6:22). Her performance leads to a rash vow by Herod and the beheading of John the Baptist (Matt 14:6-11; Mark 6:22-28).

DANEL See DANIEL.

DANIEL 1. The son of David and Abigail born at Hebron (1 Chron 3:1). He is called CHILEAB in 2 Sam 3:3.

2. The head of a Levite family that returned from Babylon with Ezra. He was a descendant of ITHAMAR (Ezra

8:2). Daniel placed his seal on the covenant document (Neh 10:6).

3. The main character and hero of the biblical book that bears his name.

DANIEL, ADDITIONS TO Three supplements to the book of Daniel appear in the ancient Greek versions: "The Prayer of Azariah (and Hymn of the Three Young Men" (inserted in Dan 3, between v. 23 and v. 24) records the words spoken by the young men in the fiery furnace. "Susanna" recounts Daniel's rescue of a falsely accused virgin from execution. "Bel and the Snake" exults in Daniel's triumph over Babylonian idols.

DANIEL, BOOK OF Counted among the prophets in the ancient Greek and modern Christian versions of the Bible, but included among the wisdom writings in the OT and modern Jewish translations, this work readily falls into two parts. It begins with six tales about the wise and heroic exploits of the young Jew Daniel and his three friends in the courts of Babylon and Media. These tales reflect a degree of acceptance of the rule of the imperial powers, over which the book believes the God of Israel is sovereign. The work concludes with three bitterly anti-imperial apocalypses (chaps. 7, 8, 10–12) and a lengthy prose prayer of penitence (chap. 9). The tales are told in the third person about Daniel and friends, and amount to a kind of "outer history" of their lives of faithful trust and obedience. The apocalypses and prayer are first person reports by Daniel of his dream-visions and his dialogues with an angelic dream interpreter. They serve as a kind of "inner history" of the seer, whose task it is to convey to the saints the answers to mysteries that have been revealed to him. Much figurative scholarly blood has been shed over the date of the book of Daniel. More traditional and conservative commentators have regarded the book's own 7th and 6th cent. BCE dates for the tales and visions as accurate; in contrast, modern critical commentators are almost unanimous in arguing that the book as we have it is the product of the early 2nd cent. BCE.

DARA Son of Zera and grandson of Judah and Tamar (1 Chron 2:6).

DARDA SOLOMON's wisdom was said to have surpassed the wisdom of four men apparently noted for their wisdom (1 Kgs 4:31). Three of the four were sons of MAHOL, one of whom was Darda.

DARIC A golden Persian coin of about 8.3 g, the daric was apparently named after Darius I, who originated it to demonstrate his power and prestige rather than for economic reasons.

DARIUS Old Persian name used by kings of the Achaemenid Empire.

1. Darius I, the Great or the Conqueror (522–486 BCE). Work on rebuilding the temple began in the second year of Darius (520 BCE; Ezra 4:24). Simultaneously, the prophets Haggai and Zechariah (see also Isaiah 56–66) innervated the community, along with Zerubbabel the governor and Jeshua the high priest, to begin the work. When opponents petitioned Darius to stop the rebuilding efforts (Ezra 5:6-17), the king responded with Achaemenid resources to support the work (6:1-12).

2. Darius II (423–405 BCE). Ochus, the illegitimate son of Artaxerxes I, took the throne upon his father's death in 423 BCE, despite two other sons with claims as successors.

3. Darius III (336–330 BCE). Artashata, also known as Codomanus, came to the Persian throne under questionable circumstances in 336 BCE and adopted the royal name Darius III. Often characterized as a weak dynast who is blamed for the loss of central authority and eventually the empire, Darius III had the misfortune of opposing Alexander of Macedon. Although Darius appears to have fought valiantly, he suffered repeated losses to Alexander's armies

and was eventually murdered by one of his generals, bringing the Achaemenid Empire to an end.

4. Darius the Mede. This 62-year-old, according to the book of Daniel, ruled the Babylonian Empire upon the death of Belshazzar (Dan 5:30-31 [Aram. 5:30–6:1]), ruled at least a year, and divided the empire into 120 satrapies (Dan 6:1 [Aram 6:2]). Babylonian, Persian, and Hellenistic sources all attribute the conquest of Babylon (539 BCE) to CYRUS the Persian. No Median king Darius is attested elsewhere, and attempts to identify him historically have failed to gain wide acceptance.

DARKON One of Solomon's servants whose descendants are among those returning from Babylonian exile in similar lists in Ezra 2:56 and Neh 7:58. See ZERUBBABEL.

DATES Fruit of the palm tree or date palm. Dates, a high-energy food source, could be eaten fresh, dried in the form of small cakes, or used for making wine and honey. Dates served as a symbol of life in the desert. In the OT, the date palm is mentioned only once as a fruit-bearing tree (Joel 1:12). However, Song 7:8 refers to the fruit of the palm tree.

DATHAN Dathan was the son of Eliab of the tribe of Reuben. He joined Korah, ABIRAM, and 250 other leaders of Israel in rebelling against the exclusive authority of Moses and Aaron in the wilderness journey from Egypt to Canaan. God condemned the rebels, and the earth opened up and swallowed them as punishment (Num 16:1-40; 26:9-11).

DAVID David means "beloved," probably the shortened form of a name meaning "Beloved of Yahweh" or "Yahweh is beloved." David was the second king of united Israel and the founder of the ruling dynasty of Judah, who was considered a model of kingship. He is a main character in 1 Sam 16–1 Kgs 2 and 1 Chron 10–29.

DAVID'S CITY 1. Jerusalem. According to 2 Sam 5:6-9 and 1 Chron 11:4-7, the fortified city of the Jebusites, also called the "fortress of Zion," was renamed "David's city" after David's conquest and occupation.

In postexilic times, the term *David's city* seems to have been used of the older parts of the city (Neh 2:14; 3:15-16, 26; 12:37), located on a triangular-shaped spur on the southeastern slope of Mount Moriah (2 Chron 3:1), south of the present-day Temple Mount, bordered on the east by the Kidron Valley and on the southwest and northwest by the Hinnom and Tyropoean valleys.

2. Bethlehem. The Gospel of Luke (2:4, 11) identifies BETHLEHEM as David's city in order to link Jesus' birthplace with the lineage of David.

DAY OF RECONCILIATION The Day of Reconciliation (Yom Kippur), celebrated annually on the 10th day of the 7th month (Tishri), comprises a series of rituals by which the high priest purifies both the sanctuary and the people, thereby restoring both as fitting receptacles for and agents of God's holy presence in the world (Lev 16).

DAY STAR This English phrase is used in the NRSV and NJB translations of Isa 14:12. The KJV translates this word as "Lucifer" and uses "Day Star" in 2 Pet 1:19. In a song of joy in Isa 14, the king of Babylon is mocked for his downfall when trying to portray himself as the "Day Star" or "MORNING STAR."

DAY'S JOURNEY The distance one might travel in the course of a day (Num 11:31; 1 Kgs 19:4; Luke 2:44; Acts 1:12).

DEACON Used in Hellenistic Greek and occasionally in the LXX (Esth 1:10; 2:2; 6:1, 3, 5; Prov 10:4; 4 Macc 9:17) for a minister, servant, agent, or representative, and in the NT with the general meaning of "servant" or "assistant" (Mark 9:35; 10:43; Matt 20:26; 22:13; John 2:5; 12:26; Rom 13:4; 15:8; Gal 2:17). The word appears as a nonspecific title in the Pauline Letters, probably with stronger associations of official agent or representative of Christ and God, as well as servant (1 Cor 3:5; 2 Cor 3:6; 6:4; 11:15, 23; Eph 3:7; 6:21; Col 1:7, 23, 25; 4:7; 1 Thess 3:2; 1 Tim 4:6). But already in Phil 1:1 and Rom 16:1 the word is beginning to be used in a more specific meaning as a title for some kind of local church position, whose exact function is not clear.

At a later stage, deacons are a group of ministers who assist the bishop in 1 Tim 3:1-13.

DEACONESS A female DEACON. The word does not occur in the NT, in spite of the confusion caused by the sometimes-mistranslation of Phoebe's title in Rom 16:1.

DEAD SEA The Jordan River's terminal basin, a narrow, land-locked, hypersaline lake lying below sea level, near the southern end of the Syrian Rift Valley. Originally called the Salt Sea, the expression "Dead Sea" occurs only in the OT (Gen 14:3; Num 34:3, 12; Deut 3:17; 4:49; Josh 3:16; 12:3, 15:2, 5; 18:19; 2 Kgs 14:25; Ezek 47:8, 18; Zech 14:8). Postexilic prophets knew it as the "eastern sea," distinguishing it from the "western sea," the Mediterranean (Joel 2:20).

The NT lacks any explicit reference to the Dead Sea.

DEAF, DEAFNESS A total lack (Lev 19:14; Mark 7:32; Luke 7:22) or partial deficiency in the sense of hearing (Ps 38:13) or understanding (Isa 42:18; 43:8). In the biblical view, God is responsible for healing and sickening (Exod 15:26), and also the senses of sight, hearing, and speech (Exod 4:11). The story of Jesus' healing of a deaf man (Mark 7:32-37) probably reflects the folk understanding of its cause (Isa 35:5) and its proper remedy (Mark 7:33-35).

DEATH The OT represents a multifaceted portrayal of death. The writers of the OT (especially the psalmists) used the language of death not just to describe the physical cessation of life, but also as a metaphor for distress and anguish.

The Gospel writers use the term *death* to refer to the literal cessation of biological life. The evangelists have variant notions about the rituals of death, for example, Jesus advises his followers to let the dead bury their own dead (Matt 8:22; Luke 9:60), but commends the woman who anoints him prior to his own death (Mark 14:3-9; Matt 26:6-13; Luke 7:36-50; John 12:1-8). In four instances, people are resuscitated from death (Mark 5:21-43; Matt 9:18-26; Luke 8:40-56; Luke 7:11-17; John 11:1-44; Acts 9:36-43), but there is no reason to believe that their physical resuscitations would be permanent.

Paul uses the concept of death theologically in both literal and metaphorical senses. In the literal sense, death is not a natural constituent of creation and is the result of sin; Jesus saves humankind from sin and, therefore, death is overcome in the afterlife (see Rom 4:25; 5:12; 6:23; 1 Cor 15:26). In his comparison of Jesus and Adam, Paul argues that the first created human was, because of his disobedience, earthly, perishable, dishonorable, weak, and physical; Christ, on the other hand, is heavenly, imperishable, glorious, powerful, and spiritual. Jesus, according to Paul, is the "last Adam" who overcomes death (1 Cor 15:42-49). Paul assures his followers that "those who have died in Jesus" will rise first (1 Thess 4:16-17).

DEBIR 1. A king of Eglon mentioned in Josh 10:3 who was part of an Amorite force that opposed Joshua.

2. A Canaanite city south of Hebron in the highlands of Judah that was conquered by Joshua. Joshua 10:38-39

describes how the Israelites "turned back" to the south and defeated Debir after other major cities in the western foothills and the Judean highlands were conquered (compare also Josh 12:3).

3. A settlement mentioned on the northern border of Judah toward Gilgal and opposite the ascent of Adummim (Josh 15:7).

4. A city mentioned in the inheritance of Gad (Josh 13:26) in the land of Gilead.

DEBORAH 1. Rebekah's nurse. She was a significant enough figure that her death rates mention (Gen 35:8).

2. A judge and prophet. An Israelite leader, Deborah ("honey bee") is introduced in Judg 4:4 with a string of designations: "Deborah, a prophet, the wife of Lappidoth [or "a woman of torches"], was a leader of Israel at that time." The only female judge and the only named prophet in Judges, she is also the only biblical individual called "a mother in Israel" (5:7).

3. Mother of Tobit's father Tobiel. She taught Tobit his scrupulous observance of tithing and instilled in him the Law of Moses after his father's death had left him an orphan (Tob 1:8).

DEBORAH, SONG OF The poem in Judg 5:2-30 (31) is commonly called the "Song of Deborah." Widely regarded as one of the oldest compositions in the OT, the song is characterized by repetitive style, vivid imagery, and a rapid montage of scenes. The related prose account in Judg 4, different in detail and emphasis, is deemed by most to be later than the poem and at least partially dependent upon it.

DEBT, DEBTOR In the ANE debts often forced people into slavery when they were unable to repay. Hammurabi's laws indicate loan interest rates at 20 percent for money and 33 percent for grain. In NT times, interest rates throughout the Graeco-Roman world ran between 10 percent and 30 percent, so people also fell into debt slavery or debtor's prison (see SLAVERY).

DECALOGUE See TEN COMMANDMENTS.

DECAPOLIS Literally means "Ten Cities" and refers to a group of Greek cities located in southern Syria, northern Palestine, and the northern Transjordan.

DECREE Announced by an authority (human or divine), a declaration or statute directing/prescribing the actions of individuals or communities, often documented in writing. Examples include Cyrus's decree to rebuild the temple (Ezra 5:13, 17) and Caesar Augustus's decree calling for a census (Luke 2:1). (See also Isa 10:1; 2 Chron 30:5; Ezra 6:1; Esth 1:20; Dan 3:10; Ps 2:7; Job 28:26; Acts 17:7.)

DEDAN 1. A son of Jokshan son of Abraham and Keturah (Gen 25:3; 1 Chron 1:32), or a son of Raamah (Gen 10:7; 1 Chron 1:9), a descendant of Ham. Both references list Sheba as Dedan's brother.

2. Ezekiel lists Dedan in an oracle against Edom (Ezek 25:13) and pairs Sheba with Dedan as trade cities (Ezek 38:13). Dedan was a prominent commercial city in the 7th cent. BCE located at a desert oasis in northwestern Arabia known today as Al Ula.

DEDICATION, FEAST OF See FEAST OF DEDICATION.

DELAIAH 1. A temple priest under David allotted the 23rd position (1 Chron 24:18).

2. One of several officials who, hearing Baruch read Jeremiah's scroll of prophecy, urged Jehoiakim not to burn the scroll (Jer 36:12, 25).

3. One of seven sons of Elioenai, a descendant of Solomon through Zerubbabel (1 Chron 3:24).

4. A family unable to prove they were

descendants of Israel (Ezra 2:60; Neh 7:62; 1 Esdr 5:37).

5. Father of Shemaiah who conspired to stop Nehemiah by closing the doors of the temple (Neh 6:10).

DELILAH A woman from the Valley of Sorek, beloved by the judge SAMSON (Judg 16:4). Unlike the former, unnamed, Philistine wife of Samson (Judg 14:1-20), Delilah bears a name but is not explicitly characterized as Philistine or Israelite. Bribed by the Philistines, Delilah tried to seduce Samson to reveal the secret of his superhuman strength. In return for obtaining this information, each of the Philistine lords had promised her 1,100 pieces of silver (Judg 16:5). Three times her attempt failed because Samson lied to her when she coaxed him to divulge his weakness. Recognizing the truth at last, Delilah summoned the Philistine lords, who this time carried with them the bribe money (Judg 16:18-19). Delilah made Samson sleep in her lap so that his head could be shaven. When she called again, "Samson, the Philistines are on you," Samson was not able to free himself since his strength had left him along with the loss of his hair (Judg 16:20). Betrayed and delivered by his mistress, he was overwhelmed by the Philistines (Judg 16:21).

DELUGE See FLOOD.

DEMAS Paul calls Demas a "coworker" (Phlm 24), but later says Demas has deserted him (2 Tim 4:10; Acts of Paul and Thecla 1; 4; 12–14).

DEMETRIUS Demetrius was the name of three Seleucid kings who interacted at one time or another with Judah.

1. Demetrius I Soter (162–150 BCE) was the son of Seleucus IV, who succeeded Antiochus V Eupator.

2. Demetrius II Nicator (145–140, 129–126 BCE). In 147 BCE the son of Demetrius I sailed from Crete to take back his father's kingdom from Alexander. With the help of Ptolemy VI's forces, he was able to defeat Alexander and establish his rulership in the year 145 BCE, to become Demetrius II Theos Nicator Philadelphus.

3. Demetrius III Eucaerus. Around 90 BCE there were four claimants to the Seleucid throne. One of these was Demetrius III Eucaerus of Damascus who had been put on the throne by Ptolemy IX about 95 BCE. Alexander Janneus (see HASMONEANS) was now high priest and king of the Hasmonean kingdom, but he had considerable opposition from among the Jews of Palestine.

4. Demetrius the silversmith was an artisan who instigated a riot against Paul for encouraging the Ephesians to refrain from buying Artemisian shrines (Acts 19:23-41).

5. Demetrius the chronographer was a 3rd-cent. BCE historian whose work, found only in fragments in Josephus's and Eusebius's writings, is the first known writing to use the LXX.

6. Demetrius of Phalerum was an Athenian rhetorician and historian (ca. 355–280 BCE).

DEMON Generally, a demon is a semidivine entity. Although indeterminate in the OT, demons in the NT are seen as evil or unclean spiritual beings with the capacity to harm life or allure people to heresy or immorality. Demons, the evil angels of Satan (Mark 3:22), can form a group and cooperate against a person (Matt 12:45; Luke 11:26), can be so numerous or multifaceted as to be described as "legion" (Mark 5:9), and a number of different ones can be said to possess a person (Luke 8:2), causing a wide range of sicknesses.

From what can be recovered of the historical Jesus, exorcisms were the most common form of healing or miracle he is said to have performed. He understood these exorcisms not only to be relieving suffering (e.g., Mark 5:1-20) but, as is most clearly shown in the so-called Beelzebul Controversy (Mark 3:22-27; Mark 9:32-34; 12:22-30; Luke 11:14-23), to be a battle with Satan, in which he plunders his possessions.

Exorcisms were a common occurrence in Jesus' time, and his contemporaries did not look on exorcism as an eschatological sign. Therefore, it is astounding that Jesus made the unique claim that his exorcisms were the operation of God's kingdom. That is, his dealing with demons was not merely preparatory to the coming of God's kingdom, nor a sign or even an illustration of its arrival, but the actual materialization of God's kingdom (Matt 12:28; Luke 11:20).

In contrast to the Gospels and Acts, Paul has little to say about evil spirits or demons (1 Cor 10:20). Much of what we can glean of Paul's ideas about evil spiritual beings is contained in his notion of "forces of cosmic darkness, and spiritual powers of evil in the heavens" (Eph 6:12). The most obvious meaning of this language is that there were supernatural motivating powers behind the pagan world order (Deut 32:8; Isa 24:21-22; Dan 10:13, 20; 1 Cor 2:6-8). However, this by no means exhausts the content of Paul's speaking of "authority and power," in relation to which Rom 8:38-39 is of particular interest (see 1 Cor 15:24; also Eph 3:10; 6:12; Col 2:15).

DEMONIAC In the NT, *demoniac*, meaning "a person having or possessed by a demon or evil spirit," is found only in the Gospels (seven of thirteen occurrences in Matthew). It is considered a distinct unspecified illness (diseases and pains, demoniacs, epileptics, and paralytics in Matt 4:24) cured by Jesus, although sometimes it is associated with violence (8:28), being blind, mute (9:32), or tormented (15:22). In John, having a demon is a charge against Jesus and is equated with madness (John 10:20-21). In Mark 3:21-22, 30 a charge of madness against Jesus is associated with having a BEELZEBUL or unclean spirit.

DEMOPHON Along with TIMOTHY, APOLLONIUS, and Hieronymus, Demophon was one of the Syrian governors in the 2nd cent. BCE in Palestine under ANTIOCHUS V, Eupator, ensuring that the Hellenistic harassment of the Jews continued unabated (2 Macc 12:2).

DENARION, DENARIA A Roman silver coin equivalent to the Greek DRACHME. Throughout the NT, the denarion (plural denaria) is referenced as an equivalent of payment for daily wages and the Greek is sometimes translated as such (Matt 20:2; 22:19; Rev 6:6). See MONEY, COINS.

DEPUTY Someone governing on behalf of a superior (1 Kgs 22:47 [Heb. 22:48]; Ezra 4:8; Jer 51:28; Acts 13:7; 18:12). See GOVERNOR.

DERBE A town in LYCAONIA, near the boundary of the Roman provinces of Galatia and Cappadocia. The town was one of Paul's destinations on his first visit to Asia Minor (Acts 14:6, 20), and a place he revisited (Acts 16:1 and perhaps 18:23; 19:1).

DESERT Although the term *desert* is often colloquially used for areas that will not sustain rain-fed agriculture, deserts are complex and diverse. Principally they vary according to altitude, temperature, precipitation, and soils, which in turn determine the amounts and kinds of plant and animal communities that inhabit these biomes.

DESOLATING SACRILEGE See ABOMINATION OF DESOLATION.

DESSAU A village in Judea where the Jews engaged in battle against NICANOR (2 Macc 14:16).

DEUEL Father of ELIASAPH, who represented the tribe of Gad during the census and the mobilization of the tribes by Moses during the exodus wanderings in the Sinai wilderness (Num 1:14; 7:42-47; 10:20).

DEUTEROCANONICAL See APOCRYPHA, DEUTEROCANONICAL.

DEUTERONOMY, BOOK OF The familiar scriptural identity of ancient Israel as a people set apart among the world's dispersed nations, discretely allied with "the Lord" (Yahweh) in covenant and unified by its commitment to live in accord with a unique legacy of Mosaic Torah, comes to mature definition in the fifth and final book of the Pentateuch, Deuteronomy. The English name derives, by way of Latin, from a compound term in Greek meaning "Second Law-giving."

DEVIL, DEVILS A slanderer, false accuser, or liar (Sir 51:2; 2 Tim 3:3).

In the OT a SATAN ("the Adversary") is a human enemy (1 Sam 29:4) or opponent (1 Kgs 11:14), or an angelic adversary acting for God (Num 22:22).

In the NT a devil is the accuser (1 Pet 5:8) and is a synonym for the evil one (Matt 13:19; Luke 8:11) and is used interchangeably with the tempter (Matt 4:1, 3), the enemy (Matt 13:39), Satan (John 13:2, 27) and, in Rev 12:7-9, is the great dragon, the ancient serpent, and the deceiver of the whole world. He can be worshipped (Luke 4:7), tempts Jesus (4:2), and is the enemy of the children of the kingdom (Matt 13:39), disabling their belief and salvation (Luke 8:12). Jesus is said to heal all who were oppressed by the devil (Acts 10:38) and his death destroys the devil (Heb 2:14). An eternal fire is prepared for the devil and his angels (Matt 25:41). In the Gospel of John, the devil is a murderer, contains no truth, lies, and is the father of lies (John 8:44). He also motivates (13:2), fathers (8:44), or is an epithet for (6:70) Jesus' opponents. Paul uses only the term *Satan*, but in the deutero-Pauline letters the devil can snare, condemn (1 Tim 3:6-7) and capture (2 Tim 2:26) believers, who are not to make room for the devil (Eph 4:27) but to stand against his craftiness (Eph 6:11; see Jas 4:7). See DEMON.

DEVOTED The NRSV, NIV, and ASV normally use devoted or "devoted thing(s)" to translate the Hebrew word for BAN. Probably the most widely known example of the ban occurs in Josh 6–7, the narrative in which Jericho is conquered and "set aside for God" (6:18 CEB) and Israel is warned "not to take some of the things reserved" (6:18 CEB). All silver, gold, and bronze are "holy to the LORD" (v. 19). Achan, however, coveted fine clothing, silver, and a bar of gold, and kept these for himself (7:21). For this he was utterly destroyed.

DIAL A (sun) dial is an instrument used to indicate the time of day by measuring the movement of the sun's shadow.

DIASPORA The Greek term for "dispersion." It is used in the LXX twelve times with the meaning "dispersion of Jews among the Gentile nations" or "the Jews as thus scattered."

DIBLAIM Father of GOMER, Hosea's wife (Hos 1:3).

DIBON A settlement located 3 mi. north of the Arnon (modern Wadi Mujib) on the plateau east of the Dead Sea. It was an area claimed by both Israel and Moab. In the Iron Age inscription of King Mesha of Moab (ca. 840 BCE; cf 2 Kgs 3).

DIBRI A Danite whose unnamed grandson blasphemed the divine name (Yahweh) in a curse during a personal fight and, with the approval of Moses, was subsequently stoned to death. The blasphemer's mother, SHELOMITH, was the daughter of Dibri, and his father was an Egyptian (Lev 24:10-16).

DIDRACHME A Greek double-DRACHME coin struck in silver.

DIDYMUS A proper name meaning "twin," and a nickname for THOMAS, one of the Twelve (John 11:16; 20:24; 21:2).

DIKLAH Son of JOKTAN (Gen 10:27; 1 Chron 1:21); also used figuratively to refer to a people or territory in Arabia.

DILAN A city with its villages allotted to the Judah tribe (Josh 15:38), possibly situated in the LACHISH district, but whose precise location is unknown.

DIMNAH Town allocated from the Zebulun territory for the Merarite Levites (see MERARI, MERARITES).

DINAH The daughter of JACOB and LEAH. She is the only daughter named in the story describing the birth of Jacob's first eleven sons (Gen 29:31–30:24). Dinah is the last of Leah's progeny. She is also the only female descendant named among Jacob's children in a genealogical list (Gen 46:15), though others are also mentioned collectively as "his . . . daughters."

Dinah is best known for her appearance in a narrative account that involves the Hivite Shechem son of Hamor (Gen 34), one of three OT narratives that explicitly recount the rape of a woman.

DIONYSIA The name of festivals of Dionysus celebrated at various localities in ancient Greece, including the spring celebration at Athens known as the Great Dionysia or City Dionysia (ca. 6th cent. BCE). As part of the Hellenizing measures brought about in Jerusalem under the Seleucid ruler Antiochus IV, the Jewish people were forced to participate in the Dionysia (2 Macc 6:7).

DIONYSIUS In the Bible, Dionysius is the name of a man present for Paul's famous MARS HILL speech at Athens who responded with faith (Acts 17:34).

DIOSCURI A term for the brothers Castor and Pollux, semidivine twin sons of Zeus, protectors of sailors and thus the figurehead on Paul's ship (Acts 28:11).

DIOTREPHES Diotrephes, meaning "cherished by God," is mentioned in 3 John 9.

DISCIPLE WHOM JESUS LOVED See BELOVED DISCIPLE.

DISCIPLE, DISCIPLESHIP These terms involve the role of pupil or adherent. The term *disciple* occurs more than 300 times in the NT, exclusively within the Gospels and Acts, and twice in the OT (Isa 8:16; 54:13).

DISHAN One of the sons of SEIR, who in turn had two sons: Uz and Aran (Gen 36:21-30; 1 Chron 1:38-42).

DISHON A descendant of ANAH, who is among the children of SEIR the Horite (Gen 36:21; 1 Chron 1:38). Dishon's clan is listed among those who inhabit the land in which Esau settles after departing from Jacob (Gen 36:6-7).

DISTRICT The English word *district* is used for several biblical terms specifying geographical regions or units of political and religious administration.

DIVIDING WALL The Temple Mount in JERUSALEM was divided into different courtyards of increasing levels of purity. The largest, outermost area was open to Gentiles, but a low partition wall, about 1.5 m high with signs in Greek and Latin warning non-Jews not to enter further or suffer immediate execution, prevented non-Jews from entering the temple itself. Some Jews erroneously thought Paul brought Gentiles into the temple and tried to kill him (Acts 21:28*b*-31). It is also the "barrier of hatred" Paul uses symbolically in Eph 2:14.

DIVINATION The process of discerning divine purpose or attaining supernatural knowledge through various devices and stratagems. Widely practiced in the ANE, divination focuses on human schemes for uncovering divine will, in contrast with prophetic insight that derives from direct revelation (conveyed through visions, dreams, and other ecstatic experiences of the divine). While the OT retains some traces of divinatory ritual, by and large it regards manipulative approaches to God with suspicion.

Moses' review of God's covenantal law, preparing Israel to possess its holy land, unequivocally forbids any engagement in sundry forms of divination, augury, and other "detestable practices" of the alien peoples of Canaan (Deut 18:9-14; quotation v. 12). Philistine, Babylonian, and Chaldean diviners also appear in a negative light (1 Sam 6:2; Isa 2:6; Jer 50:35-36; Dan 2:27; 4:7; 5:7).

DIVINE ASSEMBLY In the ANE, a common metaphor for describing the world of the divine was the "divine assembly" or "divine council." These descriptions of gods and goddesses gathered together under the leadership of a senior deity were derived, in all probability, from the activities of the royal court. The divine assembly figures prominently in 1 Kgs 22, Isa 6, and Job 1–2, as well as Pss 29; 82; and 89.

DIVINE IMAGES An object of worship or devotion ("teraphim"), often in the form of a figurine. The term is frequently associated with shrines (Gen 31:19-35; Judg 17:5; Ezek 21:21), but it would be incorrect to assume that all divine images were figurines. It is as likely that they were ancestor figures or emblems of authority for the household.

DIVINER'S OAK A place near Shechem (Judg 9:37) given as a reference point in Gaal's description of the location of Abimelech's troops. This oak was possibly a TEREBINTH, or sacred tree, perhaps the same oak mentioned in Judg 9:6.

DIVORCE Leviticus 21:7, 14; 22:13, and Ezek 44:22 prohibit priests from marrying a divorced woman. Deuteronomy 21:14 deals with provisions for a man to marry a woman taken captive in war. If the man is not satisfied with her, he is to divorce her and set her free; he is not to sell her for money or treat her as a slave. Deuteronomy 22:19 and 22:29 deal with cases in which a man may never divorce his wife. In each case, the aggrieved party is the father of the "young woman" (Deut 22:19, 28-29), to whom the man must pay a fine. These laws may also protect the woman, who would otherwise be ineligible to marry another man (see also Deut 24:1-4). Divorce is used as a prophetic metaphor in Isa 50:1; 54:5-8; Jer 3–4; and Mal 2:16. Paul argues against three specific cases of divorce in 1 Cor 7:10-16. Jesus' teachings on divorce are found in Matt 2:18-20; 5:31-32; 19; Mark 10:2-12; and Luke 16:18.

DIVORCE, CERTIFICATE OF According to the deuteronomic law code (Deut 24:1, 3), a husband "writes up divorce papers, hands them to her, and sends her out of his house." The content of the writ is not specified, although it possibly included the formula, "She is not my wife, and I am not her husband" (Hos 2:2 [Heb. 2:4]). In both testaments, the husband alone gives a certificate of divorce. It is not known if this was always the practice or required in all cases.

DIZAHAB A place mentioned in Deut 1:1 in relation to the location from which Moses delivers his final address to the Israelites.

DODAI Chief of King David's military forces in the second month (1 Chron 27:4).

DODANIM The son of Javan and grandson of Noah (Gen 10:4).

DODAVAHU The father of Eliezer, who spoke prophetically against Judean king

JEHOSHAPHAT for his alliance with King AHAZIAH of Israel (2 Chron 20:37).

DODO 1. The grandfather of TOLA and a descendant of Issachar (Judg 10:1). Tola rose to judge Israel after ABIMELECH.

2. The father of ELEAZAR, a warrior of David. Dodo was a son of Ahohi (2 Sam 23:9; 1 Chron 11:12).

3. The father of ELHANAN, a warrior of David (2 Sam 23:24; 1 Chron 11:26).

DOEG The Edomite head of Saul's shepherds (1 Sam 21:7) or of Saul's guard (1 Sam 22:17); Doeg was detained before the Lord at NOB during the time that David took the bread of the presence and Goliath's sword from AHIMELECH.

DOG At times, packs of unmanaged dogs (Ps 22:16) roamed the cities (1 Kgs 14:11; 16:4), while other dogs were used by the Israelites in herding (Isa 56:11; Job 30:1) and as watchdogs (Isa 56:10). Yet, in spite of their positive contribution they were not well treated. Jesus alluded to the lower status of dogs when he said, "Don't give holy things to dogs" (Matt 7:6) and to a woman who asked him for help: "It is not good to take the children's bread and toss it to dogs," to which she responded that even the dogs get the crumbs that fall from the master's table (Matt 15:26-27; Mark 7:27). Several biblical references to dogs have bad connotations as in the words of Hazael to Elisha: "How could your servant, who is nothing but a dog, do such mighty things?" (2 Kgs 8:13; see also Exod 22:30; Deut 23:19; 2 Sam 3:8; Prov 26:11; Eccl 9:4). Evildoers are likened to dogs in Phil 3:2 and Rev 22:15.

DOMINION Dominion translates several Hebrew, Aramaic, and Greek words for control, mastery, or sovereignty. Old Testament and NT authors concur that ultimate rule and governance of humanity and of all creation belongs to God (Pss 22:28; 103:22; see also the NT doxologies 1 Tim 6:16; Jude 25; Rev 1:6). Dominion is also used in the OT for human rule over others, whether nations over nations (Judg 14:4; 1 Kgs 4:24; 9:19), enemies over God's people (Neh 9:28; Ps 19:13), or God's chosen king over all creation (Ps 72:8). Political and military rule, however, is relativized in light of God's supreme authority (Dan 6:26; Wis 6:3).

DOORKEEPER This office seems to be the responsibility of PRIESTS AND LEVITES, although not limited to them entirely (John 18:16). Other than guarding the entrances to the temple, meeting tent, or other households, the only stated responsibilities for doorkeepers are collecting the silver brought into the temple and placing it in the collection box for temple repairs (see 2 Kgs 12:10; 22:4), or bringing contraband items out from the temple during Josiah's reform.

DOPHKAH An exodus itinerary site on the journey to Mount Sinai, described as the second stop after leaving Yam Suf, adjoining the Wilderness of Sin (Num 33:12-13).

DOR A seaport city on the Mediterranean south of the Carmel range, probably established during the Late Bronze Age, and continuously inhabited until the 7th cent. CE.

DORCAS The Greek name of Tabitha. She was brought back to life by Peter (Acts 9:36-43). Called a disciple, she was probably a woman of some financial means and significant status in the Christian communities because "her life overflowed with good works and compassionate acts on behalf of those in need" (9:36), especially among widows for whom she provided clothing (9:39).

DORYMENES Father of Ptolemy (2 Macc 4:45) who was governor of Coelesyria and Phoenicia (2 Macc 8:8), and whom Lysias appointed to attack Judah (1 Macc 3:38–4:25).

DOVE The rock dove (Columbia livia) was probably the first bird that was domesticated in Palestine. Doves, or pigeons, were bred in dovecots (Isa 60:8), probably for meat production. In addition, the dove and turtledove had an important ritual function, which was not granted other "clean" (i.e., edible) birds: They could be offered as a sacrifice (Lev 1:14). In some cases, pigeons and turtledoves were accepted as substitutes for lambs, which the poor could not afford (Lev 5:7; 12:6). In the NT period, pigeons were sold in the courtyard of the Jerusalem temple (Matt 21:12).

DRACHME, DRACHMEN A Greek silver coin that was used in many daily transactions, but varied greatly in value and purchasing power. During the 1st cent. CE, it was generally equated with the denarion, one day's wage for a laborer (see Tob 5:15; 2 Macc 4:19; 10:20; 12:43; Luke 15:8-9).

DRAGON Several ANE cultures developed myths concerning primeval chaos monsters, often depicted as dragons. Yahweh receives praise for crushing (Ps 89:10) and dismembering the monster RAHAB (Isa 51:9). In each instance the dragon refers to a chaos monster that opposes the purposes and order of God.

Revelation 12 depicts the dragon as SATAN, the adversary who pursues God's people and empowers the beast to make war against them. In Revelation the forces of the Lamb defeat those of the dragon, ending cosmic conflict and preparing the way for the new heaven and the new earth.

DRAGON'S SPRING A place by which Nehemiah passes on his inspection of Jerusalem's walls (Neh 2:13).

DREAM Dreaming is a mental activity during sleep that has fascinated humans from antiquity until the present. Dreams were considered as messages from deities, demons, or the deceased or, more recently, as spontaneous if significant eruptions from the depths of the psyche. Neither Hebrew nor Greek made a sharp distinction between dreams and visions and both considered these to be potentially revelations of God (Num 12:6; see VISION).

DRINK The primary beverages in the biblical text are water, wine, and milk (Sir 39:26). In a society with a scarcity of water resources, water, or the lack of water, forms a leading theme in texts like Exod 17 and Num 20–21. In John 4, the notion of "living water" builds on connotations of water to give and sustain life. Milk (mostly from goats) was consumed at meals and formed the basis for products like cheese and curds. Milk's significance is found in the reference to the land full of milk and honey (e.g., Exod 3:17. See also the idyllic description of the hills full of milk in Joel 3:18). Wine occurs frequently in the Bible, ranging from wine for everyday consumption (Ps 104:15; Eccl 9:7; John 2) to wine as a symbol of the final restoration (Isa 25:6; Amos 9:13). The misuse of wine is also noted in the biblical text. See, for example, the reference in Isa 5:11 to strong drink, a beverage with alcoholic content of 20–60 percent (40–120 proof). Vinegar, made from fermented wine, served as a condiment, but was also drunk in diluted form by the poor.

DROPSY Luke's exclusive use of this Greek word does not indicate that he was a physician, since it also appeared in nonmedical ancient literature. It describes the symptom (not the pathology) of a sick man at a dinner to which Jesus had been invited (Luke 14:2). Modern science suggests that the sick man had edema, excess accumulation of fluid in ankles, legs, or abdominal cavity. He would appear swollen, hence, an "abnormal swelling of the body" (CEB) is preferable to the archaic "dropsy" (RSV; NRSV).

DROSS Dross is the material by-product

extracted from alloys as they are melted down to yield pure silver.

DRUNKENNESS Intoxication appears in a variety of OT contexts: as part of the sacrificial meal (Deut 14:26), a source of pleasure (Judg 9:13; Ps 104:15; Prov 31:6-7), a metaphor for human love (Song 7:9), or an indicator of excess among the wealthy and kings (1 Sam 25:26; Esth 1:8, 10; Dan 5:2; 1 Kgs 16:9; 20:16). Prophets use drunkenness as an indicator of impending destruction (Jer 13:13; Ezek 23:33), and it produces disgrace for Noah and Lot (Gen 9:21; 19:33, 35). Priests are warned against imbibing while serving in the meeting tent (Lev 10:8-9), and proverbs caution against overindulgence (Prov 20:1; 21:17; 23:20-21, 29-35).

The NT warns against dangers associated with drunkenness: debauchery and Gentile immorality (Rom 13:13; 1 Pet 4:3), exclusion from God's kingdom (1 Cor 6:10; Gal 5:21), and disqualification from church leadership (1 Tim 3:3; Titus 1:7). See WINE.

DRUSILLA Mentioned as the wife of FELIX who came with her husband to hear Paul in Caesarea (Acts 24:24).

DUMAH 1. The sixth of twelve sons of Ishmael and eponymous ancestor of an Arabian tribe (Gen 25:13-16; 1 Chron 1:30). This Dumah likely refers to a prosperous oasis town in northcentral Arabia.

2. A town southwest of Hebron (Josh 15:52).

3. The title of an enigmatic oracle (Isa 21:11-12) set in an anti-Babylonian and Arabian context (Isa 21), possibly referencing the oasis noted in number 1 above.

DUNG Dung represents numerous Hebrew words for human or animal feces. As an unclean substance, the dung of a sacrificial animal was to be burned outside the camp (Exod 29:14; Lev 4:11), and human dung was to be buried outside the camp (Deut 23:14). A starving people under siege may have resorted to eating dung (2 Kgs 18:27) or to using human or cows' dung for cooking fuel (Ezek 4:12-15).

Dung was sometimes disposed of by burning (1 Kgs 14:10), and other times by decomposing in the open (2 Kgs 9:37; Jer 9:22).

DUNG GATE A gate of JERUSALEM (Neh 2:13; 3:13-14; 12:31) repaired under Nehemiah's direction.

DUNGEON Words meaning PIT, well, or cistern can indicate chambers used to detain prisoners. Sometimes this vocabulary functions metaphorically (e.g., Gen 41:14; Exod 12:29). Other usage (e.g., Jer 38:6-13; CEB cistern) denotes an actual subterranean container or secured room employed to incarcerate or ensure prisoners' deaths. Ancient imprisonment often did not involve buildings reserved for this purpose.

DURA A place or an architectural element in the vicinity of Babylon in Dan 3:1.

DUST Dust is used more than sixty times in the OT figuratively for judgment (Deut 28:24), abundance (Gen 13:16; 28:14; Job 27:16; Ps 78:27), humiliation, grief, and mourning (Job 2:12; 42:6; Isa 2:10; 47:1; also Rev 18:19). Six NT texts describe shaking dust off of one's feet as a sign of repudiation (Matt 10:14; Mark 6:11; Luke 9:5; 10:11; Acts 13:51; 18:6). See ADAM; CLAY; DEATH.

DYSMAS The Acts of Pilate identifies the penitent criminal crucified with Jesus as Dysmas, and the other criminal as Gestas.

Ee

EAGLE Several eagles (species of the genus Aquila) can be spotted in Israel/ Palestine, but they are relatively rare. The eagle is a powerful symbol for God in the OT; God is thus depicted as an "eagle" carrying its young on its pinions (Deut 32:11), and the faithful ones are promised that they will experience a renewal of strength and become "like eagles" (Isa 40:31). Eagle symbolism is found in Revelation (4:7; 8:13; 12:14). The description in Rev 4:6-8 of four creatures, including one "like an eagle in flight," is clearly influenced by the vision in Ezek 1:5-14. However, the descriptions of this bird indicate that it is more likely to be a vulture than an eagle. Most evidently, the eagle is not bald on its head and neck (Mic 1:16), whereas the vulture is. Further, the eagle does not feed on carrion (Job 39:27-30), but the vulture does. The reference is primarily to the majestic griffon vulture (Gyps fulvus).

EARTHQUAKE A disruptive shifting of the earth's surface, occurring throughout Mediterranean history at periodic intervals and usually at moderate levels of intensity.

The book of Amos (1:1) dates the prophet's mission "two years before the earthquake" during the kingdoms of Uzziah in Judah (783–746 BCE) and Jeroboam in Israel (786–746 BCE).

In the NT, Matthew associates earthquakes with Jesus' crucifixion and resurrection: when Jesus cried out and took his last breath, "the earth shook," splitting rocks and temple veil, releasing resurrected bodies from open tombs, and inspiring soldiers' faith in Jesus (Matt 27:50-54); at Jesus' gravesite, a "great earthquake" (Matt 28:2) signaled the arrival of a radiant angel who rolled back the tombstone and announced Jesus' resurrection to Mary Magdalene and another Mary.

In the book of Acts, a dramatic house-shaking in Jerusalem accompanies the Spirit's outpouring on the early church (4:31), and a foundation-shaking earthquake in Philippi opens prison doors and loosens the shackles of the hymn-singing Paul and Silas (16:25-27).

EAST COUNTRY The term likely refers to Babylon (Ezek 47:8; Zech 8:7), east of Israel, where Abraham sends his secondary wives' sons (Gen 25:6).

EAST GATE A gate in the Jerusalem wall, whose "keeper" and the one responsible for its repair was Shemaiah (1 Chron 26:14; Neh 3:29). References to the "East Gate" and the "outer gate that faces east" as well as the "east-facing gate" are found throughout the book of Ezekiel (10:19; 11:1; 40:6-11, 19-23, 44; 42:15; 43:1-5; 44:1-3; 46:1-3; 47:2), referring to the departure and return of the presence of the Lord from the city of JERUSALEM during the Babylonian siege.

EASTER The English word does not occur in the Bible. The NT speaks of Passover, the Jewish holiday celebrating the liberation of Israel from slavery, which the Gospels associate with the death of Jesus (see PASSOVER AND FESTIVAL OF UNLEAVENED BREAD). In the Gospels, the Last Supper occurs on the Preparation Day for the Passover, and the meal Jesus eats with his disciples is a Passover meal. Jesus' words instructing his disciples to associate his body and blood with the elements of the Passover meal point to a view in which the Lord's Supper was understood in connection to Passover (see Matt 26:1, 17-30; Mark 14:1, 12-25; Luke 22:1, 7-23). In John, the Last Supper occurs prior to Preparation Day (John 13:1), but the author explicitly associates Jesus' death with the Passover offering (John 19:14, 36).

EASTERN SEA A body of water mentioned in Joel 2:20, probably the Dead Sea, which lay eastward from ancient Israel.

EBAL 1. Son of Shobal the Horite (Gen 36:23; 1 Chron 1:40; Deut 2:12).

2. Variant for OBAL son of Joktan (Gen 10:28; 1 Chron 1:22).

EBAL, MOUNT A mountain rising 3,083 ft. above sea level in the central highlands of northern Israel (Deut 11:29; 27:4, 13; Josh 8:30, 33), adjacent to the town of Shechem and opposite Mount Gerizim (see GERIZIM, MOUNT).

EBED A proper name meaning "slave" or "servant."

1. The father of GAAL, who challenged the authority of ABIMELECH in Judg 9:26.

2. A descendant of Adin and son of Jonathan who returned from Babylonian exile under EZRA (8:6).

EBED-MELECH Ebed-melech (literally "servant of the king") was an Ethiopian EUNUCH who served in the Judahite king ZEDEKIAH's court. Ebed-melech rescued JEREMIAH from his cistern prison (Jer 38:7-13).

EBENEZER Means "stone of help."

1. A location associated with the Philistine defeat of the Israelites under Saul and the taking of the covenant chest (1 Sam 4:1; 5:1).

2. A stone set up by Samuel (1 Sam 7:12) following an Israelite defeat of the Philistines is also called Ebenezer, for, as Samuel explains, "The LORD helped us to this very point."

EBER A descendant of NOAH's son SHEM representing all the Semites in J's postdiluvian Table of Nations (Gen 10:21-32). The Priestly genealogy (Gen 11) presents the line of Eber leading directly to Abram, suggesting Eber as the eponymous ancestor of the HEBREW PEOPLE.

EBEZ Ebez was a settlement mentioned in Josh 19:20 as one of sixteen towns within the territory of the tribe of Issachar.

EBRON A city allotted to the tribe of Asher (Josh 19:28), perhaps also spelled ABDON, a Levitical town in Asher's territory (Josh 21:30; 1 Chron 6:74).

ECBATANA A city, near modern Hamadan located in the Zagros Mountains of modern Iran, mentioned in the books of Ezra, Judith, Tobit, and 2 Maccabees. In antiquity, Ecbatana was a major city in Median territory (see MEDES, MEDIA). When the Persian king Cyrus captured the city from Astyages in the 6th cent. BCE, Ecbatana became the capital of the new Persian province of Media.

ECCLESIASTES, BOOK OF The Hebrew name Qoheleth has become more common. It is also called the Book of the Preacher. Ecclesiastes is the anglicized form of a Greek word meaning an officer, or a person in charge of a congregation or assembly; this is, in turn, a rendering of the Hebrew title of the book, Qoheleth, literally, "the one who convenes an assembly." In the Hebrew canon the book belongs to the Five Megilloth, namely Ruth, Song of Songs, Ecclesiastes, Lamentations, and Esther. As such, it is located in the third part of the Hebrew canon known as the Writings, after Psalms, Proverbs, and Job and before Daniel, Ezra, Nehemiah and 1–2 Chronicles. It is traditionally read during the Feast of Booths, probably because in a number of places it invokes joy. In some early Jewish traditions the book was put together with the two other books believed to be authored by Solomon, Proverbs and the Song.

ECCLESIASTICUS See SIRACH, APOCRYPHA, DEUTEROCANONICAL.

EDEN A Gershonite who cleansed the temple during Hezekiah's reign (2 Chron 29:12), possibly the same one who tended the cities of the priests (2 Chron 31:15).

EDEN, GARDEN OF Most readers of the Bible associate Eden with Gen 2–3, yet it is important to note that the word occurs in several other places in the OT: Isa 51:3; Ezek 28:13; 31:9, 16, 18; 36:35; and Joel 2:3. From these texts one can see that Eden is a location abundantly blessed with fertility. Sterility and death have no place there.

EDER 1. A town in the south of Judah (Josh 15:21).

2. One of the sons of Elpaal (1 Chron 8:9).

3. A member of the tribe of Levi and one of the three sons of Mushi and a grandson of Merari (1 Chron 23:23; 24:30).

EDER, TOWER OF A landmark (Gen 35:21), associated today with Khirbet Siyar el-Ganam, on a ridge east of Bethlehem, likely named for flocks kept in the area.

EDNA In the book of Tobit, Edna is the wife of Raguel and mother of Sarah (Tob 7:2, 8). She welcomes the angel Raphael and Tobias, the son of Tobit, into her home (7:3-5), and later welcomes Tobias as her son (10:13) as he marries her daughter Sarah.

EDOM, EDOMITES Edom is first a geographical term, referring to the reddish-brown hills of southern Transjordan, east of the Arabah rift that runs from the southern end of the Dead Sea to the Gulf of Aqaba. The region is mountainous and semiarid, with a tribal-based pastoralism as its economic base.

EDREI 1. Major town of BASHAN (Num 21:33; Deut 1:4; 3:1, 10; Josh 12:4; 13:12, 31). In the OT, the Amorite king OG met defeat against Moses and the Israelites at Edrei, identfied with modern Der⊠a, Syria, near the Yarmuk, a major tributary of the Jordan River.

2. Town mentioned in the allotment of Naphtali (Josh 19:37), linked to a location listed in the military records of Thutmose III.

EGLAH The sixth wife of DAVID and the mother of Ithream (2 Sam 3:5; 1 Chron 3:3).

EGLON 1. A city in the western foothills of Judah. Joshua 10:1-27 tells of a coalition of Amorite kings of Eglon (King DEBIR), Jerusalem, Hebron, Jarmuth, and Lachish, who joined together to attack Gibeon after it had formed an alliance with the Israelites.

2. A king of Moab during the period of the Judges whose name means "little calf."

The judge Ehud killed Eglon, allowing the Israelites to defeat the Moabites (Judg 3:12-30).

EGYPT Egypt was one of the great ancient civilizations. Located along the Nile Valley in northeastern Africa, the land was agriculturally rich and easily defensible. A unified state first emerged in Egypt in the 4th millennium BCE. Egypt became an empire in the 2nd millennium BCE when its territory stretched from Syria to the 4th cataract of the Nile (in modern-day Sudan).

EGYPT, PLAGUES IN See PLAGUES IN EGYPT.

EGYPT, WADI OF The expression occurs in the NRSV as a geographical term for the southern boundary of the Canaanite territory (Num 34:5) and, later, of the tribe of Judah (Josh 15:4, 47; 1 Kgs 8:65; 2 Chron 7:8).

EHI The sixth-listed son of Benjamin (Gen 46:21). Ehi and the three names that follow should perhaps be read Ahiram, Shupham, and Hupham with Num 26:38-39.

EHUD 1. A left-handed Benjaminite who frees Israel from oppression by EGLON, king of Moab (Judg 3:15-30).

2. An individual listed in the genealogy of the tribe of Benjamin as the son of Bilhan and great-grandson of Benjamin (1 Chron 7:10).

EKER One of the children of Ram, the grandchildren of Jerahmeel (1 Chron 2:27). His name means "offspring," and appears in a genealogical list of Judah's descendants.

EKRON One of the cities of the Philistine pentapolis. According to Josh 19:43 it belonged to the tribal territory of Dan, while Josh 15:11 considers "the border [of Judah to go to] the slope of Ekron on the north." Whereas Josh 13:3 reckons it among the parts of the land unconquered by Joshua, Judg 1:18 claims it was conquered by the tribe of Judah. The covenant chest, captured by the Philistines, was brought to Ekron where it caused great suffering (1 Sam 5:10-11). After David's defeat of Goliath, the Israelites "chased the Philistines all the way to Gath and the gates of Ekron" (1 Sam 17:52).

EL In the Bible, El is usually a generic term for God.

EL BERITH A Shechemite temple of El Berith, "god of the covenant," appears once in Hebrew (Judg 9:46) but twice in the LXX (9:46, 50).

EL BETHEL A place-name in Gen 35:7.

EL ELOHE ISRAEL This divine epithet occurs only in Gen 33:20, and means "El, God of Israel," which suggests that El, the supreme deity of the Canaanite pantheon, was regarded as the God of Israel, the northern tribes.

EL ELYON Literally means "God, MOST HIGH" or "El, Most High." This divine epithet is associated with pre-Israelite Jerusalem (Gen 14:18-20; Ps 78:35).

EL OLAM This divine epithet means "El, the eternal God." It occurs only in association with the sanctuary at Beersheba (Gen 21:33).

EL SHADDAI According to Exod 6, God was known as El Shaddai or God Almighty prior to the revelation of the name YAHWEH to Moses (Gen 17:1; 28:3; 35:11; 43:14; Exod 6:3; Ezek 10:5).

ELA Solomon is said to have appointed Ela's son SHIMEI as governor over the district of Benjamin (1 Kgs 4:18).

ELAH 1. One of the eleven clans or chieftains of Esau (Edom) (Gen 36:41; 1 Chron 1:52). Possibly a place-name, equivalent to Elath, used here as a personal name.

2. Site of the David/Goliath battle (1 Sam 17). See ELAH VALLEY.

3. The fourth king of the northern kingdom (ca. 886–885 BCE) (1 Kgs 16:6, 8, 13-14), successor to his father King Baasha.

4. The father of Hoshea, the last king of Israel (2 Kgs 15:30).

5. The second son of Caleb (1 Chron 4:15).

6. A Benjaminite who lived in Jerusalem in the postexilic period (1 Chron 9:8).

ELAH VALLEY The conflict between DAVID and GOLIATH (1 Sam 17) is placed within the Elah Valley, or literally the valley of TEREBINTH (a type of large tree).

ELAM, ELAMITES Elam is the name of several individuals and of a nation.

1. The assumed eponymous ancestor of the nation Elam (Gen 10:22; 1 Chron 1:17).

2. An early Benjaminite (1 Chron 8:24), perhaps to be identified with Elam (3) below.

3. One or two ancestors of a group of returning exiles (Ezra 2:7, 31; 8:7; 10:2; Neh 7:12, 34). Though the text mentions "the other Elam" (Ezra 2:31; Neh 7:34), it gives precisely the same number of returnees from this Elam as from the first (Ezra 2:7; Neh 7:12), possibly suggesting this is the same individual and the same group of returnees.

4. A leader of the people (Neh 10:15).

5. A priest (Neh 12:42).

6. A priestly gatekeeper appointed by David (1 Chron 26:3).

7. Elam, located in the southwestern corner of Iran north of the Persian Gulf, was a major power during the late 3rd millennium through the first half of the 1st millennium BCE, but the area controlled by the Elamites differed considerably from period to period.

ELASA The location in Judea near Beth-horon where JUDAS Maccabeus was killed while leading his forces against the army of Bacchides (1 Macc 9:5).

ELASAH A courier for King Zedekiah, and a member of the powerful scribal family of Shaphan, who took a letter from Jeremiah to the exiles in Babylon (Jer 29:3). The name means "God has made/done" and occurs in a list of the descendants of the family Passhur (Ezra 10:22/1 Esdr 9:22).

ELATH Variant of ELOTH.

ELDAAH One of the grandsons of Abraham and his wife Keturah, through their son Midian (Gen 25:4; 1 Chron 1:33).

ELDAD Eldad and MEDAD, among seventy elders chosen to help relieve Moses' burden of leadership, remained in camp prophesying under the influence of the Spirit while the others were at the meeting tent (Num 11:24-30).

ELDER Elder appears in the OT more than 140 times. In a few passages it merely denotes persons of advanced years (Lev 19:32; Ezek 9:6; Joel 2:16; 2:28), but it more typically designates traditional but unofficial leaders of tribal communities or professional groups. Such individuals acquire knowledge and wisdom through years of experience; consequently, they gain the respect of—and typically exercise tacit authority over—the members of their community or group.

Apart from passages where "elder" refers to older persons (John 8:9; Acts 2:17 [= Joel 2:28 (LXX)]; Heb 11:2, "elders" in the sense of forebears), the elders of the NT fall into three distinct groups: Jewish elders, Christian elders, and the elders of the book of Revelation.

Jewish elders appear in the Gospels when Jesus confronts the Pharisees and legal experts about the "the rules handed down by the elders" (Mark 7:3, 5; Matt 15:2). While the phrase might mean the tradition of one's forebears (see Heb 11:2), it is more likely that "elders" refers to those who enjoyed some authority in shaping the traditions of the people. Luke mentions a delegation of Jewish elders sent to ask Jesus to heal a centurion's slave. Undoubtedly these were not simply older men but well-respected members of the Jewish community.

Ten other references to elders are to Christian elders in Jerusalem. Like their Jewish counterparts, they appear to function as a group or college of elders. Their first appearance is in Acts 11:30: the elders receive the famine relief delivered to Jerusalem by Barnabas and Saul on behalf of the church in Antioch.

The book of Revelation provides a

vision of elders who function rather differently from the elders of the NT's epistolary literature. These crowned elders take part in a heavenly liturgy. Twenty-four in number (Rev 4:4, 10; 5:8; 11:16; 19:4), they are seated on twenty-four thrones around a throne on which sits the one worthy of worship. Casting off their own crowns (Rev 4:10) and falling to the ground, the twenty-four elders worship the one who sits on the throne (Rev 4:10; 11:16; 19:4). Similarly, they fall down and worship the Lamb (Rev 5:8, 14), who stands among them (Rev 5:6). The worship of the elders includes songs of praise and thanks (Rev 4:10-11; 5:8-10; 11:16-18; 19:4). These twenty-four elders are often portrayed alongside the four living creatures (Rev 4:9-10; 5:6, 8, 11, 14; 7:11; 14:3; 19:4). Twice, they are said to be surrounded by angels (Rev 5:11; 7:11).

ELEAD A descendant of Ephraim listed in Joshua's genealogy (1 Chron 7:21).

ELEADAH The name of a descendant of Ephraim (1 Chron 7:20).

ELEALEH A Transjordanian city allotted to the tribe of Reuben (Num 32:3, 37), which appears in conjunction with HESHBON as a Moabite city in Isaiah (15:4; 16:9) and Jeremiah (48:34).

ELEASAH 1. Son of Helez and father of Sismai in the lineage of Jerahmeel (1 Chron 3:39-40). See JERAHMEEL, JERAHMEELITES.

2. Son of Raphah and father of Azel and the 10th generation from King Saul in two genealogical lists of the Benjaminites (1 Chron 8:37; 9:43).

ELEAZAR Eleven men in the OT bear this name: "El (or God) has helped." A similar name is Eliezer, "El (or God) is help."

1. The third of four sons born to Aaron and Elisheba (Exod 6:23).

2. The son of Abinadab who lived at Kiriath-jearim. When the Philistines returned the covenant chest to the Israelites, the people of Kiriath-jearim brought it to Abinadab's house and consecrated Eleazar to take charge of it (1 Sam 7:1-2).

3. The second of King David's three chief warriors (2 Sam 23:9-10; 1 Chron 11:12-14), who earned his rank by fearlessly standing his ground in a battle against the Philistines.

4. A Levite, son of Mahli and grandson to Merari the third son of Levi (1 Chron 23:21-22; 24:28).

5. One of the priests who witnessed the receipt of the treasures of silver and gold, which the exiles who returned with Ezra from Babylon brought with them (Ezra 8:33).

6. One of the Israelites who was found to have married foreign women and to have broken faith with Yahweh, according to an inquest conducted by Ezra (Ezra 10:25).

7. A priest who participated in the dedication of the wall of Jerusalem, rebuilt under Nehemiah's leadership (Neh 12:42).

8. The fourth of five sons of the priest Mattathias (1 Macc 2:5). In a battle near Beth-zechariah, Eleazar died in a heroic exploit to kill an elephant he perceived to be bearing the Seleucid king (1 Macc 6:43-46).

9. The father of Jason. Judas Maccabeus sent this Jason together with Eupolemus to Rome to negotiate an alliance against the Seleucids in 161 BCE (1 Macc 8:17).

10. An aged Judean scribe who chose a martyr's death rather than become polluted by eating pork (2 Macc 6:18-31). The text suggests a setting in 167 BCE when Antiochus IV attempted to compel Jews to abandon the Law and partake in sacrifice of swine. The same story appears again in 4 Macc 5–6, but with much more detail, including extensive speeches by Eleazar.

11. The father of Jesus who collected the proverbs in the book known as

Ecclesiasticus or as the Wisdom of Jesus, Son of Sirach (Sir 50:27).

12. An elderly Jewish priest whose prayer won deliverance for the Jews in Egypt when Ptolemy IV Philopator threatened to massacre them (3 Macc 6).

13. Ezra sent Eliezar and other leaders to find Levites to serve as priests upon the Israelites' return to Jerusalem (1 Esdr 8:43).

14. One of the men compelled to put away his wife during Ezra's expulsion of foreign women and children (1 Esdr 9:19).

ELEVEN, THE Jesus' associates after Judas' defection from the ranks (Matt 28:16; Mark 16:14; Luke 24:9, 33; Acts 1:26).

ELHANAN Meaning "God is gracious."

1. A member of David's mighty men, was noted for slaying a Philistine giant. The accounts (2 Sam 21:19; 1 Chron 20:5) differ regarding the name of the giant (GOLIATH or Goliath's brother) and the name of Elhanan's father (Jaareoregim or Jair).

2. Another of David's mighty men is Elhanan, son of Dodo of Bethlehem (2 Sam 23:24; 1 Chron 11:26). These two Elhanans could be the same.

ELI Eli is the priest at Shiloh who raises Samuel to become priest in the place of his own sons HOPHNI AND PHINEHAS. Yahweh judges the house of Eli inadequate because these two sons treat the offerings made to God with disrespect and lie with the young women who come to work at the entrance to the sanctuary. Eli himself is presented as being unacceptable as a priest because he honors his sons more than God by being unwilling to chastise them for their actions, and he benefits from their behavior regarding the meat for sacrifices (1 Sam 2:29). The judgment on the house of Eli is signaled by the deaths of both sons in a single day, and the death of old Eli when he hears that the Philistines have captured the covenant chest (1 Sam 4:13-15). The Shilonite priesthood is then replaced with Samuel, who lives at Ramah. Eli's line seems to continue in the genealogical structure in 1 Samuel as David flees from Saul. ABIATHAR, who carries the priestly vest for David, is the only survivor when Saul kills the priests at Nob. Abiathar is the son of AHIMELECH, who is the son of AHITUB, called Ichabod's brother in 1 Sam 14:3. ICHABOD is the son of Phinehas, born as his mother hears of the death of her husband (1 Sam 4:21).

ELI, ELI, LAMA SABACHTHANI In Matt 27:46 and Mark 15:34, Jesus' last words from the cross. Both versions can be rendered as "My God, my God, why have you left me?" Both are Greek transliterations of the first four words of Ps 22, but in Aramaic—the language Jesus spoke—rather than in Hebrew, the language in which Ps 22 was written. Matthew changed Mark's word for "my God" to one that sounded more like "Elijah" (Matt 27:47-49).

ELIAB 1. A leader of the tribe of Zebulun during the census of Moses and dedicatory offerings during the exodus (Num 1:9; 2:7; 7:24, 29; 10:16).

2. Father of Dathan and Abiram of the Korah rebellion (Num 16:1, 12; 26:8; Deut 11:6).

3. David's eldest brother (1 Sam 16:6, originally Elihu, 1 Chron 27:18) who fought with Saul against the Philistines and Goliath (1 Sam 17:28).

4. An ancestor of Samuel (1 Chron 6:27).

5. One of David's mighty men (1 Chron 12:9).

6. A Levite musician (1 Chron 15:18).

ELIADA 1. Tenth-listed of eleven sons of David born in Jerusalem (2 Sam 5:16); alternately the twelfth of thirteen sons (1 Chron 3:8). A parallel list reads Beeliada ("Baal knows" or "the lord knows"; 14:7), perhaps reflecting his original name.

2. Father of King REZON of Damascus (1 Kgs 11:23).

3. A Benjaminite commander of a large force of shielded archers serving King JEHOSHAPHAT in Jerusalem (2 Chron 17:17).

ELIADAS One of the descendants of Zomath who was made to divorce his wife during Ezra's expulsion of foreign women and children (1 Esdr 9:28).

ELIAHBA He was a Shaalbonite and the seventeenth-listed warrior among the heroes known as David's "Thirty" (2 Sam 23:32; 1 Chron 11:33).

ELIAKIM 1. Eliakim son of Hilkiah replaced Shebna as the governor or steward of HEZEKIAH's entire house (Isa 22:15-20).

2. The second son of JOSIAH. Upon his father's death at the hands of the Egyptians (ca. 609 BCE), Eliakim became king and was renamed JEHOIAKIM ("The Lord [Yahweh] raises up") by Pharaoh Necco (2 Kgs 23:34).

3. A priest who helped dedicate the wall of Jerusalem rebuilt under Zerubbabel (Neh 12:41).

4. In the NT, the grandson of Zerubbabel and son of Abiud within the ancestry of Jesus (Matt 1:13).

5. The son of Melea within the genealogy of Jesus in Luke 3:30.

ELIAM 1. Bathsheba's father in the report to David (2 Sam 11:3). The Chronicler calls him AMMIEL (1 Chron 3:5).

2. Son of Ahithophel the Gilonite, and one of "the Thirty" warriors in David's army (2 Sam 23:34).

ELIASAPH Means "God has added."

1. From the tribe of Gad, Eliasaph the son of Deuel, or Reuel (Num 1:14; 2:14; 7:42, 47; 10:20), was one of the tribal leaders who assisted Moses in taking a census of the Israelite congregation and led the Gadite offerings in the wilderness (Num 7:42, 47).

2. Eliasaph the son of Lael was a Levite who was head of the ancestral house of the Gershonites (Num 3:24).

ELIASHIB The name of a number of men in the OT, including:

1. A priest who lived during David's reign and received the eleventh lot (1 Chron 24:12).

2. Elioenai's second son, a descendant of King David through Jeconiah (1 Chron 3:24).

3. The high priest who worked with his brothers on the Sheep Gate (Neh 3:1), lived near the Angle (Neh 3:20-21), and fathered Jehohanan, in whose chambers Ezra slept (Ezra 10:6; 1 Esdr 9:1). His provision of space in the temple to Tobiah defiled the temple (Neh 13:4-30).

4. The head of a priestly family who fathered Joaida (Neh 12:10, 22-23).

Three men who sent away their foreign wives and children:

5. A singer (Ezra 10:24; 1 Esdr 9:24).

6. Zattu's son (Ezra 10:27; 1 Esdr 9:28).

7. Bani's son (Ezra 10:36; 1 Esdr 9:34).

ELIASIS One of Bani's descendants indicted by Ezra's council for marrying foreign women (1 Esdr 9:16-44). He does not appear in the parallel text in Ezra 10:34-37.

ELIATHAH One of the sons of Heman, a seer of King David (1 Chron 25:4, 27).

ELIDAD A Benjaminite, the son of CHISLON, to whom the Lord gave the responsibility of representing the interests of Benjamin in the allotment of land west of the Jordan (Num 34:21). Overseeing the ten men appointed to divide the land among the Israelite tribes after the conquest were JOSHUA and the priest ELEAZAR (Num 34:17).

ELIEHOENAI Means "My eyes are toward Yahu."

1. A temple gatekeeper and last-listed of seven sons of Meshelemiah the Korahite, whose allotted duties would assign Eliehoenai to the East Gate (1 Chron 26:1-3, 12-14).

2. Son of Zerahiah, a descendant of Pahath-moab and leader of an extended family returning from the exile with Ezra (Ezra 8:4; compare 1 Esdr 8:31). Eliehoenai's family is among the largest recounted in Ezra 8:1-14.

ELIEL 1. A leader within the half-tribe of Manasseh that settled east of the Jordan (1 Chron 5:24). See MANASSEH, MANASSITES.

2. Three of David's mighty men (1 Chron 11:46, 47; 12:11), although the Eliel of 12:11 may be one of the two mentioned in 11:46-47.

3. A member of the cultic musicians known as the Kohathites following the line of Elkanah and Samuel (1 Chron 6:34, possibly the ELIAB of 1 Chron 6:27).

4. Two chiefs of the tribe of Benjamin (1 Chron 8:20, 22).

5. A Levite from Hebron associated with the transfer of the covenant chest to Jerusalem (1 Chron 15:9, 11).

6. A Levite during the time of HEZEKIAH (2 Chron 31:13).

ELIENAI One of Shimei's sons whose name appears in a Benjaminite genealogy listing chiefs of clans dwelling in Jerusalem (1 Chron 8:20).

ELIEZER Means "God is help."

1. Abraham's servant, originally a resident of Damascus. Since Sarah had borne no children, Abraham assumed that Eliezer would become his heir (Gen 15:2).

2. Moses and Zipporah's second son. His name "Eliezer" recalled that God had helped Moses and the Israelites by delivering them from Pharaoh's sword (Exod 18:4; 1 Chron 23:15, 17; 26:25).

3. Becher's third son and one of Benjamin's grandsons (1 Chron 7:8).

4. A priest who played the trumpet during the celebration when the covenant chest was brought to Jerusalem (1 Chron 15:24).

5. The chief officer of the Reubenites and Zichri's son (1 Chron 27:16).

6. A prophet who foretold that Jehoshaphat's ships would be destroyed because he had allied with King Ahaziah (2 Chron 20:37).

7. A Levite priest who had been sent to Iddo (Ezra 8:16).

8. A descendant of Jeshua who sent away his foreign wife according to Ezra's instructions (Ezra 10:18).

9. A Levite who sent away his foreign wife (Ezra 10:23).

10. Harim's descendant who sent away his foreign wife and their children (Ezra 10:31).

11. An ancestor who linked Jesus with David (Luke 3:29).

ELIHOREPH One of the two sons of Shisha who served as SCRIBE to King SOLOMON (1 Kgs 4:3). The other was AHIJAH.

ELIHU 1. SAMUEL's great-grandfather (1 Sam 1:1), called ELIAB in 1 Chron 6:12 and ELIEL in 1 Chr 6:19.

2. One of the "leaders of units of a thousand" from Manasseh who joined DAVID during his flight from Saul (1 Chron 12:20).

3. A brother of David (1 Chron 27:18).

4. A Korahite who served as gatekeeper (1 Chron 26:7).

5. A man who responds to Job after ELIPHAZ, BILDAD, and ZOPHAR have finished their speeches in Job 32–37.

ELIJAH 1. Elijah was an agent ("prophet") of the Lord who lived during the dynasty of OMRI in the 9th cent. BCE and performed awesome and, at times, outrageous deeds (1 Kgs 17–19; 2 Kgs 1–2). These deeds verified that Elijah spoke for God and so authenticated the main theme of his story: sanction for toppling the Omride dynasty.

2. A descendant of Benjamin in 1 Chron 8:27. He is listed as a son of JEROHAM, but there is no indication of how Jeroham is descended from Benjamin. The genealogy in this section contains a number of family groupings assigned to Benjamin, but their relation to each other is unclear. See BENJAMIN, BENJAMINITES.

3. A priest in the line of HARIM in the postexilic period (Ezra 10:21). He is listed among those who took foreign wives, a practice decried by Ezra (Ezra 10:1-5).

4. A nonpriestly member of the postexilic community who had taken a foreign wife (Ezra 10:26).

ELIKA Elika of Harod is one of David's "Thirty" warriors (2 Sam 23:25).

ELIM A site on the exodus journey (Exod 15:27; 16:1; Num 33:9-10), Elim is, apparently, an oasis, located near or on the shore of the Reed Sea.

ELIMELECH Husband of Naomi and father of two sons, Mahlon and Chilion (Ruth 1:2). Elimelech's death leaves Naomi and her daughter-in-law RUTH to return to his homeland and family for protection (Ruth 1:22). Boaz, one of Elimelech's kin, marries Ruth (Ruth 4:1-13).

ELIOENAI Name designating six men.

1. Neariah's son, living after the exile and descending from David through Jehoiakim (1 Chron 3:23-24).

2. Leader of a clan whose members increased in numbers; settled near Gedor during Hezekiah's reign after conquering the inhabitants; and descended from Simeon, Jacob's second son borne by Leah (1 Chron 4:36).

3. One of Becher's sons who was a family head, a warrior, and a descendant of Benjamin, Jacob's second son borne by Rachel (1 Chron 7:8). His name suggests a date for the genealogy during Hezekiah's reign.

4. Priest who descended from Pashhur and dismissed his foreign wife according to Ezra's instructions (Ezra 10:22; 1 Esdr 9:22).

5. Descendant of Zattu who dismissed his foreign wife and their children (Ezra 10:27), but named Eliadas in 1 Esdr 9:28.

6. Postexilic priest who played the trumpet for dedicating the Jerusalem wall (Neh 12:41).

ELIPHAL Son of Ur and one of David's warriors (1 Chron 11:35). In the parallel text in 2 Sam 23:23-39, where these warriors are known as "the Thirty," his name is ELIPHELET, and he is identified as Ahasbai's son from the town of Maacah (v. 34).

ELIPHAZ 1. The oldest son of ADAH and Esau, who was father of several clans in Edom (Gen 36:4, 10). Genesis 36:12 lists Eliphaz as the father of Amalek, the eponymous ancestor of the Amalekites.

2. One of Job's three friends who argue with him concerning the reasons for his suffering and whether God is just. Eliphaz is always listed first among the three friends, is the first to speak to Job in each of the three cycles (Job 4; 15; and 22), and is the only one of the three friends whom God addresses directly (Job 42:7). He is called Eliphaz the Temanite, which connects him with the area of Edom.

ELIPHELEHU One of the Levites of second rank installed as singers by the Levite officers under David's order when David was about to undertake his second attempt to bring the covenant chest to Jerusalem (1 Chron 15:18). His assigned instrument was the lyre (1 Chron 15:21).

ELIPHELET 1. David's son born in Jerusalem by an unnamed secondary wife or wife (2 Sam 5:16; 1 Chron 3:6; 2 Chron 14:7).

2. Ahasbai's son, one of David's

warriors called "the Thirty" (2 Sam 23:34).

3. Eshek's third son who descended from Saul and Jonathan, both descendants of Benjamin (1 Chron 8:39).

4. A descendant of Adonikam who camped near Ahara (Ezra 8:13; see 1 Esdr 8:39-41 where the place differs).

5. One of Hashum's descendants who sent away his foreign wife and their children (Ezra 10:33; see 1 Esdr 9:33 where the father is Asom).

ELISHA Elisha was a legendary wonder-worker of the 9th cent. BCE (1 Kgs 19:16-21; 2 Kgs 2:1–10:27; 13:14-21). Elisha succeeded Elijah, and their stories in the Bible were shaped together, to support Jehu's usurpation of the Omride dynasty and founding of the longest-lasting dynasty in Israel, the house of Jehu or Nimshi (2 Kgs 9:2; see ELIJAH). As with Elijah, most of the tales about Elisha show him dealing with either kings or indigent folk; two linked episodes involve a well-regarded woman of Shunem, and her tale too begins and ends with reference to the king (2 Kgs 4:8-37; 8:1-6). Elisha was an Israelite, but his dealings with kings went well beyond political Israel to include Moab, Edom, and Syria.

ELISHAH 1. The name Elishah is found in the Table of Nations list as a descendant of Japtheth (Gen 10:4) and elsewhere as the son of Javan (1 Chron 1:7).

2. The place Elishah is referred to as a source for acquiring purple dyes (Ezek 27:7).

ELISHAMA 1. Ammihud's son and an Ephraimite chief whose tribe camped on the west side of the meeting tent (Num 1:10; 2:18; 10:22; 1 Chron 7:26).

2. One of David's sons born in Jerusalem (2 Sam 5:16; 1 Chron 3:6, 8; 14:7).

3. Jehoiakim's chief adviser who kept Jeremiah's scroll in his chamber (Jer 36:12, 20-21).

4. Ishmael's grandfather and a part of the royal family (2 Kgs 25:25; Jer 41:1).

5. Jekamiah's son and a descendant of Judah (1 Chron 2:41).

6. A priest who taught the people of Judah from the Lord's Instruction scroll (2 Chron 17:8).

ELISHAPHAT One of five commanders who conspired with the priest JEHOIADA against ATHALIAH, attempting to return Davidic kingship under JOASH (2 Chron 23:1).

ELISHEBA Aaron's wife, with whom she has four sons (Exod 6:23). Elisheba was the sister of Nahshon and daughter of Amminadab, the ancestral head of Judah whose name appears in Num 2:3.

ELISHUA One of David's children born in Jerusalem (2 Sam 5:15; 1 Chron 14:5).

ELIUD Mentioned in Matthew's Jesus genealogy (Matt 1:14-15), son of Achim and father of Eleazar.

ELIZABETH According to the first chapter of Luke, Elizabeth was the wife of the priest Zechariah and the mother of John the Baptist. She is a relative (perhaps a cousin) of Mary, the mother of Jesus.

ELIZAPHAN 1. Uzziel's son, a Levite and head of the Kohathite clan who had sanctuary duties and camped on the southern side of the meeting tent (Num 3:30). His son Shemaiah, along with his kinsman, carried the COVENANT CHEST to Jerusalem (1 Chron 15:8) and cleansed the temple under Hezekiah's reign (2 Chron 29:13). His name is Elzaphan in Exod 6:22 and Lev 10:4.

2. The son of Parnach and chief of the Zebulunite tribe (Num 34:25-29), whom the Lord told Moses to choose to divide the land among his tribe.

ELIZUR This Reubenite chief or PRINCE (Num 2:10) engages in military activities such as counting the people or leading large movements of people (Num 1:5; 10:18) and presents offerings at the meeting tent on behalf of his tribe (Num 7:30, 35).

ELKANAH 1. Jeroham's son, an Ephraimite from Ramah in 1 Sam 1:1 but a Levite in 1 Chron 6:27, 34, with two wives: Hannah, who bore him the prophet Samuel; and Peninniah, who bore him several children (1 Sam 1:2, 20).

2. A Levite descended from Kohath son of Assir (1 Chron 6:23).

3. Another Kohathite Levite, the son of Ahimoth (1 Chron 6:26).

4. Kohar's second son, descended from Levi through Kohath (Exod 6:24).

5. Two ancestors of Elkanah father of Samuel with the same name (1 Chron 6:35-36).

6. A Levite who was Asa's father and lived in a Netophathite village (1 Chron 9:16).

7. A warrior among "the Thirty" (1 Chron 12:6).

8. A Levite, a gatekeeper for the covenant chest (1 Chron 15:23).

9. King Ahaz's chief minister, whom Zichri killed (2 Chron 28:7).

ELKOSH Although other explanations have been offered, the Nah 1:1 expression, "Nahum, the Elkoshite," suggests that Elkosh was the birthplace of Nahum the OT prophet.

ELLASAR The territory ruled by ARIOCH, one of the four kings against whom the rulers of Sodom and Gomorrah revolt (only in Gen 14:1, 9).

ELMADAM Elmadam links Joseph, "adoptive" father of Jesus, to Adam (Luke 3:28).

ELNAAM Means "God is pleasantness." Father of Jeribai and Joshaviah (1 Chron 11:46), two of David's sixteen heroes whom the Chronicler lists beyond David's "Thirty" (1 Chron 11:46).

ELNATHAN 1. Elnathan was the father of Neshushta and grandfather of her son Jehoiachin (2 Kgs 24:8).

2. Possibly the same as the Elnathan in 2 Kings, an Elnathan was involved in two important incidents during the time of JEREMIAH. He was present at Baruch's reading of Jeremiah's scroll to JEHOIAKIM (Jer 36:12). He also led a group to Egypt to extract the prophet Uriah and then violently killed him by order of Jehoiakim (Jer 26:22-23).

3. The exilic return in Ezra reveals two "chiefs" and one "teacher" (person with insight) named Elnathan returning to Jerusalem from the river Ahava (Ezra 8:16).

ELOHIM The most common Hebrew term for "God/god." As a plural form it may also be used for "gods," hence also idols. See GOD, NAMES OF.

ELON 1. The Hittite (or Hivite, LXX[A]) father of one of Esau's wives (Gen 26:34, although the name of the daughter is different in 36:2).

2. A son of Zebulun in the Genesis list (46:14; Num 26:26).

3. An Israelite judge from Zebulun who led for ten years before his burial at AIJALON (Judg 12:11-12). Elon and Aijalon are spelled similarly in Hebrew and the story may explain the origin of the city's name (etiology).

4. A town in the tribal territory of Dan near Timnah, currently unidentified (Josh 19:43).

ELON-BETH-HANAN A city in Solomon's second administrative region (1 Kgs 4:9); the district corresponds approximately to the traditional allotment given to the tribe of Dan (Josh 19:40-48).

ELON-BEZAANANNIM An oak located near Kedesh where the Kenites camped (Judg 4:11).

ELON-MEONENIM A tree near Shechem associated with divination

(Judg 9:37). Some have equated it with the tree of v. 9.

ELOTH Eloth is located at the northern tip of the Gulf of Aqba. It was an important port city providing access for Judah to sea routes leading to Africa, the Arabian Peninsula, and India (1 Kgs 9:26; 2 Chron 8:17; and 2 Chron 26:2).

ELPAAL One of the two sons of Shaharaim by Hushim in Moab (1 Chron 8:11), listed among the descendants of Benjamin.

EL-PARAN A Horite city that marked the southern extent of the Elamite king CHEDORLAOMER's campaign (Gen 14:6).

EL-QUBEIBEH A modern village that is perhaps the location of the NT EMMAUS (Luke 24:13), El-Qubeibeh is located due west of Nebi Samwil and 7 mi. northwest of Jerusalem.

EL ROI The name by which HAGAR identifies the divine presence in an angel (Gen 16:13). Part of an etiology explaining the name of a well, "El roi" also connotes Hagar's surprise at experiencing benevolent attention rather than death in her divine encounter (vv. 13-14).

ELTEKEH A city within the original tribal area of Dan in the coastal region (Josh 19:44). Dan lost this land during the period of the judges and was forced to move to the north (Judg 1:34). The city was assigned to the Kohathites as a Levitical city (Josh 21:23).

ELTEKON A town in the highlands belonging to the tribe of Judah in Josh 15:59.

ELTOLAD Eltolad is contained in a list of settlements of the tribe of Simeon (Josh 15:30), but also in a list of Judahite settlements (Josh 19:4).

ELUL The sixth month of the Israelite religious calendar (August–September), characterized by high temperatures and no rain (Neh 6:15; 1 Macc 14:27).

ELUSA A city in the arid southern plain located about 20 km (12.4 mi.) southwest of Beer-sheba (M.R. 117056), Elusa appears to have been one of the earliest road stations founded by the NABATEANS along the trade route from Arabia to Gaza in the 3rd cent. BCE.

ELUZAI A Benjaminite warrior who abandoned Saul to join DAVID at ZIKLAG (1 Chron 12:5 [Heb. 12:6]).

ELYMAS Elymas, also called Bar-Jesus (Acts 13:4-12), is described by the narrator of Acts as "the sorcerer," serving the Roman proconsul of Cyprus, Sergius Paulus.

ELZABAD 1. Ninth of eleven swift, lionlike, veteran Gadite warriors proficient in pitched combat with spear and shield who joined David at ZIKLAG against Saul (1 Chron 12:11 [12]; LXX reads Eliazer).

2. Fourth-listed son of Shemiah and a gatekeeper in the Jerusalem temple (1 Chron 26:7).

ELZAPHAN Alternate form of ELIZAPHAN (Exod 6:22; Lev 10:4).

EMADABUN One of those appointed to Levitical service in the newly refounded Jerusalem temple (1 Esdr 5:56). The name Jeshua Emadabun serves to differentiate him from another Jeshua mentioned in the same passage.

EMIM, THE An ancient, mythical race of Giants that formerly inhabited Moab (Deut 2:10). Also known as the Rephaim but called Emim (terrors) by the Moabites (Deut 2:11), these giants were as tall as the Anakim. The Emim in Shaveh-kiriathaim were overrun by Chedorlaomer and his allies (Gen 14:5).

EMMANUEL See IMMANUEL.

EMMAUS According to Luke 24:13, CLEOPAS and an unnamed disciple of Jesus met the risen Lord when going to a village called Emmaus. This postresurrection encounter in Luke 24:13-35 contains a summary of Lukan theology.

EMPEROR Caesar Augustus (John 19:12, 15) and Tiberius (Luke 3:1) are both called emperor (from Latin *Caesar*), while Nero is called "His Majesty the emperor" (Acts 25:21, 25).

ENAN AHIRA A leader of the tribe of Naphtali during the wilderness period, Enan Ahira is always identified as the son of Enan (Num 1:15; 2:29; 7:78, 83; 10:27).

EN-DOR The exact location of En-dor is unknown. According to Josh 17:11, En-dor is part of Manasseh's inheritance within or near the borders of Issachar. Manassah was unable to take the city from the Canaanites.

En-dor is the home of the medium who contacts Samuel for Saul (1 Sam 28:3-25).

EN-DOR, MEDIUM IN The necromancer Saul uses the "medium in Endor" to contact the deceased SAMUEL when all the acceptable means of contacting Yahweh fail (1 Sam 28:7-25).

EN-GANNIM 1. Joshua apportioned En-gannim, located northwest of Jerusalem and in the western foothills (the Shephelah), to the tribe of Judah (Josh 15:34).

2. Joshua apportioned a town named En-gannim to the tribe of Issachar (Josh 19:21). According to Josh 21:29, the tribe of Issachar gave En-gannim to the Gershonites, a Levite family.

EN-GEDI En-gedi is the largest oasis on the western shore of the Dead Sea, located about halfway between Masada in the south and Qumran to the north. Joshua 15:62 assigns the oasis to the territory of the tribe of Judah. It was an important source of water for those in the wilderness of Judah, which explains why David took refuge there during his flight from Saul (1 Sam 24:1).

ENGRAVING Incising an image or lettering onto a hard surface such as metal, wood, stone, or precious stone.

ENOCH 1. The first son of CAIN and the father of IRAD. The first city was named after Enoch (Gen 4:17-18).

2. In the seventh generation from Adam through SETH, Enoch was the son of JARED and the father of METHUSELAH (Gen 5:18-21; 1 Chron 1:2-3; Luke 3:37). Although the text pattern in the Gen 5 genealogy says in turn that each patriarch "died," uniquely Enoch "walked with God" (Gen 5:22-24). Later interest in Enoch's nondeath is apparent as when he is cited as an example of faith (Heb 11:5) or of "a changed heart and mind" (Sir 44:16; 49:14). Much as ELIJAH's ascension stirred expectations of his return, the fact that Enoch did not die meant that he was available in the future for use by God (Jude 1:14), giving rise to an abundance of visionary and prophetic Enochic literature, including three books of Enoch.

ENOSH The father of Kenan in the Sethite genealogy of Gen 5:6-11 (also 1 Chron 1:1). The name, like ADAM, means "human being." Enosh is mentioned in Gen 4:26 along with the notice that it was in his time that human beings began to worship Yahweh.

EN-ROGEL A spring just south of JERUSALEM. From the biblical description, the spring lies in the Kidron Valley, just south of the confluence of the Kidron and Hinnom valleys. When David was near death, his son ADONIJAH had himself proclaimed king at the stone of Zoheleth beside En-rogel (1 Kgs 1:9-10).

The spring serves as one of the geographical markers for the boundary between Judah and Benjamin (Josh 15:7; 18:6).

ENROLLMENT A public and official counting, numbering, registering, or listing of people by family, tribe, genealogy, or occupation. Such enrollments occur within various social or political contexts (e.g., membership within kinship groups in kinship-based communities—Gen 46:8-27; royal enlistments by native kings—2 Sam 24:1-9; imperial registrations of populations in vassal states—Luke 2:1-5; Acts 5:37; or enrollments for ritual purposes—Num 7:1-88).

EN-SHEMESH En-shemesh ("Spring of the Sun") lay on the boundary between Judah and Benjamin (Josh 15:7; 18:17).

EPAENETUS A Christian named by Paul in Rom 16:5 as "my dear friend," Epaenetus is depicted as an émigré to Rome and the first Asian Christian convert. It is possible that Epaenetus was converted by Prisca and Aquila in Ephesus and moved with the couple to Rome since they are mentioned prior to Epaenetus (Rom 16:3-5).

EPAPHRAS Paul described his one-time fellow prisoner (Phlm 23) as "Christ's faithful minister of" (Col 1:7); "a slave of Christ Jesus" (Col 4:12); and "the fellow slave we love" (Col 1:7). Epaphras established (Col 1:5-6, 23) and correctly taught the Colossian assembly (Col 2:6) vis-à-vis others who taught unprofitable "human commandments and teaching" (Col 2:22-23). He also reported their progress (Col 1:8); worked throughout the Lycus Valley (Col 4:13); and agonized constantly in prayer for his assembly's maturity (Col 4:12).

EPAPHRODITUS A leader in Paul's assembly at Philippi who was sent by the assembly (Phil 2:25, 30) to take gifts to the imprisoned Paul (Phil 4:18). Presumably the carrier of the letter to the Philippians (cf Phil 2:25, 28), Epaphroditus was also sent back to the assembly to relieve their anxiety about the grave illness from which he had recently recovered (Phil 2:26-28).

EPHAH 1. A dry measure of capacity in the Bible (Judg 6:19; 1 Sam 1:24; 17:17; Ruth 2:17; Zech 5:6-10; etc.). According to Ezekiel (45–46) the ephah and the BATH were equal. The ephah contained ten OMER (Exod 16:36) and was smaller than the HOMER (Hos 3:2). See WEIGHTS AND MEASURES.

2. One of five sons of Midian (Gen 25:4; 1 Chron 1:33), a tribe well known for camel breeding during the period of the divided monarchy and later (Isa 60:6), appearing as a northwestern Arabian tribe in the Assyrian annals.

3. A secondary wife of Caleb (1 Chron 2:46).

4. A son of Jahdai (1 Chron 2:47).

EPHAI A Netophathite whose unnamed sons, among the commanders of Judean forces operating in the countryside following the fall of Jerusalem in 587 BCE, met with the Babylonian-appointed governor GEDALIAH (Jer 40:8). Second Kings 25:23 omits "the sons of Ephai," making Tanhumeth the Netophathite. See NETOPHAH, NETOPHATHITE.

EPHER 1. The second son of Midian and a descendant of Moses' wife KETURAH (Gen 25:4; 1 Chron 1:33) whose name was attached to a clan closely connected to the Midianites. See MIDIAN, MIDIANITES.

2. The third son of EZRA who was also a descendant of the tribe of Judah (1 Chron 4:17).

3. A chief among the "mighty warriors, famous men" of the half-tribe of Manasseh that settled east of the Jordan River (1 Chron 5:24).

EPHESIANS, LETTER TO THE No writing in the NT contains such wide-ranging, profound, and celebratory theology as this relatively short letter. Not surprisingly, it has been deeply influential in the life and thought of the church. Calvin regarded it as his favorite NT book, and Coleridge perhaps gave it the ultimate accolade when he pronounced it "the divinest composition of man." Some NT scholars have hailed it as the "quintessence" and "crown" of Paulinism. Others have been less generous, judging it a distortion of what Paul would have said, written by a later "disciple." No Pauline letter manifests such rhetorical discourse-cohesion as Ephesians. The key theme of cosmic reunification, inaugurated in the believers' union with Christ, dominates the horizon in virtually every section. This involves reinforcing repetition, yet the progress from passage to passage kaleidoscopically focuses some new perspective/outworking with each move.

EPHESUS As the capital of the Roman province of Asia, Ephesus prospered from its strategic location, banking, and commerce. It was situated at the mouth of the Cayster River, near modern Selçuk on the western coast of Turkey. Ephesus's known history begins in the 7th cent. BCE. Paul ministered in Ephesus for some three years (Acts 19:8-10; 20:31) and wrote letters to Corinth from that city.

EPHPHATHA A Greek transliteration of an Aramaic word meaning "open up" (Mark 5:41; 7:31-37).

EPHRAIM, EPHRAIMITES Ephraim is the second son of Joseph and the eponymous ancestor of the Israelite tribe that inhabited the central highlands of Palestine. The tribes of Ephraim and Manasseh, however, traced their descent to grandsons of Jacob who were born to Joseph in Egypt (Gen 41:50; 46:20). The anomaly is resolved through the story of Jacob's blessing of the two sons (Gen 48:1-22), which has been rendered to explain, first, Ephraim and Manasseh's tribal status; second, Ephraim's ascendancy over Manasseh; and third, the legitimacy of the tribes' possession of Shechem.

Ephraim occupied the country situated in the southern region of the central highlands of Israel. The "Ephraimite highlands" constituted a distinct geographical entity within early Israel (e.g., Josh 17:15; Judg 3:27; 4:5; 1 Sam 1:1; 9:4; 2 Chron 13:4). The area is topographically diverse and receives sufficient rainfall, which, along with good soil, created the conditions for an agricultural economy based on herding, raising grains, and cultivating olives.

EPHRAIM FOREST Located in the Transjordanian territory of Gilead, the Ephraim forest apparently stretched northward from the Jabbok, roughly between Manhanaim and Zaphon. It was here that David's generals meted out a disastrous defeat to Absalom's army (2 Sam 18:6-8).

EPHRAIM GATE A Jerusalem gate (2 Kgs 14:13; 2 Chron 25:23; Neh 8:16; 12:39), piercing the northern city wall (thus facing Ephraim) west of the temple courts and perhaps east of the BROAD WALL.

EPHRATHAH, EPHRATHITES 1. A town identified with BETHLEHEM (Gen 35:16, 19; 48:7; Mic 5:2 [Heb. 5:1]; Ruth 4:11; LXX Josh 15:59*a*). Several scholars have argued that Bethlehem, aka Ephrathah, was not identical with Bethlehem of Judah because Jer 31:15 allegedly situates Rachel's burial place, associated in Gen 35:19; 48:7 with both Ephrathah and Bethlehem, near RAMAH in Ephraim.

2. The father of HUR who was called "Bethlehem's father" (1 Chron 4:4).

3. The wife of Caleb, mother of Hur (1 Chron 2:19, 50; 4:4). According to LXX 1 Chron 2:24, Caleb married Ephrathah

after the death of his father HEZRON. See CALEB, CALEBITES.

4. "Ephrathite" is gentilic of Ephrathah in Ruth 1:2, and of Ephraim in Judg 12:5; 1 Sam 17:12; and 1 Kgs 11:26 (where the proper translation is, accordingly, "Ephraimite").

EPHRON 1. Ephron son of Zohar the Hittite; the individual from whom Abraham bought land to bury Sarah. All twelve references to Ephron occur in Gen 23–50 (23:8, 10, 13, 14, 16, 17; 25:9; 49:29, 30; 50:13) and relate to the land transaction.

2. Cited in Josh 15:9; 18:15 as a mountain on the border between Judah and Benjamin, near the Nephtoah Spring—approximately 7 km northwest of Jerusalem.

3. A city taken from Jeroboam by Abijah, according to 2 Chron 13:19.

4. A fortified city in Gilead of the Hellenistic era, according to 1 Macc 5:46 and 2 Macc 12:27.

EPIPHANES The Seleucid ruler ANTIOCHUS IV Epiphanes (175–164 BCE) has become one of the most notorious figures in history. He was possibly one of the most able of the Seleucid rulers; however, circumstances allowed him little room to maneuver. His was not a mission to spread Hellenism to the native peoples, but when Jason offered him a large sum of money to take the office of high priest, Antiochus was happy to accept, a question not of ideology but of valuable resources (see MACCABEES, MACCABEAN REVOLT).

He spent the first five years preparing to extend the Seleucid Empire. Antiochus successfully invaded Egypt in 170 BCE, but during a second invasion in 168, the Romans intervened and forced him to withdraw. When he heard of fighting between JASON's and Menelaus's forces in Jerusalem, he sent an army to put a stop to it, and then, for reasons that are still unclear, he authorized attempts to suppress the practice of Judaism. Thwarted by the power of Rome, Antiochus could do little in the western part of his empire. He began a series of campaigns toward the east, during which he died in late 164 BCE.

EPISTLES, APOCRYPHAL Pseudonymous letters written by or to personalities of biblical times and/or concerned with events or personalities of these times, including several by the Virgin, the Letter of Christ about Sunday, Paul to the Laodiceans, Paul to the Alexandrians, the Correspondence of Paul and Seneca, James to Quadratus, the Ap. Jas., the Letter of Lentulus, several involving Pilate, Pseudo-Titus, possibly the Epistle of the Apostles, and others contained in narrative works (e.g., two in 4 Baruch, the Correspondence of Abgar and Christ, 3 Corinthians in the Acts of Paul, several in the Pseudo-Clementines, etc.).

EPISTLES, CATHOLIC See CATHOLIC EPISTLES.

ER 1. Judah's eldest son by the Canaanitess Shua (or Bath-Shua) (Gen 38:3-7; Num 26:19; 1 Chron 2:3). Er married Tamar (Gen 38:7), but God took Er's life because of Er's unspecified evil deeds.

2. Judah's grandson through Shelah (1 Chron 4:21).

3. A third Er appears in Jesus' genealogy (Luke 3:38), twenty-five generations removed from Judah, through Judah's son Perez.

ERAN A son of SHUTHELAH and grandson of Ephraim whose name may mean "protector" or "watcher," Eran is the eponymous ancestor of the Eranites clan, a subclan of Ephraim (Num 26:36), although he is absent from the corresponding list in 1 Chron 7:20-29.

ERASTUS This name appears three times in the NT (Acts 19:22; Rom 16:23; 2 Tim 4:20), in each case referring to the same associate of Paul. In Rom 16

Paul sends greetings from several persons, among whom is Erastus "the city treasurer."

ERECH Erech is the biblical name of the ancient city of Uruk (modern Warka) on the lower Euphrates River. In Gen 10:10 it is listed, along with Babylon and Akkad, as ruled by the primeval king NIMROD in the land of SHINAR (Babylonia). In Ezra 4:9, it is one of the places from which Ashurbanipal (Osnapper) (668–627 BCE) deported people to Samaria.

ERI Among the seven sons of Gad (Gen 46:16); the eponymous founder of the Erites clan (Num 26:16). See SHUNI, SHUNITES.

ESARHADDON Esarhaddon was king of Assyria from 680 to 669 BCE (2 Kgs 19:37; Ezra 4:2; Isa 37:38).

ESAU, ESAUITES Esau is the brother of Jacob (see JACOB), the son of ISAAC and REBEKAH, ancestor of the people of Edom (see EDOM, EDOMITES). Esau and Jacob experienced significant conflict through most of their lives (Gen 25:21-34; 27; 32–33).

ESDRAS, FIRST BOOK OF The name Esdras is the Greek form of Ezra. The book Esdras A, or 1 Esdras, appears in the SEPTUAGINT just before the book Esdras B. Esdras B is a literal translation of the canonical books Ezra–Nehemiah. Esdras A appears in the Apocrypha, but unlike most books of the Apocrypha it is not included in the Roman Catholic OT. First Esdras overlaps in the gist (but not in every detail) with the end of Chronicles, with part of Nehemiah, and with Ezra.

ESDRAS, SECOND BOOK OF The Second Book of Esdras is a composite book including a pseudonymous Jewish apocalypse (written near the end of the 1st cent. CE), a Christian preface, and a Christian appendix, both added some time later.

ESDRIS A Jewish division leader in the battle against Gorgias mentioned in 2 Macc 12:36.

ESEK The well of springwater dug by Isaac's servants somewhere between Gerar and Beer-sheba (Gen 26:20). The name means "quarrel." According to the biblical account it is so named because of the quarrel over its water rights that occurred between Isaac's servants and the herders of Gerar.

ESHAN A town in the highlands of Judah, somewhere near Hebron, listed among the towns that are the tribal inheritance of Judah (Josh 15:52). This is its only reference, and thus its exact location remains unknown. See HEBRON, HEBRONITES.

ESH-BAAL SAUL's fourth son (1 Chr 8:33; 9:39).

ESHBAN A son of Dishon and grandson of Seir appearing among members of a Horite clan in Edom (Gen 36:26; 1 Chron 1:41). See EDOM, EDOMITES.

ESHCOL An ally of Abram and brother to MAMRE and Aner (Gen 14:13, 24).

ESHCOL, WADI A wadi, or dried out riverbed, near Hebron, that received its name from the extraordinary cluster of grapes the Israelite spies brought from there after having spied out the land of Canaan (Num 13:22-24; 32:9).

ESHEK A Benjaminite descended from Saul who was the father of Ulam, Jeush, and Eliphelet (1 Chron 8:39).

ESHTAOL A city in the Judean low country belonging to the tribe of Dan (Josh 19:41). The Samson narrative is situated in this area where the spirit of the Lord began to stir in Samson (Judg

13:25), and where he was buried (Judg 16:31). Eshtaol is also listed as a place from which the Danite tribe began their campaign to take Laish (Judg 18:2). It was identified as Judahite territory in Judg 15:33.

ESHTEMOA 1. A descendant of Caleb, the son of Ishbah (1 Chron 4:17). See CALEB, CALEBITES.

2. A Maacathite of the tribe of Judah, the son of Hodiah (1 Chron 4:19). See JUDAH, JUDAHITES.

3. One of the cities of refuge assigned to the Levites (Josh 21:14; 1 Chron 6:57 [Heb. 6:42]) located in the mountains of Judah near Hebron.

ESHTON The son of Mehir and father of Bethrapha, Paseah, and Tehinnah in the lineage of Judah (and perhaps Caleb) (1 Chron 4:11-12).

ESLI Father of Nahum and son of Naggai in Luke's genealogy of Jesus (Luke 3:25).

ESTHER An orphan adopted by her cousin Mordecai, Esther appears in the book that bears her name as Mordecai's ward and as one of many virgin girls rounded up as potential replacements for the exiled Queen Vashti. Vashti's crime—refusing to appear before King Ahasuerus—and the unnerved response of the king's advisers (1:16-18) set off the gender dynamics of Esther's rise to the court and her actions there. She is singled out by the eunuch Hegai, in charge of the virgins' harem, apparently for her malleablility (2:9, 15). Mordecai seems to have recommended this strategy of chameleon-like malleability (though he uses no such strategy himself) in instructing her not to reveal her Jewishness to the court (2:10, 20).

Esther's emergence as a character in her own right occurs only as she moves toward the strategic revelation of her ethnicity to Ahasuerus and to Mordecai's (and by extension, the Jews') mortal enemy Haman. Her initial incomprehension to Mordecai's act of public protest (4:4) suggests that in the process of being accepted as a Gentile at the court, Esther has lost touch with the concerns of her people. Interestingly, although the decree that the Jews be annihilated comes from the court, Mordecai hears it outside the King's Gate before Esther, tucked away under the court's wing, knows of it. She has in effect traded her ethnic identity for an intimate knowledge of how to survive at the court itself. In her exchange with Mordecai, he tells her the status of their people and she tells him the laws of entry to the court—each information of which the other was heretofore apparently ignorant (4:7, 11). The drama of Esther's character resides in her risky but successful efforts to regain her hidden Jewishness while maintaining her proximity to power.

ESTHER, ADDITIONS TO Along with the Hebrew (MT) version of Esther there exist two Greek versions of the story in the Septuagint (LXX) and the A Text. Common to these two Greek texts are six blocks of material absent from the Hebrew, commonly termed the Additions and identified by the letters A through F. The Additions were clearly introduced at a later time, and the fact that Hebrew was the original language gives an impression of differing origins for their composition. That this book exhibits such a complicated textual history suggests how significant the Esther story must have been in early Judaism, as various communities reworked and adapted the story for their use. The extra details depict the inner emotions and piety of the characters and portray the events and outcome as under divine direction. As Hebrew Esther does not mention God, the Additions make the Greek versions overtly religious.

Additions A and F describe a prophetic dream. Addition B follows Esth 3:13 and provides a verbatim text of

Haman's edict; similarly Addition E follows Esth 8:12 with Mordecai's counteredict. Lengthy and heartfelt prayers, first of Mordecai and then of Esther, comprise Addition C (following Esth 4:17). Addition D (which replaces Esth 5:1-2) presents a significantly more dramatic version of Esther's entrance before the king. A colophon appended to the LXX version attributes the translation to Lysimachus.

ETA The seventh letter of the Greek alphabet.

ETAM 1. One of the towns in the territory of Simeon (1 Chron 4:32). Its location is unknown.

2. A town mentioned in Josh 15:59*a* of LXX (not in MT) as being in the region of biblical Judah, near Bethlehem.

3. Father of Jezreel, Ishma, and Idbash, among the descendants of Judah (1 Chron 4:3). See ETAM, ROCK AT.

ETAM, ROCK AT After Samson's wife and father-in-law were burned by the Philistines, Samson "struck them, taking their legs right out from under them," and withdrew to "a cave in the rock at ETAM" (Judg 15:8). There too the men of Judah bound him to deliver him to the Philistines (Judg 15:11-13).

ETERNITY An infinite length of time (Deut 32:40; Ps 77:5; Song 3:11; 2 Esdr 8:20).

ETHAM Etham, rarely mentioned in the Bible (Exod 33:20; Num 33:6-8), is identified as the second itinerary site visited by the Israelites; first SUCCOTH, then Etham.

ETHAN 1. A wise man called the Ezrahite and used as a comparison for Solomon's wisdom in 1 Kgs 5:11, and for whom Ps 89 is dedicated (title).

2. The son of Zerah son of Judah and his daughter-in-law Tamar (1 Chron 2:6, 8).

3. An ancestor of Asaph (1 Chron 6:42).

4. A son of Kish (1 Chron 6:44).

ETHBAAL King of TYRE (ca. 887–856 BCE) who obtained kingship around age 36 through a coup d'état. In his time, Tyre was the preeminent Phoenician city, partly through his bringing SIDON under his control. Ethbaal, "Baal is with him," is referred to as the father of JEZEBEL, who married King AHAB of Israel (1 Kgs 16:31).

ETHIOPIA Ethiopia and Ethiopian(s) are terms that occur approximately forty times in the Bible, closely related to the terms CUSH, CUSHITE, a reference to the great nation that flourished between the 1st and 6th cataracts of the Nile, to the south of EGYPT and covering roughly the same territory as the Sudan.

ETHNARCH An official or dependent ruler.

ETHNI The son of Zerah and the father of Malchijah (1 Chron 6:41 [Heb. 6:26]) in the genealogy of Asaph, one of the levitical singers appointed by David who are said to have served in the meeting tent and later in the temple built by Solomon.

EUBULUS Paul's companion (2 Tim 4:21). Eubulus was a common Greek name.

EUCHARIST The term *eucharist* derives from the Greek term that means "thanksgiving." It came to be used in the early church as the primary technical term for its ritual meal of bread and wine. In the NT, however, it was used only in a generic sense, never in a technical sense.

EUNICE Eunice, whose name means "good victory," was the mother of TIMOTHY, one of Paul's closest friends and coworkers. She was from Lystra or Derbe in Galatia and had been converted to faith in Christ from Judaism, although she was apparently married to a Gentile (2 Tim 1:5; Acts 16:1, 3).

EUNUCH Although the term can designate a married royal official (Potiphar [Gen 39:1]), *eunuch* often suggests a castrated figure attending female rulers (Jezebel [2 Kgs 9:30-32], Esther [Esth 4:4-5], Candace [Acts 8:27]) or overseeing the king's harem (Esth 2:14-15). The emasculated condition of eunuchs could include a range of physiological characteristics (defective, damaged, or dismembered testicles and/or penis) resulting from inherited nature ("eunuchs who have been eunuchs from birth"), imposed mutilation ("made eunuchs by other people"—often a casualty of war or slavery), or self infliction (as with ascetics "who have made themselves eunuchs because of the kingdom of heaven") (see Matt 19:12).

While eunuchs could enjoy considerable political and economic influence (Acts 8:27), in ancient societies that placed a high premium on male virility, the eunuch embodied shame, impotence, and social deviance. Biblical law excludes men with damaged genitalia from the worshipping assembly in general (Deut 23:1) and the holy priesthood in particular (Lev 21:17-21).

Other traditions, however, paint a more hopeful picture. Isaiah and the Wisdom of Solomon envision an honored and fruitful place for faithful eunuchs in the Lord's house (Isa 56:3-8; Wis 3:14-15); Jeremiah reports the noble efforts of Ebed-melech, an Ethiopian eunuch serving the king of Judah, to rescue Jeremiah from unjust imprisonment (Jer 38:7-15; 39:15-18); and Acts 8:26-40 recounts the baptism of a Scripture-reading, God-fearing eunuch from Candace's Ethiopian court. In this latter text, the eunuch's prominent status as a chief financial officer is balanced by his apparent identification with the shorn and scorned figure from Isa 53:7-8 and his implied experience of religious ostracism ("What would keep me from being baptized?" [Acts 8:30-36]).

EUODIA Paul urges this Christian woman to agree with fellow believer SYNTYCHE so that they may live in harmony in the church in Philippi (Phil 4:2), continuing the tradition of women leaders in the church in Philippi (compare Acts 16:40). They are included in the group of "coworkers" having previously helped Paul in his evangelistic endeavors (Phil 4:3).

EUPATOR The surname of the Seleucid king ANTIOCHUS V (1 Macc 6:17; 2 Macc 10:10; 13:1).

EUPHRATES RIVER In the Bible, the Euphrates is one of the rivers of paradise (Gen 2:14). It formed the northeastern boundary of territory promised by the Lord to Israel (Gen 15:18, Deut 1:7; 11:24; Josh 1:4) and of the Israelite kingdom at its peak (2 Sam 8:3; 10:16; 1 Kgs 4:24; 1 Chron 18:3). The Euphrates and Egypt were used as idealized boundary markers of the kingdom God gave to Solomon (1 Kgs 3:13; 4:21). It is sometimes known simply as "the River" (Num 22:5) as in the province "Beyond the River" (Ezra 4:10-22; Neh 2:7-9).

EUPOLEMUS A diplomat sent by Judas Maccabeus to establish a relationship with Rome after the defeat of NICANOR (1 Macc 8:17; 2 Macc 4:11).

EUTYCHUS In Acts 20:7-12, a young man who attended an evening meeting between Paul, his missionary associates, and the leaders of the Christian movement in Troas.

EVANGELIST One who is "a preacher of the good news" (2 Tim 4:5). The two biblical uses of the term appear in Pauline-related writings and refer to preaching the gospel of Jesus Christ (Acts 21:8; Eph 4:11).

EVE The name Eve, meaning "life," appears but once in the story of Eden (Gen 2–3), near the end (3:20). At first, God creates one human without sexual differentiation. In time, the Lord God observes that the singularity of the human is not "good" and decides to make him a partner (Gen 2:18-20). God's first attempt to provide the human with a companion fails. God then puts the human to sleep, takes a part from its side, and closes up the place with flesh (Gen 2:21-25). God "builds" the part removed into "woman." The verb suggests considerable labor, but the process remains unknown. With her advent, the sexually undifferentiated human is no more. Instead, from the leftovers of the divine surgery, man the male emerges. Quoting a poem (which varies in details from the narrative), the man recognizes the simultaneity, similarity, and difference of the sexes (Gen 2:23). He uses a formula of mutuality to describe his companion as "bone from my bones and flesh from my flesh" (cf Gen 29:14; 2 Sam 5:1; 19:12).

In the subsequent scene of disobedience (Gen 3:1-7), the woman figures prominently. As spokesperson for the human couple (a departure from the strictures of patriarchy), she replies to the devious question that the serpent asks about God's command not to eat the fruit of a particular tree. To the command she attaches the prohibition "and don't touch it." Thereby she becomes a faithful interpreter of divine law, building around it "a fence" that promotes obedience. She shows intelligence and thoughtfulness as she ponders the wholesome possibilities that the fruit offers: physical nourishment ("delicious food"), aesthetic pleasure ("the tree was beautiful"), and sapiential acquisition ("the tree would provide wisdom"). Without consulting the man, "who was with her," she eats. Then, behaving like a faithful wife, she "gave some" of the fruit to him. (The verb connotes neither trickery nor seduction.) Unlike her, he ponders not at all but simply eats. Throughout the scene the strong, active, and independent role of the woman contrasts with the weak, passive, and acquiescent role of the man.

The contrast continues in a trial, with God questioning the couple (Gen 3:8-19). Though asked only about his disobedience, the man answers by betraying the woman and blaming both her and God. In her answer, the woman does not implicate the man but blames the serpent for beguiling her. God proceeds to describe (not prescribe) the consequences of disobedience. (Contrary to translations, the Hebrew verb forms are not imperatives.) The deity curses the serpent directly and the man indirectly through the ground (Gen 3:14, 17). But never does God curse the woman. The consequences (not commands) for her consist of increased pain in childbirth (a physical sign) and rule by the man (a cultural sign). Neither consequence defines her in creation.

Eve appears once more in the story, identified not by her name but as "his wife" for whom God makes clothes (Gen 3:21). But Eve returns in the next story, about Cain and Abel. Using a conventional expression for sexual intercourse, the narrator says that "the man Adam knew his wife Eve," and "she became pregnant and gave birth to Cain" (Gen 4:1). Her account differs: "I have given [also "made" or "acquired"] life to a man," she says, "with [or together with] the LORD's help." She says nothing about her husband's participation. These extraordinary words, coming in a first-person declaration, conclude Eve's life in the OT.

EVI One of the five kings of Midian killed by the Israelites as an act of the Lord's vengeance for the Midianite influence over the Israelites (Num 31:8; Josh 13:21).

EVIL The concept of evil in the OT is not limited to moral categories, but embraces a much larger concept of misfortune including natural disasters such as plagues and famines, attacks by foreign enemies, and defeat in battle. Because of this disconnect from the moral overtones, biblical authors could ascribe such evil events to God without impugning God's righteousness. God sent evil spirits to people (1 Sam 16:14), brought evil upon a nation (Isa 49:11), and caused the destruction of a city (Jer 21:10). Despite this, many biblical writers avoided ascribing evil to God, proclaiming instead that evil has no place with God (Ps 5:4).

More often, however, evil is considered an attribute of humans, though humans are not considered to be inherently evil. Judges repeatedly reproves the Israelites because they did evil in the sight of the Lord (2:11; 3:7, 12; 4:1; 6:1; 9:23; 10:6; 13:1).

In the NT, evil remains a characteristic of humans, but is never attributed to God (Jas 1:13). Evil comes from within a person, not only because of actions but also because of humanity's fallen condition (Matt 15:19; Rom 7:14-25). For Paul especially, we must be saved from our evil nature (Rom 1:28-32). Because of the new life they have been granted in Christ, Christians are to turn away from evil and pursue good (Heb 5:14; 1 Pet 3:11; 3 John 11) because their evil deeds will be judged at the end of time (2 Cor 5:10). See SIN, SINNERS.

EVIL ONE, THE A NT and early Christian term equivalent to "the devil" or "Satan."

EVIL SPIRIT See DEMON.

EXILE The biblical exilic period begins with the Babylonian deportations of Judahites in the early years of the 6th cent. BCE. While Assyria, beginning with Tiglath-pileser III (745–727 BCE), had deported many people from the northern kingdom in the 8th cent., including 27,290 from Samaria alone according to the claims of Sargon II, those exiles disappeared from history. The Judean exile, by way of contrast, played a profound role in shaping the literature and theology of the OT, and those who returned from exile exerted primary leadership in the postexilic community.

EXODUS, BOOK OF The book of Exodus tells the story of the origins of the people of Israel through the power of God: how God heard their cry as slaves in Egypt; made Godself known to them through Moses, God's appointed leader; freed them; revealed the law to them; made a covenant with them; and, in spite of their apostasy, came to dwell among them. Exodus is the second of the first five books of the Bible, the Pentateuch. The common Hebrew term for this collection is the Torah, "law, instruction." As part of Torah, Exodus is not simply a story about the past but is intended to provide a pattern and a guide for all time.

EXODUS, ROUTE OF The exodus from EGYPT is a topic around which whirl controversy, debate, and heated argument. There is no consensus regarding the date of the Israelite slavery, nor its nature, nor even its historicity. The route of the Israelite journey is also called into question in many circles. It is an area where archaeological interpretation and biblical narrative collide.

EXORCISM The supernatural expulsion of harmful spirits or demons from afflicted (possessed) persons or places. In the ANE, evil spirits were widely regarded as principal causes for physical and psychological maladies, as well as natural and environmental disasters. To ameliorate these calamities, certain sacerdotal officials and charismatic figures functioned as exorcists, invoking divine power against malignant forces through various magical incantations and demonstrations. Other exorcising techniques appear in biblical (and related) literature associated with David, Solomon, Tobias, Jesus, and Paul.

EYE Most frequently "eye" refers to the physical organ. David's eyes were "beautiful" (1 Sam 16:12), while Leah's eyes were "delicate" (Gen 29:17; or "tender, weak"). Warfare often resulted in the defeated enemy's eyes being gouged out (Judg 16:21; 2 Kgs 25:7; Jer 39:7). Loss of the right eye made one militarily worthless (1 Sam 11:2).

Eyes reveal arrogance (Prov 6:17), pity (Ezek 16:5), scorn (Prov 30:17), and respect (Ps 123:2). Bright eyes are signs of "shalom," health and well-being (Ps 38:10 [Heb. 38:11]), while dim eyes reveal ill health and age (Deut 28:65; Job 17:7; Ps 69:3 [Heb. 4]). Eyes are the portals for greed (1 Sam 2:29, 32) and lust (Ps 73:7 [Heb. 73:8]; Prov 17:24; 27:20; 2 Pet 2:14; 1 John 2:16). Open or lifted eyes symbolize alertness (Gen 13:10, 14; 18:2), while closed eyes represent lack of concern (Prov 28:27; Matt 13:15). The eyes produce tears (Ps 119:136).

Spiritual perception and comprehension are increased when the eyes are opened through God's Instruction (Ps 119:18) or by the Holy Spirit (Eph 1:18). John relates "seeing" to "believing" (John 1:50).

EZBAI Ezbai was father of Naarai, one of David's mighty warriors (1 Chron 11:37). See WARRIORS.

EZBON 1. One of Gad's seven sons (Gen 46:16); supplanted by OZNI in Num 26:16.

2. A son of Bela and grandson of Benjamin (1 Chron 7:7), although this list may be Zebulun's genealogy, given the different Benjaminite list in 1 Chron 8 and the Chronicler's omission of Zebulun otherwise.

EZEKIEL, BOOK OF The third book of the major prophets and attributed to the priest Ezekiel, son of Buzi, one of the Judeans deported to Babylonia in 597 BCE.

EZEM A town in the territorial allotment to Simeon in Josh 19:3. First Chronicles 4:29 also lists it as a Simeonite town. Simeonite territory lay entirely within the territory of Judah, and Josh 15:29 lists Ezem among Judahite towns. Its precise geographical location is unknown.

EZER Six men carry the name Ezer:

1. Sixth son of Seir and a Horite chief whose name may represent a clan who lived in Edom (Gen 36:21, 27, 30; 1 Chron 1:38-42).

2. Etam's son who founded the town Hushbah (1 Chron 4:4).

3. Ephraim's son whom the Gittites killed when he attempted to steal their cattle (1 Chron 7:21).

4. A Gadite chief who joined David's warriors at Ziglag (1 Chron 12:9).

5. Son of Jeshua, the ruler of Mizpah, and a repairman of a section of the Jerusalem wall (Neh 3:19).

6. A priest who celebrated the dedication of the rebuilt Jerusalem wall (Neh 12:42).

EZION-GEBER Ezion-geber is cited seven times in the Bible (Num 33:35, 36; Deut 2:8; 1 Kgs 9:26; 22:48 [Heb. 22:49]; 2 Chr 8:17; 20:36) and is believed to have been a port city located on the north shore of the present-day Gulf of Aqaba.

EZORA The leader of a family that heeds Ezra's call to banish non-Israelite wives and children (1 Esdr 9:34; absent in the parallel version, Ezra 10:39-40).

EZRA The story of Ezra is told in a first-person account (Ezra 7:27–8:34; 9:1-15) and a third-person account (Ezra 7:1-11; 8:35-36; 10:1-44; Neh 7:73*b*–8:18 [possibly also 9:1-5). Ezra is called a priest and a scribe of the Instruction from the God of heaven (Ezra 7:12). Despite the genealogy connecting him to the high priestly line in Ezra 7:1-5, he was not a high priest. As a scribe he was no doubt an expert in the Instruction, but some have seen in this title an indication that he was a commissioner for Jewish affairs in the Persian government.

Ezra came to Jerusalem at the direction of the Persian king Artaxerxes and in his seventh year (458 BCE if this was Artaxerxes I; 398 BCE if it was Artaxerxes II).

EZRA AND NEHEMIAH, BOOKS OF Ezra and Nehemiah were originally considered one book, under the name of Ezra. In the Greek tradition they were considered two books as early as the 3rd cent. CE. The division into two books does not appear in Hebrew manuscripts until the 15th cent. CE. These books are about the restoration of Judea after the Babylonian captivity of 597-535 BCE.

EZRAHITE Ethan the Ezrahite and his brother Heman are identified as men of wisdom and composers of songs (1 Kgs 4:31 [Heb. 5:11]; titles of Pss 88; 89).

EZRI The son of Chelub and the agricultural official in charge of fieldworkers, Ezri is listed among officers in David's bureaucracy (1 Chron 27:26).

Ff

FABLE A fable is a genre of narrative literature usually involving animals or inanimate objects who possess or exhibit human traits and interests, such as speaking and reasoning. In the OT the story of Balaam's talking donkey (Num 22:21-35) illustrates the longest example of a fable. In Judg 9:7-15 a conversation between three noble trees and a useless bramble illustrates Jotham's negative attitude toward Abimelech's kingship.

FAIR HAVENS The author of Acts is the only ancient writer to mention Fair Havens, on the southernmost tip of the island of Crete and near ancient Lasea, 12 mi. east of Matala. Paul's Rome-bound transport stopped at this bay, made up of four or five small harbors, for protection from unfavorable winds (Acts 27:8).

FAITH, FAITHFULNESS Faith and faithfulness are concepts related to both God and humans. The basic idea in the OT was "constancy" (of things) and "reliability" (of persons); thus, "that on which others can rely." From "stability" through "reliability," the concept acquires the meaning of "truth," as well as conveys more the idea of "conduct that grows out of reliability." The basic range of the term in the NT is from the sense of subjective confidence in someone/something else, to the objective basis for such confidence.

FALL, THE The identification of the story of ADAM and EVE as an account of "the fall" in Western civilization is largely due to the influence of Paul and the way he was interpreted by Augustine. In Judaism, the story of the garden of Eden does not carry quite the same weight. Nevertheless, it is clear from the final canonical form of Israel's scriptures that the stories of human rebellion in Gen 1–11 constitute the background against which God's election of Abraham (and eventually that of Israel) takes place.

FALSE APOSTLES "False apostles" and "super-apostles" are the derogatory terms Paul uses to characterize his rival missionaries in Corinth (2 Cor 11:5, 13; 12:11).

FAMINE The OT offers vivid descriptions of the suffering people experience when the food bins run dry (e.g., Joel 1–2; Lam 2:11-12; 4:3-4). In a subsistence society with limited food supplies, events such as drought, locusts, fire, and enemy invasions could be responsible for wide-ranging famine.

FARMER One who cultivates crops or breeds and raises livestock (e.g., Isa 28:24-28).

FAST, FASTING Fasting refers to a practice common in ancient Israel and postbiblical Judaism to abstain from nourishment, usually over the course of a day. In the Bible, it generally serves as a form of mourning and indicates that the individual or community is in some state of distress.

FATHER The concept of "father" in the Bible includes not only the immediate male ancestor but also more-distant ancestors. In a metaphorical sense, *father* may refer to a founder or an authority figure. Analogically, the term is applied to God, esp. in the contexts of creation and covenant.

FATHER IN HEAVEN Matthew's Jesus calls God "my [or your] Father in heaven" or "who is in heaven" twelve times (Matt 5:16, 45; 6:1, 9; 7:21; 10:32-33; 12:50; 16:17; 18:10, 14, 19); Mark's Jesus once (Mark 11:25). "Father" is a common address to God in Jewish prayers of the period (Tob 13:4; Sir 51:10*a*; 3 Macc 6:2-3; 4Q372). "In heaven" locates God as creator and ruler of the universe.

FATHER'S HOUSE In the OT, the phrase designates the smallest familial unit, a kinship designation below both tribe and clan and headed by a patriarchal figure (Gen 12:1). It occurs in the plural in census lists (e.g., Num 1:2; Ezra 2:59). In the NT, the most common referent for Father's house is the temple in Jerusalem (John 2:16; Luke 2:49).

FATLING As the choicest animal among bovines, it was raised for its use as a sacrifice (2 Sam. 6:13) or for a special celebration and therefore well fed.

FATTENED Livestock whose value for sacrifice was increased because fullness was associated with wealth and well-being. "Fattened" may be applied to a wide variety of sacrificial animals, including fowl (1 Kgs 4:23), calves (1 Kgs 1:25), and oxen ("plump" [Prov 15:17]). See SACRIFICES AND OFFERINGS.

FEAR Fear in the Bible ranges from everyday frights to terror for one's life; from fear of immediate, specific dangers to dread of unknown harm or evil. Most prominent, however, is the biblical conception of fear as a religious disposition, reflected in the expressions "fear of God" and "fear of the Lord." This complex field of meaning includes the seemingly contradictory responses of, on the one hand, dread before divine holiness, power, and mystery; and, on the other, a reverential awe that trusts in God's graciousness. Pious fear, or reverence, inspires grateful worship, ethical obedience, and the pursuit of wisdom.

FEAST OF DEDICATION Commonly known by its Hebrew designation Hanukkah, this festival may be referred to in the title of Ps 30, "A song for the temple dedication." This title may reflect the practice of singing that psalm in the second temple during Hanukkah, which begins on the 25th day of Kislev (November–December). The festival was inaugurated by Judas Maccabee in 165 BCE (1 Macc 4:36-51; 2 Macc 10:5-8) at the rededication to God of the temple on Mount Moriah.

FEAST OF WEEKS See WEEKS, FEAST OR FESTIVAL OF.

FEAST OR FESTIVAL OF BOOTHS See BOOTHS, FEAST OR FESTIVAL OF.

FEASTS AND FASTS Both feasts (festivals) and fasts were occasions for religious rites in response to events, whether favorable or unfavorable. While there were spontaneous times for celebration and grief, there were also set times for communal observances. RECONCILIATION DAY falls into both categories in that it is termed a festival as well as a fast.

Pilgrimage festivals were times when males were to appear before God at the sanctuary with an offering (Exod 23:14-17; 34:18, 22-23; Deut 16:1-17). The first of the pilgrimage holidays is the "Festival of Unleavened Bread." The second is the "Harvest Festival" or "Festival of Weeks." The third is the "Gathering Festival" or "Festival of Booths" at the last harvest.

A second category of lists, commonly attributed to priestly sources, finds expression in Lev 23 and Num 28–29. The two provide fuller enumerations that also incorporate the three pilgrimage festivals of the shorter summaries; they also date most of the festivals to specific times. They use a system of numbered, not named, months, with the sequence beginning in the spring. Later traditions added other feasts, but the basic ones endured into NT times and beyond.

Two kinds of communal fasts are connected with specific dates. The first is Reconciliation Day, which became associated with fasting. The only other dated fasts figure in the book of Zechariah. Zechariah 7:3, 5; 8:19 mention a fast in the fifth month, the month in which Babylonians destroyed Jerusalem and the temple in 587/586 BCE (2 Kgs 25:8); and Zech 8:19 makes reference to other fasts in the fourth, seventh, and tenth months.

FELIX Roman procurator of Judea, from 52 to 59/60 CE, who tried Paul in Caesarea (Acts 24).

FESTAL GARMENT Festive occasions required the use of one's best clothes. The quality of garments was determined by the type of fabric, excellence of the dye (for wool), and brilliance (especially for linen). Abundance and ability to change one's clothes also denoted power and festive quality. This was ideally a change of the customary wool mantle and tunic.

FESTIVALS See FEASTS AND FASTS.

FESTUS, PORCIUS Roman procurator of Judea from 59 to 62 CE, and the judge who sent Paul to Nero (Acts 25:12). He is known only from Josephus and Acts.

FIELD OF BLOOD The potter's field purchased with the silver Judas Iscariot received for betraying Jesus (Matt 27:3-10; Acts 1:16-19) and linked in Acts to Judas's wickedness and death. In Matthew the purchase fulfills Jeremiah's prophecy (see Zech 11:12-13; Jer 18:1-19; 32:6-15). See JUDAS.

FIG TREE, FIGS One staple of the ancient diet that provided a sweet accompaniment to other foods was the fig (*Ficus carica*). Cultivated at least since the Early Bronze Age (ca. 3000 BCE), the tree could take root in rocky soil and within seven years bear fruit for as many as fifty years. The many place-names associated with fig trees (Bethany = "house of figs"; Bethphage = "house of unripe figs" [Mark 11:1]) testify to their importance to the economy. The fig tree's pride in its flavor is chronicled playfully in its refusal to rule the other trees in Jotham's parable (Judg 9:10-11). In fact, newly ripened figs were so loved that Isaiah describes the zest with which they were eaten (Isa 28:4). Other prophets use the fig as an analogy for Israel (Hos 9:10; Amos 8:1-2; Nah 3:12). The budding or barren fig tree is a symbol of fruitfulness in some of Jesus' parables (Matt 24:32; Mark 13:28; Luke 13:6-9; 21:19-31). The fig tree begins to put on its leaves in spring and is quite lush by summer when its shade is a relief from the sun (John 1:48-50). It is also paired with the grapevine as a symbol of prosperity and peace for the farmer (Mic 4:4). Fig cakes served as rations for soldiers that could be carried on campaign or stored for later consumption in camp (1 Sam 25:18; 30:12), and were also used medicinally as a poultice for boils (2 Kgs 20:7).

FIGUREHEAD A carving on a ship's stemhead. Acts 28:11 describes an Alexandrian ship with a figurehead of the twin gods Castor and Pollux.

FIRE The phenomenon can also be described by words such as *flames* and *torch*, and it is sometimes closely related to light. Both in the OT and the NT, fire is part of everyday life. On the one hand, fire is a useful, beneficial element providing light and warmth (Isa 44:15-16; Acts 28:2), and heat for cooking (Exod 12:8; Jer 7:18) or for the work of craftsmen (Ezek 22:20). On the other hand, fire has a destructive quality and is therefore employed in war (Judg 20:48; Jer 21:10), and sometimes, though seldom, as a means of execution (Gen 38:24; Lev 20:14; 21:9; Josh 7:15). It may also refer to the scorching heat of the sun (Joel 1:19; Amos 7:4). In a figurative sense or as a metaphor it describes feelings such as extreme pain (Ps 39:4), passion of love (Song 8:6), malice (Isa 9:17), or anger (Zeph 3:8; Sir 28:10-14).

FIRE, PILLAR OF See COLUMN OF CLOUD AND LIGHTNING.

FIRMANENT In Hebrew cosmology, a dome or vault that God created on the second day to separate the waters in the heavens from the waters of the earth (Gen 1:6-8), containing small openings to allow water to fall through as rain.

FIRST AND LAST 1. A divine self-name. Three occurrences in Second Isaiah emphasize might (41:4), oneness (44:6), and power to deliver from captivity (48:12). The author of Revelation uses the term to refer to Christ's coming reign and power over death (Rev 1:17; 2:8; 22:13).

2. *First* and *last* are terms Jesus uses to describe the reversal of status in God's kingdom/heaven between those who have power and those who serve: "Many who are first will be last. And many who are last will be first" (Matt 19:30; 20:16; Mark 10:31; Luke 13:30). The one who wishes to be "first" must become "the slave of all" (Mark 10:44).

FIRSTFRUITS KJV term for the first portion of grain (Deut 18:4), fruit (Neh 10:38), oil and vegetable harvests (2 Chron 31:5); and the first (or best) batches of dough (Num 15:20-21), wine, and honey (2 Chron 31:5).

FISH GATE Gate of JERUSALEM, mentioned as part of Manasseh's refortification project (2 Chron 33:14), and repaired under Nehemiah's governorship (Neh 3:3; 12:39). This gate may have pierced the wall near the northwest corner of the temple mount, west of the Sheep Gate.

FISHERMEN Fishing was backbreaking labor with a relatively small reward. At least in ancient Israel, the fish catcher did not have to contend with crocodiles or marshlands drying up (Isa 19:8). However, the only reliable body of freshwater was the Sea of Galilee and some stretches of the Jordan River. As it flowed south the water became increasingly saline, eliminating fish habitat (note Ezekiel's eschatological vision of a rejuvenation of the Dead Sea with fishermen casting their nets from its banks from En-gedi to En-eglayim [47:8-10]). Most of what is known of the practical aspects of fishing comes from the accounts in the NT about Jesus' recruiting of his disciples from the men working the boats in the Sea of Galilee (Matt 4:18). The discovery of a 26.6-ft. wooden fishing boat near the village of Magdala provides a glimpse into the daily struggle that teams of five men (sometimes family members as in

Mark 1:19-20 and sometimes day laborers) faced sailing out each morning or evening to cast their linen nets (John 21:3). The forming of fishing cooperatives allowed families to work together and share the risks and burdens of the sea (Luke 5:7-10). Their labors did not always result in a catch (Luke 5:5), and they would have had to share what they did pull in with family members, those who provided them with loans, and the tax collector (see Levi's tax "kiosk" set near the shore in Mark 2:14). There were also the ongoing tasks of repairing, cleaning, and weaving their nets (Mark 1:19; Luke 5:2); maintaining their boats, and sorting and processing their catch.

FLESH The predominant usage of *flesh* in the OT refers to the soft (muscle) tissue of the body, human or animal, living or dead (Gen 2:21; Exod 4:7; Lev 6:3; etc.; Prov 5:11; 11:17; Ps 73:26), sometimes as distinct from bone (Job 10:11), skin (Job 10:11), or blood (Isa 49:26).

In the NT, *flesh* refers basically to the material substance that covers the bones of humans or animals—as clearly in Luke 24:39 and 1 Cor 15:39—and in the regular phrase to describe humankind as "flesh and blood" (1 Cor 15:50; Heb 2:14). Marriage has an inescapably physical character, as the union of two to become "one flesh" (Matt 19:6; Mark 10:8; 1 Cor 6:16; Eph 5:31). The point of John 6:51-56, which uses the term *flesh* rather than *body*, was to emphasize the manifest physicality of the incarnate Word (and the basic physicality of "eating" this flesh).

Consequently, flesh also stands in contrast to spirit, the spirit as a countering, positive force, but inhibited or restricted by the flesh (Matt 26:41; Mark 14:38; 1 Cor 5:5; Col 2:5). A spirit by definition does not consist of flesh and bones (Luke 24:39). There is a fundamental distinction between birth from the flesh and birth from the spirit (John 3:6). This is precisely the wonder of the incarnation: that "the Word became flesh" (John 1:14; 1 John 4:2). But although it is the flesh of the Human One, as bread of life, which must be chewed (John 6:53-54), it is also important to grasp that "the Spirit is the one who gives life and the flesh doesn't help at all" (6:63). Jesus' own transposition from the realm of flesh to Spirit (Rom 1:3-4; 1 Tim 3:16) is also the pattern for human salvation (1 Pet 3:18; 4:2). But the reconciliation takes place precisely in and through Christ's flesh (Eph 2:14; Heb 10:20).

FLINT The stone, composed of impure quartz, is abundant in the Middle East and is known for its hardness and durability (Ezek 3:9, Ezekiel's determination is harder than flint). When fractured, the stone produces sharp, elongated edges suitable for use as cutting tools. In Neolithic Age Palestine the production of various flint tools influenced all aspects of life. The flint knife was used for ceremonial "cuttings." Zipporah used "a sharp-edged flint stone" to circumcise her son (Exod 4:25), while the Israelite men's circumcision entering the promised land (Josh 5:2-3) was accomplished with "flint knives." Flint represents the steadfast determination of the Servant of the Lord (Isa 50:7). Psalm 114:8 alludes to the exodus event where the Lord "turned . . . flint stone into a spring of water."

FLOOD The biblical flood story of Gen 6–9 forms a key component of the Bible's primordial history (Gen 1–11). The flood story represents an ancient Israelite adaptation of time-honored Near Eastern lore and establishes the core theological theme of God's governance over a conflicted world.

FLOWER The landscape of ancient Canaan was brightened by the colorful blooms of olive and pomegranate trees as well as by blooming plants growing throughout the western foothills, the highlands, and the plains. In the spring the steppe regions and hillsides would have been covered with flowers. Curiously, other than the blossoms on flowering shrubs and trees such as the almond (Exod 25:33), there are only three flowers mentioned by name in the biblical text: the lily (Hos 14:5; Matt 6:28), the rose (Song 2:1), and henna (Song 1:14).

There are many references to flowering plants whose products (dyes, spices, fragrances) were imported, such as myrrh (from the Himalayas, Song 1:12-13), crocus (from Asia Minor, Isa 35:1), and saffron (from India, Song 4:14), but these were not native to Syria-Palestine.

FLY In Ecclesiastes, dead flies ruin the perfume (10:1). Flies constitute the fourth Egyptian plague (Exod 8:24). Flies kill people by biting (Wis 16:9). The Egyptian army is likened to a swarm of flies (Isa 7:18). A Philistine deity is called "Lord of the Flies" (2 Kgs 1:2), a phrase that appears in the NT as BEELZEBUL, and, more popularly, Beelzebub (see BAAL-ZEBUB). This "Lord of the Flies" is no longer god of the Philistines, but is identified with SATAN. Taken together, these verses imply a type of fly more destructive than the common housefly, which generally is aggravating but not dangerous.

FOOL, FOOLISHNESS Foolishness has a range of meanings that include "folly," "vile thing," "outrage," and "stupidity." The noun is applied to the threatened rape of the Levite and the actual rape of his secondary wife (Judg 19:23-24; 20:6, 10), Dinah (Gen 34:7), and Tamar (2 Sam 13:12). In addition, it is frequently contrasted with wisdom, especially in the Wisdom Literature. As foolishness is contrasted with wisdom, the fool is contrasted with the sage. Succinctly, a fool is everything a sage is not—imprudent, stupid, lazy, perverse in speech, even wicked (see, e.g., Prov 1:7; 14:16; 19:1; Eccl 7:25). And as wisdom is understood as divinely bestowed, the quintessential fool is the one who does not believe in God (Pss 14:1; 53:1).

In the NT, the word is also used in contrast to wisdom. For example, in Matthew, Jesus tells a parable of ten virgins—five who are wise and five who are foolish (Matt 25:1-13). In his epistles, Paul uses the word in a variety of ways including as a rhetorical device. In 2 Cor 11:1, Paul mounts a defense of his own authority by asking the community to "put up with [him while he acts] like a fool." Then, he proceeds to speak as "a fool" by boasting of his credentials, the suffering he has borne, and the dangers he has braved. Both the writers of the Gospels and Paul use the epithet "fool" and "foolish" to rebuke those who stray from the right path (Matt 23:17; 2 Tim 3:9). See WISDOM.

FOOT In ancient societies where walking was the most common means of transportation, feet were one of the dirtiest parts of the body. Thus hospitality demanded that visitors be provided with water to wash their feet (Gen 18:4; 19:2; 24:32). In wealthy homes, servants would wash their masters' and guests' feet. Jesus' washing of the disciples' feet (John 13:1-11) was intended to show that the gospel is about service, not about being served. Despite the dirtiness of feet, Moses was required to take off his sandals when he stood on holy ground (Exod 3:5). A number of idioms involve feet. For example, "to be under someone's feet" was to be under the power of that person (Ps 8:6; Eph 1:22), while "to sit at the feet" implied learning from someone (Luke 10:39).

FOOT WASHING Biblical and Greco-Roman hospitality dictated that hosts should provide water for washing guests' feet (Gen 18:4; Luke 7:44). Typically, the washing was done either by a slave (1 Sam 25:41) or by the guests themselves.

Exodus 30:17-20 requires priests to wash their feet before approaching the altar, and acting "with unwashed feet" came to suggest inadequate preparation, especially in a cultic setting (e.g., Philo, QE 1, 2).

In John 13:4-20, Jesus washes his disciples' feet, an act without recorded parallel in antiquity, where superiors did not willingly wash the feet of inferiors.

FOOTSTOOL These terms are rarely used as a literal reference to an object of furniture (2 Chron 9:18). More often, references to a footstool are metaphorical and in the context of the proper attitude of worshippers toward the deity or of dominance over enemies. In Ps 99:5,9, the Lord's footstool is identified with God's "holy mountain," a reference to Zion (cf also Lam 2:1). In Isa 66:1, the term is a metaphor for the earth, contrasted with the heavens as the Lord's throne. Jesus cites this metaphor (Matt 5:34-35) as he instructs against making oaths. Stephen cites Isa 66 to illustrate his point that God does not need a physical structure in which to dwell (Acts 7:49).

Psalm 110:1 is a metaphor for dominion over enemies, which is cited in the NT several times. In Mark 12:36 (Matt 22:44; Luke 20:43), Jesus quotes this psalm, focusing on the first phrase of the psalm to illustrate the misidentification of the Christ as literally a descendant of David. Peter quotes Ps 110:1 as proof of Jesus' ascension (Acts 2:35), and it is used again in Heb 1:13 and 10:13.

FORD A ford is a crossing place through a river or stream. The JORDAN RIVER was the main flowing water source in Israel and separated it from the Israelite tribes east of the river (Transjordan) and the nations of Moab, Ammon, and Edom (see Josh 2:7; Judg 3:28; 12:5-6; 15:28; 19:18). The ancient river was approximately 90–100 ft. wide and 5–12 ft. deep, but erosion and flooding changed its contour frequently, requiring the discovery of new fords. Jacob and his family forded (passed over) the Jabbok River (Gen 32:22 [Heb. 32:23]).

FOREHEAD The location of both marks of blessing and curse (Exod 13:9; 2 Chron 26:19; Ezek 9:4). In Revelation, both the blessed (9:4) and the cursed (13:16) receive identifying marks on the forehead. Jeremiah 3:3 suggests that a "brazen prostitute" was marked on the forehead as well. Other prophetic passages use a "hard forehead" as a metaphor for stubbornness (Ezek 3:7-9; Isa 48:4).

FOREIGN, FOREIGNER Land, customs, or people outside the land, customs, or people of context, as other than Israel or the Christian community (e.g., invaders of Israel [Obad 1:11]), foreign gods (e.g., Jer 5:19), and non-Israelites (Exod 21:8). Foreigners had few rights in ancient Israel (Exod 12:43; Deut 15:2-3; 17:15; 23:20 [Heb. 23:21]), in contrast to the sojourner, who lived in Israel and was subject to and protected by the law (e.g., Exod 12:19, 48ff.; Num 9:14; Deut 31:12).

In the NT, *foreigner* occurs less frequently (Acts 17:21; Heb 11:9, 34; Luke 17:18) due to the internationalization of Judaism. According to Eph 2:11-19, Christ has broken down the "barrier of hatred" between Jew and Gentile, so that "aliens" or "sojourners" and "strangers" can now be assimilated into the covenant by the blood of Christ (v. 13).

FORESKIN See CIRCUMCISION.

FORGIVENESS Forgiveness is the act by which an offended party removes an offense from further consideration, thereby reestablishing a basis for harmonious relations with the offender.

Forgiveness is called for when humans wrong each other (Gen 50:15-21; Matt 18:21-22). Ultimately, however, all sins—including wrongs done to other human beings—are committed against God (Ps 51:4; cf Mark 2:7) inasmuch as they represent a violation of the good order of God's creation and (in the case of those to whom God's Law has been entrusted) a transgression of God's stated will. Divine forgiveness is thus a precondition for good relations between God and God's erring creatures.

FORK 1. A "three-pronged fork," used by priests of the meeting tent to extract their portion of a sacrifice (1 Sam 2:13-14).

2. A gold or bronze sacrificial instrument at the altar of the meeting tent (Exod 27:3; 38:3; Num 4:14) and temple (1 Chron 28:17; 2 Chron 4:16).

3. A six-pronged winnowing fork for removing CHAFF from grain (Isa 30:24), used figuratively for chastisement (Jer 15:7).

4. The CEB interprets "the head of the road(s)" to mean "the fork in the road" (Ezek 21:21).

FORMER SLAVES, SYNAGOGUE OF A Jerusalem assembly of diaspora Jewish immigrants, some of whom argued with Stephen and instigated his arrest and interrogation by the high council (Acts 6:9-15). In Acts 6:9, they are identified most closely with North African (Cyrenian, Alexandrian) Jews resettling in Jerusalem; but they may also include others "from . . . Cilicia, and Asia" in the same or an affiliated synagogue.

FORT Used in the CEB to translate a variety of Hebrew and Greek words that refer to defense structures during war (1 Sam 14:15; 1 Kgs 16:16; 1 Chron 11:16). Other translations of the same terms include siege wall, siegework, stronghold, fortification, and fortress.

FORTUNATUS One of three long-standing Christian converts from Corinth (1 Cor 16:17). He traveled with ACHAICUS and STEPHANAS from Corinth to Paul in Ephesus, perhaps bringing the letter to which Paul alludes in 1 Cor 7:1. Paul states that the arrival of these three delighted him, and they raised or refreshed his spirits. Indeed they made up for his being absent from Corinth.

FORUM A center of civic life and economic exchange (Acts 28:15).

FOUNTAIN A fountain was a flow or spring of freshwater from a cavity in a hillside or valley, in contrast to a perennial stream or to a well or CISTERN used to catch rainwater. Water was a crucial factor for survival in ancient Palestine, where rainfall is limited to half the year. Ancient peoples often settled their villages based on the location of water sources. The soft limestone rock of Palestine is favorable for the natural formation of fountains, which are therefore numerous.

The fountain provided a rich metaphor for biblical writers. The Lord is a fountain (Ps 68:26), a "spring of life" (Ps 36:9) or "living water," in contrast to a cracked cistern that holds no water (Jer 2:13); the mouth of the righteous is a fountain (Prov 10:11), and the teaching of the wise (Prov 13:14), the fear of the Lord (Prov 14:27), and wisdom (Prov 16:22; 18:4) are all fountains of life. In the Minor Prophets fountains are signs of eschatological fulfillment, flowing directly from the Lord's house (Joel 3:18) and providing pardon for the royal family and the residents of Jerusalem, "to cleanse the sin and impurity" (Zech 13:1).

FOUNTAIN GATE Gate of Jerusalem (Neh 2:14; 3:15; 12:37), likely located at the south end of the city, probably named because a Pool of Siloam overflow channel ran beneath it.

FOWLER Someone who captures fowl. Indirectly, via proverbs and metaphors, the biblical texts provide information concerning fowlers' techniques. Using bait or decoys, the fowler lured small birds into a snare or trap (Amos 3:5; Ps 124:7). Alternatively, he caught them in his net (Hos 7:12). Hence, it is not surprising that cunning enemies were portrayed as fowlers (Job 18:8-10; Ps 91:3; Prov 6:5; Jer 5:26-27; Hos 9:8).

FRANKINCENSE A prized incense in the Near East and the Mediterranean prepared from the gum of several species of Boswellia (*Burseraceae*) trees and shrubs native to the Arabian peninsula (*Boswellia sacra*) and North Africa (*Boswellia papyrifera*, native to Ethiopia). The range of the frankincense tree in southern Arabia in the Hadhramaut and Dhofar follows the rain shadow of the current southwest monsoon. To obtain its resin, a deep, longitudinal incision is made in the trunk of the tree; below it a narrow strip of bark 5 in. in length is peeled off. The secreted milk-like juice hardens when exposed to the air, and within three months it is transformed into yellowish "tears" that are scraped off into baskets. The numerous references to frankincense in the Pentateuch detail its use in the formula for sacred incense in the meeting tent (Exod 30:34), in combination with grain offerings (Lev 2:2), and with the bread offering (Lev 24:7). Its aromatic values are highlighted in references to sweet fragrances (Song 3:6; 4:6), and its high price and value as a kingly gift is demonstrated in its inclusion among the gifts of the magi to the infant Jesus (Matt 2:11).

FREEDMEN, SYNAGOGUE OF THE See FORMER SLAVES, SYNAGOGUE OF.

FRIEND, FRIENDSHIP The words *friend* and *friendship* communicate a warmth of emotional closeness and common goals.

In the OT, a friend is a COMPANION or ally (Judg 7:13), or someone who is trusted like a family member (Deut 13:6). Abraham is described as a friend of God.

In the NT, Jesus calls his disciples "my friends" (Luke 12:4; John 15:14), and he is described as a friend of sinners (Matt 11:19; Luke 7:34). The early church treated this sort of intimate association with sinners as a unique feature of Jesus' behavior. As God incarnate, Jesus became a healing and forgiving presence among those who were most open to it.

The most striking use of friendship appears in the John's Gospel, when Jesus says that his disciples will no longer be called servants or slaves but friends whenever they do as he commands them; moreover, the greatest love (agape) is to lay down one's life for one's friends (John 15:12-14).

There is only one disciple whom Jesus addresses personally as "friend," and that is JUDAS (Matt 26:50), at the time of Jesus' arrest when Judas has embraced him warmly. This scene is not necessarily a display of irony or satire on the part of Jesus, as most scholars interpret. Jesus did not need to be ironic, but could be genuine and forthright in his last encounter with Judas. As Jesus affirms his friendship with Judas and offers him thanks for his obedience, the nature of friendship, as Jesus practiced it with his disciples, becomes more transparent.

FRINGE The edge of a cloth garment. The fringe on one garment had great symbolic importance in the ancient world. God commands the Israelites to make a fringe on the corners of their garments and to attach to them a thread of blue to remind them of the commandments and the exodus from Egypt. This distinctive blue dye is enormously expensive to produce, and its salient characteristic is that it never fades. The tassels on the fringe are to serve as a safeguard from sin; a visible reminder that one is a part of the "kingdom of priests" (Exod 19:6).

FROG Frogs appear in the Bible only in reference to the second plague visited upon Egypt (Exod 8:2-15; Pss 78:45; 105:30; Wis 19:10) and metaphorically in one of John of Patmos's visions (Rev 16:13).

FRUIT The fleshy and edible pulp that covers the seed of the plant or tree. The most common fruits were the olive, grape, and fig (Judg 9:7-15; Deut 8:7-8), but a rich variety of fruit was available including the almond, apricot or quince, citron, date palm, mulberry, muskmelon, myrtle, pistachio, pomegranate, olive, sycamore fig, walnut, and watermelon.

FRUIT OF THE SPIRIT This phrase is found only in Gal 5:22, though different terms and partial parallels exist in other places (cf Eph 5:9; Phil 1:11; 4:8; Col 1:6, 10; 3:12-15; 2 Pet 1:5-7). Nine qualifiers follow "fruit of the Spirit," concretely defining "fruit." These terms represent the ethical characteristics of life in Jesus through the Spirit: love, joy, peace, patience, kindness, goodness, faithfulness, gentleness, and self-control.

These fruit are contrasted with "actions that are produced by selfish motives" in Gal 5:19-21. Similar virtues and vice lists occur in other NT works and in Hellenistic (esp. Stoic thought) and Roman literature, including Jewish Hellenistic literature. Lists such as these also played a role in the literature of the church fathers and Gnosticism. The nature of these fruit in the NT takes on a significant ethical tone quite different from similar lists in Hellenistic and Roman sources.

FURNACE An enclosed chamber where fuel is converted into heat for the purpose of smelting or refining ore or to make lime. References to furnaces are most often used metaphorically to indicate God's judgment or testing.

FURNITURE The Hebrew word refers to any item that is manufactured for a specific purpose. While it is usually translated "article, utensil, implement, vessel," it often refers generally to items whose use is specified by modifying words (e.g., weapons for hunting or war [Judg 18:11, 16-17]), the equipment of oxen (2 Sam 24:22), musical instruments (Amos 6:5; 1 Chron 15:16), various implements made of metal and used as tools (1 Kgs 6:7), or the equipment used with a chariot (1 Sam 8:12). It is translated "equipment" when referring to the implements and furnishings of the meeting tent (Exod 25:9; 40:9), of the temple in Jerusalem (1 Chron 9:29), and "furniture" when describing Tobiah's or Holofernes's home furnishings (Neh 13:8; Jdt 15:11). The Greek words are used most often to mean "vessel."

FURROW A furrow is a shallow trench dug in the soil for planting. The OT presents different terms for furrows depending on their function and role.

Gg

GAAL Gaal challenged ABIMELECH's attempt to establish a hereditary monarchy during the period of the judges (Judg 9:26-41). See SHECHEM, SHECHEMITES.

GAASH, MOUNT A mountain, probably 30 km to the southwest of Shechem, to the north of which Joshua is said to have been buried in Timnath-serah in the highlands of Ephraim (Josh 24:30; Judg 2:9). One of David's fighting men hailed from the nearby Gaash ravines (2 Sam 23:30; 1 Chron 11:32).

GABAEL Son of Gabrias and brother of

Gabri from the region of Rages in Media (Tob 1:14; 4:20).

GABATHA One of two eunuchs, the other being Tharra, who conspired against King Ahasuerus until Mordecai intervened (Add Esth 1:12). The name BIGTHAN appears in the MT instead (Esth 2:21; 6:2).

GABBAI One of the Benjaminite leaders who settled in Jerusalem when Judahites and Benjaminites were repopulating it during the Persian period (Neh 11:8).

GABBATHA Gabbatha is the Greek transliteration of an Aramaic. word that refers to the elevated stone pavement upon which Pilate sat when he dispensed public judgment. The name is used only in John 19:13, a passage describing Jesus' trial before Pilate.

GABRIAS Also spelled Gabri. He appears as the brother of GABAEL in Tob 1:14, but is later described as his father (4:20).

GABRIEL Angel named twice in Daniel (8:16; 9:21) and once in Luke (1:19, 26). According to several Second Temple Jewish documents, Gabriel was one of the four archangels, along with Michael (Dan 10:13, 21; 12:1; Jude 9; Rev 12:7), Sariel, and Raphael (named more than thirty times in Tobit).

GAD, GADITES 1. Gad is the seventh son of Jacob and eponymous ancestor of the tribe of Gad. Gad's mother ZILPAH, the maidservant of LEAH, bore Gad on behalf of Leah.

2. The tribe of Gad.

3. Gad the "seer" or prophet is prominent in the David narratives (1 Sam 22:3-5; 2 Sam 24; 1 Chron 21).

4. A deity of good luck (Isa 65:11-12).

GADARA, GADARENES A town of the Decapolis, about 6 mi. southeast of the Sea of Galilee. According to Matt 8:28, two demoniacs living among the tombs met Jesus there, but Mark 5:1, Matthew's probable source, names the place "the region of the Gerasenes," (so also Luke 8:26).

GADDI 1. The spy from the tribe of Manasseh, one of twelve spies Moses sent into the land of Canaan (Num 13:11).

2. The surname of John, eldest son of Mattathias (1 Macc 2:2), who apparently played a relatively minor role in the Maccabean revolt.

GADDIEL The son of Sodi and a chieftain from the tribe of Zebulun, listed among the twelve spies whom Moses sends into Canaan from the wilderness of Paran (Num 13:10).

GADI The father of the Israelite king MENAHEM, who came to the throne after killing his predecessor SHALLUM (2 Kgs 15:14, 17).

GAHAM Of the twelve sons of NAHOR, Gaham is the second-listed of four by the secondary wife REUMAH (Gen 22:24) in REBEKAH's genealogy (vv. 20-24).

GAHAR One of several temple servants in a list of those whose descendants returned with Zerubbabel from the exile (Ezra 2:47; Neh 7:49).

GAI See HEGAI.

GAIUS 1. One of the first people baptized by Paul in Corinth (1 Cor 1:14). Probably of pagan origin, his wealth enabled him to receive "the whole church" (Rom 16:23; cf 1 Cor 14:23) for the liturgical assembly.

2. Gaius of Macedonia (Acts 19:29) was a traveling companion of Paul.

3. Gaius of Derbe (Acts 20:4) was also a traveling companion of Paul. Nothing else is known of him.

4. The apparent leader of a congregation to whom 3 John is addressed: "To

my dear friend Gaius, whom I dearly love" (v. 1).

GALAL 1. One of the Levites returning to Jerusalem after the Babylonian exile (1 Chron 9:15).

2. Descendant of Jeduthun, whom David set apart as a temple musician (1 Chr 16:41; 25:1-8); and ancestor to one of the Levites returning to Jerusalem after the Babylonian exile (1 Chron 9:16; Neh 11:15).

GALATIA The Roman province of Galatia lies in central Anatolia or modern Turkey. To the west was the province of Asia, to the southwest Lycia and Pamphylia, to the south Cilicia, to the east Cappadocia, to the north Pontus, and to the northwest Bithynia.

GALATIANS, LETTER TO THE Paul's Letter to the Galatians is one of the most significant documents in the Christian Scriptures. Paul's vigorous discussions of justification and faith are at the heart of the letter's concerns. This letter reflects an intramural debate in early Christianity. Galatians is not Paul's assessment of Judaism as a social and religious community but the apostle's response to certain Jewish Christians who sought to require observance of traditional Jewish Law in the life of the church.

GALBANUM Used in making sacred incense for the holy precincts of the meeting tent (Exod 30:34-35).

GALILEE, GALILEANS 1. The term *Galilee* refers to a district generically (e.g., Josh 13:2; Ezek 47:8), on the west side of the Sea of Galilee.

2. A Galilean is a resident or native of Galilee. Jesus is once identified as "Jesus the Galilean" (Matt 26:69). The original core of Jesus' disciples are twice called Galileans (Acts 1:11; 2:7), and could be so identified by their accents (Mark 14:70; Luke 22:59). Since in Jesus' lifetime Galilee fell under the jurisdiction of Herod Antipas, in Luke Pilate transfers Jesus to him upon learning that Jesus was from Galilee (Luke 23:6).

GALILEE, SEA OF The Sea of Galilee is a freshwater lake located in northern Palestine. At its greatest length, the present-day lake stretches approximately 13 mi.; at its widest point, it is approximately 7 mi. across. Its primary source is the Jordan River, which flows into it from Mount Hermon to the north and exits to the south toward the Dead Sea, though it is also filled by other streams and springs.

By the early 1st cent. CE, the coast of the lake was dotted with villages and small cities. On the western coast stood Capernaum, Ginnesar, Magdala (also known as Taricheae), and Hammath, famous for its hot springs. Around 20 CE, Herod Antipas built his capital city Tiberias on the lakeside, naming it after the current emperor. Another city, perhaps Philoteria, was located at Beth-yerah on the southern shore. The southeastern portion of the lake adjoined the Decapolis, an administrative district within the province of Syria, and the Decapolis city of Hippos stood directly across the lake from Tiberias. The northeastern portion of the lake, including Bethsaida, was included within the territory of the Herodian king Philip. Territorial boundaries changed throughout the 1st cent. CE; at the time of the first Jewish Revolt, for example, Tiberias, Magdala, and the former territory of Philip belonged to Agrippa II. The area west of the lake was predominantly Jewish; that to its east was mostly Gentile. Thus Jesus likely would have encountered Gentiles in his travels around the lake.

GALL, HERB A bitter-tasting herb, such as wormwood (Prov 5:4; see Deut 29:18 [Heb. 29:17]). The term is also applied metaphorically for a tragic or sorrowful condition (Lam 3:15, 19; CEB, "bitterness").

GALL, LIVER A term for the gallbladder and bile (Job 16:13).

GALLIO L. Iunius Gallio Annaeanus was PROCONSUL of Achaia while Claudius was emperor. Gallio was the adopted son of Seneca the Elder. An inscription at Delphi dates Gallio's tenure to 51–52 CE; Acts 18:12-17 describes Paul being brought before Gallio by Jews and accused of encouraging worship practices contrary to the Law.

GAMALIEL 1. Son of Pedahuzur and head of the tribe of Manasseh (Num 1:4, 10, 16; 2:20; 7:54, 59; 10:23).

2. Gamaliel I. The grandson of Hillel, Gamaliel was a prominent 1st-cent. CE Pharisaic teacher (Sotah 9.15; Acts 5.34) and is known for a number of rabbinic rulings (m. Git. 4.2-3; m. Yebam. 16.7; T. Sanh. 2.6). In Acts 5:33-40, he urges a Jewish council to show moderation toward the disciples.

GAMES The discovery of board games, rattles, whistles, and pull toys at various archaeological sites throughout Israel demonstrates that its people, as elsewhere in the Near East, enjoyed a variety of playful activities. Though infrequent in the NT, examples include a game played by children in the marketplace mentioned by Jesus (Matt 11:16-17) and what amounts to a game of chance that takes place as soldiers cast lots for Jesus' garments (Mark 15:24). Despite their absence in the NT, archaeological evidence suggests that ball and board games were part of the world of early Christianity. More common in the NT are allusions to Greek athletic competitions, such as might be seen at the games in Olympia or the Isthmian games in Corinth.

GAMUL A priest recorded as receiving the 22nd lot in the list of apportionments among the Aaronites (1 Chron 24:17).

GARDEN OF EDEN See EDEN, GARDEN OF.

GARDEN OF GETHSEMANE See GETHSEMANE.

GAREB 1. Gareb the Ithrite is listed among the warriors of David known as "the Thirty" in 2 Sam 23:38 and in the parallel text 1 Chron 11:40.

2. In Jer 31:39 the extent of the city to be rebuilt in the restoration prophecy is identified as going farther from the Corner Gate to Gareb Hill, apparently a boundary marker.

GARMITE Keilah the Garmite appears in a Judahite genealogy (1 Chron 4:19).

GAS The purported head of a family that originally returned from exile in Babylon (1 Esdr 5:34, but absent in corresponding lists [e.g., Ezra 2:57]).

GATAM A clan chief and son of Eliphaz and grandson of Esau (Gen 36:11, 16; 1 Chron 1:36).

GATH One of the cities of the Philistine pentapolis, Gath plays a particularly important role in the stories about King David. It appears first, however, in the book of Joshua, where it is listed as one of the cities where the Anakim, presumably a primordial race of giants, remained after the conquest. Later, the covenant chest was brought to Gath after it was captured by the Philistines (1 Sam 5:8-10). During his ministry, the prophet Samuel is supposed to have restored cities lying between Ekron and Gath on the border between Israel and Philistia to Israel (1 Sam 7:14). Gath's association with giants is continued in the story of David and Goliath (1 Sam 17), the latter a man of immense proportions from Philistine Gath. After the Israelites' rout of the Philistines subsequent to David's defeat of Goliath, the Israelites pursued the Philistines as far as Ekron and Gath (1 Sam 17:52), which is later the location of a series of anecdotes about the exploits of David's heroes in battle against fearsome

Philistines (2 Sam 21:15-22; 1 Chron 20:4-8).

GATH-RIMMON A town within the land that Joshua and the priest Eleazar apportioned to the tribe of Dan (Josh 19:45) and that they were required to give to the Kohothite families of the Levites (Josh 21:24). Also, the name of a town from the half-tribe of Manasseh that Joshua and Eleazar were required to give to the Kohathite families (Josh 21:25), but identified as the town BILEAM (bleam) in the par. list in 1 Chron 6:70.

GAZA A city in southwest Palestine, about 4 km (2.5 mi.) from the sea (Gen 10:19; Josh 13:3; Judg 16:2).

GAZELLE Gazelles were a supplementary meat source (Deut 12:15; 1 Kgs 4:23). In poetic texts the gazelle is often a symbol of beauty (Song 2:9, 17; 4:5; 7:3; 8:14).

GAZEZ A name possibly meaning "shearer."

1. Gazez was a son of Caleb through a secondary wife named Ephah (1 Chron 2:46).

2. A grandson of Caleb named Gazez whose father was Haran (1 Chron 2:46).

GAZZAM Head of a family of Nethinim among the returnees from Babylon (Ezra 2:48; Neh 7:51).

GEBA A town given to the Levites (Josh 21:17) in the territory of the tribe of Benjamin (Josh 18:24).

GEBAL, GEBALITES 1. A seaport city in LEBANON, best known by its Greek name Byblos (about 20 mi. north of Beirut) (Josh 13:5).

2. The Gebalites were the residents of Gebal portrayed in the Bible as highly skilled masons (Ezek 27:9).

GEBER A son of Uri; he was one of the twelve officials Solomon appointed over Israel (1 Kgs 4:19).

GEDALIAH 1. Son of Ahikam and grandson of Shaphan (2 Kgs 25:22). Nebuchadnezzar appointed Gedaliah governor of Judah (2 Kgs 25:22-26). Ishmael, an opponent of Babylonian sovereignty, killed Gedaliah (2 Kgs 25:24-26; Jer 40:13-16).

2. Son of Amariah father of Cushi, and grandfather of the prophet Zephaniah (Zeph 1:1).

3. Son of Pashhur and one of the officials of Zedekiah who conspired to accuse and imprison Jeremiah (Jer 38:1).

4. A temple singer and one of the six sons of Jeduthun; one of the temple musicians who, accompanied by lyre, sang songs of praise and thanks to God (1 Chron 25:3, 9).

5. A descendant of Jeshua the high priest, and one of the priests who divorced his foreign wife after return from Babylonian captivity (Ezra 10:18).

GEDERAH 1. A town in the lowland region of the territorial allotment of the tribe of Judah (Josh 15:36), most likely the same town from which potters in the king's service are said to have come (1 Chron 4:23).

2. The Benjaminite hometown of Jozabad, one of the warriors who joined with David at Ziklag (1 Chron 12:4).

GEDOR 1. Gibeon's son and a descendant of Benjamin, whose name may also represent his family (1 Chron 8:31). In 1 Chron 9:37, he is Jiel's son.

2. A town in Judah's highlands (Josh 15:58). The Chronicler names its founder Penuel (1 Chron 4:4).

3. A city in Judah founded by Jered. The warriors Joelah and Zebadiah were Benjaminites from Gedor, but whether the Chronicler is referring to the same city previously mentioned is uncertain (1 Chron 12:7).

4. A city that marked the boundary of the tribe of Simeon (1 Chron 4:39).

GE-HARASHIM Ge-harashim appears only twice in the OT. In 1 Chron 4:14, he is listed in a genealogy as the son of Joab. The word does seem to refer to a place in Neh 11:35 ("the valley of artisans"), as it appears in a list of cities.

GEHAZI The servant of Elisha (2 Kgs 4:12), portrayed as a man of dubious character.

GEHENNA See HELL.

GEMALLI Father of Ammiel, the spy from the tribe of Dan who was sent with eleven others to reconnoiter the land of Canaan (Num 13:12).

GEMARIAH 1. Son of HILKIAH and emissary from ZEDEKIAH to Nebuchadnezzar (Jer 29:3).

2. Son of the powerful scribe Shaphan (Jer 36:10), and brother of ELASAH.

GENEALOGY, CHRIST Extensive genealogies of Jesus are found only in Matt 1:1-17 and Luke 3:23-38. Both lists are linear, proceeding in Matthew from father to son and in Luke from son to father.

GENERATION A generation is a group of people all around the same age. One generation gives birth to the next; genealogies recount these successive generations.

GENESIS is the name of the first book of the Bible. Its English name comes from the Greek word for "origins." Genesis is the book of origins, of the beginnings of the physical world, its inhabitants, and especially of the people of Israel. Divine promises to Abraham (12:1-3) structure the stories and serve as thematic threads across the main body of the book (chaps. 12–50).

GENNAEUS The father of Apollonius (2 Macc 12:2).

GENNESARET The term may refer either to the Sea of Galilee (Luke 5:1; 1 Macc 11:67) or to a plain on its northwest side (Matt 14:34; Mark 6:53). In the latter case the area is associated in the Gospels often with the ministry of Jesus.

GENTILES Ethnic groups besides Jews.

GENUBATH HADAD, a member of the royal house of Edom, found favor in the eyes of Pharaoh, who gave him the sister of his own wife. The queen's sister gave birth to a son, Genubath, who grew up in the king's palace among Eyptian princes (1 Kgs 11:17-20).

GERA 1. Benjamin's fourth son (Gen 46:21).

2. One of Benjamin's grandsons through his oldest son BELA (1 Chron 8:3-5).

3. A son of EHUD, also called Heglam (1 Chron 8:7).

4. The father of the judge Ehud (Judg 3:15).

5. The father of SHIMEI, who cursed DAVID when he fled from ABSALOM (2 Sam 16:5-8).

GERAH The 20th part of a SHEKEL (Ezek 45:12), appearing largely in association with the shekel of the sanctuary in the Priestly Code (e.g., Exod 30:13; Lev 27:25; etc.). See MONEY, COINS.

GERAR Gerar was in the southern periphery of Canaan somewhere in the arid southern plain between Gaza and BEER-SHEBA (see NEGEB, NEGEV). After the Sarah and Abimelech event (Gen 20:2), Abraham received resident status in Gerar (Gen 20:15). Isaac sought resident status there during a severe famine (Gen 26:1). Rebekah's familiar problem with Abimelech (Gen 26:7-11) and jealousy of the inhabitants resulted in Isaac's moving out of the city into the "valley of Gerar" (Gen 26:17). Conflict with Gerar's inhabitants forced both

Abraham and Isaac to relocate to Beersheba at the kingdom's border, yet they made a treaty relationship with the king (Gen 21:31-34; 26:26).

GERIZIM, MOUNT Now called Jebel et-Tur, located on the southwest side of the city of Shechem, the mountain stands at 868 m, rising 500 mi. above Shechem. According to Deuteronomy, the Israelites were to hold a ceremony on Mount Gerizim after they had conquered the land (Deut 11:29; 27:12). Half the tribes were to stand on Mount Gerizim while Joshua read the "words of the Instruction," while the other half were to stand on Mount Ebal to hear the curses (Josh 8:30-35). See EBAL, MOUNT)

GERSHOM 1. Moses gave this name to his elder son born in Midian by his wife ZIPPORAH, to commemorate that he was "an immigrant living in a foreign land" (Exod 2:22; 18:3; 1 Chron 23:15-16; 26:24). According to Judg 18:30, Gershom's son Jonathan and Jonathan's sons served as priests for the Danite tribe.

2. Levi also gave this name to his elder son (1 Chron 6:1-2, 5, 16-17, 20, 43), whose descendants are referred to as Gershomites or the sons of Gershom (1 Chron 6:62, 71; 15:7). His name is spelled Gershon in 1 Chron 23:6-7. See GERSHON, GERSHONITES.

3. A descendant of Phinehas, who returned with Ezra from Babylon to Jerusalem, also bears this name. He is Aaron's grandson and a priest (Ezra 8:2; 1 Esdr 8:29).

GERSHON, GERSHONITES 1. The eldest of Levi's sons and the eponymous ancestor of one of the three branches of Levites (Gen 46:11; Exod 6:16; Num 3:17), Gershon was the father of Libni and SHIMEI, who probably represented two branches within the Gershonites (Exod 6:17; Num 3:18).

2. According to the schema of Leviticus and Numbers, the Gershonites were one of the three divisions of the Levites. Gershon was the oldest. In Leviticus and Numbers, however, the Gershonites are subordinated to the Kohathites, the descendants of Levi's second son.

GESHAN A Calebite of the tribe of Judah and the third son of Jahdai (1 Chron 2:47).

GESHEM Along with SANBALLAT the Horonite and TOBIAH the Ammonite, Geshem opposed Nehemiah's plans to reconstruct the wall of Jerusalem (Neh 2:19).

GESHUR, GESHURITES 1. One of the areas not conquered by Joshua (Josh 13:8-13), east of the Sea of Galilee in the southern Golan Heights, Geshur remained independent during the time of David. David's marriage to Maacah daughter of King Talmai probably indicates a treaty between the two kingdoms (2 Sam 3:3).

2. Inhabitants of an area near Philistia not conquered by Joshua (Josh 13:2) where David made raids while living with the Philistines (1 Sam 27:8-11).

GETHER A descendant of SHEM and son of Aram and progenitor of the Arameans or Syrians in the Table of Nations (Gen 10:23; 1 Chron 1:17).

GETHSEMANE An olive orchard located within the Mount of Olives. It is the site for the depiction of Jesus' agonizing prayer, Judas' betrayal, and Jesus' arrest (Mark 14:32; Matt 26:36).

GEUEL One of twelve spies Moses sent from the wilderness of Kadesh to explore the land of Canaan. This son of Machi of the tribe of Gad was among ten who advised Moses against going into Canaan (Num 13:15).

GEZER, GEZERITES A prominent mound near Ramleh, at the juncture of the central hills and central coastal plain.

GIANTS The REPHAIM were individuals of immense size and strength. GOLIATH, the Philistine giant slain by David, was noted for extraordinary height (1 Sam 17:23-54). Archaeological evidence of a giant race is minimal. Biologists note that abnormal size consistently results in sterility, thus a large assemblage of bone specimens from a race of giants is unlikely. The giant with six fingers on each hand and six toes on each foot (2 Sam 21:20) is consistent with the genetic abnormalities known in people with anterior pituitary hypertrophy.

Two types of giants are seen in the text. The NEPHILIM were offspring from divine and human relations such as the union in Gen 6:1-4 ("the ancient heroes, famous men"). A second group were giants born of human parents, such as the Rephaim (Deut 2:11, 20; 3:11, 13; Josh 12:4; 13:12; 17:15).

GIBBETHON A city originally assigned to the tribe of Dan in west-central Palestine (Josh 19:44) before they moved north.

GIBEA The grandson of Caleb by his secondary wife Maacah (1 Chron 2:49). His father was Sheva.

GIBEAH Several place-names mentioned in the OT.

1. A town in the territory of Judah listed as being south of Hebron (Josh 15:57).

2. A town in the territory of Ephraim that is the burial place of Eleazar the priest, who helped Joshua make the tribal allotments (Josh 24:33).

3. A town in Benjamin (1 Sam 13:2), which appears prominently in Judg 19–21 (cf Hos 9:9; 10:9) and has been associated with the seat of Saul's kingship (1 Sam 11:4; 15:34). Scholars disagree as to whether Gibeah was the hometown of Saul or only his seat of power. Regardless of the location of Gibeah, what is clear are the connections drawn between the rape of the Levite's secondary wife at Gibeah (Judg 19) and Saul's reign from Gibeah; these connections were possibly made to denigrate traditions about Saul's kingship.

GIBEON, GIBEONITES Gibeon is referred to primarily as a place-name in the OT. It is a strategic city in the territory of Benjamin. The Gibeonites feature prominently in the conquest narratives of the book of Joshua. While the city remains significant during the united monarchical period, it receives only scant mention in later historical periods. There are also two references to Gibeon as a personal name in the genealogies of Saul (1 Chron 8:29; 9:35).

GIDDALTI One of the sons of Heman, who, along with the sons of Asaph and Jeduthun, was commissioned by David to prophesy to the accompaniment of musical instruments (1 Chron 25:4).

GIDDEL 1. Progenitor of a family of temple servants returning after Babylonian captivity (Ezra 2:1-2, 43-54; Neh 7:49).

2. Progenitor of a family of Solomon's servants returning after Babylonian captivity (Ezra 2:1-2, 55-57; Neh 7:58).

GIDEON The story of Gideon and his family is the 4th of six told in the central section of the book of Judges (3:7–16:31). Gideon's position is pivotal in the book. The chieftains who precede him are exemplary characters who succeed in making the land "peaceful" (Judg 3:11, 30; 5:31). Gideon's story begins on a high note suggesting that he will rank not only with Othniel, Ehud, and Barak, but even with Abraham and Moses. His end, however, represents a nadir that places him instead with King Jeroboam, "because he made Israel sin too" (1 Kgs 14:16). After Gideon's death his son Abimelech only makes things worse.

And the last two chieftains, Jephthah and Samson, follow him in his successes and especially his failures. The peacefulness brought by the first four chieftains will not appear again in the book. Thus Gideon experiences a turning point in his own life and represents a turning point in the book.

GIDEONI Father of ABIDAN, the leader of the tribe of Benjamin in the wilderness (Num 1:11; 2:22; 7:60, 65; 10:24).

GIHON RIVER The second river flowing from EDEN (Gen 2:13). See GIHON SPRING.

GIHON SPRING Ancient JERUSALEM's only permanent water source, located outside the fortified city in a cave in the Kidron Valley. Gihon was a siphon-type spring, fed by groundwater that sporadically "burst forth" through cracks in the cave's floor. Depending on the season of the year, Gihon may have provided enough water to supply about 2,500 people in a day.

Solomon's coronation occurred at this site (1 Kgs 1:33, 38, 45; 2 Chron 32:30; 33:14).

GILALAI A priest and musician who participated in the consecration of the rebuilt wall around Jerusalem (Neh 12:36).

GILBOA, MOUNT Mount Gilboa is a ridge of limestone hills in the northern reaches of the central highlands extending into the eastern Jezreel Valley, rising 1,600 ft. above sea level and is south of the Moreh hill. The main OT narrative concerning Mount Gilboa relates the battle between Israel and the Philistines who were encamped in the Jezreel Valley. Israel gathered on Mount Gilboa. Saul was defeated and his three sons died with him at the hands of the Philistines (1 Sam 28:1-4; 31:1-13). Saul's headless body was hung on the walls of Beth-shan about 7 mi. away. David's lament (2 Sam 1:17-27, esp. 21) memorializes the death of Saul and Jonathan.

GILEAD, BALM IN The aromatic ointment of an unidentified plant, known in ancient times for its presumed medicinal qualities (Jer 46:11) and exported from Gilead to Egypt and Phoenicia (Ezek 27:17). Gilead's association with healing BALM became well known in the African American spiritual based on Jeremiah's rhetorical question (Jer 8:22).

GILEAD, GILEADITES The name of three individuals in the OT, a tribal designation for the inhabitants of the territory of Gilead (Gileadites, Gadites), and a place centrally located east of the Jordan between the river Yarmuk and the Dead Sea.

1. The son of Machir and grandson of Manasseh (Num 26:29-32; 36:1-2; 1 Chron 2:21, 23) who fathered six sons: Iezier, Helek, Shechem, Asriel, Shemida, and Hepher—all significant clan leaders.

2. The father of JEPHTHAH, a son born of a prostitute (Judg 11:1-2). Jephthah was exiled from his homeland by his brothers, who sought to divide his inheritance between themselves. Following the invasion of the area by the Ammonites, Jephthah was called back to Gilead years later to deliver the people from foreign oppression (Judg 10–11).

3. An ancestor of ABIHAIL and a descendant of Gad mentioned in 1 Chron 5:11-14.

4. Gilead's descendants, also called Gileadites or Gadites, dwelt in the region bounded by the Arnon in the south, the Jordan Valley on the west, Jabbok at the north and south, and the desert in the east (see GAD, GADITES).

5. According to the biblical text, Jacob settled in the region called Gilead (Gen 31:23). Moses defeated Og and Sihon, two Amorite kings controlling all Gilead and Bashan (Deut 4:47-49).

GILGAL A shrine in the early premonarchic period and the early monarchy.

GINATH The father of TIBNI, the failed rival of OMRI for the throne in Israel after the death of ZIMRI (1 Kgs 16:21-22).

GINNETHON 1. One of the priestly signatories to the covenant drawn up by Ezra (Neh 10:6).

2. Head of a priestly family listed during the tenure of Joiakim (Neh 12:4, 16), probably a reference to the same family as Neh 10:6.

GISHPA Mentioned along with ZIHA as having been in charge of the Nethinim (Neh 11:21).

GIZONITE Hashem the Gizonite is listed as one of David's warriors (1 Chron 11:34). The notice should point to Gizo as Hashem's place of birth, but no such place is known.

GLORY, GLORIFY Glory-language in the Bible has both subjective and objective senses. Subjectively, glory refers to the act of worship (e.g., "give glory to God"). Objectively, glory denotes the object of worship (i.e., God's revealed presence, God's glory). In both its subjective and objective senses, glory-language became an important marker in the development of Israel and the church's faith (monotheism) and practice (worship). What was once reserved for Israel's one true God ("giving glory to God," "glorifying God"), early Christians ascribed to the resurrected Jesus. Further, Christians claimed that Jesus was the glory of God, God's revealed presence.

Glory's most significant theological usage was as a sign of divine presence. As such, glory: (1) legitimized sacred leaders, time, and space; (2) communicated the unqualified blessing of God; (3) helped define what the eschatological future with God was to be like; (4) described the anthropomorphic depictions of the Lord in apocalyptic visions; and (5) was employed by Jesus to define his own future role as the Human One. (6) Earliest Christianity took over the hope for a future age defined by eschatological glory, and (7) effected a profound referential shift by replacing the expectation for an apocalypse of the Lord's glory with Jesus with and as the glory of the Lord. Such a shift took place because both (8) Jesus and (9) Jesus' resurrection were interpreted as an apocalypse of God's presence.

GNAT The third Egyptian plague (Exod 8:16-19) was an abundance of insects, although the exact insect is impossible to discover (CEB and NKJV, "lice"; NIV, "flies"; NEB, "maggots").

GOAD A long-handled, pointed instrument utilized by plowmen when driving or guiding their oxen. Sometimes it was tipped with metal to clean the plow (1 Sam 13:21). Shamgar used a goad, or "animal prod," to kill the Philistines (Judg 3:31).

GOAT, GOATHERD The goat was as important an animal for Israelite economy and culture as the sheep. Although goats are not very selective in their diet, they mature quickly, and are a good source of milk, meat, and hair. Goats are shorn once a year usually from May to June. Goat hair has been used for making tents, sacks, and rope.

GOD, NAMES OF The question of divine identity is a theologically critical one in the Bible, because the people of the OT and the NT worshipped neither an inanimate object nor an impersonal being, but someone with whom they related. Since in ancient Israel the name of a person signified that person's nature and character, a survey of the various names of God will give some insights about how God was understood. While *the Lord* is the distinctive name by which Israel's God was known, there are numerous other designations such as father, mother, brother, husband, holy one, mighty one, fear of Isaac, shield, and rock.

GOD-FEARER A term that designates Gentile sympathizers with Judaism (e.g., Acts 17:4). CEB has "God-worshipper."

GODLESS A person who ignores God, God's rules, and the threat of punishment for so doing (Job 8:13; Isa 10:6; 33:14).

GOD'S SON Biblical authors use "God's son" or its equivalents (e.g., "my son," "son of the Most High") with reference to a variety of persons or groups. Most famously, "God's Son" appears in the NT as a title or appellation for Jesus, and was subsequently taken up into the later christological and trinitarian debates from which it emerged as a primary component of creedal orthodoxy ("the only Son of God, eternally begotten of the Father, of one being with the Father"). Although this later development has its roots in the NT, the later use of the term should not simply be read back into the NT in disregard of the intervening stages of development.

GOG A descendant of Reuben listed only in a genealogical list in 1 Chron 5:1-10 as a brother of Shemaiah and Shemei, all sons of Joel (v. 4).

GOG AND MAGOG Gog from the land of Magog first appears in Ezek 38–39 as the archetypal evil force rising up in the eschatological age, marshaling all the enemies of Israel to attack this peaceful and defenseless people. The Lord defeats Gog and his hordes, establishing the promised covenant of peace (Ezek 34:25; 37:26). Gog and Magog also appear in Rev 20:7-10, where Magog has become a general, fighting alongside Gog.

GOLAN Moses chose the city of Golan as one of three cities of refuge east of the Jordan in the territory of Bashan allotted the half-tribe of Manasseh (Deut 4:43; Josh 20:8). Golan became a Gershonite levitical city (Josh 21:27; 1 Chron 6:71 [Heb. 6:56]).

GOLD Gold, one of the most precious of metals, is cited frequently in the Bible, both in a literal and a metaphorical sense. The traditional source of gold was OPHIR (1 Kgs 9:28, probably south Arabia or Yemen). Parvaim is also mentioned as a place of origin (2 Chron 3:6), but this has not been identified and may well be another name for Yemen, or the term may simply mean "from the east."

Gold was a synonym for wealth. Because of its intrinsic value, gold was also used as currency, although it seems to have been largely replaced by SILVER as the more common currency in the later Iron Age.

GOLDEN CALF See CALF, GOLD.

GOLDEN RULE, THE In the SERMON ON THE MOUNT, the following words are attributed to Jesus: "You should treat people in the same way that you want people to treat you" (Matt 7:12; Luke 6:31). As a summary of the Law and the Prophets, this saying functions as a concise abridgment of Jesus' message, similar to the "double commandment" in Matt 22:37-40. The Golden Rule and the "double commandment" each function as a succinct summation of the TEN COMMANDMENTS (Exod 20:13-17; Deut 5:17-21).

GOLGOTHA "The Skull." The place of Christ's crucifixion (Luke 23:33; Matt 27:33; Mark 15:22; John 19:17).

GOLIATH Philistine champion defeated by David in single combat (1 Sam 17). Though Goliath is well armed and described as a giant, David defeats him with one stone and a slingshot.

GOMER 1. Gomer the daughter of DIBLAIM was the wife of the prophet Hosea. Gomer is taken by the prophet as a living sign and becomes the mother of three symbolic children: Jezreel, "No Compassion," and "Not My People" (Hos 1:3-9).

2. Oldest son of Japheth, grandson of Noah, and the father of Ashkenaz, Riphath, and Togarmah according to the Table of Nations (Gen 10:2-3; cf 1 Chron 1:5-6). Ezekiel names "Gomer and all his troops" among the nations to be defeated as part of God's judgment on King Gog of Magog (Ezek 38:2-6).

GOMORRAH One of the cities in "the entire valley" destroyed by God (Gen 19:24-25); information in Genesis indicates that Gomorrah was located in the Jordan Valley in the Dead Sea area (Gen 13:10).

GOOD NEWS From Hebrew and Greek verbs meaning "to preach/bring glad tidings"; also translated "good tidings" or "glad tidings." In the OT's historical books, the phrase refers to news of military victory. The prophets develop theological nuances for the phrase, using it in reference to God's activity, especially God's faithfulness to God's people in exile (e.g., Isaiah). In the NT, the phrase usually indicates the activity or message of God, specifically the gospel of Jesus Christ. Reports of good news are brought by various agents including prophets, angels, Jesus, apostles, and other messengers.

GOSHEN 1. Goshen is the name given to an area believed to be in the eastern Egyptian Delta region where the Israelites resided from the time of Joseph until their sojourn from Egypt. The land of Goshen is described in Gen 46–47 as an area within EGYPT where Jacob and his sons were allowed to settle and, important, a region that was suitable for raising and shepherding livestock. Goshen is twice characterized as "the land's best location" (Gen 47:6, 11) on which the Israelites, as pastoralists, could care for both their own flocks and those of the pharaoh (47:6).

2. The land of Goshen occupied by Joshua's forces (Josh 10:41 and 11:16) is located in the southern highlands of Canaan between Hebron and the arid southern plain.

3. A city of Judah referred to in Josh 15:51, located in the highlands.

GOSPEL, MESSAGE In the NT, *gospel* is never used for a written document, but is the comprehensive term for the good news of God's saving act in Jesus Christ, communicated in a variety of images and concepts.

GOSPELS The word *gospel* is based on the Old English term *god spel*, "good news" or "good tidings." Sometime during the 2nd cent. CE, based on Mark's use of the term *gospel* to describe the content of his work, the term came to be applied to works like Mark, Matthew, Luke, and John, which were narratives of the life and teachings of Jesus. The oldest use of "gospel" for a type of literature may be the titles of the canonical Gospels themselves. These four Gospels were given similar titles when assembled in a fourfold collection, ca. 150 CE.

GOSPELS, APOCRYPHAL A general description of a large body of anonymous (i.e., the Gospel of the Ebionites and the Gospel of the Hebrews) or pseudepigraphal (i.e., the Gospel of Thomas and the Gospel of Peter), popular, extracanonical Jesus literature that arose from the early 2nd–5th cent. CE (and even later). They typically present themselves as apostolic and implicitly equal in authority to the canonical Gospels. Many of these gospels are popular in the sense that ordinary Christians wrote them, rather than scholars, and they were based on popular Jesus traditions or tried to fill in lacunae in the canonical Gospels, such as Jesus' childhood or events between his resurrection and ascension. A very few, like the Gospel of Thomas, probably preserve authentic sayings of Jesus not found elsewhere. See APOCRYPHA, NT.

GOTHOLIAH Called ATHALIAH in Ezra 8:7, he is the father of Jeshaiah, the family head of Elam who returned with Ezra from Babylon (1 Esdr 8:33).

GOTHONIEL Gothoniel was the father of Chabris, a magistrate of Bethulia, who heard the testimony of Achior against Holofernes (Jdt 6:15).

GOVERNMENT In broad terms, *government* refers to the institutions, processes, and individuals through which order is created and maintained in a given society. These institutions and processes deal primarily with the creation and enforcement of legislation, taxation, control of the economy, and military mobilization. Village chiefdoms, monarchy, and empire are the most common forms of government in biblical writings.

GOVERNOR An official empowered by a king or by an emperor with responsibilities for a particular region.

GOZAN A region and river in northwest Mesopotamia where Tilgath-Pilneser III (744–727 BCE) exiled the Transjordanian tribes (1 Chron 5:26). Then Shalmaneser V (726–722 BCE) or Sargon (721–705 BCE) also deported some Israelites there (2 Kgs 17:6; 18:11).

GRACE The word *grace* is employed frequently in the NT writings, particularly in the letters of Paul, to designate the signal demonstration of God's goodwill toward humankind in the person of Jesus Christ and the effects of that goodwill in human lives. That God shows himself gracious in his dealings with human beings is a central theme in OT and NT alike.

GRANARIES The storage of grain was a critical link to life in the marginal environment of ancient Israel. Regular droughts led to famine. The only safeguard against this possibility was to store wheat and other agricultural products in granaries and silos to tide the people over during difficult periods, but prolonged drought or insect infestations could leave these granaries empty and their villages abandoned by the starving people and animals (Joel 1:17). Underground pits lined with stones or plastered with lime and large storage jars were common in small villages. The wealthiest could have several barns to store their grain (Luke 12:18).

GREAT COMMISSION The closing pronouncement in the Gospel of Matthew (28:18-20). This is but one postresurrection directive found in the NT (see also Mark 16:15; Luke 24:47-49; John 20:21-23; Acts 1:8). Its significance in Matthew marks the shift from the ministry of Jesus to the ministry of the church.

GREECE Greece forms the southern part of the Balkans. To the east of the mainland lies the Aegean Sea, and to the west the Adriatic. The mainland stretches from Macedonia in the north down to Attica in the south; to the west, joined to the mainland by the narrow isthmus of Corinth, is the Peloponnese. Greece itself contains a large number of islands, such as Euboia, which lies just off the coast of the mainland.

GUEST A visitor or traveler to whom HOSPITALITY should be extended. Guests were dependent on the care and protection of the host (Judg 19:23). Both the OT and the NT describe guests as those invited for meals or celebratory feasts (1 Sam 9:24; 2 Sam 12:4; 1 Kgs 1:41, 49; Zeph 1:7; Matt 22:10-11), but a guest might also be anyone who needs lodging or a place to rest (Gen 18:3; 19:3). Jesus utilizes the Greco-Roman convention of "places of honor" in seating dinner guests to discuss the reversals of God's kingdom (Luke 12:37; 14:7).

GUNI 1. The second of the four sons of Naphtali (Gen 46:24; 1 Chron 7:13); eponymous ancestor of the tribe of Gunites (Num 26:48).

2. The grandfather of AHI, chief of a Gadite clan (1 Chron 5:15).

Hh

HA SHEM Leviticus 24:11 already refers to "the Lord's name," the pronunciation of which was blasphemy. Deut 28:58 refers to "the awesome and glorious name of the LORD your God." Hence, the term *Adonai* (and sometimes *Elohim*) came to be pronounced wherever *Yahweh* appeared. By rabbinic times, however, even Adonai was deemed too holy a name, and so the Tetragrammaton was simply referred to as "the name." See ADONAI, ADONAY; GOD, NAMES OF.

HAAHASHTARI A Judahite, the son of Ashhur by his wife Naarah (1 Chron 4:6). The name may also refer to a tribe, the AHASHTARITES.

HABAIAH A priest (Hobaiah [Neh 7:63]) whose descendants were among postexilic returnees to Jerusalem prevented from serving as priests due to a lack of records establishing their lineage until a priest was available to determine their ancestry by lot (Ezra 2:61; 1 Esdr 5:38).

HABAKKUK, BOOK OF The 8th book among the twelve Minor Prophets in the OT canon. Nothing is known of Habakkuk except that he is identified as a prophet in 1:1 and 3:1. His book differs from the other prophetic books in that it deals with a single subject: the question why God, whom Habakkuk believes to be the upholder of justice, seems to allow injustice to flourish without doing anything about it.

HABAZZINIAH The grandfather of the Rechabites, whose faithfulness Jeremiah tested by offering them wine to drink (Jer 35:3).

HABOR RIVER A tributary of the EUPHRATES RIVER along which the inhabitants of Samaria were settled following its conquest by the Assyrians in 721 BCE (2 Kgs 17:6; 18:11).

HACALIAH The father of Nehemiah (Neh 1:1; 10:1 [Heb. 10:2]).

HACHILAH A hill in the wilderness of Ziph where David took refuge from Saul (1 Sam 23:19; 26:1). Saul also encamped on this hill during his pursuit of David (1 Sam 26:3).

HACHMONI 1. The father of Jashobeam, one of David's warriors (1 Chron 11:11).

2. The father of Jehiel, a court official who later attended the king's sons (1 Chron 27:32).

HADAD 1. One of Ishmael's sons (Gen 25:15; 1 Chron 1:30).

2. The son of Bedad and one of the kings of Edom. He defeated the Midianites in the land of Moab and established the center of his government in the city of Avith (Gen 36:35; 1 Chron 1:46).

3. An Edomite king who succeeded Baal-hanan (1 Chron 1:50). In the Gen 36 list of the Edomite kings his name appears as HADAR (Gen 36:39).

4. A prince from the royal house of Edom, who became an adversary of Solomon (1 Kgs 11:14-22).

HADADEZER Son of Rehob, Hadadezer

was king of ZOBAH in the 10th cent. BCE (2 Sam 8:3).

HADAD-RIMMON A compound name for the ANE storm god (Zech 12:11). *Hadad* and *rimmon* both mean "thunderer."

HADAR 1. The eighth king of Edom, he succeeded Baal-hanan (Gen 36:39).

2. The eighth son of Ishmael (Gen 25:15).

HADASHAH Town listed in the allotment to the tribe of Judah (Josh 15:37).

HADASSAH The initial name the narrator supplies to identify ESTHER (Esth 2:7). The common interpretation is that Hadassah was her given Hebrew name, but that she was subsequently known as Esther.

HADES In Greek mythology, Hades is the god of the underworld.

HADLAI Either the father or the family name of Amasa, an Ephraimite chief during Pekah's reign (2 Chron 28:12).

HADORAM 1. A descendant of Joktan (Gen 10:27; 1 Chron 1:21).

2. The son of King Tou of HAMATH, sent by his father to congratulate David following his defeat of the Aramean king Hadadezer (1 Chron 18:10).

3. King Rehoboam's administrator of the department of conscript labor (2 Chron 10:18), called Adoniram in 1 Kgs 4:6; 5:14 [Heb. 5:28] and Adoram in 1 Kgs 12:18.

HAGABAH The head of a family of temple functionaries, the Nethinim, who are listed among those returning to Jerusalem from Babylon with Zerubbabel (Ezra 2:45; Neh 7:48;1 Esdr 5:29).

HAGAR Hagar's story is found in the OT in Gen 16:1-16 and 21:8-21. She was Sarai's Egyptian servant. In the NT, Hagar appears in Gal 4:21-31. She is the only named woman in the book of Galatians.

HAGGAI, BOOK OF The tenth book of the Minor Prophets (Book of the Twelve) in the OT. The book of Haggai addresses issues related to the reconstruction of the Second Temple in the early Persian period (520 BCE) in the province of Yehud. It traces the impetus of the project to the prophetic voice of Haggai and the response of the key leaders ZERUBBABEL (Davidic governor) and JESHUA (Zadokite priest) and of their community. This rebuilding project is understood as inaugurating an era of peace and prosperity for the people of God that is but a prelude to the commencement of the universal reign of Yahweh through a Davidic royal figure.

HAGGEDOLIM The father of Zabdiel (Neh 11:14), the official in charge of the priests who settled in Jerusalem after the Babylonian exile.

HAGGI, HAGGITES 1. The second-listed of seven sons of Gad and grandson of Jacob and Zilpah (Gen 46:16). Haggi was one of Zilpah's sixteen descendants among the seventy who arrived with Jacob in Egypt (Gen 46:18, 27).

2. An Israelite clan whose ancestor was Haggi (Num 26:15).

HAGGIAH A Levite among the descendants of Merari in a genealogical list in 1 Chron 6:30 [Heb. 6:15]. He is listed as the father of Asaiah and the son of Shimea.

HAGGITH A wife of David and mother of Adonijah, the fourth son of David born at Hebron (2 Sam 3:4; 1 Chron 3:2), who failed to seize the throne (1 Kgs 1:5–2:25).

HAGRITE, HAGRITES David's warrior

Jaziz, who tended David's flocks, has the epithet *Hagrite*, which identifies his residence (1 Chron 27:30).

HAIL, HAILSTONES Hailstorms are uncommon in Syria-Palestine, although they do occur during severe thunderstorms in the spring or summer. Hail is formed when raindrops freeze after having been lifted to colder regions by upward air currents. When their masses have increased to an extent that air currents can no longer support them, they fall to the ground, sometimes doing great damage (Exod 9:25).

HAIR, HAIRS Semitic men are depicted in Egyptian art as having curly hair of moderate length. They would have favored the Mesopotamians, who described themselves as "the black-headed people" in reference to their typical hair color.

New Testament evidence suggests that women typically wore their hair long. The woman who anointed Jesus' feet with oil dried his feet with her hair (Luke 7:38). Paul reflected a belief that it was shameful for a woman to shave her head (1 Cor 11:5-6), and considered it a lesson of nature that men should maintain short hair rather than wearing it long, like women (1 Cor 11:14-15).

Sorrow or the changing of one's heart or life was expressed by SHAVING the head (Isa 15:7), pulling out the hair (Ezra 9:3), or imposing dust or ashes (Josh 7:6; Job 42:6; Ezek 27:30).

HAKELDAMA Aramaic for "Field of Blood." Its scriptural origin is in Matt 27:3-10 as the potter's field bought with the blood money of Judas to bury strangers in (see Acts 1:18-19). The identification of this area with Hakeldama was made as early as the 3rd cent. CE.

HAKKATAN The father of clan chief Johanan, listed as a descendant of Azgad (Ezra 8:12; 1 Esdr 8:38), and, along with 110 other descendants of Azgad, among the returnees who left Babylon with Ezra during the reign of Artaxerxes.

HAKKOZ 1. The head of a clan of priests, descendants of Aaron upon whom the 7th lot fell when David, Zadok, and Ahimelech organized the priests for their liturgical duties (according to 1 Chron 24:10).

2. A priestly clan head whose descendants were among the returnees who left Babylon with Zerubbabel but were unable to provide documentation establishing their genealogy and were thus disqualified from serving as priests until another priest could determine their ancestry through use of the URIM AND THUMMIM (Ezra 2:61; Neh 7:63; 1 Esdr 5:39).

HAKUPHA The head of a family of temple functionaries who were among those who returned to Jerusalem from Babylon with Zerubbabel during the reign of Cyrus (Ezra 2:51; Neh 7:53; 1 Esdr 5:31).

HALAH The location where the Assyrian king deported the inhabitants of Samaria during the reign of King Hoshea (ca. 722 BCE; 2 Kgs 17:6; 18:11).

HALLELUJAH This expression is a call to praise the Lord. In the NT the Greek equivalent occurs only in Rev 19:1, 3, 4, 6, where it functions in hymns celebrating the victory of God.

HALLOHESH The father of Shallum, who governed half of Jerusalem and who, along with his daughters, helped repair the city wall (Neh 3:12). Hallohesh also appears among leaders of the people whose names were inscribed on the sealed copy of Ezra's covenant (Neh 10:24 [Heb. 10:25]).

HAM, HAMITES 1. Ham is classically understood as the second son of Noah because of the repeated secondary placement of his name "Shem, Ham, and Japheth" (Gen 5:32; 6:10; 7:13; 9:18; 1 Chron 1:4).

2. Ham or Hamites may be related to the Egyptian term for *Egypt*.

3. A town in the northern Transjordan. According to Gen 14:5, Ham was the dwelling place of the Zuzim.

HAMAN King Ahasuerus's highest adviser in the book of Esther. Haman is said to be an Agagite (Esth 3:1), and thus ancestrally set up against Mordecai and Esther—Benjaminites (see AGAG, AGAGITE).

HAMATH, HAMATHITE 1. A city-state in central Syria (2 Kgs 14:28).

2. Hamathites were citizens of Hamath, descendants of Canaan (Gen 10:18; 1 Chron 1:16).

HAMATH-ZOBAH A location mentioned in 2 Chron 8:3 as having been captured by Solomon.

HAMMATH 1. The ancestor of the Rechabites (1 Chron 2:55).

2. A fortified city of Naphtali (Josh 19:35) that was given to the Levites in Josh 21:32.

HAMMEDATHA The father of Haman, an Agagite (Esth 3:1, 10; 8:5; 9:10, 24), and the antagonist in the Esther story.

HAMMER Hammers came in various sizes and were employed for various tasks in ancient Israel. However, the claw hammer that could be used to remove nails was not invented until the Roman period when heavier iron nails were employed in construction and for crucifixions. Heavy-duty mallet-like implements were used for domestic tasks such as driving in tent pegs (Judg 4:21).

HAMMOLECHETH Gilead's sister, and mother to four sons (Ishhod, Abiezer, Mahlah, and Shemida) in the lineage of Manasseh found in 1 Chron 7.

HAMMOTH-DOR One of the levitical towns in the land allotted to Naphtali (Josh 21:32).

HAMMUEL The son of Mishma and the father of Zaccur, Hammuel appears in a genealogical list of descendants of Simeon (1 Chron 4:26) as a descendant of Shaul, the 5th son of Simeon.

HAMOR The father of Shechem, whom Simeon and Levi killed along with his son in retribution for the rape of DINAH (Gen 34).

HAMRAN One of four sons of Seir's grandson Dishon mentioned in a Horite genealogy (1 Chron 1:41).

HAMSTRING Soldiers would "hamstring" or "cripple" an enemy warhorse to disable it, meaning cut the large tendon at the tarsal joint of its hind leg (Josh 11:6, 9; 2 Sam 8:4; 1 Chron 18:4). Oxen could also be hamstrung (Gen 49:6).

HAMUL, HAMULITES 1. The younger son of PEREZ and grandson of Judah and TAMAR (Gen 46:12; 1 Chron 2:5).

2. Hamul is the ancestral head of the clan of the Hamulites (Num 26:21).

HAMUTAL Married to King Josiah, Hamutal the daughter of Jeremiah of Libnah became the mother of two kings, Jehoahaz and Zedekiah (2 Kgs 23:31; 24:18; Jer 52:1).

HANA A temple servant whose descendants with their families and possessions were escorted to Jerusalem by King Darius's horsemen to ensure their safe return (1 Esdr 5:30).

HANAEL Tobit's brother (Tob 1:21), whose son Ahikar served the kings Sennacherib and Esarhaddon.

HANAMEL The son of Shallum, Jeremiah's uncle (Jer 32:7-9). Jeremiah bought a field from this cousin at

ANATHOTH during the Babylonian siege of Jerusalem.

HANAN 1. Shahak's son who descended from Benjamin and lived in Jerusalem (1 Chron 8:23, 28).

2. Azel's son who descended from Saul, a Benjaminite (1 Chron 8:38; 9:44).

3. Maacah's son and one of David's warriors (1 Chron 11:43).

4. Head of a family of temple servants who returned to Jerusalem after the exile (Ezra 2:46; Neh 7:49; 1 Esdr 5:30).

5. A Levite who read and interpreted the Instruction for the people to understand (Neh 8:7) and whose name was included on the sealed document of the covenant (Neh 10:10 [Heb. 10:11]).

6. A leader whose name was included on the sealed covenant document (Neh 10:22 [Heb. 10:23]).

7. A leader whose name also appeared on the sealed covenant document (Neh 10:26 [Heb. 10:27]).

8. Zacur's son whom Nehemiah appointed as assistant to the temple treasurers (Neh 13:13).

9. Head of a prophetic guild, who resided in a chamber in the temple (Jer 35:4).

HANANEL, TOWER OF Mentioned in Jer 31:38; Zech 14:10; and in Neh 3:1 and 12:39 as being at the northwestern border of the newly constructed walls.

HANANI Name of several men:

1. Father of the prophet Jehu (1 Kgs 16:1, 7; 2 Chron 19:2; 20:34) and probably the seer who told King Asa of Judah the consequences of his lack of trust in God and his reliance on the king of Aram (2 Chron 16:7).

2. Son of Heman, the king's seer, who, with his brothers and father, was responsible for music in the temple and had been trained to sing (1 Chron 25:4-7, 25).

3. Descendant of Immer whom Ezra required to dismiss his foreign wife and children (Ezra 10:20; 1 Esdr 9:21).

4. Nehemiah's brother who told Nehemiah about the need for the walls and the gates in Jerusalem to be rebuilt and whom Ezra placed in charge over Jerusalem (Neh 1:2; 7:2).

5. A musician who participated in the dedication of the Jerusalem wall (Neh 12:36).

HANANIAH 1. Zerubbabel's son, father of Pelatiah and Jeshaiah, and a descendant of Solomon (1 Chron 3:19, 21).

2. Shashak's son, a descendant of Benjamin, and a tribal chief living in Jerusalem (1 Chron 8:24).

3. Son of Heman, the king's seer, and so served under his direction to provide music for the Lord's house (1 Chron 25:4, 23).

4. A commander of King Uzziah's soldiers (2 Chron 26:11).

5. Descendant of Bebai who sent away his foreign wife and their children according to Ezra's instructions (Ezra 10:28; 1 Esdr 9:29).

6. A perfumer who returned to Jerusalem to restore the wall from the Old Gate to the Broad Wall (Neh 3:8).

7. A repairman who worked near Shemaiah and was Shelemiah's son (Neh 3:30). He is possibly the same person as number 6.

8. Governor of the citadel, whom Nehemiah put in charge over Jerusalem (Neh 7:2).

9. A Levite who placed his name on the sealed covenant document (Neh 10:23).

10. A priest who played the trumpet during the celebration that dedicated the rebuilding of the Jerusalem wall (Neh 12:12, 41).

11. A false prophet from Gibeon who predicted Nebuchadnezzar's defeat, which he symbolized through breaking the yoke that Jeremiah wore (Jer 28).

12. Father of Zedekiah (Jer 36:12).

13. Grandfather of Irijah who charged and arrested Jeremiah for desertion (Jer 37:13).

14. Daniel's companion who was

renamed Shadrach by Ashpenaz, King Nebuchadnezzar's palace master (Dan 1:11, 17, 19).

15. A Levite whose descendants were among Ezra's returnees to Jerusalem (1 Esdr 8:48).

HAND Predominantly, *hand* refers to the body part in its biblical occurrences, but it also often appears as a metonym for strength and power.

HANGING According to the Bible, a criminal who was executed might then be hanged or impaled after death as a means of disgracing the criminal.

HANNAH Hannah was one of two wives of Elkanah, an Ephraimite (1 Sam 1–2). Hannah had no children, but Elkanah's other wife Peninnah did have children. During the annual pilgrimage to Shiloh, Hannah prayed at the shrine, promising that if God gave her a son she would give the son back to God. She then bore a son whom she named SAMUEL. After she weaned him she took him to Eli the priest at Shiloh in fulfillment of her promise. On that occasion she sang the hymn known today as the Song of Hannah.

HANNIEL The name of two men in the OT, both of whom are given the title of a PRINCE or chief.

1. A leader from the tribe of Manasseh. Hanniel son of Ephod was in charge of distributing the tribal inheritance among the clans of Manasseh (Num 34:23).

2. A man from the tribe of Asher (1 Chron 7:39). Hanniel son of Ulla is described as a mighty warrior and one of the leaders of the princes.

HANOCH 1. Third-listed son of Midian (Gen 25:4; 1 Chron 1:33).

2. First-listed son of Reuben, Jacob's oldest (Gen 46:9; 1 Chron 5:3), and eponymous ancestor of the Hanochite clan (Exod 6:14; Num 26:5).

In other occurrences of this name, modern translations including the CEB render the name ENOCH (e.g., Gen 4:17).

HANUKKAH The Hebrew title for the Jewish celebration known as the Feast of Dedication. Commemorated for eight days beginning on the 25th of the month of KISLEV (Nov–Dec), Hanukkah celebrates the victory of ancient Judeans over the oppressive and genocidal policies of the Seleucid king Antiochus IV Epiphanies. Antiochus, for reasons still unclear to modern scholarship, forbade the practice of Judaism and desecrated the Jerusalem temple. According to 1 Macc 4:36-61 and 2 Macc 10:1-8, a group of Judean rebels under the leadership of Judas Maccabee retook the temple on the 25th of Kislev in 165 or 164 BCE and purified the temple of the desecrations committed by Antiochus.

HANUN 1. Hanun is the name of the son of Nahash the Ammonite king, who succeeds him on the throne. David sends messengers of goodwill to him, but he humiliates them and sends them back (2 Sam 10:1-4; 2 Chron 19:2-6).

2. An individual who worked in Jerusalem under the leadership of Nehemiah helping to rebuild the temple and the walls around Jerusalem (Neh 3:13).

3. Another individual who worked under the leadership of Nehemiah (Neh 3:30).

HAPPIZZEZ A priestly clan chief upon whom the 18th lot fell when David, Zadok, and Ahimelech divided the descendants of Aaron according to their tasks (1 Chron 24:15). The clan may be connected with BETH-PAZZEZ (Josh 19:21).

HARAN 1. The personal name Haran refers to the brother of Abram who died in Ur before Terah and his sons left for the west (Gen 11–12). He was the father of Lot, who traveled with Abram when he left the town Haran for the land of promise (Gen 12).

2. Haran is also an individual listed in 1 Chron 23:9 as the son of Shimei in the tribe of Levi.

3. Haran is listed as the son of Caleb and his secondary wife Ephah (1 Chron 2:46).

4. Haran refers to a place where the family of Terah settled after leaving Ur.

HARAR Three individuals in the OT are noted as being from Harar: AGEE (2 Sam 23:11), his son SHAMMAH (2 Sam 23:33; SHAGEE in 1 Chron 11:34), and SHARAR (2 Sam 23:33; SACHAR in 1 Chron 11:35). In every occurrence the designation is somehow associated with one of David's military elite.

HARBONA One of the seven EUNUCHs serving as adviser to King AHASUERUS (Esth 1:10). He recommends the king hang HAMAN on the very gallows that Haman had arranged for Mordecai (Esth 7:9).

HARE The hare is of the Leporidae family, along with the smaller rabbit, and is native to the Near East. The rabbit is not, arriving via the Romans. The hare is on the unclean list (Lev 11:6; Deut 14:7).

HAREPH Descendant of Caleb identified as the "father" (i.e., founder) of Beth-gader (1 Chron 2:51).

HARHAIAH After returning from exile, Harhaiah's son UZZIEL participated in the Jerusalem wall repairs under Nehemiah (Neh 3:8).

HARHAS The grandfather of SHALLUM, who is identified in 2 Kgs 22:14 as the husband of HULDAH the prophetess. In the par. text, 2 Chron 34:22, the grandfather's name is HASRAH.

HARHUR The name of the head of a family of temple functionaries known as the Nethinim who returned from Babylon with Zerubbabel (Ezra 2:51; Neh 7:53).

HARIM 1. The head of a priestly family that is listed among those David organized for liturgical service (1 Chron 24:8). Members of this family appear in Ezra 2:39; Neh 7:42; and 1 Esdr 5:25 among returnees who left Babylon with Zerubbabel (see also Neh 12:15).

2. The name of a lay family listed in Ezra 2:32 and Neh 7:35. A son of Harim assisted in rebuilding Jerusalem's walls (Neh 3:11). Members of the family divorced their foreign wives according to Ezra's order (Ezra 10:31).

3. A priest who appears as signatory to Ezra's covenant in (Neh 10:5 [Heb. 6]).

4. One of the lay signatories of Ezra's covenant (Neh 10:27 [Heb. 28]).

HARIPH A Judahite family patriarch who returned after the Babylonian exile and signed the covenant (Neh 10:19 [Heb. 10:20]). According to the census, the descendants of Hariph numbered 112 "sons" (Neh 7:24).

HARNEPHER The second of eleven sons of ZOPHAH (1 Chron 7:36) listed in the Asherite genealogy in 1 Chron 7.

HAROD 1. A spring, site of the camp where Gideon and his army prepare to battle Midian (Judg 7:1).

2. The hometown of two of the men listed among David's warriors known as "the Thirty" (2 Sam 23:25). Shammah and Elika are both identified as "from Harod."

HAROEH A son of Shobal (1 Chron 2:52), possibly identified with REAIAH in 1 Chron 4:2.

HAROSHETH-HA-GOIIM The home of Sisera, the commander of the army of King Jabin of Hazor (Judg 4:2).

HARSHA The head of a family of temple functionaries known as the Nethinim who returned to Jerusalem from Babylon along with Zerubbabel (Ezra 2:52; Neh 7:54).

HARUM The father of AHARHEL, whose families were descendants of their Judahite ancestor KOZ (1 Chron 4:8).

HARUMAPH JEDAIAH son of Harumaph is listed among those who rebuilt the wall under Nehemiah's leadership (Neh 3:10).

HARUPHITE The term is used in 1 Chron 12:6 in connection with the Benjaminite Shephatiah in a list of ambidextrous warriors who joined David while he was at Ziklag.

HARUZ Perhaps meaning "golden one," Haruz was the father of MESHULLEMETH mother of King AMON of Judah (2 Kgs 21:19), and, therefore, Haruz was great-grandfather of King JOSIAH (v. 24).

HASADIAH 1. The sixth of the seven sons of Zerubbabel (1 Chr 3:20), listed along with their one sister in 1 Chron 3:19-20.

2. The father of Zedekiah and the son of Hilkiah, Hasadiah appears as an ancestor of Baruch in Bar 1:1.

HASDRUBAL The name of several different Carthaginian generals.

1. The first and most notable (d. 221 BCE), the son-in-law of Hamilcar Barca, attempted diplomatic relations with Rome.

2. The second (d. 207 BCE), the son of Hamilcar Barca and younger brother of Hannibal. These brothers were involved in the Second Punic War (218–201 BCE) against Rome.

3. Hasdrubal was in command during the initial years of the HASMONEANS.

HASHABIAH 1. A Levite whose descendant served as a musician before the tent of meeting (1 Chron 6:32, 45).

2. A Levite and ancestor of Shemaiah who returned to Jerusalem after the exile (1 Chron 9:14; Neh 11:15).

3. A Levite and one of Jeduthun's sons who played lyres, sang, and prophesied according to David's directions (1 Chron 25:3, 19).

4. Along with his brothers, a Hebronite who managed the area of Israel west of the Jordan River (1 Chron 26:30).

5. Chief officer of the Levites during David's reign (1 Chron 27:17).

6. A chief among the Levites who generously supplied lambs and kids for Passover (2 Chron 35:9; 1 Esdr 1:9).

7. A levitical priest among those whom Iddo sent to join Ezra and who transported temple treasure to Jerusalem (Ezra 8:19, 24-30). This Hashabiah may be the same one who signed the sealed covenant document (Neh 10:11) and who was a levitical leader (Neh 12:24).

8. A returnee from the exile who rejected his foreign wife (Ezra 10:25).

9. Leader and repairman of part of the district of Keilah (Neh 3:17).

10. Descendant of Asaph and a Levite (Neh 11:22).

11. A priest during the reign of Joiakim (Neh 12:21).

HASHABNAH One of the "leaders of the people" (Neh 10:14) who sealed Nehemiah's covenant (Neh 10:25 [Heb. 10:26]).

HASHABNEIAH 1. The father of Hattush, who participated in the reconstruction of Jerusalem's walls under the direction of Nehemiah (Neh 3:10).

2. A Levite who participated in a liturgical blessing of the Lord that was spoken just prior to the sealing of Ezra's covenant (Neh 9:5).

HASHBADDANAH Nehemiah 8:4 lists this individual as standing to the left of Ezra during the public proclamation of the Instruction following the return from exile.

HASHEM According to 1 Chron, "the

family of Hashem" (11:34; cf 2 Sam 23:32) are among the heroes known as David's "Thirty." See JASHEN.

HASHUBAH The third son of Zerubbabel, the postexilic descendant of the Davidic line (1 Chron 3:20).

HASHUM A postexilic name appearing as the head or eponym of one of the families returning from exile with Zerubbabel (Ezra 2:19; 10:33; Neh 7:22; 8:4; 10:18; 1 Esdr 9:33).

HASMONEANS *Hasmoneans* is the term applied to the family of Maccabees.

HASRAH 1. The grandfather of the prophet HULDAH's husband. Hasrah appears in 2 Chron 34:22.

2. Head of a postexilic temple servant family, Hasrah is named in 1 Esdr 5:31 (but not Ezra 2:49 or Neh 7:51).

HASSENUAH A Benjaminite postexilic family name (1 Chron 9:7; Neh 11:9). Judah of the Hassenuah family was second in command (behind Joel son of Zichri) over Jerusalem (Neh 11:9).

HASSHUB 1. A Levite, the father of SHEMAIAH, who was among those who settled in Jerusalem after the Babylonian exile (1 Chron 9:14; Neh 11:15).

2. Two men given assignments in the rebuilding of Jerusalem (Neh 3:11, 23).

3. A leader of the people who sealed the covenant of Ezra (Neh 10:23).

HASUPHA Eponymous head of a temple servant family, Hasupha's name appears in the list of exile returnees under Zerubbabel (Ezra 2:43; Neh 7:46; 1 Esdr 5:29).

HATHACH One of the EUNUCHs King Ahasuerus appointed to attend to Esther, Hathach served as a messenger between Esther and Mordecai, informing Esther of Haman's plan to destroy the Jews, which he had learned from Mordecai, and then informing Mordecai of her reply (Esth 4:5-6, 9-10).

HATHATH Son of OTHNIEL of the tribe of Judah, listed in a genealogy and related to craftsmen of Israel (1 Chron 4:13).

HATIPHA A descendant of the temple servants who returned from Babylon with Zerubbabel (Ezra 2:54; Neh 7:56; 1 Esdr 5:32).

HATITA A descendant of the temple gatekeepers who returned from Babylon with Zerubbabel (Ezra 2:42; Neh 7:45; 1 Esdr 5:28).

HATTIL A descendant of the servants of Solomon who returned from Babylon with Zerubbabel (Ezra 2:57; Neh 7:59).

HATTUSH 1. A descendant of David and Zerubbabel (1 Chron 3:22).

2. A descendant of David among the family heads who returned to Jerusalem with Ezra (Ezra 8:2; 1 Esdr 8:29).

3. A man who worked on Jerusalem's walls (Neh 3:10). He could be the same as number 1.

4. A priest listed among the signatories to Ezra's covenant (Neh 10:4 [Heb. 5]).

HAURAN Hauran is a fertile plateau located in the northeastern part of Transjordan. It is bounded on the north by Mount Hermon and the river Pharpar, on the east by Jabal ad-Druze, on the south by the Yarmuk River, and on the west by the Sea of Galilee and the Golan Heights. It is mentioned in the Bible only in Ezek 47:16, 18 where it is described as the northeastern boundary of the restored land of Israel.

HAVILAH It is the land surrounded by the river Pishon, noted for gold (Gen 2:11). This name is given for a son of Cush (Gen 10:7; 1 Chron 1:9), as well as for the son of Joqtan, a descendant of Shem (Gen 10:29; 1 Chron 1:23).

HAVVOTH-JAIR A group of villages in the Bashan region of Gilead. They are described as consisting of either thirty villages (Judg 10:4) or a total of sixty villages (Josh 13:30; 1 Chron 2:23).

HAWK Several hawks are found in Palestine, the most common being the sparrow hawk, often in olive groves and oases.

HAZAEL King of Aram (see DAMASCUS) from 844 to ca. 800 BCE.

HAZAIAH Hazaiah is listed among the ancestors of Maaseiah, the local leader of a postexilic Jerusalem province (Neh 11:5).

HAZARMAVETH The Semetic son of Joktan and his descendants who settled the area in south Arabia of the Wadi Hadramaut (Gen 10:26; 1 Chron 1:20).

HAZEROTH Mentioned several times in the biblical text (Num 11:35; 12:1, 16; 33:17-18; Deut 1:1), Hazeroth is most notable for being the site at which Miriam and Aaron spoke against Moses (Num 12:1-16). In Num 12:16 Hazeroth is situated adjacent to the Wilderness of PARAN, itself consistently located near Edom in the region of the arid southern plain.

HAZIEL One of three sons of SHIMEI in a list of Levites whose families David enrolled for service in the temple (1 Chron 23:9).

HAZO One of the twelve sons of NAHOR, Abraham's brother (Gen 22:22). His mother MILCAH had seven other sons with Nahor.

HAZOR Tel Hazor is the site of an ancient city located in the Hule Valley, 8.5 mi. to the north of the Sea of Galilee on the eastern foot of the upper Galilee ridge. Hazor is first mentioned in the Bible in the conquest narrative of Joshua, where it is referred to as "the head of all those kingdoms in the past" (Josh 11:10-13), and again in the prose version of Deborah's wars (Judg 4). Later, Hazor is mentioned among the cities that were built by king Solomon (1 Kgs 9:15), and again as one of the Israelite cities destroyed during the campaign of Tiglath-pileser, king of Assyria in 732 BCE (2 Kgs 15:29). The plain of Hazor is mentioned in 1 Macc 11:67.

HAZZELELPONI The only listed daughter of Etam, who also had four sons, in the lineage of Judah (1 Chron 4:3).

HEAD The head as the upper part of the body (Gen 28:11, 18; 40:16-17). People bowed their heads in worship or prayer (Gen 24:26, 48; Ps 35:13), and kings (1 Sam 10:1; 2 Kgs 9:3, 6) and priests (Exod 29:7; Lev 21:10) were installed by anointing the head with oil. Mourners put dust or ashes on their head (2 Kgs 10:21; Job 16:4); people covered their heads in shame (Jer 14:3-4); and mockers wagged their heads (2 Kgs 19:21; Ps 64:8). Lifting one's head connoted pride (Judg 8:28; Job 10:15), unless it was God who lifted it (Pss 3:3; 27:6). People's evil deeds were said to return upon their heads (Josh 2:19; 1 Sam 25:39). The head was also considered to be the seat of a person's intellect (Dan 4:5, 10, 13); and a "head" was one person counted in a census (Num 1:2, 18, 20, 22).

In the NT, *head* likewise occurs most frequently in a literal sense (e.g., Matt 5:36; 6:17; 10:30; Mark 12:4; Luke 7:38, 46), including references to Jesus' head (Matt 8:20; 26:7; 27:29; Mark 14:3; Luke 9:58; John 19:2, 30); and Revelation features several references to the heads of various apocalyptic figures (e.g., 4:4; 9:7, 17, 19). In keeping with OT usage, the expression figuratively conveys the notion of leadership or authority in Paul's writings. Hence Paul calls Christ the head of the church (1 Cor 11:3, Eph 1:22; 4:15-16; 5:23; Col 1:18; 2:10, 19).

HEAD COVERING In the OT several head coverings are mentioned. Aaronic priests, royalty, men, and women sometimes wore a turban or headband (Exod 28:40; 29:9; 39; Lev 8; 13; Isa 3:18, 20). Turbans were removed in times of mourning (Ezek 24:17, 23). Women could wear a headscarf or VEIL (Gen 24:65; 38:14). Royalty wore a crown or diadem (1 Chron 20:2).

In 2 Cor 3:13-14, Paul discusses the head covering or veil worn by Moses (Exod 34:33-35), introducing a play on words between what covers the face and what covers understanding. The meaning of 1 Cor 11:4-16 is much debated and controversial. In 1st-cent. Roman society (Corinth was a Roman colony), head covering for women indicated a "respectable" status and invited protection from the law against sexual harassment.

HEART An inner organ and a symbol for human conduct and action.

HEATHEN See NATIONS.

HEAVEN The term *heaven* is used both in an astronomical sense for "sky" or cosmic space and in a theological sense for the divine realm far above the earth.

HEAVEN, NEW See NEW HEAVEN, NEW EARTH.

HEBER "Companion, association." The name of several individuals in the OT.

1. A son of Beriah the son of Asher the son of Jacob by Zilpah, as listed in Gen 46:17-18 and Num 26:45. The genealogy is repeated in 1 Chron 7:31 and 8:17.

2. An individual listed in the extended genealogy of Judah and identified as the father of Soco (1 Chron 4:18).

3. The Kenite husband of Jael (Judg 4:11, 17; 5:24). In Judg 4, Deborah and Barak battle the Canaanite king Jabin of Hazor, and his general Sisera.

HEBREW PEOPLE The Hebrew people is considered another name or designation for Israel, but the use in the OT is generally limited to non-Israelites, or in the context of speaking to non-Israelites (Gen 39:14; 41:12; Jonah 1:9).

HEBREWS, LETTER TO THE The traditional title of this text is misleading. This text is called a "letter." Elements of a standard letter closing in 13:18-25 (request, benediction, doxology, news and travel plans, conveying greetings, and final farewell) are similar to the closings of other NT letters (see Rom 15:30–16:23; 1 Thess 5:23-28; 2 Tim 4:19-22; 1 Pet 5:10-14). Nevertheless, Hebrews lacks a standard letter opening. The author refers to his text as a "word of exhortation" (13:22), a term associated with the sermon delivered as part of a worship service in Acts 13:15, and assumes that his audience will be "hearing" his text (5:11). Hebrews is as an example of early (and expert) Christian preaching. The author is unable to present his "word of exhortation" in person (13:19, 23), and so must send the transcript in written form to be read aloud by another party. The author's question in 10:2 ("would they [the sacrifices] not have ceased being offered?") appears to presuppose that the Levitical sacrifices continue to provide the "annual reminder of sins" (10:3), suggesting a date prior to 70 CE, when the Temple was destroyed by the Roman armies.

HEBRON, HEBRONITES 1. A geopolitically important city situated at the central high point of the Judean highlands (elevation 3,050 ft.)

2. The third son of Kohath and grandson of Levi (Exod 6:18; Num 3:19; 1 Chron 6:2, 18 [Heb. 5:28; 6:3]; 23:12).

3. Hebronites are a levitical family descended from Hebron the son of Kohath (Num 3:27; 26:58; 1 Chron 26:23).

4. The son of MARESHAH, a descendant of Judah (1 Chron 2:42).

HEDGEHOG A ft.-long mammal

known for rolling its spine-covered body into a ball.

HEGAI The most prominent of the EUNUCHs in the book of Esther (also see Add Esth 2:8), Hegai is entrusted with the virgins gathered to replace Queen VASHTI.

HEIFER A young cow that has not borne a calf. Heifers were used for threshing grain (Hos 10:11) and as sacrifices and food.

HEIR In the OT, *heir* is generally used literally and having an heir, or "a surviving line," was considered crucial (Judg 21:17).

The NT often uses *heir* figuratively. Abraham's heirs are not only those who keep the Instruction but those who have faith in Jesus (Rom 4:14; Gal 3:29; Eph 3:6). Believers are heirs of God and coheirs with Christ (Rom 8:17; Titus 3:7; Jas 2:5). Jesus is the heir of all things (Heb 1:2).

HELAH One of the two wives of Ashhur, a descendant of Judah and the "father of Tekoa" (1 Chron 4:5).

HELDAI 1. Commander from Nathophah who was in charge of the army division responsible for serving King David during the 12th month (1 Chron 27:15).

2. One of the exiles from whom Zechariah is instructed to collect silver and gold to use to make a crown for the high priest Joshua the son of Jehozadak (Zech 6:10-14), who will rebuild the temple.

HELEK A descendant of Manasseh and eponymous ancestor of the Helekites, described once as descended from Manasseh through Machir and Gilead (Num 26:29-30), and alternately as among the "sons" of Manasseh receiving a clan allotment (Josh 17:1-2).

HELEM The Asherite father of Zophah, Imna, Shelesh, and Amal (1 Chron 7:35).

HELEZ 1. One of David's warriors ("the Thirty"). Additionally, 1 Chron 27 identifies him as a member of Ephraim's family.

2. The son of Azariah, a Judahite (1 Chron 2:39).

HELI The Greek form of ELI, the priest to whom Samuel ministered (1 Sam 1–4). In the NT, Heli is listed in Luke's genealogy of Jesus (Luke 3:23-38) as the father of Joseph (3:23).

HELIOPOLIS Heliopolis, located at the southern end of the Nile Delta, just north of modern Cairo, was one of the most important cities in ancient Egypt. Never politically powerful, the city's significance derived from the prominence of its solar cult.

HELKAI The head of a clan of priests (MERAIOTH) who served in Jerusalem during the time of JOIAKIM (the son of Zerubbabel's contemporary Jeshua).

HELL In the NT, *hell* occurs as postmortem punishment. There are three contexts: (1) sin leads there (Matt 5:22), to unquenched fire (Matt 5:29-30; Mark 9:43-48); (2) disciples must fear him who can throw or destroy them there (Matt 10:28; Luke 12:5); and (3) some legal experts and Pharisees and their converts are destined there (Matt 23:15-33).

HELMET A head covering used in warfare that took various shapes according to nationality but also within various armies to denote different units for the leaders to discern in the heat of battle. Materials used to construct the helmet differed according to the stature of the soldier or army. The common Israelite soldier likely wore a leather helmet (2 Chron 26:14; Jer 46:4; Ezek 23:24; 27:10; 38:5), while kings, princes, and heroes wore bronze helmets (Saul and Goliath [1 Sam 17:5, 38]). By the time of Uzziah (2 Chron 26:14), all the army of Judah wore helmets.

HELON The father of ELIAB, a Zebulunite called at the time of the Mount Sinai census to lead his tribe (Num 1:9; 2:7; 7:24, 29; 10:16).

HEM The skirt of a robe. The garment's hem that is described in most detail in the Bible is that of the high priest (Exod 28:33-34; 39:24-26).

HEMAN 1. Son of Lotan; grandson of Seir the Horite; and whose name actually should be translated as Hemam (Gen 36:22).

2. Son of Zerah and grandson of Judah and his wife Tamar (1 Chron 2:6).

3. Joel's son and the prophet Samuel's grandson (1 Chron 6:33 [Heb. 6:18]).

4. Father of Jehuel and Shimei (2 Chron 29:14).

HEMDAN A grandson of Seir the Horite and the first-listed son of the clan chief Dishon (Gen 36:26).

HEN Jesus uses the hen's care for her chickens as a powerful metaphor for protection: "as a hen gathers her chicks under her wings" (Matt 23:37; Luke 13:34; 2 Esdr 1:30).

HENADAD The eponym of a family whose members were active in the restoration of Jerusalem.

HEPHER 1. A Canaanite town probably located on the Sharon plain whose king was defeated by Joshua (Josh 12:17).

2. The eponymous head of a clan within the tribe of Manasseh, or Gilead, known as the Hepherites (Num 26:32-33; 27:1; Josh 17:2-3).

3. The son of Ashhur of Tekoa in Judah (1 Chron 4:6).

4. One of David's warriors (1 Chron 11:36).

HEPHZIBAH 1. King Manasseh's mother (2 Kgs 21:1).

2. Metaphorically, the restored city of Jerusalem in a prophetic oracle of Third Isaiah (Isa 62:4).

HERALD A herald is one who broadcasts a message on behalf of another, or more specifically, a royal official who makes public proclamations.

HERBS In addition to the cultivated grains (see Gen 41:5-7), ancient Israelites took advantage of the herbs growing wherever they dwelt, grinding their seeds to create condiments. This included both bitter (Exod 12:8; Num 9:11; chicory, eryngo) and spicy herbs (coriander, cumin, mint, dill, rue; Luke 11:42). These items provided flavoring to a bland stew (2 Kgs 4:39). Herb gardens near homes also provided fragrant odors that masked the smells associated with everyday life.

HERESH An Asaphite Levite listed among inhabitants of Jerusalem after the exile (1 Chron 9:15).

HERMAS, SHEPHERD OF An apocryphal apocalypse, *The Shepherd of Hermas* outlines moral teachings through the visions of an ex-slave, Hermas, in three books: the Visions, the Mandates, and the Similitudes. It employs allegorical language to express the ethical challenges facing ancient Christians.

HERMES 1. The Greek divinity with whom Paul is identified by the crowds at Lystra in Acts 14:8-18, while they identified Paul's traveling companion Barnabas as ZEUS.

2. A Christian greeted by name by Paul in Rom 16:14. His name would indicate that he was a Gentile and probably a slave or freedman.

HERMOGENES 1. One among "everyone in Asia," who with Phygelus "turned away" from Paul (2 Tim 1:15).

2. The name of a Platonizing Christian of the 2nd and 3rd cent. CE.

HERMON, MOUNT The southernmost peak of the Anti-Lebanon Mountains, Hermon was the northernmost reaches of Joshua's conquest (Josh 11:17; 12:1). It was also called Baal-hermon, reflecting its sacred nature to others also (Judg 3:3; 1 Chron 5:23).

HEROD, FAMILY The Idumean dynasty that played a powerful role in Judean affairs, from 37 BCE to 100 CE, and provided Rome with a number of client rulers (see IDUMEA). Herod the Great was born in the late 70s BCE, and was appointed governor of Galilee at the age of 25 (Josephus, *J.W.* 1.203; *Ant.* 14.158). In 37 BCE, three years after his nomination, Herod began his long reign as king of the Jews. In 20–19 BCE, Herod began construction on a remodeled Jerusalem temple with Greek influences, to serve as a symbol of his rule and power. Herod died ca. 4 BCE. His son Archelaus became ruler after a succession contested by his brothers, and he assumed the name Herod as well for his reign from 4 BCE to 6 CE. His brother Antipas and his grandson Agrippa II were also influential leaders in the region.

HEROD ANTIPAS Lived ca. 20 BCE–40 CE. Tetrarch of Galilee and Perea, son of Herod the Great and the Samaritan Malthace. When Herod the Great died in 4 BCE, the emperor Augustus divided his kingdom between his sons Herod Antipas, Archelaus, and Philip.

HERODIAS Daughter of BERNICE and Aristobulus, Herodias was of combined Hasmonean and Idumean descent, presumably born between 16 and 7 BCE in Judea. She divorced her first husband, with whom she had a daughter, and married HEROD ANTIPAS, her husband's half brother and tetrarch over Galilee and Perea.

Herodias is mentioned in the Gospels for two related reasons: John the Baptist apparently criticized her marriage with Herod Antipas (Matt 14:3-4; Mark 6:17-18; Luke 3:19), and in Matthew and Mark she is presented as the one who inspired her daughter to ask Herod for John's head (Matt 14:8; Mark 6:24). Outside the NT, the most important source of information for her life is Flavius Josephus, who mentions both her marriages, but identifies her first husband as Herod (called Philip according to Matt 14:3 and Mark 6:17) and calls her daughter SALOME (*Ant.* 18.135-36; but Herodias according to some versions of Mark 6:22).

HERODION Herodion is one of twenty-six persons Paul names in Romans. Herodion (Rom 16:11), Andronicus, and Junia (16:7) are named Paul's relatives. See JUNIA, JUNIAS.

HERON This bird, listed along with other waterbirds in the OT on the unclean list (Lev 11:19; Deut 14:18), may refer to the cormorant.

HESHBON Mentioned thirty-eight times in the OT—most notably as an Amorite stronghold conquered by the Israelites under Moses (Num 21:21-31; Deut 2:24; Josh 12:2; Judg 11:19-26).

HETH A son of Canaan among Noah's descendants (Gen 10:1-15; 1 Chron 1:4-13) and the eponymous ancestor of one of two groups of people called HITTITES.

HEZEKIAH 1. An 8th-cent. BCE king of Judah. The information from the OT about Hezekiah's reign is extensive and derived primarily from three major portions of texts: 2 Kgs 18–20; Isa 36–39; and 2 Chron 29–32.

2. The Hebrew name of ATER, the head of a family of ninety-eight people who returned from the exile in Babylon with Nehemiah (Ezra 2:16; Neh 7:21). He is also one of the signatories of the

covenant document of Nehemiah (Neh 10:17 [Heb. 10:18]).

3. The great-great-grandfather of Zephaniah, a 7th-cent. BCE prophet (Zeph 1:1).

HEZIR 1. A descendant of Aaron upon whom the 17th lot fell when David, Zadok, and Ahimelech organized the priests for performance of liturgical duties (according to 1 Chron 24:15).

2. One of the postexilic heads of the people who signed Ezra's covenant (Neh 10:20 [Heb. 10:21]).

HEZRO One of David's elite warrior chiefs known as "the Thirty" (2 Sam 23:35; 1 Chron 11:37). Hezro was from Carmel, a town in southern Judah.

HEZRON 1. Meaning "enclosure," Hezron was a town between Addar and Kadesh-barnea in south Judah (Josh 15:3; "Hazar-addar" in Num 34:4). A diferent town in southern Judah was named Kerioth-hezron (Josh 15:25).

2. A son of Reuben (Gen 46:9; Exod 6:14) and the eponym for the Hezronites (Num 26:6).

3. The son of Perez (Gen 46:12; Num 26:21; 1 Chron 2:5, 9, 18, 21, 24-25; 4:1). A grandson of Judah, he was an ancestor of David (Ruth 4:18-19) and of Jesus (Matt 1:3; Luke 3:33).

HIDDAI One of David's thirty mighty men (2 Sam 23:30), called Hurai in 1 Chron 11:32.

HIEL This man from Bethel is identified as the one who rebuilt the city of Jericho during the reign of King Ahab of Israel and suffered the curse of Joshua for having done so (1 Kgs 16:34; Josh 6:26).

HIERAPOLIS Hierapolis, located in southwest Phrygia, is one of three cities mentioned in Col 4:13, along with COLOSSAE and LAODICEA. If Colossians is accurate, the church at Hierapolis was probably begun by Epaphras, one of Paul's associates (Col 1:7; 4:12; Phil 23).

HIGH PLACE See SHRINE.

HIGHLANDS The Hebrew and Greek term used in the OT and the NT to describe natural elevated areas of land that are common in Palestine and the surrounding regions.

HILEN A levitical city of refuge listed in the allotment to Aaron's descendants in 1 Chron 6:58 [Heb. 6:43]. The name appears as Holon in Josh 15:51.

HILKIAH 1. The father of Eliakim, a palace administrator during the reign of Hezekiah (2 Kgs 18:18, 26, 37; Isa 22:20; 36:3).

2. Son of Shallum (1 Chron 6:13 [Heb. 5:39]; Ezra 7:1-2), or Meshullam (1 Chron 9:11; Neh 11:11), and father of Azariah. He was the high priest who discovered the Instruction scroll during the reign of King Josiah (2 Kgs 22:4-14; 23:4, 8, 24; 2 Chron 34:9-22; 35:8). He was the great-grandfather of Ezra through his son Azariah.

3. The son of Amzi and father of Amaziah, from the clan of Merari, the son of Levi (1 Chron 6:45 [Heb. 6:30]).

4. The second son of Hosah, of the clan of Merari, the son of Levi (1 Chron 26:11).

5. A levitical priest from the village of Anathoth who was the father of the prophet Jeremiah (Jer 1:1). It is possible that he was a descendant of Abiathar, the priest banished by Solomon (1 Kgs 2:26-27).

6. The father of Gemariah and companion of Elasah (Jer 29:3).

7. One of the six individuals who stood on the wooden platform beside Ezra to assist him while he read the words of the Instruction scroll to the people (Neh 8:4).

8. One of the chief priests who returned from Babylon with Zerubbabel and with Jeshua the high priest (Neh 12:7).

HILKIAH THE HASID Abba Hilkiah is said to be the grandson of Honi the Circle Drawer. The single story told about him is an elaborate one recounted more fully in the Babylonian Talmud than in the Jerusalem. He was reputed to have the same miracle-working capacity as Honi.

HILL, HILL COUNTRY See HIGHLANDS.

HIN A measure of liquid capacity (Exod 30:24; Lev 19:36; 23:13; Num 28:14; Ezek 4:11; 45:24). The biblical hin was perhaps 3 L. See WEIGHTS AND MEASURES.

HINNOM, VALLEY OF Called "Valley of Hinnom," the literal translation of the Hebrew is "Valley of the Son of Hinnom." This valley, located to the south of Jerusalem outside the Potsherd Gate, marked the boundary between the tribal territory of Benjamin and Judah (Josh 15:8; 18:16; Jer 19:2).

HIRAH A man from Adullam, near Bethlehem. Judah settled near him, became his friend (Gen 38:1, 12), and sent Hirah with payment to TAMAR, who had been disguised as a prostitute (Gen 38:20-23).

HIRAM Two individuals in the OT—both Tyrians—are named Hiram.

1. As king of TYRE in the 10th cent. BCE (ca. 969–936 BCE), and a contemporary of DAVID and SOLOMON, Hiram sent his envoys to David with material and labor for the building of his new royal PALACE (2 Sam 5:11; 1 Chron 14:1).

2. Hiram is described as a skilled artisan from Tyre who was responsible for the furnishing of Solomon's temple (1 Kgs 7:13-47; 2 Chron 2:13-16; 4:11-18). First Kings 7:14 describes him as skillful, intelligent, and knowledgeable in metalwork.

HITTITES An empire of the 14th cent. BCE centered on Babylonia and extending westward to the Mediterranean Sea. The Hittites called their land Hatti, after the population of Hattian-speakers who inhabited it at the beginning of the 2nd millennium BCE, and their capital city Hattusa.

HIVITES One of the non-Israelite populations named in the OT, the Hivites make their most frequent appearance in lists of NATIONS inhabiting the land before the arrival of the Israelites. The Hivites apparently inhabited the central and northern highlands of Palestine, in locales as far north as Lebo-hamath (Judg 3:3), down to Shechem (Gen 34:2), Gibeon (Josh 9:3, 7), and environs (2 Sam 24:7). Esau's marriage to a Hivite (Gen 36:2) suggests connections with Edom as well.

HIZKI Son of ELPAAL, listed in the genealogy of Benjamin (1 Chron 8:17).

HOBAB In Num 10:29, Hobab is defined as the son of Reuel the Midianite, the father-in-law of Moses, and Hobab is asked by Moses to guide the Israelites through the wilderness. In Judg 4:11 Hobab is identified as the father-in-law of Moses, leading some to see this as a third name for Zipporah's father, adding it to Reuel and Jethro.

HOD The seventh of the eleven sons of ZOPHAH in the Asher genealogy (1 Chron 7:37).

HODAVIAH 1. Son of Elioenai and descendant of King David through his son Solomon (1 Chron 3:24).

2. Head of a clan in the half-tribe of Manasseh (1 Chron 5:24).

3. Grandfather of Sallu in the tribe of Benjamin, who lived in Jerusalem (1 Chron 9:7).

4. A Levite and the ancestor of seventy-four Levites who returned with Ezra after the exile (Ezra 2:40; Neh 7:43).

HODESH A wife of Shaharaim the

Benjaminite, with whom he had seven sons (1 Chron 8:9). Hodesh is called Baara in the previous verse (1 Chron 8:8).

HODIAH 1. Grandfather of Keilah the Garmite and Eshtemoa the Maacathite married to Naham's sister (1 Chron 4:19).

2. A Levite who interpreted Ezra's public reading of the Instruction scroll so that the people could understand it (Neh 8:7), led the people in penitential prayer (Neh 9:5), and signed his name on the sealed covenant document (Neh 10:10 [Heb. 10:11]).

3. A Levite who also signed his name on the sealed covenant document (Neh 10:13 [Heb. 10:14]).

4. One of the leaders of the people who signed his name on the sealed covenant document along with the Levites (Neh 10:18 [Heb. 10:19]).

HOGLAH One of the five daughters of Zelophehad (Num 26:33; Josh 3:17). Zelophehad, who had no sons, died in the wilderness, and his daughters appealed to Moses for inheritance rights (Num 27:3-4).

HOHAM The Amorite king who joined a coalition with four other rulers to defeat the Gibeonites (Josh 10:3-4).

HOLOFERNES "Assyrian" general who theatens the Jews in the fictional book of Judith.

HOLY, HOLINESS In the OT, the source of holiness is assigned to God alone. Holiness is God's quintessential nature, distinguishing God from all beings (1 Sam 2:2). It acts as the agency of God's will. If certain things are termed holy—such as land (Canaan), person (priest), place (sanctuary), or time (festival day)—they are so by virtue of divine dispensation. Moreover, this designation is always subject to recall. The holy things of the Bible can cause death to the unwary and the impure who approach them without regard for the regulations that govern their usage.

The concept of holiness in the NT maintains significant continuity with the OT. Holiness primarily, but not exhaustively, refers to the pattern of activity embodied by God. The NT people of God are related to this holy God because they are beneficiaries of this activity and thereby granted a status as holy. Enabled by the Holy Spirit, they are called to express this holy status: (1) by corporately modeling God's purpose for humanity, exhibiting compassion, reconciliation, joy, and peace; (2) by embodying a pattern of activity analogous to that of their Lord, becoming channels through which God continues God's reconciling, redeeming purposes.

HOLY OF HOLIES See MOST HOLY PLACE.

HOLY ONE The epithet "holy one," without additional qualification, is used of God several times in the OT (e.g., Ps 22:3; Prov 9:10; Job 6:10; Isa 40:25; Hab 3:3; Hos 11:12 [Heb. 12:1]), along with the more common variant, "holy one of Israel" (twenty-nine times, twenty-three in Isaiah), but also "the holy one of Jacob" (Isa 29:23), and the possessive forms "my holy one" (Hab 1:12), and "your holy one" (Isa 43:15). The overwhelming majority of the occurrences are in the Isaiah tradition, which is not surprising, given the proclamation "Holy, holy, holy" in the prophet's inaugural vision of transcendent divine kingship (Isa 6:3). "Holy" denotes something or someone that is set apart, extraordinary (see HOLY, HOLINESS).

HOLY PLACE The larger of the two divisions of both the meeting tent and the temple, containing the lampstand(s) and the tables of the bread of the presence (cf Exod 25–40; 1 Kgs 6–7). "Holy place" is also used as a general term for the temple (e.g., Ezra 9:8), the inside of the temple (2 Chron 5:9), and even the temple grounds (Ezek 45:4).

HOLY SPIRIT The Hebrew and Greek words encompass a wide range of realities: divine energy and presence (e.g., Ps 51:11); the human core (e.g., Ps 77:6); breath (e.g., Isa 40:7); the waxing and waning of life itself (Job 34:14; Ezek 10:17); a disposition, as in "spirit of prostitution" (Hos 4:12); a demonic being (e.g., 1 Sam 16:16); and wind (e.g., Gen 1:2; Num 11:31; Ezek 11:1). Although Hebrew literature, for example, may play upon the overlap between spirit and wind (Num 11:31) or breath and spirit (Isa 40:7), contemporary translators are compelled to choose one English word and, at best, to relegate the other to a footnote.

There existed no single technical term for the divine spirit in Israelite, Jewish, and Christian antiquity. The expression "holy spirit" occurs only three times—and with very different connotations—in the OT. In Ps 51:11, the holy spirit ("your holy spirit") resides within the individual psalmist; in Isa 63:10-11, God places the holy spirit within the community of Israel. The spirit could, further, be identified in many ways: "spirit" without qualifiers (e.g., Num 11:17; Job 32:6; 1 Chron 12:18); "spirit of God" or "God's spirit" (e.g., Num 24:2; 2 Chron 15:1; Job 33:4); "spirit of wisdom" (e.g., Isa 11:12); "spirit of the Lord" or "the Lord's spirit" (e.g., Judg 6:34; 1 Sam 10:6; Mic 3:8); "good spirit" (Neh 9:20; Ps 143:10); "my [God's] spirit" (e.g., Isa 42:1; Ezek 39:29); and "extraordinary spirit" (e.g., Dan 5:12).

In early Jewish literature, the term *holy spirit* occurs with enormous fluidity. The Dead Sea Scrolls caution "not to defile your holy spirit," by which they mean not to forfeit one's integrity (e.g., 4Q416 2 II, 6). They speak of the "spirit of holiness" that cleanses new members of the community (1QS III, 7–8). They refer to "spirits of holiness" (1QHa XVI, 12). Josephus and Philo tend to prefer the moniker "divine Spirit" for the Spirit in Israelite literature (e.g., Philo, *Her.* 265; Josephus, *Ant.* 6.166). In the NT, the expressions "holy spirit" and "spirit of holiness" (Rom 1:4) occur alongside the more frequent use of the word *spirit* without qualifiers.

HOLY WAR "Divine warrior" refers to descriptions of the LORD as a warrior god who fights for (or even against) Israel. Holy war designates the actual or hypothetical practice of warfare as a religious activity.

HOMAM A son of the clan chief Lotan according to 1 Chron 1:39.

HOMER The largest dry measure of capacity in the Bible (Exod 8:10; Num 11:32; Lev 27:16; Isa 5:10; Hos 3:2). The homer contained 10 BATH (= 10 EPHAH; Ezek 45:10-11, 14); if so, the homer and the KOR were equal (roughly 190 L). See WEIGHTS AND MEASURES.

HOMOSEXUALITY The topic of homosexuality occasions very little attention from the biblical writers. There are basically six passages in the Bible that may refer directly to homoerotic relations, three in the OT: Gen 19:1-11; Lev 18:22; 20:13; and three in the NT: Rom 1:26-27; 1 Cor 6:9; and 1 Tim 1:10.

The famous story of the destruction of Sodom and Gomorrah in Gen 19 includes a passage stating that the men of the city wanted "to know" Lot's guests. Lot calls their desire "evil" and offers his daughters to them and says that "you may do to them whatever you wish," obviously meaning sexual relations (similar to Adam "knowing" his wife Eve in Gen 4:1). The men apparently want to rape Lot's foreign male guests by way of demeaning them. Little do the men of the city realize, of course, that their evil desire only confirms God's judgment against the city. Some scholars point to the violation of hospitality as the primary issue in the passage, but Lot's offer of his daughters suggests overtones of sexual violence as well (a similar passage is found in Judg 19:14-29).

The two passages from Lev 18:22 and 20:13 occur within the context of the Holiness Code (Lev 17–26), where the Israelites receive instructions on how they shall conduct themselves upon entering the land of promise. Both passages give clear prohibitions against same-sex relations between men, though no reason for the proscription is given. The second prohibition in 20:13 adds the punishment of death to men engaged in same-sex relations. There are many other prohibitions in the Holiness Code (e.g., crossbreeding of animals, sowing two kinds of seed in one field, wearing garments made of two different fabrics, rounding off the hair of one's temples, receiving a tattoo [Lev 19:19, 27-28; 21:5]). It appears that these various practices were perhaps markers for the previous idolatrous inhabitants of the land. In modern discussions the rationales for these various prohibitions form a significant issue of debate.

All of the NT passages come from Pauline Letters. The Rom 1:26-27 passage is the most important, as here Paul clearly views homoerotic behavior (male or female) as a consequence of idolatry, unnatural, and an expression of excessive lust. Most scholars acknowledge that Paul knew of homoeroticism indirectly and in stereotypic terms—that is, with reference to Gentile practices of pederasty and male prostitution—a view that receives support from 1 Cor 6:9, where homoeroticism is included in a typical vice-list of prohibited behaviors. Issues of translation are particularly important here, as there was no word in ancient Greek corresponding to our modern term *homosexuality* (which was coined at the end of the 19th cent.). Modern translations, however, often mislead the reader by rendering these terms as "sodomites" (reading the Sodom and Gomorrah story into the text (e.g., NRSV, NKJV, NAB) or as "homosexuals" (anachronistically reading modern understandings of sexual orientation into the text (e.g, NIV, NKJV). The passage in 1 Tim 1:10 also refers to same-sex relations in the context of a vice list, with the same overtones as in 1 Cor 6.

HONEY Honey in the ANE and the Bible referred either to a sweet substance made from such fruits as dates, grapes, or figs, or to honey from bees, either wild or domesticated. Honey appears in the Bible literally and figuratively. While the Egyptians and Hittites cultivated bees for honey, it appears Israel took several centuries to begin beekeeping.

HOPHNI AND PHINEHAS Hophni and Phinehas, the two sons of Eli, are noted for their despicable and worthless behavior. They treat the sacrificial laws with disrespect, and they have sex with the young women who work at the sanctuary door (1 Sam 2:12-17).

HOR Two mountains are named in the biblical text.

1. The most important Mount Hor is noted in the exodus tradition as the burial place of Aaron (Num 20:27; 21:4; 33:37; Deut 32:50).

2. The northern limit of Israel's territory (Num 34:7-8). Most likely the peak was part of the Lebanon Mountains, with Mount Hermon and Jebel Akkar as possible locations.

HORAM The king of Gezer who was killed by Joshua when Horam sought to assist Lachish during the conquest period (Josh 10:33). See GEZER, GEZERITES.

HOREB, MOUNT See SINAI, MOUNT.

HORI 1. Son of Lotan (Gen 36:22; 1 Chron 1:39) and grandson of "Seir the Horite" (Gen 36:20).

2. Father of Shaphat of the tribe of Simeon, Hori was one of twelve spies sent by Moses into Canaanite territory (Num 13:5). See HORITES.

HORITES The ancient inhabitants of Edom (Gen 14:6; 36:20; Deut 2:12, 20).

HORMAH A town in the arid southern plain of Judah, probably close to Arad. After the abortive attempt to invade Canaan from the south, the Amalekites and Canaanites pursued the Israelites as far as Hormah (Num 14:45).

HORONAIM Horonaim (2 Sam 13:34) was a town in southern Moab (Jer 48:3, 34; Isa 15:5), located at the foot of an ascent (Jer 48:5).

HORSE The horse appears in the Bible as a domesticated animal used for riding and pulling chariots. Unlike other similar animals such as the donkey and the mule, the horse was considered a prestigious animal used only for military purposes.

HORSE GATE A gate of Jerusalem mentioned in Jeremiah's description of a rebuilt, expanded city (31:40) that appears in association with the repairs being carried out by priests in Neh 3:28. It was located on the eastern side of the city near the temple/palace complex and opened toward the Kidron Valley.

HOSAH 1. Part of the tribe of Asher's allotment (Josh 19:29); it is most likely the biblical name for the Tyrian suburb Usu (Tell Rashidiyeh), which, according to the Annals of Sennacherib, was conquered in 701 BCE.

2. A man who, along with male family members, was appointed by David to serve as gatekeeper at the Lord's sanctuary in Jerusalem. By the casting of lots, these descendants of Levi were assigned to the western side of the holy site (1 Chron 16:38; 26:10-11, 16).

HOSANNA From Ps 118:25-26, "Save now." Mark's paraphrase, "Hosanna! Blessings on the one who comes in the name of the Lord!" (Mark 11:9), thus represents the first part of each verse of Ps 118:25-26.

HOSEA, BOOK OF Hosea was the only prophet with a book by his name who was a native of the northern kingdom of Israel and who proclaimed his message there. He began his ministry sometime around 750 BCE and ended it just prior to the Assyrian conquest of the Northern Kingdom in 722 BCE. The book by his name is the first in the Book of the Twelve. The beginning of Hosea's ministry is contemporary with that of Amos, although it extends through a much longer period of time. His message is about God's judgment on Israel, particularly for its sin of idolatry, viewed as an adulterous relationship with Canaanite religion, particularly the worship of Baal. However, his message of judgment is tempered by a strong concept of God's love for Israel and a divine willingness to redeem the relationship.

HOSHAMA Sixth son of King Jeconiah (JEHOIACHIN) of Judah, as recorded in the Chronicler's genealogy of Davidic descendants (1 Chron 3:18).

HOSHEA The name of five individuals in the OT.

1. Hoshea was the original name of Joshua, son of Nun, which Moses changed (Num 13:8, 16). In Deut 32:44, the Hebrew reads Hoshea, while many of the translations read Joshua.

2. The last king of the northern kingdom of Israel (732–722 BCE). Hoshea, the son of Elah, came to power during the course of Tiglath-pileser III's (733–732 BCE) campaign against Rezin the king of Damascus, and Pekah the king of Israel.

3. Hoshea son of Azaziah was the chief officer of Ephraim during the time of David (1 Chron 27:20).

4. A signatory on behalf of the entire community, committing the people to obedience to the covenant of God in the context of Ezra's work (Neh 10:23 [Heb. 10:24]).

5. The 8th-cent. BCE northern

kingdom prophet whose name is commonly transliterated Hosea.

HOSPITALITY The ancient custom of hospitality revolved around the welcoming and assisting of strangers or travelers. By extending hospitality to a traveler, the host generally committed himself or herself to provide the guest with provisions and protection while the guest remained in the region. Moreover, within a context of hospitality, hosts and guests often forged long-term, reciprocal relationships, which are commonly referred to as guest-friendships.

HOSTS, HOST OF HEAVEN "Hosts" is a plural noun commonly designating military service or troops. The plural form occurs as an epithet of Yahweh some 285 times as "Yahweh/Lord of Hosts." The majority of the occurrences of the epithet are in the prophetic books.

HOTHAM 1. Son of HEBER, one of the descendants of Asher (1 Chron 7:32), who seems to be the same person as HELEM (1 Chron 7:35).

2. An Aroerite (Transjordan region) and father of two of David's warriors (1 Chron 11:44).

HOTHIR One of the fourteen sons of HEMAN appointed to prophesy with instruments (1 Chron 25:4), chosen by lot (1 Chron 25:28).

HOUR A modern hour is 1/24 of the astronomical day, but ancients commonly divided daylight into twelve equal hours and night into twelve equal hours. Thus, a civic hour varied in length depending on latitude and season: in summer, an hour was about 5/4 of a modern hour, but in winter, an hour was about 3/4 of a modern hour.

HOUSE, HOUSEHOLD The word *house* is normally used to describe a physical structure in which individuals live (Mark 7:24), while *household* is a communal term that applies to a kinship group made up of current members and their ancestors. Throughout its existence a family's identity and its kinship ties are associated with its household (equaling its members, its inheritable property, and its social standing; see Exod 20:17; Num 1:20)

HOZAI The author of a chronicle on the deeds of King Manasseh (2 Chron 33:19), apparently cataloging the king's transgressions "before he submitted."

HUBBAH See JEHUBBAH.

HUL The second son of Aram and a grandson of Shem (Gen 10:23).

HULDAH A prophet of Jerusalem, and wife of Shallum (2 Kgs 22:14; 2 Chron 34:22). Huldah was consulted by the high priest Hilkiah and the officials of Josiah's court after the Instruction scroll was recovered from the temple (2 Kgs 22:8-11; 2 Chron 34:14-21). Her prophecy announced tragedy for the people of the kingdom, who had made offerings to idols, but offered a peaceful death to Josiah (2 Kgs 22:20; 2 Chron 34:28). The words of her prophecy encouraged the king to make a covenant to be obedient to the Instruction (2 Kgs 23:1-4; 2 Chron 34:29-33), and to initiate other religious reforms. Huldah's designation as a "prophetess" is shared by both Miriam (Exod 15:20) and Deborah (Judg 4:4).

HUMAN ONE *ben 'adam* (Hebrew) or *huios tou anthrōpou* (Greek) are best translated as "human being" (rather than "son of man") except in cases of direct address, where CEB renders "human one" (instead of "son of man" or "mortal"; e.g., Ezek 2:1). When *ho huios tou anthrōpou* is used as a title for Jesus, the CEB refers to Jesus as "the Human One." Jesus' primary language would have been Aramaic, so he would have used the Aramaic phrase bar enosha. This phrase has the sense of "a human" or "a human such as I." This phrase was taken over into Greek in a phrase that might be translated woodenly as "son of humanity." However, Greek usage often refers to "a son of x" in the sense of "one who has the character of x." For example, Luke 10:6 refers in Greek to "a son of peace," a phrase that has the sense of "one who shares in peace." In Acts 13:10 Paul calls a sorcerer "a son of the devil." This is not a reference to the sorcerer's actual ancestry, but it serves to identify his character. He is devilish—or more simply in English "a devil." Human or human one represents accurately the Aramaic and Greek idioms. Finally, many references to Jesus as "the Human One" refer back to Daniel 7:13, where Daniel "saw one like a human being" (Greek *huios anthropou*). By using the title Human One in the Gospels and Acts, the CEB preserves this connection to Daniel's vision.

HUPHAM, HUPHAMITES A descendant of Benjamin and the head of a clan whose members were called Huphamites (Num 26:39).

HUPPAH A priestly clan chief upon whom the 13th lot fell when David, Zadok, and Ahimelech divided the descendants of Aaron according to their tasks (1 Chron 24:13).

HUPPIM Ancestor of the Huphamites (Num 26:39). Huppim is listed as a son of Benjamin (Gen 46:21), but elsewhere he appears as a grandson or later descendant (Num 26:39; 1 Chron 7:15).

HUR The name of five men in the OT.

1. An assistant of Moses who, with Aaron, held up Moses' arms when they became tired during the battle against the Amalekites (Exod 17:8-13).

2. The grandfather of Bezalel, a Judahite in charge of making the meeting tent and the associated cultic apparatus (Exod 31:1-5; 38:22). Hur's father was Caleb and his mother Ephrath (1 Chron 2:18-20).

3. One of the kings of Midian killed by the Israelites (Num 31:8; Josh 13:21).

4. One of Solomon's officials in charge of Ephraim was called Ben-hur, "son of Hur" (1 Kgs 4:8).

5. The father of Rephaiah, an official in charge of half of Jerusalem in the postexilic period (Neh 3:9).

HURAM, HURAM-ABI 1. Huram is the name of the craftsman who made the bronze implements for the temple according to 2 Chron 4:11 (Huram-abi [4:16]).

2. The name of the king of Tyre, who is a contemporary of David and Solomon. He is first described as sending the materials and craftsmen to build the palace of David at the beginning of his reign in Jerusalem (1 Chron 14:1).

3. A Benjaminite identified as the son of Bela, who is the oldest offspring of Benjamin (1 Chron 8:1, 5).

HURI A Gadite and father of Abihail (1 Chron 5:14).

HURRIANS The Hurrians were a group of people who lived in northern Mesopotamia during the late 3rd and 2nd millennia BCE.

HUSHAH 1. A town in Judah, west of Bethlehem; two of David's commanders, Mebunnai (2 Sam 23:27) and Sibeccai (2 Sam 21:18), were associated with Hushah as Hushathites.

2. The Son of Ezer in the genealogy of Judah (1 Chron 4:4).

HUSHAI 1. Hushai is a friend of King David who remains loyal during the rebellion of Absalom (2 Sam 15–17).

2. The name of the father of Baana, one of Solomon's officials (1 Kgs 4:16).

HUSHAM The 3rd ruler mentioned in the list of nondynastic Edomite "kings"

(Gen 36:31-39; 1 Chron 1:43-51) and the first with a specified region of origin.

HUSHIM 1. Son of Aher, a descendant of Benjamin (1 Chron 7:12), possibly a plural reference.

2. Wife of Shaharaim, mother of Abitub and Elpaal (1 Chron 8:8, 11).

HYMENAEUS First Timothy identifies Hymenaeus and Alexander as Ephesian Christians who had strayed from the "sound teaching" of the gospel: they "ruined their faith because they refused to listen to their conscience" (1:10-11, 19-20; see 1 Cor 5:5). Second Timothy refers to Hymanaeus in conjunction with Philetus, contending that both had "deviated from the truth" by claiming the resurrection had already occurred (2:17-18).

HYMN A song of praise to God. OT hymns are frequent in the Psalms, and the NT contains several hymns praising Christ.

HYPOCRISY, HYPOCRITE In Greek culture, this term refers to an actor or one who plays a part or pretends. In the Synoptic Gospels, the use of *hypocrite(s)* occurs most frequently in Matthew (Mark uses the term only once; Luke 2 times; Matthew 13 times), a gospel that reflects a much more tense relationship between the synagogue and the church. Among synoptic characters, only Jesus uses the term. The clearest usage to the idea of the play-actor occurs in Jesus' references in the Sermon on the Mount: When you give alms, don't "blow your trumpet as the hypocrites do" when they give (6:2); when you pray, don't "pray standing in the synagogues and on the street corners" (6:5); and when you fast, "don't put on a sad face so people will know" you are fasting.

HYRCANUS 1. A prominent, wealthy person identified as the son of Tobias (2 Macc 3:11). When Seleucus IV Philopator sent Heliodorus to extract wealth from the temple in Jerusalem, the high priest informed Heliodorus that Hyrcanus had deposited a sum of money there.

2. John Hyrcanus I, a nephew of Judas the Maccabee, was a high priest of the Hasmonean dynasty who reigned in Jerusalem from 134 to 104 BCE.

3. Hyrcanus II was the son of the Hasmonean high priest Alexander Jannaeus and the grandson of John Hyrcanus I. See HASMONEANS.

HYSSOP A small plant of unknown identity used to apply blood to doorframes in preparation for Passover (Exod 12:22) and often associated with cleansing (e.g., Lev 14:4; Num 19:6; Ps 51:7). John reports that a sponge of wine vinegar was offered to Jesus on a hyssop branch (John 19:29).

Ii

I AM A name for the God of Israel taken from the initial revelation of the Israelite deity to Moses (Exod 3:13-15), deriving from an attempt to translate the Hebrew phrase "I am who I am," or "I will be what I will be." The deity instructs Moses to inform the Israelites that "I Am has sent me to you." In its original context, the self-description may mark a reticence on the part of the deity to reveal the precise name (as in Jacob's struggle with a preternatural entity in Gen 32:30).

The passage is important in the subsequent history of interpretation. Based on the LXX's translation, Jews during the Hellenistic period saw in the title an ontological reference: the God of Israel is "pure being." The consistent self-description of Jesus in the Gospel of John by means of "I am" sayings (e.g., John 6:35, 41, 48, 51) may also be grounded in the phrase. (See esp. the enigmatic statement of Jesus, "Before Abraham was, I Am," in John 8:58.)

IBHAR One of the sons of David born in Jerusalem. Of the thirteen sons born in Jerusalem, four were sons of BATH-SHUA (Bathsheba), and nine sons are listed without the name of the mother(s)—Ibhar is the first of these (2 Sam 5:15;1 Chron 3:6; 14:5).

IBLEAM A town in the Ephraimite highlands, south of Jezreel. Ibleam guarded the southern end of the ascent of Gur (the Jenin Pass), which leads into the highlands from the Jezreel Valley (2 Kgs 9:27). It was also on the main north-south road, then ran through the Ephraimite highlands down to Jerusalem.

IBNEIAH A Benjaminite who returned from exile, he was one of the first to resettle on his own property (1 Chron 9:8).

IBNIJAH A Benjaminite listed as the father of Reuel and the grandfather of Meshullam (1 Chron 9:8).

IBRI The son of Jaaziah and grandson of Merari (1 Chron 24:27), Ibri was among the group referred to as "the rest of the Levites" (1 Chron 24:20) who cast lots before King David and others to determine their duties as Levites (1 Chron 24:31).

IBSAM A descendant of Issachar (1 Chron 7:2).

IBZAN Ibzan was the 10th JUDGE of Israel, one of the "minor" judges (Judg 12:8-11). His seven-year term as judge was based in Bethlehem.

ICHABOD The son of Phineas the son of Eli, who was born when his mother heard that her brother-in-law and her husband were both dead and that the chest containing the covenant of God had been captured by the Philistines (1 Sam 4:19-21).

ICONIUM City in south-central Turkey (modern Konya) visited by Paul (2 Tim 3:11) and Barnabas (Acts 14:1).

IDBASH A son of ETAM of the tribe of Judah (1 Chron 4:3).

IDDO 1. Father of Ahinadab (1 Kgs 4:14).

2. A Levite and a clan descending from Gershom (1 Chron 6:21) and perhaps the same as Adaiah (1 Chron 6:41).

3. Son of Zechariah and leader of the Manasseh tribe (1 Chron 27:21).

4. A seer whose visions had recorded the acts of Solomon (2 Chron 9:29), Rehoboam (2 Chron 12:15), and Abijah (2 Chron 13:22).

5. A leader over the temple servants at Casiphia who sent levitical temple servants to Ezra to rebuild the temple in Jerusalem and serve in it (Ezra 8:17; 1 Esdr 8:45-46).

6. A priest who came up with Zerubbabel to Jerusalem after the exile ended (Neh 12:4), but may represent the name of an ancestral house (Neh 12:16).

7. The prophet Zechariah's grandfather in Zech 1:1, 7, but his father in Ezra 5:1; 6:14; and 1 Esdr 6:1.

8. A descendant of Nooma, he sent away his foreign wife and their children as Ezra directed him (1 Esdr 9:35).

IDOL From the Greek Idols were an indigenous part of ANE religions. Israel was surrounded by nations where a variety of deities were represented by anthropomorphic (human-like) and theriomorphic (animal-like) images. Idols were also common in later Greco-Roman religion. That people actually believed these images themselves were gods is unlikely (see IDOLATRY).

IDOLATRY The worship of idols, or giving divine honors to human-made objects. Since ancient Israel and Judah were surrounded by nations (i.e., Egypt, Canaan, Syria, Assyria, Babylonia) that used cultic images in their religions, one of the most persistent themes in the OT is an attack upon idolatry (Exod 20:4; Lev 19:4; 26:1; Deut 5:8; 27:15; and esp. the parodies in Jer 10:2-16; Isa 44:9-20; Ps 115:4-8). While the Gospels hardly mention the subject of idolatry, writings usually attributed to Paul are concerned with the issue. According to Rom 1:25, Paul, without using the word *idolatry*, described it as worshipping and serving "the creation instead of the creator." Elsewhere, idolaters are grouped with the greedy, robbers, sexually immoral, drunkards, and so on (1 Cor 5:9-11; Gal 5:19-21; Eph 5:3-5; note in this last passage greed and idolatry are identified as one and the same thing; cf Col 3:5-6).

The overall stance of the biblical witness seems to be that all "images" of God, whether made of wood, stone, precious metals, or even words, are incomplete and thus none can claim exclusivity.

IDUMEA A territory stretching to the west from the southern half of the Dead Sea. Its western boundary was the Mediterranean Sea. Its name probably comes from the Edomites, who began moving into this area following the destruction of Judah by Nebuchadnezzar in the early 6th cent. BCE (Mark 3:8).

IEZER Son of Gilead and eponymous ancestor of the Iezerites (Num 26:30).

IGAL 1. A spy from the tribe of Issachar among those sent by Moses to spy on Canaan (Num 13:7).

2. One of the warriors of King David called "the Thirty," and son of Nathan of Zobah (2 Sam 23:36).

3. Second son of Shemaiah and descendant of Zerubbabel (1 Chron 3:22).

IGDALIAH Father or mentor of HANAN (Jer 35:4 [LXX Jer 42:4]).

IKKESH Ikkesh of Tekoa is said to be the father of IRA, mentioned as one of David's warriors (2 Sam 23:26; 1 Chron 11:28; 27:9).

ILAI Ilai the Ahohite is mentioned as one of David's "mighty warriors" (1 Chr 11:29).

ILIADUN An ancestor of some of the Levites who rebuilt the temple after the exile (1 Esdr 5:56).

ILLYRICUM A mountainous district located east of Italy and the Adriatic Sea. The borders of this region were uncertain at times, but at the height of Roman power, by the early 1st cent. CE, it was divided into two provinces: Dalmatia (Illyricum Supericus) in the south, and Pannonia (Illyricum Inferius) in the north. These provinces would now include parts of modern Albania, Montenegro, Bosnia and Herzegovina, and Croatia.

Paul claims to have proclaimed the good news from Jerusalem to Illyricum (Rom 15:19).

IMAGE OF GOD Human beings (male and female, equally) are created in the image and likeness of God; no other creatures are so created. Such a claim regarding humankind occurs in OT and NT contexts ("our image/God's own image" [Gen 1:26-27]; "resemble God" [5:1-3]; "divine image" [9:6]; "image and glory of God" [1 Cor 11:7]; "image of God" [2 Cor 4:4]; "God's image" [Eph 4:24]; "God's likeness" [Jas 3:9]).

IMALKUE According to 1 Maccabees,

Imalkue was an Arab to whom Alexander Balas, one of the claimants to the Seleucid throne, entrusted his son ANTIOCHUS VI in 146 BCE (1 Macc 11:39-40).

IMLAH Imlah is the father of the prophet MICAIAH (1 Kgs 22:8-9; 2 Chron 18:7-8).

IMMANUEL The personal name Immanuel occurs once in the OT (Isa 7:14; but see also 8:8, 10), and once in the NT (Matt 1:23). It became for Christians a messianic title applied to Jesus. In contrast, in Jewish tradition, the name is never used as a messianic title.

IMMER 1. Ancestor of Maasi, a priest who was among the first who moved from Babylon to resettle in Judah after the exile (1 Chron 9:12; Ezra 2:37; Neh 7:40; 1 Esdr 5:24), along with Maaseiah, Sehmaiah, Jehiel, and Azariah (1 Esdr 9:21).

2. During David's reign, the priest who headed the 16th division (1 Chron 24:14).

3. Father of Zadok who repaired the portion of the Jerusalem wall opposite his own house (Neh 3:29).

4. Ancestor of the priest Amashsai (Neh 11:13).

5. Father of Pashhur who imprisoned Jeremiah because of his prophecy (Jer 20:1).

6. One of five towns whose inhabitants returned to Jerusalem, but could not provide their Israelite ancestry (Ezra 2:59; Neh 7:61). The name Immer could reference a person (1 Esdr 5:36).

IMMORTALITY *Immortality* literally means "to be immune to death" or "deathless." Biblical Hebrew has no single word to refer to the concept. Instead it calls on "the living God" and characterizes immortality as "eternal life," which is a later rabbinic doctrine.

In the cultures of the biblical world, the concept usually refers to divinities, even though there are significant numbers of divinities who die and are revived to rule once more. Their immortality includes the important condition that they periodically undergo death and revivification, which only emphasizes the eternity of the natural processes of planting and reaping or the unending cycle of the stars.

IMNA Only mentioned as one of four sons of HELEM (Hotham), of the tribe of Asher (1 Chron 7:35).

IMPERIAL COMPANY Acts 27:1 refers to the Imperial Company. The soldiers named in Acts 27:42 are probably part of this cohort. A cohort, an auxiliary unit that usually ranged from 500 to 1,000 soldiers, was an innovation of Augustus. Similar to a LEGION, it was much smaller and consisted primarily of noncitizens, with the promise of citizenship serving as the chief means of recruitment.

IMNAH 1. A son of Asher (Gen 46:17; 1 Chron 7:30) and the patriarch of the clan of Imnites (Num 26:44).

2. A Levite mentioned only as the father of KORE (2 Chron 31:14), who was in charge of the offerings to God. See BENJAMIN, BENJAMINITES.

IMRAH One of the sons of ZOPHAH mentioned only in a genealogy of the tribe of Asher (1 Chron 7:36). He and his brothers are said to be "heads of households, select mighty warriors, the heads of the princes" (1 Chron 7:40).

IMRI 1. Son of Bani and father of Omri. Imri was among those living in Jerusalem from the tribes of Judah, Benjamin, Ephraim, and Manasseh (1 Chron 9:4).

2. Father of ZACCUR, one of those rebuilding the gates of Jerusalem after the exile (Neh 3:2).

INCARNATION *Incarnation* literally means "enfleshed." In Christian tradition the term takes its meaning from John 1:14: "The Word became flesh." In its technical sense, then, incarnation expresses belief that the divine took human form, or, to be more specific, that God's Word became the human being Jesus from Nazareth.

INCENSE Incense is a material made of spices, gum, aromatic wood, or other perfumed substances burned to produce a fragrant smoke. Incense refers both to the aromatic substance to be burned and to the fragrant odor that results. In Israel and its neighboring cultures, the burning of incense was a cultic practice associated with sacrifice, offering, and worship. The burning of incense was also associated with prayer (Ps 141:2; Luke 1:10; Rev 5:8; 8:3-4). Incense, like spice, was a valuable trade commodity (Rev 18:11-13).

INDIA India is mentioned in Scripture only in the book of Esther (1:1; 8:9) and its additions (Add Esth 13:1; 16:1), where it is always part of the formalized expression "from India to Cush [Ethiopia]." The phrase indicates the vast extent of the Persian (Achaemenid) Empire, with India figuring as its easternmost province.

INHERITANCE *Inheritance* pertains to properties and rights that transfer to an heir or heirs following the death of the owner. In the OT, individual property rights can be traced to the traditions about the division of the land of Israel among the twelve tribes wherein the land was apportioned by the casting of lots before the Lord. The tribal allocations were to be distributed on an equitable basis with the result that each clan, lineage, and individual household shared in that inheritance. New Testament inheritance texts should be read against the background of the OT and Jewish traditions about Abraham. The promise of "inheriting the land," generally understood in Judaism as a reference to the literal land of Canaan, was commonly broadened to "inheriting the world," and sometimes spiritualized to refer to heaven or the re-created "new heavens and new earth."

While a few passages reflect the literal practice of inheritance (Luke 12:13; Mark 12:1-12; Matt 21:33-46; Luke 20:9-19; Gal 4:1-2; cf Heb 9:15-22), most portray figurative, eschatological ideas of salvation. Often associated with inheritance are the concepts of "election"/"choosing," believers as "sojourners," and God's promise that "I will be their/your God/father, and they/you will be my people/children" (Gen 17:8; Exod 6:7-8; Jer 31:33; Ezek 37:23; etc.).

INK A mixture of carbon, gum, and water dried into cakes used for writing on papyrus, leather, and ostraca (Jer 36:18; 2 John 12; 3 John 13). The impermanence of carbon ink (Exod 32:33; Num 5:23; and Ps 69:28 [Heb. 69:29]) may have served as the precedent for the later rabbinic objection to the use of metallic ink (m. Sotah 2:4; Sof. 1:5-6). In a series of metaphors about written texts, Paul contrasts the permanent message of God written on the heart with the impermanence of ink (2 Cor 3:3).

INNOCENTS, SLAUGHTER OF THE According to Matthew, King Herod had all male children 2 years of age and under in and around Bethlehem killed after hearing that MAGI were seeking one who was born "king of the Jews" (Matt 2:1-4, 16-18).

INSPIRATION AND REVELATION *Inspiration* and *revelation* in the biblical context are correlative terms that together evoke the unique and sacred character of the Bible as Scripture and its resulting special role in the Jewish and Christian communities. The faith community regards the Bible as the "word of God" and therefore, in some sense, divinely authored; this text as canonical

Scripture is, in some sense, true; and Scripture plays a special role in the believing community as, in some sense, uniquely authoritative and normative. The believing community interacts with this text, considered as somehow God-given and authoritative, continuously and diversely in its ongoing negotiation of matters of ultimate concern such as its identity, faith, morality, worship, and so on.

INSTRUCTION See TORAH.

IOB A son of Issachar (Gen 46:13).

IOTA The 9th letter of the Greek alphabet.

IPHDEIAH Iphdeiah is listed as a descendant of Benjamin (1 Chron 8:25). The names of his father SHASHAK and ten brothers are given.

IR In 1 Chron 7:12, the name for a descendant of Benjamin.

IRA 1. A Jairite (of the tribe of Manasseh, Num 32:41) listed as a priest of David (2 Sam 20:26).

2. One of two ITHRITEs among "the Thirty," David's mighty men (2 Sam 23:38; 1 Chron 11:40).

3. The son of Ikkesh, this Ira also served as one of David's mighty men (2 Sam 23:26; 1 Chron 27:9).

IRAD The grandson of CAIN and son of Enoch (Gen 4:18).

IRAM Iram appears only as one of the Edomite clan chiefs listed in Gen 36:40-43 and 1 Chron 1:51-54.

IRI Meaning "my city," a descendant of Benjamin, appearing only in 1 Chron 7:7.

IRIJAH The sentinel who arrested Jeremiah at the Benjamin Gate, accused him of desertion, and brought him before the authorities (Jer 37:13-14).

IR-NAHASH A city. Tehinnah is listed as the father of Ir-nahash within the descendants of Judah (1 Chron 4:12). This could mean that Tehinnah founded the town, or that his son was named Ir-nahash.

IRON 1. Iron is a metal with contradictory qualities. Iron ore is the most common of all metal ores. Iron can also be found in pure form, as meteoritic stones, containing some nickel, and these have been used to make objects of iron from earliest times. On the other hand, reduction of iron ore to pure metal is a complex process, requiring high temperatures and sophisticated techniques. Apart from that, in order to qualify for use as tools and weapons, the iron has to undergo complex treatment. But once that stage is reached, its qualities are unsurpassed by any other metal. These are the reasons why, on the one hand, iron did not become common until relatively late in human history, and on the other hand, it eventually became the most common metal for tools and weaponry. Together with other metals such as gold, silver, copper, and tin, iron was a symbol of wealth. At the same time, iron had a negative connotation, representing harshness and barrenness, as in the comparison of the heavens with iron (Lev 26:19), the earth with iron (Deut 28:23), the equation of Egypt with an iron furnace (Deut 4:20), and the rod (scepter) of iron that symbolized the merciless ruler (e.g., Ps 2:9; Rev 2:27). Even though many of the implements of the temple were made of iron, the use of iron tools in the construction of the altar on Mount Ebal or of the temple in Jerusalem was forbidden (1 Kgs 6:7).

2. Iron is a town listed as a fortified city belonging to the tribe of Naphtali and located in the hills of northern Galilee, about 9 mi. northwest of Hazor (Josh 19:38).

IRU The first-listed son of Caleb in the genealogy of Judah (1 Chron 4:15).

ISAAC Son of Abraham and Sarah (Gen 17:17). Isaac next appears in Gen 20–22. At first, he is only implicitly involved in the story, but the issue of his birth nonetheless features when Abraham attempts to pass Sarah off as his sister to ABIMELECH, king of Gerar.

The issues of Abraham's bizarre offer of his own wife to Abimelech when she was about to bear Isaac, his callous attitude toward the life of his older son (Ishmael) as well as that son's mother (Hagar), and his willingness to make covenant with a human sovereign all converge as a strong undercurrent of doubt about his character by the time Gen 22 laconically begins "After these events, God tested Abraham." Taking the chapter out of its context makes what happens seem unmotivated, an arbitrary test of loyalty arising from God's nature alone, rather than from Abraham's character. In chap. 22, Abraham is not the noble figure of later tradition, but the subject of testing, because his actions and their motivations have been dubious. God prevents Abraham from sacrificing Isaac. The story emphasizes at its climax that Abraham and his progeny will go on to live out the covenantal promise made by the Lord (vv. 16-18) and that Abraham is not to do anything whatsoever to harm Isaac (vv. 12-14). When he returns to Beer-sheba at the close (v. 19), Abraham does so on the basis of his covenant with the Lord, not with Abimelech, and with a complete dedication to Isaac as his and Sarah's son.

Abraham accordingly secures REBEKAH as a wife for Isaac, because she is not a Canaanite but a woman of Abraham's own land and kin (Gen 24). Isaac rather than Ishmael is the progeny of the covenant, not only by virtue of his residence in the land of promise, but also because of the union he came from and the marriage he entered.

ISAIAH, BOOK OF The book of Isaiah takes its name from Isaiah of Jerusalem, a prophet who lived in the latter 8th cent. and probably into the early 7th cent BCE. Its sixty-six chapters contain preaching, biographical accounts, and third-person reports from that period (the bulk of chaps. 1–39) as well as from a much later time—the second half of the 6th and possibly the early 5th cent. BCE (chaps. 40–66). In the fourfold division of the Christian OT (Pentateuch, Historical Books, Wisdom Literature, and Prophets), Isaiah heads the Prophets. In the threefold division of the Jewish Scripture, the TANAKH (Torah, [Former and Latter] Prophets, and Writings), Isaiah heads the Latter Prophets. On the basis of content, style, and historical context, modern scholars commonly divide the book into three parts—chaps. 1–39, 40–55, and 56–66, respectively, "First Isaiah," "Second Isaiah" (Deutero-Isaiah), and "Third Isaiah" (Trito-Isaiah). Despite the diverse origins of the material, scholars increasingly recognize that skilled editing has given unity and coherence to the sixty-six chapters.

ISHBAH Listed among the descendants of Judah in 1 Chron 4:17, he was the son of Mered and Bithiah, the daughter of Pharoah. He was the father of Eshtemoa.

ISHBAK The fifth son of Abraham by his secondary wife KETURAH, according to the genealogies in Gen 25:2 and 1 Chron 1:32.

ISHBI-BENOB The name of a Philistine descended from the giant who says that he will kill David, but is prevented when Abishai the son of Zeruiah comes to David's aid and kills the giant (2 Sam 21:16).

ISHBOSHETH The son of Saul who succeeded him as king over Israel (2 Sam 2:8). Abner's placement of Ishbosheth on the throne suggests that he was a minor and that the figure of 40 given for his accession age is a round number (2 Sam 2:10). His designation as king in Transjordan (Mahanaim) was evidently the result of the Philistine victory over "Gilead, the Geshurites, Jezreel, Ephraim, and Benjamin—all Israel" (2 Sam 2:9). Further pressure by David's treaty with Geshur to his north (2 Sam 3:3) and overtures to Saul loyalists in Jabesh-gilead (2 Sam 2:2b-7) compelled Ishbosheth into a losing war with David, ended by Abner's assassination and then his own (recounted apologetically in 2 Sam 3–4). Ishbosheth's two-year reign during David's seven and one-half years in Hebron (2 Sam 2:11) may indicate that David became king over Judah while Saul was living.

ISHHOD A descendant of Manasseh (1 Chron 7:18). Oddly, his mother is named in the text as HAMMOLECHETH, but there is no mention of his father, implying that his relationship to the tribe of Manasseh is traced through his mother, the sister of Gilead.

ISHI 1. A Jerahmeelite (1 Chron 2:31).

2. A Judahite (1 Chron 4:20).

3. A Simeonite whose sons led an attack on the Amalekites at Mount Seir (1 Chron 4:42).

4. A chief of the half-tribe of Manasseh (1 Chron 5:24).

ISHMA A Judahite, the son of Etam (1 Chron 4:3).

ISHMAEL, ISHMAELITES Ishmael is the name of several persons in the OT, and the designation of a desert tribe or a confederation of desert tribes.

1. The son of Abraham and Hagar, the servant of Abraham's wife Sarah, and the older half brother of Isaac.

2. The Ishmaelites were an ancient tribe who, according to the Bible, were the descendants of the eponymous ancestor Ishmael.

3. The son of Nethaniah son of Elishama, a member of the royal family (2 Kgs 25:25) and/or high official (Jer 41:1). Ishmael assassinated GEDALIAH, the Babylonian-appointed ruler of Judah, with Ammonite support probably in 582 BCE (2 Kgs 25:23-25; Jer 40:8–41:18).

4. A descendant of King Saul in the 12th generation (1 Chron 8:38; 9:44).

5. Father of Zebadiah, the "leader of Judah's house" under JEHOSHAPHAT (2 Chron 19:11).

6. Captain of a company of the royal guard, supporting Jehoiada's overthrow of Athaliah (2 Chron 23:1).

7. A priest of Ezra's times (ca. 400 BCE) who had married a foreigner (Ezra 10:22; 1 Esdr 9:22). See HAGRITE, HAGRITES; MIDIAN, MIDIANITES; PATRIARCHS.

ISHMAIAH 1. A Benjaminite warrior who participated as a leader and member of David's elite unit "the Thirty" (1 Chron 12:4).

2. Son of Obadiah and leader of the Zebulun tribe (1 Chron 27:19) during the reign of David.

ISHMERAI One of Elpal's sons, a Benjaminite (1 Chron 8:18).

ISHPAH One of Beriah's sons, a Benjaminite (1 Chron 8:16).

ISHPAN One of the eleven sons of Shashak, a Benjaminite (1 Chron 8:22).

ISHVAH Listed as one of the sons of Asher in Gen 46:17 and 1 Chron 7:30, the name is absent from the corresponding list in Num 26:44.

ISHVI 1. A son of Asher listed in a genealogy (Gen 46:17; 1 Chron 7:30). The name appears in a genealogy in Num 26:44, minus his brother ISHVAH.

2. A son of Saul mentioned only once (1 Sam 14:49). Ishvi may be another name for Esh-baal, who appears in other genealogies (1 Chron 8:33; 9:39).

ISLAND, ISLE The Hebrew word denotes either a coastal area (Ps 72:10; Isa 20:6; 23:6; Dan 11:18) or an island such as CYPRUS (Isa 23:1, 12; Jer 2:10; Ezek 27:6), Rhodes (Ezek 27:15), or Caphtor (Jer 47:4). These "shores" can represent the non-Israelite world in general (Isa 40:15; Zeph 2:11), esp. its distant peoples (Isa 41:5; 49:1; 66:19; Jer 31:10). In the Prophets, the islands/coasts are witnesses to God's actions (Jer 31:10; Ezek 26:15, 18; 27:35) and are home to the dispersed Israelites before their return (Isa 11:11; 60:9). Alternately, they can be God's arrogant opponents (Isa 41:1, 5), destined for destruction (Isa 59:18; cf Ezek 39:6; Jer 25:22).

In the NT the terms for "island" play a more modest role. In Acts Paul visits the islands of Cyprus (13:4-12), COS, RHODES (21:1), Crete (27:6-13), CAUDA (27:16), MALTA (28:1-11), and Syracuse (28:12). Titus is located on Crete (Titus 1:5), and John the seer is exiled to Patmos (Rev 1:9). Yet only in Revelation (6:14; 16:20) do the "islands" become thematically significant again, destroyed in the cosmic upheaval that precedes God's final judgment (cf Isa 42:15).

ISMACHIAH A Levite and an administrator of the temple tax under King Hezekiah (2 Chron 31:13).

ISSACHAR, ISSACHARITES 1. The 9th son of Jacob (his 5th son by Leah [Gen 30:17-18]) and eponymous ancestor of the tribe of Issachar.

2. The tribe of Issachar.

3. Levitical gatekeeper during the reign of David (1 Chron 26:5). This Issachar is listed as the 7th son of Obed-edom.

ISSHIAH 1. Son of Izrahiah of the tribe of Issachar; a chief in the fighting force of that tribe (1 Chron 7:3).

2. One of David's mighty men, a Benjaminite (1 Chron 12:6 [Heb. 12:7]).

3. Second son of Uzziel, a Levite and father of a certain Zechariah (1 Chron 23:20; 24:25).

4. Chief of the family of Rehabiah, a Levite (1 Chron 24:21) and descendant of Moses (1 Chron 23:14-17).

ISSHIJAH A descendant of Harim who returned with Zerubbabel from exile (Ezra 2:32; Neh 7:35) and was required by Ezra's reforms to divorce his foreign wife (Ezra 10:31).

ITHAI A Benjaminite warrior from Gibeah, Ithai is named among "the Thirty," a group of exceptional soldiers who supported David's early reign from Hebron and Jerusalem (1 Chron 11:31) before Saul's death.

ITHAMAR In Priestly traditions of the Pentateuch, in Chronicles, and in Ezra, Ithamar is the 4th son of Aaron and ELISHEBA (after Nadab, Abihu, and Eleazar; Exod 6:23; Num 26:60; 1 Chron 6:3 [Heb. 5:29]; 24:1), all four sons being consecrated to priestly office (Exod 28:1; Num 3:2-4). With the rejection and demise of Nadab and Abihu (Lev 10:1-3; Num 3:4; 26:61; 1 Chron 24:2), Eleazar becomes the leading figure through whom priestly descent is traced to Aaron (Ezra 7:5; 1 Chron 6:3-4 [Heb. 5:29-30]; 6:50-53 [Heb. 6:35-38]; Num 20:25-28), while Ithamar emerges as leader over all the Levites (Exod 38:21), including the Gershonites (Num 4:28) and the Merarites (Num 4:33; 7:8). First Chronicles 24, esp. in connection with 1 Sam 14:3; 22:9, suggests that the house of ELI at Shiloh descended from Ithamar, with the name AHIMELECH representing the priestly line of Ithamar. Returning to Jerusalem with Ezra was a family of Ithamarite priests who had become prominent in Babylonia (Ezra 8:2; 1 Esdr 8:29).

ITHIEL Ithiel was an ancestor of Sallu, a Benjaminite leader who returned to live in Jerusalem after the Babylonian exile during the time of Nehemiah (Neh 11:7).

ITHMAH A Moabite warrior among "the Thirty" (1 Chron 11:46).

ITHNAN A town settled by the tribe of Judah, located in the arid southern plains in the south toward the boundary of Edom (Josh 15:23).

ITHRA The father of Amasa (2 Sam 17:25), who served as commander of Absalom's army in the revolt against David. Ithra was later killed by Joab, David's commander in chief.

ITHRAN 1. A grandson of Seir the Horite and the first-listed son of the clan chief Dishon (Gen 36:26; 1 Chron 1:41).

2. Tenth-listed son of Zophah from the tribe of Asher (1 Chron 7:37).

ITHREAM Ithream was David's 6th and youngest son born in Hebron (2 Sam 3:5). He was born to EGLAH, specifically identified as David's wife.

ITHRITE A Judahite clan located at Kiriath-jearim (1 Chron 2:53). Ira and Gareb, two of the Thirty, are noted as being "from Ither" (2 Sam 23:38; 1 Chron 11:40).

ITTAI 1. A Philistine warrior who was exiled from his hometown of Gath and was loyal to David during Absalom's rebellion. He, his family, and 600 of his followers left Jerusalem with David. When David tried to turn him back because of the trials Ittai had already experienced, Ittai swore that he would remain with David, whether it meant life or death (2 Sam 15:19-22). His loyalty during Absalom's rebellion garnered him command of one-third of David's army alongside Joab and Abishai, the sons of Zeruiah (2 Sam 18:2, 5, 12).

2. The son of Ribai from Gibeah of the Benjaminites, who is listed among "the Thirty" as one of David's warriors (2 Sam 23:29; 1 Chron 11:31).

ITURAEA A region located northeast of Galilee, in the area of the Anti-Lebanon Mountains and the Beqa Valley. The only biblical reference to Ituraea is found in Luke 3:1, where Philip's territory of rule is described as "Iturea and TRACHONITIS."

IVVAH A town that was apparently conquered by the invading Assyrians under Sennacherib, cited alongside Hena, Sepharvaim, Hamath, and ARPAD, because, like those cities, neither its gods (2 Kgs 18:34) nor its king (2 Kgs 19:13) could save it.

IZHAR, IZHARITES 1. A Levite and descendant of Kohath and father of Korah (Exod 6:18, 21; Num 16:1; 1 Chron 6:18, 38 [Heb. 6:3, 23]).

2. A tribe whose eponymous ancestor was Izhar (Num 3:27; 1 Chron 26:23); he is called Amminadab in 1 Chron 6:22 (Heb. 6:7).

3. A Judahite listed in 1 Chron 4 as the son of Ashhur and Helah (1 Chron 4:7). The name might be a variant of Zohar.

IZLIAH Chief or head of an ancestral house, Izliah, a descendant of Benjamin, lived in Jerusalem and was a son of ELPAAL, who was born in Moab to SHAHARAIM (1 Chron 8:18).

IZRAHIAH According to the Chronicler, Izrahiah was the great-grandson of Issachar, one of the twelve sons of Israel (1 Chron 7:3). This family line results in "87,000 mighty warriors" (1 Chron 7:5).

IZRI A levitical singer who received the 4th lot to determine his shift of service (1 Chron 25:3, 11).

IZZIAH An Israelite who married a foreign woman during the Babylonian exile, an action declared by Ezra to have increased Israel's guilt before God. Izziah was one of those who sent away a foreign wife and children upon return to Jerusalem (Ezra 10:25; 1 Esdr 9:26).

Jj

JAAKAN A grandson of Seir the Horite and the 3rd-listed son of Ezer (1 Chron 1:42). As a clan name, Jaakan represents part of the indigenous Horite population disrupted by immigrating Esauite clans (Deut 2:12) and absorbed into historical Edom. The Jaakanite clan is likely referenced in the toponyms BENE-JAAKAN (Num 33:31-32) and Beeroth-BENE-JAAKAN (Deut 10:6).

JAAKOBAH Leader of a Simeonite clan (1 Chron 4:36) who migrated northwest into Philistia during Hezekiah's reign (1 Chron 3:39-41).

JAALA The ancestor of a family of descendants of Solomon's servants in a list of returnees who came to Jerusalem with Zerubbabel (Neh 7:58).

JAARE-OREGIM The father of ELHANAN, who slays GOLIATH the Gittite (2 Sam 21:19).

JAARESHIAH One of Jehoram's sons, a descendant of Benjamin, family leader, and inhabitant of Jerusalem (1 Chron 8:27).

JAASIEL 1. The Mezobaite listed among David's elite warriors known as "the Thirty" (1 Chron 11:47; 2 Sam 23:18-39).

2. The son of Abner (the cousin of King Saul) listed among officers who served in David's royal bureaucracy as being in charge of the tribe of Benjamin (1 Chron 27:21).

JAASU A descendant of Bani, one of the returning exiles compelled by Ezra to give up his foreign wife (Ezra 10:37).

JAAZANIAH 1. A captain of the army who came to Gedeliah at Mizpah after the first deportation by Nebuchadnezzar in 597 BCE (2 Kgs 25:23). Jaazaniah may also have been one of the men who later assassinated Gedeliah and fled to Egypt (2 Kgs 25:25-26).

2. The son of Jeremiah (not the prophet), one of the Rechabites whom the prophet Jeremiah brought into the temple as a lesson in faithfulness to the people of Judah (Jer 35:3).

3. The son of Shaphan, who appeared in Ezekiel's vision of the elders in the temple in Jerusalem (Ezek 8:11).

4. The son of Azzur, an official in Jerusalem (Ezek 11:1). When Ezekiel prophesied against him and other officials for giving wicked counsel, one of the other officials died immediately.

JAAZIAH A Levite identified as the son of Merari and the father of Shoham, Zakkur, and Ibri (1 Chron 24:26-27).

JAAZIEL A levitical singer and Levite of 2nd rank mentioned in a list of Levites who, by order of David, were assigned to make music on the occasion of David's transportation of the COVENANT CHEST from Obed-edom's house to Jerusalem (1 Chron 15:18).

JABAL The son of Lamech and Adah; said to be the ancestor of the tent-dwellers and herders (Gen 4:20).

JABBOK RIVER In the Transjordan, the Jabbok River flows north from near Amman (ancient Rabbath-ammon), turning northwest and finally due west into the Jordan River near Adam 15 mi.

north of the Dead Sea. The Jabbok is prominent in the Jacob narrative where the patriarch wrestled with a "man/ spirit" and received the name Israel (Gen 32:22-27).

JABESH The name can be understood as either a person or an area. Jabesh is noted as the father of King Shallum of Israel (2 Kgs 15:10, 13). The account of Menahem's usurpation of Shallum (2 Kgs 15:14) includes the destruction of TIPHSAH (v. 16).

JABESH-GILEAD A city in the Transjordan during the time of the Judges and the monarchy. Jabesh-gilead is found in Judg 21; 1 Sam 10; 11; 31; 2 Sam 2; 21; and 1 Chron 10. It is associated with the tribe of Benjamin, King Saul, and the rise of the monarchy.

In Judg 21, Jabesh-gilead appears as the region that did not answer the call to stand with Israel against Benjamin. The heinous rape and murder of the Levite's secondary wife (chap. 19) takes place in Gibeah of Benjamin. In this narrative, both Benjamin and Jabesh-gilead were punished for failure to answer a call to action. For the purposes of survival, the remnants of these two communities were joined.

In the narrative cycle that details Saul's ascension to the throne (1 Sam 10–11), the inhabitants of Jabesh-gilead were under siege by the Ammonites, and Saul of Benjamin called Israel to rally on their behalf. In an action that recalls the horror of Judg 19, Saul divided a yoke of oxen into pieces and sent them throughout the land to ensure that all the inhabitants of the area would join him. The united tribes prevailed over the Ammonites and delivered the inhabitants of Jabesh-gilead. This display of military prowess assured Saul's position as king over Israel (see SAUL, SON OF KISH).

JABEZ 1. A Judahite town (1 Chron 2:55).

2. A person mentioned in a Judahite genealogy (1 Chron 4:9-10).

JABIN 1. Canaanite king of Hazor who rallied other local kings against the conquering Israelites (Josh 11:1-5).

2. Canaanite king of Hazor (evidently descended from the earlier king) whose general SISERA warred against the Israelites led by the judge and prophetess DEBORAH.

JABNEEL 1. A place in the northwestern corner of the territory of Judah (Josh 15:11), also known as Jabneh or Jamnia. It is one of the cities upon which fear and dread of Holofernes falls in the face of his military campaign in the region (Jdt 2:28). The author of 1 Maccabees associates it in various places with the location of Seleucid military officers and troops (4:15; 5:58; 10:69; 15:40).

2. A town located on the southern edge of the territory included in the allotment of land to Naphtali (Josh 19:33).

JACAN A Gadite who lived in Bashan (1 Chron 5:13).

JACHIN 1.The 4th of six sons of Simeon, the 2nd son of Jacob and Leah. Jachin was founder or ancestor of the family of the Jachinites (Gen 46:10; Exod 6:15).

2. A priest who was chosen 21st by lot and who became head of the 21st division of priests in the time of David according to 1 Chron 24:17. One of his descendants by the same name returned from Babylon (1 Chron 9:10; Neh 11:10).

3. See JACHIN AND BOAZ.

JACHIN AND BOAZ Jachin and Boaz, the two bronze PILLARs erected at the vestibule of the TEMPLE OF SOLOMON, were each 27 ft. high and 18 ft. in circumference with capitals 7.5 ft. high on top. The names appear only at 1 Kgs 7:21 and 2 Chron 3:17.

JACKAL A dog-like, omnivorous, nocturnal scavenger still prevalent in the Middle East, the jackal is smaller than a wolf, looks much like a fox, and makes a distinct wailing sound (Mic 1:8). It tends to live among ruins; thus, the Bible associates the jackal with destruction.

JACOB 1. Jacob belongs to the 3rd generation of Israelites (see ABRAHAM; ISAAC; REBEKAH; SARAH) and becomes, eponymously, the ancestor of the whole group. He is one of the PATRIARCHS of Israel. His name was changed to Israel (Gen. 32:28), giving his name to the subsequent people and nation.

Jacob is the ancestor of Jesus (Matt 1:2-16; Luke 3:34-36; Acts 7). Jesus refers to Jacob as one of the three foundational patriarchs several times in his public preaching (Matt 8:11; 22:32; Mark 12:26; Luke 13:28; 20:37).

2. According to the genealogy in Matt 1, a certain Jacob was the father of Joseph, husband of Mary, mother of Jesus (Matt 1:15-16).

JACOB'S WELL The location where Jesus meets the Samaritan Woman (John 4:4-42).

JADA A Jerahmeelite, the son of Onam, brother of Shammai, and father of Jether and Jonathan (1 Chron 2:28, 32).

JADDAI A descendant of Nebo (Ezra 10:43) and perhaps the same as IDDO of 1 Kgs 4:14.

JADDUA 1. One of the heads of the people listed as signatories to Ezra's covenant in Neh 10:21 (Heb. 10:22).

2. A high priest who served during the time of Darius III and Alexander the Great (see Josephus, *Ant.* 11.302-47). He appears as the son of Jonathan and the grandson of Joiada in Neh 12:11.

JADDUS The head of a clan of priests whose descendants were among the returnees from Babylon with Zerubbabel. They were unable to provide documentation establishing their genealogy and were thus temporarily disqualified from serving as priests (1 Esdr 5:38). Jaddus is identified as the husband of Agia, Barzillai's daughter.

JADON 1. A builder of the Jerusalem walls who worked with Melatiah. Both worked under the governor's jurisdiction (Neh 3:7).

2. A prophet who confronted and judged Jeroboam. Jadon was later killed by a lion for his own disobedience (Josephus, *Ant.* 8.231–45).

JAEL Jael plays a major role in the dramatic military victory recounted narratively in Judg 4, and poetically in the Song of Deborah in Judg 5. Deborah announces that the Lord "will hand over Sisera to a woman" (Judg 4:9). Jael is the woman to whom Deborah refers. The wife of Heber the Kenite, Jael, along with many other biblical heroines, occupies the marginal space of the outsider who courageously throws her lot in with Israel.

JAHATH 1. The son of Reaiah and a great-grandson of Judah; he was the father of AHUMAI and Lathad (1 Chron 4:2).

2. The name of several Gershomites in the tribe of Levi (1 Chron 6:20, 43; 23:10-11).

3. An Izharite in the tribe of Levi (1 Chron 24:22).

4. A Levite who oversaw workers repairing the temple during the reign of Josiah (2 Chron 34:12).

JAHAZ A town on the Israelite exodus itinerary during the final stages of their journey to the plains of Moab (Num 21:23). The site lies on the Mishor east of the northern half of the DEAD SEA, north of the ARNON River.

JAHAZIEL 1. One of Saul's Benjaminite relatives who joined David's forces at Ziklag (1 Chron 12:4 [Heb. 12:5]).

2. A priest whom David assigned to blow the trumpet before the covenant chest when it was brought to Jerusalem (1 Chron 16:6).

3. The 3rd son of Hebron who appears in a Levite genealogy included in the narrative of David's assignment of the Levites to their divisions for liturgical service (1 Chron 23:19; 24:23).

4. An Asaphite Levite and son of Zechariah said to have prophesied to King Jehoshaphat before a battle against the Ammonites and the Moabites (2 Chron 20:14-17).

5. The father of Shecaniah whose name appears in a list of those who were in Ezra's group of returnees from Babylon (Ezra 8:5; 1 Esdr 8:32).

JAHDAI Descendant of Judah listed in the Caleb genealogy (1 Chron 2:47).

JAHDIEL Jahdiel and his fellow clan leaders in the half-tribe of Manasseh are described as "mighty warriors" and "famous men" who turned to idol worship and were therefore exiled by the Assyrians (1 Chron 5:24-26).

JAHDO A Gadite, the son of Buz (1 Chron 5:14) and father of Jeshishai.

JAHLEEL Ancestor of the clan of the Jahleelites, Jahleel was the 3rd son of Zebulun (Gen 46:14; Num 26:26).

JAHMAI One of the sons of TOLA, listed in the genealogy of Issachar (1 Chron 7:2) as heads of ancestral houses and mighty warriors.

JAHZEEL The first-listed descendant of Naphtali and progenitor of the Jahzeelites (Gen 46:24; Num 26:48), Jahzeel is the grandson of Bilhah, Rachel's female servant and Jacob's secondary wife, who gave birth to Dan and Naphtali (Gen 29:29; 30:3-8; 46:25).

JAHZEIAH Jahzeiah and Jonathan opposed Ezra's investigation into foreign marriages in Ezra 10:15, but 1 Esdr 9:14-15 suggests the two supported Ezra.

JAHZERAH An ancestor of Adaiah, a priest mentioned along with others among the first returnees after the Babylonian exile (1 Chron 9:12). Jahzerah is listed as the son of Meshullam and the father of Adiel.

JAIR, JAIRITE 1. A son/descendant of Manasseh (Num 32:41; Deut 3:14; Josh 13:30; 1 Kgs 4:13; 1 Chron 2:22), who took several villages in Gilead during the Israelite conquest.

2. A judge in early Israel for twenty-two years (Judg 10:3) who had thirty sons and thirty cities known as HAVVOTH-JAIR.

3. Jair the Benjaminite was the father of Mordecai, the cousin of Queen Esther and crucial in the Jews' salvation (Esth 2:5; 6–8).

4. The father of Elhanan who killed the brother of Goliath (1 Chron 20:5).

5. Gentilic name applied to IRA, the priest of David (2 Sam 20:26), denoting descent from Jair of the tribe of Manasseh.

JAIRUS 1. Identified as "one of the synagogue leaders," Jairus comes (Mark 5:22) to beg Jesus for the life of his young daughter, who is deathly ill.

2. The head of a family of returning exiles listed in 1 Esdr 5:31.

JAKEH Jakeh is referred to in Prov 30:1 as the father of Agur, a writer of proverbs.

JAKIM 1. One of the nine sons of Shimei in a list of Benjamin's descendants (1 Chron 8:19).

2. A priest allotted the 12th of twenty-four divisions of the temple's priestly order (1 Chron 24:12).

JALAM Second-listed son of Esau and Oholibamah and a clan chief of Esau/Edom (Gen 36:5, 14, 18; 1 Chron 1:35).

Jalam was born in Canaan and relocated to Seir (36:2, 6-8).

JALON Son of Ezrah, descendant of Judah (1 Chron 4:17).

JAMBRI The patriarch of a family some of whose members attacked, killed, and seized the possessions of John, a brother of Judas Maccabeus (1 Macc 9:32-42).

JAMES A name connected to the OT name Jacob.

1. James the son of Zebedee is referred to in church tradition as "James the Great/Major" (Matt 4:21; Mark 1:19; Luke 5:10). He is always among the first three in the four lists of the Twelve (Matt 10:2-4; Mark 3:16-19; Luke 6:14-16; Acts 1:13), indicating that he was remembered as important in the inner circles of Jesus' followers. His brother John was younger, to judge from the fact that James is always mentioned first. With their father Zebedee, they were fishers on the Sea of Galilee. Luke reports that they were partners with Peter and Andrew (5:10).

Jesus nicknamed both James and John "Boanerges, which means 'sons of Thunder,'" perhaps for their strong, sometime brash personalities (Mark 3:17), as shown in their violence-prone anger toward a Samaritan village that refused Jesus entry (Luke 9:51-56), and in their request to Jesus for preeminence in God's kingdom (Mark 10:35-45; but Matt 20:20-28 puts this request in the mouth of their mother).

2. James the son of Alphaeus is called "James the Less/Minor" in tradition. His patronymic "the son of Alphaeus" distinguishes him from the other, more prominent James the son of Zebedee. In the lists of the Twelve (Matt 10:2-4; Mark 3:16-19; Luke 6:14-16; Acts 1:13), he is named in the last 3rd of the lists, indicating his relative unimportance. This is confirmed by the fact that he is not mentioned elsewhere in the NT.

3. James the son of Mary was not one of the Twelve. This James's mother was the Mary who, with the other women, was a witness of Jesus' crucifixion and the empty tomb (Matt 27:56; Mark 15:40; 16:1; Luke 24:10). He does not appear in the NT as a character, only in the phrase "Mary the mother of James" to distinguish her from Mary Magdalene, also at the crucifixion and the empty tomb.

4. James the father of a 2nd Judas appears in the Luke–Acts lists of the Twelve, but not in the lists in Matthew or Mark. This Judas is called "the son of James" to distinguish him from Judas Iscariot, who follows immediately in the Lukan list.

5. James the brother of Jesus was not a follower of Jesus during his ministry, but he soon became the leader of the Jerusalem church, the traditional author of the canonical Letter of James, and a Christian martyr. Also known as James the Just. See Acts 15; 1 Cor 15; Gal 1–2.

JAMES, LETTER OF The letter of James follows the Pauline letters and Hebrews, which are identified by their destination. The author of James identifies himself as "James servant of God and Lord Jesus Christ." It is addressed "to the twelve tribes in the diaspora," rather than to a specific group such as the believers in Corinth or Rome. James is part of the corpus of Catholic Epistles each known by the name of its author. The corpus was a collection addressed to the church generally rather than to a particular local group.

James's canonical status was tied to its recognition as an epistle of the brother of the Lord, but many modern scholars question authorship by James. There is evidence in James of a Palestinian socioeconomic context (the problem of poverty and wealth) and significant contact with the teaching of Jesus in the Sermon on the Mount (Matt 5–7). Yet the epistle also has an orientation to the diaspora (1:1) and employs a more polished Greek than might be expected from an Aramaic-speaking Jerusalem community led by James. Consequently, the epistle probably reflects two stages of development. The epistle was likely formulated by a Jewish believer in the diaspora some time after the destruction of Jerusalem on the basis of tradition from James.

JAMIN 1. One of the sons of Jacob's son Simeon. His name appears in genealogical lists (Gen 46:10; Exod 6:15; Num 26:12; 1 Chron 4:24).

2. One of three sons of Ram. He appears among descendants of Jerahmeel in a Judahite genealogy (1 Chron 2:27).

3. One of the Levites who assisted Ezra by reading, translating, and expounding upon the Instruction for the Israelite people (Neh 8:7; 1 Esdr 9:48).

JAMLECH Means "reigning, asking counsel." According to 1 Chron 4:34, Jamlech was a descendant of Simeon and a clan leader in the Simeonite tribe.

JANAI A son of Gad and the chief of a Gadite family who lived in Bashan, an area east of the Sea of Chinnereth (1 Chron 5:12).

JANIM One of the towns belonging to the tribe of Judah (Josh 15:53).

JANNAI A Davidic ancestor of Jesus (Luke 3:24).

JANNES AND JAMBRES Names assigned by tradition to Pharaoh's magicians who opposed MOSES and Aaron (Exod 7:11-12, 22). Their willful and licentious behavior is cited as a warning to believers (2 Tim 3:8-9).

JAPHETH Japheth is one of the sons of Noah, usually presented as the youngest, based on the order of the names (e.g., Gen 9:18; 10:1; but cf 9:24). References to Japheth occur in Gen 5:32; 6:10; 7:13; 9:18, 23, 27; 10:1, 2-5, 21; 1 Chron 1:4-5.

JAPHIA 1. A town near the southern border of the tribal territory of Zebulun (Josh 19:12).

2. The king of Lachish who joined the coalition of five kings that attacked Gibeon to halt Israel's invasion. The attack resulted in defeat for the coalition (Josh 10:3-5) and the execution of the kings at Makkedah (Josh 10:22-27).

3. David's son born in Jerusalem during David's long reign (2 Sam 5:15; 1 Chron 3:7; 14:6).

JAPHLET, JAPHLETITES Japhlet was a great-grandson of Asher, first-listed son of Heber, and father of three sons (1 Chron 7:32-33).

JARAH According to the genealogy of the family of King Saul in 1 Chron 9:42, Jarah was the son of Ahaz and the father of Alemeth, Azmaveth, and Zimri.

JARED Son of Mahalalel of Seth's lineage (Gen 5:15-20; 1 Chron 1:2; Luke 3:37).

JARHA An Egyptian slave of Sheshan, a Jerahmeelite, who married his master's daughter and fathered Attai (1 Chron 2:34-35).

JARIB 1. The third of Simeon's sons listed in the Chronicler's version of his genealogy (1 Chron 4:24).

2. One of the individuals whom Ezra dispatched to Casiphia to ask Iddo to send temple servants when Ezra realized that his group of returnees lacked Levites (Ezra 8:18; 1 Esdr 8:44 [Heb. 8:43]).

3. One of the priests whom Ezra required to divorce their foreign wives (Ezra 10:18; 1 Esdr 9:19).

JARMUTH 1. A city in the south of Judah, identified with Khirbet el-Yarmuk, that was part of a five-city coalition of Amorite kings who joined together to attack Gibeon after it had made an alliance with the Israelites (Josh 10:1-27).

2. A city in the tribal area of Issachar that was given to the Gershonites to be a levitical city (Josh 21:29). The town is located northwest of BETH-SHAN.

JAROAH A Gadite, father of Huri and son of Gilead (1 Chron 5:14).

JASHAR, SCROLL OF Possibly a collection of songs (Josh 10:13; 2 Sam 1:18) associated with "the book of songs" (1 Kgs 8:12-13 LXX) or "the scroll of the LORD's wars" (Num 21:14).

JASHEN Jashen fathered several of David's thirty mighty men (2 Sam 23:32).

JASHOBEAM 1. In 1 Chron 11:11 "Jashobeam, a Hacmonite," is among the men of David and is described as "commander of the Thirty." "Chief of the Three" is an unusual designation. More familiar is the special group of David's army identified as "the Thirty," clearly David's closest and best warriors, as is seen in 2 Sam 23:18-39.

2. A man who joined David's cohort at Ziklag (1 Chron 12:6).

JASHUB 1. Third son of Issachar (Num 26:24; 1 Chron 7:1).

2. One of the descendants of BANI (or Mani in 1 Esdras) who was persuaded by the scribe Ezra to send away his foreign wife (Ezra 10:29; 1 Esdr 9:30).

JASON 1. The brother of Onias III the high priest, who displaced him under the rule of Antiochus IV (see EPIPHANES).

2. Jason, apparently one of the "believers"(i.e., a Christian) in Thessalonica. According to Acts 17:1-9, Paul and Silas were staying in his home when the Jews provoked a riot and took "Jason and some believers" before the city magistrates.

3. Romans 16:21 lists a Jason, named as one of the "relatives" of Paul who are sending greetings to the church at Rome.

JATHNIEL A gatekeeper of Korahite descent (1 Chron 26:2). He is listed as the 4th of Meshelemiah's seven sons.

JAZER Jazer was a town in Gilead. In some passages, Jazer refers to a region instead of a town (Num 21:32; 32:1), probably indicating the land around the city of Jazer.

JAZIZ Jaziz the Hagrite is listed in 1 Chron 27:30 (Heb. 27:31) as an official of King David's court who was in charge of the royal flocks.

JEATHERAI The son of Zerah, a Levite descended from Gershom (1 Chron 6:21 [Heb. 6:6]).

JEBERECHIAH The father of Zechariah, who was asked by Isaiah to witness a writing (Isa 8:2).

JEBUS, JEBUSITES Jebus is perhaps the name of the pre-Israelite city that David captured from the Jebusites and renamed "David's city" (2 Sam 5:6-9; see DAVID'S CITY). In the biblical tradition, it is identified with Jerusalem (Judg 19:10).

JECHONIAH See JEHOIACHIN.

JECOLIAH Mother of King AZARIAH of Judah, and one of three Jerusalemite queen mothers (2 Kgs 15:2; 2 Chron 26:3).

JECONIAH 1. An otherwise unknown individual whose descendants did not rejoice when the Philistines returned the COVENANT CHEST to Beth-Shemesh (1 Sam 6:19).

2. Alternate name of JEHOIACHIN, king of Judah exiled by Nebuchadnezzar (1 Chron 3:16).

3. Variant form of CONANIAH (1 Esdr 1:9).

4. Alternate name of JEHOAHAZ, king of Judah (1 Esdr 1:34).

JEDAIAH 1. Son of Shimri who descended from Simeon (1 Chron 4:37), one of Jacob and Leah's sons.

2. An eponym for a priestly family living during David's reign (1 Chron 24:7) and among those returning after the exile (1 Chron 9:10; Ezra 2:36; Neh 7:39; 1 Esdr 5:24).

3. One of the repairmen of the Jerusalem wall (Neh 3:10).

4. A priest who became a resident in Jerusalem after the exile (Neh 11:10).

5. The head of a priestly family (Neh 12:6, 19).

6. Another priest belonging to a family with this name (Neh 12:7, 21).

7. One of the exiles in Babylon who descended from Aaron and returned to Jerusalem, where he contributed gold and silver for making a crown (Zech 6:10, 14).

JEDIAEL 1. Jediael the Benjaminite (although the genealogy is probably of Zebulun) is described as having a single son and seven grandsons (1 Chron 7:6, 10-11).

2. One of David's mighty men (1 Chron 11:45).

3. Although possibly the same man as in 1 Chron 11:45, deserted the Mannasites to join David during David's service in Philistia (1 Chron 12:20 [Heb. 12:21]).

4. A Korahite gatekeeper at the temple in Jerusalem during the reign of David (1 Chron 26:2).

JEDIDAH The mother of King JOSIAH (2 Kgs 22:1).

JEDIDIAH Through Nathan, God told David to name the child whom Bathsheba bore Jedidiah (2 Sam 12:25).

JEDUTHUN In Chronicles, Jeduthun is portrayed as a leader of one of the guilds of the Levites (see PRIESTS AND LEVITES) that provided music for the temple service. According to Chronicles, King DAVID "set apart Asaph's family, Heman and Jeduthun, for service to prophesy accompanied by lyres, harps, and cymbals" (1 Chron 25:1). "Jeduthun" also appears in the superscription to Pss 39; 62; and 77, seemingly ascribing authorship of these psalms to Jeduthun, but the superscriptions then proceed to assign the psalm to David or Asaph (Ps 77).

JEHALLELEL 1. Jehallelel, possibly an eponym, appears in a list of descendants of Judah (1 Chron 4:16).

2. A Merarite Levite and the father of Azariah who was among those who cleansed the temple under Hezekiah (2 Chron 29:12).

JEHDEIAH 1. A Levite mentioned in a genealogy as a religious official of David's court (1 Chron 24:20).

2. The Meronothite in charge of the donkeys in David's court (1 Chron 27:30).

JEHIAH Jehiah and OBED-EDOM were two Levite gatekeepers appointed by David for the COVENANT CHEST when it was moved to Jerusalem (1 Chron 15:24).

JEHIEL 1. A Levite and a gatekeeper. He played a harp and joined in the dedication of the COVENANT CHEST that King David brought to Jerusalem (1 Chron 15:18, 20; 16:5).

2. A Levite and chief among Ladan's sons (1 Chron 23:8). Gershon's grandson and Levi's great-grandson (1 Chron 23:6-7). He managed the temple treasury during David's reign (1 Chron 29:8) and established the Jehieli priestly family (1 Chron 26:21-22).

3. Hachmoni's son who tutored or advised David's sons (1 Chron 27:32).

4. Son of King Jehoshaphat of Judah (2 Chron 21:2).

5. A Levite who assisted Conaniah in storing the offerings (2 Chron 31:13).

6. A chief officer of the temple who

gave the people, the priests, and the Levites lambs, kids, and bulls for Passover offerings (2 Chron 35:8).

7. Descendant of Joab and father of Obadiah who returned to Jerusalem with Ezra after the exile had ended (Ezra 8:9; 1 Esdr 8:35).

8. Shecaniah's father (Ezra 10:2; 1 Esdr 8:92). He dismissed his wife and their children according to God's instructions to Ezra (Ezra 10:26).

9. A priest and a descendant of Harim. He dismissed his foreign wife and their children according to God's instructions to Ezra (Ezra 10:21) and is listed as a descendant of Immer in 1 Esdr 9:21.

JEHIZKIAH Son of Shallum and one of four Ephraimite chiefs who opposed taking the Judahite captives (2 Chron 28:12-15) during the war between Pekah of Israel and Ahaz of Judah.

JEHOADDAH Son of Ahaz, descendant of Saul, and so a Benjaminite (1 Chron 8:36).

JEHOADDAN The mother of King AMAZIAH of Judah, one of three Jerusalem queen mothers (2 Chron 25:1; Jehoaddin in 2 Kgs 14:2). See JECOLIAH; NEHUSHTA.

JEHOAHAZ The name of a number of Israelite and Judahite kings.

1. Jehoahaz, son of JEHU, king of Israel, reigned 816–800 BCE. The reign of Jehoahaz was marked by pronounced military weakness, as Israel was dominated by HAZAEL of Aram-Damascus. These conditions are noted in 2 Kgs 13, where the pitiful state of the Israelite military is carefully enumerated. It is also reported that Jehoahaz entreated the Lord to save Israel from the Arameans, and that the Lord granted the Israelites a "savior" (2 Kgs 13:4-5).

2. Jehoahaz, son of JOSIAH king of Judah, reigned for three months in 609 BCE. Despite being a younger son of Josiah (possibly the youngest), he was enthroned after Josiah's death at Megiddo, at the instigation of the Judahite political faction known as the "people of the land." Based on Jer 22:11 and the genealogical data in 1 Chron 3:15, it appears that Jehoahaz was also known as Shallum.

3. Jehoahaz is once used as an alternate form of the name of AHAZIAH, son of Jehoshaphat, king of Judah (2 Chron 21:17).

4. It is also likely, based on an inscription of the Assyrian king TIGLATH-PILESER III, that Jehoahaz was the full name of the king known in the Bible as AHAZ son of Jotham, king of Judah, whose reign is described in 2 Kgs 16.

JEHOASH See JOASH.

JEHOHANAN 1. Meshelemiah's 6th son, a Korahite Levite who served as a gatekeeper during David's reign (1 Chron 26:3).

2. An army commander with 280,000 warriors under King Jehoshaphat in Judah (2 Chron 17:15).

3. Father of Ishmael, an army commander, who, along with others, joined the priest Jehoiada in the revolt against Athaliah (2 Chron 23:1).

4. The high priest Eliashib's son (Ezra 10:6; 1 Esdr 9:1), whose chamber provided sleeping quarters for Ezra and who may actually be Eliashib's grandson as mentioned in Neh 12:22.

5. A descendant of Bebai who sent away his foreign wife and their children according to Ezra's instructions (Ezra 10:28; 1 Esdr 9:29).

6. Tobiah's son who married Meshullam's daughter (Neh 6:18). Tobiah was a major opponent of the rebuilding of the Jerusalem wall.

7. Priest and head of the ancestral house Amariah during the priesthood of Joiakim (Neh 12:13).

8. A priest who participated in the dedication of the Jerusalem wall with trumpet playing (Neh 12:42). See JOANAN; JOHANAN.

JEHOIACHIN King of Judah 598–597 BCE; son and successor of JEHOIAKIM; his mother was Nehushta, daughter of Elnathan of Jerusalem. He was also called JECONIAH (1 Chron 3:16-17; Jer 24:1; 27:20; 28:4; 29:2; Esth 2:6; Matt 1:11, 12) and Coniah (Jer 22:24, 28; 37:1). He became king at age 18 but reigned for only three months (2 Kgs 24:8; three months and ten days according to 2 Chron 36:9).

JEHOIADA 1. The father of BENAIAH, who is one of the warriors of DAVID listed in 2 Sam 8:18; 20:23; 23:20; and 1 Kgs 1:8.

2. The person who replaces Ahithophel as David's adviser, according to 1 Chron 27:34.

3. The high priest who, after seven years of rule by ATHALIAH, leads the coup against the queen by producing JOASH, the legal heir to the throne (2 Kgs 11:4-20).

JEHOIAKIM 1. The king of Judah from 609 to 598 BCE; son of Josiah and Zebediah daughter of Pedaiah of Rumah in Galilee. His given name was Eliakim, but Pharaoh NECO changed his name to Jehoiakim when Neco made him king in place of his brother JEHOAHAZ, who was exiled to Egypt (2 Kgs 23:34). Jehoiakim became king at the age of 25 and reigned for eleven years (2 Kgs 23:36; 2 Chron 36:5). He was a vassal of Neco for almost four years and enjoyed a peaceful life in Egypt's shadow. This arrangement was shattered when the Babylonians under Nebuchadnezzar defeated the Egyptians at Carchemish in 605 BCE. Jehoiakim was able to remain on the throne but had to serve Nebuchadnezzar as his suzerain.

2. The son of Hilkiah and the high priest in Jerusalem at the beginning of the exile according to Bar 1:7.

JEHOIARIB 1. A priestly clan chief who is listed in 1 Chron 9:10, between Jedaiah and Jachin, among those who were the first to settle in the land after the Babylonian exile. A priest by the name of JOIARIB, probably the same person, appears in close proximity to Jedaiah (Neh 11:10; 12:6, 19).

2. A priestly clan chief who received the first lot when David divided Aaron's descendants according to their tasks (1 Chron 24:7).

JEHONATHAN 1. A Levite whom King Jehoshaphat sent with other Levites, priests, and officials to the cities of Judah to teach the people the Instruction scroll (2 Chron 17:8).

2. The priest who headed the ancestral house Shemaiah (Neh 12:18) during the time that Joiakim was high priest (Neh 12:12-21) and Nehemiah was governor (Neh 12:26).

JEHOSHAPHAT 1. Son of Ahilud. He served as the recorder during the reigns of David (2 Sam 8:16; 20:24; 1 Kgs 4:3; 1 Chron 18:15) and Solomon (1 Kgs 4:3).

2. Son of Paruah. He was one of Solomon's twelve administrative officers who served as the overseer in the province of Issachar (1 Kgs 4:17).

3. Son of Nimshi, and the father of Jehu, king of the northern kingdom of Israel (2 Kgs 9:2, 14).

4. Son of Asa. He was the 6th king of the Davidic monarchy and the 4th king of Judah after the division of the kingdom in 922 BCE. His mother was Azubah the daughter of Shilhi (1 Kgs 22:41-42; 2 Chron 20:31). Jehoshaphat was 35 years old when he became king, and he ruled in Judah twenty-five years, from 873 to 849 BCE. He followed his father Asa, who had reigned in Jerusalem for forty-one years (1 Kgs 15:10). Jehoshaphat ruled during the reigns of Omri, Ahab, Ahaziah, and Jehoram, kings of the northern kingdom of Israel.

JEHOSHAPHAT VALLEY This designation appears in the Bible only in the book of Joel (3:2, 12 [Heb. 4:2, 12]), and its context suggests that it is a figurative expression for a kind of place rather than the name of an actual valley.

JEHOSHEBA The daughter of Judah's king Joram and the sister of Ahaziah (2 Kgs 11:2). After Ahaziah's death, she hid his son Joash from Athaliah, who planned to murder all the king's children so she could reign over Judah. Jehosheba successfully concealed Joash for six years until the priest Jehoiada anointed him as king.

JEHOVAH This English name for God is derived from an older English blended transliteration of two Hebrew words for God. The transliteration appears variously in a number of English translations, such as "Iehouah" in the Geneva Bible. Nevertheless, through hymnody, translations (notably, the KJV), and the Jehovah's Witnesses, the term *Jehovah* has become a widely used name for God in the English language. The inaccurate English transliteration came about as a result of an early, Jewish practice that combined the vowels of the term *Adonai* (lit., "my Lord"), with the consonants of the tetragrammaton YHWH or the term *Yahweh*. This practice of pronunciation, which reveres the holy name for God, dates back at least to Second Temple Judaism.

JEHOZABAD 1. Son of Shomer and one of two conspiring servants who assassinated King Joash of Judah (2 Kgs 12:21; cf 2 Chron 24:26). See JOZABAD.

2. The 2nd of eight sons of Obed-edom (1 Chron 26:4) whose sixty-two male descendants were servants at the temple's south gate and storehouse (v. 15).

3. A Benjaminite commander of a large force of shielded archers serving King Jehoshaphat in Jerusalem (2 Chron 17:18).

JEHU 1. Jehu son of Hanani, a prophet who appears in 1 Kgs 16:1-4. Jehu pronounces a judgment oracle against BAASHA king of Israel, in which the Lord decrees that Baasha's house will be destroyed because of his failure to amend the religious practices of Jeroboam I.

2. Jehu son of Jehoshaphat son of Nimshi, king of Israel. His reign is chronicled in 2 Kgs 9–10.

3. Jehu son of Obed, mentioned in the genealogy of Judah (1 Chron 2:38).

4. Jehu son of Joshibiah, mentioned in the genealogy of Simeon (1 Chron 4:35).

5. Jehu of Anathoth, one of David's warriors, who joined him at Ziklag while David was pinned down there by Saul (1 Chron 12:3).

JEHUBBAH One of the sons of Shemer and a descendant of Asher (1 Chron 7:34).

JEHUCAL Court official of King Zedekiah who recommends killing Jeremiah because of the offensive nature of his preaching (Jer 37:3; 38:1-4).

JEHUDI A Cushite (Jer 36:14) officer of King Jehoiakim's court, probably a scribe, sent to summon Baruch to bring a scroll containing Jeremiah's prophecies (Jer 36:14), which Jehudi read before the king and all his officials (v. 21).

JEIEL 1. Jeiel is listed as a leader in the descendants of the tribe of Reuben in 1 Chron 5:7.

2. From the time of David, Jeiel is listed as a leader of the tribe of Levi, who lives in Gibeon and is identified as the father of Gibeon (1 Chron 9:35).

3. The son of Hotham the Aroerite and brother of Shama (1 Chron 11:44).

4. A Levite gatekeeper and musician (1 Chron 15:18, 21).

5. A Levite appointed to minister before the covenant chest of the Lord, apparently as a musician (1 Chron 16:5).

6. The name appears in the genealogy of Jehaziel, a Levite of Asaph's family in the days of Jehoshaphat, king of Judah (2 Chron 20:14).

7. The name of the secretary for King Uzziah of Judah (2 Chron 26:11).

8. A Levite who appears in the account of Josiah's Passover (2 Chron 35:9).

9. The name also appears in a list of priests from various clans in Ezra 10:43.

JEKAMEAM A Levite and the 4th son of Hebron who belonged to the Kohath class (1 Chron 23:19; 24:23).

JEKAMIAH 1. In the tribe of Judah, Shallum's son and a descendant of Jerahmeel (1 Chron 2:41).

2. Son of King Jecohiah (Jehoiachin) (1 Chron 3:18).

JEKUTHIEL A son of Mered and his Judean wife, therefore a descendant of Judah (1 Chron 4:18).

JEMIMAH Job's eldest daughter born after the restoration of his possessions. She and her sisters, alongside her brothers, inherit these possessions (Job 42:14; cf Num 27:5-11).

JEMUEL The first of Simeon's sons (Gen 46:10; Exod 6:15).

JEPHTHAH A male character in the book of Judges. The stories about Jephthah extend from Judg 10:6 to 12:7. Rather than trusting in God, Jephthah bargains with God using a vow to sacrifice the first person he sees upon returning from successful battle. When Jephthah returns home to Mizpah, his unnamed daughter, rejoicing with drums and dancing, comes forth to meet him. In language reminiscent of Isaac and his near sacrifice (Gen 22:2), the narrator observes that she "was an only child; he had no other son or daughter except her" (11:34). Upon seeing her, Jephthah blames her for the predicament he himself has set up. He declares that he cannot turn back from his vow to the Lord. In her reply the daughter echoes the understanding of her father but asks that he give her two months to wander on the hills with her female friends, to lament her virginity. Jephthah grants the request. At the end of that period, the daughter returns, and Jephthah "did to her what he had promised" (11:39).

JEPHUNNEH 1. Father of Caleb (Num 13:6; 14:6, 30, 38; 26:65; Deut 1:36; Josh 15:13; 21:12; 1 Chron 4:15; 6:56) and a Kenizzite (Num 32:12; Josh 14:6, 13-14) who belonged to the tribe of Judah (Num 34:19). Caleb son of Jephunneh and Joshua were two of the spies sent by Moses into Canaan who reported faithfully (Num 14:6-9).

2. First of three sons of Jether from the tribe of Asher (1 Chron 7:38).

JERAH Son of JOKTAN (Gen 10:26; 1 Chron 1:20) and a descendant of Shem.

JERAHMEEL, JERAHMEELITES 1. A descendant of Judah by TAMAR (1 Chron 2:3-4, 9); the oldest son of Hezron (v. 9) son of Perez (v. 5); brother of RAM and Chelubai (v. 9). His genealogy appears only in 1 Chron 2:25-41.

2. The descendants of the eponymous ancestor Jerahmeel, mentioned as inhabitants of a "southern plain" separate from Judah (1 Sam 27:10; 30:29).

3. A son of the Levite KISH (1 Chron 24:29) and a member of the Merarite clan (1 Chron 23:21), apparently Jerahmeel married the daughters of his uncle Eleazar, who had no sons (1 Chron 23:22), in order to ensure the survival of the house of Eleazar.

4. An officer in the service of King JEHOIAKIM of Judah who, along with two others, was sent by the king to arrest Jeremiah and Baruch after having heard and destroyed a scroll containing the prophecies of Jeremiah.

JERED A son of Mered and his Judean wife and therefore a descendant of Judah (1 Chron 4:18).

JEREMAI One of the returning exiles

commanded by Ezra to give up his foreign wife (Ezra 10:33).

JEREMIAH 1. A warrior who joined David at Ziklag (1 Chron 12:4).

2. Another warrior who joined David at Ziklag (1 Chron 12:10).

3. One of the warriors who joined David at Ziklag (1 Chron 12:13).

4. The head of a Mannassite family house that settled in the region of Bashan (1 Chron 5:24).

5. The father of Hamutal wife of Josiah and mother of Jehoahaz and Zedekiah (2 Kgs 23:31; 24:18).

6. The father of Jaazaniah, a Rechabite living in Jerusalem during the time of Jeremiah the prophet (Jer 35:3).

7. A priest in the list of priests who came from Babylon with Zerubbabel (Neh 12:1), as well as a priestly family (Neh 12:12).

8. The name on a seal on the covenant of Ezra (Neh 10:2).

9. A leader of Judah at the dedication of the wall of Jerusalem (Neh 12:34).

10. Jeremiah the prophet, who preaches in Jerusalem in the 7th and 6th cent. BCE.

JEREMIAH, ADDITIONS TO Two independent additions to Jeremiah, the book of Baruch and the Letter of Jeremiah, appear in the LXX but not in the Masoretic text. Baruch purports to be written by Jeremiah's secretary in exile in Babylonia, for the people of Jerusalem (Jer 32:12). The book expresses hope of restoration and return from the exile. Inspired by Jeremiah's letter to the exiles (Jer 29:1-23), the Letter of Jeremiah claims to be written by Jeremiah to those who are about to be deported.

JEREMIAH, BOOK OF The book of Jeremiah is the longest and arguably the most tumultuous of the prophetic writings in the OT. With haunting imagery and palpable emotion, Jeremiah, or more accurately, the book that bears his name, reenacts the dismantling of Israel's most cherished social and symbolic systems, including the Temple, covenant arrangements, ancestral land claims, as well as election traditions, and dynastic structures. While re-performing the collapse of Judah's once secure preexilic world, Jeremiah constructs a theology of suffering, which strives to help survivors cope with massive wreckage and imagine fresh possibilities springing forth from the ruins of war and forced deportation.

JEREMIAH, LETTER OF This diatribe against idolatry originated during the Hellenistic era (332–63 BCE). The apparent reference to the letter by the author of 2 Macc suggests a date prior to 150 BCE (2 Macc 2:1-3).

JEREMIEL Archangel who responded to Ezra (2 Esdr 4:36).

JEREMOTH 1. A descendant of Benjamin in the house of Becher (1 Chron 7:8).

2. A descendant of Benjamin through Elpaal (1 Chron 8:14).

3. A descendant of the line of Merari through Mushi during David's division of levitical duties (1 Chron 23:23), the same as Jerimoth in 1 Chron 24:30.

4. A descendant of the line of Merari during David's division of levitical duties during the reign of David (1 Chron 25:22), perhaps the same as 3 above and the same as Jerimoth in 1 Chron 25:4.

5. One of those listed as having taken foreign wives (Ezra 10:26; 1 Esdr 9:27).

6. Another of those listed as having taken foreign wives (Ezra 10:27; 1 Esdr 9:28).

7. Yet another of those listed as having taken foreign wives (Ezra 10:29; 1 Esdr 9:30).

JERIAH A son of Hebron and a Levite from the Kohathite division (1 Chron 23:19; 24:23).

JERIBAI A son of Elnaam (1 Chron 11:46) listed among King David's warriors.

JERICHO A town situated at an oasis in the Jordan Valley, just northwest of the Dead Sea, has gained a reputation for being one of the oldest cities in the world. The name Jericho is most well known for its appearance in the conquest narrative of the book of Joshua. Its position on a major road from a ford of the Jordan to the highlands placed it directly in the path of the Israelites, and it was their first conquest upon crossing the Jordan (Josh 6). In the NT, Jericho features most prominently in the Gospels in the story of Jesus restoring sight to the blind beggar(s). Only two references outside the book of Joshua, however, refer to the Israelites' conquest of the city (1 Kgs 16:34; Heb 11:30-31).

JERIEL Head of a family in the tribe of Issachar (1 Chron 7:2).

JERIJAH The head of the Hebronites (1 Chron 26:31)..

JERIMOTH 1. Son of Bela, grandson of Benjamin and a warrior (1 Chron 7:7).

2. Son of Becher, grandson of Benjamin and a warrior (1 Chron 7:8, Jeremoth).

3. Son of Beriah and a descendant of Benjamin (1 Chron 8:14, Jeremoth).

4. Warrior from the tribe of Benjamin who joined David in battle at Ziglag (1 Chron 12:5).

5. A Levite; son of Mushi and great-grandson of Levi through Merari (Jeremoth in 1 Chron 23:23; Jerimoth in 1 Chr 24:30).

6. Musician who prophesied with musical instruments; son of Heman the king's seer (1 Chron 25:4-5)

7. Azriel's son, head of the tribe of Naphtali (1 Chron 27:19).

8. One of David's sons and father of Mahalath, who became Rehoboam's wife (2 Chron 11:18).

9. Overseer who assisted Conaniah and his brother Shimei in storing the tithes and contributions (2 Chron 31:13).

JERIOTH (1) One of Caleb's wives in addition to Azubah; (2) another name for Azubah; (3) the name of Azubah's former husband; (4) the daughter of Caleb and his wife Azubah (1 Chron 2:18).

JEROBOAM 1. Jeroboam I. King of Israel (ca. 924–903 BCE) after its secession from the Davidic/Solomonic kingdom.

2. Jeroboam II. King of Israel ca. 785–745 BCE, 4th in the dynasty of JEHU, and contemporary of kings AMAZIAH and Azariah (UZZIAH) of Judah. The biblical historian offers a negative evaluation of Jeroboam II, consistent with that of the other kings of Israel, namely, that he followed in the apostasy of Jeroboam I (2 Kgs 14:24).

JEROHAM 1. Father of Elkanah the father of Samuel (1 Sam 1:1; 1 Chron 6:27, 34).

2. Priest in Jerusalem during the postexilic restoration (Neh 11:12).

3. A Benjaminite (1 Chron 8:27), who may be identified with Jeremoth (8:14).

4. Ancestor of priest in postexilic Jerusalem (1 Chron 9:12).

5. A Benjaminite of Gedor whose descendants joined David at Ziklag (1 Chron 12:7 [Heb. 12:8]).

6. Father of Azarel, a Danite leader during David's reign (1 Chron 27:22).

7. Father of Azariah, who was a leader in the army that killed Athaliah during the palace coup that returned a descendant of David to the throne in Jerusalem (2 Chron 23:1).

JEROME Jerome (ca. 340–420 CE) was born at Stridon (now in Croatia) into a Christian family and educated in classical letters and rhetoric at Rome. After conversion to an ascetic life, ordination at Antioch, residence at Rome, and some traveling in the Holy Lands, he settled in Bethlehem and founded a monastic community (ca. 386 CE). Dissatisfied with the many variant translations of the OT, he decided to learn Hebrew (from a Jewish convert) in order to make his own translations from the original language. He translated the entire OT and at least the Gospels into Latin.

JERUBBAAL This name was given to GIDEON because of his opposition to BAAL worship and his desecration of the Canaanite cult at OPHRAH (Judg 6:32).

JERUSALEM The capital city of Judah, captured by David. It remained the primary governmental city of the region into NT times.

JERUSHA The mother of King JOTHAM of Judah and daughter of Zadok (2 Kgs 15:33; 2 Chron 27:1).

JESARELAH A son of Asaph who is assigned the task of prophesying with music (1 Chron 25:14). See ASARELAH.

JESHAIAH 1. In 1 Chron 3:21, Jeshaiah is the son (or perhaps grandson, compare LXX) of Hananiah.

2. According to 1 Chronicles, one of the temple musicians appointed by David. Jeshaiah was a son of Jeduthun (25:3, 15).

3. One of the Levites serving over the temple treasury (1 Chron 26:25).

4. In Ezra 8:7, Jeshaiah is Athaliah's son and is one of the exiles who return with Ezra.

5. In Ezra 8:19, Jeshaiah is Merari's son and is a Levite who served in the temple during Ezra's time.

6. The Jeshaiah in Neh 11:7 was a Benjaminite who lived at the same time.

JESHEBEAB The priest or priestly house to whom the 14th lot fell during the organization of the priesthood under David (1 Chron 24:13), appointed to duty by the procedure established by Aaron (1 Chron 24:19).

JESHER Listed among Judah's descendants as one of the three sons of Caleb and his wife Azubah (1 Chron 2:18).

JESHIMON Means "WILDERNESS" or "wasteland."

1. A region in the southeastern part of the Judean hills, near Ziph. First Samuel (23:19-24; 26:1-3) locates this north of Horesh ("on the hill of Hachilah").

2. Possibly a district in northern Moab (Num 21:20; 23:28). The NRSV interprets this as a common noun, "the wasteland."

3. The Poriyyah ridge southwest of Tiberias, during rabbinic times (y. Kil. 9:4, 32c).

JESHISHAI A Gadite whose name appears in the lineage of ABIHAIL (1 Chron 5:14).

JESHOHAIAH A Simeonite "leader of the family" (1 Chron 4:36, 38).

JESHUA Name borne by several individuals mentioned in the postexilic canonical and deuterocanonical literature. It also appears as a place-name.

1. Identified as the head of the 9th course of the priests when the priestly courses were established under King David (1 Chron 24:11).

2. A Levite who assisted in administering the temple storehouses in Jerusalem in the time of King Hezekiah (2 Chron 31:15).

3. Jeshua son of Jehozadak, a high priest who returned from exile in the same group that included the provincial governor Zerubbabel (Ezra 2:2; Neh 7:7; 1 Esdr 5:11). In the prophetic books of Haggai and Zechariah, he is referred to as "Yehoshua, son of Jehozadak," which the CEB translates as "Joshua" (Hag 1:1; Zech 3:1). This translation is in accord with an ancient tradition evidenced in the LXX, although most scholars see this name as a variant of Jeshua.

4. Probably the name of an extended family group listed as a subpart of a

group bearing the name Pahath-moab (Ezra 2:6; Neh 7:11).

5. Name of the head of a levitical family group (Ezra 2:40; 3:9; Neh 7:43; 8:7; 1 Esdr 5:58).

6. Identified as the father of Ezer, one of the leaders who worked on repairing Jerusalem's walls when Nehemiah was governor (Neh 3:19).

7. Apparently a variation on the name "Joshua," since the narrator of the book of Nehemiah uses a reference to "Jeshua son of Nun" in a context where Joshua (also known as "son of Nun") would seem to be the indicated person (Neh 8:17).

8. A "Jeshua, Azaniah's son," is listed as one of the Levites who agreed to a covenant during Nehemiah's term as governor (Neh 10:9). He may have been a member of the levitical family of the Jeshua in #5.

9. A place-name in Judah (Neh 11:26), settled by returnees from the exile in Babylon.

JESHURUN From the Hebrew verb meaning "to be straight, right," this word is a poetic title for the people of Israel, highlighting their "upright" ideal character. Jeshurun is found in only four verses in the OT, three of which occur in Moses' final speeches in Deut 32:15; 33:5; 26, and the 4th is in Isa 44:2.

JESIMIEL A descendant of Simeon and tribal leader, literally described as "leaders in their clans" (1 Chron 4:36, 38).

JESSE The Bethlehemite father of DAVID, presumably from the Ephrathah clan in the tribe of Judah (1 Chron 2:50), although the only genealogy in the OT providing a clear connection from Judah to David is probably the Chronicler's composition (1 Chron 2:10-17; see also Matt 1:3-5; Luke 3:31-33). Jesse is also identified as the grandson of RUTH the Moabite (Ruth 4:17-22), which may account for David's choosing Moab as a refuge for his parents (1 Sam 22:3-4).

JESUS Greek version of the name JOSHUA.

1. Jesus, Sirach's son, was the author of the book of Sirach (2nd cent. BCE).

2. Jesus of Nazareth. See JESUS CHRIST.

3. Jesus BARABBAS is a variant name for the criminal released by Pilate at the Passover festival (Matt 27:16-17).

4. Jesus JUSTUS was a coworker of Paul mentioned in Col 4:11.

JESUS, BAR- A Jewish "false prophet" and magician, also known as ELYMAS, who served proconsul Sergius Paulus (Acts 13:6-11). Bar-Jesus' opposition to Paul and Barnabas resulted in Paul's inflicting blindness upon him, demonstrating Paul's power and authority in the Holy Spirit at the beginning of his first missionary trip.

JESUS CHRIST "Jesus," a name common among Jews before the rise of Christianity. The NT, including on occasion the Gospels, often adds "Christ" before or after the proper name. Followers of Jesus originally used it to designate their leader's status as the Davidic king in fulfillment of Israel's royal and eschatological expectations. The titular force, however, soon faded, and "Jesus Christ" became a personal name, as already in Paul's letters.

This historical Jesus was an itinerant missionary, a public preacher, a controversialist, a composer of parables, a healer, an exorcist, an interpreter of the Instruction, and an eschatological prophet who became, even before Easter, the focus of messianic hopes. The Gospels tell of his preaching, his followers, his rejection, his crucifixion, and his resurrection.

JETHER 1. The young son of the judge Gideon (Judg 8:20-21).

2. An Ishmaelite and the father of Amasa, a commander of the Judean army (1 Kgs 2:5, 32; 1 Chron 2:17). In 2 Sam 17:25, the name is ITHRA.

3. Son of Jada and a descendant

of Jerahmeel from the tribe of Judah (1 Chron 2:32).

4. Son of Ezrah from the tribe of Judah (1 Chron 4:17).

5. Descendant of the Asher tribe and father of Jephunneh, Pispa, and Ara (1 Chron 7:38).

JETHETH The 3rd in a list of eleven clan chiefs of Esau/Edom (Gen 36:40; 1 Chron 1:51).

JETHRO One of the names for the priest of Midian, the father-in-law of Moses (Exod 3:1; 4:18; 18:1-2, 5-6, 12). Elsewhere, the father-in-law appears as REUEL and HOBAB.

JETUR Tenth-listed of twelve sons of Ishmael (Gen 25:15; 1 Chron 1:31) and eponymous ancestor of a Transjordanian tribe defeated by Reubenites, Gadites, and the half-tribe of Manasseh (1 Chron 5:19). The Jetur tribe is linked to the Ituraeans of the ANTI-LEBANON mountains, northeast of Galilee.

JEUEL 1. One of the sons of Zerah, who lived in Jerusalem after the Babylonian exile (1 Chron 9:6).

2. A Levite who took part in cleansing the temple in accordance with Hezekiah's reforms (2 Chron 29:13).

3. One of Adonikam's three sons who returned to Israel with Ezra during the Persian king Artaxerxes' reign (Ezra 8:13).

JEUSH 1. Son of Esau and OHOLIBAMAH and progenitor of one of the clans in Seir (Gen 36:5, 14, 18; 1 Chron 1:35).

2. Son of Bilhan, a Benjaminite (1 Chron 7:10).

3. Son of Eshek, also of Benjamin and a descendant of Saul (1 Chron 8:39).

4. Son of Shimei, one of the descendants of Levi, according to a genealogy that establishes the continuity of the levitical priestly line through Levi's son Gershon (Gershom [1 Chron 23:10-11]).

5. Son of Rehoboam and Mahalath (2 Chron 11:19) and a descendant of David on both his father's and mother's side.

JEUZ A son of Shaharaim, a Benjaminite holding a high social position (1 Chron 8:9-10), and his wife Hodesh.

JEW, JEWS Originally meaning someone from the tribe of Judah. That tribe gave its name to the southern kingdom, whose capital was Jerusalem. In the Hellenistic period, the favored self-designation of Jews was "Israel," so *Jew* may have originated as a term used by outsiders. Over time, Jewish writers also referred to themselves as Jews.

JEWELRY Small pieces, usually crafted of metals, worn by men and women as part of dress customs and/or symbols of special place in society. Notable passages in the Bible deal with objects (often explicitly identifying the parts of the body on which they were worn) that carry a distinctive message. Virtually all biblical references to jewelry items are found in the OT.

JEWELS AND PRECIOUS STONES The Hebrew means "stones of delight" and "stones of/for setting," and the phrases were used in the biblical texts to refer to special minerals and stones. The general terms today refer to minerals or stones considered to be of value.

JEZANIAH Perhaps a variant of JAAZANIAH, Jezaniah is identified (Jer 40:8) as the son of the Maacathite, an army officer who went to Mizpah to join Gedaliah after Jerusalem's destruction in 587–586 BCE.

JEZEBEL 1. As one of the most despised women in the OT, Jezebel has become a symbol for uncontrolled female power and unrestrained sexuality, even though the biblical text portrays her as a devoted spouse (1 Kgs 16:31–2 Kgs 9:37). She was the daughter of King Ethbaal of Tyre and Sidon, wife of the reviled King AHAB of Israel (ca. 875–854 BCE), mother of Jehoram and AHAZIAH, and possibly the sister-in-law to Queen ATHALIAH of Judah. Jezebel's marriage to Ahab cemented the alliance between the Omride dynasty and Phoenicia.

2. Jezebel is an epithet used in the NT for the Thyatiran prophetess accused by John of seducing his servants into practicing fornication and eating food sacrificed to idols (Rev 2:18-29). As in 2 Kgs 9:22, this Jezebel is labeled a whore because she serves other gods. By aligning this woman to the Israelite queen, the author shames her and associates her with what is religiously unacceptable.

JEZER See GEZER, GEZERITES.

JEZIEL Son of Azmaveth and brother of Pelet (1 Chron 12:3); a Benjaminite leader who joined David's forces at Ziklag.

JEZRAHIAH Leader of the temple singers, present at the dedication of Jerusalem's wall (Neh 12:42).

JEZREEL, JEZREELITE 1. Jezreel is the name for a beautiful and fertile valley situated between the hills around Samaria and the hills of Galilee. Its position is a strategic point on the route from Egypt to Damascus, and the valley has seen many clashes between ancient powers.

2. The listing of towns in the tribal inheritance of Judah in Josh 15:56 includes a town named Jezreel, but its location and significance are unknown. One of David's wives, Ahinoam, the mother of Amnon, is listed as a Jezreelite (1 Sam 25:43).

3. The valley shares its name with a town located in the eastern end of the valley attested from the Iron Age forward.

4. In the genealogies that open the book of 1 Chronicles, a descendant of Judah is listed as Jezreel (1 Chron 4:3).

5. Jezreel is the symbolic name given by Hosea, the prophet of the 8th cent. BCE in the northern kingdom of Israel, to the first son born to his wife GOMER (Hos 1:4). The name symbolized the coming judgment of God on the house of JEHU, the dynasty still on the throne in the person of Jeroboam II.

JIDLAPH The 7th of eight sons of NAHOR the brother of Abraham and Nahor's wife MILCAH (Gen 22:22).

JOAB 1. Joab was David's nephew and chief military officer. In 2 Sam 2–3 is a comprehensive introduction to Joab, including not only his exceptional military prowess but also his hard-line violent tendencies and his hold over David—all of which are significant as the story of David's rule unfolds.

2. The son of Seraiah in the line of Kenaz (1 Chron 4:14).

3. The descendants of Joab of PAHATH-MOAB (Ezra 2:6; Neh 7:11) return with Zerubbabel from exile.

JOAH 1. Asaph's son and King Hezekiah's recorder (1 Kgs 18:18, 26; Isa 36:3, 11), who, along with Eliakim and Shebnah, met with the three Assyrian officials, requested that they speak in Aramaic, and reported back to Hezekiah (2 Kgs 18:37; Isa 36:22).

2. Zimmah's son and a Levite (1 Chron 6:21; 2 Chron 29:12).

3. Obed-edom's 3rd son and one of the Levite gatekeepers (1 Chron 26:4).

4. Joahaz's son and recorder for King Josiah, who sent him to repair the Jerusalem temple (2 Chron 34:8).

JOAKIM 1. Son of Zerubbabel who was among those leading the Judahites back after the exile (1 Esdr 5:5).

2. High priest of Jerusalem in the story of Judith (Jdt 4:6, 8, 14; 15:8).

3. Husband of Susannah (Sus 1:1, 4, 28-29, 63).

JOANAN The father of Joda, listed in one genealogy of Jesus (Luke 3:27).

JOANNA Joanna was the wife of Herod Antipas's steward CHUZA and was healed by Jesus of some infirmity (Luke 8:2-3). Along with other women, she traveled with Jesus and provided for him financially. In the Gospel of Luke she is also portrayed as one of the women to whom angelic beings announced Jesus' resurrection and who then told the news to the eleven disciples (Luke 24:1-10).

JOARIB Joarib was the head of the family of Mattathias and his sons, the original leaders of the Jewish resistance against the Hellenizing program of Antiochus Epiphanes (1 Macc 2:1; 14:29).

JOASH 1. The father of the judge GIDEON (Judg 6–8). Joash was apparently a landowner of some significance and influence.

2. A son of Shelah, part of the genealogy of Judah (1 Chron 4:22).

3. One of David's warriors, who joined him at Ziklag while David was pinned down there by Saul (1 Chron 12:3). This Joash appears to have been second in command of a detachment of ambidextrous archers from Benjamin.

4. A king's son of Israel, possibly the crown prince, mentioned in the prophetic story of Micaiah son of Imlah (1 Kgs 22:1-38).

5. Joash/Jehoash (both forms are used) son of AHAZIAH, king of Judah. The career of Joash is described in 2 Kgs 11–12.

6. Joash/Jehoash son of JEHOAHAZ, king of Israel, whose reign is explicitly described in 2 Kgs 13:10-25, with an additional episode related in 2 Kgs 14:8-14 and 2 Chron 25:17-24.

7. A son of Becher, part of the genealogy of Issachar. A mighty warrior and head of an ancestral household, and so, presumably, a person of some substance and standing in the community (1 Chron 7:8).

8. One of David's royal stewards, with responsibility for oil stores, mentioned among a lengthy list of David's court officials and functionaries (1 Chron 27:28).

JOB, BOOK OF Considered by many to be the crown jewel of biblical literature, the book of Job begins with a simple statement, "There once was a man in the land of Uz whose name was Job" (1:1). Forty-two chapters later, this seemingly simple story ends with an astonishing declaration that comes from none other than God. Of all those who speak in this book—Eliphaz, Bildad, Zophar, and Elihu—God says that Job alone has spoken "of me what is right" (42:7, 8). Despite the proverbial commendation of the "patience of Job," the book that bears his name offers multiple and often dissonant perspectives on vexing and enduring issues, such as God's moral governance of creation, the role of innocent suffering in the divine economy, and the requisites of faith in a world where cries for justice often go unanswered.

Whatever date may be assigned to the book of Job, it is clear that the biblical writer(s) did not create the story out of whole cloth. A variety of texts from Egypt, Mesopotamia, and Canaan confirm that the social, cultural, and historical situations that gave rise to questions about suffering, divine justice, and the meaning of life were present in the ANE at least as early as the second millennium BCE.

JOBAB 1. Son of Joktan of the line of Shem (Gen 10:29; 1 Chron 1:23).

2. Son of Zerah of the kings of Edom (Gen 36:33, 34; 1 Chron 1:44-45).

3. Son of Shaharaim and the son of Elpaal, of the tribe of Benjamin (1 Chron 8:9).

4. The son of Elpaal, of the tribe of Benjamin (1 Chron 8:18).

5. King of Madon, part of the coalition

of kings who fought against the Israelites in northern Israel (Josh 11:1; 12:19).

JOCHEBED Jochebed the wife of Amram is named in two genealogies (Exod 6:20; Num 26:59). In Exod 6:20, she is identified as Amram's aunt (his father's sister). The marriage apparently violates the law forbidding the union of a nephew to his aunt (Lev 18:12; 20:19). Both genealogies recognize Jochebed as the mother of Aaron and MOSES, underscoring their levitical origins through both parents (see Exod 2:1). The genealogy in Numbers recognizes Jochebed as the mother of MIRIAM as well.

JODA 1. The son of Illiadun and a Levite appointed by Zerubbabel to assist in the temple restoration following the return from the exile (1 Esdr 5:58).

2. The son of Joanan and father of Josech in the genealogy of Joseph (Luke 3:26).

JODAN A priestly descendant of Jozadak who divorced his wife (1 Esdr 9:19).

JOED Joed is listed in Neh 11:7 as a resident of postexilic Jerusalem.

JOEL 1. One of the sons of Samuel, whom Samuel appointed to be a judge (1 Sam 8:2; 1 Chron 6:28).

2. A leader from the tribe of Simeon in the days of King HEZEKIAH (1 Chron 4:35).

3. A man from the tribe of Reuben (1 Chron 5:4).

4. Another Reubenite, who lived in AROER (1 Chron 5:8).

5. One of the Gadites' chiefs (1 Chron 5:12).

6. The father of HEMAN (1 Chron 6:33; 15:17) the Kohathite singer appointed by David in preparation for the Jerusalem temple.

7. One of the ancestors of Heman the Kohathite (1 Chron 6:36).

8. A chief in the tribe of Issachar (1 Chron 7:3).

9. A warrior in David's army (1 Chron 11:38).

10. Chief of the Gershonites (1 Chron 15:7) and one of the Levites summoned by David to bring the COVENANT CHEST into Jerusalem (1 Chron 15:11-14).

11. A Levite grandson of Gershon through LADAN (1 Chron 23:8).

12. One of the sons of Jehieli and the nephew of Joel (#11). Joel and his brother ZETHAM were in charge of the temple treasury (1 Chron 26:22).

13. A leader of the tribe of Manasseh (1 Chron 27:20).

14. A Kohathite Levite who helped cleanse the temple during the reign of King Hezekiah (2 Chron 29:12).

15. In the postexilic period a descendant of NEBO who had married a foreign woman (Ezra 10:43).

16. An overseer of the Benjaminites in Jerusalem during the postexilic period (Neh 11:9).

17. The prophet Joel, son of PETHUEL (Joel 1:1).

JOEL, BOOK OF Joel constitutes the second writing in the Book of the Twelve. Named for an otherwise unknown postexilic prophet whose name means "the LORD is God," Joel is generally considered one of the latest prophetic books in the OT because of the complexity of its eschatological outlook, its dependence upon other prophetic writings, and internal observations. Joel's eschatological message reflects the major recurring themes of the larger corpus: a call to repentance in the face of the impending day of Yahweh, and its promises of restoration, fertility of the land, and the removal of foreign nations.

JOELAH Son of Jeroham and brother of Zebadiah, Benjaminites of Gedor who joined David's army when David resided in Gath while fleeing from Saul. Joelah and other ambidextrous Benjaminites (1 Chron 12:1-8) joined David at Ziklag, a

Philistine city King Achish gave David (1 Sam 27:1-7).

JOEZER Joezer was one of the ambidextrous Benjaminites who joined David at Ziklag during David's flight from Saul (1 Chron 12:1-7).

JOGLI The father of the Danite leader BUKKI (Num 34:22).

JOHA 1. A Tizite who, with his brother Jediael, is listed among the mighty men called "the Thirty," who supported David's rise to power (1 Chron 11:45).

2. One of the sons of Beriah, a Benjaminite (1 Chron 8:13-16). Beriah and his brother Shema drove out the inhabitants of Gath.

JOHANAN 1. The oldest son of King Josiah (1 Chron 3:15). Perhaps he died young since it appears he did not succeed his father.

2. A son of Elioenai in the Davidic family (1 Chron 3:24).

3. Son of Azariah and father of Azariah (apparently naming his son after his father), in the lineage of Levi (1 Chron 6:9-10 [Heb. 5:35-36]).

4. A Benjaminite warrior who joined David at Ziklag during his flight from Saul (1 Chron 12:4 [Heb. 12:5]).

5. A Gadite warrior who also joined David at Ziklag (1 Chron 12:12 [Heb. 12:13]).

6. The son of Hakkatan of the Azgad family; he brought 110 men to Ezra's group of returnees (Ezra 8:12; 1 Esdr 8:38).

7. A priest, or high priest, the son of Eliashib, who came up with Zerubbabel and Jeshua (Neh 12:22-23).

8. The son of Kareah, he was one of the Judean leaders who joined Gedaliah at Mizpah after the destruction of Jerusalem (2 Kgs 25:23).

JOHN 1. The father of Mattathias and grandfather of Judas "Maccabeus" (1 Macc 2:1; see HASMONEANS). The text of 1 Macc identifies him as a priest in the line of Joarib, probably the Jehoiarib mentioned in 1 Chron 9:10; 24:7.

2. Eldest son of Mattathias and grandson of John (#1). His nickname is "Gaddi" (1 Macc 2:2). John is not the leader of his younger brothers, but fought alongside his brother Judas Maccabeus (1 Macc 2:65–3:2).

3. John Hyrcanus, commander of the forces of his father Simon (brother of Judas Maccabeus; 1 Macc 13:53; 16:1-10). He eventually succeeded Simon as high priest (1 Macc 16:18-24).

4. John son of Accos secured concessions to the Jews from Antiochus III (2 Macc 4:11). Judas Maccabeus chose John's son Eupolemus as an envoy to Rome (1 Macc 8:17).

5. Envoy from Judas Maccabeus to Lysias, guardian of Antiochus V (2 Macc 11:17). The text does not give further identification of this person..

6. John 1:42; 21:15-17 refers to Peter (see PETER, THE APOSTLE) as "Simon, son of John," while Matt 16:17 identifies Peter's father as Jonah.

7. A member of the Jerusalem high council (Acts 4:6) who is otherwise unknown. Some manuscripts read "Jonathan" instead, probably identifying this person with the son of Annas, who succeeded Caiaphas to the high priesthood in 36 CE.

8. John, the late 1st-cent. Christian prophet and teacher in Asia Minor, who identifies himself as the author of Revelation (Rev 1:1, 4, 9; 22:8), came to be identified with John the son of Zebedee (see John #10) in the 2nd cent.

9. John the Baptist figures prominently in the NT Gospels and Acts. He provides the context for the ministry of Jesus. John's preaching, baptizing, imprisonment, and execution by Herod Antipas are also mentioned in Josephus's history.

10. John the son of Zebedee, one

of the twelve disciples, is traditionally held to be the author of five NT writings: the Gospel, Letters, and Revelation of John.

JOHN, GOSPEL OF The Fourth Gospel is traditionally associated with the apostle John, the son of Zebedee. The Gospel relates the story of Jesus, the incarnate Logos, descending from heaven to reveal the glory of God. Key to the narrative is the theme of acceptance of Jesus by some and rejection by others. The distinctiveness of John's story as told has captured the interest of interpreters from the 2nd cent. CE to the present.

JOHN, LETTERS OF Three NT writings bear the traditional titles First, Second, and Third Letters of John. None of the three claims to be written by JOHN, and only 2 and 3 John employ the letter form. Collectively, these three writings have some relationship to one another and perhaps to the Gospel of John, though less likely to Revelation, and hence are called the "Johannine Letters."

JOIADA 1. The son of Paseah who repaired the Old Gate with Meshullam as part of the effort to repair the wall around Jerusalem when the people returned from exile (Neh 3:6).

2. A Levite son of the high priest Eliashib (Neh 12:10) who is listed as the father of JONATHAN (Neh 12:11).

JOIAKIM An abbreviation of JEHOIAKIM, Joiakim (Neh 12:10, 12, 26) was a son of the high priest JESHUA, who supervised the building of the temple following the Babylonian exile. Joiakim was also the father of Eliashib, high priest during Nehemiah's tenure. Based on Eliashib's recorded tenure, Joiakim lived during the early 5th cent. BCE.

JOIARIB 1. A Levite with wisdom whom Ezra sent to Iddo at Casiphia to procure ministers for the Jerusalem temple (Ezra 8:16-17).

2. Ancestor of MAASEIAH from the tribe of Judah (Neh 11:4-5).

3. Father of Jedaiah (Neh 11:10); a levitical priest who returned to Jerusalem with Zerubbabel during Jeshua's days (Neh 12:1-7).

4. Name of an ancestral house headed by Mattenai (Neh 12:19) during Joiakim's days.

JOKIM Descendant of Judah (1 Chron 4:22).

JOKSHAN Second of seven sons born to Abraham and KETURAH (Gen 25:2). Jokshan is the father of Sheba and Dedan (Gen 25:3; 1 Chron 1:32).

JOKTAN Joktan was the youngest son of EBER and the brother of PELEG. His descendants migrated to Arabia, forming several Arabian tribes/groups (Gen 10:25-29; 1 Chron 1:19-23) representing the earliest inhabitants in Arabia, prior to the children of Abraham through Hagar and Keturah.

JOKTHE-EL 1. A town near LACHISH in the lowlands constituting part of Judah's inheritance (Josh 15:38).

2. Name given to the captured Edomite SELA ("the Rock") by King Amaziah of Judah when he retook Edom after slaying 10,000 in the Salt Valley (2 Kgs 14:7).

JONADAB 1. David's nephew Jonadab counseled his lustful cousin AMNON to feign illness and request that his sister TAMAR be allowed to nurse him (2 Sam 13:3-5). Amnon raped Tamar and later was murdered by her full brother ABSALOM. When rumors spread that all the king's sons had fallen, Jonadab assured David that Amnon alone had died, as the only one who had deserved death (2 Sam 13:32-33).

2. The son of Rechab. He was revered

as a spiritual guide by the Rechabites, who eschewed wine and lived as nomads according to Jonadab's command (Jer 35:6-19).

JONAH 1. The son of AMITTAI. In 2 Kgs 14:25 he is described as a prophet from Gath-hepher who prophesied the restoration of Israel's territory by Jeroboam II. The book of Jonah picks up the tradition of this prophet and connects him with a prophetic mission to Nineveh.

2. A Levite who divorced his foreign wife and offered a ram in expiation during Ezra's reform according to 1 Esdr 9:23.

JONAH, BAR In Matt 16:17, Jesus commends "Simon son of Jonah" (i.e., bar Jonah), after he identifies Jesus as "the Christ, the Son of the living God" (v. 16). In John 1:42, Simon's father is said to be John.

JONAH, BOOK OF The book of Jonah appears among the Twelve Minor Prophets. In most listings Jonah occupies the fifth place, between Obadiah and Micah. The designation "minor" for these books pertains to their relatively short length, not to their value. Jonah comes in forty-eight verses, eight of them in poetry and forty in poetic prose. Unlike the other books, it is a story, not a group of oracles; its title comes from the chief human character, not from the presumed author; and its content builds on imagination, not on history.

JONAM The grandfather of Judah and the son of Eliakim, Jonam appears in the Lukan genealogy of Jesus (Luke 3:30).

JONATHAN 1. The name of the first of Saul's sons listed in 1 Sam 14:49, along with those of two daughters. One of those daughters, Merab was probably the oldest child, and two other sons are named in other places in the OT (1 Sam 31:2; 1 Chron 9:39; 10:2).

2. A Levite from Bethlehem of Judah, son of Gershom, and direct descendant of Moses (or possibly of Manasseh, the wicked king of Judah as preserved in some manuscript traditions).

3. A priest during the reign of David who was the son of ABIATHAR.

4. David's nephew, the son of Shimei. He killed a Philistine giant at Gath (2 Sam 21:21).

5. One of David's mighty men, the son of Shammah the Hararite (2 Sam 23:32; 1 Chron 11:34 as the son of Shagee).

6. The Jerahmeelite son of Jada, brother of Jethen and father of Peleth and Zaza (1 Chron 2:32-33).

7. Son of Uzziah who was partially responsible for the treasuries along with Azmaveth who was over David's treasury (1 Chron 27:25).

8. King David's uncle. His name is included in a list of David's officers (1 Chron 27:32).

9. The father of Ebed and descendant of Adin (Ezra 8:6; 1 Esdr 8:32).

10. The son of Asahel. He opposed Ezra's reform measure of putting away foreign wives or the commission that was established to initiate the task. Against the Heb., the LXX portrays Jonathan as agreeing with Ezra (Ezra 10).

11. A Levite descendant of Asaph who was father of Zechariah (Neh 12:35).

12. A priest during the time of Joiakim who was head of the house of Malluchi (Neh 12:14), one of the priestly houses listed in Neh 12:12-21.

13. Son of Joiada and father of Jaddua who was among those who returned to Jerusalem with Zerubbabal. He is sometimes identified with Eliashib's descendant in whose house Ezra lodged (Neh 12:11, 23; Ezra 10:6).

14. A high-ranking official, whose home was used to imprison Jeremiah (Jer 37:15, 20; 38:26). He was preceded in this office by Elishama (Jer 36:12)

15. The son of Absalom and a military general who in 142 BCE was sent to Joppa by Simon Maccabeus with a large army to protect the city and to expel its inhabitants (1 Macc 13:11).

16. According to 2 Macc 1:23, Jonathan recited a prayer over the sacrifice along with Nehemiah in an account of the restoration of the sacred fire to the second temple (2 Macc 1:18-36).

17. Jonathan was the son of Mattathias and the brother of JUDAS. Jonathan succeeded his father and brother as leader of their Jewish following after their deaths. We know of Jonathan mainly from 1 Macc 9:23–12:53, though Josephus also has information (*Ant.* 13.1–212).

JORAH The head of a family who returned to Judah after the exile (Ezra 2:18).

JORAM The name of a Judean king and an Israelite king in the 9th cent. BCE.

1. Joram, also Jehoram, became king of Judah following his father Jehoshaphat (2 Kgs 8:16).

2. Joram, also Jehoram, son of AHAB, became king of Israel in Samaria (2 Kgs 3:1) following the death of Ahaziah, son of Ahab, who had no son (2 Kgs 1:17). Presumably the relationship between the two is that of brother, because AHAZIAH had no son (2 Kgs 1:17).

JORDAN RIVER The Jordan River rises at the foot of Mount Hermon, the highest point in the southern Levant. The river's headwaters flow through the Huleh Valley and the Sea of Galilee before eventually emptying into the Dead Sea. The Jordan is somewhat unique in Palestine, as it is one of relatively few perennially flowing rivers.

JORIM Jorim is the father of Eliezer and the son of Matthat in Luke's genealogy of Jesus (Luke 3:29).

JOSECH The father of Semein and the son of Joda in Luke's genealogy of Jesus (Luke 3:26).

JOSEPH, JOSEPHITES 1. Joseph belongs to the 3rd generation of descendants of Abraham and Sarah; he is the oldest son of JACOB and RACHEL (Gen 35:24) and the father of Ephraim and Manasseh. Joseph is one of the PATRIARCHS of Israel, and in some lists his name is an eponym for one of the twelve tribes.

2. The common designation for the combined tribes of Manasseh and Ephraim (Num 34:23; Josh 16:1).

3. The father of Igal, who was sent by Moses as a spy into Canaan (Num 13:7).

4. "From Asaph's family," and set apart by David as a musician (1 Chron 25:2, 9).

5. A returned exile of the time of Ezra who is listed as having taken a foreign wife (Ezra 10:42).

6. A postexilic priest of the house of Shebaniah in the time of Joiakim (Neh 12:14).

7. One of two guards who was left in charge of a unit in Judas Maccabeus's army (1 Mac 5:18).

8. A commander in the army of Judas Maccabeus, who led a division in the battle against Nicanor (2 Mac 8:22).

9. An ancestor of Joseph, husband of Mary (Luke 3:24).

10. An ancestor of Joseph son of Mary, who lived after the time of King David and prior to the rule of Zerubbabel (Luke 3:30).

11. Also known as Barsabbas, and one of two candidates to fill the place of Judas after his death (Acts 1:23). However, the lots fell in favor of the other candidate, Matthias (Acts 1:26).

12. A man called BARNABAS by the apostles (Acts 4:36-37).

13. The NT Gospels refer to Joseph husband of Mary nineteen times by name. Eleven appear in Matthew (1:16, 18, 19, 20, 24, 25; 2:13, 14, 19, 21, 22), none in Mark (omitted from Mark 6:3 for example), six in Luke (1:27; 2:4, 16, 39; 3:23; 4:22), and two in John (1:45; 6:42). All but four references appear in the infancy narratives of Matthew and Luke. Of the four remaining references, one occurs in Luke's genealogy (3:23),

and three on the lips of the Nazareth and Capernaum crowds (Luke 4:22 and John 6:42), and of Philip (John 1:45). These three instances identify Jesus as "Joseph's son."

14. Joseph is one of the brothers of Jesus, along with James, Simon, and Judas (Matt 13:55).

15. The son of one of the women present at the crucifixion of Jesus, called Mary "the mother of James and Joseph" (Matt 27:56).

16. Joseph of Arimathea is known primarily for his request to Pilate to bury Jesus' body. In Matt 27:57-60 and John 19:38-42, Joseph's wealth had not prevented him from becoming a disciple of Jesus even though Jesus had spoken of the difficulties of the rich in entering God's kingdom (Matt 19:16-26).

JOSES 1. Known also as Joseph (Matt 13:55), Joses is commonly referenced as one of the brothers of Jesus likely born later to Mary and Joseph (Mark 6:3).

2. In Mark 15:40, Joses is a brother of James, and perhaps a cousin of Jesus, born to Mary's sister.

JOSHAH Son of Amaziah and leader of his clan, listed among the descendants of Simeon in 1 Chron 4:34.

JOSHAPHAT 1. Joshaphat the Mithnite was one of David's mighty men who was added to the original list of "the Thirty" (see 2 Sam 23:8-39) by the Chronicler to demonstrate the universal support of David over Saul (1 Chron 11:43).

2. One of the priests whose job was to walk before the COVENANT CHEST, blowing the trumpet, as David brought the chest from the house of Obed-edom into Jerusalem (1 Chron 15:24).

JOSHAVIAH One of Elnaam's sons in the Chronicler's list of David's mighty men (1 Chron 11:46).

JOSHBEKASHAH One of the sons of Heman assigned the task of prophesying with music. Joshbekashah was under the supervision of Heman and led the 17th of twenty-four temple choirs (1 Chron 25:4, 24). See GIDDALTI.

JOSHIBIAH Listed as one of the descendants of Simeon, Joshibiah is the son of Seraiah and the father of JEHU (1 Chron 4:35).

JOSHUA 1. The political successor to Moses and the commander who leads the Israelite invasion of Canaan. Joshua, described as the assistant of Moses and one of his "assembled seventy men" (Num 11:24, 28), is put in command of the Israelite defensive action against the Amalekites at Rephidim (Exod 17:9). As they approach the land of Canaan, Moses includes Joshua among the spies sent to scout the land and to gauge the possibility of capturing the region from its inhabitants (Num 13:16-20). As the wilderness wanderings come to a close, God tells Moses to pass "some of" his power to Joshua "so that the entire Israelite community may obey" (Num 27:20). Moses commissions Joshua in this position of authority by placing his hands on him in front of the entire congregation. This is a sign of transference of identity and authority, as in the hand-laying ceremony in the purification offering (e.g., Lev 4:15).

2. A man who owned a field in which the covenant chest was displayed and honored (1 Sam 6:14-18).

3. The governor of Jerusalem during Josiah's reforms (2 Kgs 23:8).

4. The high priest who served with Zerubbabel during the early Persian Period (Hag 1:12).

5. An unknown man listed in Luke's genealogy of Jesus (Luke 3:29).

JOSHUA, BOOK OF The sixth book of the Bible and first book of the Former Prophets tells the story of how JOSHUA, successor of Moses, leads a unified Israel to conquer (chaps. 1–12) then allot (chaps. 13–21) the promised land.

JOSIAH 1. Josiah was king of Judah from 640 to 609 BCE; he was the son and successor of AMON and his mother was Jedidah daughter of Adaiah of Bozkath. Second Kings 22–23 reports that during the 18th year of his reign (622 BCE), he implemented reforms based on the Instruction scroll, which was found during a renovation of the temple.

2. The son of Zephaniah (Zech 6:10, 14.)

JOSIPHIAH The father of Shelomith, head of a family who returned from the Babylonian exile with Ezra (Ezra 8:10; 1 Esdr 8:36).

JOTHAM 1. A son of Gideon, who is also referred to as Jerubbaal, Jotham is the youngest of the seventy sons (Judg 9:5).

2. A king of Judah in the mid-8th cent. BCE, Jotham son of King Uzziah ruled during a time of national prosperity.

3. A descendant of the clan of Caleb whose father is identified as Jahdai (1 Chron 2:47).

JOZABAD 1. Warrior from GEDERAH and among the Benjaminites who joined David in battle at Ziklag (1 Chron 12:1-4).

2. Two Manassite military leaders who joined David in battle at Ziklag (1 Chron 12:20).

3. During Hezekiah's reign, an overseer and a Levite who assisted Conaniah the chief officer with storing contributions and tithes (2 Chron 31:13).

4. During Josiah's reign, a chief among the Levites (2 Chron 35:9).

5. Levite leader who worked on rebuilding the temple (Neh 11:16). Probably the same Levite who witnessed the weighing of precious metals and vessels (Ezra 8:33; 1 Esdr 8:63) and who taught the people God's Instruction (Neh 8:7-18; 1 Esdr 9:48).

6. Descendant of Pashhur whom Ezra commanded to dismiss his foreign wife (Ezra 10:23; but Gedaliah in 1 Esdr 9:22).

JOZACAR JEHOZABAD and Jozacar were two servants of King Joash who murdered him (2 Kgs 12:21 [Heb. 12:22]).

JOZADAK Father of Jeshua, a priest who had returned from Babylon with Zerubbabel (Ezra 3:2, 8; 5:2; 10:18; 1 Esdr 5:5, 48, 56; 6:2; 9:19; Sir 49:12). He is also the grandfather of the priest Joiakim, who served during the time of Nehemiah (Neh 12:26).

JUBAL A son of Lamech and Adah, descendants of Cain, associated with the playing of the lyre and pipe (Gen 4:21).

JUBILEE YEAR The Jubilee year is the final year of a cycle of seven "sabbatical" periods of seven years each. The name derives from the ram's horn with which the Jubilee year is inaugurated on RECONCILIATION DAY (Lev 25:10; 27:18, 23-24). Land is left fallow (Lev 25:11, 19-22), debts for fellow Israelites are forgiven (Lev 25:35-37), and Israelite slaves held by other Israelites are freed (Lev 25:39-46). Jubilee laws also include general rules governing fair commercial practices (e.g., Lev 25:14) and attention to the economically disadvantaged, particularly among one's own kin (25:35-55).

JUDAH, JUDAHITES 1. Judah, the 4th son of Jacob; born to Leah (Gen 29:35). As a character in Genesis, Judah can be seen in a sympathetic light. For instance, Judah entreats his brothers to sell Joseph rather than kill him (Gen 37:26-27), though the story reports a mercenary motive on Judah's part. Also, when Joseph threatens to imprison Benjamin in Egypt, Judah pleads for him and offers himself in Benjamin's stead (Gen 44:18-34).

2. Judah, the territory, was located

in the southern part of the Levant. Joshua 15 describes its ideal expanse: Its eastern border was the Dead Sea, and its northern boundary ran basically from the northern edge of the Dead Sea to the Mediterranean, its western border. Judah's southern border met the Mediterranean at the Wadi "or border" of Egypt, perhaps the Wadi Besor or the Wadi el-Arish.

The general area of Judah became known as Yehud in the Persian Period and eventually as Judea in NT times (see JUDEA, JUDEANS). Judah is the location of Jesus' birth according to Matt 2:6 (cf Mic 5:2). Hebrews mentions the tribe of Judah twice; once to affirm that Jesus is not a levitical priest (as he was a Judahite, Heb 7:14), and once in a quotation of Jer 31:31 [Heb. 8:8]. Revelation 5:5 symbolically refers to Jesus as "the lion of the tribe of Judah," and Rev 7:5 lists 12,000 "sealed" from Judah.

3. Judah, a Levite, appears in a list of persons who married foreign wives and were forced to give them up (Ezra 10:23).

4. Judah son of Hassenuah is a Benjaminite who is named as 2nd in charge of Jerusalem (Neh 11:9).

5. The Levite Judah appears in a list of priests and Levites who came to Jerusalem with Zerubbabel (Neh 12:8).

6. Judah is an official who participates in the dedication of Jerusalem's wall (Neh 12:34).

7. A relative of the priest Zechariah, who also participated in the dedication of Jerusalem's wall (Neh 12:36).

8. In Luke's geneaology of Jesus, a Judah son of Joseph, father of Simeon, is listed (3:30).

JUDAS Judas is the Greek name for the Hebrew patriarch Judah. In the NT, likewise, references to the patriarch (e.g., Matt 1:2; Luke 3:33) or to the traditional tribal territory of Judah (more or less synonymous with "Judea" [e.g., Luke 1:39]) appear in the Greek as Judas, but are usually translated as Judah in English.

1. Judas the Maccabee was the son of MATTATHIAS and one of five brothers who fought against the Seleucids and eventually gained political independence for Judah. He was the main leader during the Maccabean revolt proper (see MACCABEES, MACCABEAN REVOLT) and the founder of a ruling dynasty known as the Hasmoneans (see HASMONEANS). In the list of brothers (1 Macc 1:2-5) Judas is 3rd, which suggests that he was younger than JONATHAN and SIMON.

2. Judas son of Chalphi (1 Macc 11:70) is described as a commander of the army under Jonathan (Judas the Maccabee's brother), and as standing by Jonathan when most fled in battle.

3. Judas was the son of Simon and the nephew of Judas Maccabeus and Jonathan. This Judas and his brother John succeeded Simon (1 Macc 16:1-3). Judas, along with his father Simon and his brother Mattathias, was murdered at a banquet in Jericho (1 Macc 16:14-16), leaving John (Hyrcanus) to carry on the Hasmonean line.

4. Judas was the author of the letter to Aristobulus and the Jews of Egypt, introduced in 2 Macc 1:10 as being from "the citizens of Jerusalem and Judea, the council of elders, and Judas."

5. The brother of Jesus and/or James. According to several sources, Jesus had a brother named Judas (Mark 6:1-6).

6. According to some sources, the disciple of Jesus identified as "THOMAS" in the canonical Gospels was actually named Judas. The suggestion makes sense, as the word *Thomas* is an epithet meaning "twin" (e.g., John 11:16).

7. Yet another disciple named Judas is identified by the Gospels of Luke and John. In the synoptic lists of the Twelve, the figure of THADDAEUS (or, according to some manuscripts, Lebbaeus [Matt 10:3; Mark 3:18]) is replaced in Luke's list by "Judas son of James" (Luke 6:16; also Acts 1:13). The Gospel of John also refers to a disciple named Judas, present

at the Last Supper, who is described as "Judas (not Judas Iscariot)" (John 14:22).

8. Judas Barsabbas, representative of the Jerusalem church, is mentioned in Acts at the decision of the Jerusalem Council to send two leading figures of the Jerusalem church as emissaries to Antioch with Paul and Barnabas. The men are identified as "Judas Barsabbas and Silas" (Acts 15:22). They are also described as prophets (15:32).

9. Judas was the owner of a house in Damascus. According to the Acts account of Paul's call by God, after being blinded on the road to Damascus, Paul takes refuge in the Damascus house of a man named Judas who lives on Straight Street (Acts 9:11).

10. Judas the Galilean was a revolutionary around the time Judea was brought under direct Roman rule, and subjected to a census in 6 CE (see QUIRINIUS).

11. Judas Iscariot was one of Jesus' inner circle of twelve disciples (Matt 10:4; Mark 3:19; Luke 6:16; John 6:71). All the Gospels agree he played some role in Jesus' arrest, but the details about him differ widely.

JUDE, LETTER OF The letter of Jude, the penultimate book in the Christian canon, is a sermon attacking unnamed, libertine "intruders." The use of noncanonical material and unknown sayings, together with the sharp rhetoric of the epistle, caused the letter of Jude to move in and out of favor in the early church. The letter identifies the biblical figure to be understood as its author in the salutation "Jude, a servant of Jesus Christ and brother of James" (v. 1), that is, Jude, one of the brothers of Jesus (Mark 6:3).

JUDEA, JUDEANS The Greek form of the term *Judah* (Lat. *Iudaea*), the Jewish territory in the southern land of Israel, in the area surrounding Jerusalem, and its inhabitants (Lat. *Iudaean*).

JUDGE The Hebrew word for "judge" has a much broader range of meaning, including judging, conducting foreign diplomacy, leading in battle, and ruling domestically. It is also synonymous with "prince" (Isa 40:23).

JUDGES, BOOK OF The book of Judges is a mixture of heroic tales, political polemics, and horrific images of a society in chaos. Individual figures (Ehud, Deborah, Gideon, Samson) are among the most memorable of all biblical characters. Although some of these tales have well-developed plots and fully defined characters, others are quite minimal with rough edges and loose ends. In fact, some characters are barely there (Shamgar and the "minor judges").

JUDGMENT SEAT The judicial bench in a Roman city court.

JUDITH The name Judith is Semitic and is the feminine form of the Hebrew word for Judahite.

1. Judith is the wife of Esau and daughter of Beeri the Hittite and Basemath the daughter of Elon the Hittite (Gen 26:34).

2. Judith is the principal character of the 2nd-cent. BCE fictional book of Judith, which tells the story of the invasion of the eastern Mediterranean region by the Assyro-Babylonian king Nebuchadnezzar and Judith's deliverance of the Hebrew people through her assassination of the enemy general Holofernes.

JULIA A Roman Christian (the gens Julia suggests citizenship by birth or as a freed slave) greeted by Paul, paired with her husband or brother PHILOLOGUS (Rom 16:15).

JULIUS When Paul was to be sent to Rome for trial, a centurion named Julius was put in charge of him (Acts 27:1). Julius was a member of the IMPERIAL COMPANY based largely in Syria.

JUNIA, JUNIAS Junia was a Jewish Christian female whom Paul called a "prominent" apostle. She was imprisoned with him presumably because of their gospel ministry (Rom 16:7).

JUSHAB-HESED A son of ZERUBBABEL (1 Chron 3:20) whose name means "kindness will be returned."

JUSTIFICATION, JUSTIFY Normally, the noun *justification* and the verb *to justify* refer to being set right, to being vindicated by a judge, to having a debt removed, or to having a right relationship restored or granted.

JUSTUS A Latin surname suggesting a person of righteous or just character.

1. Joseph BARSABBAS, also known as Justus, was nominated (although not chosen) to replace Judas after his suicide (Acts 1:23).

2. Titius Justus (alternately, Titus Justus), a "Gentile God-worshipper," provided refuge for Paul after he was asked to leave the nearby synagogue (Acts 18:7).

3. "Jesus, called Justus" (Col 4:11), was one of Paul's few Jewish coworkers and supporters during his imprisonment.

Kk

KAB A biblical measure of capacity, mentioned only in 2 Kgs 6:25.

KABZEEL Joshua 15:21 lists this town among the inheritance of the tribe of Judah, indicating its location in the southern part of the territory toward Edom. Benaiah, son of Jehoiada and one of David's valiant men, came from Kabzeel (2 Sam 23:20; 1 Chron 11:22).

KADESH, KADESH-BARNEA A site at the southern end of Canaan from which Moses sent spies to reconnoiter the land and where Israel rebelled against God.

Assuming Kadesh and Kadesh-barnea are the same site, its first reference in the Bible is as En-mishpat ("spring of judgment"), after which it is identified as Kadesh (Gen 14:7).

KADMIEL A Levite clan head (Neh 12:24; 1 Esdr 5:26) and returnee from exile (Ezra 2:40; Neh 7:43; 12:8) who helped lead the restoration (Ezra 3:9; Neh 9:4-5; 10:9).

KADMONITE One of the groups listed as inhabitants of the land promised to Abram in the pre-Israelite period (Gen 15:19).

KAIN 1. A singular collective term used to refer to the KENITES (Num 24:22; cf Judg 4:11). The similarity between the names Kain and Kenite may suggest that "CAIN" (Gen 4:1-7) was considered the ancestor of the Kenites.

2. A town in the extreme south allotted to the tribe of Judah (Josh 15:57).

KALLAI A priest listed among those who served under the high priest JOIAKIM (Neh 12:20).

KANAH 1. A river or stream mentioned in the book of Joshua (16:8; 17:9). It marked the boundary between the tribes of Ephraim and Manasseh. The river runs westward past Tappuah and is often identified with the Wadi Qanah.

2. Part of the territorial apportionment to the tribe of Asher in Joshua (19:28).

KAREAH Father of JOHANAN, who was among the officers who served under Gedaliah (2 Kgs 25:23; Jer 40:8-16).

KEDAR 1. The name of the 2nd of Ishmael's twelve sons (Gen 25:13; 1 Chron 1:29).

2. The designation of the tribal groups in northern Arabia that were regarded as Kedar's descendants according to the OT.

KEDEMAH One of the sons of Ishmael (Gen 25:15; 1 Chron 1:31). As the last listed son, the name may be a personification of the "people of the east."

KEDEMOTH A city most likely located north of the ARNON River. Moses sent messengers to Sihon, king of the Amorites, from Kedemoth (Deut 2:26; Josh 21:37). Later it was the 3rd levitical city given to the tribe of Reuben (1 Chron 6:79 [Heb. 6:64]).

KEDESH 1. A town on the southern border of Judah (Josh 15:23). It is also known as Kadesh or Kadesh-barnea (see KADESH, KADESH-BARNEA).

2. A levitical town in Issachar given to the sons of Gershon (1 Chron 6:72 [Heb. 6:57]).

3. One of the fortified cities in Naphtali in the Galilee (Josh 19:35-38). According to Josh 21:32 and 1 Chron 6:67, it was a levitical city and served as a REFUGE CITY (Josh 20:7; 21:32). It was the home of Barak (Judg 4:6) and where Deborah and Barak rallied the ancient Israelite forces to battle Sisera (Judg 4:1-10).

KEILAH 1. A town allotted to Judah after Joshua's conquest (Josh 15:44).

2. A GARMITE grandson of Hodiah among the descendants of Judah (1 Chron 4:19).

KELAIAH A Levite, also known as Kelita, who divorced his Gentile wife and helped Ezra expound the Instruction to returning exiles (Ezra 10:23; Neh 8:7; 10:10; 1 Esdr 9:23).

KEMUEL 1. Father of Aram and son of Nahor the brother of Abraham (Gen 22:21).

2. Son of Shiphtan and a leader of the tribe of Ephraim. He is among those responsible for apportioning the land of Canaan (Num 34:24).

3. Father of Hashabiah, who was the leader of the Levites during the time of King David (1 Chron 27:17).

KENAN Great-grandson of Adam, son of Enosh and father of Mahalalel, he lived 910 years (Gen 5:9-14; 1 Chron 1:2). See CAINAN.

KENATH A city in eastern Gilead. Kenath was captured by the Manassite Nobah, who renamed it after himself (Num 32:42), and it was later captured by Geshur and Aram (1 Chron 2:23).

KENAZ, KENIZZITE 1. A grandson of Esau and Adah, born to their oldest son Eliphaz (Gen 36:11; 1 Chron 1:36). The grandsons of Esau became the chiefs of the Edomite clans after they settled in their new territory in the highlands of Seir (Gen 36:15, 42; 1 Chron 1:36, 51-53). At least some of that ethnic group must have migrated back into the southern area of Canaan, however, because the Kenizzites were listed as one of the ten people groups occupying the land the Lord promised to the descendants of Abram (Gen 15:19). The Kenizzites ultimately assimilated into the tribe of Judah.

2. The younger brother of Caleb (Judg 3:9) and father of Othniel and Seraiah (1 Chron 4:13).

3. The grandson of Caleb and the son of Elah (1 Chron 4:15).

KENITES The ancestry of the Kenites is believed to reach back to the marked and ousted brother of Abel, Cain. Some of Cain's descendants built a city while others lived in tents and had livestock, some played the lyre and the pipe and some made all kinds of bronze and iron (Gen 4:17-22).

KEREN-HAPPUCH Means "horn of antimony." Keren-happuch was Job's 3rd daughter after his fortune had been restored (Job 42:14).

KERIOTH The name of a fortified site on the Moabite plateau (Jer 48:24; Amos 2:2).

KETAB An exiled temple servant whose progeny returned to the land (1 Esdr 5:30).

KETURAH Abraham's wife following the death of Sarah (Gen 25:1). Keturah mothered six children by Abraham (Zimram, Jokshan, Medan, Midian, Ishbak, and Shuah), all of whom were sent away from Isaac after Abraham gave him the full inheritance (Gen 25:4-6). Keturah was also mentioned in the genealogical lists of the Chronicler (1 Chron 1:32-34).

KEY A key is a tool for locking or unlocking gates or doors (Judg 3:25). It is frequently used as a symbol of authority of the one who controls entrances and exits. In the OT, God promises to give a new servant the key to David's house (Isa 22:22). In the NT, Jesus accuses the legal experts of taking away the key of knowledge (Luke 11:52), and he gives Peter the keys of the kingdom of heaven (Matt 16:19). Revelation refers to the keys of "Death and the Grave" (1:18) and the keys of a sealed abyss (9:1; 20:1). Revelation reserves the key of David as God's domain (3:7), although the two witnesses in 11:6 have the power to shut heaven.

KEZIAH One of three daughters born to Job when his fortunes are restored. Job's three daughters are described as more beautiful than any other women in the land, and each is offered a share of Job's inheritance along with his seven sons (Job 42:13-15).

KIDNEY In the OT, the kidneys often represent deep and defining parts of a living being. God's absolute creative power is portrayed as the formation of the kidneys (Ps 139:13), and conversely the severest wounds reach to the kidneys (Job 16:13; Lam 3:13). Ritual texts prescribe the burning of the kidneys of a sacrificial animal along with portions of fat (Lev 3:4, 10, 15; 4:9; 7:4; Exod 29:13, 22).

KIDRON VALLEY This valley and its wadi lie between JERUSALEM to its west and the MOUNT OF OLIVES to its east and continue through the Judean wilderness where they run into the Dead Sea. Hezekiah built the SILOAM Tunnel to divert the waters of the Gihon into the fortified area of the city, where it emptied into the Siloam Pool (2 Kgs 20:20).

The Kidron Valley is first mentioned in the OT in the account of David's flight from Jerusalem during Absalom's rebellion (2 Sam 15:23): the people wept as "the king crossed the Kidron Valley." David's crossing of this traditional boundary (1 Kgs 2:37) formalized his departure from the city.

The Kidron Valley and its eastern slopes were also notorious as the location of aberrant worship. Solomon built shrines for CHEMOSH, Molech, and Moloch there (1 Kgs 11:7). The valley became the site where reforming kings deposited impure cultic items (1 Kgs 15:13; 2 Kgs 23:4, 6, 12; 2 Chron 29:16; 30:14). Jesus crossed the Kidron Valley on his way to the garden of GETHSEMANE (John 18:1), located at the base of the Mount of Olives. A number of other locations are sometimes identified with the Kidron: see JEHOSHAPHAT VALLEY; SHAVEH VALLEY.

KILAN An exile whose progeny returned to the land with Zerubbabel (1 Esdr 5:15).

KING, KINGSHIP Israel and its neighbors were often ruled by kings, but the beliefs and institutions surrounding the king and kingship varied widely.

Kingship was the main pattern of political organization in the ANE. It was understood to be part of the basic fabric of the sociopolitical order, and the king was recognized as a shepherd appointed by the god(s) to help society function in a harmonious fashion. The ubiquity of kingship among Israel's neighbors is reflected in Deut 17:14, where the people are depicted as saying, "Let's appoint a king over us, as all our neighboring nations have done" (cf 1 Sam 8:5, 20).

Certain biblical texts are typically treated as central for understanding kingship: the laws of the king in Deut 17:14-20; the explanation of "how the king will rule over you and operate" given in 1 Sam 8:11-17; the promise of an eternal dynasty to DAVID in 2 Sam 7:5-17; and the royal psalms. Like their ANE counterparts, the Israelite kings had responsibilities in four main spheres: military, judicial, cultic, and state building projects.

One of the king's sons, usually the oldest, often reigned after his father. The idea that primogeniture was not automatic is clear from 1 Kgs 1:20, where Bathsheba says to David: "the eyes of all Israel are upon you to tell them who will follow you on the throne of my master the king." In certain cases, the "people of the land," perhaps a term for a group of the landed gentry, decided who would reign (see 2 Kgs 11:14). Sometimes a foreign power removed a king and appointed his successor, but in such cases in Judah the successor was part of the royal Davidic family (e.g., 2 Kgs 24:15-17). In rare cases, there was a coregency, where the successor began to reign before his father died (e.g., 2 Kgs 15:5).

The crown and the throne were the two most important objects associated with kingship. The crown was the main royal symbol, so a fallen or removed crown may represent lost kingship (e.g., Lam 5:16; Jer 13:18), yet we have no idea what it looked like. To "sit on" the throne is equivalent to reigning (1 Kgs 1:13; 2:12; Jer 22:30). Only Solomon's throne is described in detail (1 Kgs 10:18-20; 2 Chron 9:17-19).

Ancient Near Eastern texts and reliefs suggest that the king had special clothing, though this is not described in the Bible. Second Samuel 1:10 mentions a royal "bracelet," a SCEPTER is referred to in several texts, and is even used metonymically to refer to kingship (e.g., Gen 49:10), and two texts mention a special pillar (2 Kgs 11:14; 23:3).

Kingship came to an end in 586 BCE, with the Babylonian capture of Jerusalem and destruction of the temple. Second Kings 25:7 and its parallels suggest that Zedekiah, the last king of Judah, was blinded, and his children were killed; eleven years earlier, King Jehoiachin had been exiled to Babylon. An attempt by Ishmael "from the royal family" to resurrect the Davidic monarchy failed (2 Kgs 25:25). The very end of 2 Kgs records the release of King Jehoiachin from prison in Babylon; some see this notice as reflecting the author's hope that the Davidic dynasty would be restored. It is unclear if there was an attempt to reestablish the Davidic monarchy after the return from exile.

KING OF THE JEWS In the Matthean infancy narrative, MAGI come from the east seeking the "newborn king of the Jews" (Matt 2:2). Herod, client king of Judea (who is not really a king, nor a Jew), seeks to kill this potential rival in an act of brutality that defines the sort of "king" he is (Matt 2:16; see HEROD, FAMILY; INNOCENTS, SLAUGHTER OF THE). By way of contrast, Matthew states that Jesus is the Messiah and SON OF DAVID (Matt 1:1), whose throne is established forever (2 Sam 7:16), and in fulfillment of the prophecy (Mic 5:2) that from Bethlehem will come a ruler who is to shepherd Israel (Matt 2:6).

For Matthew, Jesus is the true king who inaugurates the kingdom of heaven (4:17, 23) and fulfills the Jewish Law and the Prophets (5:17-20).

All four Gospels record that Pontius Pilate asks Jesus if he is "king of the Jews" (Matt 27:11; Mark 15:2; Luke 23:3; John 18:33). In the Synoptics, Jesus does not answer this charge, because his accusers do not understand who he is or what kind of kingdom he represents (in John 18:36-37 Jesus clarifies that his kingdom "doesn't originate from this world"). The mocking soldiers hail him as "king of the Jews" (Matt 27:29; Mark 15:18; Luke 23:37; John 19:3) and give him a "crown" made of thorns (Matt 27:29; Mark 15:17; John 19:2). Jesus is crucified with the title "King of the Jews" over his head (Matt 27:37; Mark 15:26; John 19:19, 21), an indication that his crime is insurrection against Rome. See CROWN OF THORNS; JESUS CHRIST; KINGDOM OF GOD, KINGDOM OF HEAVEN; MESSIAH, JEWISH.

KINGDOM OF GOD, KINGDOM OF HEAVEN The Scriptures of Israel and the NT portray God as king of the universe, the fundamental force behind all that is and shall be. The biblical phrases "kingdom of God" as well as "kingdom of heaven" focus on God's role in shaping human experience. At the same time, kingdom in Semitic languages, as well as in Greek, can refer to the area over which royal rule extends (see KING, KINGSHIP).

The interchangeability between "kingdom of God" or "God's kingdom" and "kingdom of heaven" in the Bible sometimes reflects a shift of emphasis, from the divine power behind the kingdom to the extent of that kingdom. In English, a kingdom might refer to a limited and local manifestation of power; in an attempt to avoid a limiting sense, alternative translations—such as "reign of God," "rule of God," and "dominion of God"—have been attempted. These attempts at paraphrase fail to observe that, although the experience of rule by kings (both foreign and domestic) was overwhelmingly negative in ancient Israel, Israelite hope remained fixed on a better kingdom, rooted in God and therefore neither limited nor tyrannical.

The promise of the kingdom is that people will at last come to realize divine justice and peace in all that they do. Jesus made God's kingdom the center of his preaching and programmatic activity, and it has proved pivotal in the development of Christian theology. Within the communities that shaped the NT, views of the kingdom of God influenced conceptions of ethical behavior and provided motivation to persist, in the face of often trying circumstances, in witnessing to the transformative power of God's action in the created world.

KINGDOMS, BOOKS OF The four books of Kingdoms in the LXX correspond to 1–2 Samuel and1–2 Kings in the Hebrew.

KINGS, FIRST AND SECOND BOOKS OF The fourth book of the middle section of the Hebrew Scriptures known as the Prophets, the last of the subsection known as the Former Prophets. In Christian Bibles, following the LXX arrangement, 1–2 Kings are the eleventh and twelfth books in the OT, the final entries among the "Historical Books."

KING'S GARDEN A garden of Jerusalem located near the Kidron Valley, the Pool of Shelah (Neh 3:15), and the gate between the double walls through which Zedekiah and his soldiers fled (Jer 39:4; 52:7). See SHELAH, POOL OF.

KING'S HIGHWAY The phrase "the King's Highway" appears twice in the account of the journey to the land of Canaan (Num 20:17; 21:22). The name probably signified that it was the main road of the region.

KIR Means "city" in Moabite and "wall" in Hebrew. Thus many place-names are formed with the prefix (e.g., Kir-hareseth; Kiriath-arba, etc.).

1. The city of Kir in Moab is noted in the oracle against Moab in Isaiah (15:1).

2. A Mesopotamian Kir (see Isa 22:6) is noted as the place of origin for the Arameans (Amos 9:7). Tiglath-pileser III of Assyria deported many inhabitants of Damascus to this Kir (2 Kgs 16:9). Amos predicted the deportation: "the people of Aram [Syria] will be forced to live in Kir" (1:5).

KISH 1. The father of King Saul. Kish was a Benjaminite and the son of ABIEL (1 Sam 9:1; Acts 13:21). Saul and his son were buried with Kish after David retrieves the Saulides' bodies from Jabesh-gilead (2 Sam 21:12-14).

2. A descendant of Jeiel and Maacah (1 Chron 8:30; 9:36). This Kish may be the same as Kish #1, but the genealogies are different (1 Chron 8:29-33; 9:35-39; cf 1 Sam 9:1).

3. A Merarite Levite. This Kish was the son of Mahli and father of Jerahmeel (1 Chron 23:21-22; 24:29).

4. A Merarite Levite and the son of Abdi. This Kish helped to cleanse the temple during the reign of Hezekiah (2 Chron 29:12-17).

5. A Benjaminite ancestor of Mordecai (Esth 2:5). Esther Rabbah does make this Kish the same as Saul's father.

6. The capital of an ancient city-state southeast of ancient Babylon.

KISHI Son of Ethan who was a singer and player of music in the temple during the time of David (1 Chron 6:44 [Heb. 6:29]); named KUSHAIAH in 1 Chron 15:17.

KISLEV The 9th month of the postexilic Jewish calendar, roughly corresponding to the months of November and December.

KISS A gesture of familiarity, affection, or respect between relatives, friends, and guests that involves touching one's lips to someone else's face or hands. To kiss someone's feet was a sign of subservience and devotion. Within early Christianity, the kiss developed into a symbol of spiritual kinship.

KITTIM A town in CYPRUS that flourished already in the Bronze Age. This term also designated its residents. The region had a Greek population at an early date. Hence, the biblical references to Kittim as a son of Javan, grandson of Noah (Gen 10:4; 1 Chron 1:7). The name Javan referred to all of Greece, apparently including the Greek isles. The 4th oracle of Balaam (Num 24:24) predicts that Asshur and Eber (probably the Hebrews) will be afflicted by ships from Kittim,

KNEAD The process used to make bread and unleavened cakes that involves mixing flour with water in a kneading bowl containing a portion of yesterday's batch (Gen 18:6; 1 Sam 28:24; 2 Sam 13:8; Jer 7:18; Hos 7:4).

KOHATH, KOHATHITE Kohath was the 2nd-born son of Levi and head of one of the three levitical divisions (Gen 46:11). The Kohathites were prominent among the Levites and were assigned the most important duties, including carrying the sacred furniture housed in the MEETING TENT, notably the COVENANT CHEST (Num 3:30-31). Because these objects were sacred, however, the Kohathites could not enter the meeting tent until the Aaronic priests had covered the objects with cloth (Num 4:15). Unlike the Gershonites and Merarites, the Kohathites were not provided with carts for their work because the sacred objects were to be carried on their shoulders (Num 7:9). They camped on the south side of the meeting tent, forming a barrier between it and the people so that the Israelites might not violate the sacred precincts (Num 3:29). The Kohathites were divided into four clans according to the sons of Kohath: Amram, Izhar, Hebron, and Uzziel (Exod 6:18; Num 3:19). Kohathites served as musicians in Solomon's temple in Jerusalem (1 Chron 6:33-43).

KOINONIA The Greek noun translated in the NT as "fellowship, participation, sharing, or contribution." The term is absent from the Gospels, but in Acts 2:42 it appears to be an essential part of the early church.

KOLA A location in the book of Judith (15:4) that may correspond to Holon (Josh 15:51; 21:15).

KOLAIAH 1. Ancestor of Benjaminites living in Jerusalem after the exile (Neh 11:7).

2. Father of Ahab the false prophet (Jer 29:21).

KOR The largest biblical dry measure of capacity, possibly equal to a homer, used for flour, wheat, and barley (1 Kgs 4:22; 5:2; 2 Chron 2:10; Ezra 7:22). See WEIGHTS AND MEASURES.

KORAH, KORAHITES 1. Son of Esau, born in the land of Canaan (Gen 36:5).

2. Clan name for one of the sons of Eliphaz, Esau's oldest offspring (Gen 36:16). In registering the clans and chieftains of Esau/Edom, Gen 36:9-20 lists the name Korah several times, but it is unclear whether all references are to the same person (cf 1 Chron 1:35).

3. Son of Hebron of the Calebite clan (1 Chron 2:43).

4. In the priestly genealogies of Exod 6:21, 24, Korah is listed as the son of Izhar son of Kohath son of Levi. Izhar was the brother of Amram, which makes Korah the cousin of Moses and Aaron. The genealogy of 1 Chron 6:22 lists the same affiliation, and Korah's lineage is simplified, though not essentially altered, in 1 Chron 6:37.

5. Korah is the eponymous ancestor of the clan of the Korahites (Num 26:58; 1 Chron 9:19; 12:6; 26:1, 19; 2 Chron 20:19). This identifies the Korah who led a rebellion against Moses and Aaron in the wilderness after the exodus from Egypt, events that are narrated in Num 16–17.

KORE 1. A Levite ancestor of the temple gatekeepers Shallum (1 Chron 9:19) and Meshelemiah (1 Chron 26:1).

2. A Levite son of IMNAH, who was in charge of the freewill offerings during the days of King Hezekiah (2 Chron 31:14).

KOZ A descendant of Judah (1 Chron 4:8) and father of Anub and Zobebah, he may be an ancestor of the priestly house HAKKOZ.

KUSHAIAH A Merarite Levite who was a sanctuary singer during David's reign (1 Chron 15:17). He is likely the same as KISHI in 1 Chron 6:44 [Heb. 6:29].

Ll

LAADAH Laadah is a descendant from the tribe of Judah in the line of Shelah (1 Chron 4:21). He is the father of MARESHAH.

LABAN 1. Rebekah's brother, Leah and Rachel's father, and the father-in-law of Jacob. Laban is the son of Bethuel, who is the son of Nahor, who is the brother of Abraham.

2. One of the places listed with Paran, Tophel, Hazeroth, and Di-zahab that marked the boundaries of the wilderness plain where Moses expounded the Instruction to the Israelites (Deut 1:1). It is sometimes identified with Libnah (Num 33:20).

LABOR The biblical words for labor convey various types and meanings of work, ranging from physical and mental toil to the labor of childbirth.

LACCUNUS One of the sons of Addi and an Israelite who had a foreign wife (1 Esdr 9:31).

LACHISH Tel Lachish, a prominent mound whose summit and slope cover an area of about 31 ac., represents the remains of biblical Lachish. It is situated in the low hill region extending between the Coastal Plain and the Hebron Hills. Water was supplied by wells, one of which was excavated on the mound. Availability of suitable land for cultivation and sufficient water contributed to the prosperity of the settlement in all periods.

LADAN 1. An Ephraimite who was the great-great-grandfather of Joshua (1 Chron 7:26).

2. A Levite descended from Gershon (1 Chron 23:7-9; 26:21) who is elsewhere called Libni (Exod 6:17; Num 3:18). See LIBNI, LIBNITES.

LAEL A Gershonite Levite and the father of ELIASAPH (Num 3:24).

LAHAD A Zorathite descendant of Judah's son Shobal (1 Chron 4:2).

LAHMI Listed in 1 Chron 20:5 as the brother of Goliath of Gath.

LAMB A young sheep, usually less than a year old. Most OT references to lambs are sacrificial. Lambs were a daily entirely burned offering in the temple (i.e., Num 15:1-13), and they were the animals offered at Passover (Exod 12:3-4). Lambs could be sacrificed as offerings for purification and reparation (Lev 4:32; Num 6:12; "purification" and "compensation" offerings). However, bulls and goats were the more common offerings for these purposes (Lev 4:1-31).

In the NT, *lamb* is used only metaphorically. The seventy disciples in Luke are sent out as "lambs" (Luke 10:3), indicating their vulnerability in a hostile environment. Jesus instructs Peter to "feed my lambs" (John 21:15); here the lambs are followers for whom Peter should provide care. Primarily, however, *lamb* in the NT is a metaphor for *Christ* (e.g., John 1:29; 1 Pet 1:19; Rev 5:6).

LAME, LAMENESS In general, lameness is a condition of physical impairment in which part or all of a limb is lacking, or a limb, organ, or mechanism of the body is injured or defective so that it does not function properly. In the ancient world, there was a high survival rate from impairment-causing injuries, so that dealing with impairment and impaired people was a common experience in daily life.

God's relationship to impaired creatures, whether human or animal, is complex. On the one hand, a priest who has a blemish, or who is lame, or has a limb too long may not offer sacrifice (Lev 21:18). On the other hand, he (Lev 21:22) and his family (Lev 22:11) are entitled to eat of the sacrifice, and his impairment did not remove him from the priesthood.

Some biblical accounts attest that physical problems were believed to be the result of divine punishment (e.g., John 9:2). However, this conclusion does not reflect the biblical evidence accurately. Throughout the ancient world, the experience of impairment was mixed, that is, it was viewed in both negative and positive ways. Some ancients considered lameness as something shameful (Zeph 3:19), a true misfortune (Prov 25:19; 26:7). Job lists among his good deeds his service as "feet to the lame" (Job 29:15). The lame could hope for eventual wholeness, because God promised to reverse shameful fortunes including lameness and its consequences (Isa 33:23). Indeed, when God's reign is decisively established, the "lame will leap like the deer" (Isa 35:10). Jesus, who announced the immanent establishment of the reign of God (Mark 1:14-15), manifested this promise in his healing.

See MIRACLE.

LAMECH There are two versions of the patriarch Lamech in Gen 4–5, in two genealogies, which are closely related.

1. According to the J source (Gen 4:19-24), Lamech was an exemplar of violence, whose children were the ancestors of various cultural occupations—herders, musicians, and metalworkers. Lamech is born from the line of Adam and Cain in the 7th generation.

2. According to the P source (Gen 5:25-31), Lamech is the father of Noah, the exemplary righteous man. Lamech is born from the line of Adam and Seth in the 9th generation. This Lamech is listed in Jesus' genealogy (Luke 3:36).

LAMENTATIONS, BOOK OF The book of Lamentations portrays Israel in lament in the historical context of the destruction of the Jerusalem Temple and the Babylonian exile of 587 BCE.

LAMPSTAND The repository or support for a light source (i.e., a lamp). When lamplight was needed above ground level, ceramic stands were sometimes used to hold lamps. These stands were typically hollow cylindrical forms, approximately three to five in. in diameter and up to a ft. high, with flaring bases. They are similar to stands used for holding incense dishes and other vessels without flat bases. Ceramic lampstands were probably not usual household items since relatively few have been recovered archaeologically. Lamps in most dwellings would have been elevated by placing them in niches in the stone walls.

Accordingly, the use of *lampstand* in the Bible refers most often to the single golden menorah of the meeting tent or the ten of the Jerusalem temple (Exod 25; 1 Kgs 7:49; cf Heb 9:2). Building on the symbolism of the golden menorahs of the OT and perhaps suggesting a temple setting, the NT (in the visions of Rev 1 and 2) refers to seven golden lampstands representing the seven churches and also to two golden lampstands (Rev 11:4; cf Zech 4:2-3).

LAODICEA Laodicea and/or its inhabitants are mentioned six times in the NT (Col 2:1; 4:13, 15, 16; Rev 1:11; 3:14). The passages in Colossians convey the depth and sincerity of Paul's concern for Christian congregations located in the Lycus Valley. The passages in Revelation contain a message from Christ scolding the Christians in Laodicea for their half-hearted efforts and lack of total commitment to the faith.

LAPPIDOTH The husband of DEBORAH, the prophetess who judged Israel (Judg 4:4).

LASHARON A city whose king was conquered by Joshua (Josh 12:18).

LAST SUPPER, THE The account of the Last Supper of Jesus is found in Matt 26:26-29; Mark 14:22-25; Luke 22:15-20; and 1 Cor 11:23-26. A variant account, without the words of institution, is found in John 13:1-20, but this is not the story traditionally indicated by the term *Last Supper*. The Last Supper has been perceived as a foundation story for the Christian communal meal, or LORD'S SUPPER, throughout Christian history, beginning with Paul (1 Cor 11:17-34).

LASTHENES A Cretan official of significant rank (perhaps that of governor) under the reign of the Seleucid king Demetrius II Nicator. Lasthenes is mentioned as the recipient of a letter of Demetrius concerning Jews, a copy of which Demetrius sent to Jonathan (1 Macc 11:31-32).

LAWYER An expert in law; in the NT, normally the Law of Moses. Except for a textual variant in Matt 22:35, "lawyer" and "teacher of the Law" appear only in Luke–Acts and the Pastorals. Luke appears to consider *legal expert*, *lawyer*, and *teacher of the Law* as equivalent terms.

LAYING ON OF HANDS The act of laying on of hands in the OT occurs primarily in the context of offering sacrifices, making appointments, giving blessings, and in receiving judgment (Lev 24:14). Persons bringing offerings are to lay or press their hands on the sacrificial animals (Lev 3:2, 8, 13; 4:4; concerning priests, Exod 29:10, 15, 19), presumably to demonstrate whom the sacrifice concerns. Aaron places both hands on the scapegoat (Lev 16:21), the bearer of sins (not a sacrifice). Laying his hands upon Joshua, Moses appoints him as his successor (Num 27:18, 23; Deut 34:9; see also the consecration of the Levites in Num 8:5-13). Jacob blesses his grandsons through this gesture (Gen 48:14), a custom that continues in the NT in Jesus' blessing of the children (Matt 19:15; Mark 10:16). Parallel to the OT, assignments to specific tasks are symbolically marked by the laying on of hands in the NT. Hence, the Twelve appoint the seven Hellenists by prayer and laying on of hands according to Acts 6:6 (see also Acts 13:3 concerning Paul and Barnabas). In the NT this gesture is also associated with the imparting of the Spirit, with spiritual gifts (Acts 8:17-18; 9:17; 19:6; 1 Tim 4:14; 2 Tim 1:6), and with healing. Thus laying on of hands is a common healing technique that Jesus and his later followers use (Mark 5:23; 6:5; 7:32; 8:22-26; 16:18; Luke 4:40; 13:13; Acts 9:12, 17; 28:8). See CONFIRMATION.

LAZARUS Two men in the NT are named Lazarus.

1. Lazarus, the poor man in the parable of the rich man (Luke 16:19-31), is the only named character in any parable of Jesus.

2. Lazarus of Bethany is a character unique to the Gospel of John (John 11:1–12:11). Lazarus is from the village of BETHANY, and is the brother of MARY and Martha (John 11:1-2), whose interactions with Jesus comprise the bulk of this story (11:20-40). When Lazarus becomes sick, the sisters send word to Jesus (11:3), believing he will heal their brother (11:21, 32). Jesus' intentional delay (11:4-5) sets up the astonishing miracle of Lazarus's resurrection (11:43-44), which occurs after Lazarus has been dead four days (11:17, 39).

LEAD, METAL Lead is mentioned in the Bible several times. In Exod 15:10 the weight of it is stressed in the victory song of Moses, when Pharaoh and his riders are compared to lead that sinks into the sea. The weight is also stressed in Sir 22:14. Lead is regularly mentioned together with other metals such as gold, silver, bronze, iron, and tin (e.g., Num 31:22; Ezek 22:18, 20). In these lists lead usually comes at the end, suggesting that it was considered the least valuable of metals. In Job 19:24 it is used for writing on a rock.

LEAH Leah, daughter of LABAN and wife of JACOB, is the 3rd matriarch. She appears only in Genesis (mostly Gen 29–30) and in a blessing in Ruth 4:11. First described as possessing "weak" or "soft" eyes (29:17, CEB "delicate"), Leah is deceitfully given to Jacob as wife instead of his dearly loved RACHEL, her younger sister. The narrator subsequently states that Leah was "unloved" but adds that God blessed her with fertility (29:31).

Competition between Leah and Rachel results in the birth of Israel's twelve tribes. Leah proves to be the fertile wife and biological mother of six children, including Israel's most important eponyms, Judah and Levi, as well as their only named sister, DINAH. The names Leah gives her children (including those of her woman servant ZILPAH) repeatedly express longing to be loved by her husband. She resents Rachel, accusing her of stealing Jacob's love (30:15). Nevertheless, Leah assists Rachel (in exchange for a night with Jacob) by letting her have mandrakes that purportedly help fertility (Gen 30:14-17).

According to Gen 49:29-31, Jacob buries Leah in the family's cave of MACHPELAH and instructs his sons to bury him with her. Yet Jacob's words and actions repeatedly indicate that he prefers Rachel.

LEATHER The first clothes mentioned in the Bible are the animal-skin garments given by God to Adam and Eve (Gen 3:21). Leather was used for waterskins or wineskins, sandals (Ezek 16:10), armor, shields, chariot harnesses, belts (2 Kgs 1:8; Matt 3:4), and parchment. Finer-quality leather was employed as coverings for the covenant chest and the other sacred objects used in the meeting tent when the Israelites were on the move (Num 4:6-25).

LEAVEN An agent that causes fermentation. In biblical times it may often have been a piece of fermented dough left from a previous batch. In addition to its literal meaning, the word developed a figurative sense as something small that, when added to another entity, produced major change, whether good or bad. In some passages there is reference to baking that did (Hos 7:4) or did not (Gen 19:3; Judg 6:19-21; 1 Sam 28:24) involve yeast. But a more frequent usage has to do with the presence or more often the absence of yeast on cultic or festival occasions. Most famously, the legislation for Passover and the Feast of Unleavened Bread (see PASSOVER AND FESTIVAL OF UNLEAVENED BREAD) stipulates that no yeast was to be consumed or found in the houses of the Israelites (Exod 12:8, 15, 17-20, 34, 39; 13:3, 6-7; 23:15; 34:18). Deuteronomy 16:3 terms unleavened bread "bread symbolizing misery," and notes that baking bread without leaven was related to Israel's hasty departure from Egypt.

Whatever may have been the reason(s) for the sacrificial regulations regarding leaven, the word took on a figurative meaning as is evident in the NT and in rabbinic literature. Leaven has a general sense of something small that works its way entirely through something larger (see 1 Cor 5:6; Gal 5:9), but it more frequently is set in an evaluative context. It could convey a positive meaning. In Matt 13:33 (par. Luke 13:20-21) Jesus tells a short parable: "The kingdom of heaven is like yeast, which a woman took and hid in a bushel of wheat flour until the yeast had worked its way through all the dough." But there are several instances of negative connotations. Matthew 16:6 quotes Jesus as warning his disciples: "Watch out and be on your guard for the yeast of Pharisees and Sadducees" (see also vv. 11-12 and Mark 8:15); in Luke 12:1 this becomes "the yeast of the Pharisees—I mean, the mismatch between their hearts and lives." Paul also employed such imagery. See also 1 Cor 5:1-7.

LEBANAH Head of a family of exiles returning from Babylon (Ezra 2:45; Neh 7:48; 1 Esdr 5:29).

LEBANON Lebanon occupies the central section of the eastern coast of the Mediterranean, forming a coastline 210 km long. In biblical times it consisted of a number of independent city-states extending to Arwad (now in Syria) in the north and Akhziv to the south (now part of Israel). It is bordered by Syria to the north and east and the modern State of Israel to the south.

Lebanon is regarded both positively (Isa 35:2; 40:16; Jer 22:6) and negatively (Isa 10:34; 33:9; Jer 22:20, 23; Nah 1:4; Zech 11:1) in the Bible. Lebanon is also mentioned in the lands of the tribes of Israel (Deut 1:7; 3:25; 11:24; Josh 1:4; 9:1; 12:7; 13:5-6; Judg 3:3).

In biblical times Lebanon was forested with cedars (*Cedrus libani*) and other evergreen trees and was valued for hunting but especially for timber. The cedars of Lebanon "high and lofty" (Isa 2:13) take a prominent place in parts of the Bible (Pss 29:5; 104:16), with many references to their majesty and beauty.

LECAH A descendant of Judah or, in the Chronicler's pattern, the name of a village (1 Chron 4:21).

LEGION The fundamental unit of the much-vaunted ancient Roman army. The number, size, and structure of the legion changed somewhat throughout Roman history. In the early 1st cent. CE, the Roman army would have had twenty-five such legions stationed throughout the empire (Cassius Dio, Rom. 55.23; Tacitus, *Ann.* 4.5). Biblical references to legion are limited to just four, and these only in the NT, all of which are figurative.

LEHABIM The Table of Nations includes Lehabim as a descendant of Ham and a direct offspring of Egypt (Gen 10:13; 1 Chron 1:11).

LEHI Samson was delivered to Lehi by his own people after he burned down the Philistine crops (Judg 15:1-8). When he arrived he was overcome with religious fervor and took the lives of a thousand Philistine men with the jawbone of a donkey (Judg 15:14-15). The place was thus called Ramath-lehi, meaning "Jawbone Hill" (Judg 15:17).

LEMUEL Usually rendered as a proper name, Lemuel appears in Prov 31:1, 4 as the conveyor of his mother's wisdom. The Hebrew text calls him king of Massa, a land unknown except as a "descendant" of Ishmael (Gen 25:14).

LENTIL Among the earliest leguminous crops to be cultivated (7th-millennium carbonized remains from Iraq), lentils (*Lens culinaris*) were served as a hearty stew (Gen 25:34) or mixed with cereal grains to make bread (Ezek 4:9). They also served as rations for soldiers (2 Sam 17:28).

LEOPARD The leopard, a close relative of the lion, is rarely mentioned in the Bible, suggesting it was not as common as the lion. Nevertheless, the leopard still exists in the region. As a night hunter it will attack humans as well as animals. It is quite fearless and ferocious and is probably the fastest mammal (Hab 1:8). The leopard's spots are its trademark (Jer 13:23) and its color tends to reflect its habitat, which in Palestine was the rocky mountainous region (Song 4:8). Isaiah, foreseeing the Day of the Lord as a time of peace and tranquillity, declared the impossible, namely that "the leopard will lie down with the young goat" (Isa 11:6).

LEPROSY Scholars agree that the condition described so extensively in Lev 13–14 and mentioned elsewhere in the Bible is not the condition known today as leprosy, that is, Hansen's disease. Instead, it is a skin condition involving scaly or rough patches of skin; these descriptions indicate conditions that may include psoriasis, ringworm, and eczema, among other maladies.

LESHEM Alternate form of Laish (Judg 18:7), ancient name of the city of Dan (Josh 19:47).

LETTER No OT document is in letter form. More than a dozen are embedded in the OT (e.g., 2 Sam 11:15; 1 Kgs 21:9-10; 2 Chron 21:12-15). In contrast to the OT, twenty-one books of the NT are in letter form: the thirteen Pauline Epistles, one anonymous letter (Hebrews), James, 1–2 Peter, 1–3 John, and Jude. In OT style, two letters are embedded in Acts (15:23-29; 23:26-30). (The "letters" in Rev 2–3 were never independent missives.) Other letters are mentioned but now lost (Acts 18:27; 1 Cor 5:9; 7:1; 16:3; 2 Cor 2:3-4; Col 4:16; 2 Thess 2:2). Extant NT letters have much in common with other Greco-Roman letters. These letters had a set structure and content, far more than letters today. Even family letters had generic greetings, set phraseology (formulas), and standardized wishes for good health. Letters had two primary purposes: to start or keep a relationship with the recipient, or to continue a conversation.

All NT letters (except 3 John) are addressed to groups. (The Pastorals speak to the church behind Timothy or Titus; Philemon includes "the church that meets in your house" (v. 2), though it deals with a personal issue.) They assume familiarity with Jewish Christian tradition, inserting OT quotations/allusions, hymnic fragments, and so on, often without explanation (or indication). These letters were to be read in front of the congregation (1 Thess 5:27). Is this why Paul replaced the typical health wish with a thanksgiving/blessing, following the custom of the synagogue and Jewish speeches, or earlier Aramaic letters? Paul's letters contained more (and more complex) thanksgivings than any other known ancient writer. His opening thanksgiving often "previewed" the letter's main topics (e.g., 1 Cor 1:4-7). His letters also contained large amounts of paraeneses (moral exhortations).

LETTERS, APOCRYPHAL Although most of the NT Apocrypha is in the Gospel or Acts genre, a few pseudepigraphical letters in the name of the apostles and others survive from the 2nd–4th cent. Among them are the Letter of Paul to the Laodiceans (see Col 4:16) and a Letter to the Corinthians (now embedded in the Acts of Paul). Letters purporting to be from Christ to King Abgar of Edessa and between Paul and Seneca have also survived.

LEUMMIM The Leummim or Leummites are listed in Gen 25:3 among the descendants of DEDAN, a grandson of Abraham and Keturah.

LEVI, LEVITES The name of four people and a tribe in the Bible.

1. In the OT Levi is the 3rd son of Jacob by Leah (Gen 29:34) and the ancestor of the tribe of Levi and all priests.

2. The OT testimony regarding Levites, the descendants of Levi, reports that they are from the line of Jacob that provided Israel's priests. The evidence of the Levites' nature, function, and destiny vis-à-vis the priesthood appears chiefly in four places: Deuteronomic texts, Ezekiel, Priestly texts, and Chronicles.

3. According to Joseph's genealogy, Levi is the son of Melchi (Luke 3:24).

4. In Luke 3:29-30 the genealogy that links Joseph back to Adam lists Levi as the son of Simeon.

5. Luke 5:27, 29 says the tax collector in whose house Jesus dined was named Levi; in Mark 2:14 he is Levi, "Alphaeus's son."

LEVIATHAN This terrible serpent of the salty sea, slain by God at the beginning (Ps 74:14) and end of time (Isa 27:1), is mentioned by name only six times in the Bible (Job 3:8; 41:1; Pss 74:14; 104:26; Isa 27:1 [twice]).

The biblical Leviathan is not all bad. Job 41:1-34 depicts the monster as the Lord's favorite playmate (see also Ps 104:25-26). In postcanonical Jewish literature Leviathan and its partner BEHEMOTH are identified with "the great sea animals" that God created on the 5th day (Gen 1:21; see 2 Esdr 6:49, 52; 1 En 60:7-10, 24; 2 Bar 29:4). After eons in hiding, they reemerge to become food for the elect at the eschatological banquet.

LEVIRATE LAW If a woman's husband dies before a son is born to the couple, it is the legally binding duty of the husband's brother to marry the widow and produce a son in his brother's name (Deut 25:5-10). If the brother-in-law does not wish to marry the widow, both parties consult with the elders, and the widow and her brother-in-law take part in a ceremony in which she removes his sandal, spits in his face, and renounces him as a man unwilling to establish a name for his brother in Israel. Once this ceremony is performed, the widow is free to marry outside her husband's family. This legal practice is the subject of Gen 38 and, arguably, Ruth 4. Later Jewish interpreters expounded upon this law, and it is the primary topic of tractate Yevamot of the Mishnah and Talmud. See MARRIAGE.

LEVITICAL CITIES, TOWNS Moses denied the Levites an allotment of land among the rest of the tribes (Num 18:20), yet decreed that they were to be given forty-eight cities, with contiguous grazing lands, when Israel took possession of Canaan (Num 35:1-8). Joshua 21:1-42 reports the implementation of the Mosaic decree and designates each of the cities within a scheme that situates the levitical clans among particular tribal groups. The Chronicler utilizes a corresponding and derivative list to conclude a section on the organization of the Levites (1 Chron 6:54-81).

LEVITICUS, BOOK OF Leviticus is the third book of the PENTATEUCH. The Hebrew title, "and He called," is the first word of the book. The LXX focuses on content and calls the book, "instructions for/by the Levites," although Numbers is more concerned with the Levites and their duties. Indeed, in Leviticus, the priestly family is limited to Aaron and his descendants. The book itself makes clear that it is addressed to both priests and non-priests in Israel (e.g., 1:2; 4:1; 7:23, 29; 11:2; 12:2; 15:2; 17:2; 18:2; 19:2).

LIBNAH 1. An unknown site in the Sinai Peninsula where the Israelites camped en route from Egypt to Canaan (Num 33:20-21).

2. A Canaanite city conquered by Joshua (Josh 10:39; 12:15), allotted to Judah (Josh 15:42), and set apart as a levitical city (Josh 21:13; 1 Chron 6:57 [Heb. 1 Chron 6:42]). Libnah rebelled during the reign of Jehoram because of the king's apostasy (2 Kgs 8:22; 2 Chron 21:10). Hamutal, Josiah's wife and the mother of kings Zedekiah and Jehoahaz, was from this city (2 Kgs 23:31; 24:18).

LIBNI, LIBNITES 1. Libni and his brother Shimei appear in Exod 6:17; Num 3:18; and 1 Chron 6:17, 20 [Heb. 6:2, 5] as the two sons of Levi's son Gershon.

2. A clan of Levites descended from Libni the son of Gershon. The Libnites were associated with the Judahite town

of Libnah, which is located about 15 km west-northwest from Hebron (Num 3:21). Numbers 26:58 lists the Libnites alongside four other clans of Levi in a different genealogical structure.

3. First Chronicles 6:29 [Heb. 6:14] lists Libni as a grandson of Gershon's brother Merari and as the father of Shimei.

LIBYA, LIBYANS In antiquity, the term *Libya* was a general designation for much of northern Africa to the west of EGYPT, a more extensive geographic domain than the modern nation of Libya. In the NT Simon of Cyrene was compelled to carry the cross for Jesus on his way to Golgotha (Matt 27:32). People from "the regions of Libya bordering Cyrene" were present at the event of Pentecost (Acts 2:10). See CUSH, CUSHITE.

LIFE Life is the fundamental gift shared between God and creation. Life is not an inherent quality possessed independently by us; it is a gift, first given in creation and then again in redemption. Without God, the cosmos would be void and lifeless; without God sinful creatures would be unable to sustain life as God intends. God gives life and the sole possibility that it might be eternal.

LIFE, SCROLL OF This is the list of people who receive the gift of life with God. Early references to "the scroll of life" (Ps 69:28) and the "scroll" that God has written (Exod 32:32) identify people who are alive and assume that being blotted out of the book means dying. In other sources, being "on the list" entails a glorious future in God's city (Isa 4:3); those whose names are "written in the scroll" are assured of resurrection to future life (Dan 12:1); being removed signifies final condemnation (1 En 108:3). People are often understood to be placed in the book through divine grace, which gives them citizenship in heaven and hope of everlasting life (Phil 3:20–4:3). As creator, God can inscribe people in the book from the foundation of the world (Rev 13:8; 17:8). Divine grace stands in tension with human accountability. At the last judgment people are accountable for their actions inscribed in the scrolls of deeds, but they are saved by grace by having their names in the scroll of life (Rev 3:5; 20:12-15; 21:27). In contrast, others regard a place in the scroll as a reward for righteous living (Herm. Sim. 2.9; Apoc. Zeph. 3:6-9). See APOCALYPTICISM.

LIGHT AND DARKNESS In ANE cultures, physical light and darkness were associated with the cycles of life, growth, decay, and death. The light emanating from the heavens symbolized life, happiness, and prosperity, while darkness was an expression of chaos and death. The light-bearing celestial bodies such as the sun, moon, and stars were often deified and worshipped.

In the OT, light is the first manifestation of God's creative word in the CREATION story (Gen 1:3-5). It is separated from darkness and declared by its creator to be good (1:4, 18). The light is associated with day and darkness with night. The appearance of God to people is often portrayed as light or fire, as in the exodus from Egypt (Exod 10:23; 13:21; Neh 9:12, 19; Pss 78:14; 104:2; 105:39; Dan 2:22). In the wisdom tradition, light and darkness are given their strongest ethical interpretation. Ecclesiastes 2:13 equates wisdom with light and folly with darkness. The wise person lives according to the light of God's Law (Ps 43:3; Prov 13:9) and is illuminated by God's presence.

Light and darkness continue in the NT as a metaphor for knowledge or ignorance of God and human lives either attuned to God or the world or the powers of evil. The ways of the nations can be described as darkness (Rom 2:19), but the completion of the apocalyptic process will result in the recognition of the light by all nations (Rev 21:24).

Although Jesus is the "light of the world" in the 4th Gospel, the synoptic tradition insists that the community of believers is also a source of illumination as they "walk in the light" (Matt 5:14-16//Luke 8:16-17; Luke 16:23; Matt 10:27//Luke 12:3; Matt 6:22-23//Luke 11:33-36). The followers of Jesus are referred to as "people who belong to/whose lives are determined by the light" and "children of light" (Luke 16:8; John 12:36; Eph 5:8; 1 Thess 5:5).

Conversion is portrayed as the movement from darkness to light (2 Cor 4:6; Acts 26:18; 1 Pet 2:9), and those who separate themselves from darkness actualize this in a new way of life (Eph 5:8-10).

LIKHI The third son of SHEMIDA in the line of Manasseh (1 Chron 7:14-19). The name may be a corruption of HELEK, a son of Gilead (Num 26:30).

LILY The lily mentioned in both the OT and NT likely refers generically to a variety of wildflower that grows naturally on the slopes of the hills and in the fields and valleys throughout much of the Sharon Plain and in the Galilee region.

LILY OF THE VALLEY The phrase "lily of the valleys" appears only in Song 2:1, in which the female voice uses it and "rose of the Sharon plain" to describe herself. Although it may be a well-known expression, no precise plant can be identified with this LILY.

LIME, LIMESTONE From the verb "to whitewash," lime is a white, alkaline powder usually derived in ancient days by smelting limestone at temperatures surpassing 1022° F (550° C). Lime was used to plaster cisterns, store bins, and walls. The intense heat needed to produce lime provides imagery to declare the fate of the unfaithful in Israel (Isa 33:12; Amos 2:1).

LINEN Linen is a product of flax, which has been cultivated since ancient times in Egypt and the Levant (Hos 2:5, 9). Cultivation of flax is mentioned in the OT in regard to Egypt (Exod 9:31). Flax was carefully pulled and dried in the field or on house terraces (Josh 2:6); retted (ideally in water rather than by dew) to decay the woody material around the fibers; and beaten and combed to separate the fibers (Isa 19:9), which were then cleaned, spun, and finally woven. Much of this work was carried out by women (Prov 31:13, 19). Families of "linen workers" are mentioned in 1 Chron 4:21. Much high-quality linen may have been imported from Egypt (Ezek 27:7).

LINUS 1. In 2 Tim 4:21, Paul sends greetings from Linus, Eubulus, Pudens, and Claudia to his companion Timothy.

2. According to Catholic tradition, Linus was the successor of Peter as the pope of Rome. Irenaeus of Lyons identifies Linus with the Linus in 2 Tim 4:21.

LION The lion (*Panthera leo* or *Felis leo*), which inhabited the ANE and is now extinct, belongs to the family Felidae. The lion was one of the largest carnivores inhabiting the land.

Biblical references suggest that the lion was prevalent both east and west of the Jordan. The lion was found in the mountains (Song 4:8), in the forests (Jer 12:8; Amos 3:4; Mic 5:8), in the thicket (Jer 4:7), near Bethel in Judah (1 Kgs 13), and near Timnah (Judg 14).

LIZARD Hebrew has several words for *lizard* that occur in two distinct contexts. In levitical dietary laws, lizards are among "the small creatures that move about on the ground" considered impure. Proverbs 30:24-28 recognizes the lizard as one of four small or insignificant entities (along with the ant, the badger, and the locust) that deserve consideration for their wisdom.

LOCUST An insect widely known in the ANE for its periodic swarming, at which times it devoured most kinds of vegetation in its path. Because of the destructiveness of locusts, biblical writers sometimes saw them as punishment from God (see Exod 10:3-20), even of apocalyptic proportions (Rev 9:1-12), while at other times they constituted a mere natural calamity on account of which Israelites were to invoke God's intervention (2 Chron 6:28). Writers could also employ locusts as symbols of military destruction (see Joel 1:4; 2:25). The dietary regulations also defined locusts, crickets, and grasshoppers as ritually clean food, suitable for human consumption (Lev 11:22).

LOG In the OT, *log* has two meanings. It commonly refers to "timber" for building, burning, or splitting (1 Kgs 5:8-10; Ezek 24:5, 10; Eccl 10:9, respectively). Log also denotes the smallest liquid measurement, as in a "log" of oil for temple sacrifices (Lev 14:10, 12, 15, 21, 24).

The NT always employs *log* figuratively. In the Sermon on the Mount/Plain material, a "log" symbolizes large personal faults set in contrast to minute flaws (speck) in others (Matt 7:3-5).

LOGOS See WORD.

LOINS The midsection of the body, often indicating the waist area. One would fasten ("gird") a belt or girdle there for the purpose of carrying something (2 Sam 20:8), in preparation for a journey (Exod 12:11; 2 Kgs 4:29), or for battle (Nah 2:1). In the Priestly literature, *loins* refers to the fatty area of an animal near its kidneys, which was to be sacrificed to the Lord (Lev 3:4, 10, 15; 4:9; 7:4).

LOIS Lois was the mother of Eunice and maternal grandmother of Timothy (2 Tim 1:5). Acts 16:1 indicates that Timothy's mother was Jewish; thus Lois probably was as well. According to 2 Tim 1:5, both converted to Christianity and were believers before Timothy.

LORD In most contemporary English translations of the OT, the word *Lord* renders the divine name. The CEB also uses the word *Lord/lord* (in noncapital letters) to translate other words referring to God (e.g., Luke 20:37).

The Lord is the personal name of Israel's God revealed to Moses in Exod 3:15. Apparently deriving from some form of the verb "to be" both its origin and that of the enigmatic self-description in 3:14 remain disputed. While the OT depicts the Lord in complex ways, Second Temple Judaism emphasized God's uniqueness, the only true God who is sole creator and ruler of all things (Deut 6:4-5; 4:35; Isa 45; Sir 18:1-2; 36:5; 3 Macc 2:1-3).

Whatever the catalyst, the use of "Lord" to refer to Jesus permeates the NT, most likely originating with the earliest Aramaic-speaking Christians (1 Cor 16:22). In many cases, the title carries no divine connotations (e.g., Matt 15:27). However, it is significant that the NT continues to use this word to refer to God (e.g., Rom 11:34; Mark 13:20; Luke 1:6), but it also draws language from certain OT texts that originally have to do with the Lord and applies it to Jesus as Lord (e.g., Rom 10:13; 2 Cor 3:15-18; Acts 2:21, 36; Mark 1:2-3; 1 Cor 1:8]).

The use of "Lord" in such ways to refer to Jesus redefines monotheism christologically. Since it predates Paul, this is indeed an early high christology whose cumulative effect is to include Jesus as Lord in the unique identity of the one God of Israel. See GOD, NAMES OF; JESUS CHRIST.

LORD OF HEAVEN The earliest attestation of the epithet "Lord of heaven" is in Dan 5:23. It is common in Tobit (6:18; 7:11, 16; 10:11, 12), and often appears as "the Lord of heaven and earth" (Matt 11:25; Luke 10:21; Acts 17:24; Tob 10:13; "ruler of heaven and earth" [Jdt 9:12]). See GOD, NAMES OF.

LORD OF HEAVENLY FORCES The

divine epithet "LORD [God] of heavenly forces" occurs more than two hundred times in the OT, making it the most common designation for God in the OT. By far, most of its occurrences are in the prophetic books, and it is absent from Genesis through Joshua, among others. A number of passages associate it directly with the Lord, noting "the LORD of heavenly forces is his name" (Isa 47:4; 48:2; 51:15; 54:5; Jer 10:16; 31:35; 50:34; 51:19; Amos 5:27). The variety of usages suggests a range of possible meanings.

The phrase is commonly associated with the concept of the Lord as commander of the armies (forces) of Israel, as is explicit in 1 Sam 17:45. Tradition also associates the Lord with the COVENANT CHEST and the shrine at Shiloh (1 Sam 1:3, 11). Thus the Lord is referred to as "the LORD of heavenly forces, who sits enthroned on the winged heavenly creatures" (1 Sam 4:4; 2 Sam 6:2; Isa 37:16). The Lord could also be depicted as the head of the heavenly bodies, including sun, moon, and stars (2 Kgs 23:5), and of the members of his heavenly forces (see DIVINE ASSEMBLY), from which prophetic authority may be claimed (1 Kgs 22:19; Jer 23:18, 22; Amos 3:7). Also counted among the heavenly forces were the angels who gave the Lord praise (Ps 148:2). See GOD, NAMES OF.

LORD'S DAY The designation of a day specifically as "the Lord's day" occurs in the NT only in Rev 1:10, which describes a day when the writer claimed to have been caught up in the spirit. Given its context within an apocalyptic document, some commentators argue that this designation does not refer to the first day of the week, but rather to Judgment Day (see Matt 12:36) based on the significance of the "day of the LORD" for the prophets (e.g., Isa 13:6; Amos 5:18; Zeph 1:14).

LORD'S PRAYER A model prayer that Jesus taught his disciples to use as a communal prayer, which reflects his relationship with God and the key themes of his teaching on God's kingdom. The Lord's Prayer is found in two versions in the NT: Matt 6:9-13 and Luke 11:2-4.

LORD'S SUPPER The congregational meal at which bread and a CUP were used to remember the death of the Lord Jesus. The phrase "Lord's Supper" ("Lord's meal" in CEB) was used by Paul in reference to a congregational meal that was not being conducted in an appropriate manner and thus was unworthy of this name (1 Cor 11:20). The phrase is not found elsewhere in the NT. The meal is discussed in 1 Cor 5; 10; and 11. Paul's wording for the meal and its ritual is closest to Luke 22:19-20 (cf Matt 26:26-29 and Mark 14:22-25, also John 13).

LORD'S WARS, SCROLL OF THE A poem mentioned in Num 21:14-15, reciting the wars of Israel in the conquest of the Transjordan.

LOT Lot is the son of Abraham's dead brother Haran. He travels and lives with his uncle, who protects him. Eventually he moves to Sodom, but his uncle's presence continues to influence his life. Lot accompanies his uncle Abraham and Sarah when they leave Haran for Canaan in response to God's promise to Abraham in Gen 12:1-3, 7. However, when they go to Egypt (Gen 12:10-20), Lot does not accompany them. When Abraham and Sarah return to Canaan, they rejoin Lot (Gen 13:1-18). The men have large flocks and their servants fight for use of the land. Abraham asks Lot to choose where he will settle and promises to move elsewhere. Lot chooses the best-irrigated land: the Jordan Valley. Lot will find difficulty in the land of his choice while God will renew his promise to Abraham in 13:14-18. Lot's choice includes the cities of Sodom and Gomorrah, which God destroys in Gen 19. Lot and his daughters are the only survivors; Abraham witnesses the destruction. Thinking that all human life has been destroyed, the daughters have sex with their father when he is drunk in order to repopulate the earth. Lot's daughters bear their father two sons: Moab and Ben-Ammi, understood to be the ancestors of the Moabites and Ammonites (Gen 19:30-38; see AMMON, AMMONITES; MOAB, MOABITES).

LOTAN One of seven sons of SEIR the Horite (Gen 36:20-29; 1 Chron 1:38), Lotan had two sons, Hori and Heman (Gen 36:22; 1 Chron 1:39). His sister TIMNA is also mentioned in his genealogies (Gen 36:22; 1 Chron 1:39).

LOTS Lots could be used for gambling (Job 6:27; Joel 3:3; Obad 1:11), but were also commonly used in the ANE as a human means for determining the divine will. In Israel, lots were cast to determine guilt (Josh 7:14; 1 Sam 14:42; Jonah 1:7), to apportion land (Num 26:55; Josh 14:2), or to select which animals should be sacrificed (Lev 16:7-10). Various ranks of temple personnel were chosen by lot (1 Chron 24:5; 25:8; 26:13), as were assignments for temple provisions in time of need (Neh 10:34 [Heb. 10:35]; 11:1). The lot could be used to decide contentious disputes in the lack of other evidence (Prov 18:18). Most notably, Israel resorted to the lot in order to choose its first king (1 Sam 10:20-21).

LOZON One of the returning exiles (1 Esdr 5:33). DARKON appears in the lists of Ezra 2:56 and Neh 7:58.

LUCIFER Latin word meaning "light-bearing" and also the name for the planet Venus. See DAY STAR.

LUCIUS 1. A Roman consul mentioned in 1 Macc 15:15-22. The passage quotes his alleged correspondence with King Ptolemy in favor of Simon Maccabeus's fight to secure the high priesthood (see SIMON).

2. A prophet at the church in Antioch named Lucius of Cyrene (Acts 13:1).

3. Paul's companion who sends greetings to the Roman church (Rom 16:21). There is some speculation that Acts and Romans refer to the same Lucius. Further, some argue that this Lucius wrote Luke and Acts, preserving his "travel diary" in the last section of Acts (Acts 16:10).

LUD, LUDIM 1. Lud was a country and/or population group in the ANE. Josephus (*Ant.* 1.144) identifies it with Lydia in west-central Asia Minor, support for which comes from Isa 66:19 where Lud is grouped with three locations that can be placed, with varied degrees of certainty, in Asia Minor: Javan (Ionia), Tarshish (possibly Tarsus), and TUBAL.

2. Ludim is mentioned as the son of EGYPT and grandson of Ham (Gen 10:13; 1 Chron 1:11). Jeremiah 46:9 describes Ludim as fighting, together with ETHIOPIA and PUT (most likely Libya), on the Egyptian side in the battle of CARCHEMISH (605 BCE), and Ezek 30:5 predicts that Nebuchadnezzar will defeat Lud together with Ethiopia ("Cush"), Put, and Arabia.

LUKE, EVANGELIST Luke according to early Christian tradition dating to the late 2nd cent. CE, was the author of the Third Gospel of the canonical NT and its sequel narrative, the Acts of the Apostles, writings that together account for more than a fourth of the NT. The formal literary preface with which the Gospel begins locates the author in the second or third generation of Christians; he mentions previous narrative accounts of the events he records and distinguishes himself from "those who from the beginning were eyewitnesses and servants of the word" and who handed on the tradition "to us" (1:2). Early Christian tradition identified Luke as a coworker of the apostle Paul (Phlm 24; Col 4:14; 2 Tim 4:11). Taking a cue from Col 4:14, centuries of tradition imagined the author to have been a physician. This biographical sketch outruns the evidence, and in any case the elusive personal identity of the author does not aid in the interpretation of the Lukan writings.

LUKE, GOSPEL OF The third Gospel in the NT canon, Luke is the longest NT writing and finds its narrative completion in the book of Acts. Probably composed between 75 and 95 CE for an audience of Gentile (and probably some Jewish) Christians living in an urban center in the Greco-Roman world, Luke accents the salvation that God brings to Israel through the ministry of the prophet and Messiah Jesus. While fulfilling ancient scriptural promise, this salvation also brings provocation, conflict, and surprise, as Jesus' proclamation and enactment of God's reign turn the existing social world and conventional cultural patterns upside down and inside out.

LUZ 1. The site where Jacob dreamed of a ladder going up to heaven. He commemorated the dream by setting up a pillar and renaming the site Bethel (Gen 28:18-19). The description of the Ephraimite border says that "it goes from Bethel to Luz" (Josh 16:2), while the boundary description of Benjamin speaks of "Luz . . . (that is, Bethel)" (Josh 18:13). It may be that Jacob's Bethel was not Luz itself, but a sanctuary in its immediate vicinity whose name eventually transferred to the town.

2. A city built in the land of the Hittites (Judg 1:26) by a man whom the invading house of Joseph spared after he "showed them the way into the city" of Bethel (v. 25).

LXX The standard abbreviation for the SEPTUAGINT.

LYCAONIA Lycaonia was a region of Asia Minor (modern Turkey) with a somewhat fluid boundary at different periods. In the NT, Lycaonia is mentioned only in Acts. It is the region where Paul and Barnabas went after being compelled to leave Iconium (Acts 14:6), and they visited Lystra and Derbe. In Lystra they heard the Lycaonian language (14:11), although they were able to make themselves understood in Greek (14:14-18).

If Paul's letter to the Galatians was written to churches in south GALATIA, it is highly likely that the Lycaonian churches of Lystra and Derbe were among the recipients.

LYCIA Lycia is a craggy, mountainous district on the southwest coast of Asia Minor bounded on the north by Phrygia and Pisidia; on the northeast by Pamphylia; on the northwest by Caria; and on the east, west, and south by the Lycian Sea. The region's earliest inhabitants were akin to the Hittites. Important Lycian ports include MYRA and Patara, both explicitly cited in Acts. Luke echoes a common practice of 1st-cent. CE sea travel: Lycian ports were convenient resting stations for ships carrying travelers and cargo from west Mediterranean ports or from the Aegean Sea to Palestine (Acts 21:1; 27:5-6).

LYDIA, LYDIANS 1. A region in western Asia Minor (modern Turkey), centered in the lower Hermus and Cayster valleys, which is named after its non-Semitic inhabitants (seemingly Indo-European), Iron Age people called the Lydians. At least since the 8th cent. BCE, Lydia's capital was SARDIS (modern Sart), positioned in the center of the Hermus's fertile plain, near the highway leading from the interior to the Aegean coast. The Lydians were the first to mint gold and silver coins (ca. 600 BCE).

2. According to the account in Acts 16:13-40, Lydia was Paul's first convert to the WAY in Europe. A woman from Thyatira, she was a dealer in purple fabric. Her trade and the use of her personal name

(unusual for a Greco-Roman woman) suggest that Lydia enjoyed high social status among free persons and merchants.

LYING Lying is a deceit that typically involves speaking. Such deceit is often represented by lying tongues (Ps 109:2), lying lips (Prov 10:18), or lying words (Isa 59:13). Lying may also come as prophecy, divination, visions (Jer 14:14), dreams (Jer 23:32), and wonders (2 Thess 2:9). In the NT, to deny Christ or to follow him in word but not action is to lie (John 8:55; 1 John 2:4).

Lying is destructive, causing justice to be turned back (Isa 59:13-14), its victims' ruin (Prov 26:28), death (Hos 4:2), and one to be flung into the fires of hell (Rev 21:8). The fruit of lies may last but a moment (Prov 12:19). Lying is against Christian teaching (1 Tim 1:10).

LYSANIAS The tetrarch of Abilene when John the baptizer began his ministry ca. 28–29 CE (Luke 3:1; see TETRARCH, TETRARCHY).

LYSIAS, CLAUDIUS The Roman tribune in Jerusalem (ca. 58 CE) when Paul made his last trip there (Acts 23:26).

LYSTRA Lystra, modern Zoldera near Hatunsaray, lies about 24 mi. south of the modern city of Konya. It was a moderately important market town in the relatively backward region of Lycaonia in south-central Turkey.

Mm

MAACAH Nine individuals, male and female, and one place are identified as "Maacah" in the OT.

1. The son of Nahor (Abraham's brother) by his secondary wife Reumah (Gen 22:24).

2. The secondary wife of Caleb (1 Chron 2:48).

3. The sister or wife of Machir of the tribe of Manasseh (1 Chron 7:15-16). First she is called "sister," then "wife."

4. The wife of the Benjaminite Jeiel, who lived in Gibeon (1 Chron 8:29; 9:35).

5. The father of Shephatiah, the Simeonite official under the Davidic aegis (1 Chron 27:16).

6. The father of Hanan, one of David's mighty men (1 Chron 11:43).

7. The father of Achish king of Gath (1 Kgs 2:39).

8. The daughter of King Talmai of Geshur, wife of David, mother of Absalom (2 Sam 3:3; 1 Chron 3:2).

9. The daughter of Absalom and favored wife of Rehoboam (2 Chron 11:20-21). First Kings 15:2 identifies her as the daughter of Abishalom and mother of Abijah, Rehoboam's short-term heir. First Kings 15:10 presents her as the daughter of Abishalom and the grandmother of Asa, whom 1 Kgs 15:8 identifies as Abijah's son.

10. A region in the north of Israel, situated north and east of the former Lake Huleh and the southeastern foothills of Hermon. The king of Maacah contributed 1,000 warriors to the coalition gathered by Hanun, king of the Ammonites, against David, in preparation for the Ammonite War (2 Sam 10:6-8; 1 Chron 19:6-7).

MAADAI Maadai son of Bani married a foreign woman and was compelled by Ezra to dismiss her (Ezra 10:34).

MAADIAH Listed among the priests who returned with Zerubbabel after the exile in order to rebuild Jerusalem and its temple (Neh 12:5). This person has been identified with MOADIAH (Neh 12:17) and MAAZIAH (Neh 10:8; variant in LXX, Neh 12:5).

MAAI A Judahite musician who participated in the dedication of the Jerusalem wall after it was rebuilt (Neh 12:36).

MAASAI One of the priests who returned to Jerusalem from the Babylonian exile (1 Chron 9:12); corresponds to AMASHSAI in a similar list in Neh 11:13.

MAASEIAH An Israelite personal name similar to Elasah, Asahel (e.g., 2 Sam 2:19-23), and Asaiah (e.g., 1 Chron 4:36; 6:30). There is also a short version of the name: Maasai (1 Chron 9:12); and a corrupted version in 1 Chron 6:40 (Heb. 6:25): "Baaseiah." The name appears in Jeremiah, but particularly in the late historical books Ezra–Nehemiah, and Chronicles, as well as on some seals. It was very popular esp. in the Second Temple period.

1. A levitical gatekeeper (1 Chron 15:18), mentioned among the second order of the Levites.

2. A levitical harp player who took part in the 2nd attempt of King David to transfer the covenant chest from the house of Obed-edom the Getite to Jerusalem (1 Chron 15:20).

3. Son of Adaiahu, one of the five captains who made a covenant with Jehoiada the high priest to replace Athaliah with Joash from Davidic descendants as king of Judah (2 Chron 23:1, add. to 2 Kgs 11:4). The captains' names are not given in the book of Kings or elsewhere in the OT. Thus, the Chronicler filled in this lacuna.

4. An official of Uzziah king of Judah (2 Chron 26:11).

5. The son and/or an official of King Ahaz of Judah, who was murdered by Zichri, "an Ephraimite warrior" (2 Chron 28:7).

6. The commandant of Jerusalem in the time of Josiah king of Judah. He was one of the officials sent by Josiah to reconstruct the temple (2 Chron 34:8; add. to 2 Kgs 22:3).

7. A priest from the family of Joshua the high priest, who is mentioned among those who had foreign wives (Ezra 10:18; 1 Esdr 9:19).

8. A priest, son of Harim, who is mentioned among those who had foreign wives (Ezra 10:21; 1 Esdr 9:21, where he is mentioned as a son of "Immer").

9. A priest, son of Pashhur, who is also pointed out among those who had foreign wives (Ezra 10:22; 1 Esdr 9:22).

10. An Israelite, son of Pahath-moab, who is listed among those who had foreign wives (Ezra 10:30; 1 Esdr 9:31: "Of the family of Addi . . . Moossias").

11. The father of Azariah who assisted in rebuilding Jerusalem's wall (Neh 3:23).

12. One of the men who stood at Ezra's side when he read the Instruction scroll to the people at Rosh Hashanah (Neh 8:4; 1 Esdr 9:43: "Baalsamus").

13. One of the persons who explained to the people the Instruction scroll read by Ezra (Neh 8:7; 1 Esdr 9:48: "Maiannas").

14. One of "the leaders of the people" who put his seal on the covenant of Nehemiah and the returnees (Neh 10:25 [Heb. 10:26]). He may be identical with #10 or #12.

15. The son of Baruch from the tribe of Judah, who resided in Jerusalem in the Second Temple period (Neh 11:5; 1 Chron 9:5: "Asaiah").

16. An ancestor of Sallu, the only Benjaminite who is listed among the residents of Jerusalem in Nehemiah (Neh 11:7; it does not appear in the par. list, 1 Chron 9:7).

17. A priest (possibly identical to one listed in #7–#9) who apparently took part in the inauguration of Nehemiah's Jerusalem wall (Neh 12:41-42).

18. A second priest (possibly identical to one listed in #7–#9) who apparently took part in the inauguration

of Nehemiah's Jerusalem wall (Neh 12:41-42).

19. The father of Zedekiah, whom Jeremiah accused of false prophecy (Jer 29:21).

20. The son of Shalom the gatekeeper (Jer 35:4), and father of Zephaniah, one of the important priests in Jerusalem in the last days of the Judean monarchy (Jer 21:1; 29:25; 37:3).

MAASMAS A leader known for understanding, he went to Iddo requesting that priests return to serve in the temple (1 Esdr 8:43).

MAATH An ancestor of Jesus who appears only in Luke 3:26.

MAAZ A son of Ram and a grandson of Jerahmeel in the list of Judah's descendants (1 Chron 2:27).

MAAZIAH 1. Descendant of Aaron and designated by David as the priest leading the 24th division (1 Chron 24:18).

2. One of the priests who placed his name on the sealed covenant document written by Ezra (Neh 10:8).

MACCABEES, FIRST BOOK OF Following a brief account of the career of Alexander the Great (1:1-9), the bulk of 1 Maccabees concerns a forty-year period of events from the rise of the Seleucid king Antiochus IV Epiphanes in 175 BCE until the death of the Jewish leader Simon in 134 BCE. In 1:16-64, various measures taken by Antiochus against the Jews are related, including the desecration of the Jerusalem Temple; the establishment of a citadel near the Temple garrisoned by Greek soldiers; and the suppression of Jewish religion. In 2:1-70, a Jewish priest named Mattathias instigates an uprising against these measures. In succession, three of Mattathias' five sons lead the Jews in the remainder of the book, together ushering in the Hasmonean Dynasty. Roman Catholic and Orthodox Christians recognize 1 Maccabees as deuterocanonical. The book is noncanonical for Protestants and Jews, though Protestants regard it as part of the Apocrypha and Jews make use of it as an explanation for the origin of Hanukkah.

MACCABEES, FOURTH BOOK OF The title of the work reflects the tendency to group this text with the other books of the "Maccabees" in the major codices of the LXX. It is a misnomer insofar as the author never actually mentions the family of Judas Maccabeus. The other title traditionally assigned to this work, "On the Absolute Power of Reason," better suits its subject matter and emphasis. Fourth Maccabees presents itself as the demonstration of a philosophical thesis, with the result that a person is able consistently to choose the virtuous and honorable path under any circumstances (see 4 Macc 1:1, 7, 15, 30; 2:24; 6:31; 13:1; 16:1; 18:2). The underlying thesis, however, is that strict observance of the Jewish law is the path to self-mastery, and thus the pious Jew best fulfills this ethical ideal. The author wrote 4 Maccabees at some point between the 1st and early 2nd cent. CE.

MACCABEES, MACCABEAN REVOLT The Maccabean Revolt—one of the most significant events in Jewish history—came about in 168–165 BCE or 167–164 BCE because the Seleucid ruler attempted to suppress the practice of the Jewish religion, the temple was polluted, and the temple service stopped. Most of the Jewish community in Palestine refused to accept Antiochus IV's measures and revolted. To the astonishment of the world, the Jews fought off the armies sent against them, retook the temple, and restored the temple service after a period of only three years or so.

When the persecution of Jews began in 168 or 167 BCE, many people fled from Jerusalem into the countryside. Armed resistance allegedly began with the Hasmonean family, initially led by MATTATHIAS. After Mattathias's death the military leadership was taken over by JUDAS Maccabees, along with his brothers. The means of fighting was by guerrilla tactics, at least in the early stages of the revolt.

Judas felt sufficiently encouraged to march on Jerusalem and retake the temple area. The rededication was accomplished on the 25th of Kislev, supposedly an exact three years after it was first polluted. It was a memorable event of Jewish history, still commemorated in Judaism today by HANUKKAH or the FEAST OF DEDICATION. Many Jews were brought back as refugees from Galilee and Transjordan.

MACCABEES, SECOND BOOK OF The book of Second Maccabees describes the revolt of the Jews, under the leadership of Judas Maccabeus, against their overlords, the Seleucid kings. It deals with the period from 175 to 164 BCE. It is called the "second book" of Maccabees because it tells in a different way events recounted in 1 Maccabees. The book itself is a composite work, as it comprises two letters and a condensed version of a much larger account of the revolt. The author, date, and point of origin of the narrative are unknown, with suggestions for date ranging from 142 BCE to the first half of the 1st cent. BCE and for place of composition from Jerusalem to anywhere in the Greek-speaking Jewish diaspora.

MACCABEES, THIRD BOOK OF An apocryphal OT writing, usually dated to around the beginning of the common era, or somewhat earlier. It relates the story of the miraculous deliverance of the Jewish community, annually celebrated in the synagogues of Egypt. Although it does not seem to have exerted much influence on Judaism or Christianity, it is an important witness to the life and thought of Egyptian Jews in the Hellenistic and early Roman periods

MACEDONIA The Roman province of Macedonia lay in the northern part of GREECE and extended beyond the historic kingdom of Macedonia, from the Adriatic eastward to Thrace. To the north lay the provinces of Illyricum and Moesia. Southward it took in the area of Thessaly (and the mountainous range around Olympus). To the southwest of Macedonia was the region of Epirus, and to the south the province of Achaia.

In the NT Paul was invited to "come over to Macedonia" in a dream, while he was at Troas in northwestern Anatolia (Acts 16:9-10). He arrived in the province at Neapolis (the modern Kavala opposite the island of Thasos), the harbor for the main Roman colony of PHILIPPI (Acts 16:11). At Philippi, Paul established a church whose members included Lydia from Thyatira (Acts 16:14). After Paul and Silas had been arrested, beaten, and imprisoned (Acts 16:19-40), the pair headed westward along the line of the Roman road, the Via Egnatia, passing through the cities of Amphipolis and Apollonia (Acts 17:1). They then arrived at the major seaport of Thessalonica, where there was a Jewish community (Acts 17). There was an uproar in response to their preaching in the city. Paul and Silas were sent westward, again along the Via Egnatia, to Beroea (Acts 17:10). Again in response to unrest, Paul was sent off by sea to Athens while Timothy and Silas remained in the city (Acts 17:14).

Timothy and Erastus were sent to Macedonia from the province of Asia (Acts 19:21-22); Paul followed on, traveling through Macedonia and continuing down to Greece (the province of Achaia) (Acts 20:1-3). He then returned via Macedonia accompanied by several Macedonians, Sopater son of Pyrrhus from Beroea, and Aristarchus and Secundus from Thessalonica (Acts 20:3-6). Aristarchus and another Macedonian, Gaius—clearly Roman in origin—accompanied Paul in Ephesus (Acts 19:29). It was perhaps during this

2nd visit to northern Greece that Paul found himself at Illyricum on the Adriatic (Rom 11:19). His departure from Philippi may perhaps be dated to the Passover of 57 CE.

Two major churches were established in Macedonia: at Philippi and Thessalonica. They were the recipients of three NT Epistles.

MACHAERUS The site of mountain fortresses built by Alexander Jannaeus and Herod the Great southwest of Madaba in modern Jordan. Josephus identifies Machaerus as the site at which Herod Antipas incarcerated and executed John the Baptist (*Ant.* 18.116–119).

MACHBANNAI Listed as the 11th warrior from the tribe of Gad who joined with David while he was at Ziklag (1 Chron 12:13 [Heb. 12:14]). David later made Machbannai and the other warriors officers over his troops (1 Chron 12:18).

MACHBENAH Son of SHEVA and member of the tribe of Judah (1 Chron 2:49), descended from Caleb son of Hezron and his secondary wife MAACAH.

MACHI The Gadite father of the spy Geuel in the list of tribal representatives sent from Kadesh to reconnoiter the land of Canaan (Num 13:15).

MACHIR 1. The eldest son of Manasseh, grandson of Joseph (Gen 50:23) and brother of Asriel. His mother was an Aramean secondary wife. He married Maacah, who gave birth to Peresh and Sheresh (1 Chron 7:16). He also had a daughter (1 Chron 2:21). Machir is noted as the father of Gilead (Num 26:29; Josh 17:1; 1 Chron 2:21; 7:14). He was a warfare expert (Josh 17:1) and the head of the Machirite clan (Num 26:29). The Machirites captured Gilead, an area east of the Jordan River, and settled it in the time of Moses (Num 32:39-42). The text further mentions that Jair settled Bashan. However, Joshua allotted Gilead and Bashan to Machir (Josh 17:1-2). An inconsistency exists as to their relationship. Numbers 32:41 lists Jair as a brother, thus a separate clan, while 1 Chron 2:21-22 lists him as a grandson, thus a family within the Machirites.

2. The son of Ammiel of Lo-debar. He harbored MEPHIBOSHETH son of Jonathan from regicide after the death of Saul (2 Sam 9:4-5). Later, Machir, Shobi, and Barzillai brought food and supplies to David at Mahanaim when David fled during Absalom's usurpation (2 Sam 17:27).

MACHNADEBAI Descendant of Binnui who dismissed his foreign wife and their children as Ezra commanded (Ezra 10:40).

MACHPELAH The burial site of Sarah (Gen 23), which the Bible refers to as the "cave in Machpelah" (Gen 23:9) and "the field of Ephron" (Gen 23:17). Comprising a field with a cave and trees, Machpelah was the burial plot for Abraham's family including Abraham (Gen 25:9-11), Isaac (Gen 35:29; 49:31), Rebekah, Leah, and Jacob (Gen 50:13).

MADAI One of Japheth's sons (Gen 10:2; 1 Chron 1:5). As is known from Assyrian monuments, the name means "middle land" or "Medes." See MEDES, MEDIA.

MADMANNAH 1. A city in southwestern Judah (Josh 15:31).

2. Grandson of Maacah and Caleb. First Chronicles 2:49 states that Maacah, Caleb's secondary wife, "gave birth to Shaaph, Madmannah's father."

MADNESS References to madness include Deut 28:28; 1 Sam 21:13; Eccl 1:17; 2:12; Jer 29:26; Jer 51:7; Hos 9:7; Zech 12:4; John 10:20; and 2 Pet 2:16.

Saul experienced what appear to be manic and depressive episodes, which were attributed to an evil spirit from the Lord (1 Sam 16:14, 23; 18:10; 19:9). An ecstatic frenzy left him raving and naked while among a band of prophets (1 Sam 19:24).

The boastful Babylonian king Nebuchadnezzar also experienced a period of madness at the hand of God before learning his lesson when his "reason returned" (Dan 4:29-37). David reportedly feigned madness to escape the Philistines (1 Sam 21:13-15). His open-mouthed drooling and scrabbling at the gate caricatured behavior expected of an ancient madman.

In the NT, mental illness is uniformly characterized as possession by demons, who could be cast out (Mark 7:26-30; Luke 4:33-35; 8:27-35; 9:42). The relation of the two is evident in John 10:20, where Jesus is accused of having a demon and having "lost his mind."

MAGADAN Magadan is the name given in Matt 15:39 to regions near the shore of the Sea of Galilee where Jesus goes after feeding the 4,000.

MAGBISH Perhaps an unidentified town in Benjamin, but may also refer to a man (and thus family) whose 156 children (sons) returned from exile (Ezra 2:30).

MAGDALA Mary "Magdalene" is understood by most scholars to mean "Mary from Magdala."

MAGDALENE See MAGDALA; MARY.

MAGDIEL A descendant of Esau and one of the chiefs of Edom (Gen 36:43; 1 Chron 1:54), perhaps also an Edomite tribe.

MAGI Persian priests who espoused Zoroastrian traditions and theology. Their ideology embraced universalism, a supreme deity (Ahura Mazda) opposed by an evil cosmic entity, concern for purity rules, angelology, a final savior who would come to establish a kingdom of righteousness, and belief in the afterlife. All these features (aside from universalism) were adopted and adapted by the Israelite Pharisees (from Persian *Parsee* meaning "party") that were part of the Persian colonial foundation of Jerusalem in Judea (see PHARISEES). The Zoroastrian fire-priests were significant in the administrative center of Babylon (Chaldea) and moved westward with the Persian armies in the 6th cent. BCE. By the Hellenistic period they could be found in a number of sites in Asia (Cappadocia, Phrygia, Pontus, Commagene, Lydia) as well as in Egypt, Parthia, and Medea.

The magi as wise men or traditional Persian fire-priests appear in the NT in Matthew's story of events attending Jesus' birth (Matt 2:1-12). Magi who expected a savior who would inaugurate God's kingdom came from the east following a celestial portent, a moving star or comet. They sought out a new king in the land over which the comet stopped. A comet commonly meant political upheaval, so Herod and Jerusalem were rightly perturbed about the moving star over their land. The magi eventually found the star over Bethlehem (see MATTHEW; STAR OF BETHLEHEM).

The magi as magicians are found in two passages in the book of Acts. First there is the incident of the Samaritan magician SIMON (Acts 8:9-24). He accepted the gospel when he heard the deacon Philip's proclamation, was duly baptized, and was amazed at the wonders wrought by Philip. Then Peter and John came to Samaria to lay on hands and give the Spirit. After experiencing the effects of the Spirit's presence, Simon wished to buy from Peter the ability to impart the Spirit of God, an ability that would be a fine thing to add to his magical repertory.

Second there is the Israelite magician Bar-Jesus, whom Paul, Barnabas, and John Mark met at Paphos on Cyprus (Acts 13:4-12). Bar-Jesus ("son of Jesus"), also known as ELYMAS, proved no match for Saul (also known as Paul), who cursed him as son of the devil and left him blinded for a time (see JESUS, BAR-).

MAGIC, MAGICIAN Magic, for an ancient observer, involved the invocation of spiritual forces for illegitimate or antisocial purposes. The practice of magic was thus regarded as subversive. A MIRACLE, in contrast, was the legitimate invocation of divine forces by those invested with the proper authority and for socially constructive ends. The difference between magic and miracle, therefore, amounted largely to a sociopolitical distinction. When a group or individual performed supernatural acts, the status of the deed would be determined by the social standing of the performer. If the person in question operated outside official channels of authority, they were regarded as a magician. Hence, much of what constituted early Christian miracle, such as the feats described in the NT, constituted magic to those in authority at the time.

The Bible designates magic as demonic rather than divine, in contrast to a miracle. The word *magician* (singular and plural) appears nineteen times in the NRSV. It appears repeatedly in Genesis (41:8, 24) and Exodus (7:11, 22; 8:7, 18, 19; 9:11) to describe the wise men and diviners in the court of Pharaoh. The word *magician* appears again in the book of Daniel (1:20; 2:2, 10, 27; 4:7, 9; 5:11), where it similarly describes a diviner or wise man in the royal court of Persia. In Acts, *magic* appears twice to describe the activities of a man named SIMON. He appears to have been some kind of miracle worker, similar to the apostles, who had attracted a large crowd of followers in Samaria who proclaimed him to be "the power of God called Great" (Acts 8:10).

One of the charges against Jesus, in addition to treason, seems to have been magic. Various statements in the NT suggest that opponents of Jesus identified the source of his power as demons rather than God, insinuating that he practiced magic (Matt 9:34; 12:24; Mark 3:22; Luke 11:15; John 8:49, 52; 10:20).

MAGISTRATE Magistrates were key figures in the administration of cities in the Greco-Roman world. Generally, magistrates were unpaid—and thus tended to be from the elites. Typically, they were over 30 years old, were freeborn citizens, were without criminal convictions, and had not worked in dishonorable occupations. In Greek cities, magistrates typically were elected for one year by an assembly of adult male citizens.

MAGNIFICAT Latin for "magnifies." Magnificat is the traditional title for Mary's hymn in Luke 1:46-55. Elizabeth declares Mary to be blessed as the mother of the Messiah, and Mary responds with a joyful hymn of praise that acknowledges this special blessing but also detects a broader saving purpose behind God's exaltation of a lowly woman.

MAGOG Land from which Gog comes to make war on God's people (Ezek 38–39). Although it appears in the Table of Nations (Gen 10:2), in Ezekiel's use Magog is not an actual nation but symbolizes the archetypal northern enemy. Magog's armies come to make war on Israel and are defeated by God. Revelation draws on Ezekiel's imagery in portraying scenes of eschatological judgment. Gog and Magog appear metaphorically as opponents of God, the "nations that are at the four corners of the earth" (Rev 20:8). The narration of their destruction by fire echoes Ezek 38:22, as does the battle scene of Rev 19:11-21 (esp. Rev 19:17-18, 21; cf Ezek 39:4, 17-20). Magog also appears in eschatological battle scenes in rabbinic writings.

MAGPIASH One among the group of officials, Levites, and priests who signed the covenant of Ezra (Neh 10:20).

MAGUS, SIMON See SIMON.

MAHALAB A town (modern Khirbet el-Makhalib) in Asher's allotment (Josh 19:29) and most likely the AHLAB or Helbah of Judg 1:31. SENNACHERIB seized Mahalab from the king of Sidon in 701 BCE, the same year he besieged Jerusalem.

MAHALALEL 1. A descendant of SETH and son of KENAN, born to him when he was 7 years old (Gen 5:12-17; 1 Chron 1:2).

2. A descendant of PEREZ, a Judahite who settled in Jerusalem after the exile at the time of Nehemiah (Neh 11:4).

MAHALATH 1. Daughter of Ishmael and one of the wives of Esau (Gen 28:9).

2. Daughter of JERIMOTH, one of David's sons. This Mahalath was one of the wives of REHOBOAM (2 Chron 11:18).

3. A musical direction (Ps 53 title).

MAHANAIM A city in Gilead in the Transjordan identified with the site of Tel edh-Dhahab el-Gharbi, it lies on the north side of the JABBOK RIVER, east of SUCCOTH and north of PENUEL. Jacob encountered God's messengers (Gen 32:1-2) and declared, "This is God's camp," hence Mahanaim ("the two camps"). Genesis 32:7-8 provides a second etiology for Mahanaim when Jacob divided his family into "two camps" in preparation for meeting Esau.

Mahanaim was the southern boundary of the territory of Manasseh (Josh 13:30), although it is also listed as part of the tribal allotment of Gad (Josh 13:26). It was given to the Merarites as a levitical city (Josh 21:38; 1 Chron 6:80). Mahanaim served as the capital for the illegal government set up by ABNER under Ishbaal after the death of Saul (2 Sam 2:8). David likewise took refuge in Mahanaim when he fled from Jerusalem during ABSALOM's revolt (2 Sam 17:27-29). It also served as the capital of one of Solomon's administrative districts (1 Kgs 4:14).

MAHANEH-DAN Between Zorah and Eshtaol and west of Kiriath-jearim, it is where 600 Danites camped as they migrated north (Judg 18:12) and also where "the Lord's spirit began to move" (Judg 13:25) (see SAMSON).

MAHARAI Maharai the man from Netophah, of the tribe Judah, was one of "the Thirty," David's mighty warriors (2 Sam 23:28; 1 Chron 11:30; 27:13). He had 24,000 in his company and was on duty in the 10th month.

MAHATH Elkanah's father and Amasai's son from the Kohathite clan within the Levite tribe. One of the priests who cleansed the temple at Hezekiah's command (1 Chron 6:35; 2 Chron 29:12, 15). He assisted Conaniah and Shimei with the temple offerings (2 Chron 31:13).

MAHAVITE, THE An epithet for Eliel, one of David's mighty men (1 Chron 11:46).

MAHAZIOTH One of the sons of HEMAN upon whom the 23rd lot fell when assigning shifts for prophecy accompanied by musical instruments during David's reign (1 Chron 25:4, 30). See GIDDALTI.

MAHER-SHALAL-HASH-BAZ Meaning "spoil hastens, plunder hurries." The Lord instructed Isaiah to give this name to his 3rd son (8:1-3) as an object lesson for King Ahaz of Judah, who was tempted to turn to Assyria for help following the invasion of Judah by Syria and Israel. The name demonstrated the brevity of the threat: Before the child was even able to say "mama" or "daddy," Assyria will have already defeated Damascus and Samaria (Isa 8:4).

MAHLAH 1. One of the five daughters of Zelophehad (Num 26:33; Josh 17:3).

Zelophehad died in the wilderness leaving no male heirs, and his daughters appealed to Moses for inheritance rights (Num 27:3-4). The Lord sided with the daughters' request (Num 27:5-12; 36:11).

2. A descendant of Manasseh (1 Chron 7:18).

MAHLI The name of two different Levites.

1. Mahli and his brother MUSHI were sons of Merari (Exod 6:19; Num 3:20), grandsons of Levi, and heads of the two divisions of Merarites (Num 3:33). Ezra 8:18 refers to Mahli as the son of Levi, but it is not uncommon for an informal list of parentage to omit a generation.

2. A grandson of Merari through Mushi (1 Chron 6:47).

MAHLON Means "sick," or "sickly." The first husband of Ruth, the eldest son of ELIMELECH and NAOMI. He married her in Moab and died there, leaving Ruth childless (Ruth 1:2, 5; 4:9-10). Elimelech and his sons were ancestors of David (1 Sam 17:12).

MAHOL First Kings 4:31 compares Solomon with "Mahol's sons," judging Solomon wisest.

MAHSEIAH Grandfather of Baruch (Jer 32:12; Bar 1:1) and Seraiah (Jer 51:59).

MAKKEDAH Makkedah is the headquarters of Joshua in the story of the defeat of the five Amorite kings who attacked the Israelite ally Gibeon (Josh 10). Although the location is unknown, Makkedah is mentioned as being near Libnah, Beth-horon, and Azekah (Josh 10:11, 29; 12:16; 15:41).

MALACHI, BOOK OF Means "the messenger or angel of Yahweh." The last book in the Minor Prophets of the Christian OT, Malachi is the third of three additions to Zech 1–8 introduced by similar headings that begin with the same three words: "Oracle the word of Yahweh." The date of the book of Malachi is debated, with most suggestions ranging anywhere from shortly after the restoration of the Temple (520–515 BCE) to the end of the 5th cent. Most scholars think that Malachi appeared during the time of Ezra and Nehemiah (i.e., mid-5th cent.) and addressed many of the problems discussed in the books bearing those men's names.

MALCAM A Benjaminite born in Moab, the 4th of seven sons of Shaharaim by wife Hodesh, after he sent away his earlier wives Hushim and Baara (1 Chron 8:9).

MALCHIEL Means "appointed by God." The son of Beriah, father of Birzaith, and eponymous ancestor of the Malchielites tribe (Gen 46:17; Num 26:45; 1 Chron 7:31).

MALCHIJAH The name of a variety of individuals. The Hebrew name is sometimes translated "Malchiah."

1. A descendant of Gershom and ancestor of Asaph (1 Chron 6:40).

2. The father of Pashhur, a priest (1 Chron 9:12; Neh 11:12) This family is possibly connected to #3.

3. The head of the 5th division of priests in Jerusalem (1 Chron 24:9).

4. A man who divorced his foreign wife according to Ezra's command (Ezra 10:25; 1 Esdr 9:26).

5. A descendant of Harim who divorced his foreign wife (Ezra 10:31).

6. A man who assisted in rebuilding the Tower of the Ovens under Nehemiah (Neh 3:11).

7. A man who helped repair the Dung Gate (Neh 3:14).

8. A goldsmith during the time of Nehemiah (Neh 3:31).

9. One who stood by Ezra during the reading of the Instruction scroll (Neh 8:4; 1 Esdr 9:44).

10. One who signed Nehemiah's covenant (Neh 10:3 [Heb. 10:4]).

11. A priest who participated in the dedication of the rebuilt wall (Neh 12:42).

MALCHIRAM Son of JECONIAH (1 Chron 3:18).

MALCHISHUA One of the four sons of Saul (1 Sam 14:49; 1 Chron 8:33), Malchishua is killed in a battle with the Philistines, along with Saul's other sons ABINADAB and JONATHAN (1 Sam 31:2; 1 Chron 10:2).

MALCHUS At Jesus' arrest, one of those with Jesus cuts off the ear of the high priest's slave (Matt 26:51; Mark 14:47; Luke 22:50; John 18:10). Only John identifies this slave as Malchus and the disciple as Peter. John also identifies one of Peter's later accusers as a relative of this slave (18:26).

MALLOTHI One of the sons of HEMAN whom David and his military officers consecrated for the liturgical function of prophesying to the accompaniment of musical instruments (1 Chron 25:4). The 19th lot fell upon him in assigning shifts for this service (1 Chron 25:26). See GIDDALTI.

MALLUCH 1. Great-grandfather of Ethan, appointed by David to sing before the meeting tent and later in Solomon's temple (1 Chron 6:44 [Heb. 6:29]).

2. Son of Bani; sent away his foreign wife at Ezra's behest (Ezra 10:29).

3. Son of Harim; sent away his foreign wife (Ezra 10:32).

4. Among the priests, Levites, and officials who signed Ezra's covenant (Neh 10:4); came with Zerubbabel from exile (Neh 12:2).

5. One of the "leaders of the people" who signed Ezra's covenant (Neh 10:27).

MALTA Malta is an island whose proximity to the narrowest point of the Mediterranean Sea has always given it a significance out of proportion to its size. It is 18 mi. (29 km) by 8 mi. (13 km) and lies 60 mi. (96 km) south of Sicily and 190 mi. (300 km) east of Tunisia. The fact that the storm in Acts 27 ends with shipwreck on Malta is no surprise, archaeologically.

MAMMON An Aramaic term of uncertain etymology denoting money, property, or wealth of some sort.

MAMRE 1. Mamre is an Amorite who, along with Eshcol and Aner, joins Abraham to fight a coalition of kings led by Chedorlaomer (Gen 14:13, 24).

2. *Mamre* appears in the composite name "the oaks (or terebinths) of Mamre," the site of Abraham's encampment (Gen 14:13; 18:1). It was near to or identical with Hebron (Gen 13:18; 23:19; 35:27), and lay just west of Machpelah, the burial site Abraham acquired from Ephron the Hittite (Gen 23:1-20; 49:30; 50:13).

MAN, SON OF See HUMAN ONE.

MANAEN Mentioned only in Acts 13:1 in early Christian literature, Manaen is one of the teachers or prophets in Antioch who sends out Barnabas and Paul on a missionary journey.

MANAHATH, MANAHATHITES 1. Ancestor of a Horite clan, son of SHOBAL and grandson of SEIR (Gen 36:23; 1 Chron 1:40).

2. According to 1 Chron 2:54, "half of the Manahathites" traced their origin to Salma, a descendant of PEREZ.

3. A locality to which a Benjaminite group (see BENJAMIN, BENJAMINITES) was exiled by another Benjaminite, Gera (1 Chron 8:6).

MANASSEH, MANASSITES 1. Eponymous ancestor of the Israelite tribe by the same name, son of Joseph and ASENATH (Gen 41:50-51; 46:20; Num 26:28) (see JOSEPH, JOSEPHITES). According to Gen 48, on his deathbed Jacob symbolically adopted Manasseh and his brother Ephraim (vv. 1-12; see

EPHRAIM, EPHRAIMITES), assigning them equal status with his sons (v. 5)—and, accordingly, allotted Joseph an extra portion of his estate (v. 22).

2. The tribe of Manasseh traced its ancestry to the oldest son of Joseph. The tribe is first mentioned in Numbers, where it is headed by Gamaliel son of Pedahzur (1:10; 2:20; 7:54-58; 10:23). Manasseh was the only tribe that had possessions on both sides of the Jordan.

3. A Judahite Israelite descendant of Pahat-moab (Ezra 10:30) whose marriage to a foreign woman was revealed by an investigation launched at the behest of Ezra.

4. A descendant of Hashum (Ezra 10:33) who sent away his foreign wife and their children.

5. Deceased husband of JUDITH. The account of his death of sunstroke or heat exhaustion while overseeing barley harvest (Jdt 8:2-3) bears certain resemblance to the beginning of the story of the Shunammite woman's son resurrected by Elisha (2 Kgs 4:18-20) and may have been influenced by it.

6. According to the scribal correction in Judg 18:30, an ancestor of JONATHAN, founder of the priestly dynasty that officiated at the sanctuary of Dan until the exile of 721 BCE.

7. Manasseh son of Hezekiah became king of Judah at the age of 12 and reigned for fifty-five years (697–642 BCE), longer than any other king in the history of ancient Israel. What is undisputed is the portrayal of Manasseh as one of the most evil kings in the Bible, guilty of various acts of injustice and apostasy (2 Kgs 21:1-18; 2 Chron 33:1-9). In particular, he reintroduced "the detestable practices of the nations" (2 Kgs 21:2) that his father Hezekiah had purged, including necromancy, consulting with mediums and wizards, and even human sacrifice (2 Kgs 21:6). He provoked God's anger as no other king had done.

MANASSEH, PRAYER OF A pseudonymous text that purports to be the prayer that King Manasseh prayed while imprisoned in Babylon by the king of Assyria (2 Chron 33:12-13).

MANDRAKE *Mandragora officinarum* (syn. *M. autumnalis*) is a perennial wild herbaceous plant with a forked taproot (resembling a human torso) surmounted by a rosette of leaves ca. 30 cm long, reminiscent of sugar beet or chard leaves. When Leah's son found mandrake fruits in a field, Rachel pleaded for them because she was barren (Gen 30:14-16), reflecting an ancient tradition that mandrake is an aphrodisiac.

MANEH See WEIGHTS AND MEASURES.

MANNA Manna is the bread that God made "rain down from the sky" (Exod 16:4) for Israel during their journey through the wilderness on the way to the land of promise. The name manna (Exod 16:31) echoes Israel's question: "What is it?" (Exod 16:15). According to v. 23, the manna could be baked or boiled to form bread that "tasted like honey wafers" (v. 31). Compare the alternative view in Num 11:8 that the manna tasted like "cakes baked in olive oil"). Moses, acting as interpreter, explained to the people that this white, fine substance that looked like coriander seed (Exod 16:14, 31) and that came every morning with the dew was the gracious gift of food that God has provided (v. 15).

Several stories in the NT build on the tradition of God's provision of manna to Israel in the wilderness. Scholars have shown connections between Exod 16 and the Gospel accounts of Jesus providing food to the crowds of followers (Matt 14:15-21; Mark 6:35-44; Luke 9:10-17). Particularly, in John 6:22-59 we find an in-depth exposition of the manna story when Jesus makes a connection between himself and the bread from heaven. Not only does Jesus provide the life-giving bread that comes from God, Jesus identifies himself as "the bread of life" (v. 35).

MANOAH The father of SAMSON (Judg 13).

MAOCH Fleeing Saul, David and his army stayed with "ACHISH, Maoch's son and GATH's king" (1 Sam 27:2). In 1 Kgs 2:39 Achish is "MAACAH's son."

MAON 1. A descendant of Caleb, Maon was a son of Shammai and the father of BETH-ZUR (1 Chron 2:45) and may have founded the town that bears his name.

2. A town allotted to the tribe of Judah (Josh 15:55), located about 7 mi. south of Hebron. David sought refuge in the "the Maon wilderness" when Saul was trying to kill him (1 Sam 23:24-25). The most famous inhabitant of Maon was NABAL (1 Sam 25:2).

MARA Means "bitter." Mara is the name NAOMI chooses for herself following the loss of her husband and sons (Ruth 1:19-21).

MARAH During the exodus, after passing through the Reed Sea and traveling three days in the wilderness of Shur, the Israelites arrived at Marah (Exod 15:22-23). This story provides the etiology for the name "bitter," stating that the Israelites could not drink the water because it was bitter. God provided a solution, making the water drinkable by having Moses throw a tree into it.

MARANATHA The Greek transliteration of the Aramaic expression "Come, Lord!" or "Our Lord has come." Paul used the term in his closing words to the Corinthian congregation (1 Cor 16:22) to emphasize his eschatological belief and to encourage them that Jesus would be returning within their lifetimes.

MARBLE Marble is limestone that has been recrystallized by geologic pressure over time. Marble is available in a variety of styles and colors, but "pure" marble is considered white. Marble is the luxury building material listed among precious metals and gemstones for the building of the temple (1 Chron 29:2). Marble is also used as one of the luxury building materials for pillars and a mosaic floor of precious stones in the Persian king's palace (Esth 1:6). In the lament over fallen Babylon and her extravagant living, it is listed among merchant cargoes (Rev 18:12). The Hebrew name may be an Assyrian loan word. White marble is similar to alabaster in appearance and translucency, so the latter term is used in many English translations for this Hebrew word (e.g., Song 5:15).

MARESHAH 1. Father of Hebron in the family of Caleb in the lineage of Judah (1 Chron 2:44).

2. A member of the clan of Shelah in the lineage of Judah (1 Chron 4:21).

3. A city, located in the Judean southern plain 35 km east of ASHKELON and 40 km southwest of Jerusalem. Mareshah (Marisa) was one of Rehoboam's fortified cities (2 Chron 11:7-9) and was listed among the cities of Judah (Josh 15:44; Mic 1:13-15); it was populated by the families of the sons of Shela (1 Chron 4:21) and the Calebites (1 Chron 2:42; see 1 and 2 above).

MARK In contrast to the common practice of body markings in the ANE, the Israelites were prohibited from making marks (tattoos) or cuttings on their bodies (Lev 19:28). Cain receives a protective mark from God (Gen 4:15), likely reflecting body markings of the Kenites, as do those persons receiving a mark on their foreheads in Ezekiel's vision (Ezek 9:4, 6; cf Exod 12:13). Drawing on this tradition, John envisions an angel marking the servants of God on their foreheads with a seal (Rev 7:3; 9:4; 14:1), whereas the people destined for destruction receive "the beast's mark" (Rev 13:16-17; 14:9-11; 16:2; 19:20; 20:4). Paul calls his scars from beatings "marks of Jesus" (Gal 6:17).

MARK, GOSPEL OF The second

Gospel in the NT canon, likely the first Gospel written, is the shortest and, in many ways, the simplest of the canonical Gospels. It presents a unique, hopeful, and unsettling story of Jesus' announcement that the kingdom of God has drawn near. Tradition has named John Mark, who was a colleague of Paul, Barnabas (Acts 13:5; 15:37-39), and Peter and was the son of a Jerusalem woman named Mary who may have been a house church leader (Acts 12:12), as the author of the Second Gospel. The Gospel makes no such claim, and John Mark's authorship has been impossible to verify. Scholarly consensus dates the composition of the Gospel between 65–70 CE.

MARRIAGE In the NT, marriage represents the cornerstone of the household. Closely related to concepts of kinship and family, marriage has important social, economic, and spiritual dimensions. Men interact publicly with each other as married heads of households. The husband's authority over his wife is closely tied to ownership of property. He has exclusive sexual access to his wife; children born in the household belong to him. As in the OT, metaphorical references to marriage in the NT explore the nature of the community's relationship with God. In the NT, however, human marriage is also at times forsaken as a sign of the dawning of God's kingdom.

MARS HILL A rocky height of 377 ft. in Athens located northwest of the Acropolis and south of the Agora. A council met there. See Acts 17:19, 22.

MARSENA One of the seven officials of Persia and Media advising King Ahasuerus who were consulted regarding Queen Vashti's disobedient actions (Esth 1:14).

MARTHA According to Luke, the sister of Mary (10:38-42); according to John, the sister of Mary and Lazarus (11:1–12:11). The 4th Gospel associates the siblings with Bethany and describes them as persons whom Jesus loved (John 11:5). Whereas both Gospels mention Martha's work, Luke's portrayal of the sisters is often read as an affirmation of Mary, who prioritizes learning at the feet of Jesus, and as a rebuke of Martha, who "was preoccupied with getting everything ready for their meal" (10:39-40). In contrast to Luke, John attributes to Martha an extensive dialogue with Jesus that sets the stage for Jesus to reveal his identity and Martha to articulate a confession of faith (11:27).

MARTYR A martyr is someone who gives witness to the strength of his or her convictions by dying rather than recanting religious or political beliefs. A martyr's death often is the end result of harassment and torture. *Martyr* derives from the Greek word for "witness" or "testimony." Those who die for their beliefs inspire others to loyalty and faithfulness under harassment and threat of death.

In the OT the martyrdom of the righteous is evident as far back as Abel (Gen 4:8), whose death is noted by Jesus as the 1st martyrdom (Matt 23:34-36). According to the Jewish canon, the last martyr was Zechariah (2 Chron 24:20-22; cf Matt 23:34-36; Luke 11:49-51). Martyrdom is a major theme of literature from the time of the MACCABEAN REVOLT.

In the NT the most notable martyrdom was that of Jesus, whose resurrection became a symbol of God's vindication of his righteousness and a promise of reward to those who remained faithful to his message. Stephen was stoned to death (Acts 7:54-60), and Herod Agrippa I executed James the brother of the apostle John (Acts 12:2). Most scholars believe that the apostle Paul was martyred in Rome sometime after he wrote the book of Romans. In Revelation, Antipas is cited as a martyr for his faith (2:13). Later stories of Christian martyrs, including some of Jesus' apostles and women such as Felicity and Perpetua, were popular reading among early Christians.

MARY The name Mary, derived from the Hebrew *Miriam*, is the name of several NT women.

1. Mary the mother of Jesus.

2. Mary Magdalene is one of the most well-known disciples of Jesus, and she appears in all four canonical Gospels. The name by which she is known indicates her association with MAGDALA, most likely the city by that name located on the northwestern shore of the Sea of Galilee.

3. Mary of Bethany was the sister of MARTHA (Luke 10:38-42; John 11:1-37; 12:1-3) and of LAZARUS (John 11:1-3, 19, 32) who lived in BETHANY.

4. Mary mother of James and Joseph/Joses was a witness to the empty tomb and the angelic announcement of Jesus' resurrection according to the synoptic tradition (Matt 28:1-10; Mark 16:1-8; Luke 24:1-10).

5. Mary the mother of John Mark was a member of the Jesus movement, most likely a widow, in whose home the community of faith regularly gathered for meetings and prayer (Acts 12:12-16). Mary "was John's mother; he was also known as Mark" (Acts 12:12).

6. Mary the wife of Clopas was a follower, perhaps kin, of Jesus (John 19:25).

MASH Aram's 4th son and Shem's grandson in the Table of Nations (Gen 10:23).

MASHAL A city along with its pasturelands that was allocated out of the Asherite tribe's properties to support the levitical clans (1 Chron 6:74).

MASIAH Servant of Solomon whose postexilic descendants returned to Jerusalem (1 Esdr 5:34).

MASKIL 1. A term found in the titles of thirteen psalms of varied genre (32; 42; 44–45; 52–55; 74; 78; 88; 89; 142; cf Ps 14).

2. A name for the elect group of the wise in Daniel (12:3), or for a leader or instructor in the Dead Sea Scrolls (1QS III, 13).

MASON Masons are craftsmen, specifically stoneworkers who build walls and structures, often listed among other kinds of builders (e.g., carpenters, stonecutters) in the OT. Masons are mentioned as building a palace for David (2 Sam 5:11; 1 Chron 14:1), building the temple (1 Chron 22:15), repairing the temple at the time of Joash [Jehoash] (2 Kgs 12:12; 2 Chron 24:12) and Josiah (2 Kgs 22:6), and rebuilding the temple in Zerubbabel's time (Ezra 3:7). Since the palace and temple were both royal building projects, masons were among the most skilled of stoneworkers.

MASREKAH The region or city of origin of SAMLAH, the 5th ruler of Edom in the list of nondynastic Edomite "kings" (Gen 36:31-39; 1 Chron 1:43-51).

MASSA Massa is listed in the genealogies of Gen 25:14 and 1 Chron 1:30 as the 7th son of Ishmael.

MASSAH One of the names given to REPHIDIM after the Israelites stayed there during their exodus from Egypt (Exod 17:1-7). The people complain to Moses because they find no water to drink.

MASSEBAH The Hebrew term for sacred stones or stone pillars found at sites of notable importance, esp. cultic activity (e.g., Gen 28:18; Deut 16:22).

MATRED In the Edomite king list, Matred was either the mother or father of Mehetabel (Gen 36:39), the wife of King Hadar ("Hadad" in 1 Chron 1:50).

MATRIARCHS In biblical studies, the

term *matriarch* usually refers to Sarah, Rebekah, and Rachel and Leah, the wives of Abraham, Isaac, and Jacob, respectively. Some scholars use the word to indicate other important biblical women who are mothers of famous men.

MATRITES A family of the tribe of Benjamin to which Saul, the first king of Israel, belonged (1 Sam 10:21).

MATTAN 1. The only named priest of Baal killed as a result of the covenant between the priest JEHOIADA, the Lord, the people, and King JOASH in the purge after ATHALIAH was overthrown in Judah (2 Kgs 11:18; 2 Chron 23:17).

2. Father of Shephatiah, one of four named witnesses to Jeremiah's unwelcome prophecies that Jerusalem was about to fall to Babylon (Jer 38:1).

MATTANIAH 1. Appointed king after the exile of Jehoiachin (597 BCE) and renamed Zedekiah (2 Kgs 24:17).

2. A Levite, son of Mica son of Zichri, who was among the first to return to Judah after the exile (1 Chron 9:15).

3. A Levite, son of Heman, a musician appointed by King David (1 Chron 25:4, 16).

4. A Levite, ancestor of the prophet JAHAZIEL who prophesied success for King Jehoshaphat (2 Chron 20:14).

5. A Levite, son of Asaph, who participated in the cleansing of the temple under King Hezekiah (2 Chron 29:13).

6. The son of Elam and a non-Levite forced to divorce his non-Israelite wife (Ezra 10:26; 1 Esdr 9:27).

7. A non-Levite who divorced his non-Israelite wife (Ezra 10:27).

8. A son of Pahath-moab who divorced his non-Israelite wife (Ezra 10:30).

9. A returnee who divorced his non-Israelite wife (Ezra 10:37).

10. A Levite, son of Mica son of Zabdi, a worship leader in the early postexilic period (Neh 11:17; 12:8).

11. A Levite, great-grandfather of the overseer Uzzi (Neh 11:22).

12. A Levite, a storehouse gatekeeper under Nehemiah (Neh 12:25).

13. Great-grandfather of a musician at Nehemiah's dedication of the wall (Neh 12:35).

14. Grandfather of the assistant treasurer appointed by Nehemiah (Neh 13:13). See MATTAN.

MATTATHA Mattatha appears only in Luke's genealogy of Jesus (Luke 3:31) as the son of Nathan and grandson of David.

MATTATHIAH One of thirteen men standing on the wooden platform with Ezra as he read the Law scroll (1 Esdr 9:43).

MATTATHIAS 1. In 1 Macc 2, Mattathias is the head of a priestly family who begins the Maccabean Revolt (see MACCABEES, MACCABEAN REVOLT).

2. A representative of Nicanor sent to Judas (2 Macc 14:18-19). Mattathias and this incident are not mentioned in 1 Macc.

3. One of Jesus' ancestors through the line of Joseph according to Luke's genealogy (3:25-26).

MATTATTAH The second of the sons of HASHUM listed among those who, after the exile, pledged to send away their foreign wives (Ezra 10:33; 1 Esdr 9:33).

MATTENAI 1. Descendant of HASHUM who sent away his foreign wife and their children according to Ezra's instructions about maintaining God's covenant (Ezra 10:33; 1 Esdr 9:33).

2. Descendant of BANI who sent away his foreign wife and their children according to Ezra's instructions about maintaining God's covenant (Ezra 10:37).

3. A priest and head of the ancestral house of JOIARIB when Joiakim was high priest (Neh 12:19).

MATTHAN Son of Eleazar, father of Jacob, and grandfather of Joseph, Matthan appears only in Matthew's genealogy linking Jesus to King David (Matt 1:15).

MATTHAT 1. The father of Heli in Luke's genealogy of Jesus (Luke 3:24).

2. The son of Levi in Jesus' genealogy (Luke 3:29).

MATTHEW 1. One of the twelve apostles of Jesus (Mark 3:18; Matt 10:3; Luke 6:15; Acts 1:13).

2. The name ascribed to the author of the 1st Gospel. In truth, the earliest manuscripts are anonymous. The tradition of Matthew as author of the 1st Gospel dates to at least the 2nd cent. CE.

MATTHEW, GOSPEL OF The first Gospel in the NT canon attributed to one of Jesus' original disciples named in all of the lists of the Twelve (Matt 10:3; Mark 3:18; Luke 6:15; Acts 1:13). It is also one of the Synoptic Gospels and the second-longest Gospel in the NT. The connection between this document and the apostle Matthew dates back at least to the middle of the 2nd cent. CE, although it is not clear that the collection of Jesus' "sayings" reportedly preserved by Matthew corresponds to this text.

MATTHEW, MARTYRDOM OF An account of the death by fire of the apostle Matthew in the Roman province of Pontus, based largely on an earlier work called the Acts of Andrew and Matthias.

MATTHIAS More than likely an abbreviated form of the Hebrew name MATTITHIAH (1 Chron 9:31) or its Greek form MATTATHIAS (1 Macc 2:1-5; Luke 3:25-26). Matthias appeared only in Acts 1:23, 26 as the replacement for Judas in the list of the Twelve.

MATTITHIAH 1. Jeduthun's son who prophesied with a lyre (1 Chron 25:3) and received the 14th lot (1 Chron 25:21). Akin to the chief of the Levites (1 Chron 15:18, 21), he ministered before the covenant chest (1 Chron 16:5).

2. A Korahite Levite, a son of Shallum, who made flat cakes for the Sabbath (1 Chron 9:31).

3. A descendant of Nebo, he dismissed his foreign wife and their children as Ezra instructed (Ezra 10:43).

4. He stood beside Ezra as Ezra publicly read the Instruction scroll (Neh 8:4; 1 Esdr 9:43).

MATTOCK One of several hand tools used in the process of plowing and cultivating fields (1 Sam 13:20-21).

MEAL Grain that was ground up, parched, and eaten in loaves of bread. Every village and town would have been familiar with the sound of millstones grinding grain into flour (Isa 47:2) or the sight of women sitting before their houses grinding meal by hand in a quern (Luke 17:35). As part of its daily provisions, every household kept a store of meal in jars (1 Kgs 17:12) that they would mix with olive oil and then fashion into unleavened cakes (Gen 18:6; Judg 6:19).

MEAL CUSTOMS The number of meals and the amount of food consumed each day depended on socioeconomic status (1 Kgs 4:22-23; 17:8-16). For many, two meals were the norm: a simple meal in the late morning (e.g., parched grain and bread dipped in sour wine [Ruth 2:14]) and the main meal in the evening after the day's work (e.g., bread and lentil stew [Gen 25:29-34]).

Many meals represented in the Bible were not typical daily meals but feasts or banquets. These meals were special occasions, usually served in the evening, and were integral parts of weddings (Gen 29:21-22; Matt 22:1-13; John 2:1-11), religious festivals (e.g., Passover; Exod 12; Mark 14:12-25), ratifications of political treaties or covenants (Gen 26:26-33; Exod 24:9-11), offers of HOSPITALITY

(Gen 18:1-8; Ps 23), or gatherings of organizations (1 Cor 10:17-33).

Distinctive meal customs were common in these cultural contexts. Jewish dietary laws specified the type of food fit for consumption and the manner in which food was to be prepared (e.g., blood is to be drained). The practice of these laws, outlined in Lev 11 and Deut 14, was associated with holiness (Lev 11:44-45; Deut 14:21) and influenced Jewish-Gentile relationships in the OT and NT (see Acts 15).

Ancient Near Eastern and Greco-Roman customs associated with formal evening meals called BANQUETs became prevalent by the 1st cent. BCE. The first part of this social event was dinner. Invitations were sent to the guests (Luke 14:10, 12, 16). When arriving, guests would have their feet washed (Judg 19:21; cf John 13:1-16) and might be anointed on the head with oil or perfume (Mark 14:3; Luke 7:46). Around the table, guests would be seated according to rank (Gen 43:33; Luke 14:7-11). Before eating, guests would wash their hands (Mark 7:1-8) and thanks would be offered (Matt 26:26-27; Mark 8:6). While at ordinary meals women and men ate together, at banquets typically only men reclined around the table, leaning on their left elbow so they could eat with their right hand (John 13:23-25).

The second part of the event, the symposium, included the drinking of wine, philosophical conversations, and various forms of entertainment such as singing and dancing (Mark 6:22). In the Last Supper, the guests drank wine after supper (Luke 22:20) and engaged in conversation (Luke 22:24-30).

Failure to follow meal customs in the ancient world might warrant a critique. Those who did not offer hospitality were condemned (Deut 23:3-4; Luke 10:10-12). Jesus admonished his dinner host for not bathing his feet, greeting him with a kiss, or anointing his head with oil (Luke 7:36-50). The wealthy who participated in luxurious dining to the exclusion or detriment of the poor were criticized (Amos 6:4-7; Luke 14:12-14; 16:19-30; 1 Cor 11:17-34). While Mark and Luke portrayed women participating in more traditional meal customs as servants or in private settings (Mark 1:29-31; Luke 10:38-42), Matthew advocated a more egalitarian, inclusive, and public role for women and children in meal settings (Matt 14:13-21; 15:32-39; 25:1-13).

MEAT In the biblical traditions, meat was considered not a basic necessity but a luxury to the majority of the population. Meat does not form part of Sirach's food list denoting the basic necessities of human life (Sir 39:26). Rather, the consumption of meat more often than not signaled a special occasion, such as King Solomon's inaugural festival in 1 Kgs 8:63-65, where 22,000 oxen and 120,000 sheep served as a sign of great festivity (see also the wedding meal in Matt 22:4 that consisted of oxen and fattened calves).

MEBUNNAI Mebunnai the Hushathite (see HUSHAH) is listed as one of "the Thirty," David's champions, in 2 Sam 23:27.

MECHERATHITE HEPHER the Mecherathite is listed among David's warriors (1 Chron 11:36).

MEDAD ELDAD and Medad, among seventy elders chosen to relieve Moses' burden of leadership, remained in camp prophesying under the influence of the Spirit while the others were at the MEETING TENT (Num 11:24-30). When Joshua complained about the usurpers, Moses defended them.

MEDAN One of the sons of Abraham and KETURAH (Gen 25:2; 1 Chron 1:32).

MEDEBA Modern Madaba. The main city on the Mishor Moab, on the high plateau east of the Dead Sea. The site is located 7 km east of Mount Nebo and 30 km south of Rabbath Ammon. The city is mentioned several times in the OT as a city conquered and occupied by the Israelites (Num 21:30; Josh 13:9, 16). According to the Mesha Stele lines 7–9 (9th cent. BCE), Mesha was able to take the city, and it is later listed as a city of Moab (Isa 15:2).

MEDES, MEDIA The Table of Nations in Genesis portrays MADAI, possibly representing the eponymous ancestor of the Medes, as a grandson of Noah and son of Japheth, as well as the brother of Gomer, Magog, Javan, Tubal, Meshech, and Tiras (Gen 10:2).

MEDITERRANEAN SEA Also known as the Great Sea or the Western Sea. When referenced in the Bible, the Mediterranean Sea is usually identified as the ideal western boundary of the land of Israel (e.g., Num 34:6; Deut 11:24; 34:2; Josh 15:12). In actuality, for most of its history Israel had no control of cities along the Mediterranean coast, and references to seagoing activity by Israel's tribes are both rare and obscure (Gen 49:13; Judg 5:17). For the most part, the coast was occupied by the PHILISTINES in the south and the Phoenicians in the north. The Mediterranean Sea, referred to as simply "the sea" in Josh 16:8, was distinguished from the SALT SEA on Israel's eastern border not only by its greater size but also in that it was teeming with life (Ezek 47:8-10). It was also noted as the home of great sea monsters (Gen 1:21) and a place of violent and dangerous storms (Jonah 1:4). The vast collection of salt waters that was the Mediterranean Sea remained an ongoing symbol of the forces of death-dealing CHAOS (Dan 7:2).

MEETING TENT The portable tent sanctuary constructed by the people of Israel in the Sinai desert according to instructions given by God to Moses on Mount Sinai after God's conclusion of a covenant with Israel (Exod 25–31; 35–40). Together with its cultic personnel and its rituals, the meeting tent is the archetype of OT worship.

MEGIDDO A prominent mound, called Tel Megiddo in Hebrew and Tell el-Mutesellim in Arabic ("the tell of the governor"), marks the site of biblical Megiddo. The mound rises about 30 m above the surrounding plain, and its summit covers about 13 ac.

MEHETABEL 1. The daughter of Matred, and one of the wives of HADAD, king of Edom (Gen 36:39).

2. Shemaiah, son of Delaiah, son of Mehetabel, was a prophet who was paid to tell Nehemiah, falsely, of a plot to kill him (Neh 6:10).

MEHIDA Ancestor of a family of temple servants who were among the first group to return to Judah from the Babylonian exile (Ezra 2:52; Neh 7:54; 1 Esdr 5:32).

MEHIR The son of CHELUB and father of Eshton (1 Chron 4:11), according to the Chronicler's genealogy of Judah (1 Chron 4).

MEHOLAH ADRIEL, husband of Saul's daughter Merab, is described as being from Meholah (1 Sam 18:19), as is Adriel's father Barzillai (2 Sam 21:8). Meholah might identify the same place as ABEL-MEHOLAH (1 Kgs 4:12).

MEHUJAEL The son of Irad, father of Methushael, and grandfather of Lamech (Gen 4:18).

MEHUMAN One of the seven eunuchs who served King AHASUERUS and was charged with bringing Queen VASHTI before the king (Esth 1:10-11).

MELATIAH Melatiah the Gibeonite was one of the people who repaired the west wall of Jerusalem (Neh 3:7) after the exile.

MELCHI The name occurs twice in Luke's genealogy of Jesus.

1. Father of Levi (Luke 3:24).
2. Father of Neri (Luke 3:28).

MELCHIEL The father of Charmis, one of the elders of Bethuliah (Jdt 6:15), to whom the Israelites brought ACHIOR. The Hebrew name is MALCHIEL (e.g., Gen 46:17).

MELCHIZEDEK Melchizedek ("Zedek's king") is the first priest mentioned in Genesis (14:18) and for that reason has been the object of speculation over the centuries despite his relatively minor role in the story of the celebration of Abram's victory over CHEDORLAOMER in Gen 14:17-20. Melchizedek was king of SALEM and priest of EL ELYON. As king, he brought out bread and wine to Abram. As priest, he blessed Abram by El Elyon, "creator of heaven and earth" (14:19). These events occurred in the King's Valley, a site possibly near Jerusalem (2 Sam 18:18; see SHAVEH VALLEY). In Ps 110:4 the king of Judah receives eternal priesthood "in line with Melchizedek."

Given the secondary role of Melchizedek in Genesis and Psalms, readers of the Letter to the Hebrews may be surprised to find that Melchizedek and his priesthood are given great significance there (Heb 5:6, 10; 6:20; 7:1, 10-11, 15, 17), providing Christ a priestly order and prefiguring its superiority to the Jewish priesthood.

MELCHIZEDEK TEXT The Qumran Melchizedek Document (11Q13) is a pesher (an eschatological commentary) on a string of texts, Lev 25:13; Ps 82:1-2; and Isa 52:7, that may derive from a Reconciliation Day liturgy. According to this text, Melchizedek and his armies will appear on the 10th Jubilee to make reconciliation for the Sons of Light (11Q13 II, 8–9). He will oppose Belial and allied spirits and rescue the redeemed from their control (11Q13 II, 12, 22, 25). An Anointed of the Spirit will come with Melchizedek in fulfillment of Daniel's prophecy (Dan 9:26) and will declare peace, comfort the congregation, and instruct them in the "ages of the w[orld]" (i.e., a ten-Jubilee schema [11Q13 II, 15–21]).

MELEA ELIAKIM's father and MENNA's son in Jesus' genealogy (Luke 3:31).

MELECH With PITHON, TAREA, and AHAZ, one of MICAH's four sons and a descendant of Benjamin (1 Chron 8:35; 9:41).

MELKON According to late tradition, Melkon (or Melchior), king of Persia, was one of the three MAGI who visited Jesus' manger in Bethlehem, expanding the canonical account (Matt 2:1-12), which does not specify the names, numbers, or genders of the visitors from the east. Later tradition commonly limited the visitors to three (the number of gifts mentioned in Matthew): Melkon, Gaspar, and BALTHASAR.

MEMMIUS, QUINTUS One of two Roman ambassadors who bore a letter to the Jews after their victory over Lysias in 164 BCE (2 Macc 11:34).

MEMORIAL, MEMORY Both the OT and the NT contain several Hebrew and Greek concepts related to divine and human remembrance as well as cultic memorials. A memorial is more than a mental image. It denotes a physical sign that functions as a reminder of an object or event of importance. In the NT, the accounts of the institution of the Eucharist clearly indicate that the saving power present in the past event is operative each time that event is "remembered" in cultic reenactment. This same idea is presumed in Hebrews, which argues that former cultic memorials were ineffective.

MEMPHIS Memphis, 13 mi. south of modern Cairo on the west bank of the Nile River, was one of the most important cities in ancient EGYPT. Administratively part of Lower Egypt (i.e., the Delta) and capital of the first nome (province) of Lower Egypt, Memphis actually lay outside the Delta proper in a narrow stretch of the Nile Valley just south of the apex of the Delta.

MEMUCAN One of seven officials of Media and Persia advising King AHASUERUS, Memucan operates as spokesperson when Ahasuerus seeks counsel concerning Queen VASHTI (Esth 1:14, 16, 21).

MENAHEM The son of Gadi, he was the 16th king to rule in the northern kingdom (ca. 745–738 BCE). See 2 Kgs 15.

MENE, MENE, TEKEL, AND PARSIN These are the famous words written by "the fingers of a human hand . . . on the plaster of the king's palace wall" (Dan 5:5-28) that terrified the putative last Babylonian king, BELSHAZZAR. In Dan 5:24-28, the Jewish sage and riddle-solver DANIEL, brought into the banquet at .the insistence of the queen (vv. 10-12), uses puns in order to create an oracle of judgment against the king.

MENESTHEUS Menestheus is the father of APOLLONIUS (2 Macc 4:4, 21), governor of Coelesyria and Phoenicia around the time of Antiochus IV Epiphanes, who is mentioned in this context in connection with his support of Simon the Benjaminite against the high priest Onias III.

MENNA Appears only in Luke's genealogy of Jesus. Menna is the son of Mattatha and the father of Melea (Luke 3:31).

MENUHOTH A half-tribe referred to by the proper name HAROEH (1 Chron 2:52) and descended from SHOBAL (Gen 36:20, 23-29; etc.).

MEONOTHAI In Judah's genealogy, one of OTHNIEL's two sons and the father of OPHRAH (1 Chron 4:13-14).

MEPHAATH One of the levitical cities (Josh 13:18; 21:37; 1 Chron 6:79) among the cities of the tribe of Reuben, east of the Dead Sea. See LEVITICAL CITIES, TOWNS.

MEPHIBOSHETH Second Samuel uses the name Mephibosheth ("out of the mouth of shame") for two characters:

1. The son of Saul and Rizpah whom David delivers to the Gibeonites for execution along with six other sons of Saul (2 Sam 21:8-9).

2. Jonathan's son and Saul's grandson, whom David spares due to his promise to treat Jonathan's family kindly (2 Sam 21:7; cf 1 Sam 20:14-15).

MERAB Eldest daughter of King Saul (1 Sam 14:49). In accordance with the promise he made before the engagement with Goliath (1 Sam 17:25), Saul betrothed Merab to David. Before that marriage Merab's younger sister MICHAL had displayed her attachment to David, so Michal married David instead of Merab. Merab was then married to ADRIEL the Meholathite, to whom she bore five sons (2 Sam 21:8).

MERAIAH According to Nehemiah's list of priests in the days of JOIAKIM, Meraiah was head of the ancestral house of Seraiah (Neh 12:12).

MERAIOTH Priestly name in the OT.

1. A high-priestly descendant of Aaron who was an ancestor of Zadok (1 Chron 6:6-7, 52) and of Ezra (Ezra 7:3).

2. Zadok's father (1 Chron 9:11; Neh 11:11), in contradiction to references to Ahitub as the father of Zadok (e.g., 1 Chron 6:8; 18:16).

3. A postexilic priestly family according to Neh 12:15.

MERARI, MERARITES 1. The 3rd-born son of Levi (Gen 46:11).

2. The group of Levites who were descended from Merari (Num 26:57). They formed the 3rd branch of the Levites and were divided into two clans named after the sons of Merari, MAHLI and MUSHI (1 Chron 6:19). According to Num 4:29-33, the Merarites were in charge of carrying the poles and bases that made up the frame of the meeting tent

3. The father of Judith (Jdt 8:1; 16:6).

MERCY, MERCIFUL *Mercy* is a synonym for *compassion* and means "to have pity" or "to feel sorry for someone."

MERCY SEAT The covering for the COVENANT CHEST. Two winged creatures faced each other and spread their wings over the elaborate gold mercy seat (Exod 25:16-21).

MERED In Judah's genealogy, one of Ezrah's four sons. He married Bithiah, Pharaoh's daughter, and an unnamed Jewish wife (1 Chron 4:17-18).

MEREMOTH 1. Uriah's son who received the silver, the gold, and the vessels that Ezra brought to the temple (Ezra 8:33; 1 Esdr 8:62).

2. A descendant of Bani who dismissed his foreign wife and their children (Ezra 10:36).

3. A participant in the community's covenant renewal whose name appeared on the sealed document (Neh 10:5).

MERES One of the seven officials of Media and Persia who occupied a high rank and advised King AHASUERUS (Esth 1:14).

MERIBAH In REPHIDIM the people complain to Moses because there is no water (Exod 17:1-7). Moses presents their complaint to God, who commands Moses to strike the rock at Horeb. Moses does so, producing water, and the name Rephidim is changed to MASSAH, "test," and Meribah, "confrontation."

MERIB-BAAL The son of JONATHAN (1 Chron 8:34; 9:40). In 1 Samuel, the name of Jonathan's son is MEPHIBOSHETH, meaning "from the mouth of shame," and is probably a constructed replacement to avoid using the name of Baal. Similar changes can be seen in the change of Ishbaal (1 Chron 9:39) to Ishbosheth (2 Sam 2:8).

MERODACH A long form of the name of the Babylonian god Marduk. It appears in Jer 50:2 and in the names of the Babylonian kings MERODACH-BALADAN (2 Kgs 20:12; Isa 39:1) and Awil-merodach (2 Kgs 25:27; Jer 52:31). The god was also known as BEL.

MERODACH-BALADAN Marduk-apla-iddina II (Akkadian) was sheikh of the Chaldean Bit Yakin tribe, whose territory lay in the marshes of southern Iraq and who profited from the camel caravan trade to Arabia. In 729 BCE, he paid tribute to Tiglath-pileser III as king of Assyria and Babylon and was recognized by him as king of the Sealand. Taking advantage of the confusion surrounding the overthrow of Shalmaneser V by Sargon II (722), he seized the throne in Babylon. Sargon II dethroned Marduk-apla-iddina (710 BCE) and besieged him in his capital Dur-Yakin (709–707 BCE), but he managed to escape and take refuge with his Elamite allies. Riding on the heels of a successful revolt against the new king Sennacherib by a Babylonian Marduk-zakir-shumi II, Marduk-apla-iddina ousted the latter and reclaimed Babylon (703 BCE). His allies included Elamites, Arabs, and Hezekiah of Judah. Isaiah strongly disapproved of the connection and warned that no good would come of it (2 Kgs 20:12-19;

Isa 39). Marduk-apla-iddina was ousted after nine months by Sennacherib. In the face of a 2nd campaign (700 BCE), he collected the gods of his land and the bones of his fathers from their graves and fled by ship to Elam, where he died (ca. 694 BCE).

MEROM, WATERS OF The Israelite army under Joshua and a Canaanite coalition of armies did battle by the waters of Merom (Josh 11:5, 7), whose actual location is unknown.

MERRAN A city along with TEMAN in Edom known for wisdom (Bar 3:23).

MESALOTH Demetrius I dispatched Bacchides to besiege Mesaloth in the west Galilean town of Arbela after the death of Nicanor (1 Macc 9:1-2).

MESHA 1. A place marking a boundary of the territory where SHEM's descendants through ARPACHSHAD lived (Gen 10:30).

2. A son of Caleb (1 Chron 2:42).

3. One of the sons of SHAHARAIM, a Benjaminite living in Moab (1 Chron 8:9), who had sent away two of his wives. Another wife, HODESH, bore him Mesha.

4. Mesha was a mid-9th-cent. BCE Moabite king known through two sources: 2 Kgs 3 and the Moabite Stone (also known as the Mesha Stele). During a period of the Israelite Omride dynasty, Moab was under Israelite domination (Mesha Stele line 5; 2 Kgs 3:4). Israel's annual tax on Mesha consisted of large quantities of sheep and of rams' wool (2 Kgs 3:4). Mesha rebelled against this domination. In the biblical text, Mesha faces a coalition of Jehoram, Jehoshaphat (king of Judah), and the king of Edom, supported by the Israelite prophet Elisha. Mesha's defeat by the coalition ends with him offering his son as an entirely burned offering on the wall of Kir-hareseth (2 Kgs 3:25-27). The Mesha Stele portrays Mesha both as successful in his endeavor to rid Moab of Israelite oppression and as a successful builder of the Moabite kingdom.

MESHACH See SHADRACH, MESHACH, ABEDNEGO.

MESHECH 1. In the Table of Nations, Meshech is listed as the 7th son of Japheth, immediately after TUBAL (Gen 10:2; 1 Chron 1:5).

2. In 1 Chron 1:17 Meshech appears among the sons of Shem.

3. A land located in east Asia Minor (modern Turkey), known from the Greek sources as Phrygia, and populated with non-Semitic inhabitants. As a result of their geographic proximity, Meshech and Tubal are mentioned together in various biblical and extrabiblical texts.

MESHELEMIAH A gatekeeper, a Levite, a descendant of Korah, and the father of seven sons, including Zechariah, who was also a gatekeeper (1 Chron 9:21; 26:1-3). Also referred to as Shelemiah (1 Chron 26:14) and may be the same as SHALLUM.

MESHEZABEL 1. Father of Berechiah, father of Meshullam who made repairs to the Jerusalem wall (Neh 3:4; compare 3:30).

2. One of forty-four leaders of the people who signed Ezra's covenant to keep the Law (Neh 10:21).

3. Descendant of Zerah and father of Pethahiah, the representative of Judean concerns to the Persian king (Neh 11:24).

MESHILLEMITH Ancestor of Jeroboam and priest listed in the genealogy of 1 Chron 9:10-13.

MESHILLEMOTH 1. Father of Berechiah, an Ephraimite chief (2 Chron 28:12).

2. Son of Immer and ancestor of Amashsai, a priest in Jerusalem in Nehemiah's time (Neh 11:13). He may

be identical to MESHILLEMITH son of Immer (1 Chron 9:12).

MESHOBAB Clan leader in the Simeonite tribe who prospered in the east side of the valley (1 Chron 4:34).

MESHULLAM 1. Grandfather of Shaphan, the secretary of King Josiah (2 Kgs 22:3; see JOSIAH).

2. One of the sons of Zadok and the father of the priest Hilkiah (1 Chron 9:11; Neh 11:11), who found the Instruction scroll (2 Kgs 22:8).

3. A Kohathite who was appointed as one of the overseers of the temple repairs (2 Chron 34:12).

4. One of three children of Zerubbabel (1 Chron 3:19).

5. A Benjaminite whose son Shallu was one of the first returned exiles (1 Chron 9:7; Neh 11:7).

6. Another Benjaminite who was one of the first returned exiles; son of Shephatiah (1 Chron 9:8).

7. Another member of the priestly family of Zadok; his great-grandson was a returned exile (1 Chron 9:12).

8. One of eleven leading men whom Ezra sent to recruit Levites to join the company of exiles returning to Jerusalem (Ezra 8:16).

9. One of four leading men who opposed Ezra's policy against marriage to foreign women (Ezra 10:15).

10. A son of Bani who had married a foreign wife and was among those who sent their wives away with their children in accordance with Ezra's policy (Ezra 10:29).

11. A son of Berechiah, he was a leader of one of the groups assigned to repair the wall of Jerusalem (Neh 3:4, 30).

12. A son of Besodeiah who helped repair the Old Gate (Neh 3:6).

13. One of the leaders who was given the honor of standing beside Ezra as he read from the Instruction scroll (Neh 8:4).

14. One of the priests who signed the covenant drawn up by Nehemiah (Neh 10:7).

15. One of "the leaders of the people" who also signed the covenant drawn up by Nehemiah (Neh 10:20).

16. The head of the priestly family of Ezra in the time of the high priest Joiakim (Neh 12:13).

17. The head of the priestly family of Ginnethon in the time of the high priest Joiakim (Neh 12:16).

18. A gatekeeper during the time of the high priest Joiakim (Neh 12:25).

19. One of the priests who participated in the dedication ceremony of the city wall (Neh 12:33).

20. A descendant of Gad who lived in Bashan (1 Chron 5:13).

21. A descendant of Benjamin, son of Elpaal (1 Chron 8:17).

MESHULLEMETH The mother of Amon, the daughter of Haruz, and the wife of Manasseh, Judah's king (2 Kgs 21:19).

MESOPOTAMIA The vast land between the Tigris and the Euphrates Rivers, the region from which international powers ruled the ancient world, including ASSYRIA AND BABYLONIA in the 1st millennium BCE.

MESSIAH, JEWISH *Messiah* means "anointed one." Kings were anointed in Israel and Judah, as were high priests. There is also limited evidence for the anointing of prophets (see ANOINT). The term refers to the legitimate king (see KING, KINGSHIP). It does not have a future or eschatological connotation in the OT. In the Second Temple period, when there was no longer a king on the throne, the term came to refer to the one who would restore the kingship. The same figure could also be designated by other terms such as "Branch of David." Ideal, even supernatural characteristics were often attributed to him.

MESSIAH, TITLE FOR JESUS See CHRIST.

METHUSELAH Methuselah, son of Enoch and father of Lamech (Luke 3:37), lived 969 years, the longest life span of anyone in the Bible, according to Gen 5:21-27. According to the chronology of Gen 5–6, Methuselah died in the 600th year of Noah, the year of the flood. See METHUSHAEL.

METHUSHAEL Descendant of Cain and son of Mehujael and father of LAMECH (Gen 4:18), this name is the equivalent of METHUSELAH (Gen 5:21-26), credited as the longest-lived human.

ME-ZAHAB Mother of Matred and grandmother of Mehetabel wife of King Hadad (II) of Edom (Gen 36:39; 1 Chron 1:50).

MIBHAR Hagri's son, one of David's mighty men called "the Thirty" (1 Chron 11:38).

MIBSAM 1. Son of Ishmael and brother of Mishma (Gen 25:13; 1 Chron 1:29).

2. A Simeonite, the son of Shallum and father of Mishma (1 Chron 4:25).

MICA 1. Mephibosheth's son and descendant of Saul. He had four sons. David provided for his father MEPHIBOSHETH as if he were his son (2 Sam 9:12).

2. A Levite; Asaph's grandson, Zichri's son, and Mattaniah's father (1 Chron 9:15; Neh 11:22).

3. A Levite who placed his name on the sealed covenant document (Neh 10:11).

MICAH 1. Resident of the highlands in Ephraim, who stole from and later returned to his mother 1,100 silver shekels. Micah's mother made an idol out of silver for his shrine. Micah placed his son as priest over the shrine, then later replaced him with a Levite from Bethlehem in Judah (Judg 17:1–18:4).

2. Son of Joel and a descendant of Reuben (1 Chron 5:5).

3. Son of Merib-baal (MEPHIBOSHETH in 2 Sam 9:12), descendant of Jonathan and Saul (1 Chron 8:33-35; 9:40-41). See MICA.

4. A Levite and the elder son of Uzziel during Solomon's reign and David's last days (1 Chron 23:20; 24:24-25).

5. Father of Abdon (2 Chron 34:20). Called MICAIAH in 2 Kgs 22:12.

6. A prophet (Mic 1:1).

7. Father of Uzziah, a magistrate (Jdt 6:15).

MICAH, BOOK OF Micah, a shortened form of Micaiah, means "Who is like Yah(weh)?" The question is rhetorical and expresses Yahweh's incomparability. Micah is the prophet associated with the Book of the Twelve—the sixth in the Hebrew collection, the third in the Greek. Micah is identified in the book's superscription (Mic 1:1) as having come from the town of Moresheth—probably the same as Moresheth-gath in 1:14—and having prophesied during the reigns of Judahite kings of the latter part of the 8th cent. BCE. In Jer 26:18, Micah is remembered for the prophecy of Jerusalem's destruction found in Mic 3:12. The book bearing Micah's name contains both oracles of judgment for the capital cities of Samaria and Jerusalem and their leaders, and visions of future restoration, vindication, and peace for Jerusalem and Jacob.

MICAIAH The name also appears in the contracted form of MICAH.

1. The son of Imlah, who prophesied about the death of Ahab in his attempt to conquer Ramoth-gilead from the Arameans (1 Kgs 22:4-28; 2 Chron 18:3-27).

2. The father of Achbor, who was one of the people sent to the prophetess Huldah to inquire of the Lord concerning the book found at the occasion of the repair of the temple (2 Kgs 22:12).

3. The daughter of Uriel of Gibeah, who was the wife of Rehoboam king of Judah, and the mother of Abijah (2 Chron 13:2).

4. One of the royal officers sent by Jehoshaphat, king of Judah, throughout all the cities of Judah to teach the people the Instruction of the Lord (2 Chron 17:7-9).

5. The son of Zaccur and a descendant of Asaph, the temple musician.

6. One of the eight levitical musicians who blew the trumpet in the temple and stood with Nehemiah, the leaders of Judah, and the priests during the ceremonies at the occasion of the dedication of the wall of Jerusalem (Neh 12:41).

7. The son of Gemariah and the grandson of Shaphan (Jer 36:11). Micaiah, a contemporary of the prophet Jeremiah, reported to the princes of Judah the words Baruch read from the scroll in the temple, at the command of Jeremiah, in the 5th year of King Jehoiakim (Jer 36:9).

MICHAEL 1. An Asherite, the father of Sethur, who was one of the twelve spies sent to reconnoiter in Canaan (Num 13:13).

2. A Gadite who settled in Bashan in the days of Jotham and Jeroboam II (1 Chron 5:13).

3. A Gadite, the son of Jeshishai and father of Gilead (1 Chron 5:14).

4. A Levite singer, the great-grandfather of Asaph (1 Chron 6:40).

5. An Issacharite, son of Izrahiah, who served as a military leader in the time of David (1 Chron 7:3).

6. A Benjaminite, son of Beraiah, who resided in Jerusalem (1 Chron 8:16).

7. A military leader from the tribe of Manasseh who deserted Saul at Ziklag and was made a commander of David's forces (1 Chron 12:20).

8. An Issacharite, father of Omri, who oversaw Issachar during David's reign (1 Chron 27:18).

9. A son of King Jehoshaphat of Judah, who was assassinated when his older brother Jehoram assumed the throne (2 Chron 21:2-4).

10. The father of Zebadiah, who led eighty men back from Babylon with Ezra, in the time of Artaxerxes (Ezra 8:8).

11. ARCHANGEL and heavenly prince. Michael and GABRIEL are the only two angels mentioned by name in the Bible. Michael is identified only at Dan 10:13, 21; 12:1, where he is described as "one of the highest leaders" or the "great leader" in charge of God's people.

In the NT, Michael is mentioned by name only twice, at Jude 9 and Rev 12:7.

MICHAL King Saul's younger daughter who loves and marries DAVID. Saul tries to use her to bring about David's death, but David uses her to become the king's son-in-law (1 Sam 18:21, 26).

MICHMASH A Benjaminite town located near the border between Benjamin and Ephraim, east of the central Benjamin plateau and the north-south ridge route that extends from Bethlehem to Shechem.

MICHRI A family head whose descendants lived in Jerusalem. He was the grandfather of ELAH and a descendant of Benjamin (1 Chron 9:8). See BENJAMIN, BENJAMINITES.

MIDIAN, MIDIANITES Abraham's descendants through Keturah (Gen 25:2) included six sons, one named Midian. Genesis 25:1-6 states that Abraham sent his six sons born by Keturah away from Canaan to the east. The Midianites became a tribal and ethnic entity whose territory consisted of the desert regions of the southern Transjordan, south and east of the Dead Sea. Thus, the Midianites are understood to be part of the ancestry and precursors of the Arabic-speaking tribes of the Western Arabian Desert.

MIGDOL A site on the exodus itinerary near PI-HAHIROTH, BAAL-ZEPHON, and the Reed Sea (Exod 14:2; Num 33:7). The biblical description places it somewhere east of SUCCOTH (Tell el-Maskuta).

MIGRON A site in the tribal area of Benjamin where Saul sat under a pomegranate tree preparing for battle with the Philistines (1 Sam 14:2). The text mentions it as on the outskirts of Gibeah.

MIJAMIN 1. During David's last days, the head of the 6th division and therefore the ancestor of a priestly family in postexilic times (1 Chron 24:9).

2. Among the descendants of Parosh who dismissed their foreign wives and children in accordance with God's command through Ezra (Ezra 10:25; 1 Esdr 9:26).

3. A priest who placed his name upon Ezra's sealed covenant document (Neh 10:7). Possibly the same as MINIAMIN (Neh 12:17, 41).

4. A priest who returned to Jerusalem after the exile with Zerubbabel (Neh 12:5).

MIKLOTH 1. A descendant of Benjamin, Mikloth is the son of Jeiel and father of Shimeam (also called Shimeah) (1 Chron 8:32; 9:37-38).

2. An officer under Dodai (see DODO) in the army of David; he led the division of the 2nd month, which had 24,000 men (1 Chron 27:4).

MIKNEIAH One of the 2nd rank of Levites chosen to play a musical instrument during David's 2nd attempt at processing into Jerusalem with the covenant chest (1 Chron 15:18, 21).

MIKTAM A term in the superscriptions of several psalms associated with David (Pss 16; 56–60).

MILALAI One of the priests and musicians who participated in the dedication of the Jerusalem wall in the postexilic reconstruction (Neh 12:36).

MILCAH 1. Abraham's niece and daughter of HARAN, who married Abraham's other brother NAHOR (Gen 11:29). She was the grandmother of REBEKAH (Gen 24:15, 24, 47).

2. One of the daughters of Zelophehad, of the tribe of Manasseh, who were involved in establishing Mosaic legislation regarding a daughter's right to inheritance in the event of no male heir (Num 27:1; Josh 17:3).

MILCOM The Ammonite god (1 Kgs 11:5, 33; 2 Kgs 23:13). See MOLECH, MOLOCH.

MILE A Roman measure of about 1,480 m (an English mile is a little over 1,600 m). Another word often translated "mile" (Luke 24:13; John 6:19) is only 185 m. Roman soldiers could compel citizens of the regions they occupied to help carry their equipment (Epictetus, Diss. 4.1.79; see Mark 15:21, where soldiers compel Simon of Cyrene to carry Jesus' cross). Jesus told his disciples to walk 2 mi. when compelled to walk 1 (Matt 5:41). In so doing, they would offer kindness to their enemies, a prominent theme in the SERMON ON THE MOUNT. See WEIGHTS AND MEASURES.

MILETUS Miletus was a seaport located on the Aegean coast 30 mi. south of EPHESUS in southwest Asia Minor, situated on a peninsula extending from the southern shore of the Gulf of Latmos. The city had four natural harbors and relied primarily on its maritime potential for growth and prosperity. Miletus is mentioned three times in the NT, each instance in reference to Paul's mission

MILL, MILLSTONE Grain (primarily wheat and barley) formed the staff of the daily diet. In order to process it into flour for loaves and cakes, the women of each household would grind it by hand between upper and lower millstones, sometimes referred to as the saddle-quern based on its concave shape (cf Num 11:8; Matt 24:41).

MILLENNIUM The term *millennium*, meaning "a thousand years," never occurs in the Bible. This thousand-year period is mentioned repeatedly in Rev 20:1-10. During that time, according to John, the named author of Revelation, SATAN is bound in the ABYSS (Rev 20:1-3, 7-10), and those martyred "for their witness to Jesus and God's word" are raised from the dead to reign with Christ (Rev 20:4-6). At the end of it, Satan is released "for a little while" (Rev 20:3) to deceive the nations and threaten the people of God once more before being consigned finally to "the lake of fire and sulfur" (Rev 20:7-10).

MILLET A type of grass whose small seeds are used for food.

MINIAMIN Meaning "from the right" or "luck; lucky person."

1. One of Kore's assistants overseeing the gathering of freewill offerings during King Hezekiah's reign (2 Chron 31:15).

2. One of the priestly houses during Joiakim's term as high priest (Neh 12:17).

3. A trumpet-playing priest present for the dedication of the Jerusalem wall rebuilt under Nehemiah's supervision (Neh 12:41). See MIJAMIN.

MINISTRY, CHRISTIAN The uncertainty over the nature of Christian ministry may reflect the diversity of the biblical witness, for the NT offers no uniform church order or nomenclature for describing Christian ministry. The roots of Christian ministry are evident in the synoptic accounts of Jesus' call to the disciples and the commission to extend his ministry in a ministry of preaching, teaching, and healing (see Matt 10:2-8). Their ministry, therefore, involved the dual aspects of being called (Matt 10:1; Mark 3:13) and sent (Matt 10:5; Mark 3:14) to act on behalf of the one who sent them. They were the representatives of Jesus with the authority to speak on his behalf (Matt 10:40; Luke 10:16) and to minister to Israel's outcasts. Those who participated in Jesus' ministry also share his precarious existence (Matt 8:18-22; 10:9-36) and take up a cross (Matt 10:38; Mark 8:34; Luke 9:23).

All three Synoptics report the disciples' struggle to define Christian ministry. When they indicate their desire for the first places in the kingdom, Jesus responds with the claim that his community has a countercultural understanding of leadership. While "the Gentiles" exercise power over others (Mark 10:42), among the disciples "whoever wants to be great among you will be your servant" (Matt 20:26; Mark 10:43). In all three synoptic accounts Jesus identifies himself as "one who serves," (e.g., Luke 22:27), making himself a model for Christian ministry and defining the mission of those who follow him in the language of being at the disposal of others.

The traditions about the apostles in Acts indicate the continuity between their role during the life of Jesus and after his departure. Under the power of the Spirit, the apostles continue the signs and wonders that they began when they were first sent out by Jesus (Acts 2:43; 4:30; see 6:8) and proclaim the name of Jesus in the presence of the authorities (4:5-12), an indication of their readiness to share the destiny of Jesus.

Because Paul does not belong to the circle of the Twelve, his need to defend his apostleship results in considerable reflection on the nature of his apostleship and Christian ministry. Using the language for those who are at the disposal of another, Paul insists that the basic requirement for ministers is that they are faithful in managing a trust. As Paul indicates in other instances (1 Cor 9:17; 1 Thess 2:4), he is at the disposal of the gospel, commissioned for the task before him.

Timothy and Titus ensure that local communities are equipped to meet the challenge of heresy and to protect the deposit of faith. According to 2 Tim 2:2, Timothy's task is to commit (lit., "deposit") what he has learned to faithful people who will teach others. In 1 Timothy and Titus, the restriction of these functions to those who meet the criteria reflects the emergence of offices in the local communities. Titus's commission to appoint elders in every city (Titus 1:5) presupposes an office that is not mentioned in the undisputed Pauline Letters (see ELDER). First Timothy mentions the qualifications for a variety of offices, including the offices of BISHOP (1 Tim 3:1-7) and deacon (1 Tim 3:8, 12), which probably reflect continuity and development from the bishops and deacons (Phil 1:1) and "those who are . . . leading you" (1 Thess 5:12) in the undisputed Pauline Letters. The elders mentioned in 1 Tim 5:17 may be the equivalent of the office of bishop in 3:1. Although the office of bishop was limited to men, the office of deacon probably included both men and women, as the reference to women who are deacons in 3:11 suggests.

MINNI Appears only in Jer 51:27 as one of three states, at that time controlled by the Medes, called to attack Babylon. It is located in the area south of Lake Urmia, a salt lake in the Azarbaijan region of northwestern Iran.

MINNITH Minnith was one of twenty Ammonite cities taken by JEPHTHAH (Judg 11:33), and, additionally, the source of wheat traded to Tyre.

MINT The Mediterranean variety of horse-mint is a fragrant, edible perennial with an erect stem and narrow, lance-shaped leaves. Jesus accused some people of being more concerned with laws of tithing, including mint, than they were with following the laws concerning justice (Matt 23:23; Luke 11:42). See PLANTS OF THE BIBLE.

MIRACLE In the OT, the LXX, and the NT, several Hebrew and Greek terms have been used to describe miracles. Most often in the OT and NT, a miracle functions as a sign, a communication of God's relationship with humankind and history.

MIRIAM 1. Miriam, one of the few women to be called a "prophet" (Exod 15:20; cf also Deborah in Judg 4:4; Huldah in 2 Kgs 22:14; Noadiah in Neh 6:14), offers a mixed portrait of female leadership in a patriarchal society (see PROPHET). Also, the sister of Moses, whom she helped to rescue in Exod 1–2. In Mic 6:4, Miriam is remembered together with Moses and Aaron as one of the leaders by whom God redeemed Israel from the house of slavery in Egypt, attesting to her significance in the collective memory of Israel. The first reference to Miriam is found in Exod 1–2.

2. Listed in v. 17 of the Judahite genealogy in 1 Chron 4 as one of three children of Bithia, Pharaoh's daughter.

MIRMAH The 7th of seven sons born to Shaharaim and his wife Hodesh in Moab, listed in the Benjaminite genealogy (1 Chron 8:10).

MIRROR A reflective device first made of highly polished stone, copper, and bronze, and later of other materials, used to observe the self.

MISHAEL 1. A Levite, the oldest son of Uzziel (Exod 6:22).

2. One of the men who stood beside Ezra when he read the Instruction scroll to the people (Neh 8:4).

3. One of the three men from Judah who was taken to Babylon to be educated along with Daniel (Dan 1:6). Mishael served in Nebuchadnezzar's court, and he assisted Daniel with the interpretation of the king's dream (Dan 1:19; 2:17-18). The palace master changed Mishael's name to Meshach (Dan 1:7). Mishael and his friends were thrown into a furnace when they refused to bow to the king's image, but they were delivered by God (Dan 3:1-30). See SHADRACH, MESHACH, ABEDNEGO.

MISHAM One of Elpaal's sons listed in Saul's genealogy (1 Chron 8:12). ELPAAL and his sons were noted for building ONO and Lod.

MISHMA 1. The 5th of Ishmael's twelve sons (and brother of MIBSAM) (Gen 25:14; 1 Chron 1:30).

2. A descendant of Simeon, Mishma was son of Mibsam and father of Hammuel and others (1 Chron 4:25-26).

MISHMANNAH The 4th of eleven Gadite commanders, expert warriors, listed in 1 Chron 12:8-13, who defected to David's side at Ziklag and became officers in his army.

MISHRAITE One of the families of Kiriath-jearim, located on the northern border of Judah, from whom the Zorathites and Eshtaolites descended (1 Chron 2:53).

MISPAR One of the leaders returning with Zerubbabel from Babylonian exile (Ezra 2:2).

MITHNITE Family name or place of origin ascribed to Joshaphat (1 Chron 11:43), one of David's mighty men.

MITHREDATH 1. King CYRUS of Persia's treasurer who inventoried the Jerusalem temple vessels taken by Nebuchadnezzar and returned them to SHESHBAZZAR, who brought the vessels with him when he returned from Babylonian exile to Jerusalem (Ezra 1:8; Mithridates in 1 Esdr 2:11).

2. A Persian officer who, along with others, sent correspondence to King Artaxerxes opposing the rebuilding of Jerusalem and the walls surrounding the city (Ezra 4:7; "Mithridates" in 1 Esdr 2:6, 12).

MIZPAH, MIZPEH Five locations in the OT are given the name Mizpah or Mizpeh, which are two variant spellings of the name.

1. A land located near Mount Hermon occupied by Hivites (Josh 11:3).

2. A town in the arid southern plains of Judah (Josh 15:38).

3. A settlement in Benjamin. This Mizpah is the only one that receives repeated and detailed references in the DtrH (Josh 18:26; Judg 20–21; 1 Sam 7; 10:17-27; 1 Kgs 15:16-22; 2 Kgs 25:23, 25), and in 2 Chron 16:6; Neh 3:7, 15-19; Jer 40–41; and 1 Macc 3:46.

4. A site in Gilead (Judg 11:29).

5. A settlement in Moab to which David traveled during his flight from Saul (1 Sam 22:3).

MIZZAH Name of Reuel's 4th son and one of Esau's grandsons (Gen 36:13, 17). Also can be understood as the name of an Edomite tribe (1 Chron 1:37).

MNASON An early Cypriot disciple and host of Paul and his companions on Paul's final visit to Jerusalem (Acts 21:16).

MOAB, CITY OF A city on the Arnon River where Balaam meets with Balak (Num 22:36-38). Probably the same as Ar (Num 21:15, 28).

MOAB, MOABITES 1. The son of Lot by one of his daughters according to the etiological account in Gen 19:30-38. The Ammonites are descended from Lot by his other daughter and are related to Moab.

2. Moab refers to a geographic region and more particularly to the plateau areas east of the Dead Sea. Moab also refers to the nation-state in that same region during the Iron Age, with political antecedents that may reach back into the Late Bronze Age. The designation Moabite, therefore, can refer either to someone living in the area of Moab or to someone attached to the political entity of Moab.

MOADIAH A priestly family whose head was listed as PILTAI when JOIAKIM was high priest (Neh 12:17).

MOLADAH A town in the extreme south toward "the border of Edom" (Josh 15:21), first said to have been allotted to Judah (Josh 15:26), then to Simeon (Josh 19:2).

MOLECH, MOLOCH Molech occurs several times in the OT as the name of a detested god associated with child sacrifice (Lev 18:21; 20:2-5; 2 Kgs 23:10; Jer 32:35; see also Isa 30:33; 57:9; Jer 7:31; 19:5; Zeph 1:5; Molech in 1 Kgs 11:7 is a slip for "Milcom," cf vv. 5 and 33).

MOLID Son of Abishur and his wife Abihail in Judah's genealogy; also a descendant of Jerahmeel (1 Chron 2:29).

MONEY, COINS Coinage is the minted form of money, standardized in various units. The Bible reflects the whole history of money from bartering, to primitive forms of bullion (precious metal in bars or ingots), to intricately produced forms of officially minted coins.

MONEY-CHANGER Money-changers facilitated economic exchange by converting coins to and from the many international currencies and denominations. In the Roman Empire, the profession of money-changer (*nummularius*) was closely related to that of banker (*argentarius*). Within the Roman cities the former specialized in assaying coins and exchanging currencies; the latter handled the more lucrative fiscal tasks, such as deposits, loans, and commodity speculation. Beyond the Roman cities, such as in Palestine, these two professions often merged.

MOREH 1. The "oak of Moreh" is more accurately the "plain of Moreh." According to Gen 12:6, Shechem was in this vicinity.

2. The hill of Moreh (Judg 7:1) is north of the Jezreel Valley, near where the Midianites encamped before they were attacked by Gideon.

MORESHETH Hometown of the prophet Micah (1:1; Jer 26:18). Moresheth-gath is possibly the same place (Mic 1:14).

MORIAH 1. Moriah is the region (the Hebrew is literally "the land of the Moriah") where Abraham is sent to sacrifice his son Isaac (Gen 22:2).

2. Mount Moriah is identified as the place where Solomon built the temple; it is the place previously revealed to David, the THRESHING FLOOR of Ornan the Jebusite (2 Chron 3:1; cf 2 Sam 24:16-24).

MORNING STAR In Revelation (2:28; 22:16), a metaphor for Christ. See DAY STAR.

MORTAR AND PESTLE The mortar and pestle were used for crushing or pounding a variety of grains, herbs, pigments, resins, and some liquids (Prov 27:22).

MOSES Moses is the leader of the people of Israel as portrayed in the OT books of Exodus, Leviticus, Numbers, and Deuteronomy. He combines characteristics of the founding ruler, judge, lawgiver, scribe, teacher, prophet, intercessor, healer, and savior for Israel. He led Israel out of slavery in Egypt in the exodus (Exod 14–15). He had a uniquely close relationship with Israel's God, speaking directly with God "face-to-face" (Exod 33:11; Num 12:8; Deut 34:10). He transmitted the Ten Commandments and other laws from God on Mount Sinai to the Israelites (Exod 19–20). He led the runaway Israelite slaves from Egypt through forty years of wilderness wandering until they reached the eastern boundary of the promised land of Canaan, a land he would see from a distance but not enter (Deut 34:4-5). He taught a new generation of young Israelites the essentials of their faith, leaving behind a written "Instruction" to be read and studied by each new generation

(Deut 31:9-13). Moses has retained his prominence and importance in both Jewish and Christian imaginations throughout their history, extending as well to Islam and the wider culture up to modern times.

MOST HIGH It often occurs as the epithet "God Most High" (or "Most High God"). See EL ELYON; GOD, NAMES OF.

MOST HOLY PLACE The inner sanctum of the temple containing the golden altar of incense and the COVENANT CHEST. The high priest alone was allowed to enter the adytum once a year, on RECONCILIATION DAY (cf Lev 16).

MOTH A moth is an insect. In the Bible all moths are cloth-eating (e.g., Job 13:28; Isa 50:9; Luke 12:33). Because the moth consumes cloth when it is in its larvae stage, sometimes the Hebrew words are translated "WORM" or "maggot."

MOUNT, MOUNTAIN *Mountain* is a relative term for a high elevation in a particular region. Named mountains in Israel range in height from about 1,600 ft. above sea level (Gilboa) to over 9,000 ft. (Hermon).

MOUNT OF OLIVES A ridge with three crests, approximately 2 mi. long, located across the Kidron Valley from Jerusalem. With the highest point reaching approximately 2,700 ft., it stands just over 100 ft. above the temple mount in Jerusalem to the east, and about 4,000 ft. above the Dead Sea to the west, thus affording dramatic views of the surrounding area. In biblical times, it supported a plentiful stand of olive trees, from which it received its name (see OLIVE, OLIVE TREE).

The name Mount of Olives appears only three times in the OT (Zech 14:4 twice); and when escaping from Absalom, David crossed the Wadi Kidron (2 Sam 15:23) and "walked barefoot up the slope of the Mount of Olives" (lit., "the ascent of the olive trees" [15:30]). References to the Mount of Olives in the NT are limited to the Jesus-tradition reported in the Gospels and Acts. Jesus' familiarity with the mount is evident from his lodging with friends in Bethany (e.g., Mark 11:11; 14:3), located on the ridge of the mount. During Jesus' final week teaching in the temple, "he spent each night on the Mount of Olives" (Luke 21:37). It is from the Mount of Olives that Jesus sends two disciples to prepare for his entry into Jerusalem, and his triumphal entry would have begun from BETHPHAGE on its summit (Matt 21:1-11; Mark 11:1-10; and Luke 19:29-40 read "Bethphage and Bethany"; see John 12:12-15). Luke adds that, on the way down the Mount of Olives, Jesus wept over the city (19:41-44). The site of ancient Bethany is probably to be identified with the modern village el-Azariyeh, but the exact location of Bethphage is contested; presumably, it was along the ridge nearer the summit. According to Matt 24 and Mark 13, Jesus warned of the eschatological destruction of the temple while seated with his disciples on the Mount of Olives.

Luke also locates the ASCENSION of Jesus on the Mount of Olives (Luke 24:50-51; Acts 1:9-11).

MOURNING The word *mourning* refers to a range of emotive responses such as sadness, grief, lamenting, and weeping in relation to someone's death or a sorrowful or distressing event.

MOZA 1. Descendant of Judah, son of Caleb and his secondary wife EPHAH (1 Chron 2:46).

2. One of Saul's descendants, the son of ZIMRI (1 Chron 8:36-37; 9:42-43).

MULBERRY, MULBERRY TREE The black mulberry, a short, stout tree with hairy, heart-shaped leaves, and deep red, edible fruits composed of a number of juicy globules, is mentioned in Luke 17:6 concerning believers' faith.

MULE The mule, hybrid of a donkey and horse, is sterile and cannot reproduce, thus it was prized. It was a working animal (1 Kgs 18:5; Zech 14:15; Ps 32:9) but also a prestigious riding animal fit for a king (1 Kgs 1:33, 38, 44) and the king's sons (2 Sam 13:29). Valued more than sheep, oxen, and horses, mules appear in booty lists. Solomon received mules as annual tribute from his vassals (1 Kgs 10:25; 2 Chron 9:24).

MUPPIM A son of Benjamin (Gen 46:21), probably known by different names elsewhere—SHEPHUPHAM in Num 26:39 and Shephuphan in 1 Chron 8:5.

MURABBAAT, WADI The Arabic name of the easternmost section of a wadi that begins east of Bethlehem and drains into the Dead Sea 11.5 mi. south of Qumran.

MURMUR In the exodus stories, the Israelites express dissatisfaction with Moses and Aaron by murmuring (CEB, "complaining") against them. Scholars often refer to the murmuring stories in the wilderness traditions found in both Exodus and Numbers. Their dissatisfaction often stems from the hunger and thirst they experience in the wilderness (e.g., Exod 15:24; 16:2; see WILDERNESS). The Israelites also murmur at the unfavorable report concerning the land of Canaan that is brought back by spies (Num 14:2). In this case, their murmuring leads to God's promise that the original generation will die in the wilderness (Num 14:27-31). Although the immediate targets for the Israelites' complaints are Moses and Aaron, murmuring is interpreted as rebellion against God (e.g., Exod 16:7-8; Deut 1:27; Ps 106:25).

In the NT, John characterizes the response to Jesus in similar terms by stating that both the Jews (John 6:41, 43) and the disciples (6:61) murmur against Jesus during his discourse on the manna (6:31-58; compare 7:12, 32). Their disbelief is thus portrayed as being like that of the Israelites in the wilderness period. Their murmuring identifies them as people who do not trust God. The word *murmur* (CEB, "complain," "mutter," or "grumble") is also used without reference to the exodus story as a general term for complaint (Phil 2:14).

MUSHI Mushi and his brother MAHLI were Levites, sons of Merari (Exod 6:19), and heads of the two divisions of Merarites (Num 3:33).

MUSTARD The smallness of the mustard seed is used in Jesus' teaching to depict God's kingdom (Matt 13:31-32; Mark 4:30-32; Luke 13:18-19; cf Gos. Thom. 20) and faith (Matt 17:20; Luke 17:6). Proverbially known as the smallest of seeds in the ancient Mediterranean world (mentioned in both Hellenistic and Jewish sources), its diameter is about 0.1 in. But the plant can normally grow 6 ft. high. When conditions are favorable, a height of 15 ft. is attainable, with the main stem as thick as a human arm. This is sufficient to hold the weight of small birds that come to eat its aromatic seeds, which have been used since ancient times as a spice.

MUSTER GATE See PARADE GATE.

MUZZLE Muzzling is closing and keeping the mouth of an animal shut with a device. The law "Don't muzzle an ox" (Deut 25:4) was applied in the NT to mean "Do not neglect to pay Christian ministers" (1 Cor 9:9; 1 Tim 5:18).

MYRA Acts 27:5-6 records that Paul and his company traveled from Caesarea on a ship of ADRAMYTTIUM to Myra, then transferred to a grain ship that had traveled from Alexandria and was bound for Rome. Myra was located about 3.5 mi. from the southwestern coast of Asia Minor in the region known as LYCIA.

MYRRH Used as an ingredient in certain perfumes, cosmetics, and medicines, myrrh is a reddish-colored resin obtained from a thorny bush that generally grows no more than 9 ft. in height. Its precious nature and expense are reflected in its being given as a gift by Jacob to Pharaoh (Gen 43:11) and by the magi to the baby Jesus (Matt 2:11).

MYSIA A region of the Roman province of Asia Minor, north of Lydia, south of Bithynia, and bordered on the east by the Aegean. In Acts 16:7-8, Luke says that Paul and his companions wanted to enter Mysia, but being prevented from doing so, "went down to TROAS" instead.

MYTH IN THE NT A story about gods. Usually in biblical scholarship, this refers to stories about gods other than the God of the OT and NT. In the NT, the word *myth* refers to false stories that corrupt true Christian teaching (1 Tim 1:4; 4:7; 2 Tim 4:4; Titus 1:14; 2 Pet 1:16).

Nn

NAAM Among Judah's descendants, he was JEPHUNNEH's grandson and Caleb's 3rd son (1 Chron 4:15).

NAAMAH 1. Daughter of Lamech and his wife Zillah; sister of Tubal-cain (Gen 4:22).

2. A town in the lowlands of Judah, near Lachish (Josh 15:41).

3. One of Solomon's Ammonite wives (1 Kgs 11:1), and mother of Rehoboam, Solomon's successor (1 Kgs 14:21, 31; 2 Chron 12:13).

NAAMAN 1. A descendant of Benjamin. Naaman appears as Benjamin's son (Gen 46:21) and as his grandson (Num 26:40). He also appears as the son of Bela, Benjamin's oldest (1 Chron 8:4). Naaman was the ancestor of the Naamites (Num 26:40).

2. The commander of the army of the king of Aram (Syria). He was healed of a skin disease through the intervention of ELISHA, a prophet of the northern kingdom (2 Kgs 5:1-27).

NAARAI Son of Ezbai and one of David's "Thirty" (1 Chron 11:37). In the par. list (2 Sam 23:24-39), the name appears as "PAARAI from Erab."

NAATHUS A descendant of ADDI, he dismissed his foreign wife and children in Ezra's reform (1 Esdr 9:31).

NABAL Nabal (meaning "fool," as suggested in 1 Sam 25:25), a wealthy Calebite sheep owner, is described as "a hard man who did evil things," and later as a "despicable man" by his wife ABIGAIL (25:3, 25). When David's troops, who had protected Nabal's shepherds, asked for food during a time of feasting, Nabal declined. David, infuriated, mustered his men to kill Nabal's men. Abigail intervened with provisions while Nabal feasted and became drunk (1 Sam 25:23-36). He died ten days later and Abigail became David's wife (25:37-39).

NABARIAH One of the witnesses who stood on the platform while listening to Ezra's reading of the Law scroll (1 Esdr 9:44).

NABATEANS People from the Arab kingdom of Nabatea (1 Macc 5:25; 9:35). The Nabateans come into prominence in the late 1st cent. BCE through a lucrative trade in frankincense, myrrh, spices, gold, precious gems, silks, and medicinal products.

NABOTH Naboth lived in Jezreel during the reign of AHAB king of Israel, and owned a vineyard adjacent to the royal palace (1 Kgs 21:1-2). Ahab desired Naboth's land for a vegetable garden, offering a better vineyard or the value of the land in money. Naboth refused to sell his property, so the king's wife JEZEBEL plotted to kill Naboth and his sons and take possession of his land.

NACON Name of the town or the owner of the THRESHING FLOOR in Judah where Uzzah died (2 Sam 6:6). The site was renamed Perez-uzzah (2 Sam 6:8; 1 Chron 13:11).

NADAB 1. The first of four sons whom ELISHEBA bore to Aaron (Exod 6:23; Num 3:2), appointed to priestly service together with his father and brothers (Exod 28:1). Nadab and Abihu "offered unauthorized fire before the LORD" and were consumed by the Lord's fire (Lev 10:1-7; Num 3:4).

2. Succeeded his father Jeroboam I as 2nd king of Israel, but after a two-year reign, he was murdered by his successor BAASHA (1 Kgs 15:25-28).

3. A descendant of Judah (1 Chron 2:28, 30).

4. A descendant of Benjamin (1 Chron 8:30; cf 9:36).

5. A guest at the wedding feast Tobit held for his son Tobias and his bride Sarah (Tob 11:18). Nadab attempted to murder his uncle Ahikar but died in the trap he had set (Tob 14:10-11).

NAGGAI Appears only in Luke's genealogy of Jesus as the father of Esli and the son of Maath (Luke 3:25-26).

NAHALAL, NAHALOL Nahalal (or Nahalol, Judg 1:30) was a levitical town within the tribal allotment of Zebulun in the northwestern portion of the Jezreel Valley (Josh 19:15; 21:35).

NAHALIEL A town between Mattanah and Bamoth on the exodus itinerary north of the Arnon River (Num 21:18-19). It was one of the last places passed by the Israelites before they arrived at the plains of Moab.

NAHAM Naham was the leader of a tribe, HODIAH's brother, and Ezrah's brother-in-law (1 Chron 4:17-19).

NAHAMANI Nahamani is listed among the prominent Jewish leaders who returned from exile in Babylon with ZERUBBABEL, according to Neh 7:7.

NAHARAI Naharai of BEEROTH was one of "the Thirty," the main body of 'David's mighty warriors. He served as Joab's armor-bearer (2 Sam 23:37; 1 Chron 11:39).

NAHASH 1. Nahash was an Ammonite ruler involved in a struggle with the Israelites under the fledgling leadership of Saul (1 Sam 11:1-13; 12:12), which seems to have influenced Israel's desire to have a king (1 Sam 12:1-25), although in 1 Sam 11:15 Saul is already designated king.

2. Nahash is mentioned as the father of Abigail in 2 Sam 17:25.

NAHATH 1. One of four sons born to REUEL, the son of Esau and Basemath. Each of these brothers is identified as the leader of an Edomite clan (Gen 36:13, 17; 1 Chron 1:37).

2. The son of ELKANAH from the priestly line descending from Levi's son Kohath (1 Chr 6:26 [Heb. 6:11]).

3. One of several priestly administrators who supervised the collection and storage of the many generous offerings provided by the Israelites in the wake

of the spiritual revival that characterized Judah during the days of Hezekiah (2 Chron 31:13).

NAHBI Nahbi son of Vophsi, from the tribe of Naphtali, was one of the twelve SPIES sent by Joshua from the wilderness of PARAN into Canaan (Num 13:14).

NAHOR 1. Genesis 11:22-25 places Nahor in the line of Shem as the 7th generation from Noah and identifies Nahor as the grandfather of Abram/Abraham.

2. The younger brother of Abram, according to Gen 11:26. Nahor, who had twelve sons (Gen 22:20-24), is identified in Gen 24 as the grandfather of Laban and Rebekah, who are subsequently in the area of Haran (Gen 28).

3. The name Nahor reflects the city of Nah(h)ur, located in the upper reaches of the Habur River.

NAHSHON The brother of Aaron's wife Elisheba (Exod 6:23) and chief of the tribe of Judah when the Israelites were wandering in the wilderness. Nahshon participated in taking the census (Num 1:7) and presenting offerings at the altar dedication (Num 7:12, 17). Nahshon appears in the genealogies of Moses and Aaron (Exod 6:14-25), David (Ruth 4:18-22; 1 Chron 2:3-17), and Jesus (Matt 1:4; Luke 3:32).

NAHUM 1. Prophesied NINEVEH's destruction (Nah 1:1; Tob 14:4; 2 Esdr 1:40).

2. Ancestor of Jesus (Luke 3:25).

NAHUM, BOOK OF Nahum is the seventh book of the Twelve Minor Prophets. It is solely devoted to a series of oracles against Nineveh, the capital of the Assyrian Empire.

NAIDUS One of those who gave up foreign wives in Ezra's reform (1 Esdr 9:31).

NAIL Nails were rare in antiquity, where construction usually used holes and pegs to attach boards.

In those few instances in which iron nails are mentioned in the construction process, the context is the decoration of the Jerusalem temple (1 Chron 22:3; 2 Chron 3:9), often relating to the extravagance of affixing gold foil or plates to the inner walls of the temple. Fifty shekels of gold were then used to overlay the heads of these small iron nails (perhaps the size of tacks). Both Jeremiah and Second Isaiah refer to the fashioning of idols using iron nails or clasps to fasten them together (Isa 41:7; Jer 10:4). To deal with the demands of heavier tasks, the Romans invented forged iron nails and the claw HAMMER to remove them. Long iron nails (7.5 in. in one recovered example) would have been used and probably reused when possible for CRUCIFIXION (John 20:25; cf Col 2:14). Arms were nailed above the wrist, the legs bent, and a nail driven through the heel bones to pin the lower torso to the cross.

NAIN The site of Nain is mentioned only in Luke 7:11 as the place where Jesus raised a young man, a son of a widow, from the dead.

NAIOTH After David flees from Saul to Samuel in Ramah, both David and Samuel settle at Naioth in Ramah (1 Sam 19:18).

NAOMI Meaning "my pleasantness." An Ephrathite (Bethlehemite) woman whose story is central to the book of Ruth.

NAPHATH-DOR Located between Carmel and Caesarea. Naphath, meaning "sand dune" or "district," refers to its coastal location or its status as district seat during Solomon's reign (Josh 12:23; 1 Kgs 4:11).

NAPHISH Eleventh of the twelve sons of Ishmael (Gen 25:15; 1 Chron

1:31); founder of an Arab tribe that was besieged and conquered by the Gadites, Reubenites, and the half-tribe of Manasseh living on the east side of the Jordan (1 Chron 5:18-19).

NAPHOTH-DOR See NAPHATH-DOR.

NAPHTALI, NAPHTALITES 1. The 6th son of Jacob who became the eponymous ancestor of the tribe of Naphtali. Naphtali and his children descend into Egypt with Jacob's family to survive the famine (Gen 46:24). His sons included Jahzeel (Jahziel in 1 Chron 7:13), Guni, Jezer, and Shillem (Shallum in 1 Chron 7:13).

2. The Naphtalites, descended from the eponymous ancestor Naphtali, received territory in the northern extremity of Israel. When the tribes of Israel left Egypt, the tribe of Naphtali provided 53,400 men of war (Num 1:42-43). By the end of the wanderings, their number had reduced to 45,400 (Num 26:48-50).

NARCISSUS Members of the household of the freedman Narcissus (Rom 16:11) formed a house church. Either Narcissus was not a Christian or he was dead, and those of his house continued to be identified with him after his death. Some believe this Narcissus was the same man as a freedman of the emperor CLAUDIUS, forced to commit suicide when Claudius died in 54 CE.

NARD An herb from the Valerianaceae family that grows in the Himalayan countries of Bhutan, Nepal, and Kashmir in India. The fragrant root and lower stems were dried and used to concoct a perfumed ointment. It was transported in the form of a dry rhizome or oil phase extract and was considered a very expensive luxury item. By including the detail that nard was contained in an alabaster flask, Mark (14:3) demonstrated the precious nature of the nard used by the woman to anoint Jesus' head (cf John 12:3). Nard has an intense, warm, musky odor that is mentioned among "the very choicest perfumes" in the description of the woman's "limbs" in Song 4:14.

NATHAN 1. Nathan, son of David (2 Sam 5:14; 1 Chron 14:4) and elder brother of Solomon (1 Chron 3:5), whose name appears in the "day of the Lord" pronouncement in Zech 12:12 and who is included in Jesus' genealogy in Luke 3:31.

2. In Samuel–Kings, Nathan the prophet has three major appearances. He is first introduced in 2 Sam 7:2, without any background information or genealogy. Nathan's next appearance is 2 Sam 12, where he delivers a severe rebuke after the Bathsheba affair and the murder of Uriah. Nathan's final appearance is in 1 Kgs 1, where he and Bathsheba orchestrate Solomon's anointing as the king of Israel.

3. Nathan of Zobah, one of David's mighty men (2 Sam 23:36) and one of the heroes in 1 Chron 11:38. He was father of Igal and brother of Joel.

4. Father of Azariah and Zabud (1 Kgs 4:5). Possibly the same Nathan as #1 or #2 above.

5. Son of Attai, a descendant of Judah from the clan of Jerahmeel. He was father of Zabad (1 Chron 2:36).

6. One of the delegates sent by Ezra to Iddo in Casiphia to recruit servants for God's house (Ezra 8:16). He is probably the same Nathan who agreed to divorce his foreign wife (Ezra 10:39).

NATHANAEL 1. A priest from the line of Pashhur whom Ezra required to divorce his foreign wife (1 Esdr 9:22).

2. An ancestor of Judith (Jdt 8:1).

3. An Israelite whom Jesus described as having "no deceit" and whom he called to become his disciple and a witness of his future glory (John 1:45-51).

NATHAN-MELECH A court official or eunuch under King Josiah (2 Kgs 23:11).

NATIONS In the OT, although Israel

is occasionally referred to as a nation rather than a people, "the nations" almost invariably refers to nations other than Israel. This usage continues in the Apocrypha and the NT, though these later writings also reflect a subsequent development in which the sense of nation gives way to that of "non-Jewish."

NAVE The largest room (CEB "main hall") in the tripartite interior of the Solomonic temple, between the holy of holies and the PORCH. Sixty ft. long, thirty ft. wide, and forty-five ft. high, with gilded wall-carvings, it contained a golden altar, ten lampstands, a table for displaying bread, and numerous small golden implements (1 Kgs 6–7; 2 Chron 3–4; Ezek 41).

NAZARENE, NAZARENES An adjective denoting origin in the village of NAZARETH that is used in the singular only of Jesus; the plural is used as a designation for Jesus' followers.

NAZARETH A village in the Roman district of Galilee identified in the NT as the home of Joseph, Mary, and Jesus (Matt 2:23; Luke 2:4, 39, 51; see GALILEE, GALILEANS).

Located in lower Galilee, Nazareth is approximately midway between the Mediterranean Sea to the west and the southern tip of the Sea of Galilee to the east. Situated on a ridge overlooking the Jezreel Valley, Nazareth had a commanding view of the large basin to the south and was in close proximity to Sepphoris the capital of Galilee, and to a major highway 3 mi. to the north.

NAZIR, NAZIRITE Nazirites appear early in the OT record and are found in both the NT period and rabbinic Judaism. Nazirites demonstrated their devotion to God through distinctive behaviors, commonly observing prohibitions against cutting the hair, drinking wine, or touching the dead. The earliest Nazirites appear to have adopted the role as a life calling. In later periods, a practice developed in which one could become a Nazirite for a temporary period as payment of a vow. Early Nazirites were either called by God or dedicated by their parents to a lifelong state of consecration to God, outwardly identified by their unshorn hair. The oldest biblical account of a Nazirite is that of SAMSON, in the period of the Judges (11th–12th cent. BCE). Before his conception, the Lord's messenger instructed Samson's mother to rear her child as a Nazirite: "Don't allow a razor to shave his head, because the boy is going to be a Nazirite for God from birth" (Judg 13:5). Samson's mother was instructed to avoid wine, strong drink, and unclean foods (Judg 13:4), but the only restriction spelled out for the child was that his hair not be cut. Samson partook in his wedding feast (which typically involved fermented drinks) "as was the custom for young men" (Judg 14:10) and had no compunction against touching dead bodies (Judg 14:19). When Delilah relieved Samson of his hair, however, he lost the supernatural strength emblematic of his special relationship with God (Judg 16:19-20). Samuel (11th cent. BCE) may also have been considered a Nazirite. When his mother Hannah prayed for a son, she vowed to return him to the Lord: "I'll give him to the LORD for his entire life. No razor will ever touch his head" (1 Sam 1:11).

NEAH A town or region in Zebulun (Josh 19:13).

NEAPOLIS Ancient Neapolis (lit., "New City") is identified with the modern town of Kavala. Neapolis is located about 10 mi. from Philippi on the other side of a mountain ridge. This town became Paul's entry port into Europe on his 2nd missionary journey. Paul sailed from Troas to the island of Samothrace and then on to Neapolis (Acts 16:11). Paul probably passed through this town again on his 2nd visit to Macedonia (Acts 20:1), and likely left from this port on his way to Troas (Acts 20:6).

NEARIAH 1. A descendant of Solomon, one of the six sons of Shemaiah and a father of three sons (1 Chron 3:22-23).

2. A Simeonite military leader during Hezekiah's reign. After the Simeonites conquered the pastureland near Gedor, Neariah helped lead an expedition to destroy the Amalekites who had escaped (1 Chron 4:42). See AMALEK, AMALEKITES; SIMEON, SIMEONITES.

NEBAI A leader whose name appears on the sealed covenant document (Neh 10:19).

NEBAIOTH Oldest son of Ishmael (Gen 25:13; 1 Chron 1:29) who had an Egyptian mother, according to Jub. 17:13-14. He was the ancestor of an Arabian tribe by the same name (Isa 60:7).

NEBAT Father of JEROBOAM I (e.g., 1 Kgs 11:26).

NEBO 1. A Babylonian deity, also known as Nabu, the city god of Borsippa, the patron deity of scribes, and the son of Marduk in Babylonian theology.

2. One of the Moabite towns conquered by Israelites (Num 32:3-4). The Reubenites and Gadites asked Moses for the land, which the Reubenites settled (Num 32:38).

NEBO, MOUNT A mount 800 m above sea level, in the territory of Madaba in Jordan. The Bible relates several episodes associated with Mount Nebo, which is identified with the peak of Pisgah (Deut 34:1): the Israelite tribes encamped "in the Abarim mountains in front of Nebo" (Num 33:47; Pisgah in Num 21:20); Balak took Balaam toward the summit of Pisgah to curse the tribes of Israel (Num 23:13-26); and Moses "hiked up from the Moabite plains to Mount Nebo, the peak of the Pisgah slope," where he was shown the land of promise (Deut 34:1). The town of Nebo appears in prophetic oracles against Moab (Isa 15–16; Jer 48) as part of the territory of Reuben (1 Chron 5:8).

NEBUCHADNEZZAR, NEBUCHADREZZAR There were two important kings of Babylon named Nebuchadnezzar, though only Nebuchadnezzar II is mentioned in the Bible.

1. Nebuchadnezzar I of the Second Dynasty of Isin ruled Babylon from 1125 to 1104 BCE. He kept Assyria at bay, but it was his successful campaign against Elam, in which he recovered the statue of Marduk, that made him great in the eyes of the Babylonians (see ELAM, ELAMITES).

2. Nebuchadnezzar II, who ruled Babylon for forty-three years (605–562 BCE), was the 2nd ruler of the Neo-Babylonian dynasty founded by his father Nabopolassar (626–605 BCE). Nabopolassar had rebelled against Assyria, seized the Babylonian throne, and begun a long seesaw struggle to drive Assyria from Babylonian territory (see ASSYRIA AND BABYLONIA). In 2 Kgs 24–25, Jehoiachin the king of Judah surrendered to Nebuchadnezzar II in 597 BCE.

NEBUSHAZBAN Nubushazban, a Babylonian official (Jer 39:13-14), helped transfer Jeremiah to Gedeliah's custody. Nebushazban is listed as the chief officer.

NEBUZARADAN One of the Babylonian officials connected with the fall of Jerusalem, Nebuzaradan was "the captain of the special guard," a high-ranking military officer. He is described as responsible for burning Jerusalem and deporting exiles (2 Kgs 25:8-11, 18-21). After the fall of Jerusalem, Nebuzaradan oversaw the transfer of Jeremiah to Gedeliah's custody (Jer 39:13-14) and was also associated with a later Babylonian deportation of Judeans in 582/1 BCE (Jer 52:30).

NECO Neco, the second PHARAOH of the 26th Dynasty of Egypt, appears in biblical accounts of the death of King JOSIAH and in contemporary oracles of Jeremiah. He is usually designated Neco II, although he was the first king of that name to rule both Upper and Lower EGYPT. His grandfather Neco I was a regional ruler based in the delta city of Sais at the end of the 3rd Intermediate Period. Neco (alternate: Necho or Nekau) II son of Psamtik I ruled Egypt from 610 to 595 BCE.

NEDABIAH The 7th son of King Jeconiah (see JEHOIACHIN) of Judah (1Chron 3:18).

NEGEB, NEGEV The word *Negeb*, which derives from a Hebrew word meaning "dry," generally designates the large area south of the highlands of Judah and northeast of the Sinai Peninsula. In its OT usage the Negeb designated the area about 15 mi. north and south of BEER-SHEBA and eastward to the Dead Sea, perhaps extending southward as far as Kadesh-barnea (see KADESH, KADESH-BARNEA).

For the OT writers, the Negeb is largely peripheral, lying outside the important areas for the story of Israel and Judah. Many of the OT stories of the patriarchs/matriarchs portray Abraham, Isaac, and their families as journeying throughout the Negeb, encountering various built-up towns, and dwelling in northern locations such as Beer-sheba and GERAR (see Gen 20:1; 21:31-34; 24:62; 26:6). Many of the exodus and wilderness stories are also set in the Negeb, where the Israelites are said to have encountered nomadic groups such as the Amalekites (Exod 17:8-16; Num 13:29; see AMALEK, AMALEKITES), dwelled for an extended period at Kadesh-barnea (Num 13:25-26; Deut 1:19), and engaged in military conflict with the city of HORMAH and the king of ARAD (Num 21:1-3; Deut 1:44). The book of Joshua also tells of the conquering of the king of Arad (Josh 12:1, 14) and assigns conquered Negeb territories to the tribes of Judah and Simeon (Josh 15:21-32; 19:1-9).

NEHEMIAH 1. One of the leaders of the exiles who returned from Babylon with Zerubbabel after 538 BCE (Ezra 2:2; Neh 7:7; 1 Esdr 5:8).

2. Son of HACALIAH (Neh 1:1); governor of the Persian province of Yehud (Judah) during the restoration (445–433 BCE, with a 2nd term sometime later). The so-called Nehemiah Memoir includes Neh 1:1–7:73*a*, parts of 12:27-43, and 13:4-31. Prior to his governorship, Nehemiah was "CUPBEARER to the king" (Neh 1:11), a trusted official of ARTAXERXES I Longimanus king of Persia (465–424 BCE). Nehemiah's major achievement is the refortification of Jerusalem. During a 2nd term as governor following a brief absence, Nehemiah carried out a 2nd series of reforms regarding the misuse of the temple (Neh 13:4-9), enforced financial support of the Levites (Neh 13:10-14), compelled observance of the Sabbath regulations (Neh 13:15-22), and required the dissolution of mixed marriages (Neh 13:23-27).

3. Son of AZBUK who ruled half the district of BETH-ZUR and helped repair the walls of Jerusalem (Neh 3:16).

NEHUM A prominent Jew returning from Babylonian exile with ZERUBBABEL (Neh 7:7).

NEHUSHTA The mother of King JEHOIACHIN of Judah (2 Kgs 24:8).

NEHUSHTAN The name of the bronze serpent that King HEZEKIAH had broken into pieces in his religious reform, attempting to destroy Canaanite forms of worship (2 Kgs 18:4, the only OT reference to the name) and centralize worship in the Jerusalem temple. The biblical author noted that the bronze serpent, which was believed to have been the one erected by Moses in Num 21:8-9 for the purpose of healing, was destroyed because the people were making offerings to it.

NEIEL A town listed along with BETH-EMEK as a northern boundary marker in the allotment to the tribe of Asher (Josh 19:27).

NEKODA 1. A temple servant whose descendants returned from Babylonia to Jerusalem after King Cyrus of Persia had ended the exile (Ezra 2:48; Neh 7:50).

2. An ancestral head of a family whose descendants had returned to Jerusalem after the exile but could not verify their descent and Israelite kinship (Ezra 2:59-60; Neh 7:62; 1 Esdr 5:37).

NEMUEL 1. Listed among the descendants of ELIAB in the Reubenite tribe (Num 26:9).

2. One of Simeon's sons and the head of one of five clans together numbering 22,200 descendants (Num 26:12; 1 Chron 4:24).

NEPHEG 1. The 2nd of three sons of Izhar and a descendant of Kohath in the genealogy of Levi (Exod 6:21).

2. A son of David, born in Jerusalem to an unnamed wife or secondary wife (2 Sam 5:15; 1 Chron 3:7; 14:6).

NEPHILIM The Nephilim are mentioned in two enigmatic passages in the Pentateuch, the ambiguity of which led to differing interpretations of the Nephilim in later Judaism.

Gen 6:4 observes that the Nephilim were on the earth when "divine beings and human daughters had sexual relations and gave birth to children." The author notes that the Nephilim also lived after this time.

The 2nd passage, Num 13:33, says nothing about either the divine beings or the human daughters. Rather, the author recounts how the spies sent by Moses into Canaan reported that the Nephilim (further characterized as the sons of Anak, who came from the Nephilim) were so large that the spies themselves seemed to be the size of grasshoppers.

NEPHISIM Family head whose descendants belonged to the Nethinim or temple servants, and returned to Jerusalem after Cyrus had ended the exile (Ezra 2:50; 1 Esdr 5:31).

NEPHTOAH, WATERS OF Means "opening." A boundary marker of Judah and Benjamin, between Mount EPHRON and the Hinnom Valley (Josh 15:9; 18:15).

NER Ner is sometimes listed as the father of Abner, Saul's uncle. In other instances, Ner is listed as the father of Kish and Abner. The question is complicated by the fact that verses in Samuel and Chronicles can be read to support either case.

NEREUS Nereus is a Roman Christian greeted by Paul in Rom 16:15.

NERGAL-SHAREZER One of the Babylonian officials who was present during and after the fall of Jerusalem (Jer 39:3, 13).

NERI Found only in Luke's genealogy as the father of Shealtiel (Luke 3:27).

NERIAH The son of Mahseiah and the father of BARUCH, the scribe and loyal friend of JEREMIAH (Jer 32:12; Bar 1:1), and SERAIAH, the quartermaster of the exiled king Zedekiah (Jer 51:59-64).

NEST In the OT, the bird's nest is a common metaphor for a place of refuge. Some passages allude to the inaccessibility of certain nests (Jer 49:16; Job 39:27). Other passages describe nests being plundered (Deut 22:6; Isa 10:14

NETHANEL The name of eight to ten men.

1. A leader of the tribe of Issachar in the wilderness period who assisted Moses with the census (Num 1:8; 2:5; 7:18; 10:15).

2. The 4th son of Jesse (1 Chron 2:13-14).

3. A priest or Levite in the time of David and one of the men appointed to blow the trumpet before the covenant chest (1 Chron 15:24).

4. The father of the scribe Shemaiah, a Levite in the time of David (1 Chron 24:6). Possibly the same as #3 above.

5. A Korahite who was gatekeeper in the temple during the time of David (1 Chron 26:4).

6. An official in the reign of Jehoshaphat who was sent to teach the Instruction in Judah (2 Chron 17:7).

7. A chief of the tribe of Levi in the time of Josiah (2 Chron 35:9).

8. A priest in the postexilic period who had married a foreign woman (Ezra 10:22).

9. A priest in the time of Jehoiakim (Neh 12:21).

10. A priest or Levite in the time of Nehemiah who celebrated the rebuilding of the walls of Jerusalem (Neh 12:36). Possibly the same as #9 above. See LEVI, LEVITES.

NETHANIAH 1. Elishama's son and the father of Ishmael who murdered Gedaliah governor of Judah at Mizpah (2 Kgs 25:23, 25; Jer 40:8, 15; 41:1-18).

2. A Levite; 2nd of Asaph's four sons, who with his three brothers received the 5th lot and prophesied with musical instruments under King David's direction (1 Chron 25:2, 12).

3. One of the Levites whom King Jehoshaphat sent to instruct the people throughout Judah about God's Instruction (2 Chron 17:8).

4. One of the descendants of BANI who gave up his foreign wife (1 Esdr 9:34; "Nathan" in the par. list of Ezra 10:39).

5. Jehudi's father and Shelmiah's son (Jer 36:14).

NETOPHAH, NETOPHATHITE 1. Town in Judah mentioned along with BETHLEHEM (1 Chron 2:54), and listed as one to which some of its residents returned after the exile (Ezra 2:22; Neh 7:26; 1 Esdr 5:18). Companies of singers lived in its villages (Neh 12:28), as did Levites after the exile (1 Chron 9:16).

2. Resident of Netophah: Maharai and Heleb, two of David's warriors who commanded military divisions, were Netophathites (2 Sam 23:28-29; 1 Chron 11:30; 27:13), as was Seraiah, Tanhumeth's son, who fought on behalf of GEDALIAH before Jerusalem fell to the Babylonians in 587 BCE (2 Kgs 25:23; Jer 40:8).

NEW HEAVEN, NEW EARTH Revelation depicts John's vision of "a new heaven and a new earth" (21:1). The old heaven and earth have departed (cf 20:11), along with the sea and its associations with CHAOS. The imagery is part of the cosmic upheaval associated with God's appearance at the end time (i.e., Rev 6:12-14). The destruction or transformation of creation is common in Jewish prophetic and apocalyptic traditions (e.g., Isa 65:17; 66:22; 1 En. 45:4-5; Jub. 1:29) and the NT (Matt 5:18; Mark 13:30; Rom 8:21; 2 Pet 3:12-13).

NEW JERUSALEM The culminating image of Revelation is John's vision of "the holy city, New Jerusalem" (Rev 21:2; cf 21:10; 3:12), a vision of God's ultimate establishment of abundance and peace. The city metaphor has multiple, overlapping meanings. Many details of the city in Rev 21:1–22:5 are familiar from the restoration of Jerusalem promised by the prophets (e.g., Isa 2:1-4; 49:18; 60–62; 65:17-25; Jer 31:38; Zech 14:6-11). The measuring of the city (Rev 21:15-21) alludes to Ezekiel's vision of the restored temple (Ezek 40–47), although in Revelation God dwells directly in the city. The city as bride evokes the notion of the marriage of the church to Christ (e.g., Eph 5:25-33).

NEW TESTAMENT Commonly refers to the twenty-seven books comprising the 2nd portion of the Christian scriptures, the first portion being the OT. The Greek phrase (1 Cor 11:25; 2 Cor 3:6; Heb 8:8, 13; 9:15) has a variant translation of "new covenant" in distinction to the covenant of Jer 31:31-34 (see COVENANT, OT AND NT). The transfer of the language from "covenant" to a body of writings reflects Paul's use of "old covenant" to refer to the writings of the Mosaic covenant (e.g., 2 Cor 3:14; see TESTAMENT).

NICANOR The name Nicanor occurs frequently in the Maccabean literature.

1. The leader of the Cyprian mercenaries (2 Macc 12:2).

2. The son of Patroclus and "one of the most important political advisers" of Antiochus IV Epiphanes (1 Macc 3:38; 2 Macc 8:9).

3. The overseer of all the war elephants in the kingdom who was made governor of Judah (2 Macc 14:12).

4. The companion of Demetrius I Soter, son of Seleucus IV, who resided with Demetrius in Rome and accompanied him to Syria in 162 BCE when Demetrius supplanted Antiochus V Eupator as king (Polybius, *Hist.* 31.14.4; see 1 Macc 7:1-4; cf Josephus, *Ant.* 12.402).

5. In the NT, one of the seven deacons appointed by the Jerusalem church to oversee the daily distribution of food, thereby leaving the apostles free to focus on more-pressing responsibilities (Acts 6:5).

NICODEMUS Nicodemus appears only in the Gospel of John (John 3:1-10; 7:45-52; 19:38-42). In Nicodemus's first appearance, he engages Jesus in debate. Jesus speaks to Nicodemus metaphorically. Jesus' words indicate that Nicodemus has not understood the metaphor (John 3:9). Yet Nicodemus's initial approach to Jesus shows understanding. He calls Jesus "Rabbi" and "a teacher who has come from God" (John 3:2). Both the appellation of rabbi and the notion that Jesus is sent from God are important to John's presentation of Jesus (e.g., John 1:38, 49; 4:31; 6:41-42; 8:4).

Nicodemus's later appearances may suggest a growing understanding of Jesus. In Nicodemus's 2nd appearance (John 7:45-52), he defends Jesus, saying the Law requires that the Pharisees give Jesus a fair hearing.

Finally, Nicodemus brings a great quantity of spices and helps Joseph of Arimathea bury Jesus (John 19:38-42).

NICOLAITANS An early Christian sect mentioned only in Rev 2:6, 15. John the seer reports that the exalted Christ commended the Ephesians because they "hate what the Nicolaitans are doing, which I also hate" (v. 6), and called on those in Pergamum to "change your hearts and lives" (v. 16), because some in that church "follow the Nicolaitans' teaching" (v. 15).

NICOLAUS One of seven men chosen to care for the neglected Hellenist widows (Acts 6:5). The last listed, he is identified as a "from Antioch, a convert to Judaism."

NICOPOLIS The city of Nicopolis is located in the region of Epirus in northwest Greece, within the Roman province of Macedonia. The name "Victory City" celebrated the victory of Octavian (later the emperor Augustus) over the forces of Marcus Antonius and Cleopatra at the naval battle of Actium in 31 BCE. Paul intended to spend the winter at Nicopolis (Titus 3:12). This perhaps hints at a journey either along the Via Egnatia from Macedonia or by sea from the Gulf of Corinth.

NIGER A Greek loanword from the Latin *niger*, meaning "black" or "dark." It is found only in Acts 13:1, as a surname for Simeon. He is listed among the teachers and prophets in the church at Antioch (see ANTIOCH, SYRIAN).

NIGHTHAWK This bird in the duplicate lists of Lev 11:16 ("any kind of hawk") and Deut 14:15 was considered unclean.

NILE RIVER At over 4,200 mi. in length, the Nile is the longest river in the world, arising south of the equator in eastern Africa and flowing north through the Sudan and EGYPT to the Mediterranean Sea. The waters of the Nile gave life to the desert climate of northern Sudan and Egypt and nourished the civilizations that emerged on its shores over 5,000 years ago.

NIMRAH See BETH-NIMRAH; LEOPARD.

NIMRIM, THE WATERS OF Referenced in only two OT texts (Isa 15:6; Jer 48:34). Both are embedded in sections of the respective prophetic compositions devoted to oracles against nations—more specifically, against Moab.

NIMROD Nimrod, son of Cush and a direct descendant of Noah, was a mighty warrior and hunter who founded Nineveh and Babylon, as well as a number of other cities including Calah (Gen 10:8-12; 1 Chron 1:10; see CUSH, CUSHITE).

NIMSHI JEHU is called "Nimshi's son" (1 Kgs 19:16; 2 Kgs 9:20; 2 Chron 22:7), but also "JEHOSHAPHAT's son and Nimshi's grandson" (2 Kgs 9:2, 14).

NINEVEH A major city in northern Mesopotamia during the Bronze and Iron Ages, and the capital of Assyria at the height of the Neo-Assyrian Empire. In the wake of its destruction in 612 BCE, the city experienced sudden reversal of political fortune, from extreme wealth and power to abject ruin.

Nineveh lay on the east bank of the Tigris River, near the confluence of the Tigris and Khosr Rivers, directly across from modern Mosul on the west bank of the Tigris. The ancient city was surrounded by a roughly rectangular double wall, approximately 2 km wide and 5 km long. With an enclosed area of 750 ha., Nineveh was truly a "great city" (Jon 1:2). Second Kings 19:36-37 (cf Isa 37:37-38) presents Nineveh as the capital city of Assyria. The verses include a composite account of Sennacherib's invasion of Judah in 701 BCE. According to v. 35, the Lord's messenger visited the Assyrian camp at night and killed 185,000 troops, and subsequently Sennacherib "departed, returning to Nineveh, where he stayed" (v. 36). There, while the king was worshipping in the temple of Nisroch, his sons murdered him "with a sword" (v. 37). The biblical writers understand Sennacherib's death as fulfillment of the Lord's pledge in 19:7*b*: "I'll have him cut down by the sword in his own land." The reach of the Lord's judgment extends to the capital city of the enemy king, even to the temple of his god in Nineveh.

The 7th-cent. BCE prophets Nahum and Zephaniah proclaim the fall of Nineveh. The postexilic book of Jonah tells the story of Jonah son of Amittai, commissioned by the Lord to prophesy against Nineveh. The OT thus presents two images of Nineveh: the arrogant city that deservedly suffers divine punishment and the repentant city that God spares. The former image is picked up in the apocryphal book of Tobit, which is the story of a pious Jew exiled to Nineveh. A similarly negative picture of the city probably is assumed in the apocryphal book of Judith.

The image of Nineveh as a repentant city surfaces in the Jesus saying in Luke 11:32 (cf Matt 12:40-41). The saying reasons that, since the Ninevites repented at the proclamation of Jonah, they are qualified to condemn the recalcitrant generation of Jesus on Judgment Day.

NIPHISH Called MAGBISH in Ezra 2:30, his descendants returned after the exile (1 Esdr 5:21).

NIPPUR A city in Mesopotamia located about 60 mi. (95 km) southeast of ancient Babylon and occupied almost continually from the early 6th millennium BCE to the 9th cent. CE. Nippur is not mentioned in the Bible.

NISAN Postexilic name for the 1st month in the Hebrew calendar, comparable to March–April (Neh 2:1; Esth 3:7).

NOADIAH 1. Son of BINNUI, who, along with Eleazar and fellow Levite Jozabad, was present when Ezra weighed the treasure for the temple into the hands of Meremoth the priest (Ezra 8:33).

2. The (false) prophetess, who along with "the rest of the prophets," intimidated Nehemiah (Neh 6:14).

NOAH 1. Noah is the protagonist of the FLOOD story in Gen 6:5–9:28 and thus is arguably the center character of the primeval history. Isaiah 54:9 mentions the covenant with Noah as an example of God's steadfast love, and Ezek 14:14, 20 depicts Noah (together with Daniel and Job) as an exceptionally righteous person whose prayer can change the fortune of an entire nation. Since Isaiah and Ezekiel seem to presuppose that their readers were familiar with Noah as a literary character, it is safe to assume that the Noah tradition was known widely in the exilic and early postexilic periods.

2. One of the daughters of Zelophehad (Num 26:33; 27:1; 36:11) who, upon the death of their father, petitioned Moses for a share of the inheritance (Num 27:1).

NOAHIC COVENANT A covenant established between God and Noah, as well as with Noah's descendants and all animals, following the flood (Gen 9:8-17). God promised never again to destroy the world by means of a flood and placed the rainbow in the clouds as a reminder of the covenant. Unlike most other covenants between God and humanity, the Noahic covenant did not impose any requirements on humans. See COVENANT, OT AND NT.

NOB DAVID flees from Saul to Nob, the city of priests, where he asks for and receives the bread of the presence and Goliath's sword from Saul's priest AHIMELECH (1 Sam 21:1-9). These are important symbols of authority: holy bread and the sword of Israel's great enemy.

NOD After God marked him for the murder of ABEL, his brother CAIN left the presence of the Lord and lived in "the land of Nod, east of EDEN" (Gen 4:16).

NOGAH One of David's sons (1 Chron 3:7; 14:6).

NOHAH 1. A location in Benjamin, mentioned in the intertribal war (Judg 20:43). See BENJAMIN, BENJAMINITES.

2. The 4th of Benjamin's five sons according to 1 Chron 8:2; absent, however, from similar lists in Gen 46:21; Num 26:38-41; and 1 Chron 7:6.

NORTHEASTER The stormy wind that struck Paul's ship on its way from Fair Havens ("Good Harbors") to Phoenix and threatened to blow the ship to the African Gulf of Syrtis (Acts 27:14).

NUMBERS, BOOK OF The name "Numbers" translates the Latin and Greek titles, both of which correlate with the book's Talmudic name, "the 'fifth' of the census totals." These names derive from the wilderness census records (Num 1–4; 26), which highlight the collective identity of the Israelites on their way to the promised land.

NURSE A nurse may be a woman who is nursing or breast-feeding her own or another's child (Exod 2:7; 2 Kgs 11:2) or a caregiver for children (Ruth 4:16). Moses, despairing of his people's protesting the manna, asks rhetorically whether he must be Israel's nurse (Num

11:12). Paul speaks of tending to the Thessalonians "like a nursing mother caring for her own children" (1 Thess 2:7). When a given nurse is identified, the one in her care is often particularly significant.

NYMPHA Owner of a house in Colossae in which Christians gathered for meetings and worship, and to whom Paul (or a Christian writing in Paul's name) sent greetings (Col 4:15).

Oo

OAK Present-day remnants of oak woodland in the moister areas of Israel indicate a much wider occurrence in biblical times. The oasis-like respite provided by clumps of oak trees meant that such places were frequent camping places or villages, as evidenced in such references as "oak of Moreh" (Gen 12:6); "Moreh Oak Grove" (Deut 11:30); "oak at Ophrah" (Judg 6:11); "oak at Tabor" (1 Sam 10:3); and "oaks of Mamre" (Gen 13:18). Solitary oak trees were often used as landmarks (e.g., Gen 12:6; 35:4; Josh 19:33; 24:26) or markers of graves (1 Chron 10:12). Offering protection from the sun, oaks were often gathering places—locations for meetings, either official or social, or even encounters with the Lord's messengers (Judg 6:11, 19; 9:6; 1 Sam 10:3). However, in some shady clumps immoral practices took place (Isa 57:5; Ezek 6:13; Hos 4:13). Absalom, David's son, was killed when he was caught in the branches of an oak tree while riding his mule (2 Sam 18:9-14). Reputedly sturdy trees, oaks are also often used metaphorically as symbols of strength (Isa 61:3; Amos 2:9).

Abimelech was made king "by the oak at the stone pillar in Shechem" (Judg 9:6). Jacob hid the foreign gods of his household beneath the oak tree near Shechem (Gen 35:4). After making a covenant with the people, Joshua set up a large stone beneath the oak at Shechem (Josh 24:22-26). All of these likely refer to the same oak, perhaps related to a shrine. See SHECHEM, SHECHEMITES.

OATH At its simplest, "swearing an oath" appears to strengthen or confirm the truth of a statement or the reliability of a promise (or threat), by invoking a divine sanction in the event that the statement proves to be false or the promise or threat proves to be empty. One who swears an oath, especially in early biblical traditions, invokes a conditional curse or malediction upon himself or herself in the event that the oath turns out to be willfully false or invalid. In effect, to break or to nullify an oath constitutes an act of perjury that invites penalties. Although Jesus (Matt 5:37) and James (Jas 5:12) insist that in everyday life "yes" or "no" should require no qualification and carry no less weight or reliability than an oath, situations of crisis, absence of confidence, or public need may invite the use of oaths to provide assurance that the speaker's statement, act of witness, or promise is sincere, reliable, truthful, and made in good faith.

OBADIAH 1. Ahab's palace manager who was so devoted to the Lord that he fed and protected a hundred prophets. As Elijah requested, he told Ahab that Elijah would meet Ahab (1 Kgs 18:3-16).

2. Arnan's son; a descendant of David through Solomon (1 Chron 3:21).

3. Izrahiah's son; a descendant of

Issachar who headed a northern clan (1 Chron 7:3).

4. Azel's son; a Benjaminite and descendant of Saul (1 Chron 8:38; 9:44).

5. A Levite and descendant of Elkanah (1 Chron 9:16).

6. A Gadite warrior and an officer in David's army (1 Chron 12:9).

7. Father of Ishmaiah and Zebulunite tribal leader during David's reign (1 Chron 27:19).

8. Official of King Jehoshaphat. He taught the Instruction to the people in the cities of Judah (2 Chr 17:7-9).

9. A Levite, Merari's son, who directed temple repair during Josiah's reform (2 Chron 34:12).

10. Jehiel's son who returned with Ezra to Jerusalem (Ezra 8:9; 1 Esdr 8:35), and perhaps the same Obadiah who signed the covenant (Neh 10:5).

11. A gatekeeper at the storehouses in Jerusalem after the exile (Neh 12:25).

12. Prophet whose vision is recorded in the book of Obadiah (Obad 1).

OBADIAH, BOOK OF Obadiah is the shortest book in the OT, with a single chapter of twenty-one verses. The book contains no information regarding the prophet's lineage and origin or about contemporary rulers. It is entirely given over to a diatribe against Judah's southern neighbor, Edom.

OBAL Eighth of the thirteen sons of Joktan (Gen 10:28), and thus a descendant of Shem, the son of Noah.

OBED 1. The son of Ruth and Boaz; the father of Jesse and grandfather of King David (Ruth 4:17, 22; 1 Chron 2:12). According to some, he was the "goel" or "next-of-kin" for Naomi and functioned as her son (Ruth 4:14-17). In the Levirate marriage (see LEVIRATE LAW), he was the son (or grandson) of Naomi's husband Elimelech (Ruth 4:3-9). In both genealogies of Jesus in Matt 1:5 and Luke 3:32, he was the son of Boaz. Because Obed is named a son of Naomi, he becomes both the son of Elimelech and the son of Boaz; both men were of Bethlehem, Judah. Through Obed, Moab entered the lineage of Jesus (Ruth 1:4; 4:6). See DAVID.

2. A descendant of Judah (1 Chron 2:37-38).

3. One of David's mighty men named in the longer list in 1 Chron 11:47, but not in 2 Sam 23.

4. A gatekeeper in Solomon's temple (1 Chron 26:7).

5. The father of Azariah, a commander (2 Chron 23:1).

6. A descendant of Adin who returned from exile (1 Esdr 8:32).

OBED-EDOM The name means "servant of (the god) Edom."

1. The "Gittite" (i.e., from GATH) at whose house David lodged the covenant chest of God when the procession to bring it to David's City (2 Sam 6:1-11; 1 Chron 13:1-14) was stopped by Uzzah's death. Obed-edom's name and origin could place him among Philistines loyal to David (2 Sam 15:18, 22).

2. Son of JEDUTHUN (1 Chron 15:18, 24; 16:38) who was gatekeeper for the covenant chest of God and also performed special service as one of the lyre players accompanying the chest into David's City (15:21; 16:5, 38).

3. Son of Korah through Kore (1 Chron 26:1, 19). Obed-edom and his sixty-two descendants were gatekeepers of the temple precinct and its related storehouses in preparation for the building of the temple under Solomon (1 Chron 23:2; 26:4-8, 15).

4. Levitical custodian of temple treasures when JOASH king of Israel defeated AMAZIAH king of Judah and sacked Jerusalem (2 Chron 25:24). He presumably served in the gatekeeper tradition of his clan (cf 1 Chron 26:4-8, 15; and #3 above). The parallel account in 2 Kgs 14:14 omits mention of Obed-edom.

The precise relationship between these individuals remains unclear due to the nature of the work of the Chronicler, who presents one or more families of temple servants claiming ties to the caretaker of the covenant chest under David and gives them levitical ancestry. The son of Jeduthun and the gatekeeper under #2 above are perhaps to be understood as separate individuals (1 Chron 16:38). See KORAH, KORAHITES; PHILISTINES; PRIESTS AND LEVITES.

OBIL Obil was an Ishmaelite placed in charge of King David's camels, one of several civic officials to steward royal property (1 Chron 27:30).

OBOTH The place the Israelites camped after the bronze serpent incident, between Punon and Iye-abarim (Num 21:10-11; 33:43-44). The name could mean "wineskins" (Job 32:19) or "necromancers" (CEB, "spirits of divination" [Lev 19:31]). See SERPENT.

OCHRAN Ochran was the father of PAGIEL, a leader of the tribe of Asher. His name occurs five times in lists of tribal leaders in the book of Numbers (1:13; 2:27; 7:72, 77; 10:26). See ASHER, ASHERITES.

ODED 1. The father of AZARIAH the prophet during the reign of Asa (2 Chron 15:1).

2. A prophet who helped persuade Israel to free the Judeans taken captive during the reign of Ahaz (2 Chron 28:8-15).

ODOMERA Bedouin chief whom Jonathan killed along with his kindred and other townspeople in Phasiron (1 Macc 9:65-66).

OFFERING FOR THE SAINTS See COLLECTION, THE.

OFFERING OF WELL-BEING A voluntary sacrifice in which the fat of the entrails, the kidneys, and the appendage of the liver are burned as an offering to God (Lev 3:1-17). The remainder of the animal is eaten by the offerand and/or the priests (Lev 7:11-18). See SACRIFICES AND OFFERINGS.

OG Og was the king of BASHAN who confronted Israel on their journey through Transjordan as they moved toward the land of Canaan (Num 21:31-35). Og is reported to have reigned in the cities of ASHTAROTH and EDREI (Deut 1:4). According to Deut 3:1-4, Og and his army were destroyed in a battle at Edrei, and that defeat, along with the defeat of King SIHON, was often cited in Israel's history as evidence of the Lord's power and protection of the people of Israel (e.g., Deut 29:7; 31:4; Josh 2:10; 9:10; Ps 135:11). Deuteronomy 3:11 lists Og as the last of the remnant of the REPHAIM, a race of giants counted among the early inhabitants of this region (Deut 2:11). His great size is supported by the reference to his iron bed as being 6 ft. wide and 13.5 ft. long.

OHAD The 3rd of six sons of Simeon and grandson of Jacob and LEAH (Gen 46:10; Exod 6:15).

OHEL Ohel is mentioned only at 1 Chron 3:20, where he is listed as the 5th child of ZERUBBABEL.

OHOLAH AND OHOLIBAH Symbolic names of SAMARIA and JERUSALEM, cities represented as unfaithful wives of the Lord, in Ezek 23.

OHOLIAB A Danite (see DAN, DANITES) appointed by the Lord to assist BEZALEL in fashioning the accoutrements for the early Israelite cult, including the MEETING TENT and its accessories (Exod 31:6; 35:34; 36:1-2). Oholiab was "a gem cutter, a designer, and a needleworker" (Exod 38:23). The two craftsmen trained others to assist them in their work; Moses alone, however, was responsible for assembling the components (Exod 40).

OHOLIBAH See OHOLAH AND OHOLIBAH.

OHOLIBAMAH A Canaanite wife of Esau and daughter of ANAH, son of Zibeon the Hivite (Gen 36:2; cf 36:20, 25). Oholibamah is the most frequently mentioned matriarch in the genealogy of Esau/Edom (Gen 36), yet she does not appear among Esau's Canaanite wives in Gen 26:34. Three Esauite clans descend from her, and an Edomite clan bears her name (Gen 36:14, 18, 41; 1 Chron 1:52).

OIL While Deut 8:7-8 lists seven products of Canaan that make it a desirable, fertile, and well-watered land (wheat, barley, grape vines, figs, pomegranates, olives, and honey) the most versatile and economically important is the olive from which oil is extracted. The economic triad of olive, grape, and wheat made life possible in ancient Canaan.

The ubiquitous nature of olive oil in ANE society is attested by the many uses to which it was put. Lighting people's paths at night, their homes, and their temples were oil lamps that were carried in the hand (Matt 25:3-8), placed on a table or in a niche (2 Kgs 4:10), or placed in a LAMPSTAND before the altar (Lev 24:2). Sacred objects and persons were set apart by anointing them with oil (Jacob's pillar at Bethel in Gen 28:18; Samuel's anointing of kings in 1 Sam 10:1 and 16:13; see ANOINT). Oil was one of the items regularly offered on God's altar (Lev 2:2-7). Wheat or barley flour were mixed with oil to produce cakes, both for sacred purposes (Exod 29:2) and for one's daily bread (1 Kgs 17:12; see SACRIFICES AND OFFERINGS).

Oil was used to anoint the sick (Mark 6:13), as medicine on sores (Isa 1:6), in the bindings of wrapped wounds (Luke 10:34), and possibly as a liniment for sore joints (Ps 109:18). Customarily, olive oil was used after bathing to maintain skin tone (Sus 1:17), to soothe the spirit (Ps 133:2), and to make "the face shine" (Ps 104:15). Cosmetics to color the eyes, lips, and hair, and perfumes used by both genders depended upon oil as a base mixed with a variety of spices, roots, and dyes. The fragrant ointments, spices, and unguents used to honor the dead and mask the smell associated with their bodies were also oil-based (Mark 16:1).

OLD TESTAMENT The Christian name for the *Tanakh* in contrast to the NT. Both terms are based on the "new covenant" and a perceived "old covenant" (Jer 31:31; Luke 22:20; 1 Cor 11:25, etc.). The OT is not a single canon, but has different formulations according to different branches of Christianity. The OT for Catholic and Eastern Orthodox churches was based on the SEPTUAGINT, the Greek translation of the Jewish Scriptures, and thus it contains books such as Judith. The Protestant OT is based on the Hebrew Jewish Scriptures and does not contain such Greek books. See COVENANT, OT AND NT.

OLIVE, OLIVE TREE The olive is perhaps the most important plant mentioned in the Bible. Olive trees typify the Holy Land and adjacent territories (cf the description of the land of promis in Deut 8:8).

The olive tree is a medium-sized orchard tree with a life span of hundreds of years. Its knobby trunk may become massive and hollow with age while it still has leafy branches. When olive trees are felled, they sprout again (see Job 14:7-9), and the shoots may be seen around the base like children around a table (cf Ps 128:3).

OLIVES, MOUNT OF See MOUNT OF OLIVES.

OLYMPAS A Christian man in Rome who receives greetings from Paul in Rom 16:15, grouped with PHILOLOGUS, JULIA, and NEREUS and his sister. Family relationships among the five are possible but not specified. Due to his Greek name, Olympas was probably a Gentile.

OMAR Second-listed son of ELIPHAZ and grandson of Esau and Adah, Omar is a clan chief of Esau (Gen 36:11, 15; 1 Chron 1:36).

OMEGA The last letter of the Greek alphabet. See ALPHA AND OMEGA.

OMER A dry measure of capacity, mentioned relative to grain in Exod 16:16-36 (Lev 23:10, 15; Deut 24:19; Job 24:10). The exact size is unknown but is probably equal to one-tenth of an ephah or 2 qts. See WEIGHTS AND MEASURES.

OMRI 1. Omri was a king of the northern kingdom of Israel in the 9th cent. BCE (ca. 882–871). Omri is hailed king after the usurper ZIMRI sets fire to his own palace and perishes in the flames (1 Kgs 16:18). Despite the mere thirteen verses dedicated to Omri's story in 1 Kings with its negative evaluation, extrabiblical texts and archaeological material reveal a ruler with an international reputation who expanded the borders of the kingdom and began an impressive building campaign.

2. The 5th son of BECHER, Benjamin's oldest offspring (1 Chron 7:8).

3. Grandfather of UTHAI, a Judahite who settled in Jerusalem following the Babylonian exile (1 Chron 9:4).

4. An officer watching over the tribe of Issachar for King David (1 Chron 27:18). See ISSACHAR, ISSACHARITES.

ON A Reubenite who participates in Korah's rebellion against Moses and Aaron (Num 16:1). See REUBEN, REUBENITES.

ONAM 1. Within the genealogy of Esau and the Horite clans of Edom, Onam is the son of SHOBAL (Gen 36:23). See EDOM, EDOMITES; ESAU, ESAUITES.

2. In the Chronicler's genealogy of the clans of Judah, Onam is the son of Jerahmeel and ATARAH (1 Chron 2:26), and he had two sons (1 Chron 2:28). See JERAHMEEL, JERAHMEELITES; JUDAH, JUDAHITES.

ONAN Son of the Canaanite "BATH-SHUA" (1 Chron 2:3) and Judah; younger brother to ER, whose wife was the Canaanite TAMAR (Gen 38:2-4). The Lord deemed Er "immoral" and killed him for it (38:7). Judah in turn told Onan, whose name may mean "vigor," to impregnate Tamar, following the code of levirate marriage (see LEVIRATE LAW), providing lineage for the deceased and family to support the widow (Deut 25:5-10). However, Onan "wasted his semen on the ground, so he wouldn't give his brother children" (Gen 38:9). Thus all such acts of "wasting" one's semen, including masturbation, became known outside the Bible as "onanism," a misunderstanding of Onan's act in the text itself. The Lord viewed Onan's behavior as "wrong," and consigned him to the same demise as Er. The narrative's conclusion (Gen 38:26) suggests that the men's egregious act was neglect of responsibility to Tamar. See MARRIAGE; SHELAH.

ONESIMUS 1. In the letter to Philemon, Paul refers to himself as having become father to one of his colleagues in the gospel, Onesimus, while Paul was in prison (Phlm 10). Traditionally, this verse has been interpreted to mean that Onesimus was the slave of Philemon, though Paul never refers to Philemon as Onesimus's master. The traditional interpretation, that Onesimus is a fugitive slave, though challenged in recent scholarship, remains dominant in scholarly and popular treatments.

2. Colossians mentions a "faithful and dearly loved brother" called Onesimus (Col 4:9) whom Paul had sent to COLOSSAE and who was apparently himself a Colossian. This may be the same Onesimus from the letter to Philemon.

3. Ignatius of Antioch writes of an Onesimus, bishop of EPHESUS, "a man of indescribable charity and your bishop here on earth" (Ign. Eph. 1.3).

4. The 4th-cent. Apostolic Constitutions mentions a Bishop Onesimus of Borea in Macedonia (Apos. Con. 7.46).

5. The medieval Byzantine Martyrdom of Saint Onesimus anachronistically conflates the figure of Onesimus in the Pauline corpus with traditions about Onesimus Leontinis of Sicily, a Christian teacher martyred during the Valerian harassment in the 3rd cent. CE. According to the Martyrdom of Saint Onesimus, Onesimus, a "house servant" and associate of Paul, was martyred in Rome under a provincial administrator named Tertullus (390 CE).

6. In 18th-cent. colonial America the Puritan Cotton Mather named his slave Onesimus, because Mather believed Paul's letter to Philemon was an exhortation for the master class to make their "Negroes" into willing servants of God. When a smallpox epidemic broke out in Boston in 1721, Onesimus told his master that as a child in Africa he had been inoculated against the disease with pus taken from the sore of a victim and rubbed into a cut on Onesimus's arm, a common West African practice. Mather convinced Dr. Zabdiel Boylston to experiment with the procedure. Public reaction to the experiment was violently hostile, but the inoculation drastically reduced the mortality rate among those exposed. Credit for the procedure, however, would go to Dr. Edward Jenner, a British physician who performed his first inoculation seventy-five years later. And Onesimus, like his biblical namesake, would be remembered, if at all, only as a slave. See SLAVERY.

ONESIPHORUS A supporter of Paul mentioned in 2 Timothy. In 1:16-17, Paul, or someone writing in his name, requests that the Lord grant mercy to the household of Onesiphorus, who often refreshed Paul and was not ashamed of his imprisonment in Rome.

ONO A city in the plain, near Lod, mentioned in the 15th-cent. BCE list of Thutmose III. According to 1 Chron 8:12 it was occupied by the Benjaminites (see BENJAMIN, BENJAMINITES).

ONYCHA An ingredient in the INCENSE used in the meeting tent (Exod 30:34; Sir 24:15).

ONYX A form of quartz having alternating black and white bands, similar to agate and sardonyx.

OPHEL The Hebrew word means "hill" or "mound" but is used in the OT as a proper noun to designate a particular area of JERUSALEM: a hill (part of a ridge) south of the temple mount. Today, the area around the Ophel is commonly designated as "David's City" and considered the oldest area of settlement in Jerusalem. On the east, the KIDRON VALLEY separates the Ophel from the MOUNT OF OLIVES and the Silwan settlement; the Hinnom Valley is to the south and the Tyropoeon (Central) Valley is to the west (see HINNOM, VALLEY OF).

OPHIR 1. Ophir refers to a geographical place where gold was obtained (Job 28:16; Ps 45:9 [Heb. 45:10]; Isa 13:12).

2. Ophir appears in the genealogy of Joktan (Gen 10:29; 1 Chron 1:23).

OPHRAH 1. A city in the territory of Benjamin (Josh 18:23) identified with modern et-Taiyibeh 4 mi. northeast of Bethel. The site is named as the destination of a Philistine raiding party (1 Sam 13:17).

2. The home of GIDEON, who is also known as JERUBBAAL.

3. The son of Meonothai in the genealogy of Judah (1 Chron 4:14).

ORACLE A direct message from God delivered through a prophet. Although the word *oracle* often carries with it the idea of a divine answer given in response to an inquiry (e.g., the Oracle of Delphi), the terms translated as "oracle" in the Bible do not necessarily carry this connotation. Some biblical oracles are given in response to a question or petition presented to the deity (1 Kgs 22:15;

2 Chron 20:5-19), a practice that is also known from Mesopotamia, and in such cases the prophetic activity often takes place within a cultic setting (1 Chron 25:1). But the means by which the majority of oracles in the OT was received is unknown, as most are presented in their canonical form without reference to the process of intermediation that produced them.

This term as used in the NT does not necessarily refer to prophetic activity. It is used in later Christian literature to refer to the sayings of Christ and the teachings of the early church.

ORDINATION, ORDAIN Typically the terms *ordain* and *ordination* pertain to a ritual by which a person is formally appointed to and invested with a ministerial function in a religious community. In the OT, for example, a ritual of clothing with priestly robes and anointing with oil was used in the consecration of Aaron (Lev 8) and subsequent high priests (Lev 21:10). The people of Israel laid their hands on Levites appointed to the service of the Lord, and afterward Aaron presented them to the Lord (Num 8:5-13). Moses imposed hands on Joshua, investing him with power and authority and appointing him to leadership (Num 27:15-23; Deut 34:9). See LAYING ON OF HANDS; PRIESTS AND LEVITES.

Jesus appointed the Twelve (Mark 3:14), whom he named apostles (Mark 3:14; Luke 6:13-16). These were given power and authority and sent out to preach (Luke 9:1-2; cf Matt 10:1-5; Mark 3:14-15).

Luke's accounts of the choice of seven from among Hellenists and of the divine selection of the prophets Barnabas and Saul to be sent on a mission of evangelization include a ritual of imposition of hands accompanied by prayer (Acts 6:6; 13:3). Prayer, rather than any specific ritual, is central to the appointment of elders in Acts 14:23. See ELDER.

Concerned with ministry in the church and with the succession of Paul, the Pastoral Epistles mention an imposition of hands on Timothy. In 1 Tim 4:14, Timothy is exhorted not to neglect the spiritual gift given to him through prophecy with a laying on of hands by the presbyterate, a council of elders. Second Timothy 1:6 mentions a spiritual gift that Timothy has through the "laying on of my [Paul's] hands." See LAYING ON OF HANDS.

OREB AND ZEEB These two Midianite captains are mentioned at the conclusion of the story of GIDEON's leading the coalition of Manasseh, Naphtali, Zebulun, and Asher against their Midianite and Amalekite oppressors during the period of the judges (Judg 7:25).

OREN Jerahmeel's son (1 Chron 2:25) in Judah's genealogy.

ORNAN The Chronicler's spelling of the name ARAUNAH. Ornan is mentioned (1 Chron 21:15-28; 2 Chron 3:1) as the Jebusite owner of a certain threshing floor (the future site of the Jerusalem temple) that David purchased to use as a place to offer sacrifices to avert God's destruction of Jerusalem.

ORPAH Orpah and Ruth were Naomi's two Moabite daughters-in-law, widowed during a famine (Ruth 1:1-14). In the narrative structure, Orpah's choice to return to her mother's house (1:8) is set in opposition to Ruth's remaining with Naomi.

ORPHAN The OT use of the term *orphan* does not distinguish between the loss of both parents (orphan) and the loss of the father. Orphaned children were given special consideration. The Instruction required remnants of the harvest to be left in the fields for the orphans to glean, and a special collection of tithes was given every 3rd year for their care (Deut 14:28-29; 24:19-21; 26:12; 27:19). Orphans found protection within the community and participated in celebrations (Exod 22:22-24 [Heb. 22:23-25]; Deut 24:17; 27:19; and see Ps 82:3; Prov 23:10).

OSNAPPAR Osnappar was probably the same as Ashurbanipal (668–630 BCE), who succeeded ESARHADDON, the last significant king of Assyria, resettling peoples he conquered into Samaria and Transjordan (Ezra 4:10). See ASHURBANIPAL, ASSURBANIPAL; EZRA; SARGON.

OSTRICH The ostrich is no longer found in the Middle East. In biblical times, this anomalous bird, which cannot fly, probably inhabited the wilderness regions south of Judah and east of the Jordan River. A rather detailed description of the ostrich's behavior is found in Job 39:13-18 in the midst of God's response to Job's relentless questions. In the context of God's infinite wisdom compared to Job's ability to comprehend, the ostrich is seen as a curiosity, a creature to which God has not given wisdom or understanding, and whose behavior exhibits that deficiency. This passage mentions the ostrich's habit of laying its eggs in the hot sand, where they are occasionally abandoned and exposed to dangers (39:14-15). It makes allusions to this bird's speed, which exceeds that of a horse and rider (39:18). Since the ostrich is omnivorous, it is not surprising that it is counted among the ritually unclean birds (Lev 11:16; Deut 14:15).

OTHNI A Levite son of Shemaiah and grandson of OBED-EDOM listed among the gatekeepers assigned to temple service under David (1 Chron 26:7).

OTHNIEL Son of Kenaz (the younger brother of Caleb) (Josh 15:17; Judg 1:13) and brother of Seraiah (1 Chron 4:13) of the tribe of Judah (Josh 15).

Apart from the so-called "minor judge" accounts, Othniel's is the shortest of the narratives, yet it is shaped by the same formulaic expressions first seen in the introductory material of Judg 2:11-19, and subsequently framing the stories of Ehud, Deborah/Barak, and Gideon.

OTHONIAH A descendant of Zamoth, and one of the returning exiles whom Ezra commanded to divorce their foreign wives (1 Esdr 9:28). Ezra 10:27 seems to identify him as MATTANIAH, a descendant of Zattu.

OVEN The dome-shaped oven used by the Israelites for baking bread was constructed of clay and straw (Exod 8:3; cf Lev 11:35), with broken pottery used as further insulating material, and was sometimes sunk into the earth. Sticks and straw were used to kindle a fire inside the oven at the bottom of the dome (Matt 6:30), and when the fire had been reduced to hot coals the loaves were affixed to the interior walls of the oven for baking. Each household had its own oven, as the description of famine in Lev 26:26 illustrates: when grain is scarce, a single oven will suffice to bake bread for ten households. Bread baked in ovens could be leavened (Hos 7:4-7) or unleavened (Lev 2:4; 7:9).

The heat of an oven was proverbial, and could serve as an image of coming catastrophe (Mal 4:1 [Heb. 3:19]). Hosea uses a heated oven as a metaphor for the hotheaded wicked (7:4-7). In Lam 5:10, the effect of famine on the exiles is compared to the effect of the heat that blackened the interior of an oven's dome: "Our skin is as hot as an oven because of the burning heat of famine." See BREAD; FURNACE.

OWL Several kinds of owls (birds of the family *Strigidae*) belong to the fauna of Israel and are likely listed among the unclean birds of prey in Lev 11 and Deut 14. One may further expect that owls should be mentioned among creatures haunting deserted places, such as in Isa 34:11-15.

OX, OXEN A working animal often referenced in association with the donkey (e.g., Exod 20:17; 22:4, 9 [Heb. 22:3, 8]; 23:4). Rest is mandated for both animals in Exod 23:12 and Deut 5:14. As a sacrificial animal, the ox was on the list of such animals that could be eaten (Deut 14:4).

Oxen were the principal draft animals of ancient Mediterranean agriculture. Although less productive than horses, oxen were cheaper and could be eaten as well as worked. Farmers frequently castrated male animals slated for work to make them docile, but castration probably disqualified the animal for sacrifice.

OZEM 1. A brother of David and Jesse's 6th son listed among Judah's descendants (1 Chron 2:15).

2. The 4th of Hezron's grandsons by his eldest son Jerahmeel listed in the aforementioned genealogy (1 Chron 2:25).

OZIEL An ancestor of Judith (Jdt 8:1). Correspondingly, UZZIEL, the Hebrew form, is listed as a descendant of Simeon in 1 Chron 4:42, as is Judith in Jdt 9:2.

OZNI The 4th of seven sons of Gad (the name is EZBON in Gen 46:16) and eponymous ancestor of the Oznites (Num 26:16).

Pp

PAARAI Paarai "from Erab" (2 Sam 23:35) was one of "the Thirty," the larger subset of David's warriors.

PADDAN-ARAM An area in northwest Mesopotamia along the great bend of the Euphrates. It is the home of BETHUEL and LABAN (Gen 25:20). The name occurs only in Genesis and is usually associated with JACOB (e.g., Gen 28:1-7; 35:26).

PADON Head of a family of temple servants who returned to Judah after the exile (Ezra 2:44; Neh 7:47; 1 Esdr 5:29).

PAGIEL Son of Ochran and leader of the tribe of Asher (Num 2:27; 10:26; see ASHER, ASHERITES). Pagiel assisted Moses in the first wilderness census (Num 1:13) and presented the offering of the Asherites at the dedication of the meeting tent (Num 7:72-77).

PAHATH-MOAB 1. A leader in the early postexilic community who signed Nehemiah's covenant to follow the Instruction (Neh 10:14 [Heb. 10:15]; cf Neh 3:11).

2. A postexilic clan. Ezra 2:6 notes that 2,812 people from this group were among the first to return to Jerusalem from the Babylonian exile, while Ezra 8:4 states that 200 descendants of Pahath-moab came to Yehud with Ezra. Members of this group were among those who had taken foreign wives (Ezra 10:30).

PALACE A royal residence. The OT makes specific reference to the palaces of Solomon, Ahab, Ahasuerus, Nebuchadnezzar, and Pharaoh, as well as more general references to palaces.

The Hasmonean rulers of Judea (134–63 BCE) built palaces near Jericho. But the premier palace-builder in Judea was clearly Herod the Great (37–4 BCE) who built magnificent freestanding palaces as well as palaces incorporated within fortresses (see HEROD, FAMILY). Among his palaces were those in

Jerusalem, JERICHO, Masada, Herodium, Alexandrium, Cypros, Machaerus, Hyrcania, Doq, and Caesarea.

PALAL Son of Uzai, and one of the builders who helped repair the wall of Jerusalem under the direction of NEHEMIAH (Neh 3:25).

PALESTINE, TERMINOLOGY FOR *Palestine* is a term of convenience used by some biblical scholars and archaeologists to designate the geographic area bounded by the Jordan River to the east, the Mediterranean Sea to the west, Lebanon to the north, and the Sinai desert to the south. Other terms used by scholars to refer to the region include the *Levant* and *Syro-Palestine*. This contemporary use of *Palestine* does not generally conform to ancient usage. In biblical studies, the word *Palestine* is normally used as a geographical designation only. The political usage of this term, especially in the context of the contemporary Israeli-Palestinian conflict, is a different issue.

PALLU, PALLUITES The 2nd of Reuben's four sons. He appears in genealogical lists in Gen 46:9 (among those Israelites who went to Egypt along with Jacob); Exod 6:14 (as the head of a Reubenite clan); and 1 Chron 5:3. Pallu is also listed in Num 26:5 as the head of the Palluite clan. In Num 26:8-9 he is mentioned as the father of ELIAB, whose sons DATHAN and ABIRAM participated in Korah's rebellion against Moses and Aaron. See REUBEN, REUBENITE.

PALM CITY Another name for JERICHO (Deut 34:3; 2 Chron 28:15). As one of the oldest cities in the world, Jericho grew up around a spring (Elisha's spring) that nourished a date-palm grove, earning the town this epithet.

PALM TREE The biblical palm tree is the date palm, which flourished in Jericho, "PALM CITY" (2 Chron 28:15), where the high temperatures suit it. Their fruit is poor and was forbidden as a firstfruit offering, according to the Talmud.

PALTI 1. Moses sent Palti the Benjaminite, son of Raphu, into Canaan as one of the spies ordered to investigate the land in advance of an Israelite invasion (Num 13:1-16, esp. v. 9).

2. Saul gave his daughter MICHAL to Palti, the son of Laish, from Gallim, although she was already married to David (1 Sam 25:44).

PALTIEL 1. Paltiel son of Azzan was a leader in the tribe of Issachar (Num 34:26) and one of twelve tribal leaders selected by Moses for the distribution of land to the ten tribes of Israel west of the Jordan. See ISSACHAR, ISSACHARITES.

2. A variant form of PALTI in the story of David's recovery of his wife MICHAL (2 Sam 3:15-16).

PAMPHYLIA A region in Asia Minor (present-day Turkey), approximately 80 mi. long and 20 mi. wide, with its southern border on the Mediterranean Sea. Pisidia borders the region on the north, Lycia on the west, and Cilicia on the east (see Acts 27:5).

PAPHOS The city of Paphos is located in the southwest corner of CYPRUS. Paul and Barnabas traveled on the Roman road on the south coast of Cyprus from Salamis to Paphos (Acts 13:6). It was here that they encountered the Roman governor of the island, Sergius Paulus.

PARABLE A comparison, used as a figure of speech, often with a moral point. Jesus, like many rabbis of his time, used parables with great effect.

PARACLETE The word *paraclete* means "someone called in assistance" or "advocate." The word does not occur in the OT and is found in the NT only in John 14:16, 26; 15:26; 16:7, translated as "Companion" (1 John 2:1 "advocate").

Biblical scholars and theologians use *paraclete* as a technical term for the spiritual form that Jesus' presence will take in and among the Johannine community after his death and resurrection, to comfort and counsel them (John 14:16).

PARADE GATE The Parade Gate, also called the Muster Gate, stood opposite "the house of the temple servants and the merchants," suggesting it and the Water Gate pierced the eastern wall of a compound enclosing the temple courts and priestly residences (Neh 3:26, 31).

PARADISE *Paradise* is a Persian loanword in Hebrew, Aramaic, Syriac, Greek, and other languages. In Old Persian, the noun denoted an enclosure; it developed to signify a beautiful garden, like a king's garden. The concept of paradise evolved so that it symbolized streams flowing with crystal clear and healthful water, and trees blooming constantly beside multicolored flowers. There is no sickness in this blessed place, and the temperature is always ideal for humans.

The concept "paradise" does not appear in the OT. In Second Temple Judaism, the images from Genesis, Isaiah, Jeremiah, Ezekiel, and Psalm 1 coalesce to produce elegant poetic imagery for God's final planting (esp. in 1QHa XVI, 1QS VIII, and CD I). In early Jewish literature, *paradise* often has become synonymous with the Garden of Eden. In 1 Enoch, the "Garden of Eden" in Ethiopia becomes *paradise* in the Greek translation (see esp. 1 En. 20:7; compare 32:3). By the end of the 1st cent. CE, paradise is perceived to be the location of "the tree of life" (Rev 2:7; 4 Ezra 8:52). (See TREE OF THE KNOWLEDGE OF GOOD AND EVIL, TREE OF LIFE.)

PARALYSIS, PARALYTIC A severe medical condition (Matt 4:24; 8:5-10; 9:1-8; Mark 2:1-12), characterized by an inability to move one's limbs.

PARAN A region in the Sinai Peninsula that is usually referred to as part of the wilderness in which the Israelites wandered after they escaped Egyptian bondage. Most of the references to the region occur in the Pentateuch with a few citations in other OT books.

PARENTS Parents include the Mother and FATHER of a child. The OT does not have a generic word for parents. Children are to honor their parents (Exod 20:12; Deut 5:16), and the actions of the children reflect on the parents (Prov 17:6; 28:7; 29:3), while the sins of the parents are sometimes visited upon the children (Exod 34:7; Num 14:18; Deut 5:9; cf Jer 31:27-30; Ezek 18:1-4).

The NT parallels modern usage (Luke 1:17; Heb 11:23; Eph 6:1-2; Matt 10:21; Mark 13:12; Luke 2:41-43; John 9:2-3; Rom 1:30; 2 Cor 12:14; Col 3:20). See CHILD, CHILDREN.

PARMASHTA One of Haman's ten sons killed by the Jews in Susa after Haman's downfall (Esth 9:9).

PARMENAS One of seven men chosen to address concerns raised by the Hellenists regarding the distribution of the community's resources (Acts 6:5).

PARNACH Mentioned in the Bible as the father of ELIZAPHAN, leader of the tribe of Zebulun. Elizaphan was chosen to help with the division of the land of promise among the tribes (Num 34:25).

PAROSH The ancestor of one of the families who returned to Jerusalem after Babylonian captivity. The descendants of Parosh numbered 2,172, according to Ezra and Nehemiah (Ezra 2:3; 8:3; 10:25; Neh 7:8; 10:14; 1 Esdr 5:9; 8:30; 9:26).

PAROUSIA *Parousia* is used widely in the NT (e.g., Matt 24:3; 1 Cor 15:23; 1 Thess 5:23; 2 Thess 2:1; 2 Pet 1:16; 1 John 2:28; cf Jas 5:7). In these passages it refers to the presence of Christ eschatologically coming on the clouds of heaven (Mark 13:26) and is sometimes called the "second coming" of Christ. Nevertheless, the ambiguity of the word should be noted, as when expectation of a public coming when "every eye will see him" (Rev 1:7) allowed for the possibility of the presence of Christ in other modes of experience, whether in worship or the lives of the apostles and ministers (Gal 2:20).

PARSHANDATHA One of the ten sons of HAMAN killed by the Jews in Susa (Esth 9:7).

PARTHIA, PARTHIANS Region and empire located in the southwest part of Asia, extending from the Euphrates to the Indus Rivers. The only biblical mention of Parthians is at Acts 2:9, where they are the 1st mentioned of the fourteen peoples said to reside in Jerusalem at the time of Pentecost, and who heard the disciples speaking their own native languages. The Parthians represent the easternmost inhabitants of this catalog of nations, which, collectively, symbolizes the presence of the Jews throughout the inhabited world—among "every nation under heaven" (Acts 2:5).

PARTRIDGE The Chukor partridge, found in mountainous regions, was probably a highly appreciated game bird already in biblical times, as indicated by the simile in 1 Sam 26:20.

PARUAH A member of the tribe of Issachar (1 Kgs 4:17) whose son JEHOSHAPHAT was one of twelve officials responsible for providing food for King Solomon and his household.

PASACH Oldest of the three sons of Japhlet and great-great-grandson of the tribal ancestor Asher (1 Chron 7:33).

PASCHAL LAMB The sacrificial offering of Passover (e.g., Exod 12:21). Jesus is portrayed as the paschal lamb (John 19:36; 1 Cor 5:7), connecting him with the lamb's role in the Passover meal and exodus. See PASSOVER AND FESTIVAL OF UNLEAVENED BREAD.

PASEAH 1. One of three children born to Eshton of the men of Recah (1 Chron 4:12).

2. One of several fathers whose descendants returned from exile in the early Persian era to participate in the service of the temple (Ezra 2:49; Neh 7:51).

3. The father of JOIADA, who rebuilt the old gate of Jerusalem together with Meshullam in the days of Nehemiah (Neh 3:6).

PASHHUR 1. Son of Malchiah (see MALCHIJAH), the prince who owned the cistern into which JEREMIAH was thrown (Jer 38:6); one of the emissaries sent by Zedekiah in 588 BCE to seek Jeremiah's intercession with God concerning Nebuchadnezzar's impending attack. Jeremiah responded by announcing that God would fight with Babylon against Jerusalem (Jer 21:1, 3).

2. Son of Immer; a priest in Jerusalem in the time of Jeremiah (Jer 20:1-6). As chief officer in charge of temple security, this Pashhur ordered Jeremiah beaten and placed in stocks following the prophet's seditious attack upon the nation and its institutions.

3. Father of GEDALIAH, one of the temple officials who left Jeremiah to die in a muddy cistern (Jer 38:1). This Pashhur may be the one mentioned in 1 Chron 9:12; Neh 11:12.

4. Ancestor of the "sons of Pashhur," a postexilic priestly family (Ezra 2:38; Neh 7:41; 1 Esdr 5:25) that returned from Babylon with Zerubbabel. The six men from this family who divorced their foreign wives are the largest priestly group to do so (Ezra 10:22; 1 Esdr 9:22).

5. Either a priest who set his seal upon the firm agreement to "live by God's Instruction" (Neh 10:29 [Heb. 10:30]), or, more likely, the family name (#4) of one of the priestly courses

presented as the personal name of such a signatory (Neh 10:3 [Heb. 10:4]).

PASSION NARRATIVES The Passion Narratives are the portions of the Gospels that tell of the suffering and death of Jesus (usually including the accounts of his burial), focused on the stories of Jesus' arrest, trial, suffering, and execution.

PASSOVER AND FESTIVAL OF UNLEAVENED BREAD The Passover and Festival of Unleavened Bread are two consecutive festivals that are treated as one holiday in some biblical passages. The traditional celebration of Passover is called the Seder.

In the lists of pilgrimage festivals (Exod 23:14-17; 34:18, 22-24) only the Festival of Unleavened Bread, not Passover, is mentioned; it is said to last seven days during which only unleavened bread is to be eaten. The festival lists in Lev 23 and Num 28–29 present a different picture: in them there are two separate but contiguous holidays. The two festivals—Passover and Unleavened Bread—are distinguished in other scriptural sources but are regularly mentioned side by side. In the narratives that introduce them in Exod 12–13, they appear in the general context of the 10th plague on Egypt, the death of all the firstborn children. The destructive event happened around midnight (Exod 11:4) in the very night when the Israelites were celebrating the first Passover. The legislation in Exod 12 highlights these divine instructions to Moses regarding the Passover.

The Passover plays a central role in the NT, and the Festival of Unleavened Bread is mentioned a few times. The most famous instance is in the accounts of the Last Supper (see LAST SUPPER, THE), which is presented as a Passover meal (Seder) in the Synoptic Gospels.

PASTORAL LETTERS The "Pastoral Letters" is a composite name for the collection of epistles that includes 1 and 2 Timothy and Titus. TIMOTHY and TITUS serve as exemplary figures with whom the reader identifies, because the letters are from an older pastor (Paul) to younger pastors (Timothy and Titus). The letters' preoccupations include church order ("how you should behave in God's household. It is the church" [1 Tim 3:15 and see 5:3-22]), preservation of apostolic teaching (1 Tim 1:3-10; 3:14–4:10; 6:3-5, 20; 2 Tim 1:11-12; Titus 1:10-16), and the church's reputation (1 Tim 2:1-2; 5:14; 6:1-12; Titus 2:1-10).

PATHROS, PATHRUSIM Pathros signifies upper Egypt, the region of the Nile Valley south of Memphis to the first cataract at Aswan and the island of Elephantine.

PATMOS Patmos is the Aegean island where the visionary called John received and recorded his vision, the book of Revelation (Rev 1:9). Patmos was probably not the backwater that is often assumed, with local cults to Apollo and Artemis.

PATRIARCHS The patriarchs are the "founding fathers" of Israel: Abraham, Isaac, and Jacob (Israel). Jacob's children were the eponymous ancestors of the twelve tribes of Israel. From this lineage the Israelites claimed their identity as a people.

PATRIARCHS, TESTAMENTS OF THE TWELVE The Testaments of the Twelve Patriarchs is an extrabiblical book that presents the fictional valedictory speeches of the sons of Jacob. Satisfying the elements of the testamentary genre, they each include an introduction in which the patriarch summons his children to his premortem speech; he offers autobiographical reflections, exhorts his children to avoid his vices and/or pursue his virtues, and predicts their descendants' future; then he dies and is buried by his survivors.

PATROBAS Patrobas is one of the Roman Christians greeted by Paul (Rom 16:14), included with Asyncritus, Phlegon, Hermes, Hermas, and "the brothers and sisters who are with them," which suggests that they were part of a house church in Rome.

PATROCLUS Father of NICANOR whom Ptolemy sent to defeat the Jews and their leader JUDAS Maccabeus (2 Macc 8:9).

PAUL, THE APOSTLE Aside from Jesus, no one shaped the development of early Christianity more than Paul. Even though he was the foremost advocate of the Gentile mission, an eloquent interpreter of a Jewish Messiah for a Hellenistic world, and a visionary whose journeys carried him through Asia Minor and beyond, he undoubtedly would have been surprised that his occasional letters would one day become Scripture alongside the Law and the Prophets.

The themes at the core of Paul's gospel were Israel's traditions, Scriptures, morality, God, and a crucified Jewish Messiah whose life, death, and resurrection expanded the people of God to include believing "pagans," inaugurating a new age that would soon be brought to a grand and even revolutionary conclusion with Jesus' return. This vision suffused Paul's mission with urgency and his letters with the intensity characteristic of a time of crisis. In a great apocalyptic drama, converts lived out their faith within a community of care and hope as well as sectarian rivalry. In Paul's letters we are witness to that conflict and to a theology in the making.

PAULLUS, AEMILIUS A statesman and military tactician (ca. 230–160 BCE) who was elected *curule aedile* in 192, proconsul in 191 and 167, consul in 182 and 168, and was praetor of Spain from 191 to 189. Aemilius defeated Perseus and ended the 3rd Macedonian War.

PAULUS, SERGIUS In Acts 13:4-12 he is the GOVERNOR of CYPRUS who seeks out Paul and Barnabas in order to learn more about their teaching.

PEDAHEL Pedahel was the son of AMMIHUD and a chieftain from the tribe of Naphtali (Num 34:28).

PEDAHZUR Known only as the father of Gamaliel, who was a leader of the people of Manasseh and aide to Moses during the Israelites' time in the wilderness (Num 1:10; 2:20; 7:54, 59; 10:23).

PEDAIAH 1. Maternal grand-father of King Jehoiakim of Judah (2 Kgs 23:36).

2. Third son of King Jehoiakin/Jeconiah (1 Chron 3:17-18), Pedaiah had two sons, Zerubbabel and Shimei (1 Chron 3:19).

3. Father of Joel from the half-tribe of Manasseh in the west of Jordan when David took a census (1 Chron 27:20).

4. Son of Parosh who helped to rebuild the Jerusalem wall during the time of Nehemiah (Neh 3:25).

5. One of those who stood on the left side of Ezra when he read the Instruction scroll before the people (Neh 8:4; 1 Esdr 9:44).

6. Father of Joed and the son of Kolaiah, Benjaminites dwelling in Jerusalem under Nehemiah (Neh 11:7).

7. A Levite and one of three treasurers of the temple storehouses appointed by Nehemiah (Neh 13:13).

PEKAH Pekah was the son of Remaliah and the 18th king of Israel. Pekah succeeded PEKAHIAH (738–737 BCE) the son of Menahem after Pekahiah had reigned two years in Samaria. Pekah assassinated Pekahiah and refused to pay tribute to Assyria. It is possible that Pekah ruled over Israel no more than five years, from 737 to 732 BCE. Hoshea the son of Elah conspired against Pekah, killed him, and became king of Israel (2 Kgs 15:30). Hoshea ruled the northern kingdom, now limited mostly to

Ephraim and Manasseh, as an Assyrian vassal.

PEKAHIAH Son of MENAHEM and 17th king of the northern kingdom of Israel (2 Kgs 15:23-26), Pekahiah reigned in Samaria two years (737–736 BCE). Pekahiah decided to continue the pro-Assyrian policies of his father. Pekah assassinated him and assumed the throne.

PELAIAH 1. The 3rd of ELIOENAI's seven sons among David's descendants (1 Chron 3:24).

2. One of the Levites who interpreted the Instruction scroll that Ezra read to the people (Neh 8:7; 1 Esdr 9:48). He also signed Ezra's covenant (Neh 10:10 [Heb. 10:11]).

PELALIAH Grand-father of ADAIAH, a priest who lived in Jerusalem after the exile (Neh 11:12).

PELATIAH 1. The first son of HANANIAH in a list of David's descendants (1 Chron 3:21).

2. One of three sons of Ishi and one of the leaders of a group of 500 Simeonites (1 Chron 4:42).

3. One of those whose names appear on the covenant the postexilic community made under Nehemiah (Neh 10:22).

4. An "official of the people" and son of BENAIAH, mentioned by Ezekiel in an oracle against the leaders of Jerusalem, at the end of which Pelatiah falls dead (Ezek 11:1, 13).

PELEG Son of EBER, brother of JOKTAN, and at the age of 30 the father of Reu, in the genealogy from Noah to Abraham (Gen 10:25; 11:16-19; Luke 3:35). According to the genealogy, Peleg lived 239 years.

PELET 1. One of the sons of Jahdai in the lineage of Caleb (1 Chron 2:47).

2. A son of Azmaveth and brother of Jeziel. Pelet and Jeziel were Benjaminite warriors, ambidextrous archers and slingers who joined David's growing army at Ziklag (1 Chron 12:3).

PELETH 1. A member of the tribe of Reuben and the father of ON, who participated in Korah's rebellion against Moses at Kadesh during the exodus wanderings (Num 16:1).

2. A son of JONATHAN, descendant of Jerahmeel, assigned to the tribe of Judah (1 Chron 2:33).

PELETHITES See CHERETHITES AND PELETHITES.

PELLA The city of Pella of the DECAPOLIS in the Jordan Valley received its name in honor of Pella in Macedonia, birthplace of Alexander the Great.

PELUSIUM A major port city at the northeastern edge of the Nile Delta known for its military, industrial, and religious complexes. In Ezek 30, the litany of Egyptian sites marked for destruction includes Pelusium (vv. 15-16).

PENINNAH According to 1 Sam 1:2, 4 Peninnah was one of two wives of ELKANAH the Ephraimite. She had children, and consequently taunted HANNAH, the favored wife who did not have children.

PENTATEUCH The Pentateuch, the first five books of Israel's Scriptures (Genesis, Exodus, Leviticus, Numbers, and Deuteronomy), constitutes the foundation of Israel's canonical collection of sacred texts. It is also known as the TORAH, Instruction, the Law.

PENTECOST Meaning "50th (day)," a Greek name for the Festival of Weeks described in the holiday lists in Exod 23:14-17; 34:18, 22-24; Lev 23; Num 28–29; and Deut 16 (see WEEKS, FEAST OR FESTIVAL OF). The name was used by Greek writers for the 2nd of the three pilgrimage festivals stipulated in the OT (Exod 23:14-17; 34:18, 22-24; Deut 16:16-17) because of the procedure arranged for determining its date. Both Lev 23:15-16 (Holiness Code) and Deut 16:9-10 say that one should count seven complete weeks from an event occurring in the 1st month around the time of Passover and Unleavened Bread (the waving of the bundle in Lev 23:15; putting the sickle to the standing grain in Deut 16:9), with the next or 50th day being the date of the festival. Because neither of these events is assigned to a specific date, the Pentateuch prescribes no exact time for the Festival of Weeks/ Pentecost; as a result, there was, at least in the Second Temple period, disagreement about when it was to be celebrated. The festival marked the beginning of the wheat harvest (Exod 34:22) and was to be the occasion for a number of offerings (Lev 23:17-19; Num 28:26-31), including two loaves made from wheat flour and "baked with leaven" (Lev 23:17). It was a day for a holy convocation, and labor was prohibited (Lev 23:21; Num 28:26). It was a popular holiday (Tob 2:1-2).

The most famous NT reference to the holiday is in Acts 2, where the HOLY SPIRIT was poured out on Jesus' first followers on Pentecost Day (see v. 1). On that day, in obedience to the Instruction, large numbers of Jews from many parts of the world had gathered in Jerusalem for the PILGRIMAGE holiday and thus provided a worldwide audience that could understand the message the disciples were suddenly and miraculously speaking in their several languages (vv. 3-11; see TONGUES, GIFT OF).

PENUEL 1. A city in Transjordan on the JABBOK RIVER (Gen 32:22-32 [Heb. 32:23-33]), east of Succoth and south of Mahanaim. At Penuel, JACOB wrestled with a "man" (Gen 32:24 [Heb. 32:25]; Hos 12:4 calls him an "the messenger") prior to his reunion with Esau. Jacob named the site Peniel (Gen 32:30 [Heb. 32:31]), meaning "face of God," claiming to have seen God "face-to-face."

2. A descendant of Judah (1 Chron 4:4).

3. A descendant of Benjamin (1 Chron 8:25).

PEOPLE OF THE LAND A term whose application changed from the premonarchic through the rabbinic periods. In the premonarchic era, *people of the land* appears to have been a general term for the free citizenry of any given place. The meaning of the expression during the monarchic period is debated and has been variously understood as the lower social classes, the elite, the free citizenry, or even a body of socially and politically important Judahites (2 Kgs 11:12, 18-20; 21:24; 23:30, 35; Jer 1:18; 34:19; 37:2; 44:21; Ezek 7:27; 22:29).

In the postexilic era, the term began to be used negatively. In Ezra 4:4, those returning from exile were called "the people of Judah," and the opposing local elites were called "the neighboring peoples." In postbiblical rabbinic texts, the term was used as a pejorative for those who were either ignorant of or did not observe the Instruction.

PEOR Site of an infamous apostasy remembered by the Hebrew writers in recounting the story of Israelite wanderings prior to entering Canaan. The prophet BALAAM is identified as the instigator of the incident in which the Israelites participated in festivities involving Moabite and/or Midianite women (Num 23:28; 25:3, 5, 18; 31:16; Deut 4:3; Josh 22:17; Ps 106:28).

PERESH Peresh appears in a list of descendants of Manasseh as the son of MACHIR and of his wife MAACAH (1 Chron 7:16).

PEREZ The son of Judah and TAMAR, Judah's daughter-in-law (Gen 38:29; 1 Chron 2:4; 4:1).

PERGA A principal city in the ancient region of PAMPHYLIA in Asia Minor, twice visited by Paul during his first missionary venture (Acts 13:13-14; 14:25) .

PERGAMUM A city in western Asia Minor where one of the seven congregations addressed by Revelation was located (Rev 1:11; 2:12).

PERIZZITES A group of pre-Israelite people who lived in Canaan. They are always mentioned in conjunction with other groups. Perizzites are included in twenty-one of the twenty-seven lists of pre-Israelite people. In the common six-name lists, the Perizzites are usually found in the 4th position (Exod 3:8; 33:2; Deut 20:17; Josh 9:1; Judg 3:5).

PERSECUTION Persecution of God's people has occurred throughout history—as Jesus noted in speaking of "the murder of all the prophets" and "the murder of every prophet—from Abel to Zechariah" (Luke 11:50-51). The Israelites often faced adversaries (Isa 14:4-6; 29:20-21; Jer 11:19; 18:18; Pss 37:32; 38:20; 42:3, 10; 74:7-8) and appealed to God to judge and punish persecutors (Deut 30:7; Ps 119:84).

Three major times of persecution occur in the OT: the exodus (Exod 1:9-10; 2:23-24), the days of the judges (Judg 2:11-16), and the events leading up to the exile, including the lives of prophets.

The book of Esther relates the story of two audacious Jews, Mordecai and Queen Esther, who upset the genocidal plans of Haman, "the enemy of the Jews" (Esth 3:1-15; quotation v. 10). The events described are placed during the reign of Ahasuerus (also called Xerxes, 486–465 BCE), king of the Persian Empire. The book is set against a hostile background and points to the inescapable nature of retributive justice (4:14), and the need for the persecuted to act boldly and astutely to ensure that justice prevails.

In the Maccabean era, intense Seleucid persecution erupted when ANTIOCHUS IV Ephiphanes (175–164 BCE) attempted to impose a program of enforced Hellenization. All the rites of the Jewish faith were ruthlessly attacked. Judas Maccabeus and his brothers put up a heroic resistance marked by terrible suffering. This persecution is reflected in the book of Daniel and culminated in "desolating monstrosities"—the sacrilegious offering of a pig on the altar of the temple in Jerusalem (Dan 9:27; 11:31; 12:11). The history of the conflict is recorded in 1 Maccabees, and the Maccabean martyrdoms are graphically portrayed in 2 Maccabees 6–7. See MACCABEES, MACCABEAN REVOLT.

The harsh treatment experienced by God's people continued into NT times, both for Jesus and the early church. Jesus had warned his followers to expect persecution (Matt 23:34-37; Luke 11:49-51; John 16:2). He himself had suffered beating, mocking, and crucifixion, as all four Gospels show. His disciples were to expect similar treatment from their enemies (Matt 24:9-14; Mark 13:9-13; Luke 21:12-19). Still hard times could be met confidently; Jesus promised the help of the Holy Spirit to empower them in dangerous situations (Mark 13:9-11; Luke 12:11-12; 21:15; Acts 1:8; 2:4; 4:8-13; 6:10; 7:55) and an advocate to comfort them (John 14:15-17; see PARACLETE).

The predicted persecution came upon the early church (Acts 5:17-42; 7:57-58; 8:1; 11:19; 14:19; 16:19-24). For a time, Saul of Tarsus was one of the most aggressive opponents of Christianity (Acts 8:3; 1 Cor 15:9; Gal 1:23). Then on the Damascus road he met the one he had so vigorously opposed (Acts 9:1-19; 22:4-16; 26:9-18; 1 Cor 9:1; 15:8; Gal 1:16). Paul admitted that he had previously acted as a persecutor of the followers of the Way (Gal 1:13; Phil 3:6; cf. 1 Tim 1:13).

PERSEPOLIS One of the five royal capitals of the Persian Achaemenid Empire alongside Babylon, Susa, Ecbatana

(Hamadan), and Pasargadae (2 Macc 9:2).

PERSIA The Persians were Iranian tribes who developed into a major empire. Their religion is commonly referred to as Zoroastrianism, after Zoroaster, the Greek form of Zarathustra, or as Mazdaism (see Ahura Mazda). This religion took shape among the Iranian tribes in Central Asia, and its oldest form is known from the Avesta sacred texts. The Persian Empire defeated the Babylonian Empire in 539 BCE, changing the ruling power over the Jerusalem area. In the OT, the Persian emperor Cyrus is praised as a victorious conqueror. According to Ezra, Cyrus was divinely inspired to rebuild the Jerusalem temple and ordered all those in exile to come to Jerusalem and help in the building, notably those in Babylon (Ezra 1–2); and, under a subsequent emperor, Darius, the original decree was allegedly found in Ecbatana (6:2-12). Persian rule continued to 333 BCE, when Alexander the Great defeated Persian forces and began the Hellenistic rule of the Palestine area.

PERSIS A Roman Christian whom Paul greets as "my dear friend Persis." Paul commends him for having "worked hard in the Lord" (Rom 16:12).

PERUDA A family head of temple servants whose descendants returned to Jerusalem with Zerubbabel after the exile (Ezra 2:55; 1 Esdr 5:33; Neh 7:57).

PESHITTA An important Syriac version of the Bible, parts of which originated in the earliest centuries CE.

PETER, THE APOSTLE The most prominent disciple of Jesus, Peter is mentioned more than 200 times in the NT. His name was Simon (in Matt 4:18) or Simeon (in Acts 15:14; 2 Pet 1:1). He is also called "bar Jonah" or "son of Jonah" (Matt 16:17) or "son of John" (in John 1:42). Jesus nicknamed him "Peter" (Mark 3:16), meaning "rock," which is "Cephas" in Aram.; Paul ordinarily uses the Aram. "Cephas" (1 Cor 1:12; Gal 1:18). He is a major character in the book of Acts, and he is also known as the author of two letters in the NT, which bear his name.

PETER, FIRST LETTER OF The second of the seven Catholic Epistles, 1 Peter presents itself as a communication from the apostle Peter. Written to churches located in the northern part of Asia Minor (modern Turkey) the letter urges readers, currently undergoing sporadic persecution for their faith, to endure persecution patiently, keeping in mind the suffering of Christ that has opened to them a new life and future. While avoiding irritating, unbelieving neighbors, Christians are to remain true to their faith in Christ, which will result in their redemption.

The Greek of this letter reflects an author who knew the theological situation in Asia Minor, a situation that fits the last years of the 1st cent. CE, some years after Peter's martyrdom in 64 CE. The language of the letter is closer to the defenders of Christianity in the 2nd cent. than to the letters of Paul. Further, the complex grammatical structures in this letter point to an educated author rather than to one who reproduced the ordinary Greek spoken in the marketplace. When the author quotes the OT, the language bears a closer resemblance to the LXX (Greek translation of the OT) than to the original Hebrew; the absence of obvious Semitisms (evidences of direct translation from Hebrew) shows that the author's native tongue was Greek.

PETER, SECOND LETTER OF One of several early works ascribed to the apostle Peter by members of the early Jesus movement. Along with 1 Peter, it was admitted, with some difficulty and hesitation, into the NT canon. This letter is one of the general or Catholic Epistles and is an important pseudonymous work of the sub-apostolic period that has much to contribute to our understanding of early Christian theological and ecclesial evolution.

PETHAHIAH 1. A priest and descendant of Aaron associated with David (1 Chron 24:16).

2. A Levite (Neh 9:5) involved in the great communal confession and covenant sealing (Neh 9:38 [Heb. 10:1]) and probably the same Pethahiah who joined others in renouncing their foreign wives and children (Ezra 10:23; 1 Esdr 9:23).

3. A Judahite son of MESHEZABEL serving in Jerusalem following the exile, who "was advising the king in all matters concerning the people" (Neh 11:24).

PETHOR The home of BALAAM, the Mesopotamian diviner hired by BALAK king of Moab to curse the Israelites as they made their way from Egypt to Canaan (Num 22:4-6; Deut 23:4 [Heb. 23:5]). Pethor, according to Num 22:5, was located on the Euphrates.

PETHUEL The father of the prophet JOEL (Joel 1:1).

PEULLETHAI A Levite, a gatekeeper in the temple in Jerusalem (1 Chron 26:5).

PHANUEL The father of the prophetess ANNA, who prophesied the greatness of Jesus (Luke 2:36-38).

PHARAKIM The ancestor of a family of temple servants who returned from Babylonian exile under ZERUBBABEL (1 Esdr 5:31).

PHARAOH A title for the king of ancient EGYPT. In biblical usage, *pharaoh* is a synonym for "king of Egypt" in conformity with 1st-millennium BCE Egyptian convention. The Egyptian king is referred to alternately as "king of Egypt," "Pharaoh," or "Pharaoh king of Egypt." Any of these formulations can be used with the king's name: Shishak king of Egypt (1 Kgs 11:40); Pharaoh Neco (2 Kgs 23:33); Pharaoh Hophra king of Egypt (Jer 44:30). The formal similarity between "Shishak king of Egypt" and "Pharaoh king of Egypt" lends the appearance that Pharaoh is the king's name.

PHARISEES The Greek term occurs for the first time in the NT (more than ninety times) and is also used by Josephus (forty-four times). The term is not found in other early Jewish texts, or in the writings of Greco-Roman authors who refer to the Jews. The Pharisees were a Jewish sect in the time of the NT; Paul was a Pharisee. The Pharisees are repeatedly described as people who transmit, preserve, and develop the tradition of the Instruction in its written and oral form. Their understanding of tradition evidently was nonexclusive, which explains their interest in Jesus: they are prepared to listen to Jesus as long as he can demonstrate the continuity between his teaching and the Instruction tradition. Pharisees were known for their piety and their strict adherence to the Instruction.

PHARPAR Pharpar was one of two rivers, along with the ABANA, named by NAAMAN as rivers of Damascus (2 Kgs 5:12).

PHICOL The commander of ABIMELECH's army. He is present on both occasions when Abimelech makes a covenant first with Abraham (Gen 21:22, 32) and later with Isaac (Gen 26:26).

PHILADELPHIA A Hellenistic name for two cities.

1. Initially named RABBAH of the Ammonites (modern Amman, Jordan), this city was known as Philadelphia in the Hellenistic era (but never in the Bible).

2. Philadelphia in Lydia (see LYDIA, LYDIANS) was located in the Roman province of Asia (modern Alasehir,

Turkey). It is to this 2nd Philadelphia that Rev 1:11 and 3:7-13 refer.

PHILEMON, LETTER TO The shortest writing in the NT, this authentic letter by Paul bears the name of its recipient, a Pauline associate and slave owner who hosts a house church. The topic is Philemon's formerly pagan slave, ONESIMUS, who departed from home (v. 15), came to Paul in prison, and is being returned—with the letter—ahead of Paul's own anticipated arrival as a guest in Philemon's house (v. 22). The letter, probably written from Ephesus in the mid to late 50s CE, has a close connection to Colossians, because both exchange greetings by the same group of people and reference Onesimus (Col 4:9-14, 17; Phlm 2, 23).

PHILETUS The author of 2 Timothy sounds a warning about the preachers Philetus and HYMENAEUS, who swerved from the truth by teaching that the resurrection had already taken place (2 Tim 2:17-18).

PHILIP 1. Philip II, king of MACEDONIA (359–336 BCE), father of Alexander the Great (1 Macc 1:1). He unified Macedonia and overwhelmed the Greek city-states except Sparta to form the Hellenic League of Corinth in 337 BCE.

2. Philip V, king of Macedonia (220–179 BCE; 1 Macc 8:5). His kingdom was invaded by the Roman armies.

3. Philip the Phrygian (see PHRYGIA), governor of Jerusalem (2 Macc 5:22). He was appointed to this position in 169 BCE after Antiochus IV Epiphanes attacked the Holy City and raided the temple for its alleged revolt on the way back from his 2nd campaign against Egypt.

4. Philip the APOSTLE (Matt 10:3; Mark 3:18; Luke 6:14; Acts 1:13). He is mentioned in the Synoptic Gospels only in the lists of the twelve disciples, but several stories that reveal his character are preserved in the Gospel of John.

5. Philip, son of Herod the Great and Mariamne II (Matt 14:3; Mark 6:17; Luke 3:19; see HEROD, FAMILY). He was the half brother of HEROD ANTIPAS and the first husband of HERODIAS. When Antipas became illicitly involved with Herodias, John the Baptist rebuked them and consequently was jailed and executed.

6. Philip the tetrarch, son of Herod the Great and Cleopatra of Jerusalem (Luke 3:1; see TETRARCH, TETRARCHY).

7. Philip the evangelist (Acts 8:5-13).

8. A companion of Antiochus IV EPIPHANES who attempted to take over the kingdom after his death.

PHILIPPI Philippi is situated in eastern MACEDONIA (northern Greece) on the Via Egnatia overlooking an inland plain to the east of Mount Pangaeus/Pangaion. Philippi is named for PHILIP II (359–336 BCE), king of Macedonia and father of Alexander the Great. Philip named the city "Philippi" after himself when the citizens asked for his help against the Thracians. Around 49–50 CE, the apostle Paul started the first church in ancient Greece at Philippi (Acts 16:11-40) following his Macedonian vision at Troas (Acts 16:8-10). Although he was shamefully treated at Philippi (1 Thess 2:2), he nevertheless had a significant ministry in the city and spoke affectionately about the church and his ministry among them (Phil 4:10-20). His best-known converts at Philippi included Lydia, in whose house he began the church; the jailer and his family (Acts 16:14-15, 27-34); EPAPHRODITUS (Phil 2:25-30); Euodia and Syntyche, who were at odds with each other after Paul's departure (Phil 4:2); Clement; and others who served with Paul and Silas at Philippi (Phil 4:3).

The Philippian church contributed substantially to Paul's subsequent missionary activity (Phil 4:15-18) and became very dear to him. He visited here at least one more time (Acts 20:1-6; 1 Cor 16:5-6; 2 Cor 2:13; 7:5), and on that visit he may have gone west to Illyricum (Rom 15:19). He may have written his letter(s) to the leaders of the church at Philippi (ca. 54–55 CE) from Ephesus or later while he was at Rome (ca. 60 CE).

PHILIPPIANS, LETTER TO THE Paul's letter to the Christians of Philippi is an exhortation to unity and steadfastness, presented as a letter of friendship that will nourish the familial relationship between people who already care deeply for one another. Philippians offers unique insight into the ways Jesus' death and resurrection have transformed Paul's own life and imagination (3:3-11), includes a hymn that is one of the most powerful and provocative expressions of early Christian convictions about Jesus (2:6-11), and makes an impassioned plea for Christian unity. Paul writes while a prisoner in Roman custody (1:7, 13-17; 4:22). Scholars have identified several locations where Paul might have been imprisoned as he wrote to the Philippians, each with implications for the dating of the letter, including Rome (61–63 CE), Ephesus (54–56 CE), Corinth (ca. 50 CE), and Caesarea (58–60 CE). None of these proposals, however, has generated consensus; the date and provenance of the letter thus remain open questions.

PHILISTINES A people located on the southern coastal strip of ancient Canaan during the Iron Age. According to the OT, the Philistines were organized in a confederation of five city-states (or Pentapolis), consisting of Ashdod, Ashkelon, Ekron, Gath, and GAZA, which were under the control of rulers referred to as "tyrants." The Philistines are presented as enemies of the Israelites, particularly during the period of the putative transition from a tribal to a monarchical society.

PHILOLOGUS A Roman Christian to whom Paul sent greetings (Rom 16:15). Philologus's name is paired with that of JULIA, who is possibly his wife or sister. With these two, Paul mentions NEREUS and his sister Olympas, and other "saints" who were perhaps part of a house church in Rome.

PHILOMETOR The coronation of King Ptolemy VI Philometor of EGYPT and his hostility to the Seleucid ANTIOCHUS IV are mentioned in 2 Macc 4:21 (see also 2 Macc 9:29; 10:13).

PHINEHAS 1. The son of Eleazar and the grandson of Aaron, the 1st Israelite high priest (Exod 6:25; Judg 20:28; 1 Chron 6:4 [Heb. 5:30]; 6:50 [Heb. 6:35]; Ezra 7:5.

2. The son of Eli and father of ICHABOD, who together with his brother Hophni ministered at the early cultic site of Shiloh. HOPHNI AND PHINEHAS abused the privileges of the priestly office (1 Sam 2:12-17, 22); as a consequence, Eli's family was deprived of the priesthood, and Phinehas and Hophni themselves were killed by the Philistines while accompanying the covenant chest on a failed military excursion (1 Sam 4:11).

3. The father of Eleazar, a priest living in Jerusalem during the time of Ezra (Ezra 8:33).

PHLEGON One of the Roman Christians whom Paul greets (Rom 16:14). Along with Asyncritus, Patrobas, Hermes, Hermas, and others, he was likely part of a house church in Rome.

PHOEBE A female resident of CENCHREAE (a seaport east of Corinth), Phoebe was the apparent deliverer of Paul's letter to the Romans. In commending her to that church (Rom 16:1-2), Paul urged them to receive her befittingly and help her in whatever she might need. This possibly involved assisting her in advance planning for Paul's intended visit to Rome and subsequent mission to Spain.

PHOENICIA People living in the coastal

fringe of the eastern Mediterranean. The territory of Phoenicia lies between the mountains of Lebanon to the east and the Mediterranean Sea to the west with a surface area that varies from 7 to 30 mi. wide.

In the Iron Age, Phoenicia was also a major supplier of craftsmen to the Israelite kingdom. Hiram's envoy is said to have been skilled "with gold, silver, bronze, iron, stone, and wood, as well as purple, violet, and crimson yarn, and fine linen. He can do any kind of engraving" (2 Chron 2:13-14). During this period, Phoenician deities were also worshipped in Israel (1 Kgs 11:5) and this endured for more than 300 years until the days of King Josiah (2 Kgs 23:13). Still a much-debated point is the territorial transfers between Solomon and Hiram (1 Kgs 9:10-14; 2 Chron 8:2). Hiram was given twenty cities in the Galilee by Solomon, but for some reason the cities did not please Hiram.

PHOENIX A harbor on the south-west coast of CRETE, Phoenix was an intended but unattained destination on Paul's voyage to Rome (Acts 27:12-14).

PHRYGIA Direct biblical references to Phrygia occur only in Acts. It is one of the territories listed in the Pentecost narrative in Acts 2:10 and one of the regions of Paul's travels mentioned along with Galatia in Acts 16:6 and 18:23. Phrygian cities mentioned in the NT include Colossae, Hierapolis, LAODICEA, Pisidian Antioch (see ANTIOCH, PISIDIAN), and arguably ICONIUM.

PHYGELUS The Asian Phygelus, along with HERMOGENES, turned away from Paul during his imprisonment (2 Tim 1:15).

PHYLACTERIES Phylacteries were small boxes, made of the leather of a kosher animal, secured to the head and forearm with leather thongs that passed through the box. Each box or capsule contained the four biblical passages concerning the commandment of phylacteries (Exod 13:1-10; 13:11-16; Deut 6:4-9; 11:13-21) written on leather slips, in remembrance of the exodus from Egypt.

Rabbinic law required males over the age of 13 to wear phylacteries; women were exempt.

PHYSICIAN A person who treats bodily injuries with medicinal substances (Jer 8:22; cf Exod 21:19), as well as embalmers (Gen 50:2).

The Greek term probably refers to a person who, for a fee, heals through naturalistic and/or religious therapies (Mark 5:26).

PI-BESETH An Egyptian city in the eastern Nile Delta mentioned along with ON in Ezekiel's oracle against Egypt (Ezek 30:17).

PI-HAHIROTH A location in the eastern Nile Delta between Migdol and the Reed Sea, east of Baal-zephon (Exod 14:2; Num 33:7). The Israelites reach Pi-hahiroth after turning back from Etham, a site probably located in the Wadi Tumilat (Exod 13:20). Pi-hahiroth was the last place the Israelites stayed before crossing the Reed Sea (Num 33:7).

PILATE, PONTIUS The Roman prefect of Judea (26–37 CE) who crucified Jesus of Nazareth.

PILATE'S WIFE An unnamed woman (Matt 27:19), but clearly the wife of Pontius Pilate, the Roman procurator of Judea (26–36 CE). She sent word to Pilate to dissociate himself from Jesus because a DREAM about Jesus had troubled her sleep.

PILDASH The 6th of eight sons born to NAHOR and his wife MILCAH, and thus Pildash was a nephew of Abraham (Gen 22:22).

PILGRIMAGE The concept of pilgrimage—a journey to a foreign or holy place—holds that space is not homogeneous and provides many societies with liminality, a marginal experience of transition and potentiality. Pilgrimage to Zion, God's royal residence (Pss 46:4 [Heb. 46:5]; 76:2 [Heb. 76:3]), offers contact with the divine, mediated through sensory experience.

Exodus 23:14-17 lists three pilgrimage feasts—the Festival of Unleavened Bread, the Harvest Festival, and the Gathering Festival—during which Israelite males must appear before the Lord, presumably at local sanctuaries (see PASSOVER AND FESTIVAL OF UNLEAVENED BREAD). In Deut 16:1-17, Passover has replaced Unleavened Bread and is celebrated in the temple; the Gathering Festival now receives its "booths" (possibly the tent camps of pilgrims to Jerusalem; see BOOTHS, FEAST OR FESTIVAL OF).

PILHA One of the leaders of the people in postexilic Jerusalem who signed Ezra's pact to divorce foreign wives (Neh 10:24).

PILLAR The term *pillar* is used in two distinct ways in the OT: as a cultic object and as an architectural feature. In the NT, *pillar* refers to an architectural feature.

PILLAR OF CLOUD AND FIRE See COLUMN OF CLOUD AND LIGHTNING.

PILTAI Head of the priestly house of MOADIAH in the time of the postexilic high priest JOIAKIM (Neh 12:17).

PIN A weaver uses a pin to fasten threads securely to the loom's beam. DELILAH attempted to use her loom as a trap, interweaving Samson's hair into the warp and tying it with a pin (Judg 16:14). Saul sought to kill David by pinning him to the wall with a spear (1 Sam 18:11; 19:10; cf 26:8).

PINE, PINE TREE Pine trees have long needles and characteristic woody cones that remain complete, unlike the disintegrating CEDAR cone. The tall, slender trunks yield soft, whitish timber. In modern times pine timber is used commonly, but in biblical times it was favored for woodwork for grand houses, royal palaces, and the holy sanctuary (Isa 60:13). Imported pine, like cedarwood, would have been expensive and was symbolic of wealth because it was not easily obtained. Pine trees were one of several resin-fragrant evergreen trees envisaged as usurping the dry, leafless desert species in Isa 41:19, an image of the bounty and richness to come.

PIRAM King Piram of JARMUTH (Josh 10:3) is one of the five kings of the AMORITES who united to attack Gibeon for making a treaty with Joshua. The Israelites defeated the Amorites, eventually capturing and executing all five kings (Josh 10:1-27).

PIRATHON The significance of Pirathon for early Israel is demonstrated by its fame as the seat of government for nearly a decade during ABDON's tenure as judge in the premonarchical era (Judg 12:13-15) and as the hometown of BENAIAH, one of David's warriors and key administrator in the days of the Davidic monarchy (2 Sam 23:30; 1 Chron 11:31; 27:14).

PISGAH, MOUNT Mount Pisgah figures prominently in the narrative descriptions of the Israelite journey from Egypt to Canaan because it is from the "top of Pisgah" that Moses views the land of promise, albeit as one prohibited from crossing over (Deut 3:27; 34:1). The same vantage point is utilized by Balaam in seeking the Lord's approval for cursing the Israelites, who are encamped within view of the peak (Num 23:14).

PISHON The 1st of four streams flowing from the river in Eden and around

HAVILAH (Gen 2:11). Sirach compares the Torah, which overflows with wisdom, to the Pishon (Sir 24:23-25).

PISIDIA A geographical region in the inland highland plateau in south-central Asia Minor mentioned in ancient texts, including two passages in the book of Acts (13:14; 14:24). Pisidia, located in the southern part of the Roman province of Galatia, was encompassed by Phrygia on the north, Lycaonia on the east, and Pamphylia and Lycia on the south and west.

Paul traveled through Pisidia two times on his 1st journey (Acts 13:14; 14:24). He announced a change in the direction of his ministry, a decision that established Antioch as a center of Christianity (Acts 13:46-47). We may assume that he traveled through Pisidia on his 2nd (Acts 16:6-10) and 3rd (Acts 18:22-23) journeys as well.

PISPA One of JETHER's four sons and a descendant of Asher, head of one of Israel's tribes (1 Chron 7:38).

PIT A hole in the ground, either naturally or humanly constructed, usually of sufficient depth that extraction is difficult or impossible. Often used literally (Gen 37:20; Matt 12:11), *pit* can also be a metaphor for destruction or disaster (Prov 26:27; Luke 6:39) or for the abode of the dead (Ps 30:3 [Heb. 30:4]; Sir 21:10).

PITCH A tarry substance. Pitch is used to seal the inside and outside of the ARK OF NOAH (Gen 6:14).

PITCHER A pitcher is a form of pottery often associated with drawing, transporting, or storing water. Pitchers were bulbous-shaped clay jars, ranging in size from 18 in. to 3 ft. in height and 12 in. to 1.5 ft. in diameter; size was appropriate to intended function.

PITHOM Pithom is one of two supply cities the Israelites built for the PHARAOH while they were slaves in Egypt (Exod 1:11), the other being RAMESES. Pithom is often associated with Tell el-Maskhuta in the Wadi Tumilat.

PITHON One of Micah's four sons; a descendant of Benjamin (1 Chron 8:35; 9:41) and King Saul (1 Chron 8:33).

PLAGUE Epidemic events resulting in deaths.

PLAGUES IN EGYPT *Plagues* is the conventional term for the succession of ten disasters befalling the Egyptians in Exod 7–12.

PLANTS OF THE BIBLE Plants served many purposes in the lives of biblical people. Cereals, herbs, spices, fruits, vegetables, and nuts supplied food; grapes were crushed to make wine; and olives were crushed to make oil for consumption, anointing, and oil lamps; resinous plants and herbs were used as medicines, ointments, and cosmetics; trees provided various kinds of wood for building frames and panels, furniture, agricultural implements, and boats; water plants were employed to make writing materials and baskets; textile plants provided material for clothing, woven mats, rope, and other useful products.

PLEIADES A brilliant star cluster located in the constellation Taurus, its appearance in and disappearance from the night sky was employed throughout the ancient world to signal the beginning or end of the rainy seasons for both agriculture and navigation. The constellation is mentioned in the OT context of the divine construction of the cosmos (Job 9:9; 38:31; Amos 5:8).

PLOW The metal blade or plowshare (1 Sam 13:20; Isa 2:4; Joel 3:10) affixed to the wooden plow, pulled by teams of oxen and guided by a human (1 Kgs

19:19; Sir 25:8), was used to create deep furrows in a cleared field that could then be sown with seed.

PLUMB LINE A string with a stone or metal weight (plumb bob) attached, used by a builder to determine whether a stone or mud-brick wall is vertical.

POCHERETH-HAZZEBAIM Pochereth-hazzebaim is among the cultic professionals returning from exile (Ezra 2:57; Neh 7:59; 1 Esdr 5:34).

POISON A poison is a substance that injures or kills through chemical interaction within the body. Natural poisons occur in both animals and plants. Ingesting a poison is oftentimes fatal (2 Macc 10:13), except that in mild doses certain poisons may act as healing stimulants.

POMEGRANATE A deciduous shrub or small tree thriving in a warm climate, with bright red flowers, ca. 3 cm in diameter. The large round fruits, ca. 7 cm in diameter, have a hard rind used for dyes and tanning leather. Inside, each of the numerous seeds is encased in delicious watery pulp. In ancient traditions the abundant seeds symbolized fertility.

PONTIUS PILATE See PILATE, PONTIUS.

PONTUS Pontus is a region in the northern part of modern Turkey. Its northern boundary is formed by the Black Sea , and to the south was the province of GALATIA. Residents from Pontus were present in Jerusalem at Pentecost (Acts 2:9), suggesting a thriving Jewish community of a type known in detail from elsewhere in Anatolia.

POPLAR A type of tree found along watersides (Job 40:22). The willow of Ezek 17:5 may also be the Euphrates poplar.

PORATHA One of Haman's ten sons killed by the Jews in Susa (Esth 9:8).

PORCH An architectural space that joins the interior and exterior of a building, with or without a roof, as on Solomon's house (1 Kgs 7:6) and the temple (Ezek 8:16).

POSIDONIUS A man sent by NICANOR along with Theodotus and MATTATHIAS to offer a treaty to JUDAS Maccabeus and his troops (2 Macc 14:19).

POST, DOORPOST Doorposts are the vertical structural elements for a doorway, with the lintel as the upper horizontal member and the THRESHOLD as the lower horizontal member. Doorposts were usually of wood or stone. Mention is made of doorposts of individual houses (Exod 12:7; Deut 6:9), the temple at Shiloh (1 Sam 1:9), the inner sanctuary of the Solomonic temple (1 Kgs 6:31), Solomon's palace (1 Kgs 7:5), and the restored temple of Ezekiel's vision (Ezek 41:21).

POTS Pots were used for cooking and were included in lists of temple items (1 Kgs 7:40; 2 Kgs 4:38-41; 25:14; 2 Chron 35:13). Probably the ceramic vessel most commonly identified as a "pot" in archaeological remains is a cooking pot.

POTIPHAR The Egyptian who purchases Joseph from the Midianites (Gen 37:36) or from the Ishmaelites (Gen 39:1).

POTIPHAR'S WIFE The wife of POTIPHAR, the Egyptian who purchased Joseph (Gen 37:36; 39:1). While she is unnamed in the biblical text, some later Jewish and Islamic sources refer to her as "Zulaikha" (with various spellings).

POTIPHERA An Egyptian priest of On (Heliopolis) and father of ASENATH

(Gen 41:45). The marriage of his daughter to the Hebrew patriarch Joseph gave Potiphera two grandsons, Manasseh and Ephraim (Gen 41:50). Potiphera is not to be confused with POTIPHAR, the official of Pharaoh's court to whom Joseph was sold in Gen 39.

POTTER'S FIELD The land bought with the blood money of Judas to bury strangers (Matt 27:3-9; Acts 1:18-19).

POUND A measure of weight (John 12:3; 19:39; Rev 16:21) or of weight equivalent for coins (Luke 19:13-25).

POVERTY In the Bible, *poverty* refers to a lack of material resources and economic power as well as to the political and social marginalization that results from this lack (Prov 10:15; 30:8; 31:7; Mark 12:44; Luke 21:4; 2 Cor 8:2, 9; Rev 2:9).

PRAETORIAN GUARD The title originally described the select group of legionnaires who guarded the praetor (commander) of a Roman army. The praetor's location was the praetorium, a structure in the center of the camp; the term came to be applied to a governor's residence (Matt 27:27; Mark 15:16; John 18:28, 33; 19:9). Philippians 1:13 refers to the Praetorian Guard, where some guardsmen have become devotees of Jesus.

PRAYER In the OT, *prayer* may describe a prayer of supplication, but may also refer to a category of prayer known as the psalm of lament, occurring some twenty-one times in the book of Psalms. In the NT, *prayer* is a technical term, a request for help made by speaking to a deity, usually in the form of a petition, vow, or wish prayer. It is also used to designate the place of prayer, and in this sense is often used in Jewish texts synonymously with the synagogue.

Prayer can be understood broadly to comprehend human communication to God, which may include words and related ritual actions (see WORSHIP).

PRAYER OF AZARIAH See AZARIAH, PRAYER OF.

PRAYER OF MANASSEH See MANASSEH, PRAYER OF.

PREACHER, THE The "preacher" in the book of Micah (2:11) refers to someone who spreads palatable teachings to the people, while they reject the warnings of Micah. Traditional translation of the word referring to the author of Ecclesiastes (1:1), alternately translated "Teacher" in the CEB.

PREACHING The telling of the ancient story of God's deliverance took varied forms in ancient Israel. Like other oral cultures, the message of redemption was often cast in story. Through narrative, values, and commitments integral to the identity and well-being of the community were communicated to successive generations. Stories were lodged in the memories of those who told and heard them. As traditions developed and as the TORAH began to take on its written form, those who told the stories developed a homiletical intention. That is, creeds and affirmations became elaborated and contextualized to meet the needs and experiences of a contemporary group of hearers. In this process are the seeds of contemporary understandings of preaching.

PREPARATION DAY The day when Jews made special arrangements to observe the SABBATH. Because the Sabbath was a day of complete rest, food had to be cooked, clothing prepared, and travel concluded before it began. To avoid profaning the Sabbath, work ceased before sunset on Friday and was prohibited until after sunset on Saturday.

According to the Gospels, Jesus was crucified on a Preparation Day. The Synoptic Gospels say people were preparing for the Sabbath (Matt 27:62; Mark 15:42; Luke 23:54), but John says they were preparing for the festival of Passover, a special Sabbath (John 19:14, 31, 42).

PRIESTS AND LEVITES In Israelite religion and early Judaism to the fall of the second temple, priests and Levites were ritual specialists and mediators between God and people.

PRINCE Very occasionally in the OT, *prince* refers to the son of a king (e.g., 2 Kgs 10:13) or to a royal figure (e.g., David in Ezek 34:24; 37:25). Mostly, though, it signifies one who exercises influence (e.g., Gen 23:6; 1 Chron 7:40) or occupies a more formal leadership position (e.g., Isa 49:7; Lam 2:9). Sometimes the Hebrew word translated as "prince" refers to a preeminent leader (e.g., 1 Sam 25:30; 2 Sam 6:21; 7:8; 2 Chron 11:22). Ezekiel uses the phrase "princes of Israel" with reference to their responsibilities toward the temple and the holy city (e.g., Ezek 45:7-9, 17; 48:21-22). The term *prince* may represent an earthly or nonearthly power. The phrase "Prince of Peace" may describe a messianic figure (Isa 9:6). Elsewhere, *prince* may carry messianic overtones and imply a link between Messiah and temple (Dan 9:25-26). In the poetic books, *prince* is often used to depict an uncomplimentary contrast between princes and the poor (e.g., 1 Sam 2:8; Ps 113:8) or the subjection of princes to God (e.g., Job 12:21; 29:10). In the Apocrypha, *prince* rarely refers to royalty (Bar 1:4 is an exception). Mostly it refers to identified leaders among the people (e.g., Jdt 5:2; 2 Macc 9:25; Sir 41:17), often occurring in parallel with "leaders," "judges," and "nobles" (Bar 1:9; Jdt 9:10; Sir 8:8). Judith 9:10 implies an ironic contrast between princes and ordinary people.

PRISCA, PRISCILLA A prominent woman in the early church, Prisca (Rom 16:3; 1 Cor 16:19; 2 Tim 4:19), or Priscilla (Acts 18:2, 18, 26), is always paired with her husband Aquila. The couple traveled both independently and with Paul, spreading the gospel to Rome, Ephesus, and Corinth. Paul particularly honored their mutual sacrifice and assistance in establishing "all the churches of the Gentiles" (Rom 16:3-4; cf 1 Cor 16:19). Priscilla and Aquila supported themselves by the trade of tentmaking, or they "worked with leather," which was easily transportable and suitable to evangelistic shoptalk with customers. Although a physically demanding occupation, there is no reason to doubt Priscilla's full participation with her husband (Acts 18:2-3). During their sojourns in major cities, they hosted a house church in their residence (Rom 16:5; 1 Cor 16:19). In this domestic domain, Priscilla likely had authority, especially (but not only) among women and children, and prime opportunity for preaching, teaching, and caring for guests. As one who "explained to [Apollos] God's way more accurately," Priscilla is the only woman in Acts depicted as an authoritative teacher (Acts 18:24-26). See AQUILA AND PRISCILLA.

PRISON Ancient legal systems allowed for incarceration of prisoners as they awaited trial, sentencing, transfer, execution, or other forms of punishment.

PROCHORUS Prochorus is chosen, along with STEPHEN, among the seven named persons, "well-respected men," charged with the care of widows who were being neglected in the distribution of food (Acts 6:3-5).

PROCONSUL A Roman official who governed a province. Paul and Barnabas encountered a proconsul named Sergius Paulus (see PAULUS, SERGIUS) who became a Christian believer (Acts 13:7-12). GALLIO, proconsul of Achaia, refused to try Paul when Jews who opposed Paul's teachings brought him before the tribunal (Acts 18:12-17). Paul escaped being brought before the proconsul in Ephesus after silversmiths of the shrines of Artemis fomented a riot in opposition to Paul's teaching that silver idols were not really gods (Acts 19:21-41).

PRODIGAL SON This is the English title of the PARABLE of the son who squanders his inheritance (while his brother remains dutiful), and is subsequently forgiven and welcomed back by his FATHER (Luke 15:11-32).

PROPHET Prophets speak on behalf of the deity to the people, as the formula "Thus says the Lord" suggests, and, on occasion, they speak on behalf of an individual or the people as a whole to the deity. The term *prophet* does not, at least by dint of etymology, mean someone who forespeaks (i.e., someone who foretells the future); nor does it signify someone who "speaks forth," though prophets may, indeed, speak truth to various elements in Israelite society. Prophets occur in the books of Samuel and Kings, and several books focus on the words of prophets: Isaiah, Jeremiah, Ezekiel, and the twelve Minor Prophets.

The terms *prophet* and *prophecy* in the NT designate a variety of phenomena, including speech that names injustice or that builds up the community, revelatory visions and ecstatic utterances, altered states of consciousness, and symbolic actions that unmask and challenge the prevailing powers. Prophetic speech is not merely predictive, but combines aspects of memory, tradition, and hope to awaken vision and resistance. Prophets arose especially in times of conflict and injustice. Women may have exercised significant leadership in the early church especially as prophets (Acts 21:9; 1 Cor 11:5; Rev 2:20).

The early Christians understood prophets to represent God's own voice, the continuing voice of the crucified and risen Jesus, or the movement of the Spirit (e.g., 1 Cor 14:26-33; 1 Thess 5:19-20). The gospel traditions present John the Baptizer and Jesus as prophets.

PROSTITUTION Female prostitution—a woman's participation in sexual intercourse outside marriage, typically in exchange for payment (but see Gen 34:31; Lev 21:14; Deut 22:21)—is well attested in the Bible and other ANE sources. Equally well attested is a profoundly ambivalent cultural attitude toward prostitution. The prostitute was stigmatized and even ostracized in the societies of the ANE. In Lev 19:29 and 21:9, for example, prostitution or being "promiscuous" is characterized as that which "defiles." Similarly, Prov 23:27 condemns the prostitute as a "deep pit." Prostitutes are at the same low level as tax collectors, who were hated and marginalized members of society (Matt 21:31-32).

However, there are positive portrayals of several prostitutes. RAHAB actually lives within the city wall of Jericho, while her house proper stands on the wall's outer side (Josh 2:15). Rahab is subsequently lauded in biblical tradition for her role in securing the Israelite conquest of Jericho, to the extent that Heb 11:31 upholds her, alongside Abraham, Jacob, Joseph, and Moses, as a paradigm of faith. Rahab is also listed alongside Abraham as a paragon in Jas 2:25. Similarly, the Bible treats the widowed TAMAR's assumption of the role of prostitute as praiseworthy. Once he discovers that Tamar's reason for taking on a prostitute's guise was to fulfill her responsibility to bear a son for her deceased husband, her father-in-law Judah even declares, "She's more righteous than I am" (Gen 38:26).

In the NT, Tamar and Rahab are two of only four women listed in Matthew's presentation of Jesus' genealogy (Matt 1:3, 5). Jesus praises prostitutes for their faith in the baptism of John and, eventually, in the message of Jesus' ministry (Matt 21:23-32), and Jesus likewise praises the faith of the sinful woman—often taken to be a prostitute—who washes and anoints his feet in Luke 7:36-50. These passages clearly reflect a positive attitude toward prostitutes.

Perhaps much of the reason so much stigma is attached to the prostitute is that she controls the financial transactions in which she engages, which contravenes the normal ANE social order, where financial transactions were typically overseen by men. However, the ability of prostitutes to control their own financial destinies means they were among the few women within the ANE who were able to function independent of male authority.

In addition to the texts that concern actual prostitutes, we find passages in the OT that metaphorically employ the terms *prostitute*, *prostitution*, *whore*, and related words to suggest that the people of Israel, if they worship other gods instead of or in addition to the Israelite God, play the prostitute by violating their covenant obligation to give the Lord their exclusive fidelity. This is always portrayed negatively. In legal materials, any Israelites who might devote themselves to other gods (e.g., Lev 17:7) are said to "prostitute themselves" (Exod 34:15-16). Likewise, in the narrative complex that runs from Joshua to 2 Kings (the so-called Deuteronomistic History), as well as in the related book of Deuteronomy, Israelite worship of other gods is condemned as equivalent of prostitution (e.g., Deut 31:16; Judg 8:33). The Chronicles narratives, too, can deploy this language (1 Chron 5:25).

In the NT, this OT metaphor of "apostasy as prostitution" continues to be deployed, although in somewhat different ways. The book of Revelation in particular draws heavily on this image in its descriptions of the "great prostitute," who is said to represent the apostasies of the Roman Empire, as well as Rome's antagonism toward the peoples of the nascent Christian movement (Rev 17:1, 15-16; 19:2). Revelation's metaphorical prostitute is, however, never portrayed as an unfaithful spouse to the Lord, as in the OT prophets. Still, she shows disregard for the Lord's authority over all the earth, she is the enemy of God's righteous ones, and she is depicted as a gaudy symbol of all sorts of abominations (Rev 17:3-6). All the nations of the earth have fornicated with her (Rev 17:2; 18:3). As in the OT, therefore, the brutal punishment of the great prostitute (Rev 18:1-24) offers a religious justification for violence in relationships between men and women.

PROVERB The word *proverb* describes various types of discourse in the Bible. Readers of the biblical text most often associate the word *proverb* with short, usually two-line sayings in Hebrew poetic parallel structure that provide basic insights into human relationships. These are frequent in the book of Proverbs as well as in other OT literature. The NT uses the term to refer to sayings as well as short stories such as parables.

PROVINCE An administrative term for a subdivision of an empire outside the imperial city or country. Ancient empires generally preferred to govern their territories through local client kings, transferring a territory to provincial status under direct imperial rule only when the region became inefficient, troublesome, or outright rebellious.

PSALM 151 Whereas the Heb. contains 150 psalms, the LXX features an additional Psalm 151.

PSALMS, BOOK OF Psalms is the Bible's longest book and the most diverse, both literarily and theologically. Nowhere else in the Scriptures is found such a varied collection of religious poetry, with 150 psalms in the Hebrew text and 151 psalms in the LXX. As the product of several centuries of ancient Israel's religious life, the Psalter features prayers, hymns, didactic poems, and even a wedding song. On the one hand, nearly every theological chord of the OT resounds throughout the Psalter. On the other hand, the Psalter consists primarily of human discourse, both joyous and anguished. In the psalms, the anthropological and the theological are inseparably wedded. The title "Psalms" means "songs accompanied by stringed instrument," or simply "songs,"

PSALTER Another name for the book of Psalms. *Psalter* can also refer to a particular version of the psalms (e.g., "Syriac Psalter"), or to a collection of psalms arranged for liturgical use.

PSEUDEPIGRAPHA Traditionally, Jewish writings from the 3rd cent. BCE to the mid-2nd cent. CE that are not part of the OT or the OT Apocrypha. The designation means "falsely attributed writings," and reflects the prevalence of pseudonymous texts in the collection.

PUAH 1. In Exod 1:15-21, Puah is a midwife (whether Hebrew or Egyptian is unspecified) who attends Hebrew women during childbirth. When commanded by Pharaoh to kill all the male newborns, Puah and her colleague SHIPHRAH defy the ruler through trickery by saying that the Hebrew women can give birth on their own. It is striking that the name of the pharaoh is never recorded, yet Puah, the humble woman who saves Israel by her courage, is mentioned by name. For their valor, God rewards the midwives with "households of their own" (Exod 1:21), a possible reference to having children, being heads of midwife guilds, or receiving divine protection.

2. Puah is a descendant of Issachar. He is listed as the son of Dodo and the father of Tola (Judg 10:1) or as Issachar's son and Tola's brother (1 Chron 7:1).

PUBLIUS From the Latin "of the people," Publius was a common first name in the Roman Empire. When Paul is shipwrecked on Malta, he comes under the care and hospitality of Publius, the "island's most prominent person," which is likely an official designation of Publius's governorship of Malta (Acts 28:7-8). In response to Publius's hospitality, Paul cures his father of a fever and dysentery.

PUDENS Mentioned with the Christians in Rome who send greetings to Timothy (2 Tim 4:21), listed after Eubulus, and followed by Linus, Claudia, and all other Christians in Rome.

PUL The name "Pul" referred to TIGLATH-PILESER III (1 Chron 5:26), the Assyrian king (745–727 BCE) who established the Neo-Assyrian Empire over Babylonia under the name of Pulu. Pul received tribute from Menahem of Israel (2 Kgs 15:19-20).

PURAH To assuage GIDEON's fears, the Lord instructed him to take his servant Purah and spy on the Midianite camp (Judg 7:10-11).

PURIM A festival in the Jewish liturgical calendar falling on the 14th day of the month of ADAR, which commemorates the Jews' deliverance from HAMAN's genocidal plot through the actions of Esther and Mordecai.

PURPLE In the ancient world, purple goods were typically made with a dye extracted from sea snails. Because of the difficult and lengthy production process, purple dye was very expensive, making purple cloth a luxury item. In the OT, the manufacture of purple textiles is often associated with PHOENICIA in general and the city of TYRE in particular (2 Chron 2:14; Ezek 27:16). As a status symbol, purple cloth was often connected with royalty (Judg 8:26; Esth 1:6; Song 3:10) and honor (Esth 8:15; Dan 5:16, 29). It is high praise to say that the wife in Prov 31:21-22 can provide such goods to her family.

Purple is also associated with luxury and royalty in the NT. When the Roman soldiers mock Jesus as a king, they place a purple robe on him (Mark 15:17, 20; John 19:2, 5). In the parable of the rich man and Lazarus, the wealth of the rich man is illustrated by his purple robes (Luke 16:19). In Revelation, the woman representing Rome is dressed in purple and scarlet (Rev 17:4; 18:16), but after her destruction the merchants mourn because Rome is no longer able to buy imported goods, such as purple cloth (Rev 18:12). Paul's first convert in Europe is Lydia, "a dealer in purple cloth" (Acts 16:14). This suggests that she was a person of some wealth, which is consistent with the fact that she may have hosted a church in her house (Acts 16:40; see LYDIA, LYDIANS).

PUT 1. The person Put is the 3rd son of Noah's 2nd son Ham (Gen 10:6).

2. A nation (Jer 46:9; Ezek 27:10; 30:5; 38:5), perhaps modern Libya or the ancient Punt. Punt was a nation to the southeast of Egypt and roughly consistent with the contemporary region of Somaliland near the Horn of Africa. Put was geographically distant from Judah and its people were known to the Judean audience of the OT primarily because of their participation in the larger Egyptian-Cushite league.

PUTHITE One of four Calebite families listed as coming from Kiriath-jearim (both a personal and place-name) (1 Chron 2:53).

PUTIEL Putiel's unnamed daughter was married to ELEAZAR, and they were the parents of PHINEHAS (Exod 6:25).

PUVAH The 2nd-named son of Issachar (Gen 46:13), listed as PUAH in 1 Chron 7:1. Puvah is also cited as the eponymous ancestor of the Punite clan (Num 26:23).

PYRRHUS Father of Sopater, one of Paul's companions (Acts 20:4), and from Beroea, where Paul had preached previously (Acts 17:10-15).

Qq

QUAIL According to the account of Israel's journey through the desert, the people craved meat. Thus, God provided them not only with manna, but with great numbers of quail as well (Exod 16:13; Num 11:31-32; recalled in Ps 105:40; Wis 16:2; 19:12).

QUARRY First Kings 5:17 describes how Solomon's workers, with Tyrian assistance, quarried the stones for the temple construction (cf 1 Kgs 6:7; 2 Kgs 12:12; 22:6; 2 Chron 34:11).

QUARTUS A Christian listed with seven others in the concluding greetings in Paul's letter to the Romans (16:23).

QUEEN In the OT, the title "queen" is used in reference to royal women of foreign countries: Sheba (1 Kgs 10:1-13; 2 Chron 9:1-12); Vashti (Esth 1:1-20); Esther (Esth 2:17); and an unnamed king's wife (Dan 5:10). The term also occurs in Jeremiah's polemic against the "QUEEN OF HEAVEN" (Jer 7:18; 44:17-19, 25) and for unspecified admirers of the woman in Song of Songs (6:8-9). The majority of biblical queens, however, are not called queen. Athaliah, for example, is the wife of a king, mother of a king, and for six years sole monarch of Judah (2 Kgs 11:3), but she is never titled queen in the text.

Various biblical passages highlight the involvement of queens in the counsel of kings and in royal administration. Proverbs 31:1-9, attributed to a King Lemuel's mother, counsels restraint and directs the king to care for the poor and needy. While the terminology related to queens and the historical details of their lives remain sketchy, the general portrait of queens that emerges depicts them as symbols of a nation. They are an integral part of the Davidic monarchy and part of the process of ruling.

QUEEN OF HEAVEN According to Jer 7:16-20 and 44:15-25, some ancient Israelites burned incense, poured out libations, and baked cakes to honor a goddess known only as the Queen of Heaven. In exchange, according to the queen's adherents, she made available plenty of food and kept them safe from enemy attack. It is particularly women, moreover, who seem devoted to the Queen of Heaven; thus they become, in Jer 44:25, the object of Jeremiah's special scorn. The Queen of Heaven may be a goddess of Israel's neighbors, such as Astarte or Ishtar.

QUEEN OF THE SOUTH The queen of the South to which Jesus refers (Matt 12:42; Luke 11:31) is most likely the Gentile queen of Sheba (1 Kgs 10:1-13; 2 Chron 9:1-12).

QUIRINIUS Publius Sulpicius Quirinius, a Roman governor, associated with a census in Luke 2:2.

QUIVER A case used to carry and store arrows. The bow and arrow were used for both hunting and warfare from as early as 3000 BCE. Since the bow was delicate, strung with animal tendons and sinews, it was kept in a quiver (Gen 27:3). As a metaphor, a quiver indicates a place for hiding and protecting an object of value.

Rr

RAAMAH 1. Raamah has traditionally been identified as one of the descendants of Cush and the father of SHEBA and DEDAN (Gen 10:7; 1 Chron 1:9; see CUSH, CUSHITE).

2. The town Raamah has become loosely identified with the southern Arabian Peninsula. In Ezek 27:22 traders from Sheba and Raamah are said to have traded with TYRE in precious stones and gold.

RAAMSES See RAMESES.

RABBAH 1. "Rabbah of the Ammonites" (Deut 3:11; 2 Sam 12:26; 17:27; Jer 49:2; Ezek 21:20) is to be distinguished from the Rabbah of Josh 15:60, a border town in the 10th district of Judah.

2. A town in the highlands of Judah named in a list of towns allotted to the tribe of Judah (Josh 15:60). It is listed after Kiriath-jearim, indicating that the towns were in close proximity to each other.

RABBI, RABBONI Throughout rabbinic literature, *rabbi* means "master" and "teacher of disciples." As such, a rabbi serves as a metaphoric "father." These meanings are still in use in the modern era. *Rabbi* derives from the Hebrew term meaning "mighty," "great," or "numerous." In the NT, rabbi is explained as "teacher" in Matt 23:8 and John 1:38 (cf John 20:16). The term *rabbi* is transliterated frequently in Mark, Matthew, and John but is absent in Luke. In almost every NT citation, the term *rabbi* refers to Jesus.

RACHEL Means "ewe." Rachel is the youngest daughter of LABAN and the sister of LEAH. As JACOB's wife, she was the biological mother of Joseph (see JOSEPH, JOSEPHITES) and Benjamin (see BENJAMIN, BENJAMINITES), and the grandmother of Ephraim (see EPHRAIM, EPHRAIMITES) and Manasseh (see MANASSEH, MANASSITES), clan heads of what became the northern kingdom of Israel.

Best known, perhaps, as the object of her cousin Jacob's great love (Jacob is smitten from the moment he sees her and immediately kisses her [Gen 29:10-11]), Rachel is depicted as a complex figure. Genesis introduces her as having "a beautiful figure" and being "good-looking" (29:17) and also as a shepherd (29:9), the only woman in the Bible who explicitly holds this position. She is portrayed on the one hand as a resourceful figure (who dares, for example, to steal her father's household divine images) and also a paradigmatic barren woman who desperately longs for children (Gen 30:1). She eventually gets her wish, but she also tragically dies young in childbirth. Jacob, who seeks refuge in her father's house, falls in love with Rachel and offers to work seven years for her father in order to marry her (Gen 29:20). At the end of those years, however, her father switches brides, and Jacob discovers in the morning that he has married her sister LEAH instead (Gen 29:23-25). Beloved Rachel becomes Jacob's bride a week later, but Jacob works for her an additional seven years.

RADDAI Raddai is listed as the 5th of seven sons of JESSE (1 Chron 2:14) and the older brother of David.

RAGES The book of Tobit places the town of Rages in Media in the mountains two days east of Ecbatana (5:6).

RAGUEL Father of Sarah with his wife Edna, and relative to Tobit (Tob 3:7).

RAHAB 1. The woman who helps Joshua's spies in Jericho (Josh 2). Although most English translations describe Rahab as a "prostitute," the exact meaning of the Hebrew description is debated. Rahab, it seems, is a woman who sells access to her body in exchange for money or goods. She owns her own house, perhaps a kind of bordello, which may have led Greek interpreters to call her an "innkeeper," which is consistent with Josephus's reference to her (*Ant.* 5.7–8).

There are three verses that mention Rahab in the NT. First, Matthew puts her in the genealogy that links Jesus to Abraham (Matt 1:5). According to Matthew, she is the mother of BOAZ (the husband of RUTH). The author of Hebrews praises Rahab for her faith (Heb 11:31), while the author of James lauds her for her works (Jas 2:25).

2. A dragon or CHAOS monster, known in ANE traditions as well as the OT (Job 26:12; Ps 89:7-13 [Heb. 89:8-14]).

RAHAM Son of SHEMA and father of Jorkeam, descendants of Hebron, one of Caleb's sons (1 Chron 2:44).

RAINBOW The OT uses the Hebrew word *bow*, meaning "the weapon," to refer to the bow-shaped object seen in the sky after rain: it is the "bow in the clouds" (Gen 9:13). After the flood (Gen 9:12-17), God hangs the bow in the sky where it will serve as a reminder of God's promise to never again destroy all flesh with a flood because of human wickedness.

According to Sirach, the rainbow encircling the vaulted sky testifies to God's work as creator (Sir 43:11). Sirach also compares the high priest Simon to a rainbow (Sir 50:7). In Revelation, a rainbow surrounds the throne on which the divine presence is seated (Rev 4:3; cf

10:1), recalling the glory of the divine presence as Ezekiel saw it (Ezek 1:28).

RAM 1. The ram (a male sheep) is a valuable animal within flocks (Gen 31:38; Deut 32:14; 2 Kgs 3:4; 2 Chron 17:11; Ezek 27:21; 34:17) and figures as an offering in inaugural and festal sacrifices (Gen 15; Exod 29; Lev 8–9; 16:3; 23:18; Num 6–7; 15:6-7; 23; 28–29; 1 Chron 15:26; 2 Chron 29; Ezek 43; 45–46) as well as in offerings that accomplish forgiveness (Lev 5:14–6:7 [Heb. 5:14-26]; 16:3, 5; 19:20-22; Num 5:5-10). The ram's skin, typically dyed red (Exod 25:5; 26:14; 35:7, 23; 36:19; 39:34), features in arrangements for the cult. To this extent, the ram stands as a metonym for the act of sacrifice. The ram also has symbolic significance in the visions of Daniel (Dan 8).

2. Ram was the great-grandson of Judah and ancestor of King David (1 Chron 2:9-10). The genealogy of Jesus in Matthew gives his name as Aram (Matt 1:3-4).

3. The oldest son of Jerahmeel (1 Chron 2:25-27).

4. The name of the clan to which Elihu belonged (Job 32:2).

RAMAH This name designates four places in the Bible. It is sometimes alternated with the related forms Ramoth and Ramathaim. The name means "shrine, high place, hill, eminence," or the like. In 2 Kgs 8:29 and 2 Chron 22:6, Ramah is a shortened form of RAMOTH-GILEAD.

1. A town in Benjamin (see BENJAMIN, BENJAMINITES) located north of Jerusalem. The biblical figure who is most prominently associated with Ramah of Benjamin is SAMUEL. Ramah is the home of Samuel's parents Elkanah and Hannah (1 Sam 1:19; 2:11), from which they journey to Bethel for Hannah's fateful encounter with Eli. In the NT, Ramah is mentioned once in Matt. 2:18.

2. A town in Simeon (see SIMEON, SIMEONITES) located in the Beersheba Valley. This Ramah appears in a toponym list (Josh 19:8) and, as "Ramoth of the arid southern plain," as one of the towns to which David gave his booty (1 Sam 30:27).

3. A town on the boundary of Asher (see ASHER, ASHERITES) somewhere in the vicinity of TYRE (Josh 19:29).

4. A town in Naphtali, in the vicinity of HAZOR (Josh 19:36). See NAPHTALI, NAPHTALITES.

RAMATHITE SHIMEI the Ramathite was in charge of David's vineyards (1 Chron 27:27). *Ramathite* likely indicates that Shimei was from one of the cities named RAMAH.

RAMESES The name of a city in the eastern delta of Egypt on the Pelusiac branch of the Nile. The town name is often transcribed as Pi-Raamses to avoid confusion with the name of the PHARAOH; some translations show "Raameses." In the book of Genesis, Rameses is listed as the region where the descendants of Jacob settled in the land of EGYPT during the famine in Canaan (Gen 47:11). It is subsequently mentioned as the starting point for the exodus (Exod 12:37; Num 33:3, 5).

RAMOTH-GILEAD Located on the plateau east of the Jordan River in the tribal territory of Gad (Deut 4:43; Josh 20:8; 21:38; see GAD, GADITES) near the border between ancient Israel and Syria.

Deuteronomy and Joshua give Ramoth-gilead a prominent place in the early stages of Israel's history in the land. Deuteronomy 4:43 records the Mosaic identification of Ramoth-gilead as the most central of the three cities of refuge on the east side of the Jordan River; Josh 20:8 has Joshua implementing the assignment of the cities. In addition, Joshua designated Ramoth-gilead as one of the forty-eight levitical cities, according to Josh 21:38. The continued importance of the city in the period of the united monarchy is indicated by its identification as the location of BEN-GEBER, one of twelve Solomonic officials assigned to organizing and providing the monthly royal cuisine (1 Kgs 4:13).

Subsequent to the late-10th cent. BCE division of the monarchy, Ramoth-gilead became part of the northern kingdom; its strategic location near the Syrian border made it something of a buffer between Israel and Syria, and, consequently, control of the city was a continuing high priority for both the Israelites and the Arameans.

RAPHAEL Meaning "God heals."

1. An ancestor of Tobit (Tob 1:1).

2. In the books of Tobit and 1 Enoch, Raphael is one of seven angels who stand in God's presence (Tob 12:15; 1 En. 20:1-7; see ANGEL). In Tobit, Raphael hears the prayers of Tobit and Sarah and comes to their assistance (Tob 3:16-17).

RAPHAH Raphah (Rephaiah in 1 Chron 9:43) is listed among the descendants of Benjamin as the son of Binea and father of Eleasah (1 Chron 8:37).

RAPHU The father of PALTI, the Benjaminite among the twelve men whom Moses charged with the task of scouting the land of Canaan to determine its fruitfulness and the strength of its inhabitants (Num 13:9).

RAVEN It is evident from Lev 11:15 and Deut 14:14 ("any kind of raven") that this term could be used in a broad, generic sense, covering all birds belonging to the *Corvidae* family, including ravens, crows, jackdaws, and rooks.

See BIRDS OF THE BIBLE.

REAIAH Three different men named Reaiah are mentioned in the OT.

1. A grandson of Judah and son of Shobal (1 Chron 4:2; named HAROEH in 1 Chron 2:52).

2. A Reubenite of the family of Joel, whose father is Micah and whose son is Baal (1 Chron 5:5).

3. The ancestor of temple servants who returned from the Babylonian exile with ZERUBBABEL (Ezra 2:47; Neh 7:50).

REAP Reaping (harvesting, gathering) was vital in agriculturally based economies (Lev 23:22; Ruth 2:9; Matt 6:26; Luke 12:24) and often served as a metaphor for divine judgment (Isa 17:5; Jer 12:13; Rev 14:15-16) and the rewards and consequences of human effort (John 4:37-38; 1 Cor 9:11; Gal 6:7-9).

REBA One of the five kings of Midian killed by Moses' army (Num 31:8; Josh 13:21).

REBEKAH Rebekah (Gen 22:23; 24:15–28:5; 29:12; 35:8; 49:31; or "Rebecca," Rom 9:10-12) is the second matriarch in the Hebrew family line after SARAH. She is the wife of ISAAC, the mother of JACOB and ESAU, and the daughter of BETHUEL, son of NAHOR and MILCAH. Rebekah is an independent, assertive, clever character who overshadows her husband Isaac, about whom we learn much less than his wife.

In the NT, Paul contends that Abraham's only true heirs are those born to him as a result of a promise (Gen 18:10). He further illustrates this concept with Sarah and HAGAR, two mothers, and with Rebekah, one mother with two sons, of whom God promises that the elder will serve the younger (Rom 9:10-12).

RECHAB, RECHABITES Rechab is the name of two men in the OT, while *Rechabites* refers to the house of Rechab, a group that follows a distinctive way of living.

1. Son of RIMMON of Beeroth, a Benjaminite city. Together with his brother BAANAH, Rechab was a military leader in the forces of Saul's son ISHBOSHETH, who had succeeded his

father as king of the northern tribes (2 Sam 4:1-12).

2. The ancestor of JONADAB, founder of the house of the Rechabites, who first appears in the account of the bloody coup waged by the future king JEHU of Israel (2 Kgs 10:15-28).

3. Over two and a half centuries after Jonadab and Jehu, the Rechabites appear in Jer 35. The Rechabites affirm that they and their families abstain from wine, do not build houses or occupy them, and do not have vineyards or fields or engage in raising crops. They live in tents (Jer 35:8-10).

RECONCILE, RECONCILIATION The word *reconciliation* indicates a change in social relationship in which two parties previously at enmity with each other exchange friendship and peace. While there is no single Hebrew word corresponding to the Greek terms for reconciliation, there are several concepts that convey the healing of relationships connoted by reconciliation: "to become acceptable" (e.g., in 1 Sam 29:4); "to cover over" (e.g., in Jer 18:23); and "to redeem" (e.g., in Isa 43:1; 44:22-23; 48:20; 52:9, where God's redemption indicates that God has already turned toward the people and no longer wishes to punish them). See COVENANT, OT AND NT; MERCY, MERCIFUL.

In the NT, reconciliation must take place between community members before bringing an offering to God (Matt 5:24). In doctrinal statements in the Christian tradition, reconciliation typically denotes Jesus' sacrifice on the cross: "Christ's death for us." Paul's use in 2 Cor 5:18-21 refers to God as agent of reconciliation as well as the one being reconciled to the world. In the biblical materials, however, the concept of reconciliation refers more broadly to various means by which particular persons (or humanity) are restored to right relationship with God. See also Rom 1:18–3:20, 5:8-11, 11:15; Col. 1:20-22, Eph 2:12-17.

RECONCILIATION DAY Reconciliation Day (Yom Kippur), celebrated annually on the 10th day of the 7th month (Tishri), comprises a series of rituals by which the high priest purifies both the sanctuary and the people, thereby restoring both as fitting receptacles for and agents of God's holy presence in the world (Lev 16).

RED HEIFER According to the book of Numbers, the ashes of a special red cow were used to purify those defiled by death, the strongest contaminant in the Israelite system of impurities. A corpse was irrevocably impure, and those who had been in contact with it were required to purify themselves under penalty of death by divine agency. If one was not properly purified, corpse impurity became a danger to the sanctuary, even if no direct contact with it was made (Num 19:2-10, 13, 20).

RED SEA See REED SEA.

REED Probably the common reed (*Phragmites communis*), the cattail (*Typha angustifolia*), or one of a variety of plants that grow primarily in marshy areas along rivers, lakes, and other bodies of water in the Near East.

REED SEA A body of water, sometimes translated "Red Sea," sometimes equivalent to the modern Gulf of Aqaba. It was the site of victory over Pharaoh's army in Exod 14–15.

REELAIAH Reelaiah was among those returning from the Babylonian exile with Zerubbabel (Ezra 2:2).

REFINING The process of removing impurities from metal, ore, WATER, or WINE.

REFUGE A shelter or protection from danger or distress, *refuge* is a common metaphor for *God* in the OT (Deut 32:37).

The word appears most frequently in the Psalms (Ps 142:5 [Heb. 142:6]), where the profession of the Lord as refuge distinguishes the righteous from the wicked (Pss 2:12; 34:8 [Heb. 34:9]; 37:39-40; 52:7 [Heb. 52:9]; 64:10 [Heb. 64:11]; cf Prov 14:32). See REFUGE CITY.

REFUGE CITY Cities of refuge were established in Israel to offer protection for those who had inadvertently killed another human being (Exod 21:12-14). The retaliatory justice of Israel's kinship system demanded a life for a life. The six cities designated in Josh 20:8-9 were strategically located so that none lay outside a day's journey from any point in Israel.

The concept of asylum in the ANE was generally associated with sanctuaries. The COVENANT SCROLL reflects this perspective through legislation that allows a killer to flee to a place appointed by God if the murder was not premeditated (Exod 21:12-14; Num 35:9-29; Deut 4:41-43, 19:1-3)

REGEM One of six sons of JAHDAI listed in 1 Chron 2:42-55, in the second genealogy of Calebites (see 1 Chron 2:18-24).

REGEM-MELECH The name of a person accompanying SHAREZER, sent to inquire of the temple priests and prophets concerning the continuation of fasting in commemoration of the temple's destruction (Zech 7:2). This visit occurred as the rebuilding of the temple neared completion in the 4th year of DARIUS, the Persian king (518 BCE).

REHABIAH The only son of ELIEZER, Rehabiah is said to have had numerous sons (1 Chron 23:17; 26:25), including ISSHIAH, one of the chiefs of the Levites (1 Chron 24:21).

REHOB 1. The father of Hadadezer, king of ZOBAH (2 Sam 8:3, 12), a people of Syrian descent (2 Sam 10:8).

2. One of the Levites who signed a covenant with Nehemiah (Neh 10:11).

3. A city at the extremity of the spies' travels within Canaan (Num 13:21). It fell within the land allotted to the tribe of Asher in northern Israel (Josh 19:28, 30) but was given to the Levites (Josh 21:31; 1 Chron 6:75). However, Canaanites maintained possession of the city (Judg 1:31). See BETH-REHOB.

REHOBOAM Son of SOLOMON and the Ammonite woman NAAMAH (1 Kgs 14:21, 31), and grandson of DAVID. Rehoboam is noted for precipitating the division of the kingdom of Israel. He retained the southern tribal areas of Benjamin and Judah under his control. These tribes survived as the kingdom of Judah until the Babylonian invasion and conquest in 586 BCE. Rehoboam lost the northern tribes, who formed their own union, Israel, which lasted until 722 BCE.

REHOBOTH Meaning "open spaces" or "plaza," the place-name Rehoboth refers to two locations in the OT.

1. The name of a well built by Isaac, etymologically defined as "The LORD has made an open space for us" (Gen 26:22).

2. Genesis 36:37 and 1 Chron 1:48 identify a Rehoboth as the place from which the Edomite king SHAUL originated.

REHUM 1. One of eleven leaders of those returning from exile in Babylon (Ezra 2:2). Nehemiah 7:7 lists Rehum as NEHUM.

2. A Persian official ("royal deputy") who wrote to Artaxerxes concerning the rebuilding of the walls in Jerusalem (Ezra 4:8-24; 1 Esdr 2:16-30).

3. A Levite, son of Bani, who helped repair the wall under Nehemiah (Neh 3:17).

4. A family leader who signed the covenant of Nehemiah (Neh 10:25 [Heb. 10:26]).

5. A priest or priestly clan associated with Zerubbabel and Jeshua.

REKEM 1. One of the five kings of Midian killed by the Israelites on their journey to Canaan (Num 31:8; Josh 13:21); it is possible, however, that this is a place-name, not a person.

2. Son of Hebron in the line of Caleb (1 Chron 2:43).

3. Son of Peresh, a descendant of Manasseh, and member of one of the Machir clans in Gilead; brother of Ulam (1 Chron 7:16).

4. A town in the territory of Benjamin (Josh 18:27).

RELIGION Respect and awe for the sacred and divine, strict observance of religious ritual, or conscientiousness in morality and ethics.

See HOLY, HOLINESS.

REMALIAH Remaliah was the father of PEKAH (2 Kgs 15:25-37; 16:1-5; 2 Chron 28:6; Isa 7:1-9; 8:6).

REMNANT While *remnant* may be used for anyone or anything left behind following a disaster, it occurs most frequently in the Latter Prophets where it is used to depict a people reduced to a vestige of its former grandeur.

REPENTANCE The OT describes repentance more with reference to action than to feelings (such as contrition). The most common verb for repentance is "to turn, return." One turned away from unrighteousness (Jer 18:11; Ezek 18:21; Zech 1:4) and turned to (2 Chron 15:4) or returned to (Isa 55:7) God, so a radical change in one's way of life was involved. In the NT repentance denotes the complete reorientation of one's whole being to God. It entails acknowledging sin and turning away from all that hinders wholehearted devotion to God's will, along with resolute turning to God with renewed trust and obedience. See CONVERSION; FAITH, FAITHFULNESS; SIN, SINNERS.

REPHAEL A son of SHEMAIAH and one of the Korahite gatekeepers at the temple in Jerusalem (1 Chron 26:7). See KORAH, KORAHITES.

REPHAH In the genealogy of Joseph's sons, Rephah is listed as an Ephraimite (1 Chron 7:25).

REPHAIAH Means "God healed."

1. One of the descendants of David: grandson of Hananiah, son of Jeshaiah, and father of Arnan (1 Chron 3:21).

2. One of the four leaders of 500 Simeonites who destroyed a remnant of Amalekites at Mount Seir and "have lived there ever since" (1 Chron 4:42-43).

3. A mighty warrior of the tribe of Issachar and a son of Tola (1 Chron 7:2).

4. One of the descendants of Saul: son of Binea and father of Eleasah (1 Chron 9:43).

5. Son of Hur and ruler of half the district in Jerusalem who led efforts in repairing the city wall (Neh 3:9).

REPHAIM 1. The term occurs eight times in the Hebrew text with reference to the underworld's inhabitants. The dead are lifeless and flaccid. They tremble before the Lord (Job 26:5) but cannot praise him (Ps 88:10; cf 6:5). They are roused by a newcomer, only to note his new weakness (Isa 14:9-11; cf Ezek 32:21).

2. The Rephaim is an ethnic term designating a people who once occupied portions of the Levant, especially the Transjordan. The translation of Rephaim as "GIANTS" is probably derived from two differing traditions. One was their association with the Anakim (see ANAK, ANAKIM, ANAKITES), a people described as exceedingly tall (Deut 1:28; 9:2). The 2nd was the identification of OG, king of Bashan, as one of the Rephaim (Josh 12:4; 13:12), whose bed was reported to have been 13.5 ft. × 6 ft. (Deut 3:11), and whose land was called "Rephaim Country" (Deut 3:13).

REPHAIM VALLEY Recognized as a fertile farming valley from the Late Bronze Age onward, this agricultural center, known in modern times as Wadi el-Ward, is located southwest of Jerusalem. The valley is named in Joshua as part of a natural geographical boundary between the tribes of Judah and Benjamin (Josh 15:8; 18:16).

REPHAN A god mentioned in Stephen's speech in Acts 7:43. Stephen is quoting from the LXX version of Amos 5:26, which refers to Moloch and Rephan. The Hebrew of Amos 5:26 instead reads SAKKUTH AND KAIWAN.

REPHIDIM A site on the exodus route between the Sin desert and the Sinai desert (Exod 17:1; 19:2). Numbers 33:12-15 establishes the order of places visited as the Sin desert, Dophkah, Alush, Rephidim, and the Sinai desert.

RESAIAH Judean leader who returned to Jerusalem after the exile (1 Esdr 5:8), the same as REELAIAH in Ezra 2:2.

RESERVOIR Storage of water was critical for urban centers like Jerusalem (Sir 50:3). In preparation for the siege of 701 BCE, Hezekiah created a reservoir that was fed by the Siloam tunnel (2 Kgs 20:20; Isa 22:11). Such man-made reservoirs or "pools," some tied to canals, were also used to water groves of trees (Eccl 2:6) and fields (Exod 7:19). See CISTERN; WATER.

RESHEPH 1. A descendant of Ephraim, son of Rephah and father of Telah (1 Chron 7:25).

2. A west Semitic deity known to both harm and heal, also regarded as a god of battle and plague, which he spread by his bow and arrows. In the OT, *Resheph* appears in poetic contexts as a supernatural agent of destruction in the service of the Lord. In this connection, Resheph is mentioned alongside hunger and pestilence ("consuming plague" [Deut 32:24]; "plague" [Hab 3:5]; "disease" [Ps 78:48]), and weapons of war (Ps 76:3 [Heb. 76:4]).

RESTORATION The basic sense of the English word *restoration* implies return to a state that had once existed but had been lost. Three primary theological restorations can be found in the biblical texts: (1) restoring the captive Jews to their land after the exile; (2) restoring the kingdom to Israel; and (3) restoring cosmic conditions to their primal state before the sin of Adam and Eve. The last two are naturally related, but the first two fit better the OT context, while the last is better suited to the NT worldview.

The threat of deportation from the land because of the sins of the people was one that is frequently mentioned in the OT. Key passages are Lev 26 and Deut 28, both of which assign rewards for obedience but concentrate on the punishments that will follow disobedience. In the end, this took place first with regard to the northern kingdom about 722 BCE, which was taken captive by the Assyrians (2 Kgs 17), and then almost a century and a half later the southern kingdom fell to the Babylonians (2 Kgs 24–25). Those who survived this destruction were often referred to as a REMNANT.

The first restoration related to the physical captivity of Israel and Judah. There was no restoration of the northern kingdom—they became the "ten lost tribes" who did not return to the land but continued to live across the Euphrates. As for the southern kingdom, after a period of about half a century (described as "seventy years") the Persian conquest of Babylon opened up the way for some of those in captivity to return to Judah and rebuild the temple, as described in Ezra 1–6; Haggai; and Zech 1–8. This return was much heralded in biblical literature. The pattern of sin–captivity–return is found in many passages (such as Lev 26 and Deut 28 cited above). The people had returned from exile and were restored to their land, as they saw it (cf Ezra 2:1; Neh 7:6).

Yet in spite of this physical restoration, Judah remained a subject nation under a succession of empires: Persian, Greek, and Roman. Only briefly, for less than a century, they were an independent nation under the rule of the HASMONEANS. Thus, a succession of literature looked forward not just to being in the land and able to worship at the temple but toward a restoration, an idealized rule. Some prophetic passages picture a nation in which people lived an idyllic existence under a restored "house of David" (cf Jer 16:14-15; 23:5-8; 30:8-9; Amos 9:8-15). A key NT passage is found in Acts 1:6, which refers to the restoration of the kingdom to Israel. In some Jewish literature, the language of restoration is used in the context of some sort of a messiah (messianic expectations varied considerably among the Jews), such as the Pss. Sol. 17–18.

The ultimate goal was the restoration of the earth to its pristine state, perhaps regarded as the state before the sin of Adam (or the fall of the angels in such writings as 1 Enoch). This seems to entail a number of ideas or images. For example, we have Mal 4:5-6 [Heb. 3:23-24] where Elijah comes before the "day of the LORD" to turn the hearts of the parents to the children and vice versa. The more graphic image, however, is to refer to "a new heaven and a new earth" (Isa 65:17-25; Rev 21:1–22:5). In some cases, this takes place gradually rather than suddenly. For example, in 2 Baruch the messiah "begins to be revealed" at a particular time, implying that he is only gradually revealed (2 Bar. 29–30). It is only when he is fully revealed that the resurrection of the dead and final judgment take place. Similarly, 4 Ezra has a temporary messianic reign of 400 years, after which the messiah dies (4 Ezra 7:26-44). Only then do resurrection and judgment take place. A heavenly Jerusalem seems to be the ultimate goal (4 Ezra 10:25-27).

RESURRECTION The concept of resurrection of the dead did not develop until after 587 BCE. The First Temple period (ca. 950–587 BCE) gives us no proof of a conception of resurrection nor of any other afterlife that can be called beatific, like paradise (i.e., a reward for good behavior on earth). It could be that there was no idea of the afterlife at all, but that would make the Hebrews unique among world cultures and especially out of place in the ANE, where elaborate ideas about postmortem existence and even more elaborate funeral rituals were everywhere part of literature, myth, and social life.

Two personages in the OT—Enoch (Gen 5) and Elijah (2 Kgs 2)—can be said to have achieved a beatific afterlife, in that they are assumed bodily into heaven without dying. Nothing suggests that this was viewed as a common fate of humanity.

The doctrine of resurrection is first securely manifested in biblical writing in Dan 12, which can be dated a bit more than a century and a half before Jesus was born (approximately 168 BCE is a well-established date for the composition of the visions at the end of Daniel). Resurrection may be generally defined as the doctrine that after death the body will be reconstituted and revivified by God as a reward for the righteous and/or faithful. But resurrection is central to Christianity in a way that it is not to any of the other 1st-cent. sects of Judaism.

Paul is the first Christian writer to express what resurrection was, apparently from descriptions of the risen Christ, which came to him in visionary experience ("a revelation from Jesus Christ" [Gal 1:11-12]). From his experience of the risen Christ, Paul writes a short treatise on the resurrection (1 Cor 15:12-58). Paul claims that our flesh will be transformed into another kind of body (1 Cor 15:42-44). He calls the physical, fleshly body, in which we live our earthly lives, a natural body, that is left behind (see FLESH). The resurrected body is an immortal and incorruptible body or spiritual body. Paul calls this process a "transformation" in several related ways (Rom 12:2; 1 Cor 15:51-52; 2 Cor 3:18; Phil 3:21). Paul understands this process to have begun with the resurrection of Christ and to continue until the final consummation of history. Thus, faith in Christ begins a process of transformation that will end in the resurrection of believers, and this explains Paul's terminology of being "in Christ."

In 1 Cor 15:51-57, Paul discloses the aim and purpose of this transformation. We shall not all fall asleep (i.e., die). At the last trumpet, presumably the trumpet of Gabriel or Michael, the archangel of God, the dead will all be raised immortal and changed. The perishable body will put on imperishability, just as the baptized puts on new clothing after the ceremony.

The Gospels' interpretation of resurrection does not in every way correspond to Paul's description. Mark, the earliest Gospel, contains no description of Jesus' resurrection, instead presenting us with an empty tomb, which signifies the mystery of Easter (Mark 16:1-8). The later Gospels expand the story of the empty tomb but do not describe the actual resurrection. The Gospels, on the other hand, stress Jesus' humanity and messiahship. So he is fully human and appears in human form, arguably even in fleshly form, after his resurrection, as he eats, walks, talks, and in these ways is indistinguishable from ordinary humans (Matt 28:9-10, 17-20; Luke 24:13-48; John 20:14-29; 21:1-24).

In Luke, the ASCENSION is a separate process, not included within the resurrection itself but placed temporally at the end of the postresurrection appearances. The story is narrated twice by Luke—once at the end of the Gospel (24:51) and again at the beginning of the Acts of the Apostles (1:9-11), also written by Luke.

Throughout the Gospels, several other aspects of resurrection become clear. The term *resurrection*, for example, appears frequently in Paul but infrequently in the Gospels. There, it is explicitly part of Jesus' polemic with the PHARISEES. Against the SADDUCEES (who are characterized as not believing in resurrection, neither as a spirit nor as an angel [Acts 23:8]), the Pharisees do believe in resurrection. Conflicts with Pharisees and Sadducees are an opportunity for the evangelists to specify what they mean by *resurrection*.

RETRIBUTION Retribution means that God gives to individuals and communities a degree of suffering that somehow corresponds to their sin or offense. The idea of retribution serves as a cornerstone for the central theological claim that God governs the world with justice.

REU An ancestor of Abraham (Gen 11:18-21; 1 Chron 1:25) and Jesus (Luke 3:35).

REUBEN, REUBENITES 1. Reuben was the 1st of Jacob and Leah's sons, the oldest of all Jacob's children (Gen 29:31-32), and the eponymous patriarch of the Reubenites.

2. A tribe whose eponymous ancestor was Reuben the son of Jacob. According to Numbers, the Reubenites and Gadites had chosen lands east of the Jordan for their inheritance, the better to graze their cattle (Num 32:1-48).

REUEL Means "friend of God" or "God is a friend."

1. One of the sons of Esau by his wife Basemath (Gen 36:4), Reuel was father of Nahath, Zerah, Shammah, and Mizzah (Gen 36:17).

2. One of the names given to Moses' father-in-law (Exod 2:18), also called Jethro (Exod 3:1) and Hobab (Judg 1:16). Other passages refer to Reuel as the father of Hobab (Num 10:29). Moses' father-in-law, a Midianite priest, was a worshipper of the Lord (Exod 18:10-12).

3. The father of Eliasaph, one of the Gadites' leaders (Num 2:14).

4. A grandfather of the Benjaminite Meshullam (1 Chron 9:8) who lived in postexilic Jerusalem.

REUMAH A SECONDARY WIFE of NAHOR, Abraham's brother, who bore four children: Tebah, Gaham, Tahash, and Maacah (Gen 22:24).

REVELATION, BOOK OF This book is also called the Apocalypse of John. It is the last book in the NT. As a collection of visions addressed to seven churches in Asia Minor, it depicts the conflict between the allies of God and the forces of evil. The visions move in cycles through series of threats that culminate in scenes of worship in the heavenly throne room. The book climaxes with the defeat of evil, a new heaven and earth, and the descent of the new Jerusalem, where the redeemed worship God and Christ the Lamb. The congregations it addressed faced challenges ranging from persecution to assimilation and complacency. The author identifies himself as JOHN, which seems to be his true name (Rev 1:1, 4, 9; 22:8). He received visions on the island of Patmos, but does not say more about his identity (1:9-11). His familiarity with local issues suggests that he had prior contact with the Christians to whom he writes. John was probably of Jewish background. He knows the OT well, assumes that Christians are true Jews (2:9; 3:9), and writes a peculiar form of Greek, which might mean that his first language was Hebrew or Aramaic. Traditionally, the author was identified as John the son of Zebedee, one of the twelve apostles of Jesus. Revelation was probably written between 80 and 100 CE. A more precise date is difficult to determine.

The beast from the sea personifies a tyrant, who is said to have died and come back to life (13:3, 12, 14). This beast resembles the emperor NERO, who persecuted Christians in Rome, committed suicide in 68 CE, and yet was rumored to be alive and preparing to return to power. Some have argued that Revelation was written in the late 60s in response to Nero's persecution, but since Revelation alludes to stories about Nero's return, the book was probably written after the end of Nero's reign.

REVENGE See AVENGE; VENGEANCE.

REZEPH A Mesopotamian city located between Palmyra and the Euphrates. The city was probably conquered and absorbed into the Assyrian Empire in the 9th cent. BCE (2 Kgs 18:22, 25; Isa 36:7, 10).

REZIN 1. The Aramean leader of the anti-Assyrian coalition consisting of Damascus, Tyre, Philistia, Israel, and perhaps Edom, ca. 738–732 BCE. See ARAM, ARAMEANS.

2. The name of one of the families of temple servants who returned from Babylonian exile (Ezra 2:48; Neh 7:50).

REZON An Aramean king. Rezon son of Eliada served under HADADEZER king of Zobah, but abandoned his master, probably when Hadadezer was defeated by David (2 Sam 8:3-8).

RHEGIUM The city is mentioned in Acts 28:13 as a stopping point on Paul's journey to Rome, located on the tip of the Italian peninsula opposite Sicily.

RHESA In Luke's genealogy (3:27) Rhesa is the son of ZERUBBABEL, postexilic governor of Judah (Ezra 3:2; Hag 1:1), but ABIUD appears instead in Matthew's genealogy (Matt 1:13).

RHODA A young woman in the home of MARY (mother of John Mark) who announces the arrival of Peter following his miraculous escape from prison (Acts 12:13). Rhoda's announcement that Peter was "standing at the gate" is treated with skepticism by those gathered (Acts 12:14-15).

RHODES Rhodes is mentioned in Ezek 27:15; Acts 21:1; and 1 Macc 15:23. In Ezek 27:15, Rhodes is listed as one of many economic powers trading with Tyre in some versions. In Acts 21:1, Rhodes is one of the cities Paul passes through en route to Jerusalem. The island of Rhodes is approximately 45 mi. long and 22 mi. wide. It is located in the southeastern portion of the Aegean Sea between Asia Minor and Crete.

RHODOCUS A soldier in Judas Maccabeus's army, who betrayed him by providing information to Antiochus EUPATOR and who was subsequently imprisoned for this deception (2 Macc 13:21).

RIBAI Ribai, a Benjaminite from GIBEAH, is listed as the father of Ittai (2 Sam 23:29) or Ithai (1 Chron 11:31), one of "the Thirty," David's inner band of warriors.

RIBLAH Two different locations are named Riblah in the OT.

1. Riblah was one of the cities bordering Canaan on the northeast in the Transjordan (e.g., Num 34:11).

2. In 2 Kings (e.g., 2 Kgs 23:33), Riblah is in the land of Hamath, situated at a very strategic crossroad in Syria.

RIGHT HAND In Hebrew, the phrase "right hand" can simply mean to the right (as opposed to left) side literally (Num 20:17) or metaphorically as departing from the commandments to the right or left (Josh 1:7). It also represents the literal right hand (Gen 48:13; 2 Sam 20:9). The right hand was apparently the main hand for giving a blessing (Gen 48:14, 17-18).

The right or strong hand represents the power of God (Exod 15:6; cf Job 40:14; Ps 20:6 [Heb. 20:7]).

Being at someone's right hand or right side is to occupy a place of honor (Ps 45:9 [Heb. 45:10]; 110:1). In the NT, being at the right hand often refers to Ps 110:1 and is used especially of Jesus at God's right hand (Matt 26:64; Acts 2:33; Heb 12:2).

RIMMON Means "pomegranate."

1. A site in lower Galilee on the northern border of the tribal territory of Zebulun. Joshua 19:13 names the site in outlining the boundaries of Zebulun's territorial inheritance.

2. Judah's southernmost district, outlined in Josh 15:21-32, includes "Ain, and Rimmon" (Josh 15:32), but perhaps should be read as "En-Rimmon."

3. The rock of Rimmon was located in the southern reaches of Ephraimite territory, a few kilometers north of the Benjaminite border. It was to this location that 600 Benjaminite warriors fled for refuge (Judg 19–21; see esp. 20:45, 47; 21:13).

4. A Benjaminite, apparently a descendant of the salvaged tribe, from the town of Beeroth south of Gibeon; the father of Rechab and Baanah, the two assassins of Ishbosheth, the son of Saul (2 Sam 4:2, 5, 9).

5. A designation for Hadad the Aramean storm deity.

RINNAH The 2nd of four sons of Shimon and a descendant of Judah (1 Chron 4:20).

RIPHATH Son of GOMER, grandson of JAPHETH, and great-grandson of Noah (Gen 10:3; 1 Chron 1:6).

RIZIA Arah, Hanniel, and Rizia are the three sons of Ulla listed among the descendants of Asher (1 Chron 7:39).

RIZPAH Rizpah was the daughter of Aiah and secondary wife of Saul who produced two sons (2 Sam 21:1-9).

ROD A stick, *rod* is often used to describe an implement used for discipline. Thus, especially in Wisdom Literature, parents discipline their children with a rod (Prov 13:24), and boys and fools are similarly corrected (Prov 22:15; 26:3). Such corporal punishment was deeply imbedded in Israelite culture: it was as natural as bridling a horse or whipping a donkey (Prov 26:3) and was felt to be so beneficial that it could save the lives of those punished from premature death (Prov 23:14). Servants were also beaten with rods (Exod 21:20).

This image could also be used of God, who used a rod to reprove the Davidic kings (2 Sam 7:14), foreign rulers (Ps 2:9), individuals (Job 9:34; "punishing stick" [21:9]), or all Israel (Lam 3:1); such uses may be metaphorical. God could even use foreign nations as a rod (Isa 10:5).

Rods had a variety of other purposes: they were used for grinding seeds (Isa 28:27), for divining (Hos 4:12), and for measuring (Ezek 40:3).

The NT uses of rod are similar to the OT. Revelation 2:27; 12:5; and 19:15 use the image of "an iron rod" from Ps 2:9. Revelation 11:1 and 21:15-16 mention a measuring rod. Acts 16:22 and 2 Cor 11:25 describe rods used to beat people. The depiction of "Aaron's rod that budded" in Heb 9:4 reflects Num 17. In addition, there are several overlapping words used in the Bible to reflect more-specialized types of rods, including the stick, STAFF, and SCEPTER.

RODANIM Rodanim, the ancestor of the nation of RHODES, is identified as the son of Javan the son of Japheth the son of Noah (Gen 10:4; 1 Chron 1:7).

ROHGAH A descendant of Asher, listed among the sons of SHEMER (1 Chron 7:34).

ROMAN EMPIRE By the 1st cent. CE, Rome's empire extended from Britain in the northwest, through (present-day) France and Spain to the west, across Europe to Turkey and Syria in the east, and to the south along North Africa. Rome ruled an estimated 60–65 million people of diverse ethnicities and cultures. The empire was hierarchical with vast disparities of power and wealth. For the small number of ruling elite, both in Rome and the provinces, life was quite comfortable. For the majority of non-elite, it was at best livable and at worst very miserable. There was no middle class, little opportunity to improve one's lot, and few safety nets in adversity. NT instances of *Rome* usually refer to the Roman Empire.

ROMAN PERIOD For the biblical world, the Roman period began when the Romans took control of the region in 63 BCE. During this period, Roman technology was put to use in extensive building projects including highways, amphitheaters, and aqueducts. Trade networks grew as imports arrived via ship from Italy and were transported along the new road system. The Jews revolted against Rome in 66–73 CE, resulting in the destruction of the second temple, and again in 132–35 CE, but were unable to drive the Romans out. The end of the Roman period is often dated to 330 CE, when Constantine moved the capital from Rome to Byzantium/Constantinople. See ROMAN EMPIRE.

ROMANS, LETTER TO THE Romans is the longest and most theologically dense letter written by Paul the apostle. Paul is looking for territory where the gospel has not yet been communicated, and his gaze is drawn to Spain, at the opposite end of the Mediterranean Sea (15:24*a*). But before heading for Spain, he must make two important visits, to Jerusalem (v. 25) and then Rome (v. 24*b*). Paul must go to Jerusalem to deliver the money he has collected from the Gentile churches to relieve the poverty of Christians in Judea. This collection was an important project of Paul's on his third missionary journey (see also 1 Cor 16:1-4; 2 Cor 8–9). But the collection was more than a relief effort. Paul also saw it as a practical means of bringing together two groups in the early church that were beginning to draw apart from each another: (mainly) Jewish Christians in the Diaspora, and Gentile Christians in Judea. This was why Paul was concerned about the way the collection would be received in Jerusalem (15:30-33). Paul does not explicitly say why he plans to stop in Rome after his visit to Jerusalem, but the verb that he uses in 15:24*b* ("to be sent on by you") implies that he hopes to secure logistical and perhaps financial support for his ministry in Spain. Paul's home base of Syrian Antioch was a long way from Spain, and he evidently felt the need to find support closer to his new missionary territory.

From these details it is clear that Paul must be writing the Letter to the Romans sometime on the third missionary journey (Acts 18:23–21:16). Other indications in Romans point more precisely to his three-month stay in CORINTH, recorded in Acts 20:2-3 (that it was Corinth where Paul stayed in "Greece" is evident from 2 Cor 13:1, 10). Phoebe, a prominent Christian woman whom Paul commends to the Romans in 16:1-2, is from Cenchreae, the port city near Corinth. The Gaius with whom Paul seems to be staying (16:23) is probably the same man whom Paul mentions having baptized at Corinth (1 Cor 1:14). And there is some reason to think that the city official Erastus (16:24) is the same Erastus who is mentioned in an inscription from Corinth. Paul, then, wrote Romans from Corinth toward the end of his third missionary journey. Establishing an absolute date depends on the overall chronology of Paul's missionary work. But 57 CE is a reasonable estimate.

ROOF The roof of an ancient house was often flat and made of mud, clay, and/or straw. The roof of a temporary shelter roof might be made of reeds or rushes. Permanent, open, flat rooftops provided cool places of rest.

ROOSTER The rooster appears only twice in the OT (Job 38:36; Prov 30:31). In the NT, references to the rooster and its crowing are concentrated in one episode: Peter's threefold denial of Jesus (Mark 14:30, 68, 72; with par. in Matt 26 and Luke 22).

ROPE Ancient ropes were twisted and braided from long plant fibers or animal hair. Rope was used to guide a plow animal (Job 39:10) or attach a cart ("cord" [Isa 5:18]). It could bind Samson but not withstand his strength (Judg 15:13-14; 16:11-12). Another type of rope was used for rescue, to lower the Hebrew spies from Rahab's window (Josh 2:15) or to maneuver Jeremiah into and out of a pit (Jer 38:6, 11-13). When replacing a belt (Isa 3:24) or wrapping around the head while one was dressed in sackcloth ("cords" [1 Kgs 20:31-32]), a rope was a sign of poverty or humility. The same word describes ropes laid as a snare (Job 18:10); employed to pull down city walls (2 Sam 17:13); used as a measuring tool (2 Sam 8:2); or tied to tent stakes (Isa 33:20).

In the NT, Jesus "made a whip from ropes" (John 2:15) when he cleansed the temple, and Acts mentions ropes used on ships (27:32, 40).

ROSH One of the ten sons of Benjamin who migrated with him to Egypt (Gen 46:21).

ROSH HASHANAH The term literally means "head of the year" and refers to the Jewish New Year festival, celebrated on the 1st day of the 7th month. Leviticus 23:24 prescribes the blowing of the shofar (ram's horn) on Rosh Hashanah, a custom preserved by modern Judaism.

RUFUS Meaning "red."

1. According to Mark, Simon of Cyrene was the father of Rufus and Alexander (Mark 15:21).

2. An associate of Paul's, to whom he

sends greeting (Rom 16:13). Paul considers Rufus "an outstanding believer, along with his mother and mine."

RUMAH The home of Josiah's wife ZEBIDAH (2 Kgs 23:36).

RUTH The Moabite daughter-in-law of ELIMELECH and NAOMI, natives of Judah who search for sustenance in Moab (see MOAB, MOABITES), and the main character of the book of Ruth.

Ss

SABACHTHANI See ELI, ELI, LAMA SABACHTHANI.

SABAOTH In the OT, *Sabaoth* is a common epithet for *God*, occurring in the phrase "the LORD [God] of heavenly forces." It is commonly understood as depicting the Lord as leader of Israel's armies (1 Sam 17:45). See GOD, NAMES OF; HOSTS, HOST OF HEAVEN.

SABBATH While the Sabbath eventually became a weekly holiday, characterized as a day of rest, this may not have been its original function. As the Mesopotamian parallel, the Shapattu festival, suggests, the Sabbath day originally marked the celebration of the full moon, and in many OT texts the word is used to mean the day of the full moon. While certain activities were prohibited on this particular day (in order to avoid provoking the gods' anger), it was not a day of general rest. Israel's Sabbath tradition may not have begun until the period of the exile, and it may have developed its full character over time. Parts of the PENTATEUCH (esp. Gen 2:2-3; Exod 16:22-30; 23:12-17), the Sabbath commandment in both versions of the Ten Commandments (Exod 20:8-11; Deut 5:12-15), and the book of Nehemiah (9:14; 10:31 [Heb. 10:32]; 13:13-22) are the most explicit witnesses to a new understanding of the Sabbath. The prophetic traditions, on the other hand, show a more ambiguous picture. Isaiah 40–55, as one of the most powerful voices of the exilic and postexilic periods, never mentions the Sabbath; in the book of Jeremiah only one brief passage thematizes it (Jer 17:19-27); and even in Ezekiel, despite numerous references (Ezek 20:12-24; 22:8, 26; 46:1, 4, 12), it is not entirely clear to what extent the Sabbath denotes a weekly holiday or whether it is still considered the full moon festival.

According to Isa 56:2, 6, keeping the Sabbath is defined as doing good deeds, serving the Lord, and loving God's name, which Trito-Isaiah does not consider as exclusively Jewish virtues but as something that every human being is, or ought to be, capable of doing. As a matter of fact, Trito-Isaiah is the only voice in the OT and beyond that defines the Sabbath as a day when all the true believers in the Lord can worship together, which cuts across national, cultural, and religious divisions.

The NT reveals that on the Sabbath, the congregation assembled in the synagogue to read from the Scriptures, a practice in which Jesus seems to have participated and that also Paul and his associates continued as part of their missionary efforts among Jews (Acts 13:14; 18:4). As a matter of fact, it seems safe to say that prior to the destruction of the temple in 70 CE, the Sabbath revolved around both the sacrificial worship at the temple and the study of Scripture in the synagogue. The most characteristic feature of the NT accounts of the Sabbath is Jesus' controversies with the Pharisees about the Sabbath, which one might label prerabbinic disputes, especially with regard to Jesus' healing on the Sabbath. Given the number of healings that Jesus performed on the Sabbath, it seems safe to say that he considered the Sabbath as the appropriate day for these healings, while his opponents categorized them as labor and thus judged that the healings had their proper place on one of the six workdays (Luke 13:14). Especially in Matthew and Luke (e.g., Luke 13:18), the healings are linked to the impending nearness of God's kingdom, which was also foreshadowed in the holiness of the Sabbath day.

While Jewish Christians kept observing the Sabbath as long as they also remained within the synagogal community, it seems that Sunday rather quickly became the day on which the Christians came together to celebrate Christ's resurrection. The significance of what was called the LORD'S DAY is attested already in texts from the 1st cent. CE.

SABBATH DAY'S JOURNEY The distance a Jew could travel on the SABBATH according to scribal interpretation (Acts 1:12). Estimates vary, but it is less than a mile.

SABBATICAL YEAR Observance of the sabbatical year is a practice to regulate slavery and agricultural land management practices for the benefit of the poor and the encouragement of piety. While Deut 15 understands the 7th year primarily as a time of manumitting slaves, Lev 25 develops ancient practices of fallowing land in rotation (see Exod 23:10-11) by connecting them to the Jubilee (see JUBILEE YEAR), a utopian scheme for ensuring just distribution of wealth in Israel.

Whether the sabbatical year was ever implemented in the Iron Age is unknown, though statewide manumission of slaves, the central feature of the year in Deuteronomy, was a common practice in antiquity, known also in ancient Israel (see Jer 34:8-16). It is difficult to see how the land-fallowing practices envisioned by Leviticus could have been achievable, especially if the Jubilee Year succeeded a sabbatical year.

SABTAH Ham's descendant and a son of Cush, Sabtah is an unidentified eponym in the Table of Nations (Gen 10:7; "Sabta" [1 Chron 1:9]).

SABTECA The fifth son of Cush (Gen 10:7; 1 Chron 1:9).

SACHAR 1. The father of Ahiam, one of David's faithful warriors (1 Chron 11:35). Sachar's designation as being "from HARAR" may suggest his provenance from the Judean hills.

2. The 4th son of Obed-edom. Obed-edom and his sons guard the temple's south gate and its environs (1 Chron 26:4, 15).

SACHIA One of the Benjaminite Shaharaim's seven sons, born to his wife Hodesh, according to the genealogy in 1 Chron 8:8-10.

SACRIFICES AND OFFERINGS The Priestly traditions provide the most detailed instructions concerning the sacrificial offerings, esp. Exod 25–40; Leviticus; and Num 5; 15. The primary sacrifices are the entirely burned offering, the grain offering, the well-being offering, the purification offering, the ordination offering, and the compensation offering. The offerer must bring sacrifices and offerings to the legitimate altar; a priest must put the blood on the altar (grain offerings are exceptions) and burn the specified parts.

Jesus participated in or referred to temple sacrifices (Matt 8:1-4; 17:24-27; Mark 1:40-45; 11:1–14:25; Luke 5:12-16), but argued that true purity was also related to inner beliefs (Mark 7:1-23; cf

Matt 15:1-20). Jesus' visit to Jerusalem near the end of his life disrupted the normal temple activities (Mark 11:15-19; 13:1-8).

The Gospels interpret the Last Supper in covenantal and sacrificial terms. This very likely expresses the efforts of the early church to make sense of Jesus' death. His death did not bring the end; it was a sacrificial death on behalf of the world.

Paul's statements concerning sacrifice are for the most part limited to theological or christological interpretations of the death of Christ (e.g., Gal 2:15-21; Rom 3:21-26; 5:18-21; 6:1-11). In Romans Paul states that "God displayed Jesus as the place of sacrifice where mercy is found by means of his blood" (3:25).

The writer of Hebrews approaches the matter in very different terms. The writer argues that God established a new covenant through the blood and death of Christ. Following his death, Jesus entered into the heavenly sanctuary, contrasted repeatedly with the earthly tent of the wilderness, and sat at the right side of God (1:3; 6:19-20; 9:1-28). God set up the heavenly sanctuary, of which the earthly one is but a sketch and a shadow (8:2-5). Jesus is high priest (4:14–5:10; 7:1-28) and makes a sacrifice of reconciliation for the sins of the people (2:17; 9:26). His sacrifice, unlike the repeated ones of the Israelite priests, was offered once (7:26-28).

SADDUCEES A religious and social party that played a dominant role in the history of the high priesthood, the temple, and Jewish Law from the Hasmonean period to 70 CE. The Sadducees are mentioned several times in the NT as among Jesus' adversaries, together with the Pharisees (e.g., Matt 3:7; 16:1, 6, 11). The Sadducees did not believe in the resurrection of the body or in the persistence of the soul after death (Matt 22:23-28; Mark 12:18-27). Sadducean high priests led the harassment of Jesus and other early Christian leaders. Joseph Caiaphas (who was the governing high priest in ca. 18–36 CE) arrested Jesus. One of the accusations with which Jesus was charged was his threat to destroy the temple (Matt 26:3, 57; Mark 14:53-65). The Sadducees, including Caiaphas and Ananus the Elder (CEB, "Annas") reportedly arrested and flogged Peter and the apostles when they preached and healed in the name of Jesus at the temple mount (Acts 4:1-22; 5:12-40). According to Acts, after Paul was arrested at the temple mount for allowing a Gentile to enter the temple's sacred precinct, he was brought before the Sanhedrin consisting of Sadducees and Pharisees (who debated the theological problem of resurrection instead of accusing Paul; Acts 22:30–23:10).

SAFFRON (*Crocus sativus*) is mentioned only in a list of fragrant ornamental shrubs and spices in a pleasure garden (Song 4:14).

SAINT A common NT designation, better translated "holy one(s)," for the members of the early Christian communities, understood as God's distinctive people in continuity with the people of Israel. Unlike later usage, *saints* in the Bible does not designate a special class of God's people.

Saints can mean "holy people" (2 Thess 1:10), disciples of Jesus (1 Cor 1:2), or "brothers and sisters" (Phil 4:21; Col 1:2). *Saints* also served as a generic term to distinguish Christians as a whole from subgroups such as "widows" (Acts 9:41; 1 Tim 5:9), "leaders" (Heb 13:24), or "apostles" (Rev 18:20). In the NT, in other words, all believers are saints.

See HOLY, HOLINESS.

SAKKUTH AND KAIWAN Sakkuth and Kaiwan are non-Israelite deities mentioned only in Amos 5:26.

SALAMIEL An ancestor of Judith (Jdt 8:1).

SALAMIS The largest city on Cyprus, located on the east end of the island. It is sometimes confused with the Greek island near Athens, where the Greeks defeated the Persians in the battle of Salamis in 480 BCE. Salamis was the first stop for Paul and Barnabas when they left Antioch (Acts 13:5). From Salamis, they traveled to the capital of Cyprus, Paphos, on the west end of the island. Salamis had a significant population of Jews.

SALECAH A city previously under the control of OG, king of BASHAN.

SALEM 1. The city of King MELCHIZEDEK (Gen 14:18), long associated with JERUSALEM. In the NT, Salem is understood as a symbolic name for Jerusalem.

2. A city situated west of the Jordan River, south of the Sea of Galilee. The city is mentioned in John 3:23 in association with AENON, where John the Baptist was baptizing in the Judean countryside (John 3:22).

SALLAI Meaning "basketmaker."

1. Eponym of a Benjaminite family who settled in Jerusalem after the return from Babylon (Neh 11:7-9).

2. A priest among the levitical families "in the days of Joiakim" the high priest (Neh 12:12, 20).

SALLU 1. Sallu and his kinsmen are the first Benjaminites to inhabit postexilic Jerusalem (1 Chron 9:7).

2. One of the leaders of the priests who returned from exile with Zerubbabel and Jeshua (Neh 12:7).

SALMON Salmon is mentioned in the genealogies of David and Jesus. According to Ruth 4:20-21, Salmon was the son of Nahshon and the father of BOAZ, the husband of RUTH. This information about Salmon is repeated in Matt 1:4-5 in the genealogy of Jesus.

SALOME Mark lists Salome as the 3rd of the three women who witnessed the crucifixion (15:40) and who came to the empty tomb (16:1). Matthew identifies "the mother of Zebedee's sons" as the 3rd witness (27:56), leading some commentators to conclude that Salome was this woman's name.

SALT Salt, as a preservative and purifying agent, has both literal and metaphorical functions in the Bible. Salt was often a part of ritual observances. In Exod 30:34-35 it is an ingredient in incense to be used in the temple (cf Ezra 6:9; 7:21-22; 1 Esdr 6:30). Salt must be added to all offerings brought to the sanctuary (Ezek 43:24; Lev 2:13). The understanding of salt as a preservative or cleanser may lie behind the story of Elisha in a town with bad water (2 Kgs 2:19-22), where he used salt to make the water wholesome. Salt is used to preserve fish in Tob 6:6 and "basic to all the necessities of human life" listed in Sir 39:26. Although salt is often a preservative, it can also destroy or render a place uninhabitable or unusable (cf Ezek 47:11; Jer 17:6). The OT refers to conquerors sowing the land with salt to destroy its fertility (Judg 9:45). God sometimes also treats the land of those who do not worship him with salt (Deut 29:22-28; Ps 107:33-34; Jer 48:9; Zeph 2:9; Sir 39:23).

These senses of salt are carried over into its metaphorical uses. Ezekiel 16:4 says infant Israel was not rubbed with salt to emphasize that only God's help allowed Israel to become a people. Numbers 18:19 refers to a "covenant of salt." In Numbers the covenant is between God and Aaron's descendants. In 2 Chronicles God gave David and his descendants the kingship of Israel forever with a covenant of salt. These instances may reflect salt's use as a preservative; it perhaps was understood as making the covenant more permanent and secure (see Lev 2:13). The Synoptic Gospels remember Jesus as referring to his disciples as "the salt of the earth" (Matt 5:13), but warning against the loss of their "saltiness" (cf Mark 9:49-50, where having "salt" in themselves allows them to be at peace with each other; Luke 14:34-35).

SALT SEA See DEAD SEA.

SALU A Simeonite whose son ZIMRI was killed by PHINEHAS (Num 25:14).

SALVATION The most fundamental meaning of salvation in Scripture is God's deliverance of those in a situation of need from that which impedes their well-being, resulting in their restoration to wholeness (see SHALOM). Beneath the OT's use of explicit salvation language lies a coherent worldview in which the exodus from Egyptian bondage, followed by entry into the land of promise, forms the most important paradigm or model. In the NT salvation is God's project of rescue and restoration effected through Jesus Christ as the climax of Israel's story and the culmination of creation itself. Salvation is God's gift of life. Salvation is a comprehensive reality affecting every aspect of existence, and it is both present and future (eschatological, having to do with end times or final things).

SAMARIA The ancient city of Samaria, whose summit rose to a height of 430 m above sea level, lay near the center of the northern kingdom of Israel at approximately 56 km north of Jerusalem. In the 9th cent. BCE, it became a capital city for the northern kingdom of Israel, until its defeat in 722 BCE. In the 5th cent. BCE, Samaria was an administrative capital for the Persian Empire. By the late 4th cent. BCE, a Samaritan temple existed on Mount Gerizim, and a deep schism existed between the Samaritans and the Jews (see GERIZIM, MOUNT). During the NT, the city of Samaria was resurgent.

SAMARITAN, THE GOOD Jesus gives the parable of the good Samaritan (Luke 10:30-36). The parable would have astonished Jesus' audience because of strong tensions between Jews and Samaritans. Jesus' answer illustrates that everyone is a neighbor and that we should act neighborly to all who need us. While this parable addresses the command to love one's neighbor (Luke 10:27*b*), the story that follows, Mary and Martha's interaction with Jesus (Luke 10:38-42), teaches how to fulfill the command to love God (Luke 10:27*a*).

SAMARITAN WOMAN A woman of Samaria who meets Jesus at a well near the city of Sychar, has an extended personal and theological discussion with him, and bears witness to his identity as prophet and Messiah before her townspeople (John 4:1-42).

SAMARITANS Sometimes used to designate all inhabitants of the northern kingdom of Israel or later province of SAMARIA first used in 2 Kgs 17:29; usually "Samarians" or "people of Samaria" in English. More commonly, Samaritans refers to a Hebrew sect focused on their Holy Place, Mount Gerizim, and the INSTRUCTION, the first five books of the Hebrew Scripture, the source of their doctrines (see GERIZIM, MOUNT). They understand their name to refer to themselves as "keepers" of the Law, rather than as a geographical designation. Historically they lived primarily in the tribal regions of Ephraim and Manasseh in northern Palestine (Samaria). In the NT period, the Samaritans were frequent opponents of the forms of Judaism practiced in Jerusalem. Today they are mainly located on Mount Gerizim and in Holon, a suburb of Tel Aviv.

SAMGAR-NEBO One of the four named Babylonian officials who took charge of Jerusalem when the city was captured in 587/586 BCE (Jer 39:3).

SAMLAH An early ruler of Edom from MASREKAH (Gen 36:36-37; 1 Chron 1:47-48).

SAMOS Samos is an island in the southeast Aegean Sea. It appears in the list of cities (1 Macc 15:23) that received a letter from Lucius the Roman consul.

SAMOTHRACE An island located in the north Aegean Sea, approximately 32 km south of Thrace, on a sea route used by Paul (Acts 16:11).

SAMSON The story of Samson, the last of the major judges in the book of Judges, occurs in chaps. 13–16.

SAMUEL Means "his name is El." Known primarily as a prophet, Samuel is presented in 1 Samuel as a transitional figure embodying the roles of prophet, priest, and judge. Outside 1 Samuel, he is mentioned in the OT seven times in Chronicles (1 Chron 6:28 [Heb. 6:13], 33; 9:22; 11:3; 26:28; 29:29; 2 Chron 35:18), where he is remembered as the seer from David's reign (drawing on 1 Sam 9:9), and once each in Ps 99:6 and Jer 15:1, both of which invoke Samuel's role as intercessor from 1 Sam 7. In the Apocrypha, Sir 46:13-20 remembers his various roles as prophet, kingmaker, seer, intercessor, and military leader. First Esdras 1:20 and 2 Esdr 7:108[38] mention him as a prophet and an intercessor respectively. Three NT texts refer to Samuel in his role as a prophet (Acts 3:24; 13:20; Heb 11:32).

In the NT, Peter and John name Samuel as one of the prophets who had predicted "these days"—that is, the suffering and glorification of God's Messiah (Acts 3:24). The apostle Paul's summation of Israel's history in the synagogue in Antioch of Pisidia notes that God gave Israel judges "until the time of the prophet Samuel" (Acts 13:20).

SAMUEL, FIRST AND SECOND BOOKS OF The books of Samuel, as this grand historical narrative has traditionally been named, constitute the core of a longer work (Joshua to 2 Kings, with the exception of Ruth). Although David is the central character in Samuel, the traditional name of the book recognizes the crucial importance of the religious leader who is, after all, the transitional figure who brings the monarchy to birth.

SANBALLAT Three governors of SAMARIA during the Persian period bear the name Sanballat.

1. Sanballat I was governor of Samaria (ca. 445–408 BCE) and one of the bitter opponents of NEHEMIAH. He, together with Tobiah the Ammonite and Geshem the Arabian, opposed Nehemiah's rebuilding of the walls of Jerusalem (445 BCE) and his other activities in Judah (Neh 2:10, 19; 4:1, 7; 6:1-2, 5, 12, 14; 13:28).

2. Sanballat II presumably was the son of Delaiah and grandson of Sanballat I, who governed in Samaria before 354 BCE.

3. Sanballat III, grandson of Sanballat II and probably the son of Hananiah, was the governor of Samaria at the time of the last Persian Achaemenid king, Darius III (Codomannus; 336–332 BCE), and Alexander the Great.

SANCTIFY, SANCTIFICATION English translations use a variety of words to render this word group (e.g., *sanctify, consecrate, dedicate, set apart, hallow, purify, make sacred/holy, be/become holy, show/display/manifest/maintain holiness, sanctification, consecration, holiness, sanctuary*). In general terms, sanctification is the act or process by which persons or objects are cleansed and/or set apart for God's purposes. In its full canonical significance, to be sanctified is to be graciously taken up into, and set apart for active participation in the saving, reconciling purposes of God.

SANCTUARY Places inhabited by or significant to deities. Sanctuaries took many forms, from locations marked by natural features in the landscape, to a portable tent (see MEETING TENT), to the temple in Jerusalem (see TEMPLE, JERUSALEM) and the temples of the Greco-Roman world, and with a diversity of shrines (see SHRINE). Most sanctuaries shared at least two basic features: the distinctive aura of holiness, which often required preparatory purification, and a hierarchy of degrees of holiness within sections of the sacred precinct.

SANDALS AND SHOES Basic footwear consisted of a sturdy leather sole tied to the foot and/or ankle (Mark 1:7). More serviceable sandals with leggings were used during construction work or heavy labor, although slaves generally were forced to go barefoot. The well-dressed individual was one who had quality sandals (Song 7:1 [Heb. 7:2]; Ezek 16:10). However, since sandals protected the feet and trod through the debris associated with the secular world, they were to be removed when one wished to enter sacred space (Exod 3:5; Josh 5:15; Acts 7:33).

SANHEDRIN In the NT often a designation for the supreme Jewish council in Jerusalem in the Second Temple period. The term can also be used to describe the local council governing the affairs of cities and towns.

SANSANNAH A town listed in the territory of Judah near the border with Edom (Josh 15:31).

SAPH Saph fought for the Philistines against David and was killed at Gob (2 Sam 21:18).

SAPPHIRA In Acts 5:1-11, Sapphira and her husband ANANIAS sell a piece of property but turn over to the apostles only a portion of the proceeds, for which they are miraculously killed. Their behavior contrasts to that of BARNABAS, who turned over the full proceeds from the sale of his property to the apostles (Acts 4:36-37).

SAPPHIRE Listed as the 5th stone in the high priest's breastpiece (Exod 28:18; 39:11); used in association with theophanies (Exod 24:10; Ezek 1:26; 10:1); as adornment for the king of Tyre (Ezek 28:13); in comparison to wisdom (Job 28:6, 16); as a metaphor for beauty (Lam 4:7; Song 5:14); in the foundation walls of the New Jerusalem (Isa 54:11; Rev 21:19); and in the gates of Jerusalem (Tob 13:16).

SARAH 1. Sarah (Gen 11:29–13:1; 16:1–18:15; 20:2–21:12; 23:1-2, 19; 24:36; 25:10, 12; 49:31; Isa 51:2; Rom 4:19; Gal 4:21-31; Heb 11:11; 1 Pet 3:6) is the first matriarch in the Hebrew line. Her original name Sarai is an earlier form of Sarah, both meaning "princess." She is renamed at the time that the birth of her son Isaac is announced (Gen 17:15). Her husband is Abram (renamed Abraham in Gen 17:5), one of the three sons of Terah. When Abram passes Sarai off as his sister to King Abimelech of Gerar, Abram claims that she is his half sister, the daughter of his father, but not of his mother.

Sarah is the first of the line of Hebrew matriarchs who has difficulty bearing a child (see BARREN, BARRENNESS). She decides to do something about the problem and gives Hagar, variously described as her female servant and her slave, to Abraham to bear a child for her, a custom known from Mesopotamian sources. The plan does not turn out as Sarah apparently intends. Once Hagar is pregnant she becomes contemptuous of Sarah. Sarah blames Abraham, who gives her free rein to deal with Hagar. She later gives birth to Isaac (Gen 17–21).

Sarah dies in Hebron, and Abraham buries her in Canaan in the cave of Machpelah. In Isa 51:2 she is described as the mother of the Hebrew people.

In the NT Sarah is mentioned along with Abraham as an exemplar of faith. In Rom 4:19 Abraham's faith in spite of his age and Sarah's barrenness are highlighted. In Rom 9:9 the focus is on the children of promise rather than of flesh (also see Gen 18:10). In the allegory in Gal 4:21-31, Sarah (referred to simply as the "free" woman) represents the new covenant; she is the one whose children will be considered the true inheritors, whereas, ironically, Hagar represents the old covenant. (See also Heb 11.)

In 1 Pet 3:6 Sarah is presented quite differently. Here she is a model for wives' obedience to husbands. See ABRAHAM; HAGAR; ISAAC; ISHMAEL, ISHMAELITES.

2. Sarah the daughter of Raguel is exorcised of the demon Asmodeus and marries Tobias the son of Tobit through the intervention of the angel Raphael (see, e.g., Tob 3:17).

SARAPH Means "burning, fiery." A descendant of Judah's son Shelah (1 Chron 4:22).

SARASADAI Ancestor of Judith (Jdt 8:1) listed as "son of Israel." A variant of ZURISHADDAI.

SARDIS Sardis, located in the Roman province of Asia (present-day Turkey), was about 60 mi. from Smyrna and Ephesus. It was the capital of the Lydian Empire (late 7th cent. to mid-6th cent. BCE) and the home of the legendary King Croesus. Croesus ruled from ca. 560 to ca. 550 BCE. Throughout ancient history, it remained an important city for succeeding empires, serving as a key city for the Persian, Seleucid, and Roman administrators. Revelation 1:11 and 3:1-6 mention the city, and Obad 20 refers to Sardis as "Sepharad."

SAREA One of five scribes, trained to write quickly, who recorded the Scriptures to be restored as God conveyed them to Ezra (2 Esdr 14:24).

SARGON Sargon II was king of Assyria (722–705 BCE). While Sargon is explicitly mentioned only once in the OT (Isa 20:1), his impact is reflected in numerous passages throughout the first part of the book of Isaiah, as well as in 2 Kgs 17:1-6, 24, 29-31 and 18:9-12.

SARID A town on the southern border of Zebulon (Josh 19:10, 12). Sarid was the closest town to Megiddo in northern Israel and thus was near the site of the battle between the Israelites and the Canaanites described in Judg 4–5.

SAROTHIE One of Solomon's servants. First Esdras 5:34 mentions his descendants among those returning from the Babylonian exile with Zerubbabel.

SARSECHIM Personal name, partial name, or title of one of the royal Babylonian officials who took control of Jerusalem from ZEDEKIAH (Jer 39:3, 13). Sarsechim's title is "chief officer" (Jer 39:3).

SATAN In the OT *satan* is a Hebrew noun meaning "adversary" or "accuser." When used to refer to one of the divine beings in the heavenly council of the Lord, it is transliterated and capitalized (Satan) in most English translations as if it were a proper name. In the NT Satan becomes more particularized as an opponent of God's intentions for humankind.

In the OT, "Satan," an adversary who opposes or obstructs another, can be either a human or divine being. The book of Numbers contains the story of Balaam, who encountered an angel of the Lord as an adversary ("satan"). The story about the upright and blameless Job in the first two chapters of the book presents a heavenly being as "the satan." Although "the satan" is rendered in most English translations as "Satan," it should not be understood as a proper name. Proper names in Hebrew are not preceded by a definite article. Rather "the satan" refers to the role enacted by one of the heavenly beings (literally "sons of God"). When the sons of God, including the satan, present themselves before the Lord (1:6), the satan's task becomes clearer in his conversation with the Lord. The Lord asks: "Have you thought about my servant Job; surely there is no one like him on the earth, a man who is honest, who is of absolute integrity, who reveres God and avoids evil?" (1:8). The satan gathers information about Job not in opposition to the Lord, but as a functioning member of the heavenly entourage. When the satan proposes to test Job by taking away his riches, the Lord agrees, giving the satan power over everything Job possesses. However, the satan is not to harm Job himself. Chapter 2 of the book concerns a 2nd encounter when the sons of God come to present themselves before the Lord, who again asks the satan, "Have you thought about my servant Job?" (2:3). The satan responds that Job has passed the test and his integrity remains. However, the satan proposes to the Lord that Job's integrity will not be sustained if he endures bodily inflictions. Again, the Lord puts Job in the satan's hands, indicating that the satan can do with Job as he pleases but that the satan is not to take Job's life. His integrity and loyalty to the Lord remain unaffected by the trials set by the satan, and the Lord "doubled all Job's earlier possessions" (42:10).

It is important to note here that the satan carries out the trials and tribulations he inflicts on Job only on the Lord's approval. However, unlike the satan who appears to Balaam, apparently only as the result of the Lord's initiative to protect Balaam, the Lord casts some blame on the satan for Job's afflictions. He says to the satan, "You incited me to ruin him for no reason" (2:3).

The satan (Satan in most English translations) also appears in a scene depicted in Zech 3. The incident needs to be understood against the backdrop of the divisions in the community when the exiles are returning to Jerusalem. The setting resembles that of a trial in which Joshua the high priest is standing beside "the messenger from the LORD" with the satan "standing by his right side to accuse him" (3:1). Here the role of the satan appears to be like that of the satan in Job who gathers intelligence about the behavior of people to be used in a kind of legal adversarial role. However, the Lord himself, who appears abruptly in the scene, cuts short the proceedings, rebuking the satan for his accusations (3:2). The angel orders the filthy clothes of Joshua to be removed and for Joshua to be dressed in rich apparel with a clean turban on his head. The story seems to suggest cleansing of any filthy conduct in which Joshua may have been involved so that he can be granted the normal privileges of a high priest. The satan appears to be rebuked because he is continuing to accuse Joshua when his guilt has been pardoned.

A final OT reference is made to a satan in 1 Chron 21:1 where it is mentioned that he "incited David to count Israel." This action angers the Lord, who punishes David. Significantly, the Lord still holds David, not Satan, responsible for his actions. In 2 Sam 24:1, a passage that recounts the same episode, it is God's anger that incites David to carry out the census. David's culpability and the alternative passage in which God's anger provokes the action suggest that in the Chronicles passage satan may be operating not as a rival to God's power, but as a member of the heavenly entourage.

Satan as a personal enemy opposed to God's reign over creation does appear in later tradition, but the lines of development are obscure. Both Jub. 7 and 1 En 6–7 relate the story of angels called the Watchers. They fail in their responsibility of supervising the earth and fall from heaven when they have sexual relations with the daughters of men whom they find to be desirable (see Gen 6:1-4).

Satan becomes more identifiable as a personified figure in the NT, but once again only fleeting glimpses are given of his identity. Satan occurs thirty-nine times in the NT. However, other names are used often interchangeably, such as the devil or "Beelzebul" (Matt 10:25; 12:24, 27; Mark 3:22; Luke 11:15, 18, 19). He is also designated as "the tempter" (Matt 4:3; 1 Thess 3:5), "the evil one" (Matt 13:19; 1 John 5:18), "the accuser" (Rev 12:10), "the ruler of demons" (Matt 9:34; 12:24; Mark 3:22; Luke 11:15), "this world's ruler" (John 12:31; 16:11), and "a destructive spiritual power" (Eph 2:2).

Mark 1:12-13 is a short account of how the Spirit drove Jesus into the desert for forty days where he was tempted by Satan. In a longer account in Matthew (4:1-11), the devil, "the tempter," tries to entice Jesus to show himself as God's Son. A similar account occurs in Luke 4:1-13. Here Satan, who is performing the role of testing faith, appears to have some connection to "the satan" who tests Job. The texts are not explicit, however, about whether God condones Satan's role or whether Satan is acting independently. That the text states that the "Spirit" leads Jesus into the desert leaves open the possibility that God was complicit in this testing. Satan is also understood in the parable in Mark 4:15 as taking away the word as soon as it is sown in individuals.

In the middle of Matthew and Mark, when Jesus tells his disciples that he is the Messiah and that he must go to Jerusalem to endure suffering, Peter attempts to persuade Jesus not to go. His response to Peter is "Get behind me, Satan. You are a stone that could make me stumble, for you are not thinking God's thoughts but human thoughts" (Matt 16:23; see also Mark 8:33). Here Peter's actions attempting to lead Jesus astray are likened to those of Satan, who tempted him in the wilderness.

Satan also enters into individuals such as Judas Iscariot, who schemes to have Jesus turned over to the authorities (Luke 22:3 and John 13:27); and into Ananias, who lies to the Holy Spirit about the sale of a piece of property (Acts 5:3). The passage in Luke 22:31, in which Jesus says to Simon Peter, "Satan has asserted the right to sift you all like wheat," suggests that Satan may be acting here with the tacit approval of God.

While it is possible to draw lines of connection between these references in the Gospels to the heavenly being in the OT who acts as God's adversary (satan), other passages suggest relationships with the fallen angels noted in the Second Temple literature. In these stories the demons enter the world when the angels engage in sexual activity with "human daughters" (Gen 6:4).

Satan is also associated with the demons who are presented in the Gospels as causing physical and psychological disabilities. Jesus frees the crippled woman whom Satan had bound for eighteen years (Luke 13:16). When Jesus heals the blind and dumb demoniac, he is accused by the Pharisees of casting out demons only by the power of Beelzebub, the prince of demons (Matt 12:24; Mark 3:22; and Luke 11:15). Jesus responds that he is not Satan, responsible for demonic possession. This is nonsense since if he were Satan he would be casting out Satan, whose kingdom would fail (Matt 12:26; Mark 3:23; Luke 11:18).

Luke 10 speaks about the seventy who return to Jesus after he sent them out to prepare the way for him. They had been curing the sick, announcing that "God's kingdom has come near." When they return they say, "Lord, even the demons submit themselves to us in your name" (10:17). Jesus responds by saying that he observed Satan falling "from heaven like lightning" (10:18). This echoes notions of the Watchers who fall from heaven in Jubilees and 1 Enoch. Paul's reference to Satan in Acts 26:18 when he speaks of opening the eyes of the Gentiles so that they may "turn from darkness to light and from the power of Satan to God" suggests what could be interpreted as a dualistic concept. Here Satan is reminiscent of Belial, who leads the army of darkness, and this reference resonates with 2 Cor 6:15 where the contrast between the believer and unbeliever is paralleled by the distinction between Christ and Belial.

In Paul's letters Satan appears as an adversary. Paul says in 1 Thess 2:18 that he and his associates wanted to return to Thessalonica on many occasions "and Satan stopped us." Paul exhorts the Corinthians not to be "taken advantage of by Satan, because we are well aware of his schemes" (2 Cor 2:11). Sexual immorality is understood to be surrendering to the temptations of Satan (1 Cor 7:5), and Paul instructs that a man who is living with his father's wife should be handed "over to Satan to destroy his human weakness so that his spirit might be saved on the day of the Lord" (1 Cor 5:5; see 1 Tim 1:20; 5:15). Paul also says, "I was given a thorn in my body. . . . It's a messenger from Satan sent to torment me so that I wouldn't be conceited" (2 Cor 12:7). Whether this is a physical illness or an opponent is not clear.

In the beginning chapters of Revelation, "Satan" is used when John writes to the angels in the seven churches. Here the phrase "Satan's synagogue" is used twice (2:9 and 3:9) for those who are slandering the members of the churches. The slanderers are falsely laying claim to being Jews. These references to the synagogue of Satan appear to be associated with Satan (2:10) as one who is testing the people in the role of an adversary. "Satan's throne" and the place "where Satan lives" (2:13) apparently refer to the specific location of a particular individual who is testing the faith of the church members. The "deep secrets" of Satan (2:24) appear to be heretical teachings that test the faith.

Although the idea of Satan as an adversary who tests faith is possible, images in the book of Revelation also emphasize the dualistic struggle between the good God and Satan as the embodiment of evil. The devil who is also called Satan is identified with the dragon that was thrown down along with the angels (12:9). This throwing down with the angels resonates with the stories of the Watchers who were thrown out of heaven. The dragon is an allusion to the monster that inhabited the chaotic waters when God created the world. In Ps 74:13-14 the Lord is praised because he "shattered the heads of the sea monsters on the waters" and "crushed Leviathan's heads" (see also Ps 89:10).

At the end of Revelation the angel will come down and bind Satan (the devil, the dragon) and throw him into the abyss for a thousand years before he is released for a short time (20:2-3, 7).

In the Bible, Satan is not a well-defined figure. There are some differences between the notion of Satan in the OT and the NT, and nowhere is there a definitive description of Satan. As a number of recent publications have pointed out, Satan is a character who continued to develop postcanonically in different directions in Christian history. See BEELZEBUL; LUCIFER.

SATHRABUZANES Official in 1 Esdr 6–7 who is called SHETHAR-BOZENAI in Ezra 5–6.

SAUL, SON OF KISH Means "one requested, asked for," likely a shortened form of a name meaning "requested of the Lord" and comparable to Shealtiel, "I requested [him] of God. Saul was the 1st king of Israel according to the book of Samuel. He was God's choice as king (1 Sam 9–11), but was rejected (1 Sam 13–15). Saul and David were rival rulers for a time (1 Sam 16–2 Sam 1).

SCALES See BALANCES.

SCAPEGOAT See AZAZEL.

SCARLET A shade of red produced by an expensive, highly prized dye. The female shield louse (*Kermococcus vermilio*), which is found on the kermes oak, is the source of scarlet dye. A single pound of dye requires the bodies of 70,000 insects. Scarlet dye was used particularly in luxury items and items associated with the cult.

The dye is colorfast and does not fade. Thus, *scarlet* is a metaphor for *sin* in Isa 1:18. The Lord promises that Israel can be purified of its sins, even though they are like the permanent red stain of scarlet. Scarlet wool was used in purification rituals (Heb 9:19; cf Lev 14).

Scarlet was used on expensive clothing, like the robe the soldiers used when mocking Jesus ("red" [Matt 27:28]), and the clothing of the woman who symbolizes Babylon/Rome (Rev 17:4). Merchants mourn when they hear that Babylon is destroyed, for they have lost the market for their luxury items, including scarlet cloth (Rev 18:11-17).

SCEPTER A scepter is a royal STAFF or ROD. As king, God possesses a scepter (e.g., Ps 110:2). The scepter represents royal power (Num 24:17), so Zechariah can say, "The scepter of Egypt will turn away," meaning it will become weak (Zech 10:11; cf Ps 89:44 [Heb. 89:45]; Isa 14:5).

In the NT, *scepter* occurs only in Heb 1:8-9 (quoting Ps 45:6-7 [Heb. 45:7-8]) in a string of quotations that apply to Christ, therefore associating him with the divine throne.

SCEVA Itinerant Jewish exorcists identified as "the seven sons of Sceva, a Jewish high priest" were active in Ephesus (Acts 19:14).

SCORPION Eight-legged arthropods that belong to the arachnid class and are known for their claws, a curved tail, and a stinger that (among certain species) delivers neurotoxin surpassed by few other toxins. Scorpions, along with poisonous snakes, symbolize the potential danger of wilderness (Deut 8:15), through which the Lord guides the Israelites. Likewise, Jesus pronounced that his disciples had authority to tread on snakes and scorpions (Luke 10:19; see SERPENT).

SCRIBE A scribe was a member of a trained class of professionals who filled a variety of functions related to reading and writing within the governmental and religious administrations of ANE societies. In the early Jewish and NT eras, a scribe was an elite scholar who specialized in the teaching and interpretation of religious texts, particularly the Instruction or Torah.

Most notably, scribes appear in the lists of officials included in the government bureaucracies of David and Solomon (2 Sam 8:16-18; 1 Kgs 4:1-6). A well-known illustration of how a scribe functioned within the royal court occurs in the description of King Josiah's reforms in 2 Kgs 22. According to this text, a scribe, or "secretary," is called to read the newly discovered Instruction scroll before Josiah to initiate the king's religious reforms. Other descriptions of scribes in Samuel–Kings suggest that they functioned as international emissaries. For instance, 2 Kings depicts scribes as some of the emissaries that Hezekiah sent to the Assyrian king Sennacherib during his campaign to Judah (18:18, 37).

There are numerous references to scribes (CEB "legal experts") in the NT. The Synoptic Gospels also depict scribes as those professionals engaged in the interpretation and teaching of the Instruction. The Gospels frequently pair scribes with Pharisees, especially in Jesus' indictment: "How terrible it will be for you legal experts and Pharisees! Hypocrites!" (Matt 23:13-33; Luke 11:39-52). It is possible that the pairing of these groups in the Gospels derives from similarities in their theological beliefs, such as belief in resurrection. Several other NT passages present scribes as questioning Jesus' actions and authority (Mark 2:13-17; 11:27-28). The frequent references to scribes in these indictments no doubt reflect the Gospel writers' efforts to depict Jesus as deeply divided against the scribes in the interpretation of the Instruction.

These depictions, which are particularly prominent in Matthew, should be understood as having a specific location within the early church's rivalry with rabbinic Judaism.

Several NT texts give us glimpses of the social status held by scribes during the Second Temple period. For instance, Mark 12:30-40 describes scribes as those who walk around in long robes expecting to be greeted in marketplaces and given good seats in synagogues and banquets (see also Matt 23:5-7). The description of scribes in this passage suggests that scribes held a high social status within Jewish society. The high social status of scribes can also be inferred from their position within the Sanhedrin, the main governing body of Judaism during the Second Temple period (Acts 4:6).

SCROLL A long, rolled piece of papyrus, leather, parchment, or metal (such as copper), inscribed with literary material in vertical columns. The Hebrew and Greek terms for scrolls are often anachronously translated "BOOK" in the NRSV and NIV.

SCYTHIANS Seminomadic tribes of horse-riding warriors who originally inhabited the steppes north and east of the Black Sea. By the 8th cent. BCE they invaded Urartu (modern-day eastern Turkey) and northwestern Iran. The ASHKENAZ (Gen 10:3; 1 Chron 1:6; Jer 51:27) are usually identified with the Scythians.

The barbaric nature and cruelty of the Scythians is well known in the ancient world (see 2 Macc 4:47; 3 Macc 7:5; 4 Macc 10:7). The Scythians as barbarians, and their potential for change, is the thrust of Paul's argument for the unifying nature of the gospel of Christ (Col 3:11).

SCYTHOPOLIS Capital of the DECAPOLIS and Greek name for BETH-SHAN. Holofernes camped between Geba and this city (Jdt 3:10), located about 75 mi. from Jerusalem (2 Macc 12:29-30).

SEA OF GLASS, GLASS SEA "Something like a glass sea, like crystal" appears in John's vision of the heavenly throne room in Rev 4:6. In Rev 15:2, John sees "a sea of glass mixed with fire." The fire here may be a reflection of the flashes of lightning that emerge from the throne (Rev 4:5).

SEA OF REEDS See REED SEA.

SEA, GREAT See MEDITERRANEAN SEA.

SEAH A dry measure of capacity used for flour and cereal. See WEIGHTS AND MEASURES.

SEALS AND SCARABS Seals were often used in the ANE in legal, economic, and political contexts. There were two major types of seals in the ANE: cylinder seals and stamp seals. Cylinder seals were very common in Mesopotamia and Syria during various periods. Cylinder seals would often be rolled onto the soft clay of a completed cuneiform tablet or on an envelope containing a cuneiform tablet. Cylinder seals were normally very small, often just 2–3 cm in length. Some cylinder seals have both writing and iconography, but some have just iconography. Stamp seals (sometimes also called scarab seals) were normally made of precious stones (e.g., carnelian, agate, dolerite) and were very common during the Iron Age.

SEBA Cush's oldest offspring (Gen 10:7; 1 Chron 1:9) and the eponymous ancestor of a people or place (Ps 72:10; Isa 43:3). See CUSH, CUSHITE.

SECACAH Located within the wilderness of Judah in the region between JERICHO and EN-GEDI (Josh 15:61), Secacah shared a developed system of fortifications with Middin and Nibshan.

SECOND ADAM Paul calls Jesus the "last Adam" in 1 Cor 15:45. He contrasts the first Adam, created as a living being (Gen 2:7), with the last Adam, who became a "spirit that gives life." Paul states that in the first Adam all die, while "everyone will be given life in Christ" (1 Cor 15:22).

SECOND COMING A belief held by many Christians that at the conclusion of history Jesus will return bodily and inaugurate God's new kingdom on a newly constituted earth. The most explicit NT sources for this belief are 1 Thess 4:16 and Rev 1:7. See PAROUSIA.

SECOND TEMPLE PERIOD The period (ca. 515 BCE–70 CE) after the Babylonian exile, when the rebuilding of the Jerusalem temple began under Zerubbabel the governor of Judah and Jeshua the high priest. The temple would have a number of transformations during this period, ultimately becoming a massive precinct under Herod the Great, until it was destroyed again (by the Romans) in 70 CE.

SECONDARY WIFE The term appears to mean a wife of lower status. Bilhah, Rachel's maid, is called both "wife" (Gen 30:4) and "secondary wife" (Gen 35:22). In Judg 19, an unnamed secondary wife's partner is called husband; the woman's father is called father-in-law. Secondary wives are named as mothers in genealogies more often than wives (Gen 22:23-24; 36:12; Judg 8:31; 1 Chron 2:46, 48; 7:14).

SECU Saul's pursuit of David found Saul at Secu, on the route between Gibeah and Ramah, seeking information from the inhabitants concerning David's whereabouts (1 Sam 19:22).

SECUNDUS One of Paul's companions on the journey from Macedonia to Jerusalem (Acts 20:4). Secundus and Aristarchus were Gentile Christians from Thessalonica, possibly delegates bearing money for Paul's collection for the Jerusalem church (Acts 24:17; 2 Cor 8:1-6). It is uncertain whether Secundus and the rest of the group traveled ahead of Paul and met him in Troas or traveled with Paul to Philippi and Troas after celebrating the Festival of Unleavened Bread (Acts 20:5-6).

SEGUB 1. The name first appears in conjunction with the rebuilding of JERICHO (1 Kgs 16:34). HIEL built the city at the cost of the lives of his two sons Segub and ABIRAM.

2. The father of Jair, son of HEZRON, and great-grandson of Judah (1 Chron 2:21-22; see JAIR, JAIRITE).

SEIR 1. Genesis 36:20-30 refers to a man named Seir, from which the region supposedly took its name. His descendants lived in Seir before the coming of Esau, who settled in Seir and became the ancestor of the Edomites (Gen 36:8-14; Deut 2:12).

2. The region east of the Arabah where Edom was located, although some texts suggest that it also included areas west of the Arabah (Deut 1:44). It is possible as well that originally Edom signified the northern section of the highlands east of the Arabah, while Seir represented the south. The area is often referred to as the highlands of Seir (Gen 14:6; Josh 24:4) or Mount Seir (2 Chron 20:10; Ezek 35:3), which may also refer to a particular mountain within the region. An intriguing reference in Judg 5:4 designates Seir as the place from which the Lord marched forth to battle. Deuteronomy 33:2 likewise connects the Lord with Seir, in parallel with Mount Sinai. This suggests that Mount Sinai was located in the same region as Seir, perhaps in the Hejaz southeast of the Gulf of Aqaba. See EDOM, EDOMITES; IDUMEA; SEIR, MOUNT.

SEIR, MOUNT Means "hairy." A mountain located at Judah's northern border (Josh 15:10), possibly Shoresh

Beth-Meir, located ca. 14.5 km west of Jerusalem. The mountain probably derived its name from its having been heavily wooded in antiquity, because of its location on the western slopes of the Judean range. When the Israelites attempted to invade the highlands from the south, this Seir appears to have been the northernmost point, which they reached before being repelled by the Amorites (Deut 1:44).

SEIRAH Meaning "forested mountain range" or "goat mountain," this word occurs only once in the Bible (Judg 3:26).

SELA 1. A city of uncertain location mentioned in Judg 1:36, which, along with the ascent of Akrabbim, defines some part of "the border of the Amorites."

2. An Edomite stronghold once conquered and renamed "JOKTHE-EL" by the Judean king Amaziah (2 Kgs 14:7; 2 Chron 25:12). The city lies near the Salt Valley where Amaziah "struck down ten thousand Edomites" (2 Kgs 14:7) before storming the city.

3. A city mentioned in Isa 16:1. Moabite refugees fleeing south are urged to send a gift of lambs from this location to "the ruler of the land" in Jerusalem. The city has not been identified.

SELED Mentioned only as the son of Nadab and brother of Appiam, Seled is a descendant of Jerahmeel in Judah's genealogical list (1 Chron 2:30).

SELEUCIA The name given to a number of Greek cities founded in the Near East in the early Hellenistic period, most or all ostensibly named for the founder of the Seleucid dynasty. According to the Roman writer Appian (Hist. rom. 9.57), Seleucus founded more than thirty cities, nine of them named Seleucia. A number of important cities were referred to as Seleucia at some time during their history, including Gaza, Gadara, and Abila. Five cities called by this name are of importance.

1. Seleucia-in-Pieria, which is also known as Seleucia-on-the-Sea (Acts 13:4; 1 Macc 11:8; see SELEUCIA IN SYRIA).

2. Seleucia-on-the-Bay-of-Issus has been identified with Seleucia-in-Pieria, but the two are probably different.

3. Seleucia-on-the-Tigris was a strategic foundation, apparently meant as the capital of Seleucus's empire. Seleucia was taken over by the Parthians about 141 BCE.

4. Seleucia-Zeugma (Seleucia the Bridge) was the major crossing point on the Euphrates, supposedly going back to Alexander, who had a bridge constructed on the spot so that his army could cross the river. Antiochus III confirmed its importance by being married there in 221 BCE.

5. Seleucia was the name given to Tralles for about a century and a half (Pliny the Elder, Nat. 5.108), probably by Antiochus I (281–261 BCE), while it was under Seleucid rule. When the city came under control of the Attalid dynasty of Pergamum (mid-2nd cent. BCE), it reverted to the name Tralles.

SELEUCIA IN SYRIA Also known as Seleucia Pieria, modern Suweydiyah [Turkey], near the mouth of the Orontes River, 25 km southwest of Antioch-on-the-Orontes (see ANTIOCH, SYRIAN).

SELEUCID EMPIRE After the death of Alexander the Great in 323 BCE, his generals (known as the Diadochi or "Successors") fought for control of his empire for the next forty years. One of the players was the commander of Alexander's elite guard named Seleucus. Within a couple of years Seleucus was recognized as having responsibility for Babylon, though he lost this in subsequent fighting. In 312 BCE, with the help of Ptolemy in Egypt, Seleucus was able to retake Babylonia (inaugurating the "Seleucid era"), and later treaties allotted him the huge territory stretching from northern Syria to the borders of Egypt, including Asia Minor. His descendants ruled over this diverse empire for the next two and a half centuries.

SEMACHIAH The 6th son of SHEMAIAH and a Korahite gatekeeper at the Jerusalem temple (1 Chron 26:7).

SEMEIN The father of Mattathias and the son of Josech in the Lukan genealogy (Luke 3:26).

SENAAH Meaning "thorny." The inhabitants or descendants of Senaah returned with Zerubbabel to Jerusalem. Depending on the report, Senaah had 3,630 (or 3,930 or 3,330) descendants (Ezra 2:35; Neh 7:38; 1 Esdr 5:23). The family of Senaah ("sons of Hassenaah") worked on the construction of the Jerusalem walls, and are mentioned as the ones that built the Fish Gate (Neh 3:3).

SENEH One of two sharp crags flanking the pass of Michmash; the other is Bozez (1 Sam 14:4). The area is located approximately 11 km northeast of Jerusalem. In 1 Sam 14, Seneh is mentioned in the detailed description of Jonathan's approach to the camp of the Philistines at Michmash.

SENIR Following the recollection in Deut 3:1-8 of how the Israelites had taken from the Amorites the land between the Wadi Arnon and Mount Hermon, Deut 3:9 notes that Senir is the Amorite name for Mount Hermon. Both 1 Chron 5:23 and Song 4:8, however, appear to make a distinction between Senir and Hermon. Ezekiel 27:5 identifies Senir as a source of cypress. See HERMON, MOUNT.

SENNACHERIB Sennacherib was the king of Assyria (704–681 BCE) who invaded Judah during the reign of Hezekiah. He was the son of Sargon II, king of Assyria (721–705 BCE). 2 Kgs 18–19 depicts Sennacherib's campaign against Jerusalem.

SENTINEL, SENTR Various terms are used for a sentinel (Isa 62:6) or sentry ("watchman" [2 Sam 18:24-27]; "guard" [Ps 127:1 and Isa 21:11-12]). In the NT, a "soldier" or "guard" (e.g., Acts 5:24; 12:6, 19) has the responsibility of watching out for, or over, something or someone to ensure their safety. In the OT in particular (e.g., Ezek 3; 33) the failure of the "lookout" to warn the people of impending judgment for their sin brings about serious condemnation by God.

SEORIM The 4th priest of twenty-four Aaronides assigned duties in the temple on King David's initiative. Seorim, possibly the descendant of Ithamar, is mentioned once in the Bible (1 Chron 24:8).

SEPHAR Mentioned only once in the Bible: the sons of Joktan inhabited the area that lies between MESHA and Sephar (Gen 10:30).

SEPHARAD A place to which some Jewish residents of Jerusalem were exiled (Obad 20).

SEPTUAGINT The Septuagint (LXX) is the Greek translation of the Hebrew Scripture, known as the "Old Testament" (OT) among Protestant Christians. Tradition holds that this translation occurred around 300–250 BCE. The Septuagint was a well-known version of the OT in NT times.

SERAH Serah the daughter of ASHER is mentioned only three times in the Bible and without any accompanying details. In Gen 46:17 she is listed as one of Jacob's descendants who went down to Egypt.

SERAIAH 1. A scribe or secretary of David (2 Sam 8:17); the name, however, is questionable because in the same list elsewhere he is called SHEVA (2 Sam

20:25), SHAVSHA (1 Chron 18:16), and Shisha (1 Kgs 4:3).

2. Son of Kenaz and father of Joab in the tribe of Judah (1 Chron 4:13-14).

3. Son of Asiel and father of Joshibiah in the tribe of Simeon (1 Chron 4:35).

4. One of the leaders of the returning Babylonian exiles (Ezra 2:2; 1 Esdr 5:8) whose grandson JESHUA was an important high priest after the return (1 Esdr 5:5).

5. The first official in a list of twenty-one priests who signed Nehemiah's covenant (Neh 10:2 [Heb. 10:3]).

6. A priest in Jerusalem after the exile (Neh 11:11); he is called "the officer of God's house." Some suggest emending the text based on a similar list in 1 Chron 9:11 where Seraiah does not appear.

7. A priest who returned from exile with Zerubbabel (Neh 12:1, 12).

8. Son of Azriel, deployed by King Jehoiakim to arrest Jeremiah and Baruch; the Lord foiled their attempt (Jer 36:26).

9. Son of Tanhumeth who joined Gedaliah at Mizpah after the destruction of Jerusalem (2 Kgs 25:23; Jer 40:8).

10. Ezra 7:1 (1 Esdr 8:1) identifies Ezra as the son of Seraiah son of Azariah; this cannot be the same Seraiah of 1 Chron 6:14, although both have an Azariah as their father (See #11 below.)

11. Chief priest who was arrested and executed by the Babylonians after the fall of Jerusalem (2 Kgs 25:18-21; Jer 52:24-27). It is likely that the Seraiah of 1 Chron 6:14 is the same Seraiah as here; if so, he is the son of Azariah and father of Jehozadak. Alternatively, he may be identified as the Seraiah of Jer 36:26 (see #9 above).

12. Son of Neriah, and brother of Baruch the scribe (cf Jer 32:12), Seraiah was the "staff officer" who journeyed with King Zedekiah to Babylon in 593 BCE (Jer 51:59-64). Jeremiah took the opportunity to send with Seraiah a word of doom against the city of Babylon, presumably meant to cheer the exiles (from 598 BCE).

SERAPH, SERAPHS Heavenly creatures, often called "seraphim," with six wings and human voices serving as divine attendants in Isaiah's throne room vision (Isa 6:2, 6-7). Elsewhere the Hebrew word designates a SERPENT ("poisonous snake" [Num 21:8]; "viper" [Isa 14:29]), thus suggesting serpentine bodies for the seraphim in Isaiah. See ANGEL.

SERED A descendant of Zebulun. In Gen 46:14, Sered is listed among "the Israelites who went to Egypt, including Jacob and his sons" (46:8) who immigrate to Egypt. Numbers 26:26 identifies Sered as progenitor of the Seredites.

SERMON ON THE MOUNT The "Sermon on the Mount" is the traditional designation for a section of Matthew's Gospel (chaps. 5–7) that presents the teaching of Jesus on matters of discipleship.

The name "Sermon on the Mount" derives from Matt 5:1, which indicates that Jesus delivered this teaching to his disciples on a mountain. About half the material in the Sermon on the Mount finds parallel in a section of Luke's Gospel in which Jesus instructs a multitude of people "on a large area of level ground" (Luke 6:17); this portion of Luke's Gospel is accordingly called the SERMON ON THE PLAIN (Luke 6:20-49).

The Sermon on the Mount contains material that has been extremely influential on the Christian religion and on secular civilization in areas where Christianity has flourished. It is here that one finds the BEATITUDES (Matt 5:3-12), the Golden Rule (Matt 7:12; see GOLDEN RULE, THE), and the LORD'S PRAYER (Matt 6:9-13). Here Jesus speaks of the humble inheriting the earth (Matt 5:5) and identifies his followers as "the salt of the earth" (Matt 5:13). He taught, "If people slap you on your right cheek, you must turn the left cheek to them as well" (Matt 5:39); and "When they force you to to go one mile, go with them two" (5:41). He refers to wolves "dressed like sheep" (Matt 7:15), serving "two masters" (Matt 6:24), collecting "treasures for yourselves in heaven" (Matt 6:20), and throwing "your pearls in front of pigs" (Matt 7:6).

SERMON ON THE PLAIN The "Sermon on the Plain" is the traditional designation given to a section of Luke's Gospel (Luke 6:20-49) that parallels the better-known SERMON ON THE MOUNT found in the Gospel of Matthew (Matt 5–7). The name derives from Luke 6:17, which indicates that Jesus spoke to his disciples and a great crowd of people "on a large area of level ground" (cf Matt 5:1, which indicates that similar teaching was presented to the disciples on a mountain).

SERON A commander of the Syrian army (1 Macc 3:13, 23). When Seron heard of Judas's success in raising an army against the Syrian kings, he gathered a large company at Beth-horon to fight against them, hoping to win fame for himself (1 Macc 3:14). While Judas's army was much smaller, it defeated Seron's army, further spreading Judas's fame among the Gentile population (1 Macc 3:26).

SERPENT There are a variety of terms used to denote snakes within the OT, variously translated as serpent, snake, dragon, poisonous serpent, fiery serpent, asp, adder, or viper. Snakes that appear in narrative contexts have magical or mythological characteristics. In Gen 3, the snake is introduced at the beginning of the chapter as "the most intelligent" (also meaning "shrewd" or "sensible") of all the wild animals that the Lord God had made. Magical snakes appear in the exodus narrative. In Exod 4:3 (part of Moses' call narrative), God turns Moses' staff into a serpent as a reassuring sign that God will be with him. This staff is alluded to again in Exod 7:15. In other references in chap. 7, Aaron's staff changes to a snake in competition with the magicians of Egypt. Aaron's staff/snake wins the competition by swallowing those of the Egyptians.

Numbers 21:4-9 describes an episode in the wilderness when the Israelites complain about the food, and the Lord responds by sending poisonous snakes that bite and kill the people.

Serpent language is used in the prophetic literature to describe God's judgment. In these instances, serpents are always depicted as dangerous or malevolent (Isa 14:29; Jer 8:17; Amos 5:19). Serpent language is also used in descriptions of hope and restoration. In these cases, serpents are still viewed as dangerous animals. In Isa 11:8 (a description of a peaceful reign under the Davidic monarch) and Isa 65:25 (a vision of a new creation), snakes, among other dangerous creatures such as wolves, leopards, lions, and bears, will live in harmony and will not be harmful to humans. Micah 7:17 describes Judah's enemies as snakes that will be in dread of God and the people of Judah.

In the NT, snakes are dangerous or evil (Matt 7:10; Luke 10:19; 11:11; John 3:14; 1 Cor 10:9; 2 Cor 11:3).

In Revelation, the devil is called "the old snake" (Rev 12:9; 20:2).

Jesus is portrayed as condemning the Pharisees and their religious practices as hypocritical with the phrase "you children of snakes" (Matt 3:7; 12:34; 23:33; Luke 3:7).

SERUG A descendant of Noah, the son of Reu, and the father of Nahor, as well as the great-grandfather of Abraham (Gen 11:20-23; 1 Chron 1:26; Luke 3:35).

SERVANT Servants are persons under a superior for whom they perform tasks. They clearly are not chattel slaves. While a number of biblical terms may be translated as "servant," there is not always a clear distinction between who is a servant and who is a slave. The terminology covers a broad semantic domain, and a translation of either servant or slave depends on the specific context.

In the OT, servants look after the affairs of individuals (Gen 24:2; Exod 24:13; Judg 7:10; 1 Kgs 19:21; 2 Kgs 4:12); are part of extensive households (Judg 19:3; 1 Sam 9:3); oversee laborers (Exod 5:15-16; Ruth 2:6; 1 Kgs 11:26; 2 Chron 13:6); serve in the military (1 Sam 22:6-10; 2 Sam 2:12-17; Isa 36:9); advise the king (1 Sam 16:15; 1 Kgs 1:2; Esth 6:3-5); and assist in the temple (1 Chron 9:2; Ezra 2:43; Neh 7:46). Conquered peoples are sometimes designated as servants of the king (2 Sam 8:2, 6, 14). The role of servants varies widely, but it is clear that these individuals are not in a restricted, permanent form of slavery. Indeed, many of them have the respect of the people they serve.

In a religious context, prominent individuals, kings, and prophets are designated as servants of God, a title that describes their humility, piety, and/or obedient performance of tasks given to them by God. Included among these are: Abraham (Gen 26:24; Ps 105:6); Moses (Exod 14:31; Num 11:11; Ps 105:26); Joshua (Judg 2:8); David (2 Sam 3:18; Ps 144:10); Hezekiah (2 Chron 32:16); Isaiah (Isa 20:3); Nebuchadnezzar (Jer 25:9); and Daniel (Dan 6:20).

The theme finds its most significant theological expression in the Servant Songs of Second Isaiah (Isa 40–55). Scholarship debates whether the servant is to be understood as a corporate or individual figure. While a number of the references clearly designate the nation of Israel as the servant, others are ambiguous and some portray the servant as an individual who will suffer on behalf of Israel (Isa 53). Both Judaism and Christianity adopted the Servant Songs as a paradigm for understanding the vicarious suffering of righteous ones as having redemptive power.

In the NT, individuals continue to understand themselves as God's servants (Luke 1:38; Jas 1:1; Titus 1:1), and with the advent of Christianity, servants of Christ (Rom 1:1; Gal 1:10; Phil 1:1). Again, a translation of either "servant" or "slave" depends on the context.

A more specific term for servant in the NT is sometimes translated as "deacon," which in ancient Greek denotes a table server, messenger, or minister. The earliest, most ample evidence for the term in early Christianity is found in Paul. Although commonly associated with the office of deacon (1 Tim 3:8-13), the majority of occurrences are less specific. Paul refers to himself and others as servants of the gospel, God, and Christ (1 Cor 3:5; 2 Cor 11:23; 1 Thess 3:2), a designation also found in the disputed Epistles (Eph 3:7; 6:21; Col 1:7, 23, 25; 4:7; 1 Tim 4:6). As servants of God, these emissaries are entrusted with the gospel (2 Cor 3:5) and have earned the right to be heard (2 Cor 6:4). On the other hand, some are the servants of Satan who oppose the servants of righteousness (2 Cor 11:14-15). Apart from individuals, Paul calls Christ the servant of the circumcision (Rom 15:8), but not of sin (Gal 2:17). Government is also the servant of God (Rom 13:4). There is early evidence that this became a more specific title for a local church office during Paul's lifetime (Rom 16:1; Phil 1:1), but the exact role of this position is unclear.

See DEACON; DEACONESS; SLAVERY.

SETH 1. Third son of Adam and Eve, who was born after Cain, the oldest, and murdered his brother Abel.

2. In Egyptian mythology, Seth is one of four siblings (Osiris, Isis, Seth, and Nephthys) born to Geb and Nut. Seth is often associated with confusion and disorder: within his family, he brings death into the world by murdering Osiris and further embodies strife in his fight with his nephew Horus. Nevertheless, Seth retains a prominent place in Egyptian civilization. Pharaohs, for example, represent Horus reconciled to Seth. In the Ramesside period (1295–1069 BCE),

Seth becomes a god of state as demonstrated by several royal names (Sety I and II and Sethnakht).

SETHUR The son of Michael and representative from the tribe of Asher who, with representatives from the other eleven tribes, was charged by Moses with the task of scouting the land of Canaan to determine its fruitfulness and the strength of its inhabitants (Num 13:13).

SEVEN WORDS FROM THE CROSS Also sometimes called the "seven last words" of Jesus, this is a traditional set of seven sayings created by conflating the four canonical accounts of the crucifixion. None of the sayings appear in all four Gospels, and most occur only in one. No single account contains all seven sayings.

According to the traditional order, the seven words are: (1) Jesus' prayer for those who are crucifying him: "Father, forgive them, for they don't know what they're doing" (Luke 23:34). (2) Jesus' promise to the repentant criminal who is being crucified beside him: "I assure you that today you will be with me in Paradise" (Luke 23:43). (3) Jesus' words to his mother Mary and to the beloved disciple: "Woman, here is your son. . . . Here is your mother" (John 19:26-27). (4) Jesus' cry of abandonment (Matt 27:46; Mark 15:34) and translated by the evangelists: "My God, my God, why have you left me?" The cry mirrors the opening words of Ps 22 (v. 1 [Heb. 22:2]), a fact that has given rise to much debate over whether Jesus spoke the words in despair or in hope. (5) "I am thirsty" (John 19:28). (6) "It is completed" (John 19:30; cf John 17:4). (7) "Father, into your hands I entrust my life" (Luke 23:46). This final phrase is a quotation from a psalm expressing trust in God's deliverance (Ps 31:5 [Heb. 31:6]).

SHAALBON The residence of Eliahba, one of David's Thirty (2 Sam 23:32; 1 Chron 11:33). It may be the same as the city called Shaalbim.

SHAAPH 1. The youngest son of Jahdai (1 Chron 2:47).

2. A son of Caleb, born to his secondary wife Maacah (1 Chron 2:49); father of Madmannah.

SHAARAIM A town in Judah (Josh 15:36), probably located along the Wadi es-Sant, near Socoh and Azekah. After defeating the Philistines, the Israelites pursued them from Shaaraim to Gath and Ekron (1 Sam 17:52).

SHAASHGAZ The eunuch responsible for the 2nd harem where King Ahasuerus's secondary wives reside (Esth 2:14).

SHABBETHAI The name derives from the noun *Sabbath* and may mean "one who belongs to the Sabbath," for example, a priest. Shabbethai was a leader of the Levites (Neh 11:16) who assisted Ezra in prosecuting Israelites who had taken foreign wives (Ezra 10:15; 1 Esdr 9:14). He also served as an interpreter when Ezra read the Instruction scroll (Neh 8:7; 1 Esdr 9:48).

SHADRACH, MESHACH, ABEDNEGO Shadrach, Meshach, and Abednego were, according to Dan 1:3-7, companions of Daniel, and were taken along with him into the court of the Babylonian king Nebuchadnezzar during the time of the Israelite exile in Babylon. They are described as being "royal descendants and members of the ruling class"; "good-looking young men without defects, skilled in all wisdom, possessing knowledge, conversant with learning, and capable of serving in the king's palace" (vv. 3-4). These four, apparently along with many other young men (Dan 1:10, 13), were to be taught the "Chaldean language and its literature" for three years in preparation for positions within the king's court (vv. 4-5). Their story is found in Dan 1–3.

Nebuchadnezzar's chief eunuch Ashpenaz changes their Hebrew names to

Babylonian names as part of the grooming process. Daniel, whose Hebrew name means "God judges," becomes Belteshazzar, an Akkadian word meaning "protect his life" or "protect the life of the king"; Hananiah, "God is gracious," becomes Shadrach, meaning "command of Aku" (a Mesopotamian lunar deity); Mishael, "who is that which God is," is called Meshach, meaning "who is that which Aku is"; and Azariah, whose Hebrew name means "God is my help," becomes Abednego, which means "servant of Nabu" (Nebuchadnezzar's personal deity).

SHAGEE First Chronicles 11:34 lists Shagee the Hararite as the father of Jonathan, one of "the Thirty" among David's mighty men. The LXX gives his name as Sola.

SHAHARAIM One of the descendants of Benjamin, although the relationship is not specified (1 Chron 8:8). Shaharaim's descendants were said to have inhabited Moab.

SHALLUM The name of several persons, most of them associated with the levitical priesthood.

1. The youngest son of Naphtali, the son of Jacob and Bilhah (1 Chron 7:13). His name appears as Shillem in Gen 46:24 and Num 26:49.

2. A descendant of Simeon and the father of Mibsam (1 Chron 4:25).

3. A Judahite, he was the son of Sismai and the father of Jekamiah (1 Chron 2:40-41).

4. The son of Zadok and the father of Hilkiah the high priest (1 Chron 6:12-13 [Heb. 5:38-39]; 9:11). He was one of the ancestors of Ezra (Ezra 7:2; 1 Esdr 8:1; 2 Esdr 1:1; Bar 1:7). His name appears as Meshullam in 1 Chron 9:11 and Neh 11:11; 12:13.

5. The son of Jabesh, he was the 16th king of the northern kingdom of Israel (745 BCE). He killed King Zechariah of Israel, the son of Jeroboam II, and assumed the throne, but he reigned in Samaria only one month (2 Kgs 15:10-15). He was killed and succeeded by Menahem.

6. The father of Jehizkiah, one of the leaders of the tribe of Ephraim (2 Chron 28:12) in the days of Ahaz king of Judah.

7. The son of Tikvah, he was the husband of the prophetess Huldah (2 Kgs 22:14) and a temple official in charge of the ritual vestment used in the temple by the priests and Levites. Shallum appears as the son of Tokhath in 2 Chron 34:22.

8. The youngest son of Josiah (1 Chron 3:15), he became king of Judah after the death of his father in 609 BCE (Jer 22:11). Known also as Jehoahaz, his mother was Hamutal the daughter of Jeremiah of Libnah (2 Kgs 23:30-31). It is possible that Shallum was his given name and that Jehoahaz, a name containing the divine name, was his throne name. Shallum reigned three months in Judah, whereupon Pharaoh Neco of Egypt deposed him and took him to Egypt, where he died (2 Kgs 23:30-34).

9. The father of Hanamel and an uncle of the prophet Jeremiah (Jer 32:7). During the siege of Jerusalem by the Babylonians, Hanamel asked his cousin Jeremiah to buy his property in their hometown of Anathoth.

10. The father of Maaseiah, a levitical priest in the days of Jeremiah (Jer 35:4). Maaseiah was "the temple doorkeeper," one who kept watch over the entrance to the temple.

11. A Levite and a descendant of Kore, he was one of the gatekeepers in the temple (1 Chron 9:17). He seems to be identical with the Shallum mentioned in 1 Chron 9:19, 31. Shallum probably was the head of a family of gatekeepers mentioned in Ezra 2:42; Neh 7:45; and 1 Esdr 5:28, whose descendants returned from the exile in Babylon. He is called Shelemiah in 1 Chron 26:14; Meshullam in Neh 12:25; and Meshelemiah in 1 Chron 9:21. He probably was the Levite and gatekeeper of the temple who married a foreign wife and was forced to divorce her (Ezra 10:24).

12. A Levite and a descendant of Binnui who had married a foreign wife and sent her away in the days of Ezra (Ezra 10:42).

13. The son of Hallohesh and a "ruler of half the district of Jerusalem," he and his daughters helped repair the walls of Jerusalem (Neh 3:12).

14. The son of Col-hozeh, he was the administrator of the district of Mizpah during the days of Nehemiah. His name is spelled as Shallun (in Hebrew), possibly a variant of Shallum. He rebuilt the Fountain Gate and repaired the wall of the Pool of Shelah located in the king's garden, as far as the stairs that go down from David's City (Neh 3:15).

SHALMAI The sons of Shalmai are recognized in Neh 7:48 and Ezra 2:46 as one of the families who returned to Judah from the Babylonian exile together with Zerubbabel in the Persian period and who participated in Israelite religious life as cultic functionaries called the Nethinim (CEB "temple servants"), a class of individuals given over to assist the Levites (Ezra 8:20).

SHALMAN Name of a king whose destruction of BETH-ARBEL is compared to the coming destruction of Israel: "as Shalman destroyed Beth-arbel" (Hos 10:14). The king and location of battle, apparently known to Hosea's audience, is otherwise unattested.

SHALMANESER Five Assyrian kings go by the name Shalmaneser, the first reigning from 1273 to 1244 BCE, and the last from 726 to 722 BCE. Of these five, two are particularly important for Israelite history—Shalmaneser III and Shalmaneser V—but only the latter is referred to by name in the OT (2 Kgs 17:3; 18:9).

SHALOM The concept has many meanings ranging from the basic notion of well-being, safety, and contentment to the more traditional understanding as a status absent of warfare and violence.

People go or travel in safety (Gen 26:29) and can die in peace (Gen 15:15). Shalom expresses greeting and personal blessing (Gen 29:6; 37:14; Num 6:26; 1 Sam 1:17; 25:6; 2 Sam 11:7), victory in warfare (2 Sam 8:10; e.g., after offering "peace" to a city, Deut 20), or "surrender" (1 Kgs 4:24).

The term comes to be used as "safety" in many contexts, suggesting freedom from animal predators or human intruders (e.g., Pss 4:8; 29:11; 85:8; 122:7; Isa 9:7; 32:18; 54:13; Jer 12:12; Nah 1:15). When used in connection with treaty-making, however, it is clear that a more political meaning of peace is intended (Deut 2:26; 1 Sam 7:14) and related to the practice of justice (Zech 8:16). *Shalom* is explicitly used in distinction to war in wisdom and prophetic literature (Eccl 3:8; Jer 12:12; Mic 3:5). The word is used increasingly as part of personal names in the postexilic period (1 Chron 2:40; 4:25; Neh 3:12).

SHAMA One of David's mighty men (1 Chron 11:44), listed in what appears to be an expansion of the original list in 11:11-41*a* and 2 Sam 23:8-39. Many of the sixteen named in the expanded list were from Transjordan.

SHAMGAR One of Israel's lesser-known judges mentioned in only two verses (Judg 3:31; 5:6). Both references to Shamgar identify him as "Anath's son."

SHAMHUTH Shamhuth, a descendant of Zerah, appears in 1 Chron 27:8 as the 5th of David's twelve commanders.

SHAMIR 1. One in a list of cities in the southwestern highlands of Judah (Josh 15:48).

2. A city in the highlands of Ephriam and the home of Tola son of Puah (Judg 10:1-2).

3. The Chronicler lists Shamir son of Micah as one of the Levites appointed by David to serve in the house of the Lord (1 Chron 24:24).

SHAMMA The 8th of eleven sons of Zophah, warriors and heads of households among the descendants of Asher (1 Chron 7:37).

SHAMMAH Variations of this name include Shimeah, Shemiah, Shimei, and Shimea. Several individuals bear this name.

1. Third son of Reuel and grandson of Esau (Gen 36:13, 17; 1 Chron 1:37).

2. The 3rd son of Jesse (1 Chron 2:13-16) who was passed over for kingship (1 Sam 16:9). He later went to battle against the Philistines (1 Sam 17:13). He is also identified as the father of Jonadab and Jonathan (perhaps the same person), whose actions carry both positive (2 Sam 13:32-33; 2 Sam 21:21; 1 Chron 20:7) and negative consequences (2 Sam 13:3).

3. One of the three mighty men of David known for holding his ground against the Philistines in a field of lentils (2 Sam 23:11). There is some confusion if Shammah the Harodite (2 Sam 23:25) is the same as Shammah the Hararite (2 Sam 23:33), but most scholars view them as the same person and locate Harod near Bethlehem.

SHAMMAI THE ELDER Shammai, who is designated by the title "Elder," lived in the early 1st cent. CE and was a forebear of the rabbinic movement. Along with Hillel, Shammai is listed in the Sayings of the Fathers as the last of the "pairs" who led Judaism before the Roman destruction of Jerusalem.

SHAMMOTH Shammoth of Harod is listed among David's warriors in 1 Chron 11:27; 27:8. In 2 Sam 23:25 his name is given as SHAMMAH of Harod.

SHAMMUA The name of several individuals in the OT.

1. Son of Zaccur, who represented the Reubenite tribe as one of the spies Moses sent to examine the land of Canaan (Num 13:4). Shammua disagreed with the report of Joshua and Caleb.

2. One of the sons of David born in Jerusalem to Bathsheba/Bath-shua (2 Sam 5:14; 1 Chron 14:4). Called SHIMEA in 1 Chron 3:5. Brother to Solomon, Shobab, and Nathan.

3. Numbered among the Levites who lived in Jerusalem after the exile (Neh 11:17). Grandson of Jeduthun, son of Galal, father of Abda. Called Shemaiah in 1 Chron 9:16.

4. Head of the priestly house of Bilgah in the time of the high priest Joiakim (Neh 12:18).

SHAMSHERAI The first of Jeroham's six sons, descendants of Benjamin, living in Jerusalem, and heads of households (1 Chron 8:26).

SHAPHAM A leader, 2nd in command in the tribe of Gad and a resident of Bashan (1 Chron 5:11-12).

SHAPHAN 1. In the Judean kingdom, Shaphan served under King Josiah as an official state scribe (2 Kgs 22:3-14; 2 Chron 34:8-20). It was Shaphan and his sons who intervened during the days of Jehoiakim and saved Jeremiah from a mob (Jer 26:24).

2. In Ezek 8:11, Ezekiel's visions reveal Jaazaniah the son of Shaphan as an inciter of popular idolatry among the exiles.

SHAPHAT 1. A Simeonite, one of the spies sent by Moses to reconnoiter Canaan (Num 13:5).

2. Father of the prophet Elisha (1 Kgs 19:16, 19; 2 Kgs 3:11; 6:31), from Abel-meholah.

3. Youngest of the six sons of Shemaiah, and a descendant of David and Zerubbabel (1 Chron 3:22).

4. A Gadite (1 Chron 5:12).

5. Son of Adlai, a herdsman in charge of David's animals (1 Chron 27:29).

6. One of the servants of Solomon who returned with Zerubbabel (1 Esdr 5:34).

SHARAI One of the returnees from

Babylon who gave up their foreign wives (Ezra 10:40).

SHARAR Sharar from HARAR was the father of Ahiam, listed in 2 Sam 23:33 as one of David's warriors.

SHAREZER 1. Son of Sennacherib king of Assyria. Sharezer conspired with his brother to murder their father (2 Kgs 19:37; Isa 37:38).

2. One of two men sent from Bethel to Jerusalem to ask if the people should continue to mourn on the anniversary of the fall of Jerusalem (Zech 7:2).

SHARON, SHARONITE 1. The coastal plain of Sharon has three sets of parallel corridors stretching from the south (Joppa) or Yarkon River to the north (Mount Carmel) or Tanninim (Crocodiles) River. The area was productive for animal husbandry. The OT and the NT record the following references to Sharon: 1 Chron 5:16; Song 2:1; Isa 33:9; 35:2; 65:10; and Acts 9:35. According to 1 Chron 5:16, Sharon is not the central coastal plain, but a region east of the Jordan River, with pasturelands associated with Bashan and Gilead.

2. A resident of Sharon, used of Shitrai, a shepherd in the pastures of Sharon (1 Chron 27:29).

SHASHAI A descendant of Binnui, one of the lay families who returned from Babylon with Zerubbabel and who agreed to divorce their foreign wives at Ezra's urging (Ezra 10:40; 1 Esdr 9:34).

SHASHAK The 7th of eight sons of Elpaal, Jerusalem Benjaminites who were heads of households (1 Chron 8:14). Shashak was the father of eleven sons (1 Chron 8:25).

SHAUL Means "one asked for" (see also SAUL, SON OF KISH).

1. The 7th Edomite king, who hailed from the region of Rehoboth. He reigned before there were kings in Israel (Gen 36:37-38; 1 Chron 1:48-49).

2. The child of Simeon whose mother was a Canaanite. This Shaul was the progenitor of the Shaulite clan (Gen 46:10; Exod 6:15; Num 26:13).

3. The descendant of Levi and one of the sons of Kohath (1 Chron 6:24).

SHAVEH VALLEY The place where Abram encountered the king of Sodom and Melchizedek after Abram routed King Chedorlaomer and his allies and reclaimed Lot (Gen 14:17; cf v. 5). See KIDRON VALLEY.

SHAVEH-KIRIATHAIM Mentioned as the location where Chedorlaomer the king of Elam defeated the Emim (Gen 14:5). The city Kiriathaim was allotted to Reuben, who fortified the city (Num 32:37; Josh 13:19).

SHAVING Israelite men usually wore beards, and shaving was limited to special circumstances. Levites prepared for their consecration by shaving their whole bodies (Num 8:7). At the completion of their vows, Nazirites shaved their heads and burned the hair (Num 6:13-20). During a visit to Jerusalem, Paul sought to show his respect for the Law of Moses by making a Nazirite vow, which included shaving his head (Acts 21:23-24; cf 18:18). Shaving was employed in the diagnosis of "scabies infection" or "skin disease" (Lev 13:31-33) and in subsequent purification (e.g., Lev 14:8-9). Forcefully shaving another's beard was a means of humiliation carried out on enemies, prisoners, or slaves (e.g., 2 Sam 10:4; Isa 7:20; Jer 48:37; cf 1 Cor 11:5-6). Occasionally the Lord commanded shaving as a sign of mourning over sinfulness (Isa 22:12; Amos 8:10).

SHAVSHA Shavsha was David's court secretary according to 1 Chron 18:16. Similar Deuteronomistic lists give his name as Seraiah (2 Sam 8:17) and Sheva (2 Sam 20:25). He is probably also the

"Shisha" whose two sons are named as secretaries in Solomon's court (1 Kgs 4:3).

SHEAL Descendant of Bani, who returned to Jerusalem after the Exile and among those whom Ezra instructed to send away their foreign wives and children in accordance with God's commandments, an attempt to cleanse the land of their polluting effect (Ezra 10:29).

SHEALTIEL In biblical and apocryphal references (1 Chron 3:17; Ezra 3:2, 8; 5:2; Neh 12:1; Hag 1:1,12, 14; 2:2, 23; 1 Esdr 5:5, 48, 56 [LXX 5:47, 54]; 6:2; Luke 3:27; cf Matt 1:12), Shealtiel is primarily recognized in his role as the father of Zerubbabel; hence, a descendant of David and forefather of Jesus.

SHEARIAH The 4th of Azel's six sons and a descendant of Benjamin (1 Chron 8:38; 9:44) and therefore also of King Saul.

SHEAR-JASHUB Isaiah's son (Isa 7:3). In Isa 10:20-21, this phrase is a prophetic statement ("a few will return"), not a name. See REMNANT.

SHEBA 1. The Table of Nations (Gen 10:7) gives evidence of a descendant of Ham, Cush, and RAAMAH known as Sheba, mentioned again in the Adam to Abraham genealogy in 1 Chron 1:9. A close reading of the narratives supports either a person or a tribe located in mountainous southwestern parts of Arabia.

2. Geographically the descendants of Sheba (known tentatively as Sabeans) were located in a lush region of the Arabian Peninsula that facilitated their trade. Sabeans were known to trade in precious stones, gold, and frankincense. The book of Job records that Sabeans also were slave traders (Job 1:15; 6:19). Isaiah 45:14 mentions "the tall Sabeans." In the OT text *Sheba* often occurs in the context with Egypt and Cush (both African countries).

3. Sheba son of Bichri led the northern tribes of Israel against David (2 Sam 20). Joab catches up with Sheba at Abel of Beh-maachah and beseiges the city. A woman of the city agrees to hand over Sheba's head in order to save the town.

4. A Gadite (1 Chron 5:13).

SHEBA, QUEEN OF The visit of an unnamed dignitary from Sheba, identified only by title, to the court of King Solomon bolsters the biblical perspective that the monarch oversaw a prosperous empire, which he ruled as a just king, renowned for his sagacity (1 Kgs 10:1-13; 2 Chron 9:1-12). The queen's acknowledgment of the God of Israel as the source of Solomon's affluence corresponds to the motif of the foreign proselyte, a concept reiterated in the NT, where she is referred to as the QUEEN OF THE SOUTH (Matt 12:42; Luke 11:31). The Islamic traditions (Qur'an 27:16-44) depict her in a similar light, as one who, in making the journey from southern Arabia, arrives at a spiritual destination.

SHEBANIAH 1. A priest who served with others as a trumpeter in the presence of the covenant chest during the Davidic monarchy (1 Chron 15:24).

2. A name associated with several individuals, mainly identified as Levites, in the era of Nehemiah's governorship (Neh 9:4-5; 10:4, 10, 12 [Heb. 10:5, 11, 13]; see 12:14). Because other names appear redundantly in Neh 10, perhaps only a single Levite named Shebaniah existed at that time.

SHEBER Sheber was the 1st son of Caleb and his secondary wife Maacah (1 Chron 2:48) in the 2nd genealogical list of Calebites in 1 Chron 2.

SHEBNA Shortened form of Shebaniah (Neh 9:4). Shebna appears on Iron Age II seals from Lachish and other sites. Shebna himself was an official during the reign of Hezekiah who was "in charge of the house" (Isa 22:15-25). He was second in command under the king and supervised affairs in the capital as well as the kingdom. The Lord announced that he would replace Shebna with Eliakim, who would bear "the key to David's house on his shoulder" (v. 22), because Shebna constructed an extravagant tomb for himself and rode in splendid chariots. It is uncertain whether a tomb discovered on the slopes of Silwan is Shebna's.

SHEBNAH See SHEBNA.

SHEBUEL 1. Son of Gershom and grandson of Moses (1 Chron 23:16). He is the "chief officer in charge of the treasuries" (1 Chron 26:24).

2. One of the sons of Heman appointed by David to prophesy with musical instruments (1 Chron 25:4).

SHECANIAH The name is confused with SHEBANIAH in certain Latin, Greek, and Syriac manuscripts of Nehemiah (see 9:4-5; 10:4, 12; 12:14). Nevertheless, at least six individuals bearing the name can be identified.

1. A priest living in the days of Hezekiah (2 Chron 31:15).

2. A priest who accompanied Zerubbabel in his return from exile (Neh 12:3) and whose name served to designate a priestly household (LXX Neh 12:14; see 1 Chron 24:11; Ezra 8:3; 1 Esdr 8:29).

3. A descendant of Zattu and son of Jahaziel, who accompanied Ezra on his journey to Jerusalem (Ezra 8:5; 1 Esdr 8:32).

4. A descendant of Elam and son of Jehiel, known from the days of Ezra (Ezra 10:2).

5. The father of Shemaiah and a member of the postexilic royal family (Neh 3:29; 1 Chron 3:21-22).

6. The father-in-law of Tobiah, an adversary of Nehemiah (Neh 6:18).

SHECHEM, SHECHEMITES 1. The son of Hamor and prince of the region in Canaan that Jacob enters with his family (Gen 33:18-19). Shechem rapes Jacob's daughter DINAH, and then demands to marry her (Gen 34:2-4). When Jacob and his sons learn of the rape, they deceitfully agree to the marriage, on the condition that Shechem and all the men of the city be circumcised (Gen 34:11-18). Dinah's brothers take advantage of the subsequent incapacitation of the men, killing Shechem and his father (Gen 34:26).

2. A male descendant of Manassseh, son of Joseph (Josh 17:2).

3. A son of Shemida, also from the family of Manasseh, but described as part of a subsequent generation from the man listed in Josh 17 (1 Chron 7:19).

4. Shechem ("shoulder") was one of the most prominent biblical locations, ca. 40 mi. north of Jerusalem. Shechem is strategically situated in Mount Ephraim in the pass between Mount Ebal and Mount Gerizim near modern Nablus.

SHEDEUR Shedeur's name appears five times in Numbers as a member of the tribe of Reuben and as father of ELIZUR (e.g., Num 2:10; 7:30, 35).

SHEERAH The daughter of Ephraim, Sheerah built Lower and Upper Beth-horon and Uzzen-sheerah (1 Chron 7:24).

SHEHARIAH The 2nd of Jeroham's six sons, Benjaminites who lived in Jerusalem and were heads of households (1 Chron 8:26).

SHEKEL The basic unit of weight in the Bible; only in postexilic periods did it mean a coin. Three types of shekel can be distinguished: (1) the "shekel of the sanctuary," mentioned in the Pentateuch and Ezekiel, containing 20 gerahs (Exod 30:24); (2) the shekel "by the royal weight" (2 Sam 14:26); and (3) the regular or common shekel, containing 24 gerahs. Inscribed stone weights from Iron Age Judah indicate that one common shekel weighed 11.33 g. See MONEY, COINS; WEIGHTS AND MEASURES.

SHEKINAH In postbiblical Jewish literature, the term *Shekinah* ("dwelling, resting") refers to God's numinous presence in the world. The term is not found in the Bible; biblical analogues are "Spirit" or "Holy Spirit," "God's creative Word," and "Woman Wisdom" (see SOPHIA). The Bible's presentation of the divine glory, resident in the wilderness meeting tent and in the temple of Solomon, provides much of the ground for the later understanding of the divine presence in the form of the Shekinah. *Shekinah* is sometimes an alternative term for *God*. Its feminine characteristics are strongly represented in Jewish mystical literature.

SHELAH 1. Son of Arpachshad and father of Eber (Gen 10:24; 11:12-15; 1 Chron 1:18, 24; Luke 3:35).

2. Youngest of the three sons of Judah and the daughter of Shua the Canaanite (Gen 38; 46:12; Num 26:20; 1 Chron 2:3; 4:21).

SHELAH, POOL OF A body of water near the King's Garden in Jerusalem (Neh 3:15).

SHELEMIAH Several individuals with this name appear in the OT, especially in conjunction with the late monarchical and early exilic periods.

1. The father of Zechariah, appointed by David to watch over the East Gate of the Jerusalem sanctuary (1 Chron 26:14).

2. The grandfather of Jehudi (Jer 36:14).

3. The son of Abdeel (Jer 36:26).

4. The father of Jehucal/Jucal (Jer 37:3; 38:1).

5. The father of Irijah (Jer 37:13).

6–7. The two individuals identified in the era of Ezra as having been illicitly married to foreign women (Ezra 10:39, 41; 1 Esdr 9:34).

8. The father of one who rebuilt a portion of the Jerusalem wall (Neh 3:30).

9. The priest commissioned by Nehemiah to help oversee the redistribution of the priestly allotment (Neh 13:13).

SHELEPH Sheleph is one of the thirteen sons born to Joktan, son of Eber and great-grandson of Shem (Gen 10:26; 1 Chron 1:20).

SHELESH An Asherite, the 3rd of four sons of Helem who were both heads of households and warriors (1 Chron 7:35).

SHELOMI One "chief" was selected from each of the tribes for the apportionment of the land in accordance with God's directions, and Shelomi is listed as the father of Ahihud, the chief from the Asher tribe (Num 34:27).

SHELOMITH Meaning "peaceful," this feminine name form was sometimes confused with the masculine SHELOMOTH (see 1 Chron 23:9; 24:22; 26:25-28).

1. A daughter of Dibri of the tribe of Dan who married an Egyptian and gave birth to a son. This unnamed son traveled with the Israelites in the wilderness as a sojourner. In a conflict with an Israelite, he blasphemed the name in a curse. His punishment was death by stoning according to the edict of Moses (Lev 24:10-23).

2. A daughter or son of Rehoboam by his wife Maacaah (2 Chron 11:20).

3. The daughter of Zerubbabel (1 Chron 3:19).

4. Son of Josiphiah who led a household of Bani and returned with Ezra from Babylon (Ezra 8:10; 1 Esdr 8:36).

SHELOMOTH A masculine plural form meaning "peaceful."

1. A Levite who was chief of the sons of Izhar (1 Chron 23:18; 24:22).

2. A Gershonite Levite; one of Shimei's sons and head of a clan (1 Chron 23:9).

3. A descendant of Moses through

Eliezer and one of the temple officials of David (1 Chron 23–26).

SHELUMIEL "God is my peace." The son of Zurishaddai and leader of the tribe of Simeon (Num 1:6).

SHEM The oldest son of Noah and the brother of Ham and Japheth. He lives through the flood, along with Noah, his brothers, and their wives. After the flood, God blesses Shem and his brothers and creates a covenant with them (Gen 9:1, 17). Shem also plays a part in the story of Noah's drunkenness, when Ham sees his father's nakedness and goes and tells his brothers. Placing a garment on their shoulders, Shem and Japheth walk backward into Noah's tent and cover him up (9:23). As a result of these actions, Ham's son Canaan is cursed, while Shem and Japheth are blessed (Gen 9:26-27).

SHEMA Meaning "sound."

1. A town in southern Judah near Hebron (Josh 15:26).

2. A Judahite, son of Hebron, father of Raham, and descendant of Caleb (1 Chron 2:43-44).

3. A Reubenite, son of Joel from Aroer, father of Azaz (1 Chron 5:8), and perhaps the same as Shemaiah in v. 4.

4. A Benjaminite, son of Elpaal who, along with his brother Beriah, was the father of a household in Aijalon and ran out the people of Gath (1 Chron 8:13). He is called Shimei in 1 Chron 8:19.

5. One of six men standing on Ezra's right side when Ezra conducted a public reading of the Instruction scroll (Neh 8:4; 1 Esdr 9:43).

SHEMA, THE The Shema is a prayer (Deut 6:4-9; 11:13-21; Num 15:37-41) that states the core beliefs of Judaism, primarily monotheistic faith: "Israel, listen! Our God is the LORD! Only the LORD!

SHEMAAH A Benjaminite from Gibeah and the father of Joash and Ahiezer. He was one of David's mighty warriors at Ziklag (1 Chron 12:3).

SHEMAIAH A personal name that means "the Lord has heard."

1. The prophet who instructs Rehoboam (1 Kgs 12:22-24; 2 Chron 11:2-4) against trying to crush the rebellion of the northern tribes led by Jeroboam because the events were sanctioned by God (1 Kgs 12:15).

2. Son of Shecaiah, father of five, and a descendant of David (1 Chron 3:22).

3. A descendant of Simeon (1 Chron 4:37), perhaps to be identified with Shimei (1 Chron 4:27).

4. Son of Joel from the tribe of Reuben (1 Chron 5:4).

5. Son of Hasshub, a Levite representing the branch of Merari (1 Chron 9:14; Neh 11:15), one of those "in charge of the outside work on God's house" (Neh 11:16).

6. Son of Galal and father of Obadiah and a descendant of Jeduthun, he is a prominent leader of a singer guild (1 Chron 9:16; Neh 11:17*b*).

7. A chief and one of the descendants of Kohath (1 Chron 15:8, 11), one of the three main levitical families ordered by David to bring the chest containing the covenant of the Lord from the house of Obed-edom (13:14) to Jerusalem (16:1).

8. A scribe, son of Nethanel, a Levite, who registered the distribution of priestly duties of the families of Eleazar and Ithamar (1 Chron 24:6).

9. A member of the Korahite lineage (1 Chron 26:4, 6-7), oldest offspring of Obed-edom and father of "sons who ruled over their household, because they were valient men" (26:6).

10. One of the Levites who composed the group of eight Levites and two priests sent by King Jehoshaphat to the cities of Judah to teach the people from the Instruction scroll (2 Chron 17:8).

11. A son of Jeduthun (2 Chron 29:14), one of the fourteen Levites representing seven levitical families who

followed King Hezekiah's command to cleanse the house of the Lord (29:15).

12. One of the six Levites who, following the order of King Hezekiah, distributed the gifts from the clergy collected in Jerusalem (2 Chron 31:15).

13. One of the six chiefs of the Levites and brother of Nethanel and Conaniah, who contributes for the Passover's offering established by King Josiah (2 Chron 35:9; 1 Esdr 1:9).

14. A descendant of Adonikam who came with Ezra from Babylon to Jerusalem (Ezra 8:13; 1 Esdr 8:39).

15. One of the leading men sent by Ezra to Casiphia to request Levites to serve in Jerusalem (Ezra 8:16; 1 Esdr 8:44).

16. A descendant of Harim (Ezra 10:21; 1 Esdr 9:21 conflates the descendants of Harim with the decendants of Immer) who was among the priests who had married foreign women, and afterward sent them away with their children (Ezra 10:18, 44).

17. A descendant of Harim (Ezra 10:31; mentioned as Sabbaias in 1 Esdr 9:32), he is counted among "Israel" (i.e., nonclergy) in the list of those who married foreign women and sent them away afterward.

18. Son of Shecaniah (Neh 3:29), keeper of the East Gate of Jerusalem who helped repair a section of the walls of the city under the direction of Nehemiah (Neh 2:17-20).

19. The son of Delaiah (Neh 6:10) hired by Tobiah and Sanballat to intimidate Nehemiah, prophesying that Nehemiah should hide in the temple to save his life (Neh 6:10-14).

20. One of the priests and head of a priestly family who came from Babylon with Zerubbabel and signed Nehemiah's pledge to adhere to the Law of God (Neh 10:8; 12:6, 18).

21. One of the priests participating in the procession led by Ezra to dedicate the walls of Jerusalem (Neh 12:34).

22. Grandfather of Zechariah and a descendant of Asaph (Neh 12:35).

23. One of the Levite musicians who followed Ezra in the dedicatory procession of the walls of Jerusalem (Neh 12:36).

24. One of the Levite musicians who followed Nehemiah in the dedicatory procession of the walls of Jerusalem (Neh 12:42).

25. Father of Uriah, who prophesied during the times of Jeremiah (Jer 26:20).

26. A false prophet from Nehelam who prophesied in Babylon to the priest Zephaniah to induce him to rebuke the prophet Jeremiah. For this rebellious act, God instructed Jeremiah to prophesy punishment on Shemaiah and his descendants (Jer 29:24-32).

27. Father of Delaiah, one of the officials present when the Instruction scroll of Jeremiah was read (Jer 36:12).

28. Father of Ananias and Nathan/Jathan, relatives of Tobias (Tob 5:14).

SHEMARIAH 1. A Benjaminite warrior who joined David at Ziklag as one of David's mighty men (1 Chron 12:5 [Heb. 12:6]).

2. A son of Rehoboam born to Mahalath (2 Chron 11:19).

3. A son of Harim and one of the Israelites who dismissed their foreign wives after returning from the Babylonian exile according to Ezra's instructions (Ezra 10:32).

4. A son of Binnui who, like the Shemariah above, put away his foreign wife after the exile (Ezra 10:41).

SHEMEBER A king of Zeboiim, listed among the kings defeated by a rival coalition of five kings in the Siddim Valley (Gen 14:2-3).

SHEMED Shemed, "who built Ono and Lod with its towns," is listed with Eber and Misham as sons of Elpaal (1 Chron 8:12) in a genealogy of descendants of Benjamin.

SHEMER 1. The owner (either an individual or a clan) of the hill that the Israelite king Omri bought to build his capital city, which was then named Samaria after Shemer (1 Kgs 16:24).

2. A Levite of the Merari lineage, who was an ancestor of Ethan, a cult singer appointed by David (1 Chron 6:46 [Heb. 6:31]).

3. A member of the tribe of Asher listed in 1 Chron 7:34, usually understood as Heber's son Shomer (7:32).

SHEMIDA A son of Gilead and head of the clan of the Shemidaites (Num 26:32). His clan belonged to the tribe of Manasseh, along with the clans of Abiezer, Helek, Asriel, Shechem, and Hepher (Josh 17:2). Their tribal allotment lay west of the Jordan.

SHEMIRAMOTH 1. A harpist from the 2nd rank of levitical musicians, appointed to accompany the covenant chest's procession from the house of Obed-edom into Jerusalem and to play before the covenant chest after its installation in the tent that David constructed (1 Chron 15:18, 20; 16:5).

2. Jehoshaphat assigned another Levite by the same name to be one among several officials who would teach throughout Judah from the Instruction scroll (2 Chron 17:8).

SHEMUEL *Shemuel* is also an alternate English spelling of *Samuel*.

1. The representative of the tribe of Simeon designated to assist in apportioning the land to the twelve tribes (Num 34:20).

2. One of the sons of Tola, a descendant of Issachar (1 Chron 7:2).

SHENAZZAR The 4th of King Jehoiachin's (Jeconiah's) seven sons (1 Chron 3:18).

SHEPHAM Town marking the northeastern boundary of the land of Canaan that the Lord had promised to Moses (Num 34:10-13).

SHEPHATIAH 1. The 5th son of David of those born to him at Hebron (2 Sam 3:2-5; 1 Chron 3:1-3).

2. A Benjaminite warrior who joined David's army at Ziklag (1 Chron 12:5) while David was hiding from Saul.

3. Son of Maacah, the leader of the tribe of Simeon during the reign of David (1 Chron 27:16).

4. A son of King Jehoshaphat of Judah (2 Chron 21:2), later killed by his brother Jehoram (21:3-4).

5. A son of Mattan (Jer 38:1) and prince in King Zedekiah's (597–586 BCE) court (Jer 38:4).

6. The ancestor of a family that returned to Judah following the exile; 372 returned with Zerubbabel (Ezra 2:4; Neh 7:9) and 81 with Ezra (Ezra 8:8).

7. A descendant of Solomon's servants who returned from the exile with Zerubbabel (Ezra 2:57; Neh 7:59).

8. The eponymous ancestor of the family of Meshullam, Benjaminites who returned to Jerusalem after the exile (1 Chron 9:8).

9. A descendant of Perez and the eponymous ancestor of a Judahite family that lived in Jerusalem during the time of Nehemiah (Neh 11:4).

SHEPHELAH From a Hebrew root word meaning "to make low" or "to humble," Shephelah designates the southern two-thirds of a 50-mi.-long region of gently sloped limestone hills and fertile valleys separating the Judean highlands from the western coastal plain. Approximately 10 mi. wide, the region extends northward from Beer-sheba to Yehem. The Shephelah is located within the boundaries of the land originally given to Dan and Judah. The CEB translates "Shephelah" as "western foothills."

SHEPHER, MOUNT A campsite (location unknown) between Kehelathah and Haradah where the Israelites stopped as they journeyed from Egypt to Canaan (Num 33:23-24).

SHEPHERD Biblical references to

shepherding reflect the agricultural environment of the ANE, in which sheep and goats (domesticated from 7000 BCE or earlier) were a primary source of food, wool, and hides. Accordingly, livestock constituted a significant component of familial wealth (so Gen 26:12-14; 1 Sam 25:2; Job 42:12; Ps 144:13; etc.).

In Scripture, the antiquity of shepherding is evident from the fact that Abel "cared for the flocks" (Gen 4:2-4), and that Abraham, Isaac, and especially Jacob (Gen 30:37-43) shared this role. When blessing Joseph, the aged Jacob declares, "God . . . was my shepherd from the beginning until this day" (Gen 48:15 cf 49:24; Ps 80:1). Moses was tending sheep when confronted by the burning bush (Exod 3:1-2), just as the Israelites were obliged to become "shepherds in the desert" during their forty-year sojourn between Egypt and the land of promise (Num 14:33). But the biblical portrait of the shepherd is indebted above all to David, who in youth cared for the family flock (1 Sam 16:11; 17:34); hence the terms of God's commission: "You will shepherd my people Israel, and you will be Israel's leader" (2 Sam 5:2; cf Ps 78:70-71). Likewise, the Davidic psalms characterize the life of faith in pastoral imagery: "The LORD is my shepherd. I lack nothing" (Ps 23:1; cf 28:9; 68:10). Such metaphors are a staple feature of Israel's worship: "He is our God," declares Ps 95:7, "We are the people of his pasture, the sheep in his hands" (similarly Pss 79:13; 100:3; 119:176).

Later prophets frequently denounce national leaders as unfaithful shepherds who abuse the flocks in their care (Isa 56:11; Jer 12:10; 23:1-2; 50:6; Ezek 34:2-10; Zech 10:2-3). This connotation in particular forms the background for Jesus' bold announcement: "I am the good shepherd. The good shepherd lays down his life for the sheep" (John 10:11; cf 10:14). His words run counter to the apparently low reputation of shepherds in his day (Philo, Agriculture 61; m. Qidd. 4:14; m. b. Qam. 10:8-9)—which also accounts for the unusual choice of shepherds as the first to learn of Jesus' birth (Luke 2:8-20). In his teaching Jesus reiterates prophetic language by characterizing previous leaders as "thieves and outlaws" (John 10:8) and God's people as lost sheep (Mark 6:34; Luke 15:4-7), with himself as their true shepherd (Matt 15:24; 25:32; Mark 14:27; cf Matt 2:6). According to John 10:16, this ministry also embraces those outside ethnic Israel: "I have other sheep that don't belong to this sheep pen. I must lead them too. They will listen to my voice and there will be one flock, with one shepherd."

In similar terms, Jesus commissions Peter to care for his followers: "Feed my lambs. . . . Take care of my sheep" (John 21:15-17); and the early church continues to use shepherding language both for Jesus (Heb 13:20; 1 Pet 2:25) and for those who pastor in his name (Acts 20:28; 1 Pet 5:2-4). Scripture's last word on this theme, however, points back to Jesus and the eternal destiny of the saints: "The Lamb who is in the midst of the throne will shepherd them. He will lead them to the springs of life-giving water, and God will wipe away every tear from their eyes" (Rev 7:17).

SHEPHI Son of Shobal (1 Chron 1:40), named SHEPHO in Gen 36:23.

SHEPHO The 4th of five sons of Shobal (Gen 36:23), whose clan belongs among the Horites in Edom.

SHEPHUPHAM See SHUPHAM, SHUPHAMITE.

SHEREBIAH 1. A Levite who returned from exile in the days of Zerubbabel (Neh 12:8).

2. A Levite who accompanied EZRA in his return from exile. Ezra was pleased to receive from Casiphia this "skillful man" (Ezra 8:18), together with his

immediate relatives and additional Levites. Sherebiah would subsequently play a significant role as a priestly leader in Jerusalem (Ezra 8: 24; Neh 8:7; 9:4-5; 10:12 [Heb. 10:13]; 12:24; 1 Esdr 8:47, 54; 9:48). He is particularly recognized for his assistance in the covenant renewal process instigated by Ezra, through which the people repented in response to the reinstitution of the Instruction (see LEVI, LEVITES).

SHERESH One of the sons of Machir and his wife Maacah (1 Chron 7:16) in the list of the descendants of Manasseh.

SHESHAI One of the three sons of Anak (Num 13:22; Josh 15:14; Judg 1:10), who were giants living in the vicinity of Hebron when the Israelites invaded Canaan.

SHESHAN A descendant of Jerahmeel of the line of Judah; he is the son of Ishi and father of Ahlai (1 Chron 2:31).

SHESHBAZZAR A person mentioned four times in Ezra (1:8, 11; 5:14, 16) and four times in 1 Esdras (2:8, 11; 6:17, 19), but not even once in any other biblical or extrabiblical sources. According to Ezra 1:7-11, he was the leader of the Jews who retuned from Babylonia to Judah (538 BCE).

SHETHAR One of the seven officials of King Ahasuerus's court, who collectively possessed the highest rank in the kingdom and had personal access to the king (Esth 1:14).

SHETHAR-BOZENAI Persian official who, along with Tattenai, sent a letter to Darius regarding the building of the temple in Jerusalem under Zerubbabel (Ezra 5:3, 6).

SHEVA 1. David's court secretary (2 Sam 20:25). The same official is identified as Seraiah in 2 Sam 8:17 and Shavsha in 1 Chron 18:16.

2. The Chronicler's genealogy lists Sheva as a son of Caleb's secondary wife Maacah, and as the father of Machbenah and Gibea (1 Chron 2:48-49).

SHIBAH The name Isaac gave to a well his servants dug (Gen 26:33). The name is provided as an etiology for BEER-SHEBA (cf Gen 21:31-33 where Abraham names the well "Well of seven" [see CEB footnote]).

SHIBBOLETH In Judg 12:1-6, after the Gileadite warrior Jephthah achieves victory over the Ammonites and sacrifices his daughter, the Ephraimites cross the Jordan eastward into Gileadite territory and a battle ensues in which Jephthah's Gileadite forces defeat the Ephraimites. The Gileadites hold the fords of the Jordan against the retreating Ephraimites; if an Ephraimite comes and denies his tribal identity, the Gileadites ask him to pronounce the word *shibboleth*, which means both "ear of corn" and "river." The Ephraimites apparently cannot pronounce the sound "sh" and say "Sibboleth" instead. As a result, 42,000 Ephraimites are killed. Idiomatically, "shibboleth" refers to any expression that serves to distinguish one set of people from another.

SHIHOR Although it is clear that the Shihor is a river, its precise identification is uncertain. Jeremiah chides the people for going to Egypt to drink the waters of Shihor, which are in parallel with Assyria and the waters of the Euphrates (Jer 2:18). As the Euphrates is the main river in Assyria, this would suggest that the Shihor is the Nile. Isaiah 23:3 strengthens this association, placing the Shihor and the Nile in parallel with each other. Joshua 13:3, however, states that the Shihor is in the east of Egypt, which might suggest it is the Pelusaic branch of the Nile, the easternmost branch in the delta.

SHIHOR-LIBNATH Possibly a river, Shihor-libnath formed part of the western boundary of the territory allotted to Asher (Josh 19:26).

SHILHI Maternal grandfather of Jehoshaphat (1 Kgs 22:42; 2 Chron 20:31).

SHILLEM In the list of those who migrated with Jacob to Egypt, Gen 46:24 lists Shillem as the youngest son of Naphtali, who was the son of Jacob and Bilhah, Rachel's maid. In another list of Naphtali's offspring, the name appears as SHALLUM (1 Chron 7:13). In the results of Moses' 2nd census Shillem appears as the ancestral head of the Shillemites (Num 26:49).

SHILOH, SHILONITE 1. A town mentioned in the Former Prophets, Jeremiah, and Psalms. In the book of Joshua, Shiloh functions as a sanctuary, repeatedly housing pan-Israelite gatherings. In Shiloh, Joshua completes the division of the land of promise among the tribes (18:1; 19:51), sets aside cities for the Levites (21:1-3), and announces to the Transjordanian tribes that they have fulfilled their military obligations and may return to their allotments (22:1-9). A different notion of Shiloh as a cultic site is operative in Jer 7:12 ("Go to my sanctuary in Shiloh, where I let my name dwell at first, and see what I did to it because of the evil of my people Israel") and Ps 78:60 ("God abandoned the sanctuary at Shiloh, the tent where he had lived with humans"). In both fragments, the location is initially favored by the Lord and abandoned not because the itinerant shrine simply moved on, but as a punishment for the people's transgressions (see esp. Ps 78:56-58).

2. A term to denote descendants of Shiloh, used of the prophet Ahijah in 1 Kgs 11:29; 12:15; 15:29; 2 Chron 9:29; 10:15. In 1 Chron 9:5 and Neh 11:5, the term most likely refers to descendants of SHELAH the son of Judah and should therefore be rendered "Shelahide."

SHILSHAH The 9th of Zophah's eleven sons, descendants of Asher who were both warriors and heads of households (1 Chron 7:37).

SHIMEA 1. Third son of Jesse (1 Chron 2:13) and older brother of David. Called SHAMMAH in 1 Sam 16:9. Father of Jonathan who slew a giant from Gath who had twelve fingers and toes (1 Chron 20:7). Called SHIMEI in 2 Sam 21:21. Father of Jonadab who schemed with Amnon to rape his sister Tamar (2 Sam 13:3, 32; here he is called Shimeah).

2. Son of David born to Bath-shua/Bathsheba in Jerusalem (1 Chron 3:5). Brother to Solomon, Shobab, and Nathan. Called SHAMMUA in 2 Sam 5:14 and 1 Chron 14:4.

3. Descendant of Merari son of Levi (1 Chron 6:30 [Heb. 6:15]).

4. Ancestor of Asaph (1 Chron 6:39 [Heb. 6:24]), one of the temple singers.

SHIMEATH Father of one of the assassins of King Joash of Judah (2 Kgs 12:21; 2 Chron 24:26). See SHIMRITH; SHOMER.

SHIMEATHITES Part of the Calebite family of Hur (1 Chron 2:55).

SHIMEI 1. A Benjaminite, the son of Gera of Saul's family, who cursed David and threw stones at him as he fled from Absalom (2 Sam 16:5, 13).

2. The grandson of Levi and son of Gershon and hence a levitical clan (Exod 6:17; Num 3:18, 21; 1 Chron 6:17 [Heb. 6:2]; 23:7, 10; Zech 12:13).

3. David's brother (2 Sam 21:21), elsewhere called SHIMEA (2 Sam 13:3, 32; 1 Chron 2:13; 20:7) or Shammah (1 Sam 16:9; 17:13).

4. An official in David's court who did not support Adonijah's bid to become king (1 Kgs 1:8).

5. The son of Ela, who served as the official in charge of the province of Benjamin in Solomon's redistricted kingdom (1 Kgs 4:18).

6. The brother of Zerubbabel (1 Chron 3:19).

7. The son of Libni and great-grandson of Merari (1 Chron 6:29 [Heb. 6:14]).

8. An individual or clan of Simeon (1 Chron 4:26-27). It is not clear whether this genealogy is linear and each name represents a generation or segmented so that Shallum, Mibsam, and Mishma are Shaul's sons and Hammuel, Zaccur, and Shimei are all Mishma's. Shimei and Mishma pun on Simeon, as all three are from the same Hebrew root (see SIMEON, SIMEONITES).

9. An individual or clan within Reuben (1 Chron 5:4); the son of Gog, the grandson of Joel, whose connection with Reuben is not clear (see REUBEN, REUBENITES).

10. One of five heads of Benjaminite families (1 Chron 8:21), called SHEMA in 8:13.

11. One of the individuals or families of levitical singers in the line of JEDUTHUN (1 Chron 25:17, and restored in v. 3). The rotation of the singers in 25:9-31 reflects regular alternation and indicates the artificiality of the claim that it resulted from lottery.

12. An official from Ramah who was in charge of David's vineyards (1 Chron 27:27).

13. A Levite of the line of Heman who helped implement Hezekiah's directive to cleanse the temple (2 Chron 29:14).

14. A Levite, the brother of CONANIAH, who was 2nd in charge of the contributions to the temple under Hezekiah (2 Chron 31:12-13). Perhaps the same as #13.

15. A Levite forced to divorce his foreign wife (Ezra 10:23; 1 Esdr 9:23).

16. A son or descendant of Hashum, who was forced to divorce his foreign wife (Ezra 10:33; 1 Esdr 9:33).

17. A son of Bani or, more likely, Binnui, based on the Greek reading (Ezra 10:38; cf 1 Esdr 9:34), who was forced to divorce his foreign wife.

18. A Benjaminite ancestor of Mordecai and descendant of Kish (Esth 2:5). Possibly the same as #1.

SHIMEON Variant spelling of Simeon (see SIMEON, SIMEONITES). A son of Harim numbered in the census taken by Ezra (Ezra 10:31), Shimeon and his brothers Eliezer, Isshijah, Malchijah, and Shemaiah are listed among the returned exiles who married foreign women.

SHIMON Head of a clan in the tribe of Judah and father of four sons (1 Chron 4:20).

SHIMRATH The genealogical list in 1 Chron 8:21 includes Shimrath, a son of Shimei, among the descendants of Benjamin. His name, along with most of the names in the list, differs from other Benjaminite lists in 1 Chron 7:6-12; Gen 46:21; and Num 26:38-40.

SHIMRI 1. Son of Shemaiah and ancestor of Ziza who was a family leader of the tribe of Simeon (1 Chron 4:37).

2. Father of Jediael and Joha, who were two of David's warriors (1 Chron 11:45).

3. Son of Hosah of the sons of Merari. The Chronicler draws attention to the fact that he was appointed chief even though he was not the oldest (1 Chron 26:10).

4. Son of Elizaphan and brother of Jeuel. One of the Levites commanded by Hezekiah to cleanse the Lord's temple (2 Chron 29:13).

SHIMRITH According to 2 Chron 24:26, Shimrith, a Moabitess, was the mother of Jehozabad.

SHIMRON 1. A son of Issachar and the ancestral tribal head of the Shimronites (Gen 46:13; Num 26:24; 1 Chron 7:1).

2. A Canaanite city during the conquest. The king of Shimron joined Jabin to oppose Joshua and was defeated by Israel (Josh 11:1; 19:15). See SHIMRON-MERON.

SHIMRON-MERON A Canaanite city whose king is listed among those whom Joshua defeated (Josh 12:20). Achshaph's association with SHIMRON in Josh 11:1 and with Shimron-meron in Josh 12:20 suggests Shimron-meron may be the city's full name.

SHIMSHAI Persian official in the province "Beyond the River," which included Jerusalem. Rehum and his adjutant Shimshai the scribe wrote to Artaxerxes from their base in Samaria, asking that the Jews be barred from rebuilding Jerusalem (Ezra 4:8-24; 1 Esdr 2:16-30).

SHINAB Shinab king of Admah (Gen 14:2) was one of five kings, including the kings of Sodom and Gomorrah, who rebelled against and were defeated by Chedorlaomer and his three allies in the Siddim Valley along the coast of the Dead Sea.

SHINAR The general area of southern Mesopotamia (modern south Iraq), known in ancient times as Babylonia. The association of Shinar with Babylon is confirmed by the frequent translation of Shinar in the LXX as "Babylon" (Isa 11:11; Zech 5:11; Dan 1:2). According to Gen 10:8-10, Nimrod's kingdom first included cites in Shinar and later extended north into Assyria, and Shinar was the location of the tower of Babel (Gen 11:2).

SHION A place in the land of promise that was divided by Joshua (Josh 18–19). Shion was one of the sixteen cities that fell to the lot of the tribe of Issachar (Josh 19:19).

SHIPHI Father of Zita and son of Allon in a genealogy of Simeon's descendants (1 Chron 4:37).

SHIPHMITE Appellation given to Zabdi, overseer of the produce in David's vineyards, indicating he came perhaps from SHEPHAM or Siphmoth (1 Chron 27:27).

SHIPHRAH A midwife (Exod 1:15-21). She and her fellow midwife PUAH were commanded by Pharaoh to kill any boys born to the Hebrew mothers they tended. The two refused and, when confronted by Pharaoh, suggested that the Hebrew mothers were delivering before the midwives could arrive. Their protective act of deception was rewarded by the Lord, who gave them families of their own.

SHIPHTAN To apportion the inheritance, the conquered land, God instructed Moses to select one leader from each of the twelve tribes, among whom KEMUEL the son of Shiphtan was selected from the tribe of Ephraim (Num 34:24).

SHISHAK The Egyptian king Shishak plays a pivotal role in the biblical accounts of the division of the kingdom after the death of King Solomon, by harboring the fugitive rebel Jeroboam (1 Kgs 11:40) and attacking Judah (1 Kgs 14:25-26; 2 Chron 12:2-9). The biblical Shishak was Sheshonq I (or Shoshenq I), the 1st king of the 22nd Dynasty who ruled Egypt 931–910 BCE or 945–924 BCE.

SHITRAI King David put Shitrai "the Sharonite" in charge of his cattle that were pastured in Sharon (1 Chron 27:29).

SHITTIM Means "acacia trees." Located approximately 14 km northeast of the Jordan River's mouth, and 13 km west-northwest of Heshbon. Numbers 25:1 has Israel staying at Shittim at the end of their forty years of wandering and prior to their entrance into the land of Canaan.

SHIZA The father of the warrior Adina, a descendant of Reuben who led thirty Reubenites in David's army (1 Chron 11:42).

SHOA In Ezekiel's oracle against

OHOLAH AND OHOLIBAH, Shoa is an unknown group of people listed with the Babylonians, Chaldeans, Pekod, Koa, and Assyrians prophesied to conquer Jerusalem (Ezek 23:23).

SHOBAB 1. Son of Caleb and his wife AZUBAH, although the role of JERIOTH is not clear (1 Chron 2:18).

2. Child born to David and BATHSHEBA in Jerusalem (2 Sam 5:14; 1 Chron 3:5; 14:4).

SHOBACH Commander of the Aramean forces under King Hadadezer, when David fought a decisive battle against them at Helam in Transjordan, which saw the Arameans routed and Shobach killed (2 Sam 10:15-19).

SHOBAI The head of a family of gatekeepers (and the name of that family) whose descendants returned to Jerusalem with Zerubbabel after the exile (Ezra 2:42; Neh 7:45; 1 Esdr 5:28).

SHOBAL The name of several individuals in the OT.

1. Son of Seir the Horite, tribal chief in the land of Edom (Gen 36:20, 23, 29; 1 Chron 1:38, 40).

2. Son of Hur, descendant of Caleb (1 Chron 2:50, 52).

3. Son of Judah and, according to the typical pattern of genealogies in Chronicles, brother of Hur (1 Chron 4:1-2).

SHOBEK One of the postexilic "leaders of the people" (Neh 10:24) who, along with Nehemiah, signed a covenant of confession and obedience (Neh 9–10).

SHOBI One of three men who provided food and shelter for David and his party when they fled Jerusalem after Absalom seized power (2 Sam 17:27).

SHOMER 1. The father of Jehozabad, one of the two servants who assassinated King Joash of Judah (2 Kgs 12:21). See SHIMEATH.

2. A son of Heber of the tribe of Asher (1 Chron 7:32).

SHRINE A structure used as a place of worship. In premonarchic Israel, the Israelites established shrines throughout the land. Though there is considerable scholarly debate on their exact nature, they were likely open-air raised platforms used for offerings and sacrifices. First Samuel 9:12-25 describes a sacrificial meal at such a shrine. Shrines contained other cultic paraphernalia, such as the priestly vest and divine images in Judg 17:5. After the monarchy and the centralization of worship at the Jerusalem temple, all other shrines were outlawed. The reforms of Hezekiah and Josiah (2 Kgs 18:1-7; 23:4-25) included destruction of the shrines, reflecting the widespread, albeit unorthodox, continued popularity of local shrines throughout ancient Israel.

SHROUD A cloth wrapper prepared for a corpse (see BURIAL; LINEN). Isaiah 25:7 states that the "shroud enshrouding all nations" will be removed when the people join in the divine feast provided by God on his holy mountain.

SHUA 1. A Canaanite man whose daughter married Judah (Gen 38:2). Shua had three grandsons (Er, Onan, and Shelah) through his daughter and Judah. Both Er and Onan died at the Lord's hand (Gen 38:7-10; cf 1 Chron 2:3), and Shua's own daughter later died (Gen 38:12). See BATH-SHUA.

2. An Asherite, the daughter of Heber (1 Chron 7:32).

SHUAH, SHUHITE 1. Shuah was one of six sons born to Abraham by KETURAH, his secondary wife (Gen 25:2; 1 Chron 1:32).

2. BILDAD the Shuhite is referenced in several passages from the book of Job (2:11; 8:1; 18:1; 25:1; 42:9).

SHUAL 1. According to 1 Sam 13:17, the "territory of Shual," near Ophrah, was the object of one of three Philistine raids designed to provoke King Saul. The area, otherwise unknown, would have been in the northern part of the Benjaminite highlands.

2. A descendant of Asher (1 Chron 7:36).

SHUHAM Apparently the only son of Dan and head of the single clan called Shuhamites within the tribe of Dan (Num 26:42). In a parallel genealogy, the name provided is HUSHIM (Gen 46:23). See DAN, DANITES.

SHUNI, SHUNITES Shuni was one of the seven sons of Gad (Gen 46:16), and the eponymous ancestor of the Shunites (Num 26:15).

SHUPHAM, SHUPHAMITE In Num 26:39, Shupham is listed as the 4th of five children in Benjamin's genealogy. This genealogy was recorded during the 2nd census by Moses and Eleazar of the Israelites who came out of the land of Egypt (Num 26:1).

SHUPPITES Members with the Huppites of Ir's family in the tribe of Benjamin (1 Chron 7:12). Shuppites and Huppites also appear in Manasseh's genealogy (1 Chron 7:15), while variants occur in Benjaminite genealogies in Gen 46:21 ("Muppim" and "Huppim"), Num 26:39 ("Shupham"), and 1 Chron 8:5 ("Shephuphan").

SHUR DESERT The DESERT crossed by the Israelites after the exodus from Egypt (Exod 15:22). Its exact location is unknown, but could have been along Canaan's southern border with Egypt.

The Israelites suffered for three days without water due to the arid climate of this region (Exod 15:22). Moses averts a crisis by transforming bitter water into potable water at MARAH (Exod 15:23-27). Numbers 33:8, however, identifies the ETHAM desert as the site of this event.

In the patriarchal accounts, Hagar flees to a well between Kadesh and Shur (Gen 16:7). Here, "on the road to Shur" could be a reference to a trade route named Darb el-Shur—a caravan route running from Hebron to Egypt. Abraham dwelt between Kadesh and Shur (Gen 20:1). Ishmael's descendants inhabited the region from Havilah to Shur, described as being opposite Egypt, in the direction of Assyria (Gen 25:18). Saul (1 Sam 15:7) and David (1 Sam 27:8) each pursue the Amalekites "all the way to Shur, which is near Egypt," which pinpoints Shur along the Egyptian border.

SHUTHELAH In Num 26:35, Shuthelah is listed as the 1st of three sons in Ephraim's genealogy. Shuthelah is the only son to have his descendant, Eran, recorded in the genealogy (Num 26:36). In 1 Chron 7:20, Shuthelah is listed as the 1st of many descendants of Ephraim.

SIA Ancestor of a family of temple servants who returned to Judah from the Babylonian exile (Neh 7:47). In the parallel passage in Ezra 2:44, the name is spelled "Siaha."

SIBBECAI Sibbecai "from Hushah" is credited with the heroic killing of a Philistine named Saph, identified as "a descendant of the Raphah [giants]" (2 Sam 21:18).

Sibbecai the Hushathite, "from the Zerahites," is also named by the Chronicler as the commander of 24,000 troops, who are listed 8th among the twelve divisions of David's army (1 Chron 27:11).

SIBMAH A town originally allotted to Reuben (Num 32:38; Josh 13:19) but later incorporated into Moab.

SICYON A city on the south shore of the Gulf of Corinth, 25 km west of Corinth. Sicyon appears in the list of cities (1 Macc 15:23) that received a letter from Lucius the Roman consul requesting kindly treatment of Jews and the return of Judean "troublemakers" to Judea.

SIDON Sidon and Tyre, the twin Phoenician cities (Jer 25:22; 27:3; 47:4; 1 Chron 22:4; Matt 11:21-22; 15:21; Mark 3:8; 7:24, 31; Luke 6:17; 10:13-14; Acts 12:20; Jdt 2:28; 1 Macc 5:15; 2 Esdr 1:11) 35 and 40 km south of Beirut, were for many centuries independent of each other. Sidon was considered from the classical period onward to be the most ancient and the most prominent of the Canaanite/Phoenician coastal cities. Sidon is mentioned in the OT as "the oldest" of Canaan (Gen 10:15; 1 Chron 1:13). The terms *Sidon* and *Sidonians* were not only used in a narrow sense of the city itself and its inhabitants but also included at times the whole of Phoenicia (Judg 10:12; 18:7; 1 Kgs 5:6; 11:1, 5; 16:31; 2 Kgs 23:13; Ezek 32:30). Early use of the names in this wider sense indicates a period in antiquity during which Sidon was powerful enough to impose her rule and her name upon large areas outside the city. Sidonian and Phoenician were at times synonymous.

Sidon's dominant position among the Phoenician coastal cities during this period seems clear. In biblical accounts (Deut 3:9; Josh 13:6; Judg 3:3; 10:12; 18:7) it is Sidon, not Tyre, which appears as a powerful city.

SIEVE An agricultural tool used to sift grain, thus separating grain from chaff or refuse (Sir 27:4). Sieving grain is a metaphor for separating the wicked from the righteous in Isa 30:28 and Amos 9:9.

SIHON The Amorite king who, when approached by Israelite emissaries, refused Israel peaceful passage through his territory, resulting in his defeat (Num 21:21-32; Josh 12:2, 5). The capital of his kingdom, which reached from the Jabbok to the Arnon Rivers (Josh 12:2, 5) was located at Heshbon (Num 21:26-28). This conquered territory subsequently became the tribal inheritance of Reuben (Num 32:33; Josh 13:10, 21, 27).

SILAS Latinized as Silvanus, both names refer to the same person. Acts retains the Jerusalem community's designation (Silas), while Paul and 1 Peter retain the name used in Greco-Roman communities (Silvanus). Silas is first mentioned in Acts wherein he is sent as a delegate (with Paul, Barnabas, and Judas Barsabbas) from the Jerusalem church to report to the church at Antioch the results of the Jerusalem conference (Acts 15:22-35). Judas and Silas, named as "prophets," are said to have "encouraged and strengthened" the believers there (v. 32) before departing, leaving Paul and Barnabas in Antioch. After Paul's split with Barnabas, Silas becomes one of Paul's missionary companions (Acts 15:40–18:5). He is imprisoned with Paul in Philippi for exorcising a slave girl; while praying and singing in prison, their bonds are loosened by an earthquake (16:16-28), and they are released after Paul identifies them as Roman citizens (v. 37; cf 1 Thess 2:1-2). Silas accompanies Paul to Thessalonica, where Paul's preaching creates an uproar; they then travel to Beroea, where Silas stays behind with Timothy when Paul departs (17:1-15). Silas and Timothy rejoin Paul in Corinth (Acts 18:5) for an extended sojourn (2 Cor 1:19). After Paul's departure from Corinth, Silas remains behind and this apparently brings to an end their missionary work together. Before departing Paul's company, Silas coauthors 1 and 2 Thessalonians (1 Thess 1:1; 2 Thess 1:1) with Paul and Timothy. First Peter also mentions Silvanus as perhaps the secretary (amanuensis) of the letter (5:12). See PAUL, THE APOSTLE; PETER, THE APOSTLE.

SILK Developed in ancient China, silk is a luxury fiber made from the cocoons of a moth. Unlike wool and cotton, silk was little known in the biblical world. Only in Rev 18:12 is there a clear reference to silk, where it appears in a list of luxury items.

SILLA Mentioned only at 2 Kgs 12:20 [Heb. 12:21] as a place relative to Beth-millo. Its precise location, as well as its significance, is unknown. Silla may have been a landmark or district located east-southeast down the slope of David's City in the Kidron Valley.

SILOAM A water reservoir or pool in the southeast corner of ancient Jerusalem that is fed by the Gihon ("Gushing") Spring, later known as the Virgin's Fountain (see GIHON SPRING). The name seems to be derived from a Hebrew term meaning "aqueduct" or "(water) channel."

In NT times, a "pool of Siloam" was a popular feature in Jerusalem. It may have been in this large pool that Jesus told a blind man to immerse himself (John 9:7, 11). Luke 13:4 refers to an otherwise unknown incident in which eighteen people "were killed when the tower of Siloam fell on them." It is reasonable to consider this tower as an architectural feature associated with the pool.

SILVER Silver appears in the Bible in two basic meanings: as a precious metal and as currency. As a precious metal it ranks in value just below gold: GOLD and silver (and sometimes BRONZE) are usually mentioned together to denominate wealth. In general, silver was used for the vessels in the temple and in the palaces of the kings.

Gods and idols were often made of silver and gold, or at least plated with it (Exod 20:23; Isa 2:20; 40:19). Refining of silver with lead was a common metaphor for spiritual purification in the OT (Jer 6:29-30).

The most common use of silver was probably for JEWELRY. Silver jewelry is regularly mentioned in the Bible. It was worn by both men and women, but it seems to have been more common for women as earrings, rings, bracelets, armlets, pendants, and beads.

Silver was also the most common currency in the biblical period. The Bible contains numerous references expressing the value of various items in weight units of silver. Common units are the gerah (.416 grams), the shekel (20 gerahs), the mana (50 shekels), and the talent (3,000 shekels). Abraham bought the field with the cave of Machpelah for 400 shekels of silver. The hill of Samaria, on which Omri built his capital, was bought for two talents of silver; in the days of Solomon an Egyptian chariot cost 600 shekels of silver, and a horse 150.

In the Persian period coins became more common as a means of payment. Silver coins from the Hellenistic and Roman periods are common all over Palestine.

SIMEON, SIMEONITES Simeon is a personal name that occurs in both the OT and the NT.

1. The most common usage of the name in the OT is to designate the tribe of Simeon. According to Gen 29:33, Simeon is the 2nd son born to JACOB and LEAH. Genesis 29:31-35 lists the birth of Jacob's and Leah's first four sons: Reuben, Simeon, Levi, and Judah. The births of two additional sons, Issachar and Zebulun, and one daughter, Dinah, are recorded in Gen 30:16-21 (see also Gen 35:23).

2. Ezra 10:31 refers to a man named Simeon son of Harim in a list of inhabitants of Jerusalem who had taken foreign wives.

3. Luke 2:25-35 contains the account of an otherwise unknown man named Simeon, described as a "righteous and devout" man who "eagerly anticipated the restoration of Israel." He blessed Mary and Joseph, and pronounced a prophecy concerning Jesus (vv. 34-35).

4. Luke 3:30 lists Simeon son of Judah in the genealogy of Jesus.

5. A certain Simeon is listed among the "prophets and teachers" in the

church at Antioch in Acts 13:1. He may have been of African origin. He was one of the five leaders who helped commission Barnabas and Paul for their first mission (13:1-3).

6. Simeon, rather than the standard Simon, is used as a designation for Peter in the context of James's speech at the council held in Jerusalem and reported in Acts 15:14. The only other time Peter is referred to as Simeon occurs in 2 Pet 1:1 in Codices Sinaiticus and Alexandrinus.

7. In 1 Macc 2:1, a Simeon is the grandfather of Mattathias.

SIMEON BEN ELEAZAR BEN SIRA The author of SIRACH as named in the early Hebrew manuscripts, although the CEB, following the Greek, names the author "Jesus, Sirach's son and grandson of Eleazar the Jerusalemite" (Sir 50:27).

SIMON Simon is the Greek form of the Hebrew name Shimeon. Several Simons are mentioned in the Bible.

1. Simon Chosamaeus was one of the men in Jerusalem who sent away their foreign wives and children in keeping with Ezra's purity law (1 Esdr 9:32).

2. Simon II the high priest (d. 198 BCE), son of Onias II, was remembered for repairing the temple and restoring its service (Sir 50:1-21).

3. Simon the Benjaminite, captain of the temple, falsely accused Onias III, the high priest, of embezzlement.

4. Simon Peter, son of Jonah (or John) and brother of Andrew, was a fisherman from Bethsaida (Matt 16:17; John 1:40-44) who became a leading disciple of Jesus and was named "Peter" (see PETER, THE APOSTLE).

5. Simon the Zealot, another disciple of Jesus (Luke 6:15), was so called either because he was enthusiastic in religious piety or because he was once associated with the resistant forces against the Roman rule in Palestine.

6. Simon Iscariot was father of Judas, the disciple who betrayed Jesus (John 6:71; 13:2, 26).

7. Simon the brother of Jesus was mentioned when Jesus was rejected by his hometown people in Nazareth who knew his family (Mark 6:3; Matt 13:55).

8. Simon the Pharisee regarded Jesus as a prophet and invited him to his house for dinner, where a woman came uninvited to wash Jesus' feet with tears, dry them with her hair, and anoint them with ointment (Luke 7:36-50).

9. Simon was a friend of Jesus in Bethany. In a dinner in his house, Jesus was anointed on the head with ointment of nard by an unnamed woman (Mark 14:3-9). This Simon was once healed by Jesus of a skin disease.

10. Simon of Cyrene was a passerby compelled by Roman soldiers to carry Jesus' cross as he was taken to Golgotha for execution (Mark 15:21; Matt 27:32; Luke 23:26). He might have been a Jew from Cyrene, the capital city of Cyrenaica in North Africa. He was the father of Alexander and Rufus (Mark 15:21) who seemed to be well known to Paul and the church in Rome (Rom 16:13).

11. Simon the tanner lived in Joppa. Peter stayed in his house (Acts 9:43) and, while praying on the rooftop, saw the vision of the unclean animals in a large sheet and heard the voice from heaven saying, "Never consider unclean what God has made pure" (Acts 10:15; see TANNER, TANNING).

12. Simon the Maccabee was the last of the Maccabee brothers (see HASMONEANS) to lead Judah during its struggle for independence in the 2nd cent. BCE. He acted as general and second in command under his brother Jonathan (see JONATHAN). When Jonathan was taken captive and executed by Tryphon ca. 143 BCE, Simon took over leadership; he was now the 3rd of the Maccabean brothers to become leader of the Hasmonean movement.

13. Simon was a popular practitioner of magical arts in Samaria encountered by Philip the evangelist and the apostle Peter in Acts 8:9.

SIN, SINNERS Israel's prophets, poets, priests, storytellers, wisdom teachers, and lawgivers reflected on sin in a variety of ways. Early Christian heirs of Israel continued that reflection on sin in the light of their experience of God's action in Christ.

The OT uses a variety of terms to label harmful or rejected behavior, and to refer to those who engage in it. It also offers an array of means for dealing with the problems caused by such behavior. It may be possible to offer a simple definition of *sin* as "behavior that offends God and impairs relationship with the divine," but such a definition may oversimplify the complex range of evildoing, its effects and its remedies. Related terms include *transgression*, *iniquity*, *missing the mark*, *disobedience*, *infidelity* (to God), *rebellion*, and *evil*.

One of the earliest strata of the Pentateuch's legal material, the Covenant Code of Exod 20:22–23:9, consists largely of case law with a strong focus on social relations. Within the code itself, the actions condemned are not explicitly labeled with one of the many words for sin and the category is not an organizing principle of this compilation. Insofar as there are remedies for sin in the Covenant Code, they are also part of the ruptured social realm. Remedies include restitution or compensation (Exod 21:19, 22, 30-32; 22:1-14) and punishment (20:20), including capital punishment (21:15-17; 22:18-20). The framing story of the divine revelation on Mount Sinai implicitly describes infractions of the code as sin, since the purpose of the revelation is to instill in Israel a fear of committing sin (20:20). That frame, with the Decalogue (Exod 20:2-17; cf Deut 5:1-22), provides the categories that will define the general contours of sin for Jewish and Christian traditions: idolatry, profanation of the divine name, infringement of the Sabbath (a capital offense: Exod 31:14; 35:2; Num 15:32-36), disobedience to parents, murder, adultery, theft, false witnessing, and covetousness.

The Priestly tradition devotes elaborate attention to sin and what may be done about it through the mechanism of cult. There are tensions in the regulations, and the cultic system certainly developed over time. Leviticus highlights two major types of sacrifice: the sacrifice for sin and the guilt sacrifice. The regulations for the former specify that it is offered to affect reconciliation for unintentional inadvertent sins of priests, rulers, or people in general (a similar restriction on the limits of cultic reconciliation appears at Num 15:22-31). The examples of sins given in Lev 5:1-4 include matters of both ritual purity and behavior. Uncleanness arising from both touching a corpse (v. 2) and touching some human substance (semen, menstrual blood are probably in view, v. 3; cf Lev 15) are easily understood as inadvertent infringements of purity codes. Failing to testify when there has been a public adjuration to do so (v. 1), or uttering aloud a rash oath (v. 4) involve behavioral matters. In all such cases, confession of the sin accompanies the offering of an appropriate sacrifice, depending on one's means (sheep, goat [v. 6]; two doves or pigeons [v. 7]; one-tenth of an ephah of flour [v. 11]).

Prophetic literature focuses on social and economic evils, denouncing the oppression of the poor, and also identifies sin as a lack of faithfulness to Israel's God. The prophets also call for repentance and, while threatening divine judgment, hold out hope for restoration. The psalms offer eloquent expression to the attempts to wrestle with sin, and echo the calls for confession and repentance found in the prophets and historians.

The traditions about the teachings of Jesus found in the Synoptic Gospels display traditional understandings of sin. The accounts of John the Baptist suggest the ethos of the revival movement out of which Jesus emerged. In view of impending divine judgment, John called for repentance and baptism, understood to be for the forgiveness of sins (Mark 1:4; Luke 3:3; cf Mark 1:5; Matt 3:6). While he reportedly preached honesty (Luke 3:7-14), John denounced the sinful character of the religious leaders of his generation, calling them "children of snakes" (Matt 3:7; Luke 3:7). A major focus of his critique was the tetrarch Herod Antipas and his marriage to his brother's wife, which led to his arrest and execution (Matt 14:1-12; Mark 6:14-29; Luke 9:7-9; cf Mal 2:15-16).

The ministry of Jesus is understood by the Evangelists to involve salvation from sin (Matt 1:21; John 1:29). As the Human One he claimed have power to forgive sin a claim contested by his adversaries as blasphemous (Matt 9:6; Mark 2:1-12; Luke 5:17-26). Jesus himself seems to have welcomed people conventionally considered to be sinners and developed a reputation as their friend (Matt 9:10-13; 11:19; Mark 2:13-17; Luke 5:27-32; 7:34). He is portrayed as admonishing those whom he heals not to sin again (John 5:14).

Three of the most probing theologians of the NT explore the theme of sin and its remedies. Paul offers the most complex treatment of sin, its pervasive reality, and its effects. Not all of his writing is on that level of reflection. He can at times reproduce simple lists of vices and sinful behavior from which his converts have been liberated (Rom 1:29-31), or from which he warns them (Rom 13:13; 1 Cor 5:2-11; 6:9-10; 2 Cor 12:20-21; Gal 5:19-21). Such lists, mirroring concerns of Hellenistic moralists, focus more on personal moral behavior than on prophetic denunciations of social sin. The Galatians list, for example, notes that "the actions that are produced by selfish motives are obvious, since they include sexual immorality, moral corruption, doing whatever feels good, idolatry, drug use and casting spells, hate, fighting, obsession, losing your temper, competitive opposition, conflict, selfishness, group rivalry, jealousy , drunkenness, partying, and other things like that." Paul's most reflective letter, Romans, offers the most elaborate treatment of sin. The letter's overarching goal is to explain to the Roman community Paul's understanding of the Law and Israel in God's plan for humankind. His first move is to insist on the universal reality of sin (Rom 1–3), which God's action in the sacrifice of Christ was designed to counter (Rom 3:25-26). In developing this theme, Paul uses the testimony of the psalms (Pss 14:1-3; 53:1-3 at Rom 3:10-18), as well as imaginative personification and lively dialogue. In the process, following in the footsteps of the prophetic tradition, and Hellenistic Jewish literature such as Wis 13–15, he identifies the fundamental sin as idolatry, from which all other sins flow. Among these Paul features prominently the sin of same-sex intercourse, echoing the taboos of Leviticus (Rom 1:26-27; cf Lev 18:22; 20:13). Of even greater prominence in the diatribe is the act of hypocritical judgment (Rom 2:17–3:8) by those who would share the basic perspective of Paul's analysis. Whatever the particulars of individual sins, Paul, citing texts from the psalms (Rom 3:9-18, including Pss 5:9; 10:7; 14:1-3; 53:1-3; 140:3), summarizes his sketch of the unredeemed human condition as one in which sin is universal and all, Jew and Gentile alike, "fall short of God's glory" (3:23).

Against that universal reality of sin, Paul, probably drawing on a traditional formula, suggests that God has provided relief through Christ, whose death is imaged as a sacrificial offering that expiates or makes reconciliation for sin.

Paul alludes elsewhere to the Christ event in terms of its effects on sin, although in each case without fully developing the theme. Thus, in 2 Corinthians, while celebrating his ministry as a continuation of God's work in Christ, he describes the process of reconciliation: "God caused the one who didn't know sin to be sin for our sakes so that through him we could become the righteousness of God" (2 Cor 5:21). Paul may have in mind the notion of the scapegoat of Lev 16, or a simple identification of the death of Christ as a "compensation offering" for sin (Lev 5), but the point is the same. God has effectively dealt with the reality of sin in order to liberate and empower those who are now "in Christ."

Paul in Romans continues his reflection on sin and its power through a meditation on the sin of the first human being. In a passage influential for Christian notions of original sin, Paul notes that as Adam sinned, so, by imitation, did all who have descended from Adam (Rom 6:12).

Examination of sin's universal power reaches its climax in Paul's attempt in Rom 7 to explain how he can recognize the Law as holy and good and, at the same time, claim that it does not provide a vehicle for a saving relationship with God. The answer, he argues, is in the fundamental character of human nature, "the flesh," which is beset by the force of passionate desire that overcomes the rational recognition of what is right. Paul's argument moves through two stages. In the first, using a fictive "I" to describe the experience, he evokes the scriptural command not to covet (7:7). Paul's adopted persona may be that of the primordial pair Adam and Eve, whose response to the divine prohibition Paul evokes. Using that persona, Paul suggests a psychological insight, that prohibitions, far from preventing negative behavior, can actually stimulate it.

The 2nd stage of Paul's argument probably owes much to Greco-Roman discussions of weakness of the will. In language echoing poetic archetypes, Paul describes a self divided between the good that the mind acknowledges and the evil that the will pursues (Rom 7:16-20). Against such a force, he claims, God's Law is powerless.

Paul's answer to this predicament is the result of Christ's death and resurrection, a new life mediated through baptism, in which the believer becomes identified with Christ (cf Rom 6:1-11). That identification makes possible life "in the spirit," which transforms the self, making it "dead to sin" (6:11; 8:10), and enables the appropriate alignment of mind and heart, spirit and will. All of this may be inspired by the hopes for interior transformation expressed by Jeremiah and Ezekiel. Paul celebrates that eschatological transformation in the following chapter (8:1-17), while recognizing that it is still a work in progress (8:18-30). The condition of sinful humanity has not been obliterated by the life of the spirit, which lives within believers and "is groaning" (8:22) with the faithful in expectation of the completion of the process of renewal.

The Johannine corpus offers a fundamental reinterpretation of the category of sin. The theme first appears when John the Baptist identifies Jesus as the Lamb of God who takes away the sins of the world (John 1:29). The proclamation foreshadows the crucifixion, particularly John 19:36, where a scriptural citation, Exod 12:46, identifies Jesus as the paschal lamb. The identification already presumes a development in the understanding of the function of the sacrifice of Passover, which initially was simply an apotropaic symbol to ward off the angel of death. The requirement that blood be smeared on the lintels and doorposts of Israelite residences perhaps absorbed connotations of cleansing from rituals such as that of Yom Kippur (Lev 16:16, 19), and popular tradition may have assimilated the Passover sacrifice to sacrifices for sin. Such traditions, as well as the interpretation of the death of Jesus as a Passover sacrifice, attested in 1 Cor 5:7, was certainly a Christian tradition before the composition of the 4th Gospel.

As it does with other traditions, the 4th Gospel probes the affirmation for its deeper meaning, although sin generally plays a limited role in John. It is an issue in the interpolated pericope of the adulteress (John 8:1-12), in some polemical remarks about Jesus and sin (8:21, 34, 45), in discussion of the status of the man born blind (9:2, 34, 41) or the sinfulness of his opponents (15:22, 24), and in the prediction that the Paraclete, the Holy Spirit, would come to convict the world of sin (16:8-9). The last remark is significant for the way in which the Gospel ultimately treats the issue of sin.

The 3rd major theological reflection on sin in the pages of the NT appears in the Epistle to the Hebrews, which exhibits structural similarities and thematic differences from Paul and John. In the process of exhorting to renewed fidelity a community in danger of slipping away from commitment to Christ (Heb 2:1), this anonymous author offers a bold reinterpretation of the significance of Christ's death. That reinterpretation builds on the kind of cultic understanding of that death evident in the traditional formula found in Rom 3:25-26. Here, however, there is no doubt about the derivation of the interpretive framework. The author of Hebrews portrays the death of Christ as the ultimate Yom Kippur sacrifice, designed to affect lasting and effective reconciliation for sin (Heb 8–10). The development of the theme exhibits a polemical edge, in its rhetorical contrast of between the "old" and the "new." The Yom Kippur sacrifice of the meeting tent involved the "blood of goats and bulls" (9:13), and could effect only a superficial cleansing and not the elimination of sin. Lurking behind this critique may be both prophetic charges against the superficiality of cultic sacrifice and contemporary rationalistic critiques of religious practice. In any case, the true sacrifice of Christ, consummated in the "greater and more perfect meeting tent" (9:11), not with animal blood but "by his own blood" (9:14), has the effect of cleansing "consciences" (9:14) from sin, and thereby "he perfected the people who are being made holy with one offering for all time" (10:14). Sin, therefore, is implicitly understood to be what weighs on the conscience, a category then receiving significant attention among Hellenistic moralists.

SIN DESERT The Sin desert (not to be confused with the ZIN DESERT). is mentioned four times as part of the exodus itinerary (Exod 16:1; 17:1; Num 33:11-12). The Israelites' complaints about food shortages result in the appearance of manna and quail in the desert.

SINAI, MOUNT Mount Sinai is the mountain in the wilderness at which God appeared to the Israelites and gave them laws and a covenant on their way from Egypt to the land of promise of Canaan in the books of Exodus, Leviticus, and Numbers.

SINAI PENINSULA The Sinai Peninsula is a large triangular desert region that lies east of ancient Egypt and south of Canaan. The Mediterranean coastal plain in the northern part of the peninsula formed a land bridge that connected northern Africa with southwest Asia, providing a major trade route between Egypt and other nations of the ANE.

See SINAI, MOUNT.

SINITES Designation for a people group and a geographic region. The Sinites are mentioned in the Table of Nations (Gen 10:17; 1 Chron 1:15) among the eleven peoples descending from Canaan—all are situated in Asia Minor, the northern Levant, and the southern Levant.

SIRACH This long wisdom writing (sometimes called Ecclesiasticus) was composed in Hebrew in Jerusalem by a scribe named Ben Sira in the early 2nd cent. BCE. Because it was included in the SEPTUAGINT but excluded from the rabbinic canon, it is classed as one of the Apocrypha books. The work combines theological and practical teaching on many topics, ranging from the fear of

God and divine retribution, to friendship and conduct at banquets.

SIRAH, WELL AT The cistern of Sirah was a well that Josephus locates north of Hebron (*Ant.* 7.34). ABNER went there when David dismissed him after a raid, and the messengers of JOAB retrieved Abner at the cistern and took him back to Hebron, where Joab killed him (2 Sam 3:26).

SIRION The Sidonian (i.e., Phoenician) name for Mount Hermon (Deut 3:9; see HERMON, MOUNT).

SISERA Sisera, the general of the Canaanite king Jabin's army, appears in Judg 4 and 5. Judges 4 offers a narrative account of the same events recorded in Judg 5 in poetic form. According to Judg 4:3, Sisera had cruelly oppressed the Israelites for twenty years before he met his match in Jael the wife of Heber the Kenite.

SISINNES Governor of Coele-Syria and Phoenicia (1 Esdr 7:1) who objected to Darius about the Jews' rebuilding of the temple (1 Esdr 6:3, 7). When a search of the royal archives yielded the decree from Cyrus, Darius ordered Sisinnes to comply and reconstruction resumed (1 Esdr 6:27).

SISMAI Of the tribe of Judah, he was son of Eleasah and father of Shallum (1 Chron 2:40).

SITHRI The genealogy in Exod 6:14-25 lists Sithri as a great-grandson of Levi and grandson of Kohath (v. 22). His father Uzziel was the brother of Amram, the father of Moses, Aaron, and Miriam, and thus Sithri was their cousin.

SITNAH Second of three wells dug by Isaac's servants in the valley of Gerar (Gen 26:21). The herders of Gerar feuded with Isaac's herders over the water rights, so the well was named Sitnah ("accusation").

SIX HUNDRED SIXTY-SIX The number of the beast (Rev 13:18). Over the centuries popular interpreters have identified countless persons and institutions with this eschatological mystery, but two lines of interpretation have won endorsements from critical interpreters. A symbolic interpretation posits that 666 conveys an emphatic sense of imperfection. In Revelation, seven frequently indicates perfection, so the repetition of "six" could imply absolute corruption; however, the only other occurrence of "six" reveals the number of wings on the four living creatures (Rev 4:8; cf Isa 6:2), hardly suggesting imperfection.

A 2nd line of interpretation emphasizes 666 as the number of a person, as Revelation dares its audience to "calculate" the riddle. One theory identifies this person as the emperor Nero. In Hebrew *gematria* (numerical symbolism), the value of the name Nero is 666. This interpretation is extremely complicated, suggesting that Revelation takes the less common Hebrew form of a Latin name, calculates its value, then presents the riddle in Greek.

SLAVERY Slavery is not simply owning a human being as property (chattel), the equivalent of forced labor, the denial of civil rights, or the loss of freedom. Its distinctiveness lies in the permanent and violent domination of persons alienated from birth who live in a general state of dishonor. This preliminary definition from historical sociology offers a useful model of slavery as "social death."

In the OT, the Hebrews experienced slavery in Egypt, and this is the consistent framework for understanding the limits to be placed on slavery. Slavery was usually the result of a debt and was rarely related to race. The Roman Empire in the NT used slaves gathered from conquest throughout the known world, and slaves were common in all levels of the economy and society. Paul frequently uses slavery as a metaphor, calling himself a "slave of Christ Jesus," an apostolic designation (Rom 1:1; Phil 1:1; Gal 1:10; see 1 Cor 9:16-18), and "a slave to all people," a commonplace trope of servant leadership (1 Cor 9:19-23; see 2 Cor 4:5).

SLEDGE, THRESHING A machine pulled by animals over grain many times until the grain was separated from the stalks. It consisted of wooden planks into which sharp stones or metal had been inserted into holes underneath to facilitate the separating process (Isa 28:27; "threshing boards" [2 Sam 24:22]; "threshing tool" [Isa 41:15]). See THRESHING.

SLIME The secreted mucus of an animal, such as a snail. In Ps 58:8 [Heb. 58:9], the psalmist, imagining that snails "dissolve" into slime, uses the image to express the hope that the wicked will perish. See SNAILS.

SLING Among the many ANE implements of warfare, the sling was considered one of the most important "long-range" weapons, 2nd only to the bow and arrow. The sling was composed of two thongs, usually leather, and the "pouch," in which the projectile was placed (1 Sam 25:29). The sling was used primarily for military purposes, but also for hunting, with a potential for great accuracy (Judg 20:16). The sling is well attested both in biblical and extrabiblical literature, but is not mentioned in the NT.

SMYRNA Smyrna, the modern city of Izmir, Turkey, was at the foot of Mount Pagros at the mouth of the Melas River on the southern shore of the Gulf of Izmir. It is mentioned in Rev 1:11 and 2:8-11. Smyrna was an independent and powerful city under Roman rule.

SNAILS The Hebrew word translated "snail" is related to a word meaning "fluid." The name may refer to the creature's high moisture content, the wet trail it leaves behind, and its propensity to melt away. In Ps 58:8, the psalmist wishes that her or his enemies would disappear "like the snail that dissolves into slime." This context seems to describe the gastropod mollusk we call "snail" but could perhaps indicate a slug or worm. Snail shells were widely used in the ANE as a source of purple dye.

SNOW With the exception of Mount Hermon in the north, modern-day Israel does not experience snow on an annual basis. Occasionally, however, snow does fall on other mountainous regions, including the hills of Jerusalem. Psalm 147:16 acknowledges its presence in the environs of Jerusalem as one of the provisions of the Lord. Elsewhere, snow epitomizes spiritual purity and exemplifies the color white. Thus, Isa 1:18 and Ps 51:7 utilize snow to illustrate the state of cleanness that results from the removal of sin's stain.

SO The pharaoh whom King Hosea of Israel asked for assistance against Shalmaneser of Assyria a few years before the destruction of Israel in 721 BCE (2 Kgs 17:4). King So is likely Pharaoh Osorkon IV, the last king of the 23rd Dynasty, who ruled Egypt until 724 BCE.

SOAP A cleansing agent, usually symbolizing moral or spiritual purification. For example, Mal 3:2 describes the refinement of the Levites by God's messenger, who is compared to a cleaner's soap. Jeremiah portrays Judah's iniquities as unable to be cleansed with soap (Jer 2:22).

SOCO, SOCOH 1. A descendant of Judah (1 Chron 4:18), perhaps the person for whom the town of Socoh was named.

2. A town in Judah, according to Josh 15:35, where it is listed with Jarmuth, Adullam, and Azekah (1 Sam 17:1-3; 2 Chron 11:17; 28:18).

3. A town by the same name mentioned in Josh 15:48 is located in the 5th district of Judah together with the sites

Shamir, Jattir, and Dannah and identified with Khirbet Shuweikah southwest of Hebron.

4. A town in the central highlands cited as the center of Solomon's 3rd district (1 Kgs 4:10) is generally identified with Shuweiket er-Ras near the pass leading to Shechem.

SODI From the tribe of Zebulun, the father of Gaddiel, whom Moses charged with the task of scouting Canaan to determine its fruitfulness and the strength of its inhabitants (Num 13:10).

SODOM, SODOMITE Sodom is first mentioned in the list of nations in Gen 10:1-32. It appears in a geographical description of Canaan (10:19) and as the land of the cursed descendants of Noah's son Ham, the Canaanites (9:22-27). One boundary extends to the southeast in the direction of "Lasha," as far as, but not including, "Sodom, Gomorrah, Admah, and Zeboiim" (10:19; cf Gen 13:10, 12-13; 14:2, 8). These four cities, with a 5th, "Bela," later called "Zoar" (13:10; 14:2, 8; 19:22-23, 30), form a region known collectively as the "cities of the valley" (Gen 13:12).

These cities play an important role in the Abraham cycle in Genesis, effectively offering the patriarch an alternative mode of existence to that which he is to bequeath to his descendants. They are notable for their attractiveness (to Lot and to later Israelites), their proverbial wickedness (as homes to every sin), and their deserved destruction (an ever-present threat to an "evil and sinful" people of God [Gen 13:13]). In subsequent texts, the cities (in different combinations) will reappear as exemplars to be shunned.

SOLEMN ASSEMBLY Also known as a "holy occasion" "holiday," or "celebration," a special cultic period of repentance, often lasting seven or eight days (Exod 12:16; Lev 23; Num 28:18, 25-26; 29:1, 7, 12, 35; Deut 16:8; 2 Chron 7:9; and Neh 8:18). Isaiah 1:13 and Amos 5:21 employ expressions of divine displeasure over the nation's assemblies when accompanied by iniquity or absent of justice.

SOLOMON The 3rd monarch of Israel and son of David, Solomon reigned, according to the Bible, in the mid-10th cent. BCE, and was a main character of 1 Kings and 2 Chronicles. The biblical stories about Solomon emphasize his connections with the building of the Jerusalem temple, and his efforts at centralizing political power in the monarchy. While the historicity of some of the stories about him is debatable, it seems clear that his reign marked a transition in the development of Israelite political life.

SOLOMON'S PORCH The court of Herod's temple was surrounded by colonnaded porches or porticoes. Tradition attributed the eastern porch to Solomon (Josephus, *Ant.* 20.221). While the line of the eastern porch may follow that of Solomon's temple mount and some of its foundations may date back to Nehemiah, Herod the Great probably built the porch.

Jesus identified himself as the Messiah while walking in Solomon's Porch (John 10:22-29). The early followers of Jesus worshipped in the temple (Luke 24:52-53), and according to Luke the apostles met regularly in Solomon's Porch in executive council (Acts 3:11; 5:12). See JERUSALEM; TEMPLE, JERUSALEM.

SON OF DAVID In the OT, the phrase "David's son" primarily refers to SOLOMON (2 Chron 1:1; 13:6; 35:3; Prov 1:1; cf Eccl 1:1) or a descendant of DAVID (2 Chron 11:18; cf Matt 1:20; Luke 3:31). It subsequently became a title referring to the royal Messiah, stemming from the promise God made to David regarding the eternal reign of David's offspring (2 Sam 7:12-16; see MESSIAH, JEWISH).

In the NT, the title "Son of David" is applied to Jesus, exclusively in the Synoptic Gospels (e.g., Matt 1:1; 9:27; 12:23; 20:30-31; see also Luke 1:32; John 7:42; Rom 1:3). Jesus never explicitly claimed to be the Son of David, perhaps because of the nationalistic and militaristic overtones. The title refers to Jesus' earthly life and is subordinated to other christological titles, especially "CHRIST" and "GOD'S SON."

SON OF GOD See GOD'S SON.

SON OF MAN See HUMAN ONE.

SONG OF SONGS is the original love poem in the Western literary tradition. Love poetry was also a common staple of the ANE literary tradition, with fine exemplars from Mesopotamia and Egypt in particular. The dating of the Song itself remains debated. The only truly tractable datum is the language of these poems, and on present evidence it appears to be a variety of late biblical Hebrew, most likely originating sometime between the late 4th and early 2nd cent. BCE. The initial line (or *incipit*) of the Song is most often construed as assigning authorship to Solomon—"the Song of Songs, which is Solomon's." If so (the syntax of the Hebrew may be interpreted in other ways as well) it is of this latter kind of attribution, since the late date of the language alone makes genuine Solomonic authorship unlikely—neither is Solomon a speaker, subject, or center of interest in any of these poems.

SONS OF THUNDER See BOANERGES.

SOPATER Sopater, the son of PYRRHUS, was a companion of Paul, mentioned in Acts 20:4 as traveling with Paul from Greece back to MACEDONIA. His name—meaning "savior of his father"—indicates that Sopater introduced his father to Christianity. Sopater may be the same as SOSIPATER (Rom 16:21).

SOPHERETH Means "scribe." Head of a family of temple servants who returned from the Babylonian exile with Zerubbabel and Jeshua ("Hassophereth" [Ezra 2:55]; Neh 7:57; 1 Esdr 5:33).

SOPHIA Wisdom, personified as a woman, is an important, if somewhat puzzling, construct in the OT. There, "Wisdom" is grammatically feminine in gender, as are most abstract concepts in the Hebrew language. One must distinguish whether the text is referring to Woman Wisdom, the character and patron of the sages, or the overall concept of knowledge, learning, and skill. Within Proverbs and elsewhere, both uses are found: at times, Woman Wisdom is speaking to those who scorn her, love her, or might be advised to seek her (Prov 1:20-33; 3:19; 8:1-36; 9:1-6); in other places, the skill of the specially trained is meant (Exod 28:3; 31:3; 35:31; 1 Kgs 2:6; 4:29-34 [Heb. 5:9-14]; Prov 14:8; Isa 29:14).

SOREK VALLEY The sole biblical reference to this valley comes in the description of Samson's love for Delilah, who resided there (Judg 16:4). "Sorek" primarily refers to a relatively broad valley approximately 13 mi. west of Jerusalem, principally running between the towns of Zorah and Timnah. Since Samson was born in Zorah, he too is from this Sorek area (Judg 13). The tribe of Dan migrated out of the Sorek Valley to Laish (Judg 18).

SOSIPATER 1. A general under Judas Maccabeus in his battle against Timothy's army (2 Macc 12:19, 24).

2. One of the persons from whom Paul sends greetings to the Christians in Rome. Paul describes Sosipater as his relative or compatriot, along with Lucius and Jason (Rom 16:21). He is often considered to be the same person as Sopater in Acts 20:4.

SOSTHENES 1. The ruler of the

synagogue in Acts 18:12-17 who initiated charges against Paul.

2. In 1 Cor 1:1, Sosthenes is included in Paul's greeting as cosender of the letter. Some argue that Sosthenes was Paul's scribe.

SOTAI Head of a family of SOLOMON's servants, who returned from the exile to Jerusalem with Zerubbabel (Ezra 2:55; Neh 7:57).

SOUL For much of the Christian tradition, *soul* has referred to the spiritual part of a human distinct from the physical or as an ontologically separate entity constitutive of the human person. However, the biblical sources almost unanimously depict the human as a single unified being, not as split between body and soul.

SOW, SOWER In the OT, sowing is not merely the planting of crops. Sowing defines the parameters of Israel's covenant relationship with God. As a result, the law lists several restrictions about the sowing or planting of seed including: when, what kind, and how often (Exod 23:10; Lev 19:19; 25:11, 22; Deut 22:9). The connection between God and farming is emphasized by the number of times that the sowing of seed is either blessed or cursed depending on Israel's faithfulness to God (Ps 107:37; Isa 30:23; 55:10; Mic 6:15; cf Isa 19:7; Jer 50:16).

In the NT, the imagery is used either metaphorically or as part of a parable. Paul reiterates the OT aphorism that a person reaps what was sown (Gal 6:7-8). Sometimes he describes his ministry through the imagery of sowing (1 Cor 3:6-8; 9:11). More significant, however, is Paul's adaptation of sowing imagery to describe the resurrection. The picture of sowing a seed is correlated with the death and burial of the human body. Just as a seed is buried and brings forth a crop greater than the original seed, so too the resurrected body will be greater than the former (1 Cor 15:36-44; cf John 12:24). Paul uses sowing imagery when encouraging the Corinthians to give generously toward the Jerusalem offering. Although they are not under compulsion, Paul reminds them that God loves a generous giver and will reward them according to the amount they have sown (2 Cor 9:6-10).

SPARROW In the NT period, sparrows were sold in great amounts and at very low prices in the market places. The saying in Matt 10:29-31 and Luke 12:6-7, where Jesus underlines God's care for each sparrow, should be understood against that background.

SPICE Given the pungent odors that permeated human dwellings and cities, it is not surprising that the ancient world put a high premium on fragrant spices that could mask the smells associated with both life and death. Some of these products (BALM, CUMIN, dill, MINT) could be obtained in Israel, but the more exotic formed a lucrative portion of the caravan trade throughout the ANE (ALOES from southwest Arabia, calamus from Asia, cinnamon from Sri Lanka). For example, when the Queen of Sheba visited Solomon, her camels were laden with valuable presents including an unheard-of quantity of spices (1 Kgs 10:2, 10). Trading networks are mentioned in the lament for Babylon in Rev 18:13, which describes vast commercial interests that trafficked in cinnamon, spices, and incense as well as ivory, grain, and slaves (cf the lament for Tyre's trading network in Ezek 27:22). The high value attached to spices is demonstrated by Hezekiah's boasting display of his storehouses for the envoy sent by the Babylonian king Merodach-baladan, which featured among his most precious possessions a large quantity of spices (2 Kgs 20:13).

SPIES The Bible primarily describes spies in an official, military context where they are sent out to reconnoiter enemy towns prior to a military encounter (Gen 42:9 [Joseph accuses his brothers of being spies]; Josh 2:1 [spies sent into Jericho]) and to track enemy movements (1 Sam 26:4 [David's spies track Saul]; 1 Macc 12:26 [Jonathan's spies watch Demetrius's forces]). Of note are the spy narratives in Num 13:1–14:45 and Josh 2:1-24 (cf Heb 11:31).

Spies are sent by the scribes and chief priests to trap Jesus concerning paying taxes in an effort to hand him over to the civil authorities (Luke 20:20). One should be careful choosing friends because the proud can be like spies (Sir 11:30). Paul says the "false brothers and sisters . . . slipped in to spy on our freedom" (Gal 2:4).

SPIRITUAL GIFTS Spiritual gifts are a characteristic feature of the apostle Paul's theology. The early church in Corinth experienced controversy over these abilities, ranking some of them as better or more spiritual than others and creating a divide among the believers. In response, in 1 Cor 12–14 Paul redefines these abilities as "gifts" given by the Holy Spirit in their midst. Thus, while conceding the spiritual nature of these extravagant abilities, Paul insists that they are free gifts given by God the giver, so that the Corinthians have no ground to boast. In the NT, the term *spiritual gift* occurs only in Paul's letters, in writings influenced by him (1 Tim 4:14; 2 Tim 1:6), and in 1 Pet 4:10.

If the same Spirit stands behind all forms of power, then these are nothing more than manifestation of the one Spirit. As such, they are designed to fulfill the purpose intended by the Spirit—"for the common good" (12:7). Paul contends that everyone has gifts (cf 7:7 and Rom 12:6), even if not everyone has the same gift (12:14-21).

SPONGE A sponge was placed at the end of a stick to transfer sour wine from the ground to the dying Jesus' lips (Matt 27:48; Mark 15:36; John 19:29). This ties Jesus' death to a psalm for help during harassment, where the sufferer is given vinegar to drink by the harassers (Ps 69:21).

SQUAD A group of four Roman soldiers (Acts 12:4).

STACHYS A Christian whom Paul greets in Rom 16:9 as "my dear friend."

STAFF A variety of Hebrew and Greek words with a variety of functions are reflected in the CEB "staff." In some cases (e.g., Zech 8:4; Heb 11:21), a staff is used by the elderly like a cane. Often, however, staffs function as walking sticks (e.g., 1 Sam 14:43). Shepherds used staffs (Mic 7:14) to negotiate difficult terrain, count their sheep (Lev 27:32), and hit their flock to guide them (cf Num 22:27). This image is inverted in Ps 23:4, where the Lord's staff "protect[s]" the individual. Staffs could be highly individualized and recognizable as belonging to a particular person (Gen 38:25).

As an everyday object, the staff, or "shepherd's rod," could be used to perform miracles, as in the case of Moses and Aaron. Moses' staff turned into a snake (Exod 4:1-5), initiated plagues against Egypt, split the Reed Sea (Exod 14:16), and brought forth water from the rock (Num 20:2-13). As such, it is twice called "the shepherd's rod from God" (Exod 4:20; 17:9). This suggests that a prophet's staff had magical powers and explains why Gehazi tried to use his master Elisha's staff to revive a dead child (2 Kgs 4:29-31). Staffs were typically made of dead wood from sturdy trees—hence the miraculous flowering staff of Aaron (Num 17:1-11 [Heb. 17:16-26]; see AARON'S STAFF), and the image of Egypt compared to a "broken reed," which is both weak and sharp (e.g., 2 Kgs 18:21). See ROD.

STAR OF BETHLEHEM In Matt 2:1-12, Magi, Zoroastrian priests, observed this star "in the east" (Matt 2:2). To relate a star to a newborn king in Israel, the star would have to appear in the constellation governing the "land of Israel" (Matt 2:20-21), that is, the Roman province of Syro-Palestine. This constellation was Aries, the springtime constellation, the first-created, celestial Lamb of God. Further, spring marked the onset of the dry season, offering the possibility of night travel.

STEPHANAS Mentioned only in 1 Cor 1:16 and 16:15-18, Paul remembers baptizing Stephanas's household in Corinth but does not recall whether he baptized anyone else there (1 Cor 1:16). While Paul's ministry was not to baptize but to proclaim good news (1 Cor 1:17), the apostle points proudly to Stephanas's household as the "first crop" of his work in Achaia, commending their service to the Corinthian Christians (1 Cor 16:15). According to 1 Cor 16:17, Stephanas, FORTUNATUS, and ACHAICUS had recently visited Paul in Ephesus.

STEPHEN One of the seven Hellenists (Greek-speaking Jews) and the first martyr (Acts 7:60) in Luke's depiction of the early Jesus movement in Jerusalem. As one of the seven (Acts 6:3), Stephen is initially appointed to resolve an internal problem (the neglect of Greek-speaking Jewish widows in the daily distribution of food [6:1]). His work extends, however, beyond "[serving] tables" (6:2) and includes the performance of "great wonders and signs" (6:8), a feat evoking both the work of the apostles in the earlier part of Acts' narrative (2:43; 5:12; cf 4:30) and ultimately that of MOSES (Deut 7:19; 11:3; 28:46; 29:2; cf Stephen's speech [7:36]). Though the narrative does not indicate the reception of Stephen's deeds, the powerful force of his words (6:10) leads to an external problem, because members of the Synagogue of Former Slaves, with whom Stephen had disputed (6:9), bring him before the Jerusalem Council (6:12) on the false charge of blasphemy against Moses and God (6:11), that is, speaking words against "this holy place" (the temple, 6:13-14), the Law (6:13), and the "customary practices" of Moses (6:14). Thereafter, and repeatedly, his words (including a long speech) are met with outright rejection (7:54, 57), with the result that he is stoned to death (7:58), the levitical punishment for blasphemy (Lev 24:16; see STONING), and buried by devout men (8:2).

STOICS, STOICISM A Greek philosophical school named after the colonnades (stoa) at the porch where they met.

The Stoics envisioned the universe as a unified material being, a continuum with active and passive aspects. The Stoics identified God as the active principle that gives structure and purpose to the universe, pictured as a living body governed by reason. The whole world was providentially created for the benefit and use of those endowed with reason. Stoics believed in predetermination, in that the world was designed to be as rational as possible. As rational beings, humans are free at any given moment to accept or resist the will of God as it plays out in the world—much as a dog, tied to a moving cart, can choose whether to walk along willingly or be dragged.

The Stoics accepted the traditional Greek philosophical identification of the basic goal of life as happiness. In Stoicism, though, "happiness" means specifically bringing one's own will into conformity with the will of God, one's own reason into harmony with the "right reason" that providentially governs the world as divine law. The basic aim of Stoic ethics, then, was "living harmoniously" with the providential world-order as it unfolds, or, put another way, living in accord with nature.

The Stoics identified virtue as the consistent and unshakable disposition of the soul characterized by right reason. Vice, conversely, represented the alternative: a soul characterized not by right reason but "passion," which they defined as "excessive impulse" (i.e., an impulse to achieve or avoid some end that goes beyond what right reason dictates).

Acts 17:16-34 places Paul in the Athenian agora, engaged in a stereotypically Athenian activity of philosophical debate with, among others, Epicureans and Stoics (17:18). The significance of Stoicism for the Bible extends well beyond this singular reference in Acts 17. The portrayal of the cosmic figure of Wisdom in the Wisdom of Solomon and other sources owes much to the Stoic notion that the cosmos is pervaded and fashioned by a rational force (e.g., Wis 1:7; 7:22, 24; 8:1, 4-6)—a notion that also stands rather clearly in the background of the Gospel of John (see esp. John 1:1-4).

STONING A type of capital execution via pelting of stones. It typically involved transport of a person outside the camp or the city (Lev 24:14; Deut 17:5), where the person was stoned initially by witnesses of the offense and, if death did not ensue, by onlookers (Deut 17:7). In biblical times, it was one of three types of judicial punishments, the others being burning and hanging. Stoning was exacted as the punishment for several infractions, including idolatry or seduction of others to idolatry (Lev 20:2; Deut 13:6-10); BLASPHEMY (Lev 24:14); and breaking the Sabbath (Num 15:32-36). Both Stephen (Acts 7:58) and Paul (Acts 14:19) were stoned, the former with a fatal end. A woman also escaped a possible stoning by virtue of Jesus' challenges to her accusers (John 8:7). In the Talmud, stoning is listed (with strangling, death by sword [including beheading], and burning) as an appropriate form of capital punishment (e.g., y. Sanh. 22d; 23b–c). Stoning was also prominent among the Persians and the Greeks.

STORK A bird included in the lists of ritually unclean birds (Lev 11:19; Deut 14:18). It is assumed by several modern translations (e.g., CEB) that the stork, famous for its conjugal loyalty, is intended. From the few and fragmentary OT references, this bird is a migrant (Jer 8:7); nests in treetops (Ps 104:17); and has large wings (Zec 5:9). This description applies to the white stork (*Ciconia alba*), but also to the common HERON (*Ardea cinerea*). See BIRDS OF THE BIBLE.

STRANGER Conceptions of stranger in the Bible relate to the differing cultural, sociopolitical, and, to some extent, socioreligious classes among people. The term may also refer to the manner in which a person exists, lives, or resides (e.g., in a city). Other connotations of "stranger" pertain to the avoidance or limitation of association with someone or the lack of kinship relations with another person.

STUMBLE, STUMBLING BLOCK "Stumble" can refer literally to tripping or falling while walking or running, as in Lev 26:37; Job 12:25; Isa 59:10; and Lam 5:13. Metaphorically, money, idols, other people, or even the Lord can cause people to "stumble" (Ezek 3:20; 33:12; Zech 12:8; Matt 11:6; Rev 2:14). Paul instructs believers to avoid putting stumbling blocks before each other (Rom 9:32-33; 11:9; 14:13). A stumbling block might be an obstacle to faith, such as when Peter says Jesus should not suffer (Matt 16:21-23). Jesus is often referred to as a rock or stone that causes stumbling (e.g., Luke 20:17-18, citing Ps 118:22-23, and 1 Pet 2:8, quoting Isa 8:14).

SUAH The first son of ZOPHAH in the lineage of Asher. The name is found only in the military census (1 Chron 7:36).

SUBAS Head of a family descended from Solomon's servants that returned to Jerusalem with Zerubbabel (1 Esdr 5:34).

SUCATHITES One of three families of

scribes, along with the Tirathites and the Shimeathites, who resided in Jabez in Judah (1 Chron 2:55).

SUCCOTH The name of two cities in the OT.

1. A city in the Transjordan near the Jabbok River. Succoth lies on the "way of the plain" (2 Sam 18:23), a north-south road on the east side of the Jordan River. Jacob lived in Succoth after meeting his brother Esau. Succoth fell within the territory given to the Gadites after the conquest (Josh 13:27). When Gideon was pursuing the Midianites, he requested supplies from Succoth but was turned down (Judg 8:4-9).

2. A city or region in the eastern delta of the Nile. Succoth was the first place the Israelites reached during the exodus after they had left the cities of Pithom and RAMESES where they worked (Exod 12:37; Num 33:5).

SUCCOTH-BENOTH A deity worshipped by Babylonian colonists in Samaria after Assyria's resettlement of the territory (2 Kgs 17:30).

SUDIAS A Levite (1 Esdr 5:26), possibly the same as HODAVIAH (Ezra 2:40; 3:9).

SUICIDE Although the biblical text does not explicitly prohibit suicide, several references suggest that suicide is against God's will and purpose for one's life. The OT prohibits killing in general (Exod 20:13; Deut 5:17), and in the NT Paul teaches that it is wrong to destroy one's body, which is a temple of the Holy Spirit (1 Cor 3:17; 6:19). In addition, Jer 29:11 indicates that God plans a future filled with hope for each person.

Nevertheless, several biblical figures do kill themselves: Samson (Judg 16:30); Saul and his armor-bearer (1 Sam 31:4-5); Ahithophel (2 Sam 17:23); Zimri (1 Kgs 16:18); and Judas (Matt 27:3-5; cf Acts 1:18). The mortally wounded Abimelech requests his armor-bearer to kill him (Judg 9:54). Paul convinces his desperate jailer not to kill himself (Acts 16:27-28).

Also, several figures wish for death as a release from suffering, most notably Job (6:8-13; 14:13). The prophets Moses (Num 11:15); Elijah (1 Kgs 19:4); and Jonah (Jon 4:3, 8) also express a wish to die. Paul longs for death, not to evade suffering but in order to be with Christ (Phil 1:20-26). Finally, according to Revelation, in the trials of the last days "people will seek death, but they won't find it" (9:6).

SUKKITE A member of a group reported to have accompanied Shoshenq I on his campaign against Jerusalem in the 10th cent. BCE (2 Chron 12:3; see SHISHAK).

SUSA Susa was one of the most prominent cities in the ancient region of Elam (modern Khuzistan, in southwest Iran). After the rise of the Achaemenid Empire under Cyrus (559–530 BCE), Susa became the winter capital of Darius I and his successors. During this period, Susa was a cosmopolitan city, located on the Royal Road, connecting it to the west as well as to the other capitals of Ecbatana and Persepolis. Darius I began building new palaces, and the construction of the residential palace is well documented in inscriptions found during excavation. The archaeological data regarding Xerxes's palace corresponds with the description given in Esther, demonstrating the author's awareness of the palace architecture. Susa is mentioned in the books of Ezra (4:9); Nehemiah (1:1); and Daniel (8:2); as well as in the book of Jubilees (8:21; 9:2). The city was captured by Alexander the Great in 331 BCE.

SUSANNA 1. Susanna is one of three additions to Daniel found in Greek versions of the Bible, namely, the LXX, where it appears as the 13th chapter of Daniel.

2. Susanna was one of the women

among those who accompanied Jesus and supported his ministry financially in Luke 8:3.

SUSI The father of Gaddi, who represented the tribe of Joseph (i.e., Manasseh) in the mission to spy out the land of Canaan (Num 13:11).

SWALLOW The swallow is used as an image only infrequently in the Bible. It represents a constituent part of wildlife, as well as the settings and instincts that wild animals recall. For instance, the swallow can elicit images of homemaking (Ps 84:3 [Heb. 84:4]) or be an example of animals knowing their proper place and role in creation (Jer 8:7). The swallow is also known for its agility and restlessness, so that it can be used as an image for things that do not or cannot come to rest (Prov 26:2; Isa 38:14). See BIRDS OF THE BIBLE.

SWINE The domesticated pig, a descendant of the wild boar, is probably the only animal domesticated solely for consumption.

In biblical tradition, the pig is singled out as an unclean animal with special prohibitions against eating its meat and touching its carcass (Lev 11:7; Deut 14:8). The date of origin of this prohibition is hard to determine, but the negative attitude also expressed in Isaiah (65:4; 66:3, "pork" [66:17]) suggests that in the postexilic Jewish community the pig was considered unclean. This attitude underlies Prov 11:22: "Like a gold ring in a pig's nose is a beautiful woman who lacks discretion." It continues in the NT in such instances as the admonition not to throw pearls "in front of pigs" (Matt 7:6); Jesus' exorcism of the Gerasene demoniac when he sent the unclean spirits into a herd of pigs (Mark 5:1-13); and the prodigal son, who found himself so desperate that he took a job feeding pigs (Luke 15:15-16). See HOLY, HOLINESS.

SWORD In the Early Bronze Age, the sword was short and straight, a dagger. In the Middle Bronze Age the sword became broader and longer. Half the uses of sword occur in the prophets Isaiah, Jeremiah, and Ezekiel to announce God's imminent judgment on Israel/Judah or the nations (e.g., Jer 25:27-31; Ezek 23:25, 47). Another 1/4 occur in Joshua–Kings and Chronicles, mostly with literal connotation, a weapon to injure and kill. Sword may also connote "guarding" (Gen 3:24) or be used figuratively to describe violence generally (Gen 27:40; 49:5). The twenty uses in Psalms occur in outcries to God to save from the sword (22:20), to deliver from (17:13) or destroy the wicked by the sword (7:12). The wicked that live by the sword will die by the sword (Ps 37:14-15). Since military imagery for God is metaphorical and human use of the sword is descriptive, Scripture's violent imagery does not endorse human use of the sword or violence. While God's defeat of Egypt may be viewed as a triumph of war (Exod 15:3), it was achieved not by the sword (Ps 44:3-6). The weapons of war the Lord uses to overthrow his enemies or punish Israel include catastrophes in the natural order. This frequent use of military analogies for God's judgment precipitated dangerous perceptions of God as violent and wrathful. Nonetheless, character descriptions of God's steadfast love and faithfulness abound.

In Eph 6:17 *sword* is used metaphorically to describe the believers' spiritual armor to withstand evil. Echoing God's armor in the OT (Isa 7:9b; 11:4-5; 49:2; 52:7; 59:17), believers are instructed to "stand with the belt of truth around your waist, justice as your breastplate, and put shoes on your feet so that you are ready to spread the good news of peace. Above all, carry the shield of faith so that you can extinguish the flaming errors of the evil one. Take the helmet of salvation and the sword of the Spirit, which is God's word" (6:14-17). The single Gospel use of *sword* outside the Passion Narrative is Matt 10:34: "I haven't come to bring peace but a sword." Luke clarifies by substituting *division* for *sword*, indicating that Jesus' statement does not mean military war (12:51). See WAR, IDEAS OF.

SYCAMORE The sycamore (or sycomore) fig (*Ficus sycomorus*). Old sycamore trees have massive trunks with clusters of small fig fruits growing through the bark of the trunk and branches. They are edible but not as delicious as the common fig. The young fruits are pollinated by certain wasps, some of which die inside and pollute the ripe fruit, so an ancient technique of cutting the young fruits was used to hasten their ripening and purity. As a "trimmer of sycamore trees," Amos performed this work (7:14). Luke 19:3-4 narrates how Zacchaeus, the short tax collector, climbed up a sycamore to see Jesus; the tree's low branches made it easy to climb. Sycamore timber is soft and white, unlike harder and reddish cedarwood, but was appreciated in Palestine where wood was in short supply (1 Kgs 10:27; Isa 9:10). In ancient Egypt the timber was important for sarcophagi, but the frosting of sycamore fruits was a calamity (Ps 78:47). See FIG TREE, FIGS; FRUIT; PLANTS OF THE BIBLE.

SYCHAR A city in Samaria that is "near the land Jacob had given to his son Joseph" (John 4:5; see Gen 33:18-20; 48:22). The unknown site is thought to be located either at the village of Khirbet Askar (Iskar) or at Shechem. The story indicates that the location was on the road north from Jerusalem at the point where the route passes between Mounts Ebal and Gerizim. In the Gospel of John this is the setting for the extended story of the Samaritan woman who came to believe in Jesus, along with "many Samaritans in that city" (4:39). The story reports that Jesus rested here, near Jacob's well, and this became the setting for his statements about "living water" (4:10).

SYENE Egyptian town found on the east bank of the first cataract of the Nile, opposite Elephantine, now known as modern Aswan. Mentioned twice in the Bible (Ezek 29:10; 30:6), Syene represents the far south of EGYPT.

SYMEON The Greek form of the name Simeon.

SYNAGOGUE A Jewish community, a gathering of people, the area or edifice in which the people gather, or all three. In particular, the synagogue was (and is) an assembly drawn together for purposes of religious worship and study, with distinct emphasis on the public reading and explication of Scripture.

All four of the canonical Gospels report that Jesus taught in synagogues (Matt 4:23; 13:54; Mark 1:21-22; Luke 4:16; 6:6; John 6:59; 18:20) and that he also healed there (Matt 4:23; Mark 1:23-27). The Gospel of Luke introduces Jesus' ministry with the pronouncement—in the synagogue in Nazareth—that he had come to fulfill the prophet Isaiah (Luke 4:16-21).

According to the Acts of the Apostles, Paul went to the synagogues in all the towns he visited to try to persuade Jews (and Gentile converts to Judaism) to follow Jesus as the Messiah (e.g., Acts 9:20; 13:5, 14-16; 14:1; 17:1-2, 10, 17; 18:4, 7-8, 19, 26; 19:8). Even though Paul's own letters do not confirm this practice (indeed, Paul says he went to the Gentiles, not Jews), Acts provides literary evidence of the many synagogues throughout the Mediterranean area in the 1st cent. CE, their function as a central gathering place for Jews (including sojourners like Paul), and the attendance of Gentile seekers.

In the 1st–2nd cent. CE, the growing tension between Jews who believed Jesus was the Messiah and those who did not sometimes took place in the context of the synagogue. For example, while one leader of the synagogue was receptive to Jesus (Mark 5:22-24, 35-42; cf Matt

9:18-19, 23-25), another questioned his authority (Luke 13:10-14). The book of Acts describes both positive and negative responses to the gospel message preached in synagogues (Acts 13:42-50; 14:1-2; 17:1-9; 19:8-10).

By the time the Gospel of John was written (late 1st cent. CE), evidence of a rift within the synagogues becomes greater, as John refers to adversaries of Jesus collectively as "the Jewish authorities" and reports that those who proclaim Jesus to be the Messiah risk being expelled from the synagogue (John 9:22; 12:42; 16:2). In the book of Revelation, the author bitterly claims that the people "who say they are Jews (though they are not)" are "from Satan's synagogue" (2:9; 3:9). These conflicts within and around the synagogue need to be understood as disagreements among 1st-cent. CE Jews who were grappling with great complexity of belief and not as a condemnation of Jews or Judaism.

SYNOPTIC GOSPELS "Synoptic Gospels" refers to the first three canonical Gospels, Matthew, Mark, and Luke, which are universally recognized as having some kind of interdependent literary relationship.

SYNTYCHE A female leader in the Philippian community who may have presided over a house church and who probably also evangelized nonbelievers (Phil 4:2-3). Paul encourages her to "come to an agreement in the Lord" with her coworker Euodia (Phil 4:2).

SYRACUSE The city of Syracuse (modern Siracusa) is located in the southeast corner of Sicily on one of the largest natural harbors in the Mediterranean. The ship taking Paul from Malta to Italy stopped at Syracuse for three days (Acts 28:12).

SYRIA Syria in biblical times is roughly equivalent to the present-day state of Syria, covers an area from the northeastern Mediterranean coast and the mountains that border it. Many different states and civilizations existed in this region during biblical times.

See ARAM, ARAMEANS.

SYRTIS The Greek name for two gulfs off the northern coast of Africa between Cyrene and Carthage: the Greater Syrtis, now called the Gulf of Sidra; and the Lesser Syrtis, now called the Gulf of Gabes. Ancient sailors feared these treacherous shallow waters. Acts 27:17 states that while Paul was being taken to Rome, a storm struck the ship near Crete, and the sailors feared running aground "on the sandbars of the Gulf of Syrtis."

Tt

TAANACH Taanach occupies a commanding position on the last line of ridges of the central highlands along the Esdraelon Plain's south edge, commanding three major travel and communication routes. In the early Iron Age, Taanach remained a Canaanite town connected with the Canaanite urban centers in the Esdraelon Plain. According to the writers of Joshua, the Israelites defeated Taanach's king and those of the nearby Canaanite centers Megiddo and Jokneam (Josh 12:7-24). Taanach and several neighboring cities (Beth-shan, Ibleam, and Megiddo) were included in the tribal territory of Manasseh but remained Canaanite strongholds that the Israelites were not able to control until the time of David (Josh 17:7-13; Judg 1:27-28; 1 Chron 7:29). The early Iron Age Song of Deborah (Judg 5:19, 21) refers to Taanach and the nearby Kishon River, locating the battle between the Israelites under Barak and Deborah and the army of the northern Canaanite kings led by Sisera there. When Israel grew more powerful under David, Taanach and the Esdraelon Plain towns were brought under Israelite control.

TABBAOTH A temple servant (see Nethinim) whose descendants returned to Judah with Zerubbabel following the Babylonian exile (Ezra 2:43; Neh 7:46; 1 Esdr 5:29).

TABEEL 1. An Aramean official in Samaria who, along with his colleagues Bishlam and Mithredath, coauthored a letter to Artaxerxes I in a successful attempt to halt Jewish reconstruction of the walls of Jerusalem (Ezra 4:7; 1 Esdr 2:16 [LXX 2:12]).

2. The father of an unnamed individual whom kings Pekah and Rezin hoped to place on the Judean throne as a puppet king, in place of Ahaz, during the Syro-Ephraimite war (ca. 735–734 BCE; Isa 7:6).

TABERNACLE See MEETING TENT.

TABLET In the Bible, *tablet* usually refers to the two hewn stone tablets (Exod 34:1; Deut 10:1) that Moses received at Mount Sinai (e.g., Exod 24:12; 31:18; Deut 4:13). A biblical tradition affirms that these tablets were placed in the covenant chest (Deut 10:5; 1 Kgs 8:9; 2 Chron 5:10; Heb 9:4). Inscribing in stone would normally require the use of a hammer and a chisel. Clay tablets were the most common medium for writing cuneiform texts. A writing stylus was used to impress the clay. Tablets could vary in both size and shape. Tablets needed to be moist at the time of writing; afterward, they were dried in an oven, or more commonly dried in the sun. The earliest clay tablets date to the late 4th millennium BCE.

TABOR, MOUNT Mount Tabor is a dome-shaped outcropping in lower Galilee rising to approximately 1,850 ft., lying about 11 mi. southwest of Tiberias and overlooking the Jezreel Valley at the intersection of the tribal territories of Zebulon, Issachar, and Naphtali.

The word *Tabor* occurs twelve times in the OT, with half of these instances referring to place-names other than the mountain: towns in tribal boundary lists that were near the mountain (Josh 19:12, 22, 34); a levitical city in Zebulon (1 Chron 6:77); a Transjordanian site (Judg 8:18); and an oak near Bethel (1 Sam 10:3). Mount Tabor itself figures prominently in the narrative of Deborah's victory over Sisera (Judg 4:6, 12, 14). The remaining three references are in poetic (Ps 89:12 [Heb. 89:13]) and prophetic (Jer 46:18; Hos 5:1) texts. The etymology of Tabor as a proper name is not completely certain, but some scholars suggest a possible Phoenician derivation from the name of a Semitic god, who is known in Greek as Zeus Atabyros (Manns).

TADMOR An important caravanserai about 150 mi. northeast of Damascus on the trade route between that city and Mesopotamia. In Hellenistic and Roman times, the site was known as Palmyra.

TAHAN A son of Ephraim and clan leader (Num 26:35). First Chronicles 7:25 apparently refers to a later descendant of Ephraim, Tahan son of Telah, who was also an ancestor of Joshua son of Nun.

TAHASH One of the children born to Reumah, the secondary wife of Abraham's brother Nahor (Gen 22:24).

TAHATH 1. A place (location unknown)

where the Israelites camped during their wilderness wanderings (Num 33:26-27).

2. A son of Assir and descendant of Kohath (1 Chron 6:24 [Heb. 6:9], 37 [Heb. 6:22]), who was a descendant of Levi (Gen 46:11).

3. Son of Bered of the tribe of Ephraim (1 Chron 7:20).

4. Son of Eleadah, and grandson of Tahath son of Bered, of the tribe of Ephraim (1 Chron 7:20).

TAHPENES Personal name or title of an Egyptian queen, the wife of a pharaoh who ruled during the 21st Dynasty of Egypt. According to 1 Kgs 11:19-20, Tahpenes was the wife of the pharaoh who sheltered Hadad the Edomite, the only member of Edom's royal family who survived the campaign led by David and Joab. Hadad and some of his father's royal officials fled to Egypt. The king of Egypt gave them asylum (1 Kgs 11:14-18). He also gave Hadad a wife, the sister of Tahpenes. Hadad and his wife had a son, Genubath, whom Tahpenes raised in her household.

TALENT In the OT, a measure of weight approximating 75 lbs.; in the NT, a monetary unit roughly equal to 6,000 drachmen (greater than sixteen years' wages for a laborer). See WEIGHTS AND MEASURES.

TALITHA KOUM Greek transliteration of the Aramaic sentence "Young woman, get up" in Mark 5:41.

TALMAI 1. One of the Anakites, who were giants living in the area of Hebron (Num 13:22). According to Josh 15:14, Caleb defeated Talmai, whereas Judg 1:10 states that the Judahites defeated him.

2. Son of Ammihud and ruler of Geshur, a small kingdom east of the Sea of Galilee. David married Talmai's daughter Maacah, apparently as part of a treaty arrangement, and she became the mother of Absalom (2 Sam 2:3; 1 Chron 3:2). After Absalom arranged the murder of his half brother Amnon, he sought refuge with Talmai in Geshur (2 Sam 13:37).

TALMON A returnee from exile and head of a house of levitical gatekeepers (1 Chron 9:17; Ezra 2:42; Neh 7:45; 1 Esdr 5:28).

TAMAR 1. In Genesis 38, Tamar is the wife of Judah's oldest son ER, then the wife of Judah's 2nd son ONAN, and then the mother of Judah's twin sons Perez and Zerah. The story tells of Tamar's persistence in seeking justice after the wickedness or neglect of the men in Judah's family. Her name is used as a blessing in Ruth 4:12, and she is listed as an ancestor of Jesus in Matt 1:3.

2. Second Samuel 13 describes the rape of Tamar, King David's beautiful daughter, by her half brother AMNON.

3. The daughter of Absalom (2 Sam 14:27), most likely named after her aunt Tamar of 2 Sam 13. Like her aunt, this Tamar is also a "beautiful" woman.

4. Town located on Israel's southern border (Ezek 47:19; 48:28). Second Chronicles 20:2 identifies Hazazon-tamar with En-gedi, and Roman sources have understood Tamar as Tamar Mesad.

TAMARISK A tall, shady tree with deep roots, particularly suitable to the sandy soil of the Sinai, Dead Sea, Israel, and Jordan. Various natural explanations for MANNA (Exod 16:14) have been connected with species of tamarisk, the closest of which may be a honeylike substance excreted from the tamarisk bush that is called "manna" by Bedouin.

TAMMUZ The Hebrew name for the Sumerian deity Dumuzi, the lover of Inanna or Ishtar, goddess of sex and war. In Ezek 8:14, women are said to be "performing the Tammuz lament" in the entrance of the North Gate of the temple.

TANHUMETH Means "consolation." Tanhumeth, a Netophathite, was the father of SERAIAH, who was a captain when Babylonia conquered Jerusalem (2 Kgs 25:23; Jer 40:8).

TANNER, TANNING Tanning is the complex process by which animal skins are made usable for garments, tents, parchment, and other items. The tanning process includes curing the skin, removing the hair, and then actually tanning the skin using liquids known as tannins, generally made from vegetable matter. Under the Mosaic law, touching a dead thing made one unclean. Therefore, a tanner would have been almost perpetually unclean.

While the act of tanning is not mentioned in the OT, Exodus specifies that tanned ram skins were to be used in the construction of the meeting tent (Exod 25:5; 26:14; 35:7, 23; 36:19; 39:34), along with LEATHER. According to Acts 9:43, Peter stayed with a tanner named Simon in Joppa. Peter was staying with Simon (19:6, 32) when he had the vision of the sheet full of clean and unclean animals (10:9-16).

TAPHATH BEN-ABINADAB's wife, who was Solomon's daughter (1 Kgs 4:11).

TAPPUAH 1. A place-name that occurs six times in the Bible: Josh 12:17; 15:34; 16:8; 17:8 (twice); 1 Chron 2:43. (See BETH-TAPPUAH.) In Josh 12:17 its king appears in a list of kings defeated by the Israelites. In Josh 16:8 it appears as one of the boundaries of the territory of the tribe of Ephraim. In Josh 17:8 the land around the town was assigned to the tribe of Manasseh while the town itself was given to Ephraim. The site is Tell Sheikh Abu Zarad about 8 mi. southwest of modern Nablus and 5 mi. northwest of biblical Shiloh. Joshua 15:34 apparently refers to a different place by this name since it is among the lowland towns allocated to the tribe of Judah. The Judean town may be identified with Beit Nettif 3 mi. southeast of Azeqah.

2. The 2nd of four sons of Hebron among Judah's descendants (1 Chron 2:43).

TAREA A Benjaminite, son of Micah (1 Chron 8:35; spelled "Tahrea" in 9:41).

TARSHISH 1. A reference to the coastland settlements in the Table of Nations (Gen 10:4-5; 1 Chron 1:7) as those descended from Jephthah through Javan (see KITTIM).

2. One of Benjamin's descendants (1 Chron 7:10).

3. The name of one of the seven counselors of Ahasuerus in Esther (1:14).

4. A geographic reference to an ancient site whose location is uncertain, probably a coastal city on the Mediterranean Sea. Jonah's flight from God's mission to Nineveh began as a journey to Tarshish (Jon 1:3; 4:2). The region was well known for its trade in silver and other metals and as a trading broker in general (Jer 10:9; Ezek 27:12; 38:13).

TARSUS A major port city on the river Cydnus near the Mediterranean Sea, directly north of the eastern tip of Cyprus. Paul's hometown was Tarsus (Acts 9:11, 30; 11:25; 21:39; 22:3).

TARTAK Tartak and Nibhaz were deities of the Avvites, one of the peoples whom the Assyrians settled in Samaria sometime after the fall of the northern kingdom (2 Kgs 17:24, 31).

TARTAN The 2nd-ranking officer after the king in the Assyrian army as of the Middle Assyrian period. As such, he gave his name to a year.

TASSELS The FRINGE or twisted threads on a garment's corners are referred to as tassels in Deut 22:12. The Hebrew word also refers to decorations on the capitals of pillars in Solomon's temple (1 Kgs 7:17).

TATTENAI Governor of the western half of the Persian province or satrapy, Beyond the River during the time of Haggai and Zechariah (Ezra 5:3, 6; 6:6, 13).

TAVERNS, THREE See THREE TAVERNS.

TAX COLLECTOR A "tax" or (preferably) "toll" collector was usually stationed at a "toll booth" and was responsible for collecting the toll, tariff, or customs duty on transported goods. Other tax collectors secured payments for farm production. Generally, many people hated and despised toll collectors since they were able to exploit the toll collection system to their own advantage. This negative attitude is present in the Gospels, where tax collectors are frequently grouped with "sinners."

TAXES, TAXATION The biblical traditions constantly engage and reflect the structures and daily realities of aristocratic-controlled empires. In empires, ruling elites claim taxes, tributes, rents, and forced labor by peasants. Taxation does not benefit the common good. Rather, it supports the privileged lifestyle of elites.

TEBAH First son of Reumah, Nahor's secondary wife (Gen 22:24).

TEBALIAH Third son of Hosah and one of the temple gatekeepers in David's time (1 Chron 26:11).

TEHINNAH Descendant of Judah and father/founder of IR-NAHASH (1 Chron 4:12).

TEKOA 1. A town on the edge of the Judean desert, located about 10 km southeast of Bethlehem and 16 km south of Jerusalem. To the east the land slopes down toward the Dead Sea in a series of desolate hills called the Tekoa wilderness (2 Chron 20:20; 1 Macc 9:33). Seasonal sheep grazing is possible in this area, whereas to the west enough moisture falls during the rainy season to sustain some agriculture. The prophet Amos was from Tekoa, which was also the home for a WISE WOMAN OF TEKOA (2 Sam 14:2).

2. A descendant of Judah through the lineage of Hezron. His father Ashhur was born after his grandfather died (1 Chron 2:24).

TELAH A descendant of Ephraim and an ancestor of JOSHUA (1 Chron 7:25).

TELEM 1. Variant for Telaim (Josh 15:24).

2. A gatekeeper who dismissed his foreign wife (Ezra 10:24; 1 Esdr 9:25).

TEMA 1. Ninth of the twelve sons of Ishmael (Gen 25:15; 1 Chron 1:30; see ISHMAEL, ISHMAELITES).

2. A city known for its trading caravans (Job 6:19) and associated with DEDAN (see Isa 21:13-14; Jer 25:23) and the Sabeans (Job 6:19; see SHEBA).

TEMAH An ancestor of temple servants among the exiles who returned from Babylon (Ezra 2:53; Neh 7:55; 1 Esdr 5:32).

TEMAN 1. One of the descendants of Esau and father of an Edomite tribe (Gen 36:9-11).

2. The name Teman is sometimes used as a synonym for *Edom* (Jer 49:7, 20; Obad 9; see EDOM, EDOMITES), but other texts seem to depict Teman as a region within Edom (Ezek 25:13).

3. An inhabitant of Teman, in Edom near Petra; and a descendant of Esau. Job's countryman Eliphaz was a Temanite (Job 2:11; 4:1; 15:1; 22:1; 42:7, 9).

TEMENI Judahite son of Ashhur and his wife Naarah (1 Chron 4:6).

TEMPLE, JERUSALEM In its long history Israel built numerous sanctuaries and temples for its God, the Lord, but of these, the historically most important were the three chronologically successive temples built on the same site in Jerusalem. The first was built by Solomon in the mid-10th cent. BCE. This temple continued with minor and major repairs and alterations until it was looted in 598 BCE, and then utterly destroyed in 587 BCE. The second temple was built by Zerubbabel, the Persian appointed governor of Judea, on the site of the ruins of the first temple between 520 and 516 BCE. This temple endured various vicissitudes during its almost 500-year history, but it remained standing until Herod the Great tore it down ca. 20 BCE in order to make way for his new temple. Herod rebuilt the temple proper in only a year and six months, but his work on the larger temple precincts, which he massively enlarged and adorned with elaborate structures, lasted some eight and a half years (Josephus, *Ant.* 15.380, 420–21). His work was so significant that the Jerusalem temple of the 1st cent. CE is usually referred to as Herod's temple. Nonetheless, work actually continued on the complex well after Herod's reign, until ca. 63 CE, during the reign of Herod Agrippa II and the procuratorship of Albinus. Herod's temple was destroyed in 70 CE when the Romans sacked Jerusalem at the end of the Jewish War.

TEMPLE OF SOLOMON King Solomon built the 1st permanent temple for the Lord in Jerusalem in the mid-10th cent. BCE, thus completing his father David's program of turning Jerusalem into the religious as well as political capital of the united kingdom of Israel and Judah. David began this process when he appointed two high priests in Jerusalem from rival priestly families from the different halves of his kingdom, and he furthered it when he brought into his new capital the covenant chest, the most revered cultic object of the earlier Israelite league. David sought divine permission to build a permanent temple to house the chest, the symbol of the Lord's presence, which would have completed his transformation of Jerusalem into the permanent religious center of his kingdom, but his plan was temporarily thwarted by Nathan's negative oracle (2 Sam 7). Though David was not allowed to build the temple, he may have begun collecting material for its construction, as the Chronicler claimed (1 Chron 22; 28–29). It was Solomon, however, who actually built the temple, beginning its construction in the 2nd month of his 4th year and completing it in the 8th month of his 11th year (1 Kgs 6:1, 37-38). See TEMPLE, JERUSALEM.

TEMPLE TAX Israelite males were required to pay a half shekel annually to support the Jerusalem temple (Matt 17:24).

TEMPTATION OF JESUS Accounts of Jesus' temptation or "testing" appear only in the three Synoptic Gospels (Matt 4:1-11; Mark 1:12-13; Luke 4:1-13). Though the devil instructs Jesus to do things Jesus accomplishes in his ministry (supply food [Matt 14:13-21]; rule the world [Matt 28:18; Luke 1:33]), Jesus refuses the devil's orders. The scenes follow God's identification of Jesus as God's Son in the baptism (Matt 3:13-17; Mark 1:9-11; Luke 3:21-22). Jesus' refusal and the location of the scenes in the Gospel narratives highlight that this scene is not so much concerned with what Jesus does as whether he will remain faithful to God's will.

TEN COMMANDMENTS Literally "the ten words" (Exod 34:28; Deut 4:13; 10:4), which is the source of the alternative designation "Decalogue." A body of divine instruction in the form of eight prohibitions and two positive commandments preceded by a brief self-presentation formula on the part of the deity: "I am the LORD your God who brought you out of Egypt, out of the house of slavery" (Exod 20:2; Deut 5:6).

The Ten Commandments appear in two versions: Exod 20:1-17, where they are the Lord's direct address to all the people of Israel at Mount Sinai after they have escaped from Egypt; and Deut 5:6-21, where the commandments are repeated, though not precisely in the same form as in Exod 20, this time by Moses on the plains of Moab prior to Israel's entering the land of Canaan.

TENT Portable dwelling used by nomads, shepherds, and armies. The structure consisted of poles held upright and connected with cords stretched between them and grounded with wooden pegs hammered into the ground using a wooden mallet. Hand-woven goat's hair, animal skins, or other materials served as covering for the roof and sides (Judg 4:21; Song 1:5; Isa 40:22; 54:2; Jer 10:20). Tents would usually be pitched near shade and a water supply (well, river, lake, etc.; Gen 18:1, 4). Less well-to-do families shared a tent, with a divider separating men's quarters from that of the women (Judg 15:1). Wealthier families had separate tents for wives, children, and servants (Gen 31:33). Furnishings were generally sparse, with coarse straw mats, goat's hair, or wool rugs sometimes used to cover the ground, and straw mats used for beds and chairs (Judg 4:18-21). A piece of leather spread on the floor served as the table (Ps 23:5; Isa 21:5). Cooking was done on stoves and ovens often consisting of nothing more than a few stones placed at the entrance of the tent or simply a hole in the ground. The head of the family sat in the entrance to guard his family and belongings as well as to watch for travelers (Gen 18:1; Exod 33:8; Judg 4:20).

After settling in Canaan, the Israelites generally lived in houses, although soldiers camped in tents during military expeditions (1 Sam 29:1). *Tent* sometimes was used to refer to the more permanent "home" (1 Kgs 8:66). Prior to the construction of the Jerusalem temple, the Israelites utilized a movable sanctuary called the "meeting tent of" or simply the "tent" (Exod 33:7-11; cf 2 Macc 2:4-5).

In the NT, *tent* often has this OT concept of tent in view. Hebrews 8–9, in which approximately half the occurrences of the term are located, for example, compares the earthly tent constructed by Moses and the true or heavenly tent (see also Acts 7:43-44). The NT also speaks of tents as the portable dwellings of the ancestors Abraham, Isaac, and Jacob (Heb 11:9) and metaphorically as the "fallen tent" or house/kingdom of David (Acts 15:16; cf Amos 9:11 [LXX]). In addition, the transfiguration scenes in the Synoptic Gospels all have Peter asking about putting up tents (CEB, "shrines") for Jesus, Moses, and Elijah, a reference to movable shelters as well as an allusion to the Jewish Festival of Booths (Matt 17:4; Mark 9:5; Luke 9:33). In 2 Cor 5:1-5 the apostle Paul contrasts the metaphorical "tent that we live in on earth" that the Corinthians live in now with the "building from heaven" with which God will clothe them, and for which the Spirit was sent as a guarantee. See BOOTH; BOOTHS, FEAST OR FESTIVAL OF.

TERAH 1. The father of Abram/Abraham, Nahor, and Haran (Gen 11:24-28, 31-32; Josh 24:2; 1 Chron 1:26). He is mentioned in Luke's genealogy of Jesus (3:34).

2. The name of a place on the Israelites' exodus journey (Num 33:27-28).

TERAPHIM See DIVINE IMAGES.

TEREBINTH A tree, similar to an oak.

TERESH A guardian of the king's threshold who, along with BIGTHAN, became angry with King Ahasuerus and plotted to assassinate him (Esth 2:21; 6:2).

TERTIUS In Rom 16:22, the only

passage in which his name appears, Tertius identifies himself as the one who wrote Romans—meaning that, as Paul's amanuensis or secretary, he wrote it down. Paul's reliance on secretaries is implied by 1 Cor 16:21 and Gal 6:11. Tertius adds his own greeting, which suggests that the Roman Christians knew him.

TERTULLUS The spokesman or attorney representing Jewish leaders from Jerusalem as they bring charges against Paul before the governor Felix (Acts 24:1-9).

TESTAMENT The word *testament* does not occur in the CEB, other than in footnotes.

In its traditional Greek usage, the term *testament* refers to a will or testament whereby a person arranges for the disposition of his or her property after death. This is the sense in which testament is used to refer to a literary genre that emerged, and continued to be used, in the Second Temple period. The OT contains several farewell discourses delivered by exalted figures before they die, such as Jacob (Gen 49), Moses (Deut 33), and Joshua (Josh 23–24); in the Apocrypha, Mattathias father of Judas the Maccabee delivers such a discourse (1 Macc 2:49-68), as does Tobit (Tob 14:3-11). Such speeches usually contain blessings and directions for future behavior. Testaments as independent literary works include, for example, the Testaments of the Twelve Patriarchs, the Testament of Job, and the Testament of Moses. The genre often contains blessings, ethical teaching, and predictions of the future.

TESTIMONY Throughout the Bible the idea of testimony is prominent. Terms like *testimony* and *witness* occur often in religious settings and have special meaning there, culminating in the development of the Greek word for "witness" into the English *martyr*.

The Law of Israel was often referred to as "decrees" or "testimonies." A copy of these divine instructions was placed in the "ark of the testimony" (Exod 30:6, 26; 31:7; 39:35; 40:3, 5, 21; NRSV, "ark of the covenant," "testimony" in footnotes) and called "The Testimony" (Exod 16:34; 25:21; NRSV and CEB, "covenant").

One of the principal uses of *testimony* or *witness* is in a forensic context, and this proves to be of considerable importance in both testaments. The testimony of two or three witnesses was necessary to establish a case, and this was insisted upon in cases involving a death sentence (Deut 17:6; 19:15; Num 35:30). Witnesses were expected to take the lead in carrying out the sentence (Deut 17:7; cf 13:9; 1 Kgs 21:13; Acts 7:58). False testimony was strictly prohibited by the Decalogue (Exod 20:16; Deut 5:20), but was clearly not unknown (Exod 23:1-2; cf Ps 35:11; Prov 6:19). If convicted as a malicious witness, a person guilty of false testimony would be subject to the same punishment he meant to inflict (Deut 19:16-19; cf Prov 19:5, 9). Despite the prohibitions, false testimony was common in both the OT and the NT (Ps 27:12; Prov 12:17; 24:28; Matt 26:60; Mark 14:55-59; Acts 6:13; cf 21:27-28).

TETRARCH, TETRARCHY *Tetrarch* originally meant "one of four rulers," but it came to describe a ruler with less autonomy or status than a king. This specialized hierarchy of royal titles is evident among the successors of Herod the Great (see HEROD, FAMILY).

THADDAEUS One of the twelve disciples of Jesus according to Matt 10:3 and Mark 3:18.

THEBES Thebes is the Greek designation for the Egyptian city Waset. Thebes was located in Upper Egypt about 350 mi. south of Memphis in the 4th nome, Waset, the name that also applied to the city.

THEBEZ A fortified city, identified with the modern town of Tubas, located about 11 mi. northeast of Shechem in the fertile highlands of Ephraim.

THEOPHILUS The individual to whom the author of Luke–Acts addresses and presumably dedicates both volumes of his work (Luke 1:3; Acts 1:1).

THESSALONIANS, FIRST LETTER TO THE First Thessalonians appears in the NT as the eighth of the thirteen letters attributed to Paul. It is generally judged to be the earliest of Paul's surviving letters, likely written from Corinth in the early 50s CE, at least a decade after Paul began proclaiming Jesus. Paul's primary purpose in writing 1 Thessalonians is to encourage the Jesus-believers to persevere and make progress in their faith. In so doing, Paul addresses a number of issues about which the Thessalonians have expressed concern, such as sexual morality (4:1-8), the nature of brotherly love (4:9-12), the fate of believers who have died before Jesus' return (4:13-18), and signs preceding Jesus' return (5:1-11).

THESSALONIANS, SECOND LETTER TO THE Second Thessalonians appears in the NT as the ninth of the thirteen Pauline letters. Unlike 1 Thessalonians, there is considerable debate over Paul's authorship of the letter. Nevertheless, it contains numerous Pauline themes and thus must have originated in "Pauline" circles. Its primary purpose is to bring hope to those who are experiencing persecution, to alleviate their anxiety and confusion over the return of Jesus, and to correct behavior that is disrupting the community. Clear emphasis lies on God's faithfulness to those who believe in Jesus and the need for believers to remain faithful to God in the face of persecution, anxiety, and community disruption.

THESSALONICA Thessalonica, modern Thessaloniki or Salonika, was founded by Cassander (one of Alexander the Great's generals) in 315 BCE. From its beginning (ca. 500 BCE), Thessalonica was strategically located on important trade routes, especially on the Roman Via Egnatia, where it was the most important port. Thessalonica became the capital of the 2nd district of Macedonia and the seat of the Roman governor in 167 BCE. In 146 it became the capital of the reorganized province of Macedonia. Cicero described abuses by provincial governors during his exile there (58 BCE; Att. 3.15).

Once Paul reached Thessalonica he engaged in a brief ministry before being driven out by Jewish opposition (Acts 17:1-13; cf 1 Thess 1:8-9). The response to his message was the establishment of a strong church. After Timothy's report that the new congregation remained strong despite harassment, Paul wrote 1 Thessalonians. The city is mentioned elsewhere in the NT in Acts 20:4; 27:2; Phil 4:16; and 2 Tim 4:10.

THEUDAS A Judean who led an unsuccessful rebellion against the Romans, possibly ca. 6 CE (Acts 5:36), but more probably ca. 44 CE (Josephus, *Ant.* 20.97).

THIGH The thigh is mentioned in the Bible in three contexts. First, it features in key patriarchal stories. Second, it is simply a body part referenced descriptively. Third, in the cult, it is offered to God and then shared by the priests.

Abraham and Jacob ask those making promises to place their hands under the thigh of the one asking a commitment and swear to their words. Scholars presume that the thigh is a euphemism for the male reproductive organs, suggesting that placing the hand there is a sign of trust. Abraham has his servant swear that he will not take Isaac off the land to find a wife, even should the servant fail to accomplish this task when he visits Abraham's kin (Gen 24:2). Jacob has Joseph promise that he will not bury his father in Egypt but in the ancestral land (Gen 47:29). And a thigh muscle is a place of injury sustained by Jacob while struggling with an angel on his way back to meet his brother Esau after a long estrangement. The narrator reports that, from that time on, Israelites did not eat that particular portion of an animal's haunch (Gen 32:32).

Some narratives simply name the thigh to explain a detail: the place where a warrior's sword rests (Judg 3:16; Ps 45:3 [Heb. 45:4]; Song 3:8); a place where one strikes oneself to express strong negative feeling (Jer 31:19; Ezek 21:12); a portion of an animal to be eaten (1 Sam 9:24; Ezek 24:4); and the place where God's Word has engraved the name "King of kings and Lord of lords" (Rev 19:16).

Cultic passages describe the ordination ceremony of Aaron and sons, where the thigh is their portion of the sacrifice (Exod 29:22; Lev 7:32-34; 8:25-26; 9:21; 10:14-15), or general circumstances where the thigh is their portion or serves as analogy for portions due them (Num 6:20; 18:18).

THIRD DAY In OT narrative, a stereotypical phrase marking the passage of a few days (e.g., Gen 22:4; 31:22; 34:25; Judg 20:30; 1 Kgs 3:18). In ritual contexts, it is more specific: meat from sacrifices must be consumed before the 3rd day (Lev 7:17-18; 19:6-7), and certain purification rites must occur on the 3rd day (Num 19:12, 19).

According to early Christian tradition, Jesus "rose on the third day in line with the scriptures" (1 Cor 15:4; cf Matt 16:21; 17:23; 20:19; 27:64; Luke 9:22; 18:33; 24:7, 21, 46; Acts 10:40). According to the Markan passion predictions, Jesus will be raised "after three days" (8:31; 9:31; 10:34; cf Matt 27:63; note John 2:19-22: "Destroy this temple [i.e., Jesus' body] and in three days I'll raise it up"). In the LXX and Josephus, "after three days" and "on the third day" are used synonymously. The early church may have preferred "on the third day" because it echoes Hos 6:2.

THISTLE, THORN One of the most obvious features of the diverse flora of the Middle East is the number of well-armed plants, a survival mechanism for grazing pressure. The Bible does not always distinguish among these. Three of the most prominent are the crown of thorns, thornbush, and a group of plants collectively known as thistles.

THOMAS One of the twelve disciples of Jesus (Matt 10:2-4; Mark 3:16-19; Luke 6:14-16; Acts 1:13), often referred to as "doubting Thomas" because of his initial refusal to believe in Jesus' resurrection (John 20:25). The apocryphal Acts of Thomas reports that he was the first missionary taking the gospel to India with miracles and was martyred there.

THREE TAVERNS Or "three shops," refers to a way station 30 mi. south of Rome, a frequent gathering place and stop for relays along the Appian Way, located near the city of Cisterna. Acts 28:15 records that believers from the Three Taverns came to meet Paul while he was traveling to Rome.

THRESHING Threshing is the process of beating grain in order to release the individual seeds. Once the fields of grain were harvested, farmers brought their stalks of wheat and barley to a communal threshing floor (Job 5:26; Matt 3:12). Laid upon this flat, open surface, the stalks were crushed under the hoofs of cattle (Hos 10:11) yoked to a wooden threshing sledge (2 Sam 24:22; see SLEDGE, THRESHING).

The process lent itself to prophetic metaphor, especially as an image of savage warfare.

THRESHING FLOOR The threshing floor was an open space, often on or near the top of a hill, where grain would be threshed and winnowed. The open space allowed oxen or other draft animals to pull the threshing sledge over the grain and break up the stalks from the heads of grain. In the winnowing process, the higher ground permitted the wind to blow the lighter straw and chaff a distance away while the heavier heads of grain fell to be gathered from the ground. See SLEDGE, THRESHING; THRESHING.

THRESHOLD A threshold is an architectural element, usually of stone, that lies at the entrance of a building or gate. The threshold often forms the base against which a door closes. The threshold marks the boundary between what is inside and what is outside the structure.

THRONE A throne is the seat of a monarch. Usually the term *throne* is reserved for the ceremonial seat used for official, administrative, or diplomatic functions. *Throne* also refers to the sovereignty of the kingdom or empire.

THUMMIM See URIM AND THUMMIM.

THUNDER, SONS OF See BOANERGES.

THYATIRA Thyatira (modern Akhisar), a city of ancient Lydia, was at the junction of the roads between PERGAMUM and SARDIS (see LYDIA, LYDIANS). Thyatira's vulnerable position on an open plain made it an easy victim for repeated military conquests throughout its history. The city is mentioned in Acts 16:14 (cf 16:15, 39) and in Rev 1:11; 2:18-29.

TIBERIAS A city founded by Herod Antipas on the west coast of the Galilee Sea. He established Tiberias as the new capital of the region of Galilee between 17 and 20 CE. The city was named for Tiberius CAESAR, the Roman emperor (14–37 CE). It remained the capital until 61 CE when it was annexed to the region of Herod Agrippa II, who ruled from Caesarea Philippi. The city is mentioned in passing in John 6:23 ("Some boats came from Tiberias"). Twice the 4th Gospel refers to the Galilee Sea as the Tiberias Sea (6:1; 21:1). No other reference to the city is made in the NT, but the early history of the city is well known from Josephus (see below) and the Talmud (e.g., b. Ber. 8a; y. Shev. 9:38d; y. Pesah. 4:2).

TIBERIAS SEA See GALILEE SEA OF.

TIBERIUS CAESAR Emperor of Rome from 14 to 37 CE, Tiberius Claudius Nero's reign marks the consolidation of AUGUSTUS's imperial government and represents the larger historical context for the events of Jesus' adult life.

TIBHATH City of Hadadezer the Aramean king of Zobah (1 Chron 18:8); perhaps the same as Betah (2 Sam 8:8). Bronze seized in Tibhath was used in the construction of the temple vessels.

TIBNI According to 1 Kgs 16:15-22, Tibni son of Ginath lost a three- to five-year civil war against King OMRI of Israel after the death of the usurper ZIMRI, who assassinated ELAH. Josephus reports that Omri's supporters killed Tibni (*Ant.* 8.311–12).

TIDAL In Gen 14:1, 9, Tidal is the king "of Goiim," who, with King Amraphel of Shinar (Babylon), Arioch of Ellasar, and CHEDORLAOMER of Elam, goes to war against five other kings.

TIGLATH-PILESER III Three Assyrian kings were named Tiglath-pileser: (1) Tiglath-pileser I (1114–1076 BCE), whose campaigns reached Lebanon; (2) Tiglath-pileser II (966–935 BCE), an insignificant king of whom little is known; and (3) Tiglath-pileser III (r. 745–727 BCE), the only one of the three mentioned in the Bible, who in 733–732 BCE conquered and annexed most of the northern kingdom of Israel, deporting significant elements of its population (2 Kgs 15:19, 29; 16:7, 10; 2 Chron 28:20).

TIGRIS RIVER The Tigris River, 1,150 mi. long, arises in the Taurus Mountains of eastern Turkey and flows in a southeasterly direction through northern Iraq, the heartland of ancient Assyria. Near Baghdad in central Iraq it takes up a roughly parallel course with the Euphrates River as it flows through the territory of ancient Babylon and then ancient Sumer. The Tigris is mentioned six times in the OT and Apocrypha. According to Gen 2:14, the Tigris, which passed east of Assyria, was one of the four rivers flowing out of Eden. Sirach compares the flow of these rivers to the flow of wisdom from the Torah (24:25). Daniel is standing on the banks of the Tigris when he receives the final revelation of the book (Dan 10:4). Tobias follows the course of the Tigris when he travels from Nineveh to Rages (Tob 6:2-3), and he cures his father's blindness with the gall of the fish he takes from the river, on the advice of Raphael. In Jdt 1:6, the Tigris basin is part of the territory allied to or controlled by Nebuchadnezzar.

TIKVAH 1. The father of Shallum, husband of the prophetess Huldah of Jerusalem, who authenticated the Instruction scroll found during the reign of Josiah (2 Kgs 22:14).

2. The father of Jahzeiah, who was one of the small minority that opposed Ezra's plan to dissolve the Judean marriages with foreign women (Ezra 10:15; 1 Esdr 9:14).

TILGATH-PILNESER See TIGLATH-PILESER III.

TILON Head of a Judahite clan and the 4th of Shimon's four sons (1 Chron 4:20).

TIMAEUS Father of BARTIMAEUS, a blind beggar whom Jesus heals en route to Jerusalem (Mark 10:46).

TIMNA 1. Sister of the Horite tribal leader Lotan (Gen 36:22; 1 Chron 1:39). She is listed as the secondary wife of Eliphaz the son of Esau, who bore him Amalek (Gen 36:12). The parallel passage in 1 Chron 1:36 lists Timna as one of the sons of Eliphaz, but the LXX of 1 Chron 1:36, which reads "and from Timna, Amalek," agrees with Gen 36:12 in treating Timna as a woman and the mother of Amalek.

2. A tribal leader listed among the tribes descended from Esau (Gen 36:40).

TIMNAH, TIMNITE 1. A town in Judah, between Beth-shemesh and Ekron (Josh 15:10-11). Timnah was ideally situated for agriculture and was a cultural and commercial link between the coastal plain and the highlands. It was assigned to the tribe of Dan (Josh 19:43) but held for a time by the Philistines (Judg 14:1-5; cf 2 Chron 28:18). Judah had flocks at Timnah (Gen 38:12-14) and Samson married a Timnite woman (Judg 14:1-8; 15:6).

2. A town in the highlands of Judah (Josh 15:57).

TIMNATH-HERES, TIMNATH-SERAH A city of Joshua's inheritance and place of his burial (Josh 19:50; 24:30; Judg 2:9). Joshua 19:50 says the Israelites gave Joshua the city at the Lord's command and he built it up and lived there.

TIMON One of seven men commissioned by the twelve apostles to attend to the daily distribution of food in the Jerusalem community (Acts 6:5).

TIMOTHY 1. Leader of an Ammonite army who fought against Judas Maccabeus and his army on several occasions around 164 BCE (1 Macc 5:6-8; 2 Macc 8:30-33; 9:3; 10:24-38; 12:2-9). The Maccabees found him hidden in a cistern at the fortress of Gazara and killed him.

2. In the NT, Timothy is a close associate of the apostle Paul and the apparent recipient of two of the Pastoral Epistles. In the Acts of the Apostles, Timothy figures prominently in Paul's 2nd and 3rd missionary journeys. He remains

with Silas in Beroea with a plan to go on to Athens to meet Paul (Acts 17:14-15). Acts 18:5 reports that he arrives in Corinth. Paul sends him to Macedonia with Erastus (Acts 19:22), and he later travels with Paul through Macedonia and Greece and is with him in Corinth on the eve of his journey to Jerusalem (Acts 20:4; Rom 16:21). As related in Paul's Epistles, Timothy serves as Paul's representative.

Timothy appears frequently in the Pauline Epistles where he is referred to as Paul's "coworker," a term frequently used for Paul's fellow missionaries (Rom 16:21; 1 Thess 3:2), as well as his "brother" (i.e., in the faith, 2 Cor 1:1; Col 1:1; 1 Thess 3:2; Phlm 1:1); "son" (Phil 2:22); "true child in the faith" (1 Tim 1:2); and "dear child" (2 Tim 1:2).

Although their authorship is far from certain, two of the Pastoral Epistles are addressed from Paul to Timothy. Many scholars think they are pseudonymous works of the late 1st to early 2nd cent. It is difficult to imagine that the seasoned associate of Paul's correspondence would require the instructions in church leadership found in 1 Timothy.

TIMOTHY, FIRST AND SECOND LETTERS TO Two letters that present Paul as an elder and authoritative teacher instructing Timothy on the conduct of community life, probably written well after the death of Paul, and that may incorporate information from Titus (Marshall). Though the canonical order places Titus after 1 and 2 Timothy, many scholars think that Titus was composed before these two epistles.

TIPHSAH 1. A city mentioned in a phrase ("from Tiphsah to Gaza") that expresses the geographical extent of Solomon's empire (1 Kgs 4:24 [Heb. 5:4]).

2. A city in the Ephraimite highlands attacked by Menahem (2 Kgs 15:16).

TIRAS A son of Japheth, son of Noah (Gen 10:2; 1 Chron 1:5), who represents a people who probably dwelled in Asia Minor near the Caspian Sea.

TIRATHITES The Tirathites were a Kenite clan living in JABEZ, a city in Judah. They were associated with scribal activity (1 Chron 2:55). See KENITES.

TIRHAKAH Tirhakah is an Egyptian ruler mentioned in the Bible, often identified as Taharqa, the 4th king of the Kushite 25th Dynasty, a dynasty whose earlier rulers united Egypt under Napatan rule. Taharqa led an aggressive twenty-six-year reign (690–664 BCE) marked by considerable building activity, war, and the end of his dynasty. In the Bible, "Cush's king Tirhakah" is said to have fought against the Assyrian king SENNACHERIB during the reign of HEZEKIAH of Judah (2 Kgs 19:9; Isa 37:9).

TIRHANAH One of several sons of Caleb and his secondary wife Maacah in the listing of Judah's descendants (1 Chron 2:48).

TIRIA Judahite head of a clan, the 3rd of Jehallelel's four sons (1 Chron 4:16).

TIRZAH 1. One of the five daughters of ZELOPHEHAD from the tribe of Manasseh (Num 26:33; Josh 17:3). Zelophehad had no male heirs; after his death, his daughters successfully petitioned Moses to pass the inheritance on to them (Num 27:1-5). Their claim set a precedent for inheritance among all the Israelites (Num 27:6-11; see also Num 36:5-11).

2. A town in Canaan whose king the Israelites killed in the conquest (Josh 12:24) and which then was apparently allotted to the territory of Manasseh (Josh 17:3-13; see MANASSEH, MANASSITES). JEROBOAM son of Nebat made Tirzah one of the capitals of his kingdom when it seceded from Judah (1 Kgs 14:17), and the site served as Israel's capital through the reigns of BAASHA

(1 Kgs 15:21), ELAH (1 Kgs 16:8), and the abbreviated reign of ZIMRI (1 Kgs 16:15). OMRI besieged the city during Zimri's reign, and Zimri committed suicide through arson as he destroyed the palace (1 Kgs 16:17-18). Omri continued to rule from Tirzah for the first six years of his reign, and he then moved the capital to SAMARIA (1 Kgs 16:23-24). Tirzah was apparently the hometown of MENAHEM (2 Kgs 15:14), one of the last kings of Israel.

TITHE A gift of a 10th of an object's value, usually to a sanctuary or for other religious purposes. While Deut 12:6, 11 make clear that tithing is necessary, vv. 7 and 17 also certify that the person making the tithe consumes it, but must do so in the presence of the sanctuary. When Israelites live so far from the sanctuary that bringing tithes in their material form would be impracticable, Deut 14:22-27 permits them to convert the tithes into money to be carried more easily to the temple; there they were to purchase with the money whatever foodstuffs they wished to consume in the presence of the sanctuary as their tithes. Deuteronomy 14:28-29 requires that Israelites also set aside a tithe every 3rd year in their towns to feed the Levites, widows, orphans, and sojourners among them (cf Deut 26:12).

The Priestly tradition shifts the focus to the sanctity of tithes to the temple and the devotion of their proceeds to the priestly class. Numbers 18:21-24 demands a yearly tithe for the Levites (but not for orphans, widows, and sojourners; cf Deut 14:28-29; 26:12) because it is their due since they have no allotment of land and they approach God in the sanctuary on behalf of all Israel. Numbers 18:25-29 decrees that the Levites must give from their tithe the best 10th to the altar priests, Aaron and his descendants.

The NT Gospels mention tithing only a handful of times. In Matt 23:23 (par. Luke 11:42), Jesus echoes Amos 4:4, accusing the Pharisees of ensuring payment of tithes while disregarding mercy and justice. Luke redeploys this Jesus saying in the parable of the Pharisee and the tax collector (Luke 18:9-14). Hebrews 7:4-10 also takes up tithing. The author recalls the Melchizedek episode to argue that as a priest of the order of Melchizedek Jesus' priesthood is superior to that of the Levites: not only does Gen 14 indicate that priests of the order of Melchizedek are unbegotten and eternal; Melchizedek also received tithes from Levi inasmuch as the latter was "still in his ancestor's [Abraham's] body when Abraham paid the tenth to Melchizedek" (Heb 7:9-10).

TITUS 1. Titus was a traveling companion of Paul by the time of the visit to Jerusalem recorded in Gal 2:1 (identified as either Acts 11:27-30; 12:25; or 15:1-29). From a Gentile background (Gal 2:3), possibly in Antioch, he may have come to faith in Christ through Paul (Titus 1:4). He accompanied Paul for some years on his travels. Paul speaks of him with great affection as "my brother" (2 Cor 2:13) and "my partner and coworker" (2 Cor 8:23), terms that Paul rarely or never uses for others.

2. Titus Flavius Vespasianus (39–81 CE) became emperor as the elder son of his predecessor Vespasian, the founder of the Flavian Dynasty. He was a popular ruler whose reign lasted just over two years (79–81 CE) until his death (almost certainly) from natural causes.

TITUS, LETTER TO A letter that presents Paul instructing his representative, Titus, on how to order the communal life of Pauline churches on Crete.

TIZITE A designation given to JOHA, son of Shimri and brother of Jediael, one of the mighty men of David's army. The term *Tizite* occurs only in 1 Chron 11:45.

TOAH An ancestor of Heman, a Kohathite musician (1 Chron 6:34).

TOB-ADONIJAH One of several Levites sent by Jehoshaphat to teach in the cities of Judah (2 Chron 17:8).

TOBIAH 1. The head of a family in Zerubbabel's group of returnees from exile, mentioned in par. lists in Ezra 2:60; Neh 7:62; and 1 Esdr 5:37. They were among those who were unable to prove their Israelite descent using genealogical records.

2. An Ammonite by birth and/or the Persian governor over Ammon. Mentioned frequently in the book of Nehemiah, Tobiah was a prominent figure in the restoration period, who, along with SANBALLAT, opposed Nehemiah's efforts to rebuild Jerusalem's walls (Neh 2:10, 19; 4:3, 7 [Heb. 3:35; 4:1]; 6:1-19). He took up residence in the temple while Nehemiah was away from Jerusalem, but Nehemiah evicted him upon his return (Neh 13:4-9).

TOBIAS 1. Tobias, the only son of Tobit and Anna.

2. Tobias, ancestor of Hyrcanus (2 Macc 3:11), who deposited money in the temple during the high priesthood of Onias II (mid-3rd cent. BCE).

TOBIEL Father of Tobit (Tob 1:1), who died while Tobit was still a child (Tob 1:8).

TOBIJAH 1. A Levite whom King Jehoshaphat sent along with other Levites, priests, and royal officials throughout Judah to teach the people from the Instruction scroll (2 Chron 17:8).

2. One of the Babylonian returnees who donated some of the silver and gold used to make a crown that symbolized the participation of the Jewish Diaspora in the rebuilding of the temple (Zech 6:10-14).

TOBIT, BOOK OF The book of Tobit, which tells the story of two families united through marriage, is both an adventure story and a moral tale. Two faithful people pray to God out of deep distress: Tobit, who has been blinded, and Sarah, whose bridegrooms are killed by a demon. In answer to their prayers, God sends the angel Raphael, who guides Tobit's son Tobias on a dangerous quest and teaches him how to heal both sufferers. The book of Tobit is clearly a Jewish book. Its characters are Jewish; it promotes Jewish values and was found among the manuscripts at Qumran. But the book of Tobit was not included in the final listing of books in the Hebrew canon. It did not become part of the Protestant canon of the OT, but it is included in the Roman Catholic canon. A likely date for composition is the early 2nd cent. BCE.

TOGARMAH The genealogy of Gen 10 presents Togarmah as the descendant of Gomer the son of Japheth the son of Noah (10:3).

TOHU The father of Elihu and the son of Zuph, an eponymous ancestor of the region (1 Sam 1:1) and a forebear of Samuel.

TOI Toi ruled the Neo-Hittite kingdom of Hamath, approximately 120 mi. north of Damascus, during the period of David's ascendancy in the 10th cent. BCE. After David crushed an Aramean coalition that included Hamath's neighbor and perennial enemy Hadadezer of Zobah (2 Sam 8:3-7), Toi sent his son with gifts of gold, silver, and bronze to congratulate David and presumably to sue for peace (2 Sam 8:9-10). David accepted the gift and apparently did not invade Hamath, leaving it as a buffer between David's growing empire and the Mesopotamian kingdoms to the east.

TOLA 1. The eldest of Issachar's four sons (Gen 46:13; 1 Chron 7:1) and ancestor of the Tolaites.

2. A judge (Judg 10:1-2), the first in a list of five so-called minor judges (Judg 10:1-5; 12:8-15).

TONGUE The muscular organ in the mouth of the human body that extends from the throat to the teeth and lips, providing the facility to speak words. However, *tongue* is most often used as a metonym for *speech*. This extends beyond speech capacity, however, to the differentiation of human speech into distinct languages (Deut 28:49) and the use of this for counting the diversity of tribes and nations (Gen 10:5; Rev 5:9; 7:9; 10:11; 11:9; 13:7; 14:6; 17:15). See TONGUES, GIFT OF.

Human speech, symbolized by the tongue, is always ethical, and thus can be good or bad, a frequent topic of wisdom literature.

TONGUES, GIFT OF Speaking in tongues (glossolalia) is a gift of the spirit (1 Cor 12–14) in which a person who is inspired or who is in an ecstatic state begins to utter words in another language. The Corinthian church experienced conflict over the distribution and use of this practice.

TOPHETH Topheth's location, according to 2 Kgs 23:10 and Jer 7:31, is "in the Ben-hinnom Valley," which is well established to be located at the southwest corner of Jerusalem's old city, at the base of Mount Zion (see HINNOM, VALLEY OF). Referenced only nine times in the OT, Topheth was notorious because of its identification with child sacrifice to the god Molech (2 Kgs 23:10; Jer 7:31; see MOLECH, MOLOCH).

TORAH A Hebrew word meaning "instruction," "teaching," and "law." It is the OT's general term for God's commandments to Israel. It often refers to specific instructions, but it came to typify the literary corpus that contains those commandments (i.e., the first five books of the OT—Genesis, Exodus, Leviticus, Numbers, and Deuteronomy—otherwise known as the PENTATEUCH), as well as the divine will for Israel in general.

TOWER A tower is a building constructed for agricultural purposes or as a fortress or stronghold, sometimes as part of a city wall. Stone towers of various shapes and sizes dot the landscape of the Levant and seem to have served a variety of purposes, but chief among them were defense and agriculture. It is against such background that the metaphorical use in reference to the Lord occurs (Ps 61:3 [Heb. 61:4]).

TRACHONITIS A region in northern Transjordan ruled by Herod Philip. It is mentioned in the Bible only in Luke 3:1, a passage that establishes the chronological setting of John the Baptist's ministry.

TRANSFIGURATION The traditional name of an episode found at Matt 17:1-9; Mark 9:2-9; Luke 9:28-37; and summarized in 2 Pet 1:16-18.

TRAY A utensil associated with the meeting tent's LAMPSTAND (Exod 27:3; 38:3; Num 4:9). Like the lampstand, the trays were made of pure gold.

TREASURE, TREASURER, TREASURY A form of wealth, often concealed, or something that is stored up or hoarded.

TREE OF THE KNOWLEDGE OF GOOD AND EVIL, TREE OF LIFE The "tree of the knowledge of good and evil" and the "tree of life" both appear in Gen 2–3. "The tree of life" connotes life, longevity, fertility, and in certain occurrences, wisdom. The book of Revelation uses OT imagery of the tree of life planted by streams of living water, to describe the New Jerusalem (Rev 22:2; see also v. 14).

TRIBE In the social system of ancient Israel, about a dozen large groupings called "tribes" constructed and expressed affinity among clans and their constitutive families ("father's house").

The institution of the tribe preceded state formation in Israel but continued to function alongside the monarchy. As a way of organizing affiliations and resources, tribes share functions with states but have few if any institutions and minimal hierarchy. The effective unit of organization above the family level was not the tribe but the clan. Both legal and narrative texts indicate that clans functioned as independent, active entities. Clans were territorial, economic, and biological associations of families claiming descent from a common ancestor. Marriage was to be outside one's family and inside one's clan.

TRIBUNE A high-ranking military officer (Acts 24:22; 25:23). The official whom Paul encounters while in Jerusalem (Acts 21:31-40; 22:22-30; 23:10-22) appears to be a *tribunus militum*, a Roman military commander in charge of a cohort (approximately 600 soldiers). CEB translates it as "commander."

TRIBUTE Payment by a ruler or people to a superior foreign king, indicating political submission or loyalty. Tribute is voluntary in that it is given, not forcibly seized. At the same time, however, it is compulsory, since the superior king usually expects the payment and regards the failure to give it as a punishable offense.

TROAS The city of Troas was situated on a gently sloping coastal plain in northwestern Asia Minor, about 20 km (12 mi.) southwest of ancient Troy (Ilium).

According to Acts, Paul visited Troas twice. While passing through the city during his travels in Asia Minor, he experienced a night vision calling him to Macedonia (Acts 16:8-11). Later, Paul stopped for a week in Troas en route to Jerusalem (Acts 20:5-12). It was during this visit that EUTYCHUS, while listening to Paul speaking at length in an upper room, fell asleep and tumbled from a window to his death, only to be revived by Paul.

TROGYLLIUM A promontory on the western shore of Asia Minor between EPHESUS and MILETUS, and a possible point of anchorage on Paul's 3rd missionary journey. Trogyllium projects westward from Mount Mycale toward the island of SAMOS. Paul and his companions on the return trip to Jerusalem "sailed to Samos" and on the next day "came to Miletus" (Acts 20:15).

TROPHIMUS Along with TYCHICUS, one of two persons (Acts 20:4) who accompanied Paul for at least part of the final journey to Jerusalem (Acts 19:21–21:17), probably as representatives of the Asian churches in the collection for the poor in Jerusalem (1 Cor 16:1-4). Upon arrival in the city, Trophimus became embroiled in the controversy that led to Paul's arrest.

TRUSTEE A manager or administrator of an estate or household (Gal 4:2).

TRUTH In the OT, the word translated "truth" means "reliability." In the NT, the Greek word can mean "reality," "accuracy," and "honesty." Its sense is sometimes influenced by OT usage, however, to become "faithfulness" or "reliability." Writers in both the OT and the NT value "truth" in the sense of correspondence between words and reality. Yet they also often use words metaphorically, sacrificing some descriptive correspondence in order to communicate realities difficult to grasp with "literal" language.

TRYPHAENA AND TRYPHOSA In Rom 16:12, Paul describes these women as "workers for the Lord." Elsewhere (e.g., 1 Cor 16:10) Paul uses similar language for Timothy's ministry, and his own. Evidently, Tryphaena and Tryphosa had prominent roles in the early church.

TUBAL The 5th son of Japheth son of

Noah, listed in the Table of Nations (Gen 10:2; see also 1 Chron 1:5). His brothers include Gomer, MAGOG, Madai, Javan, MESHECH, and Tiras.

TUBAL-CAIN Son of Lamech and ZILLAH, and the half brother of Jabal, the ancestor of tent dwellers and herds, and Jubal, the ancestor of lyre and pipe players. He also had a sister named NAAMAH. Tubal-cain is associated with the origins of metalworking, specifically the manufacture of implements of bronze and iron.

TUMORS Swollen sores, inflicted by the Lord on the Philistines after they captured the covenant chest (1 Sam 5:6, 9, 12). To appease the Lord, the Philistines offered gold tumors and mice as a sacrifice (6:4-5, 11, 17).

TUNIC An ankle-length linen garment worn next to the skin with a sash and a robe (Exod 28:39-40; Lev 8:7; Job 30:18).

TURBAN A head covering for men made of cloth that was wrapped around the head. A turban was generally a sign of status and was worn by people of wealth or on special occasions, and could be a sign of office (Ezek 21:26 [Heb. 21:31]). Turbans are listed in Isa 3:23 as one of the pieces of finery that the Lord will remove from the people in the day of punishment.

Priests in ancient Israel were required to wear turbans made out of linen when they ministered before the Lord (Exod 28:4, 39). Wool garments were not allowed (Ezek 44:17).

TWELVE, THE The Gospels describe the Twelve as disciples whom Jesus chose to accompany him during his ministry and to whom he gave authority to preach, to heal, and to cast out demons (Matt 10:1-3; Mark 3:14-19; Luke 6:13-16; 9:1-2). In Mark and Luke they are selected from among a larger group and are usually identified simply as "the Twelve," without the addition of "disciples" or "apostles" (see APOSTLE; DISCIPLE, DISCIPLESHIP). The number represents the twelve tribes of Israel (Matt 19:28; Luke 22:30). Acts recounts the selection of Judas's replacement Matthias (1:15-26).

TYCHICUS According to Acts 20:4, Tychicus was one of two persons (the other was TROPHIMUS) who accompanied Paul for at least part of the final journey from Ephesus through Macedonia and Achaia and on to Jerusalem (Acts 19:21–21:17). It is likely that Tychicus and Trophimus undertook this journey as representatives of the Asian churches in the collection for the poor in Jerusalem (1 Cor 16:1-4).

TYRANNUS HALL Paul removed his students from the hostility of the Ephesian synagogue and began to lecture in the Tyrannus lecture hall (Acts 19:8-9).

TYRE An important Phoenician island city just off the coast of southern Lebanon, about 80 km (50 mi.) south of Beirut. References to Tyre also appear some forty times in the OT, often in contexts of condemning materialism and pride. In any case, Tyre, "queen of the seas," represents one of the most significant historical sites in the entire Mediterranean littoral; as the prophet Ezekiel acknowledged, "Your territory is in the depth of the sea, and it's your builders who made you beautiful" (Ezek 27:4).

The Tyrian "golden age" was the 10th cent. BCE, with the accession of Hiram I to the throne (ca. 980 BCE). Friend to both kings David and Solomon of Israel, this king apparently built no less than three lavish temples in Tyre. A later king, ETHBAAL I (ca. 878–847 BCE) succeeded in reestablishing his dominion over the entire southern territory of Phoenicia; JEZEBEL, his daughter, was married to King Ahab of Israel.

Condemnatory references to Tyre are found in Joel 3:4 [Heb. 4:4]; in Amos

1:9-10; and in Zech 9:2-3. In Amos and Joel, Tyre is accused of social sin (enslaving peoples), and of ostentatious wealth in Zechariah. In Isa 23, and especially in Ezek 26–28, Tyre infamously symbolizes proud, willful opposition to the God of Israel, and its inevitable doom is celebrated at length. The prophet Ezekiel also holds up Tyre to condemnation (Ezek 26:1-21; 27:1-36; 28:1-19).

Uu

UEL One of the descendants of BANI who divorced his foreign wife as part of Ezra's postexilic reforms (Ezra 10:34). The name is peculiar and may be a corrupted or shortened form. The parallel text in 1 Esdr 9:34 lists Joel instead. Bani can be assumed to be the BINNUI of Neh 7:15; thus Uel was part of a family who returned from exile under Zerubbabel.

ULAI The "canal" that Daniel stood beside in his vision of a conflict between a two-horned ram representing the kings of Media and Persia and a he-goat representing the king of Greece (Dan 8:2). A voice from the middle of the Ulai called out to the angel Gabriel with instructions to interpret the vision to Daniel (8:16). Scholars believe the Ulai to have been an artificial canal that flowed on the northern side of the ancient Elamite capital city of Susa, connecting the Choaspes (present-day Kerkha) and Coprates (present-day Abdizful) Rivers.

ULAM 1. Father of Bedan and one of two sons of Sheresh, a descendant of Manasseh (1 Chron 7:16-17).

2. A warrior and archer, the oldest son of Eshek, a Benjaminite (1 Chron 8:39-40).

In both cases, the name can be understood as an eponym for a clan.

UNDERWORLD, DESCENT INTO THE Mythic journeys to and from the realm of the dead are widespread in Near Eastern and classical antiquity, and are found also in early Jewish and Christian literature. They bear witness to some degree of cultural connection, yet their frequency should be attributed not to a mythic archetype but instead to basic factors of the human experience such as the universal problem of death, the common belief in a partition between the living and the dead, and curiosity regarding the fate of the dead. In the ancient world, Sumerian tales of Ur-Nammu, Gilgamesh, and Inanna bear some relation to OT images of an underworld, as does the Egyptian story of Isis and the Greek stories of Hercules.

Descriptions of death in the OT often incorporate images reflective of burial with its idea of descending (e.g., Gen 37:35; 42:38; Ps 22:30; Isa 38:18). The resurrection and ascension of Jesus that are described in 1 Pet 3:18-20 allude to an underworld descent; however, they are referenced only in brief and left unexplained. The descent of Christ is commented on in Eph 4:7-11, yet it is not explicated in detail. As a result, the passage has long remained a source of debate regarding what this descent means (from the grave or from the underworld) along with its implications for christology.

See IMMORTALITY.

UNFORGIVABLE SIN At three points in the NT, reference is made to a sin that "won't be forgiven": in the Synoptic Gospels, Jesus speaks of unforgivable sin against the Holy Spirit (Matt 12:32; Mark 3:29; Luke 12:10); Hebrews denies a 2nd repentance to apostates (Heb 6:4-6); and 1 John distinguishes between sins that "result in death" and sins that "don't result in death" (5:16-17). Believers are discouraged from praying for persons who commit the former, but are assured of the life-giving power of prayers of intercession on behalf of fellow Christians who commit the latter.

Jesus refers to unforgivable sin when religious authorities attribute his exorcising ministry to demonic power at work within him (Matt 12:22-32; Mark 3:19*b*-30; Luke 11:14-26; 12:1-12). To deny that the Spirit at work within Jesus is God's own saving power is to blaspheme and to cut oneself off from the very source of forgiveness. Thus, Jesus warns his accusers that it is "a sin with consequences that last forever" (Mark 3:29). God's power to forgive is by no means limited (see Mark 3:28), but some prove unable to receive it.

Hebrews stresses the impossibility of restoring apostates again to repentance (Heb 6:4-6; see also 10:26-31; 12:15-17) as it addresses a serious pastoral crisis: believers have grown weary in the Christian way and are in danger of abandoning their Christian vocation (see 2:1-3; 3:12; 6:11-12; 10:23-25; 12:12). The severe words of warning, denying the possibility of a 2nd repentance, aim to dissuade them. Sin in general is not in view, but rather the specific and extreme sin of apostasy, that is, the continuing, public, and defiant repudiation of Christian faith by baptized believers who have experienced the grace of God in Jesus Christ.

UNKNOWN GOD, ALTAR TO AN In his speech on MARS HILL in ATHENS, the Lukan Paul refers to having observed an altar in the city bearing the inscription "to an unknown god" (Acts 17:23). Paul proceeds to make the proclamation of this unknown god the theme of his speech. Archaeologists have not yet found an altar dedicated "to an unknown god," nor is there any mention of such an inscription in surviving Greco-Roman literature.

The church father Jerome suggested that Paul was paraphrasing an inscription that actually read, "To the gods of Asia, Europe, and Africa, to the unknown and foreign gods." If Paul invented a singular form of a similar plural inscription to introduce his speech, this might well have impressed rather than scandalized his rhetorically sophisticated audience.

UNLEAVENED BREAD Unleavened bread figures in several contexts in the OT. Since bread of this type lacked a leavening agent and therefore did not require time for the dough to rise, it was convenient to prepare for a visitor, especially an unexpected one. Scriptural examples are Lot, who served the two angels who came to Sodom (Gen 19:3); Gideon, who presented it to his angelic guest (Judg 6:19-22); and the medium of Endor, who baked it for Saul (1 Sam 28:24).

The most familiar references to unleavened bread occur in the context of the exodus from Egypt. Exodus 12 provides the legislation for both the Passover meal, which included unleavened bread (12:8), and the Festival of Unleavened Bread when, for the seven days after Passover, unleavened bread was to be eaten and no leaven was to be found among the Israelites (12:15, 17-20; 13:1-6; see also Exod 23:15; 34:18; Lev 23:6; Num 28:17; Deut 16:3-4, 8, 16; Ezek 45:21; see PASSOVER AND FESTIVAL OF UNLEAVENED BREAD). Eating unleavened bread was also the rule at the 2nd Passover (Num 9:11; 2 Chron 30:13, 21).

The other context in which unleavened bread plays a role is the priestly legislation regarding the grain offering. Leviticus 2 provides the rules covering the different forms these sacrifices could take. If the offering is prepared in an oven, there is to be "unleavened flatbread mixed with oil or unleavened wafers spread with oil" (2:4); there was also to be unleavened bread if it is heated on a griddle (vv. 5-6; see also 1 Chron 23:29). The implication appears to be that there is something objectionable about leaven (and honey) with its fermenting properties in a sacrificial context; exactly what is objectionable about it is not explained here (cf Matt 16:6-12, where Jesus warns the disciples against "the yeast of the Pharisees and Sadducees"). See also Lev 6–8.

In 1 Cor 5:8, the apostle Paul contrasts "the unleavened bread of honesty and truth" with "the yeast of evil and wickedness" in admonishing the Corinthians to "clean out the old yeast" (v. 7). See LEAVEN.

UNNI, UNNO 1. A Levite of secondary rank mentioned in 1 Chron 15:18, 20. The name appears in a list of Levites who were charged with providing musical accompaniment during David's 2nd attempt to transport the covenant chest from the house of Obed-edom to Jerusalem.

2. A Levite listed among those who returned from exile with Zerubbabel and Jeshua in Neh 12:9.

UNPARDONABLE SIN See UNFORGIVABLE SIN.

UPPER ROOM A room in an upper story of a private house or multiunit housing. In Mark 14:12-16 (cf Matt 26:17-25; Luke 22:7-13), two disciples enter Jerusalem to prepare a Passover meal in an upstairs room (Mark 14:15; Luke 22:12) where Jesus and the Twelve will eat what becomes their final meal together. The room is described as large and furnished, possibly indicating couches spread out for guests to recline at a banquet. The house was probably a two-story private urban home, where second-floor rooms were often used as living areas or dining rooms while first-floor rooms might be work spaces, living areas, or shops.

Acts uses a different Greek word for an upper-story room. After the eleven male apostles witness Jesus' ascension, they return to Jerusalem and gather in an upper room. Shown to be united and in prayer (v. 14), Jesus' followers regroup during this transition stage as they await the Holy Spirit (1:5, 8; cf 1:21-26). The women's presence correlates with recent archaeological studies arguing that household space was dynamic and not clearly divided by gender. The diverse group assembled suggests the inclusiveness of the early church and its leaders. This may be the same upper room where the disciples ate the Passover meal (see also Acts 2:1; 12:12).

In Acts 9:36-43, Tabitha, a disciple and benefactor, is laid in a room upstairs after her death where Peter prays for her: "Then he called God's holy people, including the widows, and presented her alive to them." Later in Acts, Eutychus falls out of a window from the third story of an apartment house where Paul is meeting with others to break bread and preach (Acts 20:7-12).

See BANQUET; HOSPITALITY; ROOF.

UR 1. Ur was a very ancient and important city of lower Mesopotamia, located at modern Tell el-Muqayyar, a few kilometers southwest of the modern city of Nasiriyah, Iraq. Though Tell el-Muqayyar lies in the desert at some distance from the Euphrates and quite removed from the head of the Persian Gulf, this is due to changes in the course of the Euphrates and to a receding coastline. An ancient bed of the Euphrates runs along the western and northern walls of Ur, and in its heyday Ur was served by both a western and a northern harbor on the right bank of the river. Ur was a large and powerful city for ca. 4,000 years.

The Bible mentions Ur four times as the original home of Abraham, always in the expression "Ur of the Chaldeans" (Gen 11:28, 31; 15:7; Neh 9:7). Abraham first emigrated from Ur to Haran (Harran in cuneiform sources) in upper Mesopotamia and eventually from there to Canaan. See AMORITES; ASSYRIA AND BABYLONIA; CHALDEA, CHALDEANS; ELAM, ELAMITES; ERECH; HARAN; NEBUCHADNEZZAR, NEBUCHADREZZAR.

2. The father of Eliphal (1 Chron 11:35). Eliphal's name appears in a list of warriors in the service of David. In a parallel list in 2 Sam 23:34, a person named Ahasbai appears as the father of the warrior Eliphelet, presumably a variant form of the name Eliphal.

URBANUS One of many individuals greeted by Paul at the end of Romans (16:9), but only one of four mentioned in the letter who are explicitly identified as being a "coworker" of Paul, the others being Prisca and Aquila (16:3) and Timothy (16:21). Urbanus was most likely a Gentile Christian, although there is still debate as to whether his name indicates that he was freeborn or slave-born.

URI 1. A Judahite, father of Bezalel, one of the builders of the meeting tent (Exod 31:2; 35:30; 38:22; 2 Chron 1:5). He is a grandson of Caleb according to the genealogy of Judah in 1 Chron 2:20.

2. Father of Geber, the district officer in Gilead under Solomon (1 Kgs 4:19).

3. A gatekeeper who was compelled to divorce his foreign wife in the days of Ezra (Ezra 10:24).

URIAH Means "The Lord is light (or fire)."

1. A Hittite and an officer of DAVID's army who died because of David's betrayal. He was named in a list of an elite group of officers in the Israelite army (2 Sam 23:24-39), and the fact that his house was near the king's house may indicate that he was from a prominent member of the royal-military circles that antedated David's conquest of Jerusalem. He was on the battlefield against the Ammonites at Rabbah when David took advantage of his wife BATHSHEBA in his absence and, as a result, she became pregnant (2 Sam 11:1-5).

2. A priest in the reign of Ahaz of Judah and a contemporary of the prophet Isaiah. While in Damascus to meet Tiglath-pileser, king of Assyria, Ahaz sent him detailed descriptions of the altar in Damascus (2 Kgs 16:10). He built the altar before Ahaz returned from Damascus. When Ahaz arrived in Jerusalem, the king gave the priest instructions for the use of the altar (2 Kgs 16:15), and the priest "did everything that King Ahaz commanded" (2 Kgs 16:16). Apparently, this Uriah was one of the two "trusted people" whom Isaiah called upon to witness an oracle against Damascus and Samaria (Isa 8:1-2).

3. A prophet from Kiriath-jearim, son of Shemaiah. He prophesied against Jerusalem in words similar to Jeremiah's temple sermon (Jer 26:20). Jeremiah's life was spared by the intervention of Ahikam son of Shaphan (Jer 26:24), but no one intervened on behalf of Uriah. He fled to Egypt, but Jehoiakim sent an envoy to bring him back, struck him down with the sword, and threw his body into the common graveyard (Jer 26:23).

4. The father of the priest Meremoth who returned to Jerusalem with Ezra (8:33; cf 1 Esdr 8:62) and partook in the rebuilding of the Jerusalem wall under Nehemiah's leadership (Neh 3:4, 21). He was remembered in his son's good deeds.

5. One of the leaders who was given the honor of standing at the right side of Ezra on a wooden platform made for the occasion of the public reading of "the Instruction scroll from Moses" (Neh 8:4; 1 Esdr 9:43).

URIEL 1. A Levite whose name appears in a list of the descendants of Kohath in 1 Chron 6:24 (Heb. 6:9). He appears again in 1 Chron 15:5 and 1 Chron 15:11 as the head of the Kohathite clan during the reign of David, and he is listed among those Levites who participated in the transportation of the covenant chest to Jerusalem from the house of Obed-edom.

2. A man from Gibeah who is mentioned in 2 Chron 13:2 as the maternal grandfather of the Judahite king Abijah and whose mother was Micaiah. Elsewhere in the Hebrew and the LXX of 2 Chron 13:2, Micaiah's name appears as "Maacah." Uriel's paternity is somewhat unclear, because Micaiah appears as the daughter of Absalom in 1 Kgs 15:2 and 2 Chron 11:20. She is generally believed to be Uriel's daughter and Absalom's granddaughter.

3. An angel ("God's flame") who appears to Ezra and instructs him about the end of the age (2 Esdr 4:1; 5:20; 10:28). In 1 Enoch, he is Enoch's guide and reveals astrological knowledge, whereas in the Sibylline Oracles he leads souls from the grave to judgment, which is also his role in the Apocalypse of Peter. For the rabbis, Uriel was one of the four angels around God's throne (Num. Rab. 2:10) and one of the four wise (angelic) teachers who laid Moses to his final rest (Tg. Ps.-J. Deut 34:6). See GABRIEL; MICHAEL; RAPHAEL.

URIM AND THUMMIM *Urim* and *Thummim* are words of uncertain etymology. Some suspect that the terms come from the words for "light" and "truth," and in that way signal their obviously divinatory character. Others argue that they are formed from the roots for curse and faultlessness, and thus signal two possible outcomes of using the Urim and Thummim to judge a person. Still others suggest that they form a merism, denoting the first and last letters of the Heb. alphabet, *alef* and *tav*, and therefore the instruments referred to with the name "Urim and Thummim" would actually be the letters of the alphabet, from which the user would derive oracular meaning. None of these etymologies have found sufficient following to obtain the status of anything approaching a consensus.

Though few in number, occurrences of the pair of terms (or of one of them singly) do provide some useful information (but still less than one might hope). From the occurrences in the Priestly source in the Pentateuch we learn where the Urim and Thummim are kept (in the breastpiece attached to the high priest's vest; Exod 28:30; Lev 8:8), that they can serve as a means of judgment exercised by the high priest (Exod 28:30), and that the judgment might be more expansive than merely providing a yes or no answer to a question (Num 27:21; Urim only). One might also argue that the Priestly source limits the locus of the use of the Urim and Thummim by the high priest to the most holy place ("when he goes into the LORD's presence" in Exod 28:30; Num 27:21).

None of these passages tell us what the Urim and Thummim were, nor do they indicate how their users consulted them. Scholars have made many suggestions, including sticks, dice, or colored stones. Josephus, *Ant.* 3.216–18, may be read to suggest that the Urim and Thummim were the twelve stones on or in the chest pendant of the high priest, and that they simply shone to give a favorable response from God regarding a decision to march against enemies. It is not merely the lack of certainty regarding the nature of the Urim and Thummim that prohibits clarity on their use; it is the diversity of testimony as well.

When did the Urim and Thummim cease to serve their purpose? The evidence of Ezra 2:63 (Neh 7:65) implies that already in the Second Temple period they had gone out of use (or there was no priest to use them effectively): there simply was no priest to give Urim and Thummim to settle the priestly status of claimants to the office. By contrast, the description of the contemporary high priest in Sir 45:7-13 (early 2nd cent. BCE) insists that he still possessed the "oracle of judgment," and Josephus says that the stones of the chest pendant (really the Urim and Thummim?) still shone until nearly the end of the 2nd cent. BCE (*Ant.* 3.218).

UTHAI 1. The son of Ammihud, of the Judaite clan of Perez (1 Chron 9:4). Uthai was the head of his ancestral house (v. 9) and settled in Jerusalem with other exiles returning from Babylon (vv. 2-3). The meaning of his name is highly disputed. The alternatives include: (1) "The Lord has shown himself surpassing" or "The Lord has surpassed himself"; (2) a variant of ATHAIAH, "pride of the Lord" or "The Lord is my pride"; (3) a shorted form of ATHALIAH, "The Lord has shown himself preeminent"; and (4) "The Lord succors."

2. One of the descendants of Bigvai, who, with seventy males, accompanied Ezra from Babylon under Artaxerxes (Ezra 8:14; 1 Esdr 8:40).

3. One whose descendants returned from Babylon under Zerubbabel as temple servants (1 Esdr 5:30).

UZ 1. Son of Aram (Gen 10:23).

2. Son of Nahor, Abraham's brother (Gen 22:21).

3. Son of the Horite chief Dishan (Gen 36:21, 28).

4. The homeland of Job, east of Israel but of an uncertain location (Job 1:1). One tradition places Uz in Edom. Lamentations 4:21 parallels Uz and Edom. Uz is listed in the Edomite genealogy (Gen 36:28) and several personal names in the book of Job are Edomite. Furthermore, the LXX appendix to the book of Job places the city between Idumea and Arabia, which supports an Edomite location. See EDOM, EDOMITES.

UZAI Uzai is the father of PALAL, an individual who helped rebuild the walls and towers of Jerusalem ca. 447 BCE (Neh 3:25). The name may be a shortened form of a name meaning "Yahu has heard."

UZAL The son of Joktan, a descendant of Shem, and the eponymous ancestor of a tribe in south Arabia (Gen 10:27; 1 Chron 1:21). The site is traditionally associated with Azal, which is Sanaa, the modern capital of Yemen. Other scholars connect Uzal with a site near Medina named Azalla, based upon the similarity of these names, as well as the similarity of the names of nearby villages (Yarki and Hurarina) to those of Uzal's brothers, Jerah and Hadoram. Ezekiel 27:19 also apparently mentions Uzal in a list of nations and towns that were trading partners of Tyre, but the meaning of the Hebrew text is uncertain.

UZZAH 1. The son of Abinadab, involved with his brother Ahio in the transport of the covenant chest under the aegis of David. As the new cart on which the chest was being transported began to falter on uneven terrain—thereby jeopardizing the chest—Uzzah reached out to steady the sacred chest. Upon touching it, he was struck dead by God (2 Sam 6; 1 Chron 13). The disastrous covenant chest scenario apparently provides the etiological background for the name given to the location: Perez-uzzah.

2. The garden of Uzzah is identified as the burial place for both Manasseh and his son Amon (2 Kgs 21:18, 26, respectively); the parallel Chronicles account does not record this detail (2 Chron 33:20, 24).

3. A Levite, of the sons of Merari, specifically, the son of Shimei (1 Chron 6:29 [Heb. 6:14]).

4. A Benjaminite of Geba, descendant of Ehud and Gera (1 Chron 8:6-7; CEB, "Uzza").

5. Descendants of Uzza, listed among the temple servants who were among the returnees under the leadership of Zerubbabel (Ezra 2:49; Neh 7:51; 1 Esdr 5:31).

UZZEN-SHEERAH A town named Uzzen-sheerah (perhaps meaning "ear of Sheerah") is mentioned in 1 Chron 7:24; its location is unknown. SHEERAH was the daughter of either Ephraim or his son Beriah (1 Chron 7:23). She is the only woman credited in the Bible with building a city, and she is said to have built three: Uzzen-sheerah itself, as well as Lower BETH-HORON and Upper Beth-horon.

UZZI A shortened form of UZZIAH or UZZIEL, meaning "the Lord/God is my strength."

1. Son of Bukki and a descendant of Eleazar in the line of Aaron (1 Chron 6:5-6, 51 [Heb. 5:31-32; 6:36]; Ezra 7:4; 1 Esdr 8:2).

2. Grandson of Issachar and son of Tola (1 Chron 7:2-3).

3. Grandson of Benjamin and son of Bela (1 Chron 7:7).

4. Son of Michri and father of Elah who was a member of a family of Benjamin (1 Chron 9:8).

5. Son of Bani who was an overseer of the Levites after the return from exile (Neh 11:22).

6. The head of the priestly family of Jedaiah during the time of the high priest Joiakim (Neh 12:19).

7. A priest, perhaps a musician, who participated in the dedication of the walls of Jerusalem (Neh 12:42).

UZZIA Meaning "My strength is the Lord." An Ashterathite named among the sixteen Reubenites from Transjordan added by the Chronicler to the list of David's thirty mighty men (1 Chron 11:44).

UZZIAH Means "The Lord is my strength." Five individuals in the OT bear this name.

1. An early 8th-cent. king of Judah. Uzziah (twenty-five times) is also called Azariah ("the Lord is my help") nine times in the OT. The two names differ by a single consonant in Hebrew and are therefore much more similar than they appear in English. However, it has been suggested "Uzziah" was the king's throne name and "Azariah" his personal name, to which he reverted when disease forced him off the throne. This suggestion is based on the fact that the prophets use "Uzziah" exclusively (Isa 1:1; 6:1; 7:1; Hos 1:1; Amos 1:1; Zech 14:5).

The brief description of Azariah's reign in 2 Kgs 15:1-7 portrays him as a basically righteous king except for his failure to take away the "shrines," but whom the Lord also struck with a skin disease (probably not what is known today as leprosy, i.e., Hansen's disease) that forced him to live in a "separate house," perhaps a euphemism for a sanatorium (2 Kgs 15:5). The very different version of Uzziah's reign in 2 Chron 26 is the result primarily of theological considerations. The Chronicler was compelled to account theologically for both Uzziah's longevity and his disease, which indicated opposite divine judgments, according to his worldview.

The accounts of Uzziah's reign in Kings and Chronicles agree in attributing to him a fifty-two-year reign, beginning at age 16 (2 Kgs 15:1; 2 Chron 26:3). The reign of Uzziah appears to have been a relatively peaceful and prosperous time for Judah. This is largely because it overlapped with Jeroboam II of Israel, with whom Uzziah was at peace and by whom Judah was probably overshadowed if not dominated. An indication of Uzziah's success is the note in 2 Kgs 14:22 that he rebuilt and restored Elat to Judah.

2. Father of Jonathan, an official over David's outlying treasuries (1 Chron 27:25).

3. A Levite of the Kohathite branch (1 Chron 6:24 [Heb. 6:9]).

4. One of the priests commanded by Ezra to divorce his foreign wife (Ezra 10:21).

5. Father of Athaiah, a postexilic Judahite resident of Jerusalem (Neh 11:4).

UZZIEL Meaning "God is my strength."

1. The son of Kohath and grandson of Levi, who had three sons (Mishael, Elzaphan, and Sithri) and whose nephews were Aaron and Moses (Exod 6:18-22; Lev 10:4; Num 3:19; 1 Chron 6:2 [Heb. 5:28]; 23:12, 20). The Kohathites were charged with the care of the covenant

chest, the table, lampstands, altars, sanctuary vessels, and the screen (Num 3:27-31). When King David reorganized the cultic personnel, Amminadab led 112 of Uzziel's descendants (1 Chron 15:10), and as David's death drew near, the king's reorganization of the Levites found Micah as the chief of Uzziel's clan and Isshiah as his lieutenant (1 Chron 23:10; 24:24-25).

2. One of the sons of Ishi, a Simeonite, who led 500 of their tribesmen to destroy the survivors of the Amalekites at Mount Seir and then settled there (1 Chron 4:42).

3. The son of Bela, a Benjaminite who was a warrior. With his four brothers (Ezbon, Uzzi, Jerimoth, and Iri), he led 22,034 men of the tribe (1 Chron 7:7).

4. A Levite who served with his thirteen brothers as temple musicians under the direction of their father Heman, who was King David's seer (1 Chron 25:4). Uzziel's name is given as Azarel in 1 Chron 25:18, perhaps a scribal error.

5. A Levite, son of Jeduthun and brother of Shemaiah (2 Chron 29:14), who joined others of the tribe in obedience to King Hezekiah's command that they sanctify themselves, cleanse the temple, and reinstitute the faithful service of God there (2 Chron 29:3-19).

6. A goldsmith who was the son of Harhaiah and who participated in the rebuilding of Jerusalem's walls under Nehemiah's leadership (Neh 3:8).

Vv

VAIN The modern use of *vain* to describe an attitude toward one's personal appearance is not found in the Bible. Rather, vain is typically used to translate a cluster of words that carry the sense of being useless, ineffectual, or empty. It is frequently employed in the adverbial expression "in vain," as when God complains of having punished Israel "in vain" (Jer 2:30). The root meanings of these words involve falsehood and emptiness, respectively, but these and similar verses refer primarily to ineffectuality (e.g., Job 9:29). This meaning of vain also applies to worship that is directed toward the wrong object or does not come from the heart. See VANITY.

VAIZATHA One of Haman's ten sons, killed by the Jews in Susa and later impaled on a stake (Esth 9:9, 14). The Jews also struck down 500 men in addition to Haman's sons as retribution for Haman's plan of annihilation.

VALLEY Because they are more conducive to agriculture and urban life than the surrounding arid hills, valleys are the center of much material and metaphorical action in the biblical text. Used most commonly in the physical sense to refer to a low place between mountains or other geographical depression, the term is also used symbolically to indicate situations of divine judgment and human difficulty. The topography of Israel contains innumerable valleys, so they occur frequently as place references in the text. Valleys represent agricultural abundance, described as places of grain (Isa 17:5); orchards (Song 6:11); and cattle (Isa 63:14). Many battles are fought in valleys, both human (Gen 14:8; 2 Sam 5:22; 2 Kgs 14:7; 2 Chron 14:10) and divine (Isa 22:5; Ezek 39:11, 15; Hos 1:5; Zech 14:4-5). The transformation of valleys is a sign of the coming of the Lord (Isa 40:4; Mic 1:4). Valleys serve as a place for divine visions (Isa 22:1; Ezek

3:22; 37:1-2), while the "darkest valley" (Ps 23:4) represents the low places of human existence. Several Hebrew and Greek words are translated as "valley," some of which are alternatively translated "plain," "vale," "gorge," "wadi," or "ravine."

VALLEY OF THE SHADOW, DARK VALLEY The term is familiar from its use in Ps 23:4, where the CEB translates it as "darkest valley." Elsewhere it is translated "deepest darkness" (e.g., Ps 44:19 [Heb. 44:20]; Amos 5:8) or "darkness and deep gloom" (e.g., Ps 107:10, 14).

God's creative powers are described in terms of control over deep darkness (Job 12:22; 34:22; 38:17; Jer 13:16; Amos 5:8). The term often appears in contexts expressing hope (e.g., Isa 9:2 [Heb. 9:1], which promises that light will shine on those who live in "a pitch-dark land"); or comfort (e.g., Jer 2:6, where the Lord guided Israel "through the wilderness . . . in a land of drought and darkness"). The term may also express despair, however, and thus is a favorite of Job (16:16; 24:17; 28:3), who wishes that the day of his birth would be turned into deep darkness (3:4) and hopes for the darkness of death (10:21-22).

VANIAH A descendant of Bani and returnee from exile, who is listed among Israelites who had to divorce their foreign wives (Ezra 10:36). He appears in a parallel list in 1 Esdr 9:34. Variations in the spelling of the name raise questions about whether Vaniah is a proper name.

VANITY The word occurs in Ecclesiastes in most English versions. It opens and closes the book in 1:2 and 12:8: "Vanity of vanities, says the Teacher, vanity of vanities! All is vanity." The phrases "all is vanity" and "this is (also) vanity" form a refrain throughout the book (1:14; 2:11, 17, 23, 26; 4:4, 16; 5:10; 6:2, 9; 7:6; 8:14; 9:2).

In Jerome's 425 CE Vulgate, he translated this as *vanitas*, a word that means in Latin "unsubstantial," "empty," or "illusory." The KJV translated the word as "vanitie." Modern English translations (e.g., ASV, RSV, NASB, NKJV, NRSV) render the Hebrew word as "vanity." The CEB translates it as "perfectly pointless."

VASHTI Esther's predecessor as queen (Esth 1:9–2:4). Vashti holds a banquet for the women, which echoes the king's lavish banquet for the men. King Ahasuerus commands her to leave the women's space for the men's, to show off her beauty. Her refusal, for reasons unstated, sets up Esther's entrance into the court and the story and emphasizes that the boundary between women's and men's space is a treacherous one.

VEIL Since the earliest church, it has been a common practice for Christian women to cover their heads in worship, and many continue to do so, largely citing 1 Cor 11:5-15. This passage is the subject of debate since Paul on the one hand affirms the interdependence of the genders and on the other hand the hierarchy that places the man (or husband) as the head of the woman (or wife). In ancient Mediterranean culture most married women covered their heads to indicate that a husband protected them. Paul thus seems to reassert the Corinthian women's marital and social status, even while assuming that these same women lead worship.

In OT narratives, the practice of covering face and body is often associated with mistaken identity and unlikely sexual union (Gen 38:14-19; cf 29:23-25). Removing a veil can indicate humiliation or mourning instead of luxury or wedding celebration (Isa 3:23; 47:2; see also Sus 32; 3 Macc 4:6). The facial veil can highlight the outlines of what it covers as though it enhances, rather than conceals, the beauty beneath (Song 4:1, 3; 6:7). Similarly, Moses' unusual use of the veil in Exod 34:33-35 seems to emphasize the divine glow of his face after speaking with the Lord, while it also shields the Israelites from the apparent danger. The veil as protection from divine power echoes a general fear of seeing the face or glory of God, like the veil that shields the covenant chest and the most holy place in the temple (see VEIL OF THE TEMPLE). Paul, on the other hand, portrays Moses' veiling as the latter's attempt to hide the fading of the divine presence and uses the veil as a metaphor for the blindness of non-Christian Jews in reading the Jewish Scriptures (2 Cor 3:13-16). See HEAD COVERING.

VEIL OF THE TEMPLE In Zerubbabel and Herod's temple, a curtain or veil blocked the entrance into the shrine from the central nave (Josephus, *J.W.* 5.219). Another elaborately decorated curtain hung inside the massive doors that led from the open vestibule into the central nave (*J.W.* 5.212–14; Sir 50:5). These curtains have a precedent in the curtain and screen of the MEETING TENT (Exod 26:31-37).

Solomon's temple had wooden doors between the shrine and the nave (1 Kgs 6:31) and between the nave and the vestibule (1 Kgs 6:33-34), but no curtains are mentioned. Second Chronicles 3:14 mentions a curtain, not a door, before the shrine, but this may reflect the layout of the second temple. Nonetheless, many scholars think that a curtain hung behind the doors into the shrine to veil the shrine when the doors were open (see 1 Kgs 8:8, which suggests that a curtain blocked a direct view of the chest from the open doorway, but the gap between the doorway and the ends of the curtain permitted a view of the ends of the long poles).

The NT claims that the curtain between the nave and the shrine was mysteriously torn from top to bottom at the time of Jesus' crucifixion (Matt 27:51; Mark 15:38; Luke 23:45), indicating that access into the presence of God had been provided for all the followers of Jesus by his self-sacrifice (Heb 6:19; 10:20). See TEMPLE, JERUSALEM.

VENGEANCE While the word *vengeance* and its verbal form *AVENGE* have a pejorative connotation in English (that of excessive, indiscriminate force driven by a desire to restore someone's honor and humiliate the other), Hebrew does not have that connotation. Most occurrences of *vengeance* are ascribed to God in the OT, and in most cases, the noun has the nuance of RETRIBUTION.

Sometimes Israel is the recipient of God's vengeance (Lev 26 and Deut 32). The Lord also threatens Israel's adversaries with vengeance, often through Israel (Num 31:3; Isa 47:3; Ps 149:7).

Vengeance sometimes refers to human retaliation, such as that of a husband against the lover of his unfaithful wife ("revenge" [Prov 6:34]). New Testament examples of human vengeance include the punishment of wrongdoers by governmental authorities (Rom 13:4; 1 Pet 2:14) and self-inflicted punishment (2 Cor 7:11). See AVENGE.

VERMILION Vermilion designates a shade of red. Paint was given this color by adding a pigment obtained from iron-bearing ocher or from cinnabar, a naturally occurring compound of mercury and sulfur. Biblical examples suggest that vermilion paint was used in homes of wealth and prestige (Ezek 23:14; "red" [Jer 22:14]).

VILLAGE Historically, the largest percentage of the population of ancient Israel lived in small, unwalled agricultural villages (1 Sam 6:18; Ezek 38:11). The average size of these settlements in the highlands of Judah and Samaria during the Iron Age was no more than 5 ac. with a population of between 75 and 100 persons. Their inhabitants, like the prophet Amos, engaged in a mixed economy of herding and farming that provided them a basic subsistence level and perhaps a small surplus for trade or to pay their taxes (Amos 7:14).

VINE, VINEYARD From earliest memory, vineyards were essential to the well-being of the people of the Levant; according to tradition, Noah planted a vineyard after the flood subsided (Gen 9:20). Grapevines thrived in arid climates and provided much of the community's subsistence. The fruit was dried and stored for later consumption, used as a source of sugar, or pressed to make wine. Vineyards also provided food for the poor, widows, orphans, and sojourners, who were allowed to pick behind the harvesters (Lev 19:10; Deut 24:21; see 4 Macc 2:9). Extended family and friends helped pick and tread grapes during the short time between the fruit's ripening and rotting on the vine. Jesus' parable about an owner who goes out to hire more laborers up to the last moment may reflect such harvesttime pressures (Matt 20:1-9).

The vineyard's importance in the community was evidenced by the mandate to choose vine tending over military service (Deut 20:6). It was traumatic for a family to lose its vineyard, its inheritance, as illustrated by Naboth's refusal to part with his to Ahab and Naboth's subsequent murder by Ahab and/or Jezebel (1 Kgs 21; 2 Kgs 9:25-26). Vineyards were tended by generations of family members. The centrality of the vineyard to the families of Israel made the vineyard a likely symbol for the nation of Israel and its people: "Israel is a growing vine that yields its fruit" (Hos 10:1; see also Ps 80:8-11; Isa 5:1-7; Jer 2:21; 2 Esdr 5:23). Christians adapted the vine imagery for their new community united with Jesus, as Jesus becomes the vine and his followers the branches that bear fruit (John 15:1-6).

The vine was a metaphor for peace (Mic 4:4; Zech 3:10; cf 2 Kgs 18:31; Isa 36:16) and prosperity (Ps 128:1-6). Prophets often turned to the image of the fruitless vine to illustrate religious and economic disorder (Isa 32:10-15; 34:4; Jer 8:13; Joel 1:11-12; 2 Esdr 16:26, 30). Isaiah's "song of the vineyard" (Isa 5:1-7; 27:1-6) refers to unjust and unfaithful Israel as a vineyard bearing "rotten grapes" (Isa 5:2). Jesus adapts Isaiah's language for a parable of unfaithful vineyard workers who try to gain the vineyard for themselves (Matt 21:33-46; Mark 12:1-9; Luke 20:9-19). Burning or uprooting the vines is a metaphor for divine judgment (Ezek 15:1-7; 17:1-10). Harvesting and pressing the grapes serve as imagery for eschatological judgment, when an angel gathers "the clusters in the vineyard of the earth" and throws them into the "great winepress of God's passionate anger" (Rev 14:18-20).

The fertility of the vine and imagery of luscious, juicy grapes might have inspired the poet(s) of the Song of Songs to apply the vineyard and vine metaphorically to represent the woman's sexuality: "They made me a caretaker of the vineyards—but I couldn't care for my own vineyard" (Song 1:6*b*; see also 2:13; 6:11; 7:8, 12; 8:11-12). Likewise, personified "Wisdom" praises herself, saying, "Gracious favor was the leaf that I put forth like a vine. . . . Come to me, you who desire me, and take your fill of my produce" (Sir 24:17-19).

VINEDRESSERS Vinedressers planted and tended vines for the production of wine (Joel 1:11). Vineyards required great care if they were to remain fruitful, and the Babylonian conquerors of Judah appointed "some of the land's poor people" to "work the vineyards" (2 Kgs 25:12; 2 Chron 26:10; Jer 52:16).

See FARMER.

VINEGAR When wine is exposed to air, it turns to vinegar (cf Num 6:3, "wine vinegar"). In Ps 69:21 [Heb. 69:22], the psalmist receives vinegar as a thirst quencher, along with "poison for food." In Prov 25:20, forcing a grieving person to listen to songs is compared to "putting vinegar on a wound"; cf Prov 10:26, which likens the effect of vinegar on the teeth to that of smoke on the eyes.

In all four Gospels (Matt 27:48; Mark 15:36; Luke 23:36; John 19:29), just before his death, Jesus is offered a sponge filled with "vinegar" or "sour wine." In John, Jesus drinks and then says "It is completed" (v. 30); his action seems to be portrayed as a fulfillment of Ps 69:21 [Heb. 69:22]. See DRINK; WINE.

VIOLET A shade of PURPLE mentioned in a description of embroidery yarns used in the furnishings of Solomon's temple (2 Chron 2:7, 14; 3:14).

VIPER A viper is a type of snake, usually venomous. *Viper* and the more general word *serpent*, used metaphorically, symbolize evil or danger (e.g., Rom 3:13). Most species of snakes in Israel are not poisonous.

VIRGIN The term *young woman* or *virgin*, or its related abstract noun *virginity*, occurs more than fifty times in the OT.

In the OT the term refers generally to a nubile young woman. As suggested by its frequent pairing with "young man" (Deut 32:25; 2 Chron 36:17; Pss 78:63; 148:12; Isa 23:4; 62:5; Jer 51:22; Lam 1:18; 2:21; Ezek 9:6), the primary meaning of the noun is not focused on virginity. When the text wants to emphasize the virginal state of a girl, it adds the phrase, "hadn't known a man intimately" (Gen 24:16; Judg 11:39; 21:12). Thus *virgin* most often refers to a young, unmarried woman.

As is the case with the OT, the term in the NT has been the subject of debate as to whether it refers only to youth or also to sexual inexperience. The most well-known NT occurrences refer to Mary the mother of Jesus. The infancy narratives of both Matthew and Luke portray Mary as a virgin; emphasis on Mary's virginity underscores Jesus' extraordinary conception (see VIRGIN BIRTH). Whereas the Matthean parable of the ten virgins (Matt 25:1-13; "ten young bridesmaids" CEB) emphasizes the marital, not the sexual, status of the young women in the story, Rev 14:4 uses the term to emphasize the cultic purity of the faithful 144,000.

In the NT Epistles, Paul uses the term twice, the 1st time in 1 Cor 7:34 and the 2nd time in 2 Cor 11:2.

See MARRIAGE.

VIRGIN BIRTH "Virgin birth" is an imprecise reference to the manner of Jesus' conception, who is regarded in the Gospels of both Matthew and Luke and in the creedal tradition as having been conceived without the biological contribution of a human father and born of a human mother who had not had sexual relations with a man. A more accurate designation, therefore, would be "virginal conception."

In 1st-cent. Judaism, marriage ordinarily followed the completion of a marriage agreement, including the payment of a bride price and a period of betrothal during which a woman continued to live in her father's household, but was legally bound to her husband-to-be. This period of Joseph and Mary's betrothal is signified in Matt 1:18: "before they were married." Accordingly, Matthew's text would read that Mary was found to be with child "before their engaging in sexual intercourse." Having ruled out the biological contribution of Joseph, the Evangelist goes on to assert that Mary's pregnancy was the consequence of divine agency, "conceived by the Holy Spirit" (v. 20), referring to the inexplicable exercise of creative power by God. Using terminology employed in 1:16 and 18, an angel reports to Joseph that Mary's pregnancy has occurred apart from a father and is a result of divine intervention.

Luke emphasizes Mary's status as a "virgin," identifying her in this way twice in 1:27 and observing further that she was "engaged" to Joseph. This would identify Mary as a young woman having just achieved puberty, perhaps 12 or 13 years old. That Luke refers not simply to Mary's relative youth but also to her lack of prior sexual activity becomes obvious in 1:34.

Outside the birth narratives of the Gospels of Matthew and Luke, we find in the NT no explicit references to the virginal conception of Jesus. The enigma of the virginal conception of Jesus does not prove the incarnation, but serves as its sign.

VISION A mystical revelatory experience involving a visual dimension. The OT narrates both waking visions and night visions. Visions often include auditory components and are usually, but not always, associated with prophetic activity or apocalyptic revelation. Visions occur throughout the OT, though in the NT most are clustered in Acts and Revelation.

Various Hebrew and Greek words translated "vision" encompass a range of meanings and literary forms. God establishes the covenant with Abraham through a vision that includes both a conversation and a dream (Gen 15:1-21). In a night vision Daniel receives the interpretation of Nebuchadnezzar's dream (2:17-45). The Hebrew word can serve as a generic introduction to prophetic books (Isa 1:1; Obad 1:1; Nah 1:1) or units (2 Sam 7:17; 1 Chron 17:15; Ezek 7:13; Hab 2:2-3), even as it applies to visions generally (e.g., 1 Sam 3:1; Ps 89:19; Lam 2:9; Hos 12:10). Visions may convey messages from God, introduce the seer to mysteries such as heavenly and eschatological beings and places (1 Kgs 22:19-23; Isa 6; Ezek 40–48; Amos 9:1-10; Revelation includes visions of the risen Jesus, the heavenly court, and the New Jerusalem), provide images that require interpretation (Ezek 1; Amos 7–8), or even require participation on the part of the visionary (Ezek 8:1-18; Rev 10:8-10). Some visions rely upon wordplays (Jer 1:11-12; Amos 8:1-3).

Visions play an especially important role in Acts, particularly legitimating the inclusion of the Gentiles. Peter's Pentecost sermon alludes to Joel's prophecy concerning visions and dreams in the last days (Joel 2:28-32 [Heb. 3:1-5]; Acts 2:17-21). Through a visionary encounter with the risen Jesus, Saul turns from one who harasses the church into its most prominent missionary to the Gentiles (Acts 9:1-9; 22:1-21; 26:2-23). A vision also convinces Peter to evangelize the Gentile Cornelius (10:9-16; 11:1-18). The effectiveness of these visions depends upon complementary visions received by Ananias (9:10-19) and Cornelius (10:1-8). Paul appeals to his visionary and apocalyptic experiences in defending his authority (2 Cor 12:1-10; Gal 1:11-17).

Among the Synoptic Gospels, Matthew alone describes the transfiguration as a vision (17:9). Both biblical apocalypses, Daniel and Revelation, narrate sequences of visions. Visions constitute an essential component for the definition of classical literary apocalypses such as 1 Enoch, 2 Esdr 3–14 (4 Ezra), 2 and 3 Baruch, and the Shepherd of Hermas (Vision). See APOCALYPTICISM; DREAM; PROPHET.

VOPHSI According to Num 13:14, he was the father of Nahbi, the Naphtalite leader sent with other tribal leaders by Moses to spy out Canaan.

VOW A speech act similar to promise and OATH. More specifically, a person's explicit commitment to perform a favor for a deity if the deity will respond to his or her request for a favor.

VULGATE From Latin *vulgatus*, "common," the standardized Latin version of the Bible ascribed to JEROME (342–420 CE) and used by the Christian church as an authoritative translation for more than 1,000 years..

VULTURE Since vultures are notorious carrion eaters, several species are mentioned in the lists of unclean birds. Because *vulture* carries negative connotations for modern readers, many translations use the translation EAGLE when positive images of the bird are presented (Exod 19:4; Deut 32:11). Various passages indicate the bird's swiftness ("as fast as the eagle flies" [Deut 28:49]; "swiftly, like an eagle" [Hab 1:8]); its aeries found in inaccessible cliffs (Jer 49:16); its powerful wings (Isa 40:31); its exceptional sight (Job 39:29); or its care for its young (Deut 32:11). See BIRDS OF THE BIBLE.

Ww

WADI A valley or canyon carved by running water. Wadis usually contain rivers created by runoff during the rainy season but are dry during other parts of the year (1 Kgs 17:7). Flash flooding can occur rapidly in wadis, turning them into dangerous torrents. The term can also refer to the dry riverbed at the bottom of a valley.

WAFERS Pieces of thin, unleavened bread that served as offerings in the Israelite cult. The Levites were responsible for assisting in the preparation of "wafers of unleavened bread" for the temple (1 Chron 23:29). The regulations for baked grain offerings prescribed unleavened wafers made of choice flour and spread with oil (Lev 2:4). Unleavened wafers were among the cereal gifts offered during the consecration of Aaron and his sons as priests (Exod 29:2, 23; Lev 8:26). Wafers were prescribed for typical thanksgiving offerings (Lev 7:12), as well as for the offerings required of persons completing a Nazirite vow (Num 6:15, 19). Manna is said to have tasted "like honey wafers" (Exod 16:31). See NAZIR, NAZIRITE; SACRIFICES AND OFFERINGS.

WAGES In the OT, words translated as "wages" cover a far broader area than contemporary English use. They include any reciprocation for services rendered, whether contracted for or not, such as a benefaction, reward, or retribution, depending on context. As benefaction or retribution, the words refer to a form of generalized reciprocity not based on obligation ("I give with no expectation of specific repayment").

A frequent lament among biblical writers, aimed at elites, is that daily wage earners were deprived of the pay owed to them (Lev 19:13; Deut 24:14-15; Jer 22:23; Mal 3:5; see also Jas 5:4).

Later, another word for wages emerged among Greek speakers. This originally referred to soldier's pay (for food) in the Hellenistic period (see 1 Esdr 4:56; 1 Macc 3:28; 14:32; Luke 3:14; 1 Cor 9:7). It eventually was used to refer to any pay or wages for a contracted job, as the outcome of an interaction of balanced reciprocity based on mutual obligation (see 2 Cor 11:8). Paul's well-known statement in Rom 6:23, "The wages that sin pays are death," presumes the reader understands that sin here is a personified entity. Romans personified Victory, War, Health, and the like, and even built temples in their honor. Paul understood Sin as such an entity. Personified Sin functioned as a cultural value of willingness to challenge God's honor. Sin was like a person who claimed worth for dishonoring God, for claiming superiority to God. The quality here is enveloped in an attitude of feeling superior to God and God's honor, a willingness to shame God and anybody else, a willingness to stand up to God, a willingness to put oneself over and opposite God. To serve and honor Sin was a task deserving of recompense, in this case death. On the other hand, endless life in Christ Jesus is the outcome of generalized reciprocity, the unearned, free gift of God (Rom 6:23).

WAR, IDEAS OF The Bible presents diverse ideas of war.

In Genesis, the political ideal is not world unity but rather a plurality of peoples. Often, groups solve conflicts (especially over land) by going in separate directions. The patriarchs are, however, not pacifists. Abram goes to war in order to defend his southern Canaanite neighbors against external aggression (chap. 14). Overall, the book of Genesis contradicts view of ancient Israel as a militant people. The books of Exodus through Joshua, however, tell of a formative war in Israel's history, beginning with liberation from Egypt and continuing through military conquest of the land they would inhabit. The Israelites now wage war in order to wipe out the land's former inhabitants. Moreover, this work attributes military success to divine rather than human heroic action. In these stories, all Israel is expected to fight (see esp. Num 1–3). The book of Deuteronomy sets forth a Law code to regulate life, including war (chap. 20). Among the various blessings, Israel is promised military success and political strength. Failure to keep the commandments will be punished with defeat on the battlefield and exile, which are described at greater length.

In Deuteronomy and Joshua, the idea of the BAN is not only prevalent (cf, e.g., Deut 2:34; 3:6; and Josh 2:10 with the accounts in Numbers), but also the Israelites are required to wipe out the prior inhabitants of the land (the "seven nations") in order to avoid their cultic influence (Deut 7:1-5; 20:15-18). The ban in these two books is therefore not elicited by anger or desire for retribution, although such vengeance is required for other peoples (see, e.g., Deut 25:17-19). In contrast to Deut 7:2-5, which treats the ban together with prohibitions of intermarriage and alliances, the passages 2:34; 3:6; and 20:15-18 make it clear that all men, women, and children were to be annihilated.

The book of Judges depicts an era of a plurality of other gods (e.g., 2:12). This, in turn, leads to suffering in war: the Lord withdraws protection so that Israel is both assaulted by her enemies and no longer witnesses success on her military campaigns (2:15-16). The stories of the judges themselves seem to consist in large part of older regional legends of war heroes. The most important message of Judges is that the generations after Joshua must fight wars because they have sinned. It thus presents a punitive conception of war rather than identifying it as an unavoidable condition of the nation's existence.

While the book of Judges presents war as the means through which Israel forfeits the unity enjoyed in the age of Joshua, the book of Samuel portrays war as the path to Israel's political consolidation. In recounting the emergence of the monarchy, 1–2 Samuel emphasizes the changes this institution would bring to Israelite society—not least in the areas of warfare and the military. Samuel describes in his address to the Israelites the chariot-warfare and the weapons industry that will accompany the establishment of a kingdom (1 Sam 8:11-12). When pleading for a monarchy, the people refer to the king's role in battle (8:20), and beginning with Saul's first battle against the Ammonites (chap. 11), it is this role that dominates the account of the monarchy in the rest of Samuel and Kings. Both Judges and Samuel are critical of Israel's natural impulse to crown human military heroes: the Lord is responsible for all victory and is therefore Israel's king.

The descriptions of war in the book of Kings have many themes in common with Samuel (even though Kings presents war for the most part as a divine punitive measure). Thus, the most problematic wars for both are the civil wars. In Samuel these internal battles are fought between father and son (2 Sam 15–19) as well as political opponents (2 Sam 2–4; 20). Kings refers often to the wars between Israel and Judah (see, e.g., 1 Kgs 14:30), and recounts how Israel or Judah even entered into alliances with other nations to fight against each other (e.g., 1 Kgs 15:16-22; 2 Kgs 16:5-9).

War looms large in Isaiah, Jeremiah, and Ezekiel. Although they mirror a variety of perspectives on war, they have much in common—not least a will to perceive divine judgment in the destruction and to pinpoint exactly what elicited the judgment. By identifying the ills in the society that is threatened to be wiped out in war, they already lay the groundwork for its restoration after war. A recurring notion in these books is that Israel's God inflicts war upon Israel because she has strayed from divine teachings. Accordingly, war is caused not merely by international political dynamics but also and primarily by internal socioeconomic injustices and religious violations.

Within the book of Psalms, war represents a central theme. The king prays for deliverance from his enemies, who threaten not only him but also his people (Ps 3). Reflecting upon the destruction wrought by war, the book of Lamentations cries out in anger against Israel's God for wiping out Jacob and Zion without mercy.

Compared to the OT, the topic of war plays a relatively minor role in the NT. This fact is closely tied to its origins in nonterritorial, multiethnic communities living with the context of the Pax Romana. But war is nevertheless an important subject within the NT.

Although the Gospel of Luke presents Jesus as the successor to warriors from the OT such as Gideon, Samson, and David (see esp. chap. 1), it regards his kingdom as spiritual in nature (e.g., 17:20-21) and thus eschews the use of the sword (Luke 22:49-51; see, however, 22:36-38). Elsewhere Jesus teaches nonretaliation (Matt 5:39; Luke 6:29) and love for one's enemy (Matt 5:43-48). Similarly, Paul distinguishes between the "authority of the government" that bears the sword, on the one hand, and the community to which he writes (Rom 13:1-10), on the other. The spiritual nature of the kingdom does not preclude the possibility of Christians serving as soldiers (Acts 10). Without an army of its own, however, the church did not develop a doctrine of war until much later. In general, war is considered to be a common feature of the former, passing world; it is thus taken for granted just as much as other social and natural phenomena, such as famine and earthquakes (Mark 13:7-8).

Most warfare in the NT is not physical. Paul tells the Corinthians, "Our weapons that we fight with aren't human, but instead they are powered by God for the destruction of fortresses" (2 Cor 10:4). These strongholds are identified with "arguments, and every defense that is raised up to oppose the knowledge of God" (2 Cor 10:4-5). The author of Ephesians develops this Pauline idea into the notion of "the full armor of God" (6:10-17). Furthermore, Timothy is exhorted to "wage a good war" (1 Tim 1:18), and Peter urges his readers to "avoid worldly desires that wage war against your lives" (1 Pet 2:11). The wide acceptance of this spiritual-warrior identity is indicated by the popular use of "soldier" for the ideal Christian (Phil 2:25; 2 Tim 2:3; Phlm 2). This notion of spiritual warfare is closely related to the war fought within the individual Christian: James refers to a war of inner cravings (4:1-3); and describing the body of death, Paul speaks of another law warring with the law of his mind and making him captive to the law of sin (Rom 7:21-24).

Physical warfare nevertheless does occupy a place in the descriptions of the eschaton. In the so-called Olivet discourse, Jesus refers to the apocalyptic wars that will be fought between nations and kingdoms as signs of the end of the age (Matt 24:9-28; Mark 13:7-13; Luke 21:12-24). At this point, the Human One will come in a cloud with power and great glory, sending out his angels to gather the elect from the four winds.

WARRIORS In the ancient world, male character was often defined on the field of battle. Warriors displayed both physical and moral courage. Joshua and the judges, as well as the kings of Israel and Judah, were evaluated at least in part based upon their success as warriors. David's reputation in particular is built on his battle prowess (1 Sam 18:7), and, as with many ancient warrior-leaders, he surrounds himself with like-minded characters, such as "the Thirty" (2 Sam 23:23-39).

Exodus 15:3 claims that the Lord is a warrior, and in the hymn that follows—together with numerous psalms and prophetic poems—the character of a savior God (Isa 43:3); liberator God (2 Sam 22:2); a conqueror of enemies (Ps 18:48); and a compassionate (Ps 86:15), faithful God emerges. This God bears all the marks of a victor in battle (Isa 42:13; Pss 18:46-48; 83; 89:10), who teaches Israel the arts of war (Ps 18:34-42).

In the NT the characteristics of the warrior are desired of the church leader. By placing the struggles of the church's life within the context of "spiritual warfare" (2 Cor 10:1-5), Paul invites the comparison of leaders with warriors. In 1 Tim 1:18 and 2 Tim 2:3-4 the comparison is explicit. Members of faith communities are identified as "fellow soldier[s]" (Phil 2:25; Phlm 2); and the scars from following Christ are now battle wounds (2 Tim 2:3). The writer of Eph 6 encourages the warrior-believer to be armed for conflict, changing the foundational metaphor of the Christian life from the transformed family to the army.

WARS OF THE LORD, BOOK OF A poem mentioned in Num 21:14-15, reciting the wars of Israel in the conquest of the Transjordan.

WATCHTOWER A tall stone or brick structure built as a lookout post and fortification. Farmers built watchtowers in their fields so that the owners or workmen could guard their crops from looters or animals (Isa 5:2; Matt 21:33; Mark 12:1). Often watchtowers had a lower room that would serve as the workers' living quarters during harvest season.

Watchtowers were also part of the fortification system. Some stood alone on hills as observation posts such as those Jotham built in Judah ("towers" [2 Chron 27:4]; cf 2 Kgs 17:9; Isa 21:8; 32:14; Lam 4:17). Others were built into city walls as a part of city defenses. These served as strongholds and observation posts for defenders. Often they jutted out from the city walls, thus allowing the defenders to observe the base of the outside walls (Neh 3:25-27). See TOWER.

WATER Water is essential for human, animal, and plant life, and securing a sufficient supply represented a major part of life activities in the time of the OT and the NT. Water was often limited and costly, thus a close link between divine blessings and an ample supply of water (and thus food) existed in the minds of the authors of the Bible. Drought, and in consequence, hunger, was understood to be the result of idolatry—the illegitimate relationship of the people (or an individual) with other gods—and could be remedied by God (2 Chron 6:26-31), if there was a change of relationship. Water was also essential in ritual and religious activities in both the OT and the NT and thus carried important theological connotations.

WATER HEN A bird such as the coot or rail (family *Rallidae*) that inhabits marshlands. The animal is listed among the abhorrent or unclean animals forbidden as food for the Israelites (Deut

14:16). The CEB translates the same Hebrew term as "chameleon" in a list of swarming land animals (Lev 11:30).

WATER OF BITTERNESS A potion created by a priest out of water, dust from the floor of the sanctuary, and the washed-off ink that spelled out adulterous accusations against a wife (Num 5:18, 19, 23-24). According to the law of Num 5:11-31, a woman who drank this and suffered miscarriage, sterility, or deformity of her reproductive organs was considered guilty; a woman who had no physical consequences was deemed innocent. In 5:24 the potion is called "the water of bitterness that brings the curse." Thus "bitterness" referred to the outcome of the ritual for one who was judged guilty and perhaps to the taste of the brew as well. The bitter water ordeal began with a jealousy offering from the accusing husband (Num 5:15-16). The priest disheveled the wife's hair, had her hold the offering, and made her take an oath that the curse would betray her guilt or innocence. The priest then washed the ink of the written oath into the potion, and, having burned the offering, made her imbibe the concoction to determine the verdict and sentence at once.

WAY In both the OT and the NT, *way* has both literal and figurative meanings. It indicates a road or path (e.g., Gen 38:21; 2 Sam 18:23; Matt 2:12; Luke 10:31) or denotes direction toward something (i.e., Ezek 21:2: "face Jerusalem"; cf Matt 4:15). In the OT, *way* also commonly refers to God's deliverance of Israel: God "makes a way in the sea" (Isa 43:16; cf Ps 77:19; Isa 51:10).

Way also has a number of metaphorical uses. God's customary actions or habits are also referred to as God's "ways" (e.g., Exod 33:13; Ps 119:3; 128:1; Isa 42:24; Mark 6:52).; God's ways are beyond human understanding (e.g., Job 26:14; Rom 11:33) and contrast with human ways (i.e., "my ways" vs. "your ways" [Isa 55:8-9]). However, God's ways are also made available to humans by following the Law. God's commandments are known as "the path the LORD your God commanded you to take" (Deut 13:5; cf Exod 32:8). Isaiah 30:21 advises, "This is the way; walk in it." Following the logic of the metaphor, those who do not live according to God's Law or wisdom "turn from the path" (Deut 9:12; cf Deut 11:28; Job 31:7) or "stumble" (Jer 18:15).

In the NT, *way* often appears in a direct quotation of the OT. John the Baptist is described as "the voice of one shouting in the wilderness, 'Prepare the way for the Lord'" (Matt 3:3//Isa 40:3; cf Matt 11:10//Mal 3:1; Acts 2:28//Ps 16:11). The OT quotation communicates that the "way for the Lord" that has been known to Israel before is present in the person of Jesus.

Acts uses "the Way" as a description or name for the early Christian church (Acts 9:2; 18:25-26; 19:9, 23; 22:4; 24:14, 22). Because it is also called "God's way" (Acts 18:26), it seems that Acts also claims that "the way" God showed people in the Jewish Scriptures is now embodied in those who follow Jesus.

WEEKS, FEAST OR FESTIVAL OF The Festival of Weeks is one of the three scripturally mandated pilgrimage festivals in the OT. Exodus 23:16, part of the Covenant Code, mentions a "Harvest Festival for the early produce of your crops that you planted in the field," while the parallel in Exod 34:22 (J) provides its name and identifies the crop: "the Festival of Weeks, for the early produce of the wheat harvest." Neither of these texts specifies a date for the festival; only in Deut 16:9-12 and Lev 23:15-16 are there instructions for determining when it was to be celebrated. According to Deuteronomy, one should count seven weeks, beginning from the time the sickle is set to the standing grain, and then celebrate the Festival of Weeks with a freewill offering and rejoicing by all the population, free or slave, native or sojourner. Leviticus 23 also mentions the seven weeks but adds other details; see also 28:26-31.

WEIGHTS AND MEASURES Weights and measures are an important key for understanding the economy of ancient societies. Economy before the invention of coins (ca. 600 BCE) was different from ours.

A. Measures of Weight

Most ancient weights were made of stone. Most OT references on weighing of gold, silver, or copper involve huge sums, related to the royal court and to big events such as taxes on, or booty from, entire kingdoms.

As in other Semitic cultures, the biblical systems were based upon the shekel as the basic unit of weight. The shekel is not only the most frequently mentioned unit of weight but also holds a central position in the systems, while larger units are multiples of it. Shekels could be divided into gerahs, which may be 1/20 of a shekel (Exod 30:13) or 1/24 of a shekel. A BEQA is half a shekel (Gen 24:22; Exod 38:26).

The Apocrypha mentions shekels, manehs, and talents (1 Macc 10:40; 1 Esdr 1:36; 5:45). By the time of the NT, weighing lost its special role in favor of a monetary economy. The DARIC was made of gold and weighed 8.3–8.4 g (1 Chron 29:7; Ezra 8:27). The talent was used for large sums of money or weight (Matt 18:24; 25:15-22; Rev 16:21).

B. Measures of Capacity

The homer was the largest dry measure, mentioned for barley and wheat (Lev 27:16; Num 11:32; Isa 5:10; Hos 3:2). The EPHAH was the most common unit of capacity. The seah was a smaller unit. For liquids, the KOR was a large measure of capacity, equivalent to a homer. Smaller units include the bath and the hin.

C. Measures of Length

Simple measures of length used organs of the human body as approximate units, which later developed into more formal measures. Hence, many measures of length were named after human limbs. In the OT, distances are sometimes given by approximations, such as the distance of the flight of an arrow (Gen 21:16) or a day's walking (Gen 30:36; 31:23). Distances were often measured with a rope, rod, or a flaxen cord (1 Kgs 7:15; Ezek 40:3; Zech 1:16; Rev 11:1; 21:15-16).

The cubit was the basic unit of length. It was the distance between the tip of the middle finger and the point of the elbow. The cubit continued to be used in later periods, but the exact length is uncertain (Matt 6:27; Rev 21:17). During the Sabbath, Jews could travel to a limited distance (Acts 1:12), usually 2,000 cubits (about 1 km).

The span was the distance between the tip of the thumb to the tip of the little finger, when the fingers are set wide apart. Because similar units based on body parts existed in Mesopotamia and in Egypt, perhaps the relations were similar, namely: 1 rod = 6 cubits = 12 spans.

A stadion (often translated as "mile" or "furlong") was approx. 607 ft. (e.g., 2 Macc 12:9-10; Luke 24:13). About 8 stadia would equal one Roman mile.

WELLS Access to underground WATER required extensive human labor to produce and to draw the precious resource from the ground. Therefore, wells were highly valued and coveted throughout the ancient world. While springwater was preferred, often well water was necessary to supplement the water resources of towns and villages (1 Sam 19:22; 2 Sam 23:15; John 4:6). Due to the intensive labor, wells were dug to deliver water for human and animal sustenance (Gen 29:2) rather than irrigation.

Wells in the biblical world were dug in cities (Gen 24:11; 2 Sam 17:18) and in various topographical locations such as valleys (Gen 26:17) and fields (Gen 29:2). In the nomad's world of the wilderness, possession of wells was literally a life-and-death issue. Conflict over wells among nomadic peoples (Gen 26:20-21) has continued throughout time.

Moses' request for the Israelites to pass through Edom on their way to the land of promise included a promise not to drink from any well in Edom (Num 20:17), and then he added that any water the people or animals did consume would be purchased (Num 20:19; Deut 2:27-28). The enormous value of water in the arid biblical lands comes into view in the request and in the denial by Edom.

In the biblical texts women usually performed the difficult task of drawing water from a well. Biblical writers display the qualities of individuals in stories involving wells. Eliezer arrived in Nahor seeking a wife for Isaac son of Abraham. Willingness to draw water for Eliezer and his camels was the sign of the right woman. Rebekah's actions revealed character. She was to be Isaac's wife (Gen 24:10-50). Moses drew water for the flocks of the priest of Midian after defending his daughters from shepherds, and Moses' marriage to Zipporah resulted (Exod 2:15-22). The account of Jesus and the Samaritan woman at the well (John 4:6-15) reveals the woman's desire for water she does not draw. The tedious and difficult task of drawing water is implied along with the revelation of her questionable character.

The word *well* can depict a cistern (2 Sam 17:18) or a pit. Oxen can fall into a pit (Luke 14:5). Often a pit was thought to reach the underworld (Pss 55:23 [Heb. 55:24]; 69:15 [Heb. 69:16]). In the ancient world wells were sometimes thought to be the home of spirits (see, e.g., Gen 16:14). In frightening imagery, the term is defined as a bottomless pit with smoke pouring from the underworld (Rev 9:1-6) teeming with locusts rising to plague the earth.

Names of many places were based upon an event at a well. At Beer-sheba ("seven wells" or "well of seven"), Abraham requested King Abimelech to make an oath over seven lambs proclaiming Abraham's ownership of the well (Gen 21:30-31). Other sites include Beer-lahai-roi (Gen 16:14); Beer in Moab (Num 21:16); Beeroth in Sinai (Deut 10:6); Beer in Israel (Judg 9:21); Beeroth in Benjamin (Josh 9:17); and Beer-elim (Isa 15:8).

WESTERN SEA See MEDITERRANEAN SEA.

WHALE The word often translated "whale" in Jonah, means "fish" (as in the CEB).

WHEAT There are a number of distinct species (based on chromosomal patterns and characteristics) of wheat cultivated in the ANE: emmer (*Triticum dicoccum*); bread wheat (*Triticum aestivum*); and hard wheat (*Triticum durum*; most common in the Roman period throughout the Mediterranean area). Susceptible to saline soils, it grows best in clay-loam at moderate temperatures, and requires 500–700 mm of rain per year (a rainfall amount common in the Jezreel and Upper Jordan valleys). Based on the discovery of carbonized remains, it is clear that emmer was more common in Egypt, while bread wheat was the principal variety cultivated in Canaan/Israel during the Iron Age. Winter wheat was sown from the end of October to mid-December, taking advantage of seasonal rains (Deut 11:14), and then harvested with hand sickles (Deut 16:9) between the end of April and the end of May (Gen 30:14; 1 Sam 12:17). The celebration of this event included the covenantal requirement of setting aside a portion of the threshed and winnowed grain as part of the offering of the first portions of crops (Deut 18:4) and the Festival of Booths (Deut 16:13-15), rejoicing in the bounty provided by God. The mounds of grain piled on the threshing floor represented life to the community (Ruth 3:7) and an apt metaphor for beauty (Song 7:2).

Because it was so much a part of everyday life, wheat and its processing fit well into metaphorical usage: Satan "sifting" each person's soul like wheat to test them (Luke 22:31) or in the parable of the weeds sown among the wheat (Matt 13:24-30). Even the name for an "ear of grain" (see SHIBBOLETH) becomes the basis for a dialectic test in Jephthah's conflict with the Ephraimites (Judg 12:1-6). Wheat also played a role in the prophets' injunctions on social justice and honest behavior. Amos, for instance, chides grain merchants for complaining that the Sabbath restrictions hurt their business, and condemns those who cheat their customers by selling "garbage [sweepings] as grain" (Amos 8:5-6). See BREAD; SACRIFICES AND OFFERINGS.

WHEEL The wheel's invention represents a pivotal point in cultural advancement. It was known and used in the ANE as early as the 4th millennium BCE. Twenty-five of the thirty-five uses of wheel appear in Ezekiel, mostly in Ezek 1 and 10. Although ambiguity in the description and uncertainty regarding the function of the wheels in the Ezekiel visions call for caution on the part of the interpreter, current consensus seems to understand Ezekiel's "wheels" as depicting the wheels of a sacred chariot or cart. In an Ezekiel-like vision alluded to in Enoch, a "wheeled-throne" is described (1 En. 14:18).

Texts other than Ezekiel that clearly refer to chariot wheels include Exod 14:25, which references the Egyptian chariot wheels, and Nah 3:2. The proverb of Prov 20:26 associates a wheel with the threshing process, perhaps the wheel of a threshing cart (see also Isa 28:27).

Jeremiah 18:3 employs the term in reference to the potter's wheel.

WHIRLWIND The word *whirlwind* designates the furious and potentially destructive wind, tempest, or windstorm associated either with the northwest sea-gales common in the rainy winter season or with the less destructive, "scorching hot wind" of the southeastern sirocco (Ps 11:6) that was commonly associated with cyclonic dust devils ("swirling storm" [Ps 77:18] [Heb. 77:19]; "like tumbleweeds before a storm" [Isa 17:13]) or sand/palm-columns (Song 3:6) that come from the Syro-Arabian desert (Isa 21:1) during the spring harvest season (cf Luke 12:55).

God frequently appears in a whirlwind, which symbolizes the sovereign wisdom and power (Job 38:1; Ps 77:18 [Heb. 77:19]; Nah 1:3; Hab 3:14; Sir 43:17) by which God rides and yokes the four winds (cf Pss 18:10 [Heb. 18:11]; 104:3; Isa 19:1; Ezek 1:4) to serve him (cf Mark 4:35-41).

WHITE THRONE Found only in Rev 20:11, "a great white throne" is associated with God's final judgment. A white throne contributes not only to the spectacle of Rev 20:11-15 but also speaks to the purity and righteousness of the judgment proceeding from it.

WHORE OF BABYLON Among the many fantastic apocalyptic images in the book of Revelation is the vision of a woman clothed in purple and scarlet, adorned with gold, jewels, and pearls, who is seated on a scarlet beast with seven heads and ten horns (Rev 17:1-4). On her forehead is written "Babylon the great, the mother of prostitutes and the vile things of the earth" (17:5). This symbolic woman is commonly known as the "Whore of Babylon." An angel explains that the seven heads of the beast that the woman rides represent seven mountains, and its horns are ten kings (17:9-12). The 1st-cent. reader would recognize that the "seven mountains" are the seven hills of Rome, and the ten kings the emperors of the Roman Empire. Thus *Babylon* is a code word for Rome, known for its wealth and power as well as its cruelty and oppression (cf 1 Pet 5:13).

WIDOW A childless widow could be returned to her father's house (Gen 38:11; Lev 22:13) or to her mother's house (Ruth 1:8) until such time as she could remarry (Ruth 1:9). Alternatively, a childless widow could be subject to Levirate marriage (Deut 25:5-10) in order to procure children to carry on her husband's name (see LEVIRATE LAW). Evidently, a widow could bring her deceased husband's estate into a Levirate marriage (e.g., Ruth 4:10). Conditions for remarriage are mentioned only a few times in the OT. In addition to Ruth 4:5-10, discussed above, a priest may not marry a widow or divorced woman (Lev 21:14; Ezek 44:22).

The OT portrays Israel's God as the special helper and refuge of widows, along with strangers, orphans, and the poor (e.g., Exod 22:21-24; Deut 10:18; 27:19; Pss 68:5; 146:9; Jer 49:11). Job included his treatment of widows as evidence for his righteousness (Job 29:13; 31:16). Widows were allowed to glean in the fields (Deut 24:19-22; Ruth 2:1-23) and to share in the tithe (Deut 14:28-29; 26:12) and meals at public festivals (Deut 16:11, 14). In spite of these protections, the widow's plight was sometimes serious, as Elijah's encounter with the starving widow of Zarephath (1 Kgs 17:8-24) and Elisha's encounter with the prophet's widow whose children were to be sold into slavery to pay a creditor (2 Kgs 4:1-7) indicate. The cause of the widow was a particular example of the poor and powerless (Isa 1:17; Jer 7:6; 22:3; 49:11; Zech 7:10; Mal 3:5).

The Gospel of Luke portrays a widow's spiritual task as waiting and praying for the fulfillment of God's promises, as did the prophet Anna, a widow who never left the temple, "but worshipped God with fasting and prayer night and day," and who spoke about Jesus as the expected redeemer (Luke 2:36-37). Widows are prominent in the ministry of Jesus. As a pious Jew, Jesus was concerned for those for whom God was concerned. Jesus felt compassion for a widow in Nain whose only son had died, and like Elijah and Elisha, he restored the young man to life (Luke 7:11-15; cf 1 Kgs 17:8-24; 2 Kgs 4:1-7). Jesus uses a widow as a positive example of the constancy of prayer (Luke 18:1-8), an activity with which widows are associated in the NT (see also Luke 2:36-37; 1 Tim 5:3-16). Jesus also highlights a widow's generosity (Mark 12:41-44; Luke 21:1-4), and he attacks those who "eat widows out of their homes" (Luke 20:46-47).

In the Acts of the Apostles, widows are a recognized group within the Christian community. Care of Hebrew widows who became Christians precipitated the "division of labor" in 6:1-7, so that "there were no needy persons among" the Christians (4:34). The care for widows in Acts serves to illustrate that "true devotion, the kind that is pure and faultless before God the Father is this: to care for orphans and widows in their difficulties" (Jas 1:27). The Pastoral Epistles confirm that widows not only had a claim to benevolence from the early church but also that they had status and privilege; they were a category of leader with prescribed duties, an office with special responsibility for prayer (1 Tim 5:3-16).

Paul mentions "those who are single and widows" among whom he numbers himself as a celibate person (1 Cor 7:8). Paul suggests the widow should remain single, although as a concession (as indeed, is marriage in general for Paul), noting "It's better to marry than to burn with passion," he allows remarriage (1 Cor 7:8-9, 39-40; cf Rom 7:1-3).

WIDOW OF ZAREPHATH An unnamed woman who fed and sheltered the fugitive Elijah during the drought he predicted (1 Kgs 17:8-24). She was a Phoenician who lived in Zarephath, near Tyre and Sidon. Her desperate economic situation (v. 12) mirrors that of other widows in the Bible (see WIDOW), but her hospitality to the Israelite prophet is miraculously rewarded with an abundance of grain and oil (vv. 15-16) and the reviving of her dead son (vv. 17-24). Jesus alludes to the incident (Luke 4:24-27) when arguing that "no prophet is welcome in the prophet's hometown." See ZAREPHATH.

WILDERNESS *Wilderness* denotes a range of landscapes, from open plains and rugged mountains offering seasonal pasturage, to scrub or nearly barren desert, to scorched, toxic land incapable of supporting vegetation. The term typically refers to unsettled and uncultivated land, the natural habitation of wild animals but not of humans, a place through which shepherds and Bedouin pass following pasturage and travelers hasten to safer havens.

Wilderness usually designates a place, but it is also an evocative symbol with layers of meaning. The Bible never romanticizes the wilderness. Except when using it for pasturage or travel, biblical characters seek out the wilderness primarily as a refuge from harassment or as a place to prepare for the advent of God's kingdom. The wilderness is preeminently the place of Israel's forty-year sojourn between Egypt and the land of promised, and the most frequent and significant references to wilderness in the OT pertain to Israel's experiences there.

In the Gospels, the writers record that Jesus withdraws to the wilderness to teach ever-growing crowds (Mark 1:45), to rest alone (Matt 14:13; Luke 4:42; John 6:15) or with his disciples (Mark 6:31-32), or to pray (Mark 1:35// Luke 5:16; "up onto a mountain" [Matt 14:23; Mark 6:46; Luke 6:12]).

WILLOWS, VALLEY OF THE Willows are a genus of trees that thrive near waterways; thus Isa 44:4 refers to "willows by flowing streams." The Valley of the Willows is thought to be on the ancient frontier of Moab, part of the modern Wadi el-Hesa. Isaiah 15:7 describes the Moabites fleeing to the Valley of the Willows, carrying their belongings.

WIND In the OT, the wind is a creation of God and is subject to God's command (2 Kgs 3:17; Prov 30:4; Jer 4:12; 10:13; 51:16; Ezek 13:13; Hos 13:15; Amos 4:13; Jonah 1:4; 4:8; it is implied in Job 1:19 and Ps 148:8). The north wind is responsible for bringing rain to the land (Prov 25:23), while the east wind is of a particularly destructive nature (Ezek 17:10; 27:26; Hos 12:1; 13:15; Jon 4:8). Likewise, in the NT, winds can be natural (e.g., Matt 14:24, 32; Mark 4:37; Luke 8:23; John 6:18; Jas 3:4; Jude 1:12) or can refer to the breath of God or other spiritual entities (e.g., spirit of God, Matt 3:16; the Holy Spirit, Luke 11:13; spirit of Christ, 1 Pet 1:11; spirit of Jesus, Matt 27:50; spirit of the Lord, Acts 8:39; unclean spirit, Mark 7:25; demonic spirit, Luke 9:39; spirit of prophecy, Rev 19:10; deceitful spirit, 1 Tim 4:1). See WHIRLWIND.

WINE In ancient Israel, where water was frequently scarce or contaminated, wine was the most commonly consumed beverage. The Mediterranean climate of the land of Israel with its winter rains and summer drought offered favorable conditions for producing wine (similar to contemporary wine-producing regions such as Italy, France, and California). Wine can be seen as life-giving, but it can also be dangerous in inebriation. As a metaphor, wine can represent judgment or joy.

WINGED CREATURES Also called "cherubim." Winged beings, part animal, part human (Ezek 10:14; 41:18-19), associated with transporting the Lord (2 Sam 22:11), the divine throne (Ezek 1; Rev 4:8-10), and in sacral garden contexts (Gen 3:24; Ezek 28:14). Their images were carved on the covenant chest, the meeting tent (Exod 25:18-22; 26:1), and Solomon's temple (1 Kgs 6:23-28). See ANGEL; COVENANT CHEST.

WINNOW Winnowing is an activity designed to separate the grain from the CHAFF after THRESHING takes place. Winnowing is done at the THRESHING

FLOOR, usually located outside the settlement where the wind can be utilized in the process (Jer 4:11). Sometimes it can be done at night when the proper wind is available (Ruth 3:2). The mixture of grain and chaff is thrown into the air with a special fork, usually made of wood. The wind separates the mixture according to the weight of the components and various piles are formed, first the grain, which is heaviest, then the straw, and lastly the chaff. Further cleaning of the grain by throwing it up with a wooden shovel and letting the wind continue to separate follows this. The final activity utilizes sieves of different sizes. Winnowing is often used metaphorically (Prov 20:8; Luke 3:17).

WISDOM Wisdom is a concept that finds expression in nearly every culture, in every time and place. Persons with particular insights into human motivations and interactions, those with exceptional abilities at artisanship and the crafting of words, and those with encyclopedic knowledge are called "wise." Society often identified wise people and honored them, relying on them to teach others. Several books of the Bible represent wisdom traditions, including Proverbs, Job, and Ecclesiastes; other books depict wise persons or wisdom influences. In the NT, many of Jesus' sayings are examples of wisdom, and the letters also depict wisdom sayings.

WISDOM OF SOLOMON, THE A 1st-cent. BCE document written in Greek, is also in the Apocrypha. Although attributed to Solomon, its eschatological nature is a far cry from the kind of wisdom Solomon excelled in (see 1 Kgs 4:29-32). It praises Wisdom and elevates her to an attribute of the divine and so makes the theological leap from seeing Wisdom as a mediator but strictly created, to a hypostasis of God, hence preexistent and coexistent with God (Wis 7:2–8:1).

WISE WOMAN OF TEKOA The unnamed woman of TEKOA collaborated with Joab, convincing David to bring Absalom home (2 Sam 14:1-20).

WITHERED HAND Jesus' healing of a man's withered hand in a synagogue occurs in Mark 3:1-6 and the other Synoptics (Matt 12:9-14; Luke 6:6-11, stating it was the right hand). The focus of the scene is whether Jesus will heal on the Sabbath.

WITNESS *Witness*, a juridical term, originally signified a person who had personal knowledge about something and could speak about it before a court of law. Witnesses appear in the Bible in a number of ways. They function to attest contracts and confirm proceedings (Ruth 4:9-11; Jer 32:10, 12). Sometimes inanimate objects act as witnesses of an agreement (Gen 31:44-54; Josh 22:27; 24:27).

False or malicious witness was forbidden (Exod 20:16; 23:1-3) but was common (Prov 6:19; 12:17) and punishable (Deut 19:15-19; Prov 19:5, 9). In the NT false witnesses are noted in the trials of Jesus and Stephen (Matt 26:60; Acts 6:13; 7:58).

Witness terminology is applied metaphorically to the role of Israel and later to Jesus and his followers. "You are my witnesses," God says to Israel, referring to its task to bear witness to God as God's chosen servant (Isa 43:10, 12; 44:8). Israel was to take the Lord's side and serve as a witness to the only true God, the Lord of history, and Israel's savior and redeemer. This is an innovative use of lawsuit or controversy language.

In Acts, emphasis is placed on the witness of the apostles (1:8, 21-22; 4:33; 10:38-43) and Paul (22:14-15; 26:16). The key point of their testimony is the resurrection of Jesus (2:32; 3:15; 5:30-32; 13:30-31; cf 1 Cor 15:3-11).

John's Apocalypse depicts witness against the background of harassment. Jesus is "the faithful and true witness" (Rev 1:5; 3:14) who sets the pattern for believers (1:9). They offer testimony as they follow Christ (6:9; 12:11, 17). Faithfulness to Jesus may entail martyrdom, as it did for ANTIPAS (2:13; cf Acts 7:54-60). See TESTIMONY.

WOLF The wolf (*Canis lupus*), ancestor of the domestic DOG, is a fierce animal of prey (Gen 49:27; Jer 5:6; Ezek 22:27; John 10:12) still prevalent in the Middle East and known to attack domestic animals as big as cattle. Depicting peaceful coexistence as when "the wolf will live with the lamb" (Isa 11:6; 65:25) is a striking metaphor for the end of days.

WOOD Wood was one of the primary materials for construction in the ANE, along with stone and mud brick. Rough-cut timber was used vertically as pillars or columns to support the roof or second story of a house; it was used horizontally as beams and to hold the ceiling, the floor above, or the roof. Sawn and squared wood beams were used for monumental structures such as palaces and temples. Monumental structures often had a course of wooden beams placed after several courses of hewn stone (Ezra 6:4).

Wood was a major fuel for fire, so it is often mentioned in the context of entirely burned offerings (Gen 22:3-9; Lev 1:7-17; 1 Kgs 18:23-38).

WOOL Sheep herding and the attendant shearing of the sheep for their wool was an industry common in the ANE (Gen 31:19; 2 Kgs 3:4; Isa 53:7). Wool was the substance of most of the everyday garments fashioned by the women of the household (Prov 31:13; Ezek 34:3; Hos 2:9). Once the fleece was cleaned and dried (Judg 6:37), the wool was carded. Strands of yarn were spun into fabric on looms and sown together using elaborate running stitches. Some woolen strands were dyed and used as embroidery thread (Exod 28:39); however, the mixing of wool and linen was prohibited except for the priestly class (Deut 22:11). The white color of wool is used metaphorically to equate with purity (Isa 1:18), snow (Ps 147:16), and the shining white hair of the deity (Dan 7:9; Rev 1:14).

WORD *Word* in the Bible denotes the means of communication between subjects, and it also connotes that activity. Between persons, words are associated with actions, impacting reality: one's word conveys integrity and promise; the word of the authentic prophet comes true; the sharing of words implies receptivity and responsiveness between parties; one's word communicates oneself. Between God and humanity, God's word is the source of creation; God's revealing word guides discerning individuals; God's written word, Scripture, is inspired and sustaining; God's incarnate Word, Jesus Christ, is the agent of both creation and redemption; the fulfilled word of Jesus shows that he is authentically sent by the Father; the word of the gospel is the message preached by the apostles. Indeed, the only hope for humanity is a believing response to the divine initiative—the word of God received by faith and expressed in faithfulness.

WORM The worm plays various roles in the Bible. Sometimes the worm is portrayed as an instrument of God; most explicit in this regard is the divinely appointed worm of Jonah 4:7. The worm as symbolic of death and decay is present in texts such as Job 21:26.

WORMWOOD Plants of the genus *Artemisia*, especially lowly *A. herba-alba* in stony gray desert, the taller *A. judaica* in sandy desert, and the bushier *A. monosperma* in coastal sands. They belong to the daisy family, having small heads of inconspicuous compound flowers. Their whitish hairy leaves yield a bitter infusion traditionally used in medicine.

WORSHIP Throughout ancient Israel and early Christianity, worship of God formed an important part of religious experience and social life. A variety of aspects of worship existed throughout the centuries and cultures. Understanding the biblical evidence of worship can be difficult because the writers and readers of the Bible tended to assume their own worship practices rather than describing them.

Worship of God occurred in formal settings such as sanctuaries, temples, and synagogues, but also in homes and other public and private settings. Some of these events occurred at predetermined times, such as annual festivals or monthly and weekly meetings; worship could also be spontaneous. Activities of worship often included sacrifices, pilgrimages, gifts or exchanges, acts of justice or provision, music, gestures, touches, feasts, fasts, and sacred meals. Worship involves the expressions of ideas and emotion such as psalms, prayers, readings, recitations, songs, sermons, instruction, confession, ecstatic utterance, silence, discussion, blessing, and benediction. Worship could be inclusive, leveling differences between people, and at the same time exclusive, drawing a distinction between the worshipping community and others. In all of these ways, worship embodies human longing for and experience of God, as well as human connection between worshippers.

Both the OT and the NT deal also with instances of the worship of other gods, and other types of false or improper worship.

WRATH The personal disposition of anger, often expressed by means of violence. Wrath may be expressed by human beings, by governing authorities, by God, and by other supernatural beings, such as Satan. Wrath often indicates the impulsive acting out of anger, though some biblical authors describe wrath as something God stores up for the last days (e.g., Zeph 1:15, 18; Rom 2:5; 1 Thess 1:10). One of the Hebrew words often translated "wrath" derives from the verb "to snort" (see Ps 18:7-8 [Heb. 18:8-9]), indicating wrath's primal nature. Another word is often translated "wrath" but has a related meaning of "overflow" or "outburst." Greek thinkers often described wrath as a natural force that wells up and breaks forth.

Greco-Roman authors debated the moral value of wrath. Some proposed that "righteous wrath" motivated persons to great deeds, while others regarded wrath as a personal weakness (Jas 1:20). Hence, some ancient persons attributed wrath to the gods, while others did not. Biblical authors typically regard wrath as a failing for human beings but an appropriate disposition for the deity. In the Bible, God is the subject of the great majority of occurrences of the term *wrath*. God demonstrates wrath particularly in response to idolatry, wickedness, and injustice. God also visits wrath against the enemies of God's people. Metaphorically, God's wrath is most often expressed in terms of pouring out and burning up, consuming all that stands in its path.

WRESTLING A struggle or contest, either physical or spiritual. The encounter between Jacob and God at Peniel (Gen 32), as Jacob was returning from Mesopotamia with his clan, is the chief story of wrestling in a literal, physical way in the OT.

Of similar interest is the earlier, and related, narrative of Rachel's agonizing over her barrenness. When her servant Bilhah bore a second son to Jacob, Rachel said, "I've competed fiercely with my sister, and now I've won" (Gen 30:8). She named the child Naphtali, which means "my competition" or "my wrestling."

The NT uses a variety of terms to refer to spiritual struggling or wrestling in different life settings. Paul says that Epaphras "wrestles" in his prayers (Col 4:12) and speaks of "fighting" against the powers of darkness (Eph 6:12). The writer of Hebrews recognizes their "struggle against sin" (Heb 12:4; see also Col 1:29; 1 Tim 4:10) and with the reality of suffering and public ridicule (Heb 10:32).

Xx

XERXES 1. Xerxes I was the 4th king in the Persian Empire. He is reflected in the biblical tradition as Ahasuerus at Ezra 4:6 and in the book of Esther. The son of Darius I and Atossa, Xerxes was born in 518 BCE. With his father's death in 486 BCE, Xerxes ascended to the throne.

2. Xerxes II, son of Artaxerxes and grandson of Xerxes I, reigned a mere forty-five days in 423 BCE before being assassinated by his half brother Secydianus.

YAHWEH The distinctive name of Israel's God, originally consisting of only four consonants, YHWH, and consistently translated "(the) Lord." The pronunciation is a scholarly reconstruction based on Greek transcriptions of the name. See GOD, NAMES OF; LORD.

YOKE The term *yoke* has a wide range of uses, both literal and metaphorical, and is much more common in the OT. A literal yoke was a device that bound animals together and controlled them, enabling them to perform productive work. Animals are yoked (1 Kgs 19:19-21; Job 1:3; 42:12) or unyoked (Num 19:2; Deut 21:3). The majority of references, though, involve the sociopolitical realm. Most frequent are uses of *yoke* to denote harsh rule. Solomon and Rehoboam's harsh rule/yoke over Israel involved forced labor, taxation, and violence (1 Kgs 12:4, 9-11, 14; 2 Chron 10:4, 9-11, 14). That is, the term commonly designates the dominant imperial powers of the biblical tradition: Egypt, Assyria, Babylon, the Greeks. The contexts of these passages show that their rule was often exploitative and oppressive.

In this context, Jesus' invitation in Matt 11:29-30 to "put on my yoke" is best read as offering people a way of life that is an alternative to Rome's rule.

YOM KIPPUR See RECONCILIATION DAY.

Zz

ZAANANNIM May mean "travelers." "The oak in Zaanannim" is a point on the southern boundary of Naphtali (Josh 19:33), near Kedesh; its location is uncertain. Some scholars identify the site with Khan et-Tujjar, a caravan stop on the road from Beth-shan to Damascus, approximately 4 mi. southeast of Adam (Khirbet Damiyeh). Others associate the site with Lejjun, a site approximately 2 mi. north of Taanach, between Megiddo and Tell Abu Qedeis. Another possible location is Khirbet Bessum, approximately 3 mi. northeast of Mount Tabor.

This same site is mentioned in Judg 4:11 under the name ELON-BEZAANANNIM, which literally means "the oak in Zaanannim." Heber the Kenite camped here, and here his wife JAEL killed Sisera (Judg 4:17-22).

ZAAVAN A grandson of SEIR the Horite and the 2nd-listed son of the clan chief EZER (Gen 36:27; 1 Chron 1:42). As a clan name, Zaavan represents part of the indigenous Horite population disrupted by immigrating Esauite clans (Deut 2:12) and eventually absorbed into historical Edom (see EDOM, EDOMITES).

ZABAD 1. Nathan's son and Ephlal's father in a genealogy that traces Elishama back to Jerahmeel in the tribe of Judah (1 Chron 2:36-37).

2. Tahath's son in a genealogy that traces Joshua back to Ephraim (1 Chron 7:21).

3. Ahlai's son and one of the warriors in David's armies (1 Chron 11:41).

4. Son of Shimeath the Ammonite and one of King Joash's servants. With JEHOZABAD, he killed King Joash in his bed because King Joash had demanded that Zechariah son of the priest Jehoida be stoned to death (2 Chron 24:20-26). In 2 Kgs 12:21, his name is JOZACAR, although some manuscripts and later editions have the name as Jozabad. The Chronicler, however, has abbreviated Jozabad to Zabad.

5. Descendant of Zattu. He dismissed his foreign wife and their children in accordance with the covenant God made with Ezra (Ezra 10:1-5, 27). In 1 Esdr 9:28, he is a descendant of Zamoth.

6. Descendant of Hashum. He dismissed his foreign wife and their children in accordance with the covenant God made with Ezra (Ezra 10:1-5, 33; 1 Esdr 9:33).

7. Descendant of Nebo. He dismissed his foreign wife and their children in accordance with the covenant God made with Ezra (Ezra 10:1-5, 43).

ZABBAI Possibly means "gift."

1. A descendant of Bebai listed among the Israelites who had married foreign wives upon their return from exile in Babylon. Following Ezra's decree condemning intermarriage with the people of the land, he joined the others named in sending away their foreign wives and children (Ezra 10:28; 1 Esdr 9:29).

2. Father of Baruch, who helped to repair a section of the wall around Jerusalem from the Angle, near the armory, to the door of the high priest Eliashib's house (Neh 3:20).

ZABDI 1. A Zerahite of Judah, whose grandson Achan was stoned for violating the ban at Jericho (Josh 7:1, 17-26).

2. A Benjaminite, the 3rd son of Shimei (1 Chron 8:19; or Shema, v. 13).

3. A Shiphmite, one of twelve stewards appointed by King David, who supervised the produce of the vineyards (1 Chron 27:27).

4. A Levite, son of Asaph, listed in Neh 11:17 in the genealogy of Mattaniah, who lived in Jerusalem in the time of Nehemiah. First Chronicles 9:15 reads "Zichri" instead of "Zabdi," suggesting that either Nehemiah or 1 Chronicles has miscopied the name.

ZABDIEL Means "My gift is God."

1. The father of Jashobeam, one of David's military leaders (1 Chron 27:2), descended from Perez, a Judahite tribe (Gen 38:29).

2. The overseer of a group of priests residing in Jerusalem (Neh 11:14) after the exile. He is called the son of "Haggedolim," which means "the great ones." It is unclear if this is a personal name or a title.

3. The Arab leader who decapitated the Seleucid king Alexander Balas when he sought refuge from the Egyptian king Ptolemy VI Philometer. Zabdiel sent Alexander's head to Ptolemy (1 Macc 11:16-17). Zabdiel may have operated in the Palmyra desert area or in Lebanon.

ZABUD A son of Nathan, and a priest and king's friend (i.e., counselor) in Solomon's time (1 Kgs 4:5).

ZACCAI Head of one of the lay families who returned to Jerusalem with Zerubbabel from Babylon. According to Ezra 2:9 and Neh 7:14, the family had 760 members. This large number, like the others in the lists, suggests a political or theological purpose to the lists.

ZACCHAEUS Meaning "pure, righteous."

1. An officer in the Maccabean army (2 Macc 10:19).

2. In Luke 19:1-10, Zacchaeus was the wealthy, paradigmatic "ruler among tax collectors" resident in Jericho.

ZACCUR Means "remembered" or "is mindful"; perhaps "(God) has remembered."

1. A Reubenite whose son Shammua was among the spies Moses sent into Canaan (Num 13:4).

2. A Simeonite, son of Hammuel and father of Shimei (1 Chron 4:26).

3. A Levite, son of Jaaziah and grandson of Merari (1 Chron 24:27).

4. Son of Asaph and head of a group of twelve kinsmen who were singers in the temple (1 Chron 25:2, 10; Neh 12:35).

5. Son of Bigvai and brother of Uthai, who followed Ezra back to Judah from Babylon (Ezra 8:14).

6. Son of Imri, who led his kinsmen in rebuilding a section of Jerusalem's wall (Neh 3:2).

7. A Levite, one of those signing a covenant to obey the Law of God and separate themselves from Gentiles (Neh 10:12 [Heb. 10:13]).

8. Father of Hanan, appointed by Nehemiah to assist in the distribution of provisions to the Levites and priests (Neh 13:13).

9. A temple singer who divorced his foreign wife (1 Esdr 9:24).

ZADOK, ZADOKITES The name Zadok is mentioned more than forty times in the Bible. The "Zadokites" are mentioned three times.

1. Zadok, along with ABIATHAR, was a priest for David (2 Sam 15–19; 1 Kgs 1), and he was Solomon's highest-ranking priest (1 Kgs 2).

Zadok and Abiathar remained loyal to David during Absalom's rebellion (2 Sam 15). David ordered Zadok and Abiathar to carry the covenant chest of God into the city of Jerusalem (2 Sam 15:24-29). Zadok and Abiathar conspired with Hushai the Archite against Absalom (2 Sam 17:15-16), and after Absalom's death, David sent Zadok and Abiathar a message about his return to Jerusalem (2 Sam 19:11-12).

First Kings 1:8 mentions "Zadok

the priest," who remained loyal to David during the struggle for the succession to David's throne (1 Kgs 1:26-45). David ordered Zadok and the prophet Nathan to anoint Solomon as king (1 Kgs 1:26-45). When Solomon took the throne, he put Zadok "in Abiathar's position" (1 Kgs 2:28-35; however, cf 1 Kgs 4:4, where both Zadok and Abiathar are priests).

All other Samuel–Kings references to the priest Zadok include him in a list or name his children. Zadok is listed as son of Ahitub (2 Sam 8:17) and father of Ahimaaz (2 Sam 15:27, 36; 18:19, 27). Another list of David's officials names Zadok, Abiathar, and Ira as David's priests (2 Sam 20:23-26). A list of Solomon's officials includes Zadok's name twice (1 Kgs 4:1-6). First Kings 4:2 lists Azariah as son of Zadok, somewhat surprisingly, given the evidence from 2 Samuel (above).

Zadok appears in several genealogies in 1 Chronicles. The genealogies in 1 Chron 5:24–6:15 place Zadok among the sons of Levi in the line of Aaron (6:8). In 1 Chron 18:16, Zadok son of Ahitub is a priest alongside Abiathar. First Chronicles 24:1-6 presents the divisions of the sons of Aaron; Zadok is "from Eleazar's family." Of the remaining occurrences of the name Zadok, some may be the same as this Zadok, or the same as one another.

2. Zadok was the father of Jerusha, the mother of King Jotham of Judah (2 Kgs 15:33; 2 Chron 27:1).

3. First Chronicles 9:11 lists Zadok as son of Meraioth and father of Meshullam. The six priestly houses in Neh 11 include Zadok as grandson of Ahitub, son of Meraioth, and father of Meshullam (v. 11).

4. Zadok, "a young man, a mighty warrior," brought twenty-two men from his father's house to David at Hebron (1 Chron 12:28).

5. Zadok is chief officer for Aaron in 1 Chron 27:17.

6. Ezra's Aaronite genealogy lists Zadok as son of Ahitub and father of Shallum (Ezra 7:2).

7. Zadok son of Baana worked on the walls of Jerusalem (Neh 3:4).

8. Zadok son of Immer helped build Jerusalem's walls (Neh 3:29).

9. Zadok is among the officials, Levites, and priests who signed a covenant (Neh 10:21).

10. A scribe named Zadok is one of four treasurers over the storehouses (Neh 13:4-14).

11. Zadok appears several times in the Dead Sea Scrolls. The Damascus Document tells of a book of the Instruction that was sealed, unopened even by David and remaining unopened until Zadok (CD-A V, 2–5). This reference to Zadok may reveal the importance of Zadok to the writer(s) of the Damascus Document or could have an obscure meaning.

12. The Copper Scroll speaks of Zadok's tomb and Zadok's garden but gives no indication about his identity (3Q15 XI, 2–6).

13. Zadok is listed in Matthew's genealogical list for Jesus (Matt 1:14). This text names Azor as the father of Zadok and Zadok as the father of Achim.

14. References to Zadokites are more obscure. The final eight chapters of Ezekiel provide four references to the "Zadokites" or "descendants/family of Zadok" (Ezek 40:45-46; 43:18-19; 44:6-16; 48:9-11), the only biblical references. Some scholars consider the Zadokites to be the founders of the Qumran community, associated with the Dead Sea Scrolls.

ZAHAM One of Rehoboam's three sons by his wife Mahalath (2 Chron 11:18-19).

ZAIR The location of an unsuccessful attack by King Joram of Judah and his chariotry against the Edomites, who had recently revolted against Judah's rule (2 Kgs 8:21; 2 Chron 21:9). That "Jehoram, along with all his chariots, crossed over to Zair," suggests that Zair lay somewhere in Edomite territory, but its location is uncertain. Some have proposed identifying Zair with the Zior of Josh 15:54, near Hebron, but placing

Zair in Judah raises the question of what Joram and his army "crossed over" to reach the place. A perhaps more plausible solution is identifying Zair with Zoar (Gen 13:10; 14:2, 8; 19:22-23, 30), at the southeastern tip of the Dead Sea.

ZALAPH Father of Hanun, who helped repair the walls of Jerusalem after the return from exile (Neh 3:30). Hanun was one of two workers assigned to the detail, thought to be along the eastern wall of the city, overlooking the Kidron Valley.

ZALMON 1. Mount Zalmon appears in Judg 9:48 as a mountain near SHECHEM. 2. Psalm 68:14 [Heb. 68:15] speaks of a Mount Zalmon that may have been one of the peaks of the Bashan range in what is now northern Jordan. "When the Almighty scattered the kings there, snow fell on Mount Zalmon," possibly describes the fleeing kings as swirling about like snowflakes.

3. Zalmon from Ahoh appears in 2 Sam 23:28 as one of David's inner circle of warriors known as "the Thirty" (v. 24), but is not mentioned in the Chronicler's parallel list (1 Chron 11:26-47), and is otherwise unknown.

ZALMONAH An encampment on the Israelites' wilderness journey from Kadesh to the plains of Moab (Num 33:41-42), between Mount Hor and Punon. Though its exact location is unknown, Zalmonah was probably in the Arabah, 20–30 mi. south of the Dead Sea.

ZAMZUMMIM According to Deut 2:20-23, this was the name given to the Rephaim by the Ammonites, perhaps because of their muttering or indiscernible speech. The Lord destroyed the Zamzummim so that the Ammonites could inhabit their territory. Many commentators equate the Zamzummim with the similarly named Zuzim of Gen 14:5, but this is not certain.

ZANOAH 1. A Judean city in the western foothills (Josh 15:34), perhaps to be identified with Khirbet Zanu (about 2 mi. southeast of Beth-shemesh). The founder of this city (or less likely, another city by the same name in the Judean highlands) is identified in Chronicles as JEKUTHIEL (1 Chron 4:18). The city was resettled by Jews returning from exile (Neh 11:30), and its inhabitants worked with Hanun to reconstruct Jerusalem's city wall, rebuilding the Valley Gate and about 500 yards ("fifteen hundred feet") of the wall, as far as the Dung Gate (Neh 3:13).

2. A city in the Judean highlands near Maon (Josh 15:56), perhaps to be identified with Khirbet Beit Amra (about 1 mi. east of Juttah).

ZAPHENATH-PANEAH According to Gen 41:45, the pharaoh of the Joseph account presents the former slave with an Egyptian name to correspond to his new position: Zaphenath-paneah.

ZAPHON A city east of the Jordan River that was part of the kingdom of Heshbon, ruled by King SIHON (Josh 13:27). Along with several other cities in the Jordan Valley, Zaphon was included in the land given to the tribe of Gad (Josh 13:24-28). The men of Ephraim met Jephthah there to challenge his campaign against the Ammonites (Judg 12:1). The toponym *Zaphon* in Job 26:7 and Isa 14:13 may not refer to a specific locality but could simply mean "north." Scholars have identified Zaphon with several sites north of the Jabbok River in modern-day Jordan, including Tell es-Saidiyeh, Tell el-Qos, and Tell el-Mazar. See GAD, GADITES; ZAPHON, MOUNT.

ZAPHON, MOUNT Zaphon has several, possibly related meanings: (1) "north"; (2) the place-names Zaphon on the eastern side of the Jordan River (Josh 13:27; Judg 12:1) and BAAL-ZEPHON in the eastern delta of Egypt

(Exod 14:2, 9; Num 33:7); (3) a mountain residence of God (Ps 48:2 [Heb. 48:3]; Isa 14:13).

ZAREPHATH A town on the Phoenician coast approximately 14 mi. north of TYRE and 8 mi. south of SIDON. Most biblical references to the site occur in connection with the prophet Elijah, who found refuge there after the Cherith Brook dried up in the land of Gilead (1 Kgs 17:9-10). A widow of Zarephath gave him sanctuary and sustained him while he was a refugee in Phoenicia. In return for her kindness, the Lord sustained her and when her son died, Elijah was instrumental in his restoration (1 Kgs 17:11-24; cf Luke 4:22-30).

ZARETHAN A city or region near the Jordan River, between Adam and Succoth. When the Israelites crossed the Jordan, "the water of the Jordan coming downstream stood still. It rose up in a single heap very far off, just below Adam, which is the city next to Zarethan. The water going down to the desert sea (that is, the Dead Sea, was cut off completely" (Josh 3:16). See ZERERAH.

ZAZA A Jerahmeelite, son of Jonathan and brother of Peleth (1 Chron 2:33). He is mentioned only in the genealogy of Jerahmeel (1 Chron 2:25-33), of the tribe of Judah.

ZEALOT The Zealots were Jewish revolutionaries in the 1st cent. CE. Zealots resisted compromise but remained faithful to the Instruction in the face of persecution and even death.

ZEBADIAH Meaning "the Lord has given."

1. Son of Beriah, a Benjaminite leader who dwelled in Jerusalem (1 Chron 8:15).

2. Son of Elpaal, a Benjaminite leader who dwelled in Jerusalem (1 Chron 8:17).

3. Son of Jeroham of Gedor, a Benjaminite archer who defected to David at Ziklag and supported him, rather than following King Saul and his Benjaminite kinsmen (1 Chron 12:1-7).

4. A Levite gatekeeper of the Korahite clan, the 3rd son of Meshelemiah (1 Chron 26:1-2).

5. One of King David's commanders, who served in the 4th month of the twelve monthly rotations. He was the son of Asahel, Joab's brother, and his contingent included 24,000 men (1 Chron 27:7).

6. A Levite whom King Jehoshaphat sent throughout Judah with other Levites, princes, and priests to teach the Law of God to the people (2 Chron 17:7-9).

7. Son of Ishmael and governor of Judah who presided over levitical judges in royal matters during the reign of King Jehoshaphat. His counterpart was the priest Amariah, who presided over the judges in matters related to God (2 Chron 19:8-11).

8. Son of Michael of the clan of Shephatiah, who, along with eighty of his kinsmen, followed Ezra back to Jerusalem from Babylonian exile (Ezra 8:8). First Esdras 8:34 misspells his name as Zeraiah and numbers his kinsmen at seventy.

9. Son of Immer, who was a priest and at the command of Ezra divorced his foreign wife (Ezra 10:20; 1 Esdr 9:21).

ZEBAH AND ZALMUNNA The Midianite kings Zebah and Zalmunna are mentioned in the books of Judges (8:4-21) and Psalms (83:11 [Heb. 83:12]).

ZEBEDEE The name means "gift of the Lord." Zebedee was the father of two core members of the Twelve, JAMES and JOHN. He is mentioned solely in the Gospels and in relation to these two sons (Matt 4:21; 10:2; 26:37; Mark 1:19-20; 3:17; 10:35; Luke 5:10; John 21:2). He was a fisherman from the Capernaum area (Matt 4:12-22) with a boat (owned or leased) and hired hands (Mark 1:20).

ZEBIDAH Zebidah was the mother of

Judah's king JEHOIAKIM (2 Kgs 23:36) and daughter of Pedaiah.

ZEBINA The 4th in a list of seven sons of Nebo found in Ezra 10:43.

ZEBOIIM One of the "cities of the valley" (Gen 13:12; 19:25, 29) destroyed with Sodom, Gomorrah, and Admah (Deut 29:23 [Heb 29:22]).

See GOMORRAH; SODOM, SODOMITE.

ZEBOIM 1. A valley near Michmash in the territory of Benjamin, approximately 7 mi. northeast of Jerusalem (1 Sam 13:18).

2. A village in the territory of Benjamin where Jews who had returned from the Babylonian exile with Zerubbabel were known to live (Neh 11:34).

ZEBUL The governor of Shechem, appointed by Abimelech son of Gideon. Zebul warned Abimelech about Gaal's plans to lead an insurrection and urged him to bring an army to lie in wait outside Shechem (Judg 9:30-33).

ZEBULUN, ZEBULUNITE 1. Zebulun is the personal name given to the 6th son of LEAH and JACOB (Gen 30:20; 35:23), the eponymous ancestor of one of the twelve tribes of Israel. Throughout the OT, Zebulun most frequently refers to the people or territory of the tribe bearing this name.

2. Zebulun is listed among the names of the tribes of Israel (e.g., Exod 1:3; 1 Chron 2:1). Joshua 18:1-10 reports that Joshua allocated land to Zebulun and six other Israelite tribes who had not yet been assigned territory in Canaan (see TRIBE). Zebulun is situated in the hill country of the upper Galilee, due west of the Sea of Galilee. Zebulun is landlocked, surrounded by Asher to the northwest, Naphtali to the northeast, Issachar to the southeast, and Manasseh to the southwest (Josh 19:10-16).

According to the census in Numbers, Zebulun was the 4th largest tribe both at the beginning of the wilderness journey (Num 1:31) and at the end (Num 26:27).

In the NT, much of Jesus' life and ministry is situated in Galilee, a region that includes, but is not limited to, the territory of Zebulun (Matt 4:13). Drawing upon the words of Isaiah (9:1-2 [Heb. 8:23–9:1]), the Gospel of Matthew speaks of Zebulun (and neighboring Naphtali) as "the people who lived in the dark [who] have seen a great light" in reference to the advent of Jesus' ministry in Galilee (Matt 4:14-16). In Rev 7:8, 12,000 people from the tribe of Zebulun—along with 12,000 from each of the other eleven tribes—are sealed as God's servants. The seal apparently serves to protect them from the punishments to come.

ZECHARIAH A common name in biblical texts. The long form of the Hebrew name means "the Lord has remembered." This name is used for as many as thirty people in the OT and NT. It is especially common in the books of Chronicles and Ezra–Nehemiah.

1. A monarch in the northern kingdom of Israel (2 Kgs 14:29; 15:8-12), the 5th and final member of the longest reigning northern dynasty (2 Kgs 10:30; 15:12), established by JEHU (2 Kgs 9:1-13).

2. A Reubenite (1 Chron 5:7).

3. A levitical gatekeeper and son of Meshelemiah/Shelemiah/Shallum (1 Chron 9:17-22; see 26:14).

4. A Gibeonite (1 Chron 9:37).

5. A Levitical musician commissioned by David (1 Chron 15:18, 20; 16:5).

6. A priestly trumpeter commissioned by David (1 Chron 15:24).

7. A Levite and son of Isshiah who cast the lot during David's time (1 Chron 24:25).

8. A levitical gatekeeper and son of Hosah from the clan of Merari during David's reign (1 Chron 26:11, 16).

9. The father of Iddo from the tribe of Manasseh (1 Chron 27:21).

10. A Judean official in Jehoshaphat's court who taught the Instruction among the towns of Judah (2 Chron 17:7-9).

11. A levitical prophet and father of Jahaziel who announced victory for Jehoshaphat (2 Chron 20:14).

12. A son of the Judean king Jehoshaphat who was assassinated by his brother Jehoram (2 Chron 21:2).

13. The son of Jehoiada and a prophet through whom the spirit of the Lord spoke a message of condemnation against Joash and his people (2 Chron 24:17-22). Zechariah's father JEHOIADA was the high priest who had rescued the Judean king Joash from the lethal hands of Queen Athaliah (2 Chron 22–23). The death of Zechariah is mentioned in Matt 23:35 and Luke 11:51, even though his lineage in Matthew is traced through an individual named Berechiah (see #27).

14. A Levite from the clan of Asaph who assisted Hezekiah with his reforms (2 Chron 29:13).

15. A levitical musician from the clan of Kohath who assisted Josiah with his temple restoration (2 Chron 34:12-13).

16. An administrator of the temple during Josiah's reign (2 Chron 35:8; see 1 Esdr 1:8).

17. A leader of the clan of Parosh (Ezra 8:3).

18. A leader of the clan of Bebai (Ezra 8:11).

19. One of the leaders sent by Ezra to Iddo to ask him to send ministers for the temple (Ezra 8:16).

20. A layperson from the clan of Elam who agreed to divorce his Gentile wife (Ezra 10:26).

21. A layperson standing beside Ezra as he read the Instruction to the assembly in Jerusalem (Neh 8:4).

22. An ancestor of Athaiah, a Judahite who volunteered to live in Jerusalem in the early Persian period (Neh 11:4).

23. An ancestor of Maaseiah, another Judahite who volunteered to live in Jerusalem (Neh 11:5).

24. An ancestor of Adaiah, a priest who volunteered to live in Jerusalem (Neh 11:12).

25. A priestly trumpeter and son of Jonathan who was commissioned by Nehemiah for the dedication of the wall (Neh 12:35, 41).

26. A Judean man who, together with Uriah the priest, served as a witness to Isaiah's prophecy of the birth of a son named Maher-shalal-hash-baz (Isa 8:2). Uriah is identified by his social role (priest), but Zechariah is identified by his lineage, suggesting that he was a layperson (son of Jeberechiah). It is possible—though not certain—that this Zechariah is the maternal grandfather of King Hezekiah (see 2 Kgs 18:2; 2 Chron 29:1) and possibly also the godly prophetic mentor of Uzziah (2 Chron 26:5).

27. The son of Berechiah son of IDDO (Zech 1:1, 7; see Ezra 5:1; 6:14; Neh. 12). This prophetic figure traces his lineage to a priestly clan. His ancestor Iddo returned to the land with Zerubbabel and Jeshua around 520 BCE. Zechariah was the supposed author and central character of the book of Zechariah. The books of both Ezra and Zechariah identify Zechariah as a figure who prophesied near the beginning of the reign of the Persian king DARIUS (Zech 1:1, 7 [520 BCE]; 7:1 [516 BCE]).

28. The father of John the Baptist and priest from the clan of Abijah during the reign of Herod the Great and Caesar Augustus (Luke 1:5; 3:2; see 1 Chron 24:10). Zechariah's wife was Elizabeth, the elderly barren woman whose womb God miraculously opened in order to bear the prophet John the Baptist, forerunner of Jesus Christ (Luke 1:5-7). Zechariah is depicted as an active priest whose division cared for the temple for part of the year (Luke 1:8-10). Chosen by lot to burn incense in the temple, Zechariah is confronted by the angel from the Lord who presages the birth and ministry of John (Luke 1:11-17). Because of his unbelief, the angel strikes Zechariah mute until the child is born and named John (Luke

1:18-25, 39-45, 57-66). Immediately upon naming his son, Zechariah is filled with the Holy Spirit and his mouth opens to prophesy a song of praise to the Lord for raising up John as a prophet of the Most High (Luke 1:64, 67-79).

ZECHARIAH, BOOK OF The eleventh book of the Minor Prophets in the OT. The book of Zechariah addresses issues related to the Jewish community in the early Persian period (520–400 BCE) in the province of Yehud. The book begins with a description of a penitent community seeking to avoid the mistakes of past generations (1:1-6). Such penitence is rewarded through prophetic promises delivered through a series of night visions with accompanying oracles (1:7–6:15). Among these promises, however, there are indications of enduring problems in the province (see Zech 5). Chaps. 7–8 put restoration on hold because of insincere repentance. Chaps. 9–14 trace the demise of initial hopes for Davidic leadership with the emergence of inappropriate leadership. The darker universal tone of chaps. 12–14 reveals that the answer lies in the direct action of Yahweh as divine warrior and king.

ZEDEKIAH 1. The son of Chenaanah. Zedekiah was a false prophet in Samaria who lived in the days of Ahab king of Israel (1 Kgs 22:11, 24; 2 Chron 18:10, 23).

2. The 20th and final king of Judah (r. 597–587 BCE). Zedekiah was placed on the throne after Nebuchadnezzar deported JEHOIACHIN, Zedekiah's nephew, to Babylon in 597 BCE.

3. A son of Jehoiakim king of Judah (1 Chron 3:16).

4. One of the officials in the postexilic community (Neh 10:1 [Heb. 10:2]).

5. The son of Maaseiah. Zedekiah was a false prophet who was taken into exile in Babylon at the time of the deportation of Jehoiachin, king of Judah in 597 BCE.

6. A son of Hananiah and a royal officer of Judah in the days of Jehoiakim king of Judah (Jer 36:12).

7. The great-grandfather of BARUCH, Jeremiah's scribe and friend (Bar 1:1).

ZELEK Zelek the Ammonite is listed among "the Thirty," David's mighty warriors (2 Sam 23:37; 1 Chron 11:39). In these lists, names of warriors are given formulaically with their places of origin, clear evidence that David's most skilled fighters were mercenaries. See AMMON, AMMONITES.

ZELOPHEHAD Zelophehad is listed among the descendants of Manasseh through Makir, Gilead, and finally Hepher (Num 27:1; 1 Chron 7:15). When he died in the wilderness without a male heir, his five daughters—Mahlah, Noah, Hoglah, Milcah, and Tirzah—appealed to Moses for an inheritance of property so that their father's name might not perish. When Moses brought the matter before God, Yahweh affirmed their request and decreed that the five receive their father's inheritance and that this become the rule for other such circumstances in Israel (Num 27:1-11).

ZEMIRAH A Benjaminite, the son of Becher and grandson of Benjamin (1 Chron 7:8).

ZENAS Zenas is mentioned only in Titus 3:13. The instruction to send him and Apollos on their journey well provisioned suggests that they are the bearers of the letter to Titus.

ZEPHANIAH 1. Son of Maaseiah, a priest during the reign of Zedekiah, who sent Zephaniah to inquire of the prophet Jeremiah concerning the Babylonian crisis (Jer 21:1; 29:25, 29; 37:3). After the destruction of Jerusalem, Zephaniah was put to death by the Babylonians (2 Kgs 25:18-21; Jer 52:24-27).

2. A Kohathite (1 Chron 6:36 [Heb. 6:21]).

3. A prophet in Jerusalem during

the reign of Josiah king of Judah (Zeph 1:1; 2 Esdr 1:40), and a contemporary of Jeremiah.

4. Father of Josiah, a priest who returned from the Babylonian exile (Zech 6:10, 14).

ZEPHANIAH, BOOK OF A collection of speeches attributed to ZEPHANIAH, an otherwise unknown prophet, addressing the city of Jerusalem during the reign of JOSIAH of Judah (640–609 BCE). It is the ninth book in the collection of Minor Prophets known as the Book of the Twelve. Its major theme is the Day of the Lord, an event that portends calamitous judgment for Judah's religious and moral corruption and promises renewal for a chastened and obedient remnant.

ZEPHO Third-listed son of ELIPHAZ and grandson of Esau and Adah, Zepho is also a clan chief of Esau (Gen 36:11, 15).

ZEPHON, ZEPHONITES The oldest son of Gad (Num 26:15), elsewhere spelled ZIPHION (Gen 46:16). He was the progenitor of the clan of the Zephonites.

ZERAH, ZERAHITES The name Zerah appears twenty-one times in the OT and once in the NT, as well as on a 6th-cent. clay seal.

1. A son of Reuel and grandson of Esau (Gen 36:13, 17; 1 Chron 1:37).

2. The father of JOBAB, a king of Edom (Gen 36:33; 1 Chron 1:44).

3. A son of Simeon. His descendants are called "Zerahites" (Num 26:13; 1 Chron 4:24). In Gen 46:10 and Exod 6:15, Simeon's son is called "Zohar."

4. A son of Judah by his daughter-in-law Tamar (Gen 46:12; 1 Chron 2:4) and the ancestor of the Judahite clan of the Zerahites (Num 26:20; Josh 7:17; 1 Chron 27:11, 13) or "Zerah's son(s)" (Josh 7:24; 22:20; 1 Chron 2:6; 9:6; Neh 11:24). He was the twin brother of PEREZ, the ancestor of David (and so is mentioned in Matt 1:3). According to a folk etymology in Gen 38:27-30, Zerah's name comes from the scarlet thread tied around his wrist by the midwife to mark him as the oldest before his hand was pulled back into the womb and his brother forced himself out first.

According to 1 Chron 2:6, Zerah had five sons. The name of the first son comes from Josh 7:1, 18 (though Chronicles has "ZIMRI" instead of "ZABDI," reflecting a scribal error in one of these sources). The names Chronicles gives for the other four sons of Zerah come from 1 Kgs 4:31 [Heb. 5:11], reading "Ezrahite" as "Zerahite," and ignoring the historical context of the passage in Solomon's reign, as well as the phrase "children of Mahol."

5. A Levite in the Gershomite line (1 Chron 6:21 [Heb. 6:6]).

6. A 2nd Levite in the Gershomite line who is the ancestor of ASAPH (1 Chron 6:41 [Heb. 6:26]).

7. A Cushite who attacked Judah during the reign of ASA (911–870 BCE; 2 Chron 14:9-15 [Heb. 14:8-14]). The account in Chronicles is exaggerated (Zerah's 1,000,000 troops are met by Asa's 580,000), but the conflict itself is probably historical. If Cush here refers to Ethiopia, Zerah may be a mercenary for Pharaoh SHISHAK, left behind with a contingent of Ethiopian troops (see 2 Chron 12:3 for Ethiopians in Shishak's army) to defend Egypt's northern frontier. But if Cush refers to CUSHAN in northern Arabia (Hab 3:7), Zerah may simply be an Arab raider, a possibility supported by the mention of tents and camels in the description of Asa's victory (2 Chron 14:15 [Heb. 14:14]).

ZERAHIAH Meaning "the Lord has arisen/shone forth."

1. A Levite descendant of Aaron, he is the son of Uzzi and the father of Meraioth (1 Chron 6:6 [Heb. 5:32], 51 [Heb. 5:36]), and an ancestor of Ezra (Ezra 7:1-4).

2. A member of the family of Pahath-moab, whose son Eliehoenai led 200 of

his kinsmen to return to Palestine with Ezra (Ezra 8:1-4; 1 Esdr 8:31).

ZERED Numbers 21:12 identifies the Zered ravine as the place where the Israelites camped after leaving Iye-ibarim. From there, they traveled "across the Arnon" (Num 21:13). According to Deut 2:13-14, the Israelites' crossing of the Zered ravine was the event that marked the end of thirty-eight years of wandering in the wilderness. The ravine served as the northern boundary of Edom and the southern boundary of Moab.

ZEREDAH 1. In 1 Kgs 11:26, Zeredah is referenced as the hometown of the first king of the northern kingdom: Jeroboam, from the half-tribe of Ephraim.

2. According to 2 Chron 4:17, Solomon had the bronze objects for the Jerusalem temple cast in the Jordan Valley at an unspecified location between Zeredah and Succoth. The verse is paralleled by 1 Kgs 7:46, where ZARETHAN (cf Josh 3:16) appears instead.

ZERERAH A place-name in the Jordan Valley, called Gargatha in the LXX. It was 25 km southwest of Nablus in the highlands of Samaria near Beth-shittah and Abel-meholah. The locale is mentioned in Judg 7:22. In the narrative setting of this verse, Zererah was along the route from the Jezreel Valley to Succoth. The toponym is likely a variant spelling of ZEREDAH, which appears in 1 Kgs 11:26 and 2 Chron 4:17. Another location, ZARETHAN, appears to be an alternate name of the same place (Josh 3:16; 1 Kgs 4:12; 7:46).

ZERESH Wife of Haman, Mordecai's antagonist in the book of Esther. Zeresh encourages Haman to destroy Mordecai (5:10-14) but later predicts her husband's downfall before Mordecai, because Mordecai "is of Jewish birth" (6:13).

ZERETH A descendant of Judah, and the 1st of three sons of Ashur by one of his wives, HELAH (1 Chron 4:7).

ZEROR A Benjaminite, the father of Abiel and the son of Becorath. He is the grandfather of Kish and thus the great-grandfather of King Saul (1 Sam 9:1).

ZERUAH Mother of JEROBOAM and widow of Nebat (1 Kgs 11:26).

ZERUBBABEL Zerubbabel was a Jewish governor of Judah in the early postexilic period under Persian rule (beginning no later than 520 BCE) and a major leader in the reconstruction of Jewish life after exile. His name (common in Babylonia) implies that Zerubbabel was born in Babylon. He is a main character in the books of Haggai, Zechariah, Ezra, and Nehemiah.

Zerubbabel appears in Jesus' genealogies. Both Matthew (1:12-13) and Luke (3:27) record him as Shealtiel's son (albeit with a transliterated version of the name) but with different grandfathers (Jechoniah in Matthew; Neri in Luke).

ZERUIAH First Chronicles 2:16 states that Zeruiah and Abigail were sisters of the sons of Jesse, and that Zeruiah had three sons: Abishai, Joab, and Asahel.

ZETHAM Jehieli (see JEHIEL), Zetham, and Joel were sons of the Levite LADAN (1 Chron 23:8). However, 1 Chron 26:21-22 lists Zetham and Joel as sons of Jehieli and grandsons of Ladan.

ZETHAN The 5th of seven sons of BILHAN and grandsons of JEDIAEL, descendants of Benjamin (1 Chron 7:10).

ZETHAR One of the seven eunuchs who served King Ahasuerus and were charged with bringing Queen Vashti before the king (Esth 1:10-11).

ZEUS In Greek mythology, Zeus is the primary member of the Greek pantheon, for he possesses more power than any other immortal, gives order to the universe, and assigns dominions to other gods. The Bible reflects resistance to attempts to associate Zeus and the God of Israel. In the middle of the 2nd cent. BCE, the Seleucid king Antiochus IV (Epiphanes) tried to have the Jerusalem temple renamed in honor of "Olympian Zeus" and the Samaritan temple on Mount Gerizim renamed in honor of "Zeus-the-Friend-of-Strangers." According to 2 Macc 6:2, this act contributed to the defilement of these sites, even though the verse may also scornfully allege that the Samaritans were amenable to this name.

In Acts 14:11-13, some residents of Lystra respond to the healing of a man who could not walk by identifying Barnabas as Zeus and Paul as Hermes. See DIOSCURI.

ZIA A Gadite clan/clan leader among the sons of ABIHAIL (1 Chron 5:13).

ZIBA A servant or retainer of the house of Saul, Ziba plays a somewhat duplicitous role. When David inquired after survivors of the house of Saul, Ziba revealed the existence of Jonathan's lame son Mephibosheth (Meribbaal), who was brought to Jerusalem to be cared for under David's watchful eye. Ziba was subsequently put in charge of Mephibosheth's holdings (2 Sam 9).

Ziba next appears during Absalom's revolt. While David was fleeing Jerusalem, he encountered Ziba and inquired after his master. Ziba replied that Mephibosheth was using Absalom's revolt to further his own anti-Davidic agenda. In return for Ziba's loyalty, David rewarded him with all of Mephibosheth's holdings (2 Sam 16:1-4).

When David returned to Jerusalem following Absalom's defeat, Ziba rushed to greet David (2 Sam 19:17*b*-18*a*). Shortly thereafter Mephibosheth also came out to greet David, protesting his innocence of any treachery (2 Sam 19:24-30).

ZIBEON Father of Aiah and Anah (Gen 36:24; 1 Chron 1:40), son of Seir (Gen 36:20; 1 Chron 1:38), and grandfather of Esau's wife Oholibamah (Gen 36:2, 14). As a Horite clan name (Gen 36:29), Zibeon represents part of the indigenous population disrupted by immigrating Esauite clans (Deut 2:12).

ZIBIA The 2nd of seven sons of SHAHARAIM, a Benjaminite, by one of his wives, Hodesh (1 Chron 8:8-10).

ZIBIAH Zibiah of Beer-sheba was the mother of King JOASH (Jehoash) of Judah (2 Kgs 12:1 [Heb. 12:2]; 2 Chron 24:1).

ZICHRI Perhaps meaning "remembrance" or an abbreviated form of the name Zechariah. Twelve men in the OT bear this name.

1. The son of Izhar, a Kohathite (Exod 6:21).

2. A Benjaminite whose father was Shimei (1 Chron 8:19-21).

3. A Benjaminite whose father was Shashak (1 Chron 8:23-25).

4. One of the six sons of Jeroham, a Benjaminite (1 Chron 8:27).

5. A Levite, the son of Asaph and father of Mica (1 Chron 9:15). The name may be a corruption of ZABDI (cf Neh 11:17).

6. A Levite whose family cared for the treasuries under King David (1 Chron 26:25).

7. The father of Eliezer, chief officer of the Reubenites under King David (1 Chron 27:16).

8. A Judahite whose son, Amasiah, commanded 200,000 troops under King Jehoshaphat (2 Chron 17:16).

9. The father of Elishaphat, one of five military commanders who entered into a plot to overthrow Queen Athaliah (2 Chron 23:1).

10. The Ephraimite hero who slew Maaseiah the son of King Ahaz, as well as Azrikam and Elkanah, two of Ahaz's officials (2 Chron 28:7).

11. The father of Joel, who oversaw the Benjaminites in Jerusalem after the return from exile (Neh 11:9).

12. A priest who led his clan in the postexilic period (Neh 12:17).

ZIHA The descendants of Ziha are mentioned in Ezra 2:43 and Neh 7:46 among several groups of people who returned from the exile and functioned as the temple servants.

ZIKLAG A town on the southern edge of the western foothills originally allotted to the tribe of Simeon (Josh 19:5) and later assimilated into the territory of Judah (Josh 15:31). The Chronicler notes that descendants of Simeon still lived in Ziklag (1 Chron 4:30).

ZILLAH Zillah and ADAH were the two wives of LAMECH (Gen 4:19) in the lineage of Cain. Zillah bore TUBAL-CAIN and his sister NAAMAH (Gen 4:22).

ZILLETHAI 1. In 1 Chron 8:20, Zillethai is one of the heads of a family within the tribe of Benjamin living in Jerusalem.

2. In 1 Chron 12:20, Zillethai is one of seven chiefs of the tribe of Manasseh who deserted Saul and became warriors and commanders in David's army at Ziklag.

ZILPAH One of the servant women whom Laban gave as a servant to Leah when she married Jacob (Gen 29:24). Later, Leah gave Zilpah, whose name means "trickling," to Jacob as a surrogate mother; she bore two sons, Gad and Asher (Gen 30:9-13; 35:26; 46:18), who tended Jacob's flocks with Rachel's son Joseph (37:2). See ASHER, ASHERITES; GAD, GADITES; TRIBE.

ZIMMAH A Levite musician descended from Gershom. The details are not clear, as he is the son of Jahath and the father of Joah according to 1 Chron 6:20 [Heb. 6:5] and 2 Chron 29:12, but the grandson of Jahath in 1 Chron 6:42-43 [Heb. 6:27-28].

ZIMRAN The 1st of six sons born to Abraham and Keturah (Gen 25:2; 1 Chron 1:32); the sons' names correspond to tribes or regions in Arabia.

ZIMRI The name of four persons and one location in the OT.

1. Zimri son of Salu, a head of a Simeonite lineage, whom the priest PHINEHAS slew along with a Midianite woman for participating in the worship of Baal Peor (Num 25:14).

2. The 5th king of Israel (ca. 880 BCE). According to 1 Kgs 16:9-20, Zimri was a courtier and general of chariotry under King Elah. He reigned only a week because the army supported its commander OMRI, who besieged the capital, Tirzah, and took the throne after Zimri had set fire to the royal palace compound after the city fell.

3. Zimri the son of Zerah and grandson of Judah and thus the nominal ancestor of a Judahite clan (1 Chron 2:6).

4. The great-great-great-great-grandson of King Saul (1 Chron 8:36; 9:42), who would have lived in the mid- to late 9th cent. BCE.

5. An otherwise unknown kingdom listed alongside Elam and Media (Jer 25:25) and thus probably located in western Iran.

ZIN DESERT The "Zin desert" is used in the OT to refer to some portion of the desert wasteland that lies south of the arid southern plains on the Sinai Peninsula. It is described as lying west of Edom and north of the PARAN desert. See SIN DESERT.

ZINA See ZIZA.

ZION In both the OT and the NT, the term *Zion* is used in various ways: as a name for the city of Jerusalem or occasionally Judah, as a name for a particular part of Jerusalem, as a name for the inhabitants of the city, and as the name of the entire people of God.

Most often in the Bible, the term

Zion refers to the city of Jerusalem and its environs or part of the city or to the country of which the city is capital. A careful evaluation of usage provides helpful insight into the connotations of the name in various contexts. In both the OT and the NT, Zion is always used as a proper name. In the OT, Zion is used over 150 times, often with an addition or parallel (Daughter of Zion, Mount Zion, Zion = Jerusalem). More than half of its occurrences can be found in the books of Isaiah and Psalms. In expansion of its geographical usage, Zion often refers to the entire city of Jerusalem.

Zion is frequently used as a description of the place of the Lord's seat or throne, thus suggesting a cultic center. As the dwelling of the deity, perfection and beauty underscore its nature. Zion is where Israelites go to worship or praise God. The temple itself is referred to as Zion, and that is where the Lord dwells and is enthroned (Ps 9; see TEMPLE, JERUSALEM). In addition to the geographic and cultic aspects, Zion is often used in reference to the people. "Daughter Zion" refers to the people twenty-seven times in the OT and two times in the NT. In Jer 4:31 and Mic 4:10, "Daughter Zion" is suffering as a woman in labor suffers. "Young woman, daughter Zion" is used three times in the OT (2 Kgs 19:21; Isa 37:22; Lam 2:13). In addition, "daughters of," "women of," "sons of," and "people of Zion" are used for the inhabitants of Zion, Jerusalem, Judah, and even the whole land.

In the NT, *Zion* is used seven times—five times in relation to texts from the OT. Matthew 21:5 (Isa 62:11; Zech 9:9) and John 12:15 (Isa 62:11) refer to the Daughter of Zion. Romans 9:33 (Isa 8:14-15; 28:16) and 1 Pet 2:6 (Isa 28:16) refer to a stone in Zion. Romans 11:26 (Ps 14:7; Isa 59:20) refers to salvation coming from Zion. The two remaining occurrences are found in Heb 12:22, which refers to Mount Zion, the city of the living God; and Rev 14:1, which depicts the Lamb standing on Mount Zion. In Revelation Mount Zion becomes the place of eschatological preservation.

ZIPH, ZIPHITES 1. A town in the extreme south of Israel near the boundary of Edom (Josh 15:24).

2. Another town in the extreme south near the boundary of Edom, belonging to Judah (Josh 15:55). During David's flight from Saul, he and his men spent time in the Ziph wilderness (1 Sam 23:14).

3. The father of Mesha, a Calebite (1 Chron 2:42).

4. A family or clan of the tribe of Judah (1 Chron 4:16).

ZIPHAH Second of four sons of the Judahite Jehallelel (1 Chron 4:16). Ziphah is a feminine form of Ziph, the oldest son; perhaps Ziphah is a daughter.

ZIPHION The 1st of seven children of Gad, who are grandchildren of Jacob (Gen 46:16). He is named ZEPHON in Num 26:15.

ZIPPOR Father of Balak king of Moab; Zippor presumably reigned at the time of the exodus (Num 22:2, 4, 10, 16; 23:18; Josh 24:9; Judg 11:25, always "Zippor's son," identifying Balak).

ZIPPORAH Zipporah was the daughter of the Midianite priest REUEL (Exod 2:18-21; cf Exod 4:18; 18:2, daughter of Jethro), the wife of Moses, the mother of GERSHOM (Exod 2:22), and the mother of at least one additional son (Exod 4:20; two total in 18:3).

Zipporah saved either Moses or Gershom through the act of circumcision when the Lord tried to kill one of them along the way to Egypt (Exod 4:24-26).

ZIZA The name of two men in the OT. The name means "shining."

1. A son of Shiphi, a man in the tribe of Simeon (1 Chron 4:37). He was

a leader in his family during the time of King Hezekiah.

2. The 3rd son of Rehoboam through Maacah, his favorite wife (2 Chron 11:20). Ziza's brother Abijah became king of Judah after his father's death (2 Chron 12:16).

3. The 2nd son of Shimei, a Gershonite (1 Chron 23:11). Ziza is among the Levites whom David registers for temple service.

ZOAN Biblical name of the Egyptian capital of the 21st and 22nd Egyptian dynasties. The city is located ca. 47 km south of the Mediterranean in the eastern delta.

ZOAR A city lying in the plain of the Jordan near the Dead Sea, best known for its association with Sodom, Gomorrah, Admah, and Zeboiim, the so-called "cities of the valley" or "Five Cities" (Gen 13:12; Wis 10:6; see SODOM, SODOMITE). In Genesis, Zoar appears in stories related to the fate of LOT. When Abraham offered his nephew Lot a choice of where to pasture his flocks, Lot's eyes fell upon the well-watered "Jordan Valley," which was "well irrigated, like the garden of the LORD, like the land of Egypt, as far as Zoar" (Gen 13:10).

In the well-known story of the destruction of Sodom and Gomorrah (Gen 18–19), Lot begged the angels to let him flee to nearby Zoar. Very soon, however, Lot decided Zoar was unsafe and retreated with his daughters to a cave in the nearby hills (see LOT).

ZOBAH A powerful Aramean kingdom of southern Syria during the 11th cent. BCE, also called Aram-zobah. Zobah was located in the north Beqa' Valley of modern Lebanon. According to 1 Sam 14:47-48, Saul fought against and routed "the king of Zobah." Further hostilities between Israel and Zobah are reported in 2 Sam 10:1-19.

ZOHAR 1. Father of Ephron the Hittite, who sold the cave of MACHPELAH to Abraham for Sarah's burial (Gen 23:8). Abraham was buried there later (Gen 25:9).

2. The 5th of the six sons of Simeon (Gen 46:10; Exod 6:15). Elsewhere the name is Zerah (Num 26:12-13; 1 Chron 4:24). See ZERAH, ZERAHITES.

ZOPHAH Son of Helem and father of eleven sons, listed among the descendants of Asher (1 Chron 7:35-36).

ZOPHAR Zophar the Naamathite was one of Job's three friends who, after hearing of the disaster that had befallen him, traveled to Uz to console him (Job 2:11). Zophar is the 3rd speaker in the three cycles of speeches offered by Job's friends (chaps. 11; 20—he offers no words in the 3rd cycle).

ZORAH, ZORATHITES A village located in the Sorek Valley, 21 km west of Jerusalem and 3 km north of Beth Shemesh.

ZORITES A clan or family in Judah, descended from Salma (1 Chron 2:54). See ZORAH, ZORATHITES.

ZUAR The father of NETHANEL, a leader in the tribe of Issachar (Num 1:8; 2:5; 7:18, 23; 10:15).

ZUPH Means "honeycomb."

1. An Ephraimite ancestor of Elkanah, Samuel's father (1 Sam 1:1). The Chronicler makes him—and by extension Samuel—a Kohathite from the tribe of Levi, the line from which David appointed men for the musical ministry in the temple (1 Chron 6:35 [Heb. 6:20]). See PRIESTS AND LEVITES.

2. A district in Israel where Saul and his servant searched for his father's donkeys (1 Sam 9:5). Its location is uncertain, but it probably lay within

the highlands of Ephraim, perhaps near Ramah (cf 1 Sam 1:19).

ZUR 1. A Midianite ruler, variously identified as "a tribal leader" in Num 25:15, as a "king" in Num 31:8, and as a "leader" and a "prince" in Josh 13:21. He is named among the five Midianite kings (Num 31:8) or leaders/princes (Josh 13:21) slain by the Israelites prior to their entrance into the land allotted to the Reubenites. Zur was the father of Cozbi (Num 25:15). See MIDIAN, MIDIANITES.

2. Second son of the Benjaminite Jeiel, who lived in Gibeon (1 Chron 8:30; 9:36).

ZURIEL Zuriel son of Abihail (Num 3:35) was the chief or prince of the levitical clans of Merari (the Mahlites and the Mushites).

ZURISHADDAI The father of SHELUMIEL, who was the leader of the ancestral tribe of Simeon at the time of the exodus.